Issues of the Seventies

WADSWORTH CONTINUING EDUCATION SERIES
Leonard Freedman, General Editor

ARMAMENT AND DISARMAMENT: THE CONTINUING DISPUTE
edited by Walter R. Fisher
University of Southern California
and Richard D. Burns
California State College, Los Angeles

CONTEMPORARY COMMUNISM
edited by Howard R. Swearer
and Richard Longaker
University of California, Los Angeles

CONTEMPORARY LABOR ISSUES
edited by Walter R. Fogel
and Archie Kleingartner
University of California, Los Angeles

CONTEMPORARY MORAL ISSUES, Second Edition
edited by Harry K. Girvetz
University of California, Santa Barbara

CONTEMPORARY RELIGIOUS ISSUES
edited by Donald E. Hartsock
University of California, Los Angeles

ISSUES OF THE SEVENTIES
edited by Leonard Freedman
University of California, Los Angeles

METROPOLIS: VALUES IN CONFLICT
edited by C. E. Elias, Jr.
Fresno State College
James Gillies
York University
and Svend Riemer
University of California, Los Angeles

THE NEW TECHNOLOGY AND HUMAN VALUES
edited by John G. Burke
University of California, Los Angeles

POVERTY: AMERICAN STYLE
edited by Herman P. Miller
U.S. Bureau of the Census

PROBLEMS AND PROSPECTS OF THE NEGRO MOVEMENT
edited by Raymond J. Murphy
University of Rochester
and Howard Elinson
University of California, Los Angeles

TENSION AREAS IN WORLD AFFAIRS
edited by Arthur C. Turner
University of California, Riverside
and Leonard Freedman
University of California, Los Angeles

TWENTIETH CENTURY: THE GREAT ISSUES
edited by William R. Hitchcock
University of California, Santa Cruz

Issues of the Seventies

edited by

LEONARD FREEDMAN

University of California, Los Angeles

Wadsworth Publishing Company, Inc., Belmont, California

L. C. Cat. Card No.: 76-112599

Printed in the United States of America

1 2 3 4 5 6 7 8 9 10—74 73 72 71 70

Preface

Issues of the Seventies is the sequel to the two editions of *Issues of the Sixties*. It comprises an entirely new set of readings. This complete change is not to suggest that everything about the last edition of *Issues of the Sixties*, published in 1965, is now obsolete. Some of the same issues obstinately persist, essentially unresolved, and many of the selections written in the mid-60s are still relevant.

Still, in a book on contemporary issues, it is clearly preferable to select pieces that take into account the changes in content which are being forced on us at such an extraordinarily rapid pace. Moreover, the definition of some of the issues has changed dramatically, some growing in importance, others declining. Thus, there was no chapter in the 1965 book on the university; a public policy reader without this topic today would be inconceivable. There are also new chapters on crime, the environment, power, and intervention abroad. Conversely, there is much less in this book than in its predecessor on the prospects for the development of international institutions; the nation state may well be obsolete, but it will be all too much in evidence in the 1970s. The omission of a chapter on the city this time is not because the problems of urban life have declined. On the contrary, they have become so massive that they could not be contained within a single chapter and constitute a considerable portion of four of the chapters which follow.

Despite the fact that a clean sweep has been made, the basic principles underlying the two editions of *Issues of the Sixties* are unchanged. First, the dominant, pressing problems of the time have been selected—not all of them, of course, for space would not allow real comprehensiveness, but enough to reflect the major preoccupations of politicians, scholars, political writers, and those new and vigorous shapers of opinion, college students.

Second, the problems have been presented as arenas of public policy controversies, and more than one point of view is presented on each. This is not to say that there is a direct reply to every statement on every question dealt with in the book. Sometimes, as in the debates over the Crime Bill, the National Commitments Resolution, and racial separatism, there is a clear-cut confrontation of views. In other cases, the joining of issues is more oblique. Nonetheless, conflict is inseparable from the American political process, and the conflict of ideas is clearly in evidence in each chapter.

Third, the intention is to provide a great deal of solid information and a high level of analysis. A few of the statements do not measure up to this standard but are included to illustrate how an issue is expounded in the context of political life. In most cases, however, the selections reflect the fact that they are the product of scholars and writers of substantial reputation.

Finally, since the issues of our age cannot be contained within any one discipline, several fields of study are brought together in this book—especially political science, economics, history, sociology, and psychology.

The organization of the book is straightforward. The introductory chapter looks back to the decade of the 60s, selects technology as the most important force of our era, and explores the implications of technological change for the 70s. Part I deals with six of the crucial domestic issues which will be strenuously debated in the years immediately ahead. In Part II the context is extended to the international arena, focusing on those aspects most likely to demand decisions from the American people. Finally, the concluding chapter considers the question of whether the American political system can survive the intense pressures imposed upon it by the problems examined in this book.

I have been greatly helped in the preparation of this material by Mr. Ronald Hart, a graduate student in political science at UCLA. I am grateful, too, for the invaluable comments of Professor John Burke of UCLA's History Department on the draft of Chapter 1 and for his suggestions on Chapter 5. Finally, I want to express warm thanks to Miss Magdalen Suzuki for her extremely capable handling of the arduous tasks of checking many of the sources and assembling and preparing the manuscript.

Contents

Issues of the Seventies

Introduction: Technology and the Legacy of the Sixties

An incredible national achievement spanned the 1960s. In 1961 John F. Kennedy sent a message to Congress in which he said:

> I believe that this nation should commit itself to the goal, before this decade is out, of landing a man on the moon and returning him safely to earth. . . . A preliminary analysis of this project shows more than 2,000 tasks that must be accomplished, ranging from the development of new large boosters and the launching facilities necessary to send them into space, to experiments on the biological effects of the radiation encountered in space and the study of satisfactory methods of protection, and the engineering development of heat shields for reentry speeds as high as 25,000 miles per hour . . .

Accomplishing all these tasks cost more than $24 billion and the lives of three astronauts. Yet, in 1969, Neil Armstrong took his "one small step for man, one giant leap for mankind," and the world applauded, marveling at this apotheosis of science and technology and at the ultimate technological society, the United States.

Nor was this the only achievement of American technology in the 1960s. For it was technology organized by the American industrial system which produced an extraordinary surge in the quantity of goods and services. During the 1960 presidential campaign Kennedy had argued that the economy was stagnating. "I think it's time America started moving again," he declared. And in the 60s the economy did move at rates of growth significantly higher than in the previous decade. By 1969 the Gross National Product had passed $900 billion. Early in the 70s ours will be a trillion dollar economy—a system annually producing goods and services valued at a thousand billion dollars. Moreover, within these gross figures the emphasis has shifted from consumer goods to services, including more and more educational and recreational facilities. Thus, we move into what Daniel Bell has called the "post-industrial society," characterized by the creation and dissemination of knowledge, by the enhancement of the quality of life, and by the productive uses of leisure.

Nor, thus far, has the move toward post-industrialism been accompanied by the crisis widely predicted during the early and middle 60s. A number of writers were then arguing that the rapidly increasing use of computers and other technologies would bring the "cybernetic revolution," in which machines would replace men on a scale far surpassing any previous experience. Conceivably this will begin to reveal itself during the 70s, and there are some who claim that only Vietnam has delayed the impact. Still, unemployment in the late 60s was below 4% most of the time. The central economic problem was not unemployment but inflation; and most economists insisted that, in the foreseeable future, technological change would create as many new jobs as it eliminated.

Here, it might seem, is reason to be optimistic about the future—a nation adventurous enough to seek to conquer space, abundant enough to build a new kind of society freed from the grinding necessities of economic survival.

Yet, to persist in this vein, to declare that the legacy of the 60s is one of untarnished accomplishment, is to become fatuous. The pervasive mood at the turn of the decade is not one of triumph but one of deep uneasiness, sometimes giving way to profound alarm. While conflict is the normal condition of a democratic polity, the intensity of current dissensions—the upheaval in politics, the arts, sex, language, dress, manners—creates a sense of things coming apart at the seams, of bewilderment, of disorientation. It can be argued that the transformation of our national style during the 60s may be a clearing away of cant, the removal of irrelevant dogmas and taboos, the necessary precursor of more open and honest patterns of behavior. For the present, however, an atmosphere so permeated with rancor and bitterness, so prone to violent eruptions, does not bespeak a healthy society.

To examine what has gone wrong we must go back again to technology; for if technology is not the only force shaping American society, it is certainly the dominant one. And the fact that the national mood is not a buoyant reflection of technological triumphs can be traced in large measure to two basic shortcomings of technology: the threat to human welfare that it harbors and its inability to solve human problems.

Technology as Threat

A generation growing up under the constant danger of nuclear holocaust needs no reminder of the menace technology can represent. But this is not the only respect in which man is threatened by technology. The beneficent effects of medicine, combined with the use of pesticides and other techniques for raising food production, have unleashed the Malthusian nightmare. World population, now about 3.5 billion, will rise to about 7.5 billion by the year 2000 if present fertility and mortality rates continue; should economic development reduce fertility rates, the total may be held down to a mere 7 billion.[1] For the economically poor countries of the world, where the larger part of the increase will occur, the result may well negate any gains in productivity and produce catastrophic famines. But even the affluent nations are likely to find themselves afflicted by increased pollution, congestion, urban sprawl, and other ailments. Indeed, the combination of rising population and widening affluence is arousing profound concern about the future of the human environment.[2] Man is defiling his planet with the waste products of his technology. The ecology of earth, the balance of nature, is being destroyed. The very atmosphere, the fortuitous and delicate relationship of elements that makes life possible, is damaged. And by altering the carbon cycle, we may be causing a general rise in temperatures which, among other things, could shrink the polar ice caps and glaciers. "I am advising all my friends," says Lord Ritchie-Calder, "not to take ninety-nine-year leases on properties at present sea level."[3]

[1] United Nations Association of the USA, "World Population," 1969.

[2] See Chap. 5 and also the United Nations report in Chap. 9.

[3] "Polluting the Environment," *The Center Magazine*, Vol. II, No. 3 (May 1969), p. 11.

Beyond the question of survival, there are other human values being eroded by technological change. Earlier invasions of privacy—wiretapping, electronic eavesdropping, compulsory polygraph testing—are increasing in frequency. But now the advent of mass communications enhances the possibility of mass manipulation by elites who control the communications systems through wealth, military power, or technological expertise. Moreover, technology, as Jacques Ellul has pointed out,[4] is not merely the machine and its methods but a system of imposed uniformity and standardization. The final expression of this is the current proposal for a National Data Center, which would amalgamate the records of several government agencies into a single information data bank. This would contain all kinds of information—legal, tax, credit, educational, employment, medical, security—about every citizen. Even the establishment of the most rigid rules governing access to the files could not allay fear of centralized control, of the all-knowing and all-powerful bureaucracy. It is hardly surprising that, confronted by the accelerating trend toward standardization and bureaucratization, the young in America and many other countries regard the proponents of such a system as an alien "Establishment" and value spontaneity over order, feeling over rationality. They are not enthusiastic about the prospect that, if man does not blow himself up during the 70s, he will emerge on the other side into Orwell's *1984.*

Technology's Inability to Solve Social Problems

Philosophers have long insisted that technology cannot give us the wisdom needed to deal with the ultimate questions of man and society. For those with the *hubris* to challenge this view, the 60s provided a chastening experience. Our cities—the characteristic environment of technological society—struggled with multiplying inefficiencies, seethed with unrest, and verged on being ungovernable. Economic growth reduced the numbers living in poverty; yet the welfare rolls grew sharply. The statistics on the living conditions of black people in America showed important improvements, but the racial crisis worsened. University

[4] *The Technological Society*, translated by John Wilkinson (New York: Alfred A. Knopf, Inc., 1964).

students rose up in fury against the institutions that are the pride of the technological system and the key to its future.

As for the international situation, the 60s were years of profound discouragement. Technology, it has often been said, makes nationalism obsolete. Yet nationalism obstinately refused to go away and even became resurgent. Though the partial test ban treaty of 1963 did portend a degree of sanity in great power relationships, there was no comfort to be found in the ferocity of events in the Middle East, Nigeria, and, above all, Vietnam. The war in Vietnam, indeed, provided the supreme example of the failure of technology to solve problems in international politics; the United States, applying the overwhelming preponderance of power made available by its enormous productive machine, was unable to bring order to a small, poor, essentially pre-industrial country.

Thus, in the 1960s technology, spectacularly successful in some areas, failed to find answers to problems of social planning. We discovered that, even in the context of problems essentially technical in nature, it was increasingly difficult to adjust technology to higher orders of complexity: thus, the great electric power breakdown in New York and New England in 1965, the growing crisis of air traffic control, and mounting complaints about telephone service. But these problems do not compare in complexity with any one of the issues dealt with in this book—poverty, race, crime, power, and national rivalries—issues that have plagued man throughout his history and remain as an ominous agenda for the next decade.

Technology and the Future

Traditionally, the charges just presented—technology is a threat to human values, technology is incompetent in alleviating the social problems it helps to create—have been leveled by the humanist against the scientists and technocrats who blindly pursue their experiments without concern for their social impact. Yet there are at least some in the scientific and technical communities who, deeply aware of the dangers and the limitations of their calling, have been among the most articulate and vigorous spokesmen on this subject. It was a group of scientists, for example, who applied some of the most significant pressure for the nuclear test ban treaty. Others warned against the crises of population and pollution. Such men would generally concede that, despite the successes in space and industrial productivity, the balance sheet on technology in the 1960s is not a favorable one.

What they would not concede, however, is that it must always be thus. A number of writers in this field are pointing to new developments which suggest that science and technology may invent the essential instruments to resolve social problems.

First, they insist that technology can save us from the Malthusian disaster. Increases in industrial and agricultural productivity are indispensable to the alleviation of world poverty and hunger, and these increases will result from several kinds of technological advance. One of these is the prospective availability of abundant cheap energy from nuclear power. This would make economically feasible, even for poor countries, the conversion of sea water into fresh water and of nitrogen in the atmosphere into nitrate fertilizer.[5] It would also facilitate the extraction of minerals from common rock and from the ocean.[6] The second pivotal area of technological advance is that of the electronic computer. The basic capacity of computers has been increasing over the past fifteen years by a factor of ten every two or three years.[7] Together with improvements in input-output devices and other aspects of the total computer system, even a much slower pace of improvement in capacity would justify the description of the computer as "the most basic tool of the last third of the twentieth century."[8] The implications in such fields as education, communications, medicine, transportation, and weather prediction and control are far-reaching; and the increased application of computers to industry in the form of automation will boost productivity tremendously.

[5] Dramatic increases in agricultural productivity are also being achieved by new strains of wheat and other cereals.

[6] Harnessing nuclear fusion would be the best way to accomplish this, but that prospect is still uncertain. However, Alvin M. Weinberg estimates that breeder reactors, applying nuclear fission to nearly inexhaustible supplies of uranium and thorium from granitic rocks, will soon be available to produce all the cheap power the world needs. *Reflections on Big Science* (Cambridge, Mass.: M.I.T. Press, 1967), pp. 22-24.

[7] Herman Kahn and Anthony J. Wiener, *The Year 2000* (New York: The Macmillan Company, 1967), p. 88.

[8] Kahn and Wiener, p. 91.

The other side of the Malthusian nightmare, high birthrates, can also be brought within manageable bounds by technology. It is too late to prevent a very large increase in world population before the end of the century. But the birth control pill and the intrauterine device provide the means to keep the total world population in the year 2000 down to 5.5 to 6 billion, as against the 7 to 7.5 billion indicated by present trends.[9]

Of course, the existence of the technology does not guarantee that it will be adequately utilized. Atomic energy and computers are not easily grafted onto pre-industrial cultures. The production of birth control techniques is much easier than the task of persuading masses of people to use them. Even in highly developed economies, strong cultural resistance inhibits the full utilization of the new technological tools which succeed each other at such breathtaking speed. But in this respect, too, there are scholars who point hopefully to the future, suggesting that perhaps the most important breakthroughs of all will occur in the field of using new technologies for social change. For the first time, says Daniel Bell, we have the possibility of "large-scale 'controlled experiments' in the social sciences," which will enable us "to plot 'alternative futures,' thus greatly increasing the extent to which we can choose and control matters that affect our lives."[10]

In addition to the computer, new tools becoming available both for "controlled experiments" and for application to current social problems include the management technique of operations research and the fiscal control device known as program budgeting. And pulling together all the different kinds of available expertise is the concept of the "systems approach," which attacks complex social problems through a total, integrated plan instead of the fragmented, piecemeal methods prevailing till now.[11]

[9] United Nations Association of the USA, "World Population."

[10] "Notes on the Post-Industrial Society (I)," *The Public Interest*, No. 6 (Winter 1967), p. 30.

[11] The systems approach has been described as essentially the method of common sense, aided by the computer and other technologies for gathering and analyzing information. The process first carefully states goals, next proposes alternative ways of achieving the goals, selects the most promising program, marshalls the necessary data, then finally brings together in a coordinated scheme the combination of men and machines best designed to reach the declared goals.

Moreover, widespread acceptability of the solutions made possible by these various techniques may be increasingly possible. For one thing, as Emmanuel G. Mesthene has argued, at least some of the most angry controversies over public policy "derive from ignorance of information bearing on an issue or from lack of the means to analyze fully the probable consequences of alternative courses of action."[12] To the extent that the computer and the new techniques of engineering and social science can prove what evidence is available and relevant and can set forth alternatives clearly and without prejudice, discussion of problems can be shifted from the area of opinion and ideology to the realm of fact, and a consensus can be more readily achieved.

Then, too, decisions will increasingly be made by men who have scientific or technical training and who are likely to base their decisions on a rational assessment of the available data. Beyond the circle of decision-makers, there will be a growing number of people whose higher education has equipped them to engage in and respond to reasoned analysis. And the new technologies in mass communications and education can play a crucial part in disseminating the findings which emerge from the new tools of analysis. Although an important factor in industrialized countries, this is even more significant in less developed nations, where it can help motivate the masses of people to work toward broader social goals.

All of this adds up to an impressive case. Of course, it is highly speculative. A degree of skepticism about some of the more enthusiastic claims is called for. Not everyone will be happy about the increasing influence of what Dwight Eisenhower called the "scientific-technological elite." And if it is true that improved means of collecting, analyzing, and disseminating information will reduce ideological wrangling, it is also likely that scientific and technological discoveries will generate other issues for impassioned debate.[13]

[12] "How Technology Will Shape the Future," *Science*, Vol. 161 (July 12, 1968), p. 142. Mesthene advances this idea tentatively and recognizes that irrationality, vested interests, and deep-seated value conflicts are not easily eradicated.

[13] Thus, the impending revolution in bio-engineering, making possible the manipulation of human genes, will confront mankind with choices—what kind of people do we want to produce? what characteristics do we want to eliminate?—that could place intolerable burdens on a democratic political system.

Still, we may have little choice but to invest heavily in the social promise of the new technologies. The results may be uncertain and may present new dangers to human values; but perhaps the techniques of the future may repair some of the damage caused by the techniques of the past, and perhaps experience has better equipped us for the dangers to come. Man, after all, is the maker and user of tools; he is symbiotically linked to his technology. Although a few may withdraw into communes in the desert, for most of us there is no escape from technology; our task is to learn how to use it without becoming its slave.

Even if this be true, however, and we decide to risk vast investments in the emerging technologies, one unfortunate difficulty remains. Most of the prospective benefits will not be immediately available. Full development of the plentiful cheap power from nuclear breeders is not here yet.[14] Though economic growth will continue in most of the world, the short-range prospect is that population increases in the less developed countries will absorb most of their gains in productivity, widening the gap between the rich and the poor nations even further. Nor are the social sciences ready now to undertake the kind of large-scale controlled experiments that could lead to fast and impressive results. As for the systems approach, Donald N. Michael points out that we are far from ready to use it;[15] and Simon Ramo, a leading advocate of the systems approach, admits that it may well be a full decade before the method is substantially applied to social problems.[16]

Thus, our difficulties may not be caused solely by the much-discussed problem of cultural lag—the time elapsing before a society can adapt its beliefs and behavior to changed conditions. No less pressing is the task of finding solutions to the puzzle of technological lag—the gap between the first confident claims for a new technique and the fulfillment of

[14] There is also the problem of safely disposing of increasing amounts of nuclear wastes—though Weinberg believes this can be handled.

[15] "We do not at present have the data or the theory to make adequate system models which represent interacting human beings with all of the human characteristics you are familiar with." U. S. Joint Economic Committee, Subcommittee on Urban Affairs, *Urban America: Goals and Problems, Hearings*, 90th Congress, 1st Session, 1967, p. 37.

[16] *Cure for Chaos* (New York: David McKay Co., Inc., 1969), p. 115.

its promise. Consequently, however willing we are to accept the predictions of what technology can do for us and however ready we are to commit our resources to those predictions, salvation is likely to be some distance away. We shall have to face the issues of the 70s with the knowledge that technology will continue to cause more problems than it solves. And we shall have to try to get by as best we can with only modest improvements in the tools available to determine and implement public policy.

Will the American system survive this interim period? Perhaps the inability to solve problems with present methods could build frustrations and hostilities to the point at which our public life disintegrates into chaos. Or, the fear of chaos could provoke authorities to clamp a vise of repression on the American polity. Fortunately there are some developments which suggest a more favorable outcome. The end of the Vietnam war would probably lower the level of tensions. Continuing economic growth will help. And it may be that an increasing proportion of the American electorate—especially its younger, college-educated segment—will refuse to accept the clichés and shibboleths of the past, bringing a new vitality to our political order. Other favorable omens may be gleaned from the various readings in this book. But so will the predictions of further and deepening troubles. Social science cannot prove which of these two trends will prevail. We shall have a clearer view, perhaps, when the second edition of *Issues of the Seventies* appears. Meantime, each reader will have to arrive at his own judgment on the question.

Part One

National Issues

2

Poverty

One of the startling discoveries made by the American people in the 60s was that a considerable amount of crushing poverty existed amidst the burgeoning affluence. Of course, the poor had been there all along, but the middle classes were scarcely aware of their presence. For one thing, the poor lived in a different part of town or region of the country. They were a minority—itself a remarkable accomplishment of the American system, but placing those who remained poor in a position of·social and political isolation. This isolation reinforced the attitudes implicit in what Oscar Lewis has called the "culture of poverty"—a culture or subculture characterized by a sense of inferiority, marginality, dependence, and resignation. The political apathy endemic among the members of this culture seemed to perpetuate the political weakness to which their poverty and minority status condemned them.[1]

Why, then, with the poor so weak politically, did politicians launch a "War on Poverty"? There were a number of reasons. Writers like Michael Harrington, Dwight MacDonald, and Leon Keyserling brought the issue to public

[1] However, there is now considerable debate among scholars as to whether there is a distinctive, deep-rooted, almost universal culture of poverty or rather just certain characteristics, varying from group to group and society to society, which disappear rapidly when economic conditions improve. The latter position leads to a more optimistic view of the prospects for an early end to poverty in America.

attention. Democratic Presidents, in need of activist programs to establish their reputations and build momentum, took up the issue. Black people stopped acquiescing in their poverty, and the emergence of the Negro movement changed the balance of political forces. And economic conditions were favorable; the announcement of the War on Poverty followed on the heels of a tax cut, so the majority could be compassionate without having to pay very much.

How much success was achieved by the Office of Economic Opportunity, the agency charged with the conduct of the anti-poverty war, is still debatable. But high levels of employment and continued economic growth had a major impact on the problem. The proportion of the American people living in poverty fell. Even their absolute numbers declined, and the decline continues.

Consequently, says Norman Macrae, if we continue along the same lines, if we emphasize full employment and high rates of growth, the remaining poverty in America can be all but abolished. It is true, he concedes, that something drastic must be done about the numbers of people on the Aid for Families with Dependent Children (AFDC) program; but the replacement of this system with such new devices as the negative income tax can solve that difficulty. He recognizes that there will be strong resistance to the necessary policies, but he believes that, in time, it can be overcome.

The organizers of the Poor People's Campaign are less sanguine that their demands will be met. And Michael Harrington, revisiting the "other America" which the poor inhabit, is far from optimistic. He agrees that the extent of poverty has declined, but he believes that it is more pervasive than the official figures suggest and that the gains are precarious. He also questions whether the men who control economic and political decisions, inclined to fear inflation more than unemployment, will support the expansionist policies advocated by Macrae.

Harrington also points out that the Vietnam war has taken away the budgetary leeway which made it easy to obtain support for the first stages of the War on Poverty. There are a great many people in America who, while not considered poor, have been squeezed between rising taxes and inflation. Former Under Secretary of Housing and Urban Development Robert C. Wood described the man in this category:

> He is a white employed male ... earning between $5,000 and $10,000. He works regularly, steadily, dependably, wearing a blue

collar or white collar. Yet the frontiers óf his career expectations
have been fixed since he reached the age of thirty-five, when he
found that he had too many obligations, too much family, and
too few skills to match opportunities with aspirations.[2]

This definition of the "working American" involves almost
23 million American families. It is this American, not
educated beyond the high school level but owning his own
home, who is unlikely to support additional government
outlays to help families with less than $3,500 a year.
Candidates on all points of the political spectrum are now
wooing his vote, but Eugene Davidson believes and hopes
that he is tending strongly toward a new conservatism.

Among the social inventions favored by Macrae,
Harrington, and the Poor People's Campaign is some form of
income guarantee or supplement. Many professional economists, as their statement in this chapter makes clear, are
adopting the concept as part of their conventional wisdom.
Henry Hazlitt argues against the guaranteed income and the
negative income tax as being both economically and morally
unsound. President Nixon, however, coming to office as the
apostle of the forgotten American, has proposed to scrap the
existing welfare program and replace it with something that
looks rather like a negative income tax. Some conservatives
are hostile to the proposal, suggesting that it would cost
much more than the $4 billion a year estimated by the
Administration. A number of liberals are critical on the
grounds that the proposed minimum annual payment is only
$1,600 for a family of four; that fully half of the total funds
would go to the South; that the work requirement could be
too easily used to deny payments, especially in the South;
and that there may not be enough jobs available. So the
proposal was bound to be fiercely contested. Yet, a program
emanating from so cautious an Administration, clothed in
such conservative rhetoric, and reflecting a growing consensus
among the experts was likely in time to find acceptance, even
though some changes in its form might occur.

The final essay of this chapter sets the question of
poverty in a broader context. Herbert Gans proposes that the
revolt of the poor against their lot should be seen as part of a
many-sided uprising against all kinds of inequity. If, indeed,
discontent grows among other groups—students, women,
industrial workers—the poor might win allies and escape their

[2] Many of the resentments and anxieties of Wood's "working
Americans" are shared by what columnist Joseph Kraft calls "Middle
America," which includes people in the $9,000 to $15,000 range.

isolation. Thus, the outcry in 1969 against the unfairness of the tax system—which, for example, allowed almost 400 families earning over $100,000 a year to pay no federal income tax at all—indicated that some middle-income people felt they were being victimized by the rich rather than the poor.

Still, Gans is not sure of the outcome. The 70s could bring the last, conclusive effort to abolish poverty in America. Or the forgotten American of whom Davidson writes could refuse to support programs designed for any but his own neglected interests. Much depends on the extent to which the economy expands. For, as several writers in this chapter point out, only with an economy of extraordinary abundance can the political system provide for everybody.

THE ABUNDANT ECONOMY

Norman Macrae

Mr. Macrae is the deputy editor of The Economist *of London. These excerpts are from a series of articles resulting from a visit to the United States in 1969.*

The big story in the United States is the approach to economic consummation. Median family income there is now well over $8,000 a year, and even for oppressed black Americans it is close to $5,500. This last figure contrasts with Britain's average family income in 1967 of $4,414, if one converts at the $2.40 exchange rate. But the really important inheritance from the 1960s is that most informed Americans now appear to be confident that their country knows how to go on expanding its real gross national product by between 3 and 5 per cent per annum compound. In the next 15 years, when the labour force should be expanding by between 1 and 2 per cent a year, they should be able to get an average annual growth in gnp of around or over 4 per cent quite easily. Simply by applying existing technology, sober corporate planners and backroom government projectionists presume that America will be able to push its median family income to about

From "The Neurotic Trillionaire," *The Economist* of London (May 10, 1969, pp. 19, 25, 51, 61-62.

$25,000 a year, in terms of today's prices, by around the turn of the century—say, by about the time that any baby born this week is in the main family-rearing stages of his own working life.

This is not only by far the farthest man has advanced in all his long struggle from unending hunger and toil to the threshold of comfort and leisure. As a definition of arrival at comfort and leisure, it will quite simply do. The trail from here to material sufficiency has therefore been mapped out, and the main job of economists now is to read that map. . . .

The Forgotten Feudalism

. . . I suspect that the United States is one of the few countries where history is very important, chiefly because it has so little of it. You can forget everything about the 1860s. It was in the next three generations that the United States was created, as the great grandfathers and grandfathers and fathers of most of today's leading men swarmed over from Europe in the great migrations. Cries the Statue of Liberty:

> Give me your tired, your poor,
> Your huddled masses, yearning to breathe free.
> The wretched refuse of your teeming shore,
> Send these, the hopeless tempest-tossed, to me.

in one of the finest first examples of brilliantly mendacious American public relations prose the connoisseur could hope to collect. What Europe sent instead was its best inaugurators, men who were to some extent rebelling against a social and economic inferiority which Europe's class system battened down on them, and heavily weighted with those who had enough ability to want to drive on and up.

We know from modern sociology that the influence of the home moulds a child far more closely than the influence of a school; and it is not therefore surprising that so many even of today's Americans are still twitching under the murmur of recent ancestral voices down these two or three bare generations. Those voices have been telling them that, in a land free of European residues of feudalism, all can and should drive forward to get things done—and should then hope in turn to see their children automatically surpass them in education, occupation and prosperity. To this should be added the point (heretical though it sounds to Europeans) that America had until recently a very good way of bringing up children in the home, breeding perky self-reliance; while Europe had a very bad one, expressing parental or class dominance.

The probability is that Europe will now manage to narrow
the gap, partly because Europe really is becoming a progressively less
feudal continent, and partly because of the appearance of two
possible cankers on America's bud. One of these cankers is that the
American Negro has never hitherto been fitted into the American
dream of up-thrusting equal opportunity for all; he has been, as
Dr. James Tobin has put it, "the victim of America's own brand of
feudalism and permitted inferiority." Now that he is rising, the
American people are reacting with extraordinary political inefficiency to this emergence of an old-fashioned European class problem
in their midst. I do not suggest that this is liable to tear the whole
nation permanently apart. As the bumbling old European aristocracy
eventually managed, by a limping process of condescension, concession and reform, to integrate into a more-or-less decent society
the 95 per cent hitherto-oppressed majority called the lower classes,
it seems impossible to believe that the very educated modern
American democracy can really fail eventually to integrate this last
11 per cent minority of its people called blacks. But it does now
seem likely that the present troubles will leave behind them some of
the sediments that class struggles have left behind in European
politics and moods. They have not been particularly useful sediments
in Europe. The main one—the yielding of the left wing in politics
from an attemptedly liberal party to an attemptedly social democratic one—often makes the election of either an anti-innovative or
an inferiority-complexed government more frequent, and by this and
other means impedes growth.

The other possible canker is the new attitude of some of
America's youth. To the horror of old-fashioned Americans, the
universities have recently been reporting a sharp increase among
freshmen students in stated preferences for careers in teaching or
government service, and a decline of interest in careers in business.
This un-American trend is variously attributed by the older generation to the rebelliousness of youth, the fading down the years of
those ancestral voices, or to the fact that this is the first generation
that has been brought up from birth not on the principles of
self-reliance, but on television-watching and the precepts of that
treacherous Dr. Spock. Once again, one doubts whether a whole
course of history will really be changed by this. The most reasonable
and moderate guess is perhaps that among these new generations
there may be some diminution of America's hitherto superbly
successful go-getting mentality—but the diminution is coming at a
time when America has fortunately already nearly gone and got.

Ten years ago, it seemed doubtful whether the United States
would go and get quickly enough. The trouble was that, as has
happened before in American history, its governmental mechanism

for economic affairs seemed to be lagging so far behind the vibrant genius of its people. The great achievements of the 1960s are that this governmental mechanism has been reformed, and that the country has been set on a course of what many optimists now consider to be semi-automated economic expansion. I am inclined half to agree with this: in the sense that I believe that government management of American economic policy is now much more nearly idiot-proof. . . .

The War on Poverty Is Easy

. . . It is a misconception to suppose that the key economic problem for black Americans today is poverty. The key problems are the need for dispersion and the worrying underemployment of young members of the black underclass. By contrast, the war on black poverty should be dead easy to win. That will sound controversial, but fainthearts should look at the figures of incomes—and how they have been changing in recent years.

In 1966, some 28 per cent of the 5 million black American families had incomes of over $7,000 a year, and thus enjoyed a middle class or upper class standard of living by any other nation's standards, and a median standard of living by America's own; the proportion of black American families above this real income level has doubled since 1960. Another 41 per cent of black families had incomes between $3,000 and $7,000 a year; this left them disadvantaged compared with the average white American, but their standards of consumption (as distinct from their environmental jungle) are on a par with those of working class west Europeans. There remains, it is true, the bottom third of non-white families— often the larger ones, containing in 1967 8.3 million people, or 53.3 per cent of black Americans (plus other non-whites, such as American Indians and Eskimos)—who were below the official American definition of the poverty line. In 1966, some 17.6 million white Americans (usually older ones) were also below this poverty line, and they represented 10.2 per cent of the white community.

But two qualifying points should be made straightway. First, America draws its poverty line at levels that would be considered generous abroad. Amid all the sad statistics poured forth about the ghettos, it is worth remembering that in 1967 some 88 per cent of black American families had television sets. The poverty line in America is defined by saying that nobody can be expected to spend more than about a third of his income on food, and then studying the cost of a nutritionally adequate diet of the sort of food that the poor actually eat ("they don't eat grits, they do eat hamburgers, so it's hamburgers that are in," says one official). The result is a calculation that a four-person non-farm family is poor if its annual income is less than $3,335 at 1966 prices of consumer goods, with adjustments made for people who do not happen to belong to four-person non-farm families in fairly obvious proportions.

The second—and even more striking—point is that by 1967 a transfer of only $9.7 billion a year to the poor would have been needed to lift every American above this generously defined poverty line. This amounts to only about a quarter of a single year's normal increase in real gnp. It is rather less than the yield of the 1968 surcharge on income tax—the special tax increase made by President Johnson last year—which Mr. Nixon has recommended should be halved after January 1st next.

Moreover, the war on poverty is not only easy to win. It has been in process of being won during this last decade. The last report of the Democrats' CEA was able to say with justice:

> If the 1961-68 reductions in the number of poor persons could be continued, poverty would be eliminated entirely in about ten years. If the record of 1968 could be continued, poverty would be eliminated in about 5½ years.

It is true that a general rise in prosperity will not be enough to keep up this rate of progress. This is because 59 per cent of poor families are now headed by either women with children, or the disabled, or the elderly—and most of these will need help through some reform of the social services, such as by advance to a negative income tax. But with under $10 billion a year needed to close the entire poverty gap, this reform really is not beyond America's grasp. It is also required by America's conscience. Although the general figures of the war on poverty are comforting, there still remain in this richest country of the world—particularly among the rural Negro poor in the south— some pockets of dreadful malnutrition, which only occasionally emerge into the headlines and manage to shock the nation. . . .

Employment Is the Key

. . . America would be wise in the next decade to give almost an overstrained priority to maximum economic growth and the further expansion of full employment, even though this will mean tolerating more inflation than the middle classes will wish. One can see all the objections. It is easy to say that if one ran the economy for the next ten years at 4 per cent official unemployment instead of 3 per cent, and still aimed at 4 per cent annual growth from there, one should be able to keep price inflation to a tolerable 2 per cent per annum or so; and that the only macro-economic cost of thus bringing inflation down might be this once-for-all reduction of 1 per cent in capacity working—so that, e.g., the country would reach in December of 1980 the level of production that it would otherwise reach in September of 1980. If America had no Negro problem, one would agree that this small price for curbing inflation would be infinitely well worth paying.

But America does have a Negro problem, and nice calculations of this kind therefore miss the whole nasty point. This nasty point is that any rise in unemployment is likely to hit disproportionately hard at militant Negro youth, who already have an underemployment rate far higher than the official unemployment figures suggest and whose numbers are due to rise by 40 per cent in the decade to the mid-1970s. The Kerner report last year defined the typical Negro rioter in 1967 as:

> a teenager or young adult, a lifelong resident of the city in which he rioted, a high school drop-out—but somewhat better educated than his Negro neighbour—and almost invariably underemployed or employed in a menial job. He was proud of his race, extremely hostile to both whites and middle-class Negroes and, though informed about politics, highly distrustful of the political system and of political leaders.

The key points there are "somewhat better educated than his Negro neighbour" and "almost invariably underemployed or employed in a menial job." The first of these points gives the lie to the widespread white American belief that the black unemployed today are the unemployable. The second emphasizes that even the great economic growth of the 1960s has managed to stop short at precisely the point where increased employment is most vital. Unfortunately, however, there is no denying that greater employment of this sub-class would be inflationary; no doubt they would be somewhat less efficient than the average of existing workers, so that marginal costs (and the bargaining power of existing workers) would rise.

If the objection to risking inflation to absorb these people is internal, then objectors should look at the alternatives. If the objection to inflation is its effect on the balance of payments, then America needs to press forward all the more urgently with the projects for greater international liquidity and for more freely floating exchange rates, in which the most progressive men of the Nixon administration in any case believe. It is not wise to say that a one per cent diminution in the annual rate of inflation is well worth purchasing at the cost of letting race war in America blaze.

Negative Income Tax

The second great economic and social need in the United States is the dispersion of population from the ghettos. A major requirement here is to get deserted welfare mothers and their large families out of the city centres, instead of ridiculously saying that they can draw higher benefits only if they stay there. The need is to nationalise the welfare system, replacing it by a negative income tax. . . .

The United States is proving to be fortunate that it is the only major industrial country that is not operating a system of children's allowances. This has allowed American economists, armed as usual with computers, to study dispassionately what would be the most efficient welfare system to have. More and more, expert opinion is agreeing that it would be some version of a negative income tax. Certainly the arguments one commonly hears in Britain—such as that negative or credit income taxes would have a greater disincentive effect than the existing British welfare system, or that it would be difficult to pay a negative income tax save at yearly intervals—are shown by American research to be off target.

Under the simplest proposal (by Earl Rolph and others) every man, woman and child might be entitled to receive, say, $750 a year from the federal government—which, at least in some countries, could presumably be issued in weekly or monthly cheques or whatever—and would then have to pay a tax equal to one-third of income, not including the $750. The result is that any family with an income of under $2,250 a head would actually be getting a net sum from the government: over that figure it would be paying a net tax, but the marginal rate of tax would always be a third, so that there would be no addition of new disincentives. The basic method of payment can be varied in many ways, under proposals ranging from those of the conservative Milton Friedman (which might cost about $3 billion a year) to more ambitious schemes that would lift every American above the officially defined poverty line and help a lot of the near-poor besides (at a cost of about $25 billion a year).

It seems to me that it would be entirely possible—and immensely desirable—for America to move to one of these more ambitious schemes in the next five years. If President Nixon's team aims for rather over 4 per cent per annum real economic growth (risking some price inflation), and if it manages to close down the Vietnam war (which would probably save $20 billion a year, with a four-year lag before full effect), then the ordinary fiscal dividend should allow one of the $25 billion a year schemes to be brought into effect somewhere in the period between 1972 and 1974, even if Mr. Nixon insists on retaining some tax money for more traditionally Republican priorities. . . .

Decline and Fall?

There is no point in pretending that I have great hopes that the policies recommended here will be remotely akin to those followed by any American government in the 1970s. Nothing that has been suggested in this survey is new, but almost every view in it is going rapidly out of fashion. The right wing of America's establishment will say that the expansionist argument gravely underestimates the evil that will be done to the United States if inflationary psychology is allowed to catch hold. The left wing will say there is something beautiful in the fact that black Americans are now imbibing a dose of nationalism and pride in their own race and that the great need is to "keep up a conversation" with those who are being "driven to violence."

The reasons why the United States is proving so bad at handling its fairly normal historical crisis are rooted, I believe, in the fact that it has always been lucky enough to be a predominantly bourgeois-plus-yeoman society. Its right wing has never had reason to reflect, as we in Europe have done, that the awkward stage of history when an indigenous underclass has just been sucked by an industrial revolution into the mess and insecurity of urban society is a stage which it is crucial to dash through at maximum economic pace. America's urban underclass in years past has consisted of the most progressive types of immigrants, chasing upwards after the American dream, in conditions of natural boom which their own energetic arrival has helped to create. Meanwhile, America's left wing does not understand, as we in Europe most grimly learned in Germany and Italy between the wars, that violent nationalism is a heady drug that it is unsafe for an indignant and despairing urban lower middle class to see peddled among its young even in the smallest doses; and it is among the young lower middle class Negroes—not the pure underclass—that the most dangerous figures are now arising. This is another reason why the view of middle class white liberals, that we must hold a conversation with those "driven to violence," seems to me to be essentially lacking in compassion, because those who are really hurt by this are the humble souls who then have to live with violence as a neighbour.

Does this mean that anybody with my views should be desperately worried at the prospects ahead? At times in Washington in February, when apparently sober people told me of the rifles they kept at home "in case trouble comes," I did feel that the most appropriate texts for a reporter on America in 1969 might be found in the story of the decline and fall of another mighty empire that Gibbon started as he wandered round another Capitol. The pertinent, though scattered, phrases seem to abound.

> The decline of Rome was the natural and inevitable effect of immoderate greatness. Prosperity ripened the principle of decay. . . . The most potent and forcible cause of destruction, the domestic hostilities of the Romans themselves. . . . At such a time . . . when none could trust their lives or properties to the impotence of law, the powerful citizens were armed for safety, or offence, against the ˉdomestic enemies whom they feared or hated. . . . The nobles usurped the prerogative of fortifying their houses. . . . It was once proposed to discriminate the slaves by a peculiar habit; but it was justly apprehended that there might be some danger in acquainting them with their own numbers.

They are acquainted with their own numbers in the cities of America in 1969; the rallying symbol is black.

Even on cool reflection, I do not entirely dismiss these dangers. We have seen several times in the last year—for example, in France and Pakistan—the extraordinary pass to which riotous and even unarmed minorities of youth can bring a country. In the United States, where the cohorts of dissatisfied 16- to 25-year-old Negroes in the cities are due to increase so massively in the next few years, it is by no means certain that the rioters will be unarmed. Some time, I suspect, the guns may go blazing. And yet, even as one apprehends this, the point recurs that, according to all public opinion polls and all secret ballot elections, one is talking here about revolutionaries among a tiny minority within the minority of the black oppressed and the emotional young. As the not exactly conservative, but nowadays rather likeable, Mr. Mohammad Ali (ne Cassius Clay) said to a bespectacled television interviewer: "For black people to start shooting in their fight against American society would be as silly as for you to get up and start hitting me."

And perhaps the final antidotes to despair are to go into America's heartland, behind the troubled coasts, where families still sleep at night with all the outside doors of their homes unlocked; or else, within the greatest urban jungle of all, to mount the Empire State building and look on that well-known skyline once again; or (although this sounds a strange place in which to soothe the nerves), to pause once more among the computers of Wall Street. For this after all—and probably in the end above all—is the society in which the last important stage of man's long economic revolution is succeeding. Somehow, in the farthest recesses of one's intellect, where presumably judgment lies, one doubts whether the United States is really liable to lose its foothold on this last, steep, 30 years' climb before the country reaches what all except the most neurotic of the status-afflicted should regard as material sufficiency for all its inhabitants.

DEMANDS OF THE POOR PEOPLE'S CAMPAIGN

The Poor People's Campaign is led by the Southern Christian Leadership Conference, of which Mr. Ralph David Abernathy is President.

Major Unmet Demands of Chapter I, Poor People's Campaign (1968)

1. That hunger in America be eliminated.
2. That the Department of Labor support a jobs bill guaranteeing employment to every person able to work.
3. That a federal standard of welfare be enacted; that the "freeze" on AFDC recipients be repealed and that welfare assistance to unemployed fathers be made mandatory on the states.
4. That federal civil rights statutes covering jobs, schools, housing, hospitals, etc., be vigorously enforced by the Department of Justice.
5. That HUD provide a specific 5-year plan to build low-income housing units and vigorously enforce the 1968 open housing act.
6. That a priority on comprehensive health services for the poor be adopted by HEW.
7. That segregation and discrimination in Department of Agriculture programs be eliminated.

Chapter II Demands

The poor people's campaign (chapter II) makes the following ten demands upon the administration, the Congress and the country on behalf of the black, white, Mexican-American, Puerto-Rican and Indian poor:

1. That hunger be wiped out in America now. All persons with incomes of less than $3,000.00 per year should be provided free food stamps. A minimum of $2½ billion additional monies for fiscal 1970 should be immediately appropriated in order to insure an adequate diet to every needy person.

2. That an adequate Federal standard of welfare be immediately implemented, and that legislation be enacted to guarantee an annual income above the poverty level for every poor person. We also demand immediate repeal of the "freeze" on AFDC recipients and we demand the mandatory adoption by states of welfare assistance to unemployed fathers.

3. That a comprehensive jobs bill be adopted to provide 3 million new jobs in the private and public sectors for the unemployed. We also strongly demand that the federal government effectively enforce Executive Order 11246 and stop spending billions of federal tax dollars annually to foster racial segregation and discrimination through federal contracts.

4. That every poor child be provided a quality education. And that Title I and other education funds be appropriated on an equal basis to white and black, rich and poor. That HEW insure that local school districts comply with Title VI by completely ending the dual school system by the fall of 1969.

5. That the Vietnam war be ended promptly and that rising military expenditures be drastically cut back so that desperately needed funds can be shifted to the crying domestic needs that are tearing this nation apart. We also demand that the projected ABM expenditures be abandoned and that the military draft be changed so as not to discriminate against the poor.

6. That Title VII of the Civil Rights Act of 1964 and the National Labor Relations Act be expanded to cover employment by State and local governments and private non-profit institutions and that the rights of public employees and farm workers be protected by collective bargaining.

7. That full appropriations originally authorized be provided for the Housing and Urban Development Act of 1968, and that a housing trust fund be established which will guarantee a continuous supply of decent housing for the poor and the prompt and orderly reconstruction of our cities and rural areas. That fair housing laws be vigorously implemented to provide true housing choice for the poor and for Americans now deprived of such choice because of skin color or race.

8. That a national health program for the poor be implemented.

9. That 18-year-olds be granted the right to vote.

10. That increases in public assistance benefits and social security benefits be based on the cost of living index. And that fundamental tax reform measures be enacted to redistribute the burden the poor and the non-poor carry under the present discriminatory tax system.

THE OTHER AMERICA REVISITED

Michael Harrington

Mr. Harrington writes for a number of journals and is author of The Other America, Toward a Democratic Left, *and other books.*

The Other America was published in March, 1962. Now, almost seven years later, the condition that book described is objectively not quite as evil as it was; politically and morally, it is worse than ever. For despite a long, federally induced boom and an "unconditional" war on poverty, tens of millions of Americans still live in a social underworld and an even larger number are only one recession, one illness, one accident removed from it.

Ironically, perhaps the most dramatic single breakthrough of the government's anti-poverty effort is the increase in our official knowledge of the needless suffering that we tolerate. President Johnson's program did not achieve full employment for all nor provide impoverished children and aging people with an income but it did generate a tremendous amount of research, seminars, discussions, and even mass-media reports. So, since the poor have become less invisible, for we know they are there, the society has become even more guilty; now it knows its callousness.

Revisiting the other America in 1969 is easier than going there in the late fifties and early sixties. Now Washington has produced some revealing maps of misery. In general, the official figures show some progress in eliminating poverty, but the accomplishment is so modest that one economic downturn would annul it—and the powerful voices urging a calculated increase in unemployment so that the price stability of the affluent can be protected would bring just such a downturn. Even if that does not come to pass, there is a disturbing potential in the other America of 1969 that particularly menaces both the young and the black poor. In looking at these trends statistically, one must remember that, even though

"The Other America Revisited," *The Center Magazine,* a publication of the Center for the Study of Democratic Institutions (January 1969), pp. 36-41.

the definitions and the percentages are much more precise than in 1962, there is an enormous margin of error which usually favors understatement and over-optimism. Not very long ago, the government triumphantly announced that there had been a major decrease in deteriorated housing. Then in the summer of 1967 it turned out that the gains had actually been negligible or even nonexistent; and in the 1968 Report of the Council of Economic Advisers the Administration admitted that housing deterioration in big-city slums had actually increased. These inaccuracies were not the result of a conscious attempt to delude. They were honest mistakes—but they were often seized upon by those who want to minimize the problem of poverty in America.

More generally there is a real invisibility of the poor. The Bureau of the Census has only recently discovered that it had not counted a significant minority of the adult Negro males in the ghetto. Some years before this acknowledgment, Bayard Rustin had told me that there were more blacks in America than the government figured. He pointed out that there were special problems in a place like Harlem—for instance, people doubling-up in apartments, a fair number of individuals who feared any contact with The Man, even with the census-taker—which could lead the professionals to err. I thought that Rustin had created an amateur's fantasy until the hard data began to come in (for instance, the 1967 Manpower Report of the Department of Labor found an "undercount" of twenty per cent of the adult men in the slums). This means that there are several million Americans whose conditions of life are so mercurial that they do not even qualify to be a statistic.

With this understanding that the government's numbers are too sanguine, we should take a closer look at them. One of the most imaginative students of the "poverty line" is Mollie Orshansky of the Department of Health, Education, and Welfare. For some time now rightists, like William F. Buckley, Jr., have tried to discredit concern for the poor by arguing that all of the definitions are totally subjective and relative. There is unquestionably an historic element in the setting of such standards—hungry Americans are certainly better off than starving Indians—but it is Miss Orshansky's merit that she emphasizes the objective determinants of misery in the other America. She takes the Department of Agriculture's low-cost diet plan ($5.90 a week for a four-person family in January, 1964) and the "economy" plan (for "temporary or emergency use when funds are low" at $4.60 a week, or twenty-two cents per meal per person, in January, 1964) and puts them at the center of an imagined budget. Neither diet guarantees adequacy, but if a family falls below them it is certain that they will miss important nutrients.

Miss Orshansky then worked out the rest of the poverty budgets in relation to these food costs. In this way, anyone who falls below the poverty line will have less than a minimum diet for health or, more generally, will have to choose between necessities. (The 1968 Report of the Citizens' Board of Inquiry into Hunger and Malnutrition in the United States concluded that "malnutrition among the poor has risen sharply over the past decade.") Using the Orshansky approach, the Social Security Administration came up with a figure of $3,130 for an urban family of four as the upper limit of impoverishment.

By 1966, the poverty line had risen to $3,335. (While this index went up by nine per cent, the average income of four-person families in America had increased by thirty-seven per cent, so the new criterion meant that the poor had even less of a share of affluence.) As a result, 17.8 per cent of the people were under the line in 1966 as compared to twenty-four per cent in 1959. This statistic allows the celebrators of America to claim that the other America is disappearing at a reasonable rate. It is that claim which I want to challenge here.

There is no point in denying that there has been some progress. We are now in the seventh year of an unprecedented prosperity which was purchased, in considerable measure, with a twenty-billion-dollar tax subsidy that disproportionately favored the rich individuals and corporations. At the same time, the official unemployment figures have been reduced to under four per cent—but have not gone down to the three per cent goal that John F. Kennedy set as the mark of "full employment" when he became President. The first several years of this boom did not aid the unskilled workers and the hard-core unemployed, although eventually a few of the crumbs of good times trickled down to them.

Pride, in short, must be somewhat restrained. The poverty line, is, after all, an artificial, if extremely useful, construct. Miss Orshansky herself has pointed out that millions hover just above the definition (Daniel Patrick Moynihan calls them the "at risk" population). In 1966, there were more than three million families with incomes between $3,000 and $4,000; most of them were not officially classified as poor but all of them were in danger of becoming so with one bad break in the national economy or in their private lives.

Indeed, as Robert C. Wood of the Department of Housing and Urban Development has pointed out, the "average" American who works and earns between $5,000 and $10,000 a year "owes plenty in installment debts on his car and appliances. He finds his tax burden heavy, his neighborhood services poor, his national image tarnished, and his political clout diminishing. This, too, is alienation." And the Bureau of Labor Statistics said that, in late 1966, it took $9,191 a year for a four-person urban family to maintain a "moderate standard of living." If life for the organized, theoretically well-paid working class is still this precarious, one is probably justified in including as well all Americans in 1969 with family incomes (for four, in a city) of less than $5,000 within the magnetic field of poverty. This has explosive implications if the proposal of the top corporate executives to "trade off" an unemployment increase for an inflation decrease are put into action. It also means that the ambiance, if not the precise dimensions, of the other America has changed little since 1962 even though the society has produced unprecedented wealth.

In two particularly tragic cases it is not necessary to speculate about the numbers. The children and the blacks among the poor are worse off than when the war on poverty began. "All told," writes Mollie Orshansky, "even in 1966, after a continued run of prosperity and steadily rising family income, one-fourth of the nation's children were in families living in poverty or hovering just above the poverty line." This fact, of course, has the most disturbing and dangerous implications for the future. On the one hand, poverty more and more becomes a fate because the educational, economic, and social disadvantages of life at the bottom become progressively more damaging; and, on the other hand, the poor still have more children than any other group. Present evidence points to the melancholy conclusion that the twenty-five per cent of the young who are poor, or near-poor, will have large families very much like the ones of which they are now members. If this is true, the current incidence of poverty among children will guarantee that, short of radical political decisions, the next generation in the other America will be even more numerous than this one.

With Negroes, the problem is more a relative position than an absolute increase in indignity, but this is still a politically explosive fact. In 1959 the Social Security Administration fixed the black percentage of the other Americans at twenty-five per cent; by 1966, the proportion had risen to thirty-three per cent. This, of course, still shows that the scandal of poverty actually afflicts more whites than blacks, but it also indicates that discrimination even applies to the rate at which people escape from beneath the poverty line. During these years of prosperity even the worst off of the white Americans have had a special advantage, compared to the Negroes.

It is important to add to this brief survey of the federally certified dimensions of needless economic and social suffering in this country the remarkable "sub-employment" index of the Department of Labor. The index was developed in order to get a more accurate picture of the working—and non-working—lives of people in the slums. Whereas the official definition of unemployment, which currently is fixed at about 3.5 per cent for the nation as a whole, only counts those who are out of work and looking for work, the notion of sub-employment is much more comprehensive. It gives weight to part-time unemployment, to the fact that many people have to toil for poverty wages, to the twenty per cent of the "invisibles" in the slums, and to those who do not look for a job because they are sure they will not find one.

On this basis, the Labor Department discovered sub-employment rates in November, 1966, that ranged from around thirty per cent in the New York ghettos to near fifty per cent in New Orleans. The full significance of this analysis did not become apparent until the winter of 1967 and the report of the National Commission on Civil Disorders. For it was then that the nation learned that the typical rioter was not the least educated, most impoverished, and chronically unemployed citizen of the ghetto. Rather, he was a high-school dropout and a teen-ager and he had worked—but at a menial job. In other words, the frustrations of sub-employment—most particularly of laboring long hard hours without any real hope of advancement—are perhaps more likely to incite a man to violence than the simple despair of having no job at all.

To sum up—by courtesy of the government's card file (and computer tapes) on outrages in this nation—there has been modest progress in the official figures: a drop in the poverty population from twenty-five per cent to around eighteen per cent. Nevertheless, those who crossed the line are still very close to the world of hunger and hovels. There are signs that the present-day children of the poor will become the parents of even poorer children in the immediate future. Black Americans are falling further and further behind the whites. And the sub-employment statistics indicate a depression while the official jobless rates are cited to show that there is full employment.

What of the quality of life among the poor? Here, I think, the reality is more optimistic, but it is very easy to visualize a reversal of the positive trends.

The war on poverty was never more than a skirmish and the provisions for "maximum feasible participation of the poor" were quickly subverted by hysterical mayors. In theory, the country wants the disadvantaged to stand up and fight for their rights as all the immigrant groups did; in practice, we have knocked people down for taking that pious myth seriously. And yet, there has been a significant growth in local insurgency. It was given an impetus, a public legitimacy, by the anti-poverty efforts of recent years. To a degree, then, the other America has become less passive and defeated, more assertive. This is an enormous gain, for it is the psychological precondition for political and economic advance.

In saying this, I do not wish to suggest for a moment that the poor constitute a latter-day proletariat in the socialist sense of the term (a group goaded to solidarity and struggle by the common conditions of working life). Romantics who held such a theory have been shocked by the seemingly low rates of participation in various community elections. The industrial plant, which assembles large groups of people under a single discipline and with similar grievances about wages and working conditions, is very different from a slum. The company and its assembly line provide an institutional spine for union organizers, but in the world of the tenements there is no such unifying experience and people turn upon one another more than they join together. As the President's Crime Commission reported, the main victims of violence by the black poor were the black poor.

Once this crucial point is understood, the militancy of recent years becomes important. In the South, the dramatic struggles of a mass movement in the street have led to the registration of more than a million new black voters. In the ghettos of the North, where the enemies of Negro freedom are more subtle than Governor Wallace and the disintegrative power of poverty more compelling, there have been urban *Jacqueries*, spontaneous, unplanned riots, and the emergence among the ghetto young of a new pride of race. No one knows how deep these organizational efforts go (my impression is that the black militants have still to reach the majority of the black poor in any systematic fashion) and yet there is no doubt that there is more movement and thought and less despairing acceptance of social wrongs.

The Negroes are not alone in their insurgency. In California, some Mexican-Americans have organized economically in unions and exercised powerful political impact during the 1968 Democratic primary. In New York, Puerto Ricans have provided a mass base for unions in hospitals and public employment, and so have Negroes. Throughout the country, there are organizations of mothers on welfare demanding an end to the bureaucratic humiliations that are carefully structured into public assistance in America. And in Appalachia, poor whites have even had some limited success in the struggle against strip mining.

Yet, as I argued at some length in the book, *Toward a Democratic Left*, even if these rebellious movements grow in size and cohesion, even if they reach out to a majority of the poor, they will not be able to transform the society by themselves. Therefore the future of activism in the other America depends, in a considerable measure, upon what the non-poor do. This is certainly true if one thinks in terms of the need to create a vast majority coalition, for only such a movement would be capable of initiating the radical changes that are required if poverty is to be abolished in America. Paradoxically, the more fundamental and thoroughgoing an economic and social program, the more heterogeneous and inclusive must its supporters be. This is a truth not always appreciated by some of the sincerely self-righteous on the American Left. Even more immediately, insurgency among the poor is profoundly affected by the movement of the national economy. This fact leads to some larger generalizations about the dynamic of the other America in 1969.

When the Kennedy Administration began, the poor, with the exception of some Southern Negroes, were largely passive and pessimistic. This was partly a reflection of the daily life of the Eisenhower years: chronic unemployment and recession, official indifference, the invisibility of forty to fifty million people. The blacks made the first breakthrough below the Mason-Dixon line, and under the leadership of Martin Luther King, Jr., a general climate of hope developed. There was even the governmental policy of having the poor participate in the anti-poverty program. The economic and political upswing and the success of the black freedom movement in the South created the base for the beginning of a new spirit in the other America.

But, as that spirit expressed itself in various forms of militant protest, a new period began in 1965. The war in Vietnam began to dominate American domestic politics and the thirty billion dollars or more invested annually in that tragedy precluded any serious attempt at an "unconditional" war on poverty. The modest impact of the new economics was felt at the bottom of the American economy but in every way the tax cut was inversely—and perversely—related to need; the rich got the most benefit and profit, the poor the least. So the demands for change did not end. There was a great danger in this situation and it came to the fore in the Wallace campaign of 1968. When the struggle against poverty was part of a broad strategy of domestic economic expansion, white workers and members of the lower middle class had a certain common interest with blacks and the rest of the other America, even if they did not lose their prejudices. But when, because of Vietnam, the fight against want seemed to take on the aspect of a competition between the have-nots and the have-littles for scarce private and public goods, there were backlashers who feared that their own jobs, homes, and public places were being threatened.

At the beginning of 1969 it is uncertain what the next period will bring. In any case, I have no intention of indulging in prophecy.

But it is not difficult to imagine how certain changes in government policy would affect the other America. If there is an economic downturn, the new activism of the poor—those tentative essays in hope which we have seen—will be turned into despair, most of it passive, some of it dangerously angry. If the talk of "trading off" a little unemployment in return for increased price stability becomes more than talk, and joblessness, as a result, rises to five or six per cent, the extremely modest employment gains of our recent efforts would be abolished and the nation would return to the *status quo ante*, or worse. Up to now, when the private sector has hired marginal workers, even with federal inducements, it has done so only because a relatively tight labor market had made it economically feasible to take a few—a very few—risks on the hard-core jobless; the moment the official unemployment rate hits five per cent it will become economically imperative for corporations to fire those men and women.

This would drastically affect the quality of life in the other America. It would deprive the poor of part of their already meager economic resources (the richer a union, or a community organization, the longer it can strike). It would confirm the suspicion, which is never dispelled in the minds of the poor, that the political order of the larger society is systematically rigged against those in it who are the worst off. And most terrible of all, it would teach those who had dared to be hopeful that America was only kidding and that cynicism is the better part of valor. Under such circumstances, a few would become even more militant; the many would sink back into apathy.

Sometimes, when I contemplate this possibility, I think the leaders of the United States have acted as Trotsky said the German Communists did before the rise of Hitler: they have infuriated all classes and won none. The poor were given promises that were not fulfilled, but the rhetoric made many workers and middle-class people fearful that they were being slighted, and the resulting political standoff alienated many of the most idealistic and active among the young. Politically, the entire society moved to the Right, and in the other America the fifth anniversary of the declaration of the war on poverty was a mockery.

The scenario need not be written this way. It is possible to make the massive planned social investments that would create the setting in which the poor would become more organized and determined to control their own political and economic destiny. But, as 1968 came to an end, the happy beginning was still not very imminent. It is not just that the statistical progress in abolishing poverty has been so modest or that the position of the "at risk" population of impoverished children and of blacks is so precarious and even explosive. It is more than that: there is a very real possibility that the spiritual gains of the poor—their new sense of dignity, their awareness that they need not forever be excluded from the democratic political process—are in danger. Looking back to the other America of 1962, it may be that in the years that have passed since then we have raised up the hopes of the most abused people of this land only in order to knock them down.

THE NEW CONSERVATIVES

Eugene Davidson

Mr. Davidson is the editor of Modern Age, *a quarterly review.*

In the early years of the twentieth century William Graham Sumner wrote an essay which has become far better known by its title than by its content. It was called "The Forgotten Man" and it referred to the part of the nation that uncomplainingly went about its business, paying taxes and bills, doing its job, demanding no handouts or government subsidies either directly or in the form of high tariffs—the people in short who never got into the newspapers or the halls of congress with their petitions and lobbyists, but who carry the charities, the work load, the lame, the halt, and all those in need as well as free loaders and those who live by good deeds and a fast buck. Franklin D. Roosevelt liked the title of the Sumner essay and used it in a speech referring not to the patient citizens Sumner was writing about but to the third of a nation which then in the deep depression he declared to be ill housed, ill clad, and ill fed. In the election of 1968 the phrase was revived again, this time by Mr. Nixon who said it applied to the hard working people of the suburbs, those who joined no television demonstrations, took part in no riots, who presumably mowed their lawns and washed their cars and themselves. Nixon was closer to the original text than Mr. Roosevelt had been

From "The New Conservatives," *Modern Age* (Winter 1968-69), pp. 2-6.

and he was in fact praising a segment of the population that is vastly larger than a suburban habitat would support and that represents in its power and influence a revolutionary change in American life.

The 1968 presidential election made manifest in the combined Nixon-Wallace vote and in shifting emphases in the Democratic party as well a new pattern not only of voting but also of social-economic stratification and habits of thought. What had been for years a seemingly unbreakable alliance of ethnic, racial, and religious minorities, plus labor unions, plus the liberal intellectuals of the media and the universities has been broken into by long dammed up torrents of public sentiment that have swept aside many of the leaders and policies dominant since 1932. It is an *ad hoc* coalition that has replaced this old alliance, a coalition of millions of blue collar workers and Southern agrarians, of people from small towns, clerks, storekeepers, Middle and Far West farmers, employees, enterprisers and pensioners, a vast, partly new middle class that is rapidly becoming for the first time in history the class of a majority of those who have taken pride in being gainfully employed. It is a class that cuts across historical cleavages and symbols of status and color and in its proportion to the population and in its potential influence it may be far more powerful than the massed activists of the Kremlin and Mao Tse-tung. For these are the legions of the wage earners, the working people, the makers, they are the squares, the anti-hippies, the anti-pot and acid heads and millions of them have had it up to here with the give away programs and the burnt offerings of the liberal voodoo. Not all of them have broken with their traditional political allegiances but the yeast of change is in them all.

Although many of them are critical of the Negro, they include Negroes and a respect for Negroes who have joined their ranks. And make no mistake about it, Negroes have joined their ranks in increasing numbers as the opportunity has been open to them. A recent newsreel of a housing development on the outskirts of Cleveland recorded interviews with a number of the Negroes who live in a well-kept suburban middle class section they had created. Their indignation at Mayor Stokes' plan to move slum Negroes out from the city to a government subsidized housing development that would be next to their tidy home sites would have matched any backlashes in Cicero, Illinois or London, England. The interviews were most revealing, one neatly dressed Negro woman said flatly: "We don't want any of those project people in this neighborhood, we've come away from the project by the sweat of our brows, we know what it means to have the handout people at your doorstep." Or words to that effect. These Negroes may still follow the voting habits established during the depression but their sentiments are different now and they too are the unmistakable signs of the new wave, of an artisan middle class that has spread out over the stratifications of the nineteenth century and over the educational gaps that were often more apparent than real, for the children who use the going vocabulary of easy learning with its words like dialogue, communication, power-structure, charismatic, alienation, cultural deprivation, and such are not so much better educated than their parents as they are the parroters of a vocabulary diffused by a swinging technology.

All this is not to be explained in purely economic terms. Many, most in fact, of the rioters in Detroit and Watts were employed, some of them at high wages. The disaffected youth have come from all strata of society; the battle in Chicago was fought far more by the sons and daughters of the conventional middle, middle class people in the suburbs than by the inhabitants of the ghettoes. It is the rich who have been conspicuous among the leaders in the fight for bussing, for integration, for open housing, for increased benefits to the fecund mothers of dependent children. It is also the rich, and the comfortably affluent liberals who, having paraded in the civil rights demonstrations and agitated for all the benefactions of the Great Society from bussing to Black Power, continued to live untouched by them in their personal and domestic life. A few years ago one of my liberal friends, an historian, who was doing research in Germany and slowly making his way back home to the city of Washington, told me he was dreading his return. His children were of school age and most of the liberals he knew—this was in 1962 or 1963—were taking their children out of the Washington public schools, including those who a few years before had been most enthusiastic for integration. And this remark of my historian friend has long since been borne out by the statistics which show that only two or three of the children of members of the House of Representatives or of the Senate now attend Washington public schools which became black far more quickly than the general population of the city as parents voted one way in public and another in private.

An even more striking example of this is to be seen in the behavior of the very rich liberals, especially of those in public life. The Kennedys and Rockefellers have no immediate prospect of being forced by open housing laws to accept Negroes as neighbors or by the policies of school integration to bus their children to a school in the slums. Their passion for the integrated society can be expressed on their own terms and in graceful ways with chosen representatives of any of the races that meet their fancy. Otherwise they are threatened by no invasion of project housing or of people furnished with rent subsidies; their children are not forced into schools where they are regularly chased home at the end of the day by gangs demanding money as has happened day after day in integrated schools in Chicago.

But things are different with the blue collar workers and with the moderately well-off middle classes. Much of what they have in the world's goods and in pride is centered in the house they live in, in their neighborhood. They have fewer options, be they black or white, than the people with the acres of rolling lawns and a wide choice of private boarding or local day schools. It was the way of life of this middle group that was being threatened at every hand by the coercive society of the liberals who told them through the courts and federal and local governments they had better get to like the new era or else. And it may be noted too that the rich and the very affluent were not in the least affected in their standard of living by the costly enterprises of the Great Society. The rich liberals suffered the deprivation of not one trip abroad or one ball less; they were no Lord Buddhas retiring from the fleshpots of the world; no St. Francises or Simone Weils sharing the life of the poor and distressed. However high their pulses beat for the *Lumpenproletariat* and all the dispossessed they made not the slightest move to dispossess themselves. It was the middle class they called on to bear the burden of their welfare state and it was millions of the members of the middle class that said they had had enough.

This enormous middle class is a truly modern phenomenon; more modern than the hippies who in other disguises have long been with us, more modern than the pot and acid heads, for the drug takers too have a long and disorderly history. But for a great class of wage earners to live well, even opulently with short work weeks, the opportunity for a higher education open to them, aided if they have any talent for the higher learning or technology by private corporations that will pay their way; with art, literature, music, theater on their dials or down the street if they want them; this is something the planet has never seen before. Luxuries that a few years ago were available only to a handfull now are taken for granted by the masses who have earned the right to have them. And it was these hard earned material goods that were being defended together with the even more important feeling of having made it, of status, of being a full-fledged citizen who also had the right to say no, to dissent from union leaders, from politicos who had given them little enough choice among all the legislative panaceas and court decisions that had cascaded over their heads. They wanted no more of the facile promises that bigger doses of spending and more welfarism would at long last make it safe to walk on the streets, to use a park or public transportation after dark. They were not on the receiving end of the public cornucopia; it was mainly they who were pouring in the taxes on behalf of a war for which they had no enthusiasm and for the welfare programs they knew were supporting too many people as able to work as they were. Their revolt was based on a revulsion against the collapsed liberalism that has been dominant over so many decades far more than it was a crusade for a new politics, a new society, or the call of new leadership toward a transcendent order.

The conservative alliance is a loose conglomerate of many factions, sentiments, and beliefs. Like many other mass movements it is mainly an alliance against something, a repudiation of measures that have not worked and could not work, a denial of the proposition once overwhelmingly agreed upon that it is the state that should provide, the state that must create the great and good society, and the conviction that if enough money is shoveled out on the public sector we may have it. The fallacies in these arguments have been long exposed in a few places; in a few, very few universities, in scattered publications, by a relatively few economists, and still fewer social scientists and writers. The overwhelming majority of these pundits were on the other side but they too have been disenchanted, many of them, and from their advance guard curiously enough have come recently the most vehement denunciations of the facile liberal formulations of the last years. Some of these disillusioned liberals have joined this precarious conservative coalition, but only a few because it is always the intellectuals who are most reluctant to give up their prejudices or to admit that they exist. . . .

This middle class of the new conservatives may not be cast in a heroic mold. It has engaged in no Long Marches nor does it aspire to, nor in fact did those who followed and fought with Mao over the six thousand miles of the March want to do that either. It could be that the heroic demands of the modern world are of another order although these people too may be called on to fight and die as they have been before in the recurring wars in Europe and the Far East. But another kind of virtue may be needed to live and do one's job in this world of the Great Technology—it may demand above all the ability to participate in the automated society as its master with something more, much more than the satisfaction of spiralling material wants as the goal to be sought. The United States continues to be the leading power among those who keep communist imperialism from further conquests, the crisis of the cities and of other enclaves of poverty has still to be met, the plight of the *Lumpenproletariat* to be dealt with, and aid afforded to those who cannot provide adequately for themselves without depriving these recipients of the incentives and means for climbing out of their dependency. . . . This middle class conservatism is basically a reaffirmation that a society is made not by government but by its people and its institutions and that the individual not the government is responsible for his actions, that it is to his own efforts he must turn and that law and order must invoke the sanction of force when the other sanctions fail and the burnings begin. But whether this loose coalition will provide more than a stop gap against the forces set in motion in this century under the banners of the Left will depend on the fortitude and integrity with which it proceeds. It is one kind of victory to take over from a specious liberalism; it will need more than the notion that what is good for General Motors is good for the United States to go on from here.

ECONOMISTS FOR INCOME GUARANTEES

The sponsors of this statement were John K. Galbraith, Robert Lampman, Paul A. Samuelson, James Tobin, and Harold Watts. More than 200 economists at 143 institutions of higher learning endorsed the statement (June 1968).

The undersigned economists urge the Congress to adopt this year a national system of income guarantees and supplements.

The Poor People's Campaign in Washington is demanding a guaranteed minimum income for all Americans. The Kerner Commission on Civil Disorders called for a national system of income supplements. A group of business leaders recently advocated a "negative income tax." These proposals are all similar in design and purpose.

Like all civilized nations in the twentieth century, this country has long recognized a public responsibility for the living standards of its citizens. Yet our present programs of public assistance and social insurance exclude millions who are in need and meet inadequately the needs of millions more. All too often these programs unnecessarily penalize work and thrift and discourage the building of stable families.

The country will not have met its responsibility until everyone in the nation is assured an income no less than the officially recognized definition of poverty. A workable and equitable plan of income guarantees and supplements must have the following features: (1) Need, as objectively measured by income and family size, should be the sole basis of determining payment to which an individual and/or family is entitled. (2) To provide incentive to work, save and train for better jobs, payments to families who earn income should be reduced by only a fraction of their earnings.

Practical and detailed proposals meeting these requirements have been suggested by individual sponsors of this statement and by others. The costs of such plans are substantial but well within the nation's economic and fiscal capacity.

As economists we offer the professional opinion that income guarantees and supplements are feasible and compatible with our economic system. As citizens we feel strongly that the time for action is now.

FALLACIES OF THE GUARANTEED INCOME

Henry Hazlitt

Mr. Hazlitt is the author of several books, mainly on economics. He was formerly a Newsweek *correspondent and an editorial writer for the* New York Times; *currently he writes a weekly newspaper column.*

. . . Proposals for a guaranteed income have differed regarding what the exact amount should be. The general range suggested has been between $3,000 and $5,000 for a family of four. A social security board estimate has fixed the minimum "poverty line" figure at $3,335 a year for such a family. Several guaranteed-income proposals have adopted this figure as the standard.

The first thing to be said about this scheme economically is that if it were put into effect it would not only be enormously expensive to the taxpayers who are forced to support it, but that it

Statement before the Subcommittee on Fiscal Policy of the Joint Economic Committee, Congress of the United States, *Hearings on Income Maintenance Programs*, 90th Congress, 2nd Session, June 1968, Volume I, pp. 302-305.

would destroy the incentive to work and production on an unparalleled scale. As one commentator has put it: "Those who believe that men will want to work whether they have to or not seem to have lived sheltered lives."

Who, in fact, let us ask ourselves, would be willing to take the smelly jobs, or any low-paid job, once the guaranteed income program is in effect? The guaranteed-income sponsors propose to pay, say, $3,300 to a family without any income, but to families already earning some income they would pay only the supplementary sum necessary to bring the total up to $3,300.

Now, suppose, say, that you are a married man with two children, and your present income from some nasty and irregular work is $2,800 a year. The government would then send you a check for $500. But it would soon occur to you that though you now had $3,300, you could have got this $3,300 anyhow without doing a stroke of work. You would conclude that you would be very foolish to go on working at your nasty job or series of odd jobs for $2,800 when you could get $3,300 without doing any work at all.

So the 30 million population now judged to be below the poverty line would stop producing even most of the goods and services that it is producing now.

The money cost of the guarantee, of course, would be enormously greater than any of its sponsors calculate, because these sponsors all assume that those who are getting less than the guaranteed income of $3,000 or $4,000 would nonetheless continue to work for the smaller incomes that they are already earning.

Not only would the scheme destroy the central incentive to work, not only would it drastically undermine even the incentives of those earning more than the $3,300 guarantee—because of the heavy taxes imposed on them to pay the guarantee—but the scheme is indefensible on grounds of fairness and equity. . . .

. . . The Government has nothing to give to anybody that it doesn't first take from someone else. The whole guaranteed-income proposal is a perfect modern example of the shrewd observation of the French economist Bastiat more than a century ago: "The state is the great fiction by which everybody tries to live at the expense of everybody else."

None of the guaranteed-income advocates explicitly recognize that real "income" is not paper money that can be printed at will, but goods and services, and that somebody has to produce these goods and services by hard work. The proposition of the guaranteed-income advocates, in plain words, is that the people who work must be taxed to support not only the people who can't work but the people who won't work. . . .

This is an inequitable and immoral proposition. It is also self-defeating. Any attempt to enforce it would destroy incentives and gravely diminish the amount of wealth and income produced. There would be less for everybody. There would be a smaller pie to divide among everybody.

I should like now to turn to the so-called negative income tax. This seems to me a misleading name for what should more accurately be called a tapered-off guaranteed income. The negative income tax tries to escape the complete destruction of the monetary incentive to work implicit in the straight guaranteed income. But it merely jumps out of the frying pan into the fire.

Under the negative income tax, a man or a family would receive from the Government a subsidy of 50 percent, say, of the amount by which the family income fell below the so-called poverty line of, say, $3,300 a year. This means that if the family had no income at all it would receive a subsidy of $1,650. If it already had an earned income of $1,650, it would receive a Government subsidy of $825. If it already had an earned income of $3,000, it would receive a subsidy of only $150, and so on.

To put the matter another way, instead of taxing the subsidized family's self-earnings 100 percent, like the guaranteed income proposal, the negative income tax would tax them only 50 percent.

I fully agree that a subsidy calculated in this way—that is, one that would be reduced by only $1 for every $2 additional that the recipient was able to earn for himself—would not be as completely destructive of incentives as the type of subsidy under which it would be pointless for the recipient to earn more on his own account. In fact, some 30 years ago I put forward a similar proposal myself . . . What I suggested was a relief payment that would be reduced by only $1 for every $2 of self-earnings by the relief recipient.

I abandoned that proposal, however, shortly afterward when I came to recognize that it led into a serious dilemma. This is precisely the dilemma of the negative income tax. Either it is quite inadequate at the lower end of the scale of self-earnings or it is unjustifiably excessive at the higher end.

The problem that the negative income tax evades is the problem of the individual or family with zero income. If that family gets only $300, the figure suggested in Prof. Milton Friedman's original proposal in 1962, nobody would regard this as nearly adequate—particularly if, as Professor Friedman also proposed, negative income tax were made a complete substitute for all other forms of relief and welfare. If the negative income tax payment for a family of zero income is set at $1,650, no advocate of the guaranteed income would regard it as adequate to live on in decency and dignity. So if the negative income tax were ever adopted, the political pressure would be irresistible to make it provide the minimum "poverty line" income of $3,300.

The basic subsidy would therefore be as great as under the guaranteed income. But if it were, then under negative income tax families would continue to get some Government subsidy until their incomes reached $6,600. But this is higher than the median family income for the whole country in 1963. In brief, this would be fantastically expensive.

In addition, it would raise serious problems of equity. When the subsidized family was earning $6,598 income it would still be getting a $1 subsidy. When it earned $6,602 would it fall off the gravy train entirely, and have to wait until its income fell below $3,300 before it could get on again? And what about the family that was earning $3,302 all along, and had never got on the gravy train?

Both the straight guaranteed income and its tapered-off form known as the negative income tax are attempts to escape the allegedly humiliating and administratively troublesome means test. But if the Government wishes to protect itself from massive chiseling and swindling, under any giveaway program, it cannot avoid a conscientious investigation case by case, and applicant by applicant. The guaranteed income and negative income tax proposals do not solve the administrative problem; they simply shut their eyes to it.

The guaranteed income and negative income tax are proposed by some of their sponsors as a complete substitute for all existing forms of relief and welfare. But does anyone seriously believe the present beneficiaries of social security benefits, or unemployment benefits, or medicare, or veterans' benefits, or training programs, or educational grants, or farm subsidies, are going to give up what they have already gained? The new handouts would simply be piled on top of everything else.

The welfare bill is already staggering. Federal aid to the poor, under that official label, has risen from $9.5 billion in 1960 to $27.7 billion in the fiscal year 1969. But if we add up all the welfare payments in the 1969 budget—farm subsidies, housing and community development, health, labor, and welfare, education, and veterans' benefits, we get an annual total in excess of $68 billion. Even this is not all. We must add a social welfare burden on the States and localities of more than $41 billion, making a grand total of $110 billion. This load has already brought not only very burdensome taxation, but chronic deficits and inflation that are undermining the value and integrity of the dollar and bringing social insecurity for all of us.

I have talked here only of what should not be done, and have left myself no time to discuss what should be done. But if I may take the liberty of stating, as I see it, the problem that faces your distinguished committee—I should put it this way: How can the Government mitigate the penalities of failure and misfortune without undermining the incentives to effort and success? I do not wish to underrate the importance of the first half of this problem, but it seems to me that the second half deserves much more earnest attention than it has recently received.

A NEW FAMILY ASSISTANCE SYSTEM

Richard M. Nixon

. . .Whether measured by the anguish of the poor themselves, or by the drastically mounting burden on the taxpayer, the present welfare system has to be judged a colossal failure.

Our states and cities find themselves sinking in a welfare quagmire, as case-loads increase, as costs escalate, and as the welfare system stagnates enterprise and perpetuates dependency. What began on a small scale in the depression 30s has become a monster in the prosperous 60s. The tragedy is not only that it is bringing states and cities to the brink of financial disaster, but also that it is failing to meet the elementary human, social and financial needs of the poor.

It breaks up homes. It often penalizes work. It robs recipients of dignity. And it grows.

Benefit levels are grossly unequal—for a mother with three children, they range from an average of $263 a month in one state, down to an average of $39 in another state. So great an inequality is wrong; no child is "worth" more in one state than in another. One result of this inequality is to lure thousands more into already overcrowded inner cities, as unprepared for city life as they are for city jobs.

From the text of President Nixon's speech on welfare and other domestic matters, August 1969.

The present system creates an incentive for desertion. In most states, a family is denied welfare payments if a father is present— even though he is unable to support his family. In practice, this is what often happens: a father is unable to find a job at all, or one that will support his children. To make the children eligible for welfare, he leaves home—and the children are denied the authority, the discipline and the love that come with having a father in the house. This is wrong.

The present system often makes it possible to receive more money on welfare than on a low-paying job. This creates an incentive not to work; it also is unfair to the working poor. It is morally wrong for a family that is working to try to make ends meet to receive less than the family across the street on welfare. This has been bitterly resented by the man who works, and rightly so— the rewards are just the opposite of what they should be. Its effect is to draw people off payrolls and onto welfare rolls—just the opposite of what government should be doing. To put it bluntly and simply—any system which makes it more profitable for a man not to work than to work, and which encourages a man to desert his family rather than stay with his family, is wrong and indefensible.

We cannot simply ignore the failures of welfare, or expect them to go away. In the past eight years, three million more people have been added to the welfare rolls—all in a period of low unemployment. If the present trend continues, another 4 million will have joined the welfare rolls by 1975. The financial cost will be crushing; the human cost will be suffocating.

I propose that we abolish the present welfare system and adopt in its place a new family assistance system. Initially, this new system would cost more than welfare. But unlike welfare, it is designed to correct the condition it deals with and thus to lessen the long-range burden.

Under this plan, the so-called "adult categories" of aid— aid to the aged, the blind and disabled—would be continued, and a national minimum standard for benefits would be set, with the federal government contributing to its cost and also sharing the cost of additional state payments above that amount. But the program now called "Aid to Families with Dependent Children"—the program we normally think of when we think of "welfare"— would be done away with completely. The new family assistance system I propose in its place rests essentially on three principles: equality of treatment, a work requirement and a work incentive.

Its benefits would go to the working poor, as well as the nonworking; to families with dependent children headed by a father, as well as to those headed by a mother; and a basic federal minimum would be provided, the same in every state.

I propose that the federal government build a foundation under the income of every American family with dependent children that cannot care for itself—wherever in America that family may live.

For a family of four now on welfare, with no outside income, the basic federal payment would be $1,600 a year. States could add to that amount and most would do so. In no case would anyone's present level of benefits be lowered. At the same time, this foundation would be one on which the family itself could build. Outside earnings would be encouraged, not discouraged. The new worker could keep the first $60 a month of outside earnings with no reduction in his benefits, and beyond that his benefits would be reduced by only 50 cents for each dollar earned.

By the same token, a family head already employed at low wages could get a family assistance supplement; those who work would no longer be discriminated against. A family of five in which the father earns $2,000 a year—which is the hard fact of life for many families—would get family assistance payments of $1,260 for a total income of $3,600. A family of seven earning $3,000 a year would have its income raised to $4,360.

Thus, for the first time, the government would recognize that it has no less of an obligation to the working poor than to the nonworking poor; and for the first time, benefits would be scaled in such a way that it would always pay to work.

With such incentives, most recipients who can work will want to work. This is part of the American character.

But what of the others—those who can work but choose not to?

The answer is very simple.

Under this proposal, everyone who accepts benefits must also accept work or training provided suitable jobs are available either locally or at some distance if transportation is provided. The only exceptions would be those unable to work, and mothers of preschool children. Even mothers of preschool children, however, would have the opportunity to work—because I am also proposing along with this a major expansion of day-care centers to make it possible for mothers to take jobs by which they can support themselves and their children.

This national floor income for working or dependent families is not a "guaranteed income." Under the guaranteed income proposal, everyone would be assured a minimum income, regardless of how much he was capable of earning, regardless of what his need was, regardless of whether or not he was willing to work.

During the presidential campaign last year I opposed such a plan. I oppose it now, and will continue to oppose it. A guaranteed income would undermine the incentive to work; the family assistance plan increases the incentive to work. A guaranteed income establishes a right without responsibilities; family assistance recognizes a need and establishes a responsibility. It provides help to those in need, and in turn requires that those who receive help work to the extent of their capabilities. There is no reason why one person should be taxed so that another can choose to live idly.

In states that now have benefit levels above the federal floor, family assistance would help ease the states' financial burdens. But in 20 states—those in which poverty is most widespread—the new federal-floor would be above present average benefit levels, and would mean a leap upward for many thousands of families that cannot care for themselves. . . .

THE "EQUALITY" REVOLUTION

Herbert J. Gans

Dr. Gans is Professor of Sociology and Planning, Department of Urban Studies and Planning at the Massachusetts Institute of Technology.

Someday, when historians write about the nineteen-sixties, they may describe them as the years in which America rediscovered the poverty still in its midst and in which social protest, ranging from demonstrations to violent uprisings, reappeared on the American scene. But the historians may also note a curious fact, that the social protest of the sixties has very little to do with poverty. Most of the demonstrators and marchers who followed Martin Luther King were not poor; the college students who have been protesting and sitting-in on campus are well-to-do, and even the participants in the ghetto uprisings of the last few years—although hardly affluent—were not drawn from the poorest sectors of the ghetto.

The social protest of the nineteen-sixties has to do with *inequality*, with the pervasive inequities remaining in American life. So far the demand for greater equality has come largely from the young and the black, but I wish to suggest that in the years to come, America will face a demand for more equality in various aspects of life from many other types of citizens—a demand so pervasive that it might well be described as the "equality revolution."

This demand will take many forms. Some will ask for *equality*, pure and simple; others will press for more *democracy*, for greater participation in and responsiveness by their places of work and their governments; yet others will ask for more *autonomy*, for the freedom to be what they want to be and to choose how they will live. All these demands add up to a desire for greater control over one's life, requiring the reduction of the many inequities—economic, political and social—that now prevent people from determining how they will spend their short time on this earth.

Ever since the Declaration of Independence decreed that all men are created equal, Americans have generally believed that they were or could be equal. Of course, the Constitution argued by omission that slaves were unequal, and we all know that many other inequities exist in America. Undoubtedly, the most serious of these is economic.

About a fifth of the country lives on incomes below the so-called Federal "poverty line" of $3,300 for an urban family of four, and the proportion is higher if the population not counted by the last census (14 per cent of all Negro males, for example) is included. An additional 7 per cent of households, earning between $3,300 and $4,300 a year, are considered "near poor" by the Social Security Administration. Altogether, then, probably about a third of the country is living at or below the barest subsistence level—and about two-thirds of this population is white.

Moreover, despite the conventional description of America as an affluent society, few of its citizens actually enjoy affluence. The Bureau of Labor Statistics estimates that an urban family of four needs $9,376 a year (and more than $10,000 in New York City) for a "modest but adequate standard of living"; but in 1966, 69 per cent of American families with two children were earning less than $10,000. (Their median income was $7,945, although a recent City University study showed the median income of New York families in 1966 to be only $6,684—and those of Negroes and Puerto Ricans to be $4,754 and $3,949 respectively.)

Even $9,400 is hardly a comfortable income, and it is fair to say that today the affluent society includes only the 9 per cent of Americans who earn more than $15,000 a year. Everyone else still worries about how to make ends meet, particularly since the standards of the good life have shot up tremendously in the last two decades.

Of course, income levels have also risen in the last 20 years, and an income of $9,400 would classify anyone as rich in most countries. Even the earnings of America's poor would constitute affluence in a country like India. But comparisons with the past and with other countries are irrelevant; people do not live and spend in the past or in other countries, and what they earn must be evaluated in terms of the needs and wants identified as desirable by the mass media and the rest of American culture. Undoubtedly an advertising man or a college professor who earns $15,000 is in the richest 1 per cent of all the people who ever lived, but this fact does not pay his mortgage or send his children to school. And if *he* has economic problems, they are a thousand times greater for the poor, who have much the same wants and hopes, but must make do with $3,000 a year or less.

The extent of economic inequality is also indicated by the fact that the richest 5 per cent of Americans earn 20 per cent of the nation's income; but the bottom 20 per cent earn only 5 per cent of the income. Although this distribution has improved immeasurably since America's beginnings,[1] it has not changed significantly since the nineteen-thirties. In other words, the degree of economic inequality has not been affected by the over-all increase in incomes or in gross national product during and after World War II.

There are other kinds of economic inequality in America as well. For example, most good jobs today require at least a bachelor's degree, but many families still cannot afford to send their children to college, even if they are not poor. Job security is also distributed unequally. College professors have tenure and are assured of life-time jobs; professionals and white-collar workers earn salaries and are rarely laid off, even in depressions; factory workers, service workers and migrant farm laborers are still paid by the hour, and those not unionized can be laid off at a moment's notice.

Economic inequality goes far beyond income and job security, however. Some executives and white-collar workers have a say in how their work is to be done, but most workers can be fired for talking back to the boss (and are then ineligible for unemployment compensation). Generally speaking, most work places, whether they are offices or factories, are run on an autocratic basis; the employee is inherently unequal and has no more right to determine

[1] For example, University of Michigan historian Sam Warner reports in "The Private City" that among the minority of Philadelphians affluent enough to pay taxes in 1774, 10 per cent owned 89 per cent of the taxable property.

his work, working conditions or the policy of his work place than the enlisted man in the Army. He is only a cog in a large machine, and he has about as much influence in deciding what he will do as a cog in a machine. Our schools are similarly autocratic; neither in college nor in elementary and high school do students have any significant rights in the classroom; they are unequal citizens who must obey the teacher if they are to graduate.

The poor suffer most from these inequalities, of course. They hold the least secure jobs; they are least often union members; if they are on welfare, they can be made penniless by displeasing the social workers in charge of their cases. And being poor, they pay more for everything. It is well known that they pay more for food (sometimes even at supermarkets) and for furniture and other consumer goods; they also pay more for hospital care, as a recent study in New Haven indicates. They even pay more when they gamble. Affluent Americans can gamble in the stock market, where it is difficult to lose a lot of money except in the wildest speculation. The poor can afford only to play the numbers, where the chance of a "hit" is about 1 in 600, and if they prefer not to participate in an illegal activity, they can play the New York State Lottery, where the chance of winning is only about 1 in 4,000. Political inequality is rampant, too. Although the Supreme Court's one-man, one-vote decision will eventually result in voting equality, the individuals who contribute to a candidate's election campaign will have far more political influence than others.

Ordinary citizens have few rights in actual practice; how many can afford to argue with policemen, or hire good lawyers to argue their cases, or make their voices heard when talking to their elected representatives? . . . Rank-and-file delegates (including those named by political bosses or rigged state conventions) have little say in the choosing of Presidential candidates or platforms. Even the person who is included in a sample of the now-so-important public-opinion polls cannot state his opinion if the pollster's questions are loaded or incorrectly worded.

Finally, there are many kinds of inequality, autocracy and lack of autonomy of which most Americans are not even aware. In many cities, for instance, high-speed mass-transit lines rarely serve poorer neighborhoods and really good doctors and lawyers are available only to the wealthy. Rich or poor, not many people have a say in the choice of TV programs they are shown or in the rates they are charged by electric companies; and who can escape from the poisons in the air?

In a large and complex society, inequality and the lack of control over one's life are pervasive and are often thought to be inevitable byproducts of modernity and affluence. We are learning, however, that they are not inevitable—that there can be more equality, democracy and autonomy if enough people want them.

In the past, when most people earned just enough to "get by," they were interested mainly in higher incomes and did not concern themselves with equality or autonomy in their everyday lives. For example, the poor took—and still will take—any jobs they could get because they needed the money to pay for the week's food and the month's rent. Working-class and lower-middle-class people were, and are, only slightly more able to choose; they take whatever job will provide the most comfortable lives for themselves and their families. But in the upper-middle class, the job is expected to offer personal satisfactions, and upper-middle-class people gravitate to the jobs and careers that provide more equality and autonomy. The huge increase in graduate-school enrollments suggests that many college students want the personal freedom available in an academic career; their decreasing interest in business careers indicates that they may be rejecting the autocracy and lack of autonomy found in many large corporations.

Today, as more people approach the kind of economic security already found in the affluent upper-middle class, they are beginning to think about the noneconomic satisfactions of the job and of the rest of life; as a result, aspirations for more equality, democracy and autonomy are rising all over America.

Some manifestations of "the equality revolution" are making headlines today, particularly among students and blacks. Whatever the proximate causes of college protests and uprisings, the students who participate in them agree on two demands: the right to be treated as adults—and therefore as equals—and the right to participate in the governing of their schools. Though the mass media have paid most attention to the more radical advocates of these demands, equality and democracy are sought not just by the Students for a Democratic Society but by an ever-increasing number of liberal and even conservative students as well.

Similar demands for equality and democracy are being voiced by the young people of the ghetto. Only a few years ago, they seemed to want integration, the right to become part of the white community. Today, recognizing that white America offered integration to only a token few and required with it assimilation into the white majority, the young blacks are asking for equality instead. When they say that black is beautiful, they are really saying that black is equal to white; when the ghetto demands control of its institutions, it asks for the right to have the same control that many white neighborhoods have long had.

And although the call for "participatory democracy" is voiced mainly by young people of affluent origins in the New Left, a parallel demand is manifesting itself among the young blue-collar supporters of Governor Wallace. What they are saying, in effect, is that they are tired of being represented by middle-class politicians; they want a President who will allow the working class to participate in the running of the Federal Government and will get rid of the upper-middle-class professionals who have long dominated the formulation of public policies, the people whom the Governor calls "pseudo-intellectuals."

Many other instances of the equality revolution are less visible, and some have not made the headlines. For example, in the last two generations, wives have achieved near equality in the family, at least in the middle class; they now divide the housework with their husbands and share the decision-making about family expenditures and other activities. Today, this revolution is being extended to the sexual relationship. Gone is the day when women were passive vessels for men's sexual demands; they are achieving the right to enjoy sexual intercourse.

Children have also obtained greater equality and democracy. In many American families, adolescents are now free from adult interference in their leisure-time activities and their sexual explorations, and even preteens are asking to be allowed their own "youth culture."

Man's relationship to God and the church is moving toward greater equality, too. The minister is no longer a theological father; in many synagogues and Protestant churches, he has become the servant of his congregation, and the unwillingness of many Catholics to abide by the Pope's dictates on birth control hides other, less publicized, instances of the rejection of dogma that is handed down from on high. The real meaning of the "God is Dead" movement, I believe, is that the old conception of God as the infallible autocrat has been rejected.

In the years to come, the demand for more equality, democracy and autonomy is likely to spread to many other aspects of life. Already, some high school students are beginning to demand the same rights for which college students are organizing, and recipients of public welfare are joining together to put an end to the autocratic fashion in which their payments are given to them. Public employees are striking for better working conditions as well as for higher wages; teachers are demanding more freedom in the classroom and—in New York—the right to teach where they choose; social workers want more autonomy in aiding their clients, and policemen seek the right to do their jobs as they see fit, immune from what they call "political interference." The right of the individual to determine his job is the hallmark of the professional, and eventually many workers will seek the privileges of professionalism whether or not they are professional in terms of skills.

Eventually, the equality revolution may also come to the large corporations and government agencies in which more and more people are working. One can foresee the day when blue-collar and white-collar workers demand a share of the profits and some voice in the running of the corporations.

Similar changes can be expected in the local community. Although the exodus to suburbia took place primarily because people sought better homes and neighborhoods, they also wanted the ability to obtain greater control over governmental institutions. In the last 20 years, the new suburbanites have overthrown many of the rural political machines that used to run the suburbs, establishing governments that were responsive to their demands for low taxes and the exclusion of poorer newcomers. In the future, this transformation may spread to the cities as well, with decentralized political institutions that respond to the wants of the neighborhood replacing the highly centralized urban machines. New York's current struggle over school decentralization is only a harbinger of things to come.

Consumer behavior will also undergo change. The ever-increasing diversity of consumer goods represents a demand for more cultural democracy on the part of purchasers, and the day may come when some people will establish consumer unions and cooperatives to provide themselves with goods and services not offered by large manufacturers. Television viewers may unite to demand different and perhaps even better TV programs and to support the creation of UHF channels that produce the types of quality and minority programming the big networks cannot offer.

It is even possible that a form of "hippie" culture will become more popular in the future. Although the Haight-Ashbury and East Village hippies have degenerated into an often-suicidal drug culture, there are positive themes in hippiedom that may become more acceptable if the workweek shrinks and affluence becomes more universal; for example: the rejection of the rat race, the belief in self-expression as the main purpose of life, the desire for a more communal form of living and even the idea of drug use as a way to self-understanding. In any case, there is no reason to doubt that many people will want to take advantage of a "square" form of the leisurely hippie existence—now available only to old people and called retirement—while they are still young or middle-aged. This day is far off, and by then marijuana is likely to have achieved equality with liquor as America's major elixir for temporary escape from reality and inhibition.

These observations suggest that the future will bring many kinds of change to America, producing new ideas that question beliefs and values thought to be sacrosanct. Who, for example, imagined a few years ago that the ghetto would reject the traditional goal of integration or that college students would rise up against their faculties and administrations to demand equal rights? Thus, nobody should be surprised if in the next few years adolescents organize for more freedom in their high schools or journalists decide that their editors have too much power over their work.

These demands for change will, of course, be fought bitterly; protests will be met by backlash and new ideas will be resisted by old ideologies.

Today many argue that college students are still children and should not be given a voice in college administration, just as many say that women do not really need orgasms or that men who help their wives at home are becoming effeminate. Undoubtedly, the defenders of outmoded traditions will argue sincerely and with some facts and logic on their side, but processes of social change have little to do with sincerity, facts or logic. When people become dissatisfied with what they have and demand something better they cannot be deterred by facts or logic, and the repression of new ideas and new modes of behavior is effective only in the very short run.

But perhaps the most intense struggle between new ideas and old ideologies will take place over America's political philosophy, for a fundamental change is taking place in the values which guide us as a nation. In a little-noticed portion of the "Moynihan Report," Daniel P. Moynihan pointed out that the civil rights struggle, which had previously emphasized the achievement of liberty, particularly political liberty from Jim Crow laws, would soon shift to the attainment of equality, which would allow the "distribution of achievements among Negroes roughly comparable to that of whites."

Moynihan's prediction was uncannily accurate with respect to the civil rights struggle, and I would argue, as he does, that it will soon extend to many other struggles as well and that the traditional belief in liberty will be complemented and challenged by a newly widespread belief in the desirability of equality.

Since America became a nation, the country has been run on the assumption that the greatest value of all is liberty, which gives people the freedom to "do their own thing," particularly to make money, regardless of how much this freedom deprives others of the same liberty or of a decent standard of living. Whether liberty meant the freedom to squander the country's natural resources or just to go into business for oneself without doing harm to anyone else, it was the guiding value of our society.

Today, however, the demand for liberty is often, but not always, the battle cry of the "haves," justifying their right to keep their wealth or position and to get more. Whether liberty is demanded by a Southern advocate of states' rights to keep Negroes in their place or by a property owner who wants to sell his house to any white willing to buy it, liberty has become the ideology of the more fortunate. In the years to come, the "have-nots," whether they lack money or freedom, will demand increasingly the reduction of this form of liberty. Those who ask for more equality are not opposed to liberty *per se*, of course; what they want is sufficient equality so that they, too, can enjoy liberty now virtually monopolized by the "haves."

The debate over liberty vs. equality is in full swing, and one illuminating example is the current argument about the negative income tax and other forms of guaranteed annual incomes for the underpaid and the poor. The advocates of guaranteed annual incomes want greater equality of income in American society; the opponents fear that the liberty to earn as much as possible will be abrogated. However, neither side frames its case in terms of equality or liberty. The advocates of a guaranteed annual income rely on moral argument, appealing to their fellow Americans to do away with the immorality of poverty. The opponents charge that a guaranteed annual income will sap the incentive to work, although all the evidence now available suggests that professors and other professionals who have long had virtually guaranteed annual incomes have not lost their incentive to work, that what saps incentive is not income but the lack of it.

Being poor makes people apathetic and depressed; a guaranteed income would provide some emotional as well as economic security, raise hopes, increase self-respect and reduce feelings of being left out, thus encouraging poor people to look for decent jobs, improve family living conditions and urge their children to work harder in school. A guaranteed annual income may reduce the incentive to take a dirty and underpaid job, however, and at the bottom of the debate is the fear of those who now have the liberty to avoid taking such jobs that less-fortunate Americans may be given the same liberty.

In the years to come, many other arguments against equality will develop. We have long heard that those who want more equality are radicals or outside agitators, seeking to stir up people thought to be happy with the way things are. This is clearly nonsensical, for even if radicals sometimes lead the drive for more equality, they can succeed only because those who follow them are dissatisfied with the status quo.

Another argument is that the demand for more equality will turn America into a society like Sweden, which is thought to be conformist, boring and suicidal, or even into a gray and regimented society like Russia. But these arguments are non-sensical, too, for there is no evidence that Swedes suffer more from ennui than anyone else, and the suicide rate—high in all Scandinavian countries save Norway—was lower in Sweden at last counting than in traditionalist Austria or Communist Hungary and only slightly higher than the rate in *laissez-faire* West Germany or pastoral Switzerland. And current events in the Communist countries provide considerable evidence that the greater economic equality which some of these countries have achieved does not eliminate the popular desire for freedom and democracy.

But perhaps the most frequently heard argument is that the unequal must do something to earn greater equality. This line of reasoning is taken by those who have had the liberty to achieve their demands and assumes that the same liberty is available to everyone else. This assumption does not hold up, however, for the major problem of the unequal is precisely that they are not allowed to earn equality—that the barriers of racial discrimination, the inability to obtain a good education, the unavailability of good jobs or the power of college presidents and faculties make it impossible for them to be equal. Those who argue for earning equality are really saying that they want to award it to the deserving, like charity. But recent events in the ghettos and on the campuses have shown convincingly that no one awards equality voluntarily; it has to be wrested from the "more equal" by political pressure and even by force.

Many of the changes that make up the equality revolution will not take place for a generation or more, and how many of them ever take place depends on at least three factors: the extent to which the American economy is affluent enough to permit more equality; the extent to which America's political institutions are able to respond to the demands of the unequal, and—perhaps most important—the extent to which working-class and lower-middle-class Americans want more equality, democracy and autonomy in the future.

If the economy is healthy in the years to come, it will be able to "afford" more economic equality while absorbing the costs of such changes as the democratization of the workplace, increased professionalism and more worker autonomy. If automation and the currently rising centralization of American industry result in the disappearance of jobs, however, greater equality will become impossible and people will fight each other for the remaining jobs. This could result in a bitter conflict between the "haves" and the "have-nots" that might even lead to a revolution, bringing about formal equality by governmental edict in a way not altogether different from the Socialist and Communist revolutions of the 20th century. But that conflict between the "haves" and the "have-nots" could also lead to a right-wing revolution in which the "haves," supported by conservatives among the "have-nots," would establish a quasi-totalitarian government that would use force to maintain the existing inequalities.

Although the likelihood of either a left-wing or a right-wing revolution is probably small, even a gradual transformation toward greater equality is not likely to be tranquil. More equality for some means a reduction in privilege for others, and more democracy and autonomy for some means a loss of power for others. Those who have the privilege and the power will not give them up without a struggle and will fight the demand for more equality with all the economic and political resources they can muster. Even today, such demands by only a small part of the black and young population have resulted in a massive backlash appeal for law and order by a large part of the white and older population.

Moreover, whenever important national decisions must be made, American politics has generally been guided by majority rule or majority public opinion, and this has often meant the tyranny of the majority over the minority. As long as the unequal are a minority, the structure of American politics can easily be used to frustrate their demands for change. The inability of the Federal Government to satisfy the demands of the Negro population for greater equality is perhaps the best example. In the future, the political structure must be altered to allow the Government to become more responsive to minority demands, particularly as the pressure for equality grows.

Whether or not such governmental responsiveness will be politically feasible depends in large part on how working-class and lower-middle-class Americans feel about the equality revolution. They are the ruling majority in America, and if they want more equality, democracy and autonomy, these will be achieved—and through peaceful political methods. If the two classes remain primarily interested in obtaining more affluence, however, they will be able to suppress demands for equality by minorities, especially those demands which reduce their own powers and privileges. No one can tell now how these two classes will feel in the future, but there is no doubt that their preferences will determine the outcome of the equality revolution.

Still, whatever happens in the years and decades to come, the equality revolution is under way, and however slowly it proceeds and however bitter the struggle between its supporters and opponents, it will continue. It may succeed, but it could also fail, leaving in its wake a level of social and political conflict unlike any America has ever known.

What I have written so far I have written as a sociologist, trying to predict what will occur in coming generations. But as a citizen, I believe that what will happen ought to happen, that the emerging demand for more equality, democracy and autonomy is desirable. Too many Americans, even among the nonpoor, still lead lives of quiet desperation, and the good life today is the monopoly of only a happy few. I think that the time has come when unbridled liberty as we have defined it traditionally can no longer be America's guiding value, especially if the right to liberty deprives others of a similar liberty. But I believe also that there is no inherent conflict between liberty and equality; that the society we must create should provide enough equality to permit everyone the liberty to control his own life without creating inequality for others, and that this, when it comes, will be the Great Society.

3

Race

The Civil Rights Acts of 1964 and 1965 were the culmination of a long and bitter struggle. The Supreme Court had moved into a political vacuum in 1954 with its ruling against school segregation; but not till ten years later did the President and Congress take action to put the full weight of the government behind the ideal of racial equality.

The architects of this victory were given no time to savor their triumph, for in 1965 Watts erupted; and in the years that followed, city after city was shaken by violence in the ghettos. In the first selection in this chapter, the Kerner Commission, examining the causes of the violence, sets forth a grim catalogue of economic and social ills. Then psychiatrists William Grier and Price Cobbs describe the psychological factors behind the rage expressed in the riots—rage which, despite the evidence of progress pointed to by Nathan Glazer, has not yet been assuaged.

Black Americans are now voicing their grievances in two kinds of demands not heard during the earlier years of the civil rights struggle. The first is the demand on white America for *reparation*—recompense for all the grim years of slavery, exploitation, and humiliation. Thus, in April 1969 a National Black Economic Development Conference convened in Detroit and issued "The Black Manifesto." This statement, couched in apocalyptic language, demanded "of the white Christian churches and Jewish synagogues which are part and parcel of the system of capitalism, that they begin to pay reparations to black people in this country." The Manifesto asked for $500 million (later amended to $3 billion), which was to be used to establish publishing enterprises, TV networks, research and training centers, a black university, and "cooperative businesses in the United States and in Africa, our Motherland," as well as to help organize welfare recipients and black workers. The concept of reparation as a right, and the peremptory way in which James Forman and others initially presented the Manifesto, evoked a generally hostile reaction in the white community; yet a number of churches began to consider whether they might not be capable of a greater effort to redress the grievances of black people.

The second demand presented by some black leaders is for *separation*, the major issue to be considered in this chapter. For some leaders, the demand is a temporary expedient to help black people gain a sense of identity, self-confidence, and power; for others, it is a permanent solution involving a separate black state, necessitated by the unredeemable nature of white society. The issue is examined from various points of view here by Robert Browne, Bayard Rustin, Grier and Cobbs, and Glazer. The question posed is whether the whole direction of public policy, turned toward integration after years of arduous toil by the civil rights movement, should now be reversed. Opinion polls in 1969 indicated that, within the black community, there was still strong support for integration and thus impatience with the pace of desegregation in the schools. On the other hand, these same polls indicated that whites who believed that school integration was proceeding too slowly were far outnumbered by those who felt it was going too fast. It is true that other surveys reveal a long-term decline of prejudice among whites in America. But continued reluctance by whites to accept the full logic of the legislation of 1964 and 1965 may well give increased credence to black separatist programs.

WHITE RACISM

National Advisory Commission on Civil Disorders

Otto Kerner, at that time Governor of Illinois, was Chairman of the Commission.

. . . Race prejudice has shaped our history decisively; it now threatens to affect our future.

White racism is essentially responsible for the explosive mixture which has been accumulating in our cities since the end of World War II. Among the ingredients of this mixture are:

Pervasive discrimination and segregation in employment, education, and housing, which have resulted in the continuing exclusion of great numbers of Negroes from the benefits of economic progress.

Black in-migration and white exodus, which have produced the massive and growing concentrations of impoverished Negroes in our major cities, creating a growing crisis of deteriorating facilities and services and unmet human needs.

The black ghettos, where segregation and poverty converge on the young to destroy opportunity and enforce failure. Crime, drug addiction, dependency on welfare, and bitterness and resentment against society in general and white society in particular are the result.

At the same time, most whites and some Negroes outside the ghetto have prospered to a degree unparalleled in the history of civilization. Through television and other media, this affluence has been flaunted before the eyes of the Negro poor and the jobless ghetto youth.

Yet these facts alone cannot be said to have caused the disorders. Recently, other powerful ingredients have begun to catalyze the mixture.

Frustrated hopes are the residue of the unfulfilled expectations aroused by the great judicial and legislative victories of

From *Report of the National Advisory Commission on Civil Disorders* (Washington, D. C.: U. S. Government Printing Office, 1968), pp. 5-7.

the civil rights movement and the dramatic struggle for equal rights in the South.

A climate that tends toward approval and encouragement of violence as a form of protest has been created by white terrorism directed against nonviolent protest; by the open defiance of law and Federal authority by state and local officials resisting desegregation; and by some protest groups engaging in civil disobedience who turn their backs on nonviolence, go beyond the constitutionally protected rights of petition and free assembly, and resort to violence to attempt to compel alteration of laws and policies with which they disagree.

The frustrations of powerlessness have led some Negroes to the conviction that there is no effective alternative to violence as a means of achieving redress of grievances, and of "moving the system." These frustrations are reflected in alienation and hostility toward the institutions of law and government and the white society which controls them, and in the reach toward racial consciousness and solidarity reflected in the slogan "Black Power."

A new mood has sprung up among Negroes, particularly among the young, in which self-esteem and enhanced racial pride are replacing apathy and submission to "the system."

The police are not merely a "spark" factor. To some Negroes police have come to symbolize white power, white racism, and white repression. And the fact is that many police do reflect and express these white attitudes. The atmosphere of hostility and cynicism is reinforced by a widespread belief among Negroes in the existence of police brutality and in a "double standard" of justice and protection—one for Negroes and one for whites . . . .

The Formation of the Racial Ghettos[1]

Throughout the 20th century the Negro population of the United States has been moving steadily from rural areas to urban and from South to North and West. In 1910, 91 percent of the Nation's 9.8 million Negroes lived in the South and only 27 percent of American Negroes lived in cities of 2,500 persons or more. Between 1910 and 1966 the total Negro population more than doubled, reaching 21.5 million, and the number living in metropolitan areas rose more than fivefold (from 2.6 million to 14.8 million). The number outside the South rose elevenfold (from 885,000 to 9.7 million).

[1]The term "ghetto" as used in this Report refers to an area within a city characterized by poverty and acute social disorganization and inhabited by members of a racial or ethnic group under conditions of involuntary segregation.

Negro migration from the South has resulted from the expectation of thousands of new and highly paid jobs for unskilled workers in the North and the shift to mechanized farming in the South. However, the Negro migration is small when compared to earlier waves of European immigrants. Even between 1960 and 1966, there were 1.8 million immigrants from abroad compared to the 613,000 Negroes who arrived in the North and West from the South.

As a result of the growing number of Negroes in urban areas, natural increase has replaced migration as the primary source of Negro population increase in the cities. Nevertheless, Negro migration from the South will continue unless economic conditions there change dramatically.

Basic data concerning Negro urbanization trends indicate that:

Almost all Negro population growth (98 percent from 1950 to 1966) is occurring within metropolitan areas, primarily within central cities.[2]

The vast majority of white population growth (78 percent from 1960 to 1966) is occurring in suburban portions of metropolitan areas. Since 1960, white central-city population has declined by 1.3 million.

As a result, central cities are becoming more heavily Negro while the suburban fringes around them remain almost entirely white.

The 12 largest central cities now contain over two-thirds of the Negro population outside the South, and almost one-third of the Negro total in the United States.

Within the cities, Negroes have been excluded from white residential areas through discriminatory practices. Just as significant is the withdrawal of white families from, or their refusal to enter, neighborhoods where Negroes are moving or already residing. About 20 percent of the urban population of the United States changes residence every year. The refusal of whites to move into "changing" areas when vacancies occur means that most vacancies eventually are occupied by Negroes.

The result, according to a recent study, is that in 1960 the average segregation index for 207 of the largest U.S. cities was 86.2. In other words, to create an unsegregated population distribution, an

---

[2] A "central city" is the largest city of a standard metropolitan statistical area, that is, a metropolitan area containing at least one city of 50,000 or more inhabitants.

average of over 86 percent of all Negroes would have to change their place of residence within the city.

Unemployment, Family Structure, and Social Disorganization

Although there have been gains in Negro income nationally, and a decline in the number of Negroes below the "poverty level," the condition of Negroes in the central city remains in a state of crisis. Between 2 and 2.5 million Negroes—16 to 20 percent of the total Negro population of all central cities—live in squalor and deprivation in ghetto neighborhoods.

Employment is a key problem. It not only controls the present for the Negro American but, in a most profound way, it is creating the future as well. Yet, despite continuing economic growth and declining national unemployment rates, the unemployment rate for Negroes in 1967 was more than double that for whites.

Equally important is the undesirable nature of many jobs open to Negroes and other minorities. Negro men are more than three times as likely as white men to be in low-paying, unskilled, or service jobs. This concentration of male Negro employment at the lowest end of the occupational scale is the single most important cause of poverty among Negroes.

In one study of low-income neighborhoods, the "sub-employment rate," including both unemployment and under-employment, was about 33 percent, or 8.8 times greater than the overall employment rate for all U.S. workers.

Employment problems, aggravated by the constant arrival of new unemployed migrants, many of them from depressed rural areas, create persistent poverty in the ghetto. In 1966, about 11.9 percent of the Nation's whites and 40.6 percent of its nonwhites were below the poverty level defined by the Social Security Administration (in 1966, $3,335 per year for an urban family of four). Over 40 percent of the nonwhites below the poverty level live in the central cities.

Employment problems have drastic social impact in the ghetto. Men who are chronically unemployed or employed in the lowest status jobs are often unable or unwilling to remain with their families. The handicap imposed on children growing up without fathers in an atmosphere of deprivation is increased as mothers are forced to work to provide support.

The culture of poverty that results from unemployment and family breakup generates a system of ruthless, exploitative relationships within the ghetto. Prostitution, dope addiction, and crime create an environmental "jungle" characterized by personal insecurity and tension. Children growing up under such conditions are likely participants in civil disorder.

Conditions of Life in the Racial Ghetto

A striking difference in environment from that of white, middle-class Americans profoundly influences the lives of residents of the ghetto.

Crime rates, consistently higher than in other areas, create a pronounced sense of insecurity. For example, in one city one low-income Negro district had 35 times as many serious crimes against persons as a high-income white district. Unless drastic steps are taken, the crime problems in poverty areas are likely to continue to multiply as the growing youth and rapid urbanization of the population outstrip police resources.

Poor health and sanitation conditions in the ghetto result in higher mortality rates, a higher incidence of major diseases, and lower availability and utilization of medical services. The infant mortality rate for nonwhite babies under the age of 1 month is 58 percent higher than for whites; for 1 to 12 months it is almost three times as high. The level of sanitation in the ghetto is far below that in high-income areas. Garbage collection is often inadequate. Of an estimated 14,000 cases of rat bite in the United States in 1965, most were in ghetto neighborhoods.

Ghetto residents believe they are exploited by local merchants; and evidence substantiates some of these beliefs. A study conducted in one city by the Federal Trade Commission showed that higher prices were charged for goods sold in ghetto stores than in other areas.

Lack of knowledge regarding credit purchasing creates special pitfalls for the disadvantaged. In many states, garnishment practices compound these difficulties by allowing creditors to deprive individuals of their wages without hearing or trial . . . .

BLACK RAGE

William H. Grier and Price M. Cobbs

William H. Grier, M. D., and Price M. Cobbs, M. D., are with the University of California Medical Center as Assistant Professors of Psychiatry and are psychiatrists in private practice.

History may well show that of all the men who lived during our fateful century none illustrated the breadth or the grand potential of man so magnificently as did Malcolm X. If, in future chronicles, America is regarded as the major nation of our day, and the rise of darker people from bondage as the major event, then no figure has appeared thus far who captures the spirit of our times as does Malcolm.

Malcolm is an authentic hero, indeed the only universal black hero. In his unrelenting opposition to the viciousness in America, he fired the imagination of black men all over the world.

If this black nobleman is a hero to black people in the United States and if his life reflects their aspirations, there can be no doubt of the universality of black rage.

Malcolm responded to his position in his world and to his blackness in the manner of so many black boys. He turned to crime. He was saved by a religious sect given to a strange, unhistorical explanation of the origin of black people and even stranger solutions to their problems. He rose to power in that group and outgrew it.

Feeding on his own strength, growing in response to his own commands, limited by no creed, he became a citizen of the world and an advocate of all oppressed people no matter their color or belief. Anticipating his death by an assassin, he distilled, in a book, the essence of his genius, his life. His autobiography thus is a legacy and, together with his speeches, illustrates the thrusting growth of the man—his evolution, rapid, propulsive, toward the man he might have been had he lived.

The essence of Malcolm X was growth, change, and a seeking after truth.

Alarmed white people saw him first as an eccentric and later as a dangerous radical—a revolutionary without troops who threatened to stir black people to riot and civil disobedience. Publicly, they treated him as a joke; privately, they were afraid of him.

After his death he was recognized by black people as the "black shining prince" and recordings of his speeches became treasured things. His autobiography was studied, his life marveled at. Out of this belated admiration came the philosophical basis for black activism and indeed the thrust of Black Power itself, away from integration and civil rights and into the "black bag."

Unlike Malcolm, however, the philosophical underpinnings of the new black militancy were static. They remained encased within the ideas of revolution and black nationhood, ideas Malcolm had outgrown by the time of his death. His stature has made even his earliest statements gospel and men now find themselves willing to die for words which in retrospect are only milestones in the growth of a fantastic man.

Many black men who today preach blackness seem headed blindly toward self-destruction, uncritical of anything "black" and damning the white man for diabolical wickedness. For a philosophical base they have turned to the words of Malcolm's youth.

This perversion of Malcolm's intellectual position will not, we submit, be held against him by history.

Malcolm's meaning for us lies in his fearless demand for truth and his evolution from a petty criminal to an international statesman—accomplished by a black man against odds of terrible magnitude—in America. His message was his life, not his words, and Malcolm knew it.

Black Power activism—thrust by default temporarily at the head of a powerful movement—is a conception that contributes in a significant way to the strength and unity of that movement but is unable to provide the mature vision for the mighty works ahead. It will pass and leave black people in this country prouder, stronger, more determined, but in need of grander princes with clearer vision.

We believe that the black masses will rise with a simple and eloquent demand to which new leaders must give tongue. They will say to America simply: "GET OFF OUR BACKS!"

The problem will be so simply defined.

What is the problem?

The white man has crushed all but the life from blacks from the time they came to these shores to this very day.

What is the solution?

Get off their backs.

How?

By simply doing it—now.

This is no oversimplification. Greater changes than this in the relations of peoples have taken place before. The nation would benefit tremendously. Such a change might bring about a closer examination of our relations with foreign countries, a reconsideration of economic policies, and a re-examination if not a redefinition of nationhood. It might in fact be the only change which can prevent a degenerative decline from a powerful nation to a feeble, third-class, ex-colonialist country existing at the indulgence of stronger powers.

In spite of the profound shifts in power throughout the world in the past thirty years, the United States seems to have a domestic objective of "business as usual," with no change needed or in fact wanted.

All the nasty problems are overseas. At home the search is for bigger profits and smaller costs, better education and lower taxes, more vacation and less work, more for me and less for you. Problems at home are to be talked away, reasoned into nonexistence, and put to one side while we continue the great American game of greed.

There is, however, an inevitability built into the natural order of things. Cause and effect are in fact joined, and if you build a sufficient cause then not all the talk or all the tears in God's creation can prevent the effect from presenting itself one morning as the now ripened fruit of your labors.

America began building a cause when black men were first sold into bondage. When the first black mother killed her newborn rather than have him grow into a slave. When the first black man slew himself rather than submit to an organized system of man's feeding upon another's flesh. America had well begun a cause when all the rebels were either slain or broken and the nation set to the task of refining the system of slavery so that the maximum labor might be extracted from it.

The system achieved such refinement that the capital loss involved when a slave woman aborted could be set against the gain to be expected from forcing her into brutish labor while she was with child.

America began building a potent cause in its infancy as a nation.

It developed a way of life, an American ethos, a national life style which included the assumption that blacks are inferior and were born to hew wood and draw water. Newcomers to this land (if white) were immediately made to feel welcome and, among the bounty available, were given blacks to feel superior to. They were required to despise and depreciate them, abuse and exploit them, and one can only imagine how munificent this land must have seemed to the European—a land with built-in scapegoats.

The hatred of blacks has been so deeply bound up with being an American that it has been one of the first things new Americans learn and one of the last things old Americans forget. Such feelings have been elevated to a position of national character, so that individuals now no longer feel personal guilt or responsibility for the oppression of black people. The nation has incorporated this oppression into itself in the form of folkways and storied traditions, leaving the individual free to shrug his shoulders and say only: "That's our way of life."

This way of life is a heavy debt indeed, and one trembles for the debtor when payment comes due.

America has waxed rich and powerful in large measure on the backs of black laborers. It has become a violent, pitiless nation, hard and calculating, whose moments of generosity are only brief intervals in a ferocious narrative of life, bearing a ferocity and an aggression so strange in this tiny world where men die if they do not live together.

With the passing of the need for black laborers, black people have become useless; they are a drug on the market. There are not enough menial jobs. They live in a nation which has evolved a work force of skilled and semi-skilled workmen. A nation which chooses simultaneously to exclude all black men from this favored labor force and to deny them the one thing America has offered every other group—unlimited growth with a ceiling set only by one's native gifts.

The facts, however obfuscated, are simple. Since the demise of slavery black people have been expendable in a cruel and impatient land. The damage done to black people has been beyond reckoning. Only now are we beginning to sense the bridle placed on black children by a nation which does not want them to grow into mature human beings.

The most idealistic social reformer of our time, Martin Luther King, was not slain by one man; his murder grew out of that large body of violent bigotry America has always nurtured—that body of thinking which screams for the blood of the radical, or the conservative, or the villain, or the saint. To the extent that he stood in the way of bigotry, his life was in jeopardy, his saintly persuasion notwithstanding. To the extent that he was black and was calling America to account, his days were numbered by the nation he sought to save.

Men and women, even children, have been slain for no other earthly reason than their blackness. Property and goods have been stolen and the victims then harried and punished for their poverty. But such viciousness can at least be measured or counted.

Black men, however, have been so hurt in their manhood that they are now unsure and uneasy as they teach their sons to be men. Women have been so humiliated and used that they may regard womanhood as a curse and flee from it. Such pain, so deep, and such real jeopardy, that the fundamental protective function of the family has been denied. These injuries we have no way to measure.

Black men have stood so long in such peculiar jeopardy in America that a *black norm* has developed—a suspiciousness of one's environment which is necessary for survival. Black people, to a degree that approaches paranoia, must be ever alert to danger from their white fellow citizens. It is a cultural phenomenon peculiar to black Americans. And it is a posture so close to paranoid thinking that the mental disorder into which black people most frequently fall is paranoid psychosis.

Can we say that white men have driven black men mad?

An educated black woman had worked in an integrated setting for fifteen years. Compliant and deferential, she had earned promotions and pay increases by hard work and excellence. At no time had she been involved in black activism, and her only participation in the movement had been a yearly contribution to the N.A.A.C.P.

During a lull in the racial turmoil she sought psychiatric treatment. She explained that she had lately become alarmed at waves of rage that swept over her as she talked to white people or at times even as she looked at them. In view of her past history of compliance and passivity, she felt that something was wrong with her. If her controls slipped she might embarrass herself or lose her job.

A black man, a professional, had been a "nice guy" all his life. He was a hard-working non-militant who avoided discussions of race with his white colleagues. He smiled if their comments were harsh and remained unresponsive to racist statements. Lately he has experienced almost uncontrollable anger toward his white co-workers, and although he still manages to keep his feelings to himself, he confides that blacks and whites have been lying to each other. There is hatred and violence between them and he feels trapped. He too fears for himself if his controls should slip.

If these educated recipients of the white man's bounty find it hard to control their rage, what of their less fortunate kinsman who has less to protect, less to lose, and more scars to show for his journey in this land?

The tone of the preceding chapters has been mournful, painful, desolate, as we have described the psychological consequences of white oppression of blacks. The centuries of senseless cruelty and the permeation of the black man's character with the conviction of his own hatefulness and inferiority tell a sorry tale.

This dismal tone has been deliberate. It has been an attempt to evoke a certain quality of depression and hopelessness in the reader and to stir these feelings. These are the most common feelings tasted by black people in America.

The horror carries the endorsement of centuries and the entire lifespan of a nation. It is a way of life which reaches back to the beginnings of recorded time. And all the bestiality, wherever it occurs and however long it has been happening, is narrowed, focused, and refined to shine into a black child's eyes when first he views his world. All that has ever happened to black men and women he sees in the victims closest to him, his parents.

A life is an eternity and throughout all that eternity a black child has breathed the foul air of cruelty. He has grown up to find that his spirit was crushed before he knew there was need of it. His ambitions, even in their forming, showed him to have set his hand against his own. This is the desolation of black life in America.

Depression and grief are hatred turned on the self. It is instructive to pursue the relevance of this truth to the condition of black Americans.

Black people have shown a genius for surviving under the most deadly circumstances. They have survived because of their close attention to reality. A black dreamer would have a short life in Mississippi. They are of necessity bound to reality, chained to the facts of the times; historically the penalty for misjudging a situation involving white men has been death. The preoccupation with religion has been a willing adoption of fantasy to prod an otherwise reluctant mind to face another day. We will even play tricks on ourselves if it helps us stay alive.

The psychological devices used to survive are reminiscent of the years of slavery, and it is no coincidence. The same devices are used because black men face the same danger now as then.

The grief and depression caused by the condition of black men in America is an unpopular reality to the sufferers. They would rather see themselves in a more heroic posture and chide a disconsolate brother. They would like to point to their achievements (which in fact have been staggering); they would rather point to virtue (which has been shown in magnificent form by some blacks); they would point to bravery, fidelity, prudence, brilliance, creativity, all of which dark men have shown in abundance. But the overriding experience of the black American has been grief and sorrow and no man can change that fact.

His grief has been realistic and appropriate. What people have so earned a period of mourning?

We want to emphasize yet again the depth of the grief for slain sons and ravished daughters, how deep and lingering it is.

If the depth of this sorrow is felt, we can then consider what can be made of this emotion.

As grief lifts and the sufferer moves toward health, the hatred he had turned on himself is redirected toward his tormentors, and the fury of his attack on the one who caused him pain is in direct proportion to the depth of his grief. When the mourner lashes out in anger, it is a relief to those who love him, for they know he has now returned to health.

Observe that the amount of rage the oppressed turns on his tormentor is a direct function of the depth of his grief, and consider the intensity of black men's grief.

Slip for a moment into the soul of a black girl whose womanhood is blighted, not because she is ugly, but because she is black and by definition all blacks are ugly.

Become for a moment a black citizen of Birmingham, Alabama, and try to understand his grief and dismay when innocent children are slain while they worship, for no other reason than that they are black.

Imagine how an impoverished mother feels as she watches the light of creativity snuffed out in her children by schools which dull the mind and environs which rot the soul.

For a moment make yourself the black father whose son went innocently to war and there was slain—for whom, for what?

For a moment be any black person, anywhere, and you will feel the waves of hopelessness that engulfed black men and women when Martin Luther King was murdered. All black people understood the tide of anarchy that followed his death.

It is the transformation of *this* quantum of grief into aggression of which we now speak. As a sapling bent low stores energy for a violent backswing, blacks bent double by oppression have stored energy which will be released in the form of rage—black rage, apocalyptic and final.

White Americans have developed a high skill in the art of misunderstanding black people. It must have seemed to slaveholders that slavery would last through all eternity, for surely their misunderstanding of black bondsmen suggested it. If the slaves were eventually to be released from bondage, what could be the purpose of creating the fiction of their subhumanity?

It must have seemed to white men during the period 1865 to 1945 that black men would always be a passive, compliant lot. If not, why would they have stoked the flames of hatred with such deliberately barbarous treatment?

White Americans today deal with "racial incidents" from summer to summer as if such minor turbulence will always remain minor and one need only keep the blacks busy till fall to have made it through another troubled season.

Today it is the young men who are fighting the battles, and, for now, their elders, though they have given their approval, have not joined in. The time seems near, however, for the full range of the black masses to put down the broom and buckle on the sword. And it grows nearer day by day. Now we see skirmishes, sputtering erratically, evidence if you will that the young men are in a warlike mood. But evidence as well that the elders are watching closely and may soon join the battle.

Even these minor flurries have alarmed the country and have resulted in a spate of generally senseless programs designed to give *temporary summer jobs!!* More interesting in its long-range prospects has been the apparent eagerness to draft black men for military service. If in fact this is a deliberate design to place black men in uniform in order to get them off the street, it may be the most curious "instant cure" for a serious disease this nation has yet attempted. Young black men are learning the most modern techniques for killing—techniques which may be used against *any* enemy.

But it is all speculation. The issue finally rests with the black masses. When the servile men and women stand up, we had all better duck.

We should ask what is likely to galvanize the masses into aggression against the whites.

Will it be some grotesque atrocity against black people which at last causes one-tenth of the nation to rise up in indignation and crush the monstrosity?

Will it be the example of black people outside the United States who have gained dignity through their own liberation movement?

Will it be by the heroic action of a small group of blacks which by its wisdom and courage commands action in a way that cannot be denied?

Or will it be by blacks, finally and in an unpredictable way, simply getting fed up with the bumbling stupid racism of this country? Fired not so much by any one incident as by the gradual accretion of stupidity into fixtures of national policy.

All are possible, or any one, or something yet unthought. It seems certain only that on the course the nation now is headed it will happen.

One might consider the possibility that, if the national direction remains unchanged, such a conflagration simply might *not* come about. Might not black people remain where they are, as they did for a hundred years during slavery?

Such seems truly inconceivable. Not because blacks are so naturally warlike or rebellious, but because they are filled with such grief, such sorrow, such bitterness, and such hatred. It seems now delicately poised, not yet risen to the flash point, but rising rapidly nonetheless. No matter what repressive measures are invoked against the blacks, they will never swallow their rage and go back to blind hopelessness.

If existing oppressions and humiliating disenfranchisements are to be lifted, they will have to be lifted most speedily, or catastrophe will follow.

For there are no more psychological tricks blacks can play upon themselves to make it possible to exist in dreadful circumstances. No more lies can they tell themselves. No more dreams to fix on. No more opiates to dull the pain. No more patience. No more thought. No more reason. Only a welling tide risen out of all those terrible years of grief, now a tidal wave of fury and rage, and all black, black as night.

THE CASE FOR TWO AMERICAS—
ONE BLACK, ONE WHITE

Robert S. Browne

Robert S. Browne is Assistant Professor of Economics at Fairleigh Dickinson University and a member of the executive committee of the Black Power Conference. His article derives from a debate with Bayard Rustin before the National Community Relations Advisory Council.

A growing ambivalence among Negroes is creating a great deal of confusion both within the black community itself and within those segments of the white community that are attempting to relate

"The Case for Two Americas—One Black, One White," *The New York Times Magazine* (August 11, 1968), pp. 12, 13, 50, 51, 56, 60, 62. © 1968 by The New York Times Company. Reprinted by permission.

to the blacks. It arises from the question of whether American Negroes are a cultural group significantly distinct from the majority culture *on an ethnic* rather than a socio-economic basis.

If one believes the answer to this is yes, one is likely to favor the cultural distinctiveness and to vigorously oppose efforts to minimize or submerge the differences. If, on the other hand, one believes there are no cultural differences between blacks and whites or that the differences are minimal or transitory, then one is likely to resist emphasis on the differences and to favor accentuation of the similarities. Those two currents in the black community are symbolized, perhaps oversimplified, by the factional labels of separatists and integrationists.

The separatist would argue that the Negro's foremost grievance cannot be solved by giving him access to more gadgets— although this is certainly a part of the solution—but that his greatest need is of the spirit, that he must have an opportunity to reclaim his group individuality and have that individuality recognized as equal with other major cultural groups in the world.

The integrationist would argue that what the Negro wants, principally, is exactly what the whites want—that is, to be "in" in American society—and that operationally this means providing the Negro with employment, income, housing and education comparable to that of the whites. Having achieved this, the other aspects of the Negro's problem of inferiority will disappear.

The origins of this dichotomy are easily identified. The physical characteristics which distinguish blacks from whites are obvious enough; the long history of slavery and the post-emancipation exclusion of the blacks from so many facets of American society are equally undeniable. Whether observable behavioral differences between blacks and the white majority are attributable to this special history of the black man in America or to racial differences in life style is arguable. What is not arguable, however, is that at the time of the slave trade, the blacks arrived in America with a cultural background and life style quite distinct from that of the whites. Although there was perhaps as much diversity among these Africans from widely scattered portions of their native continent as there was among the settlers from Europe, the differences between the two racial groups was unquestionably far greater, as attested by the different roles they were to play in the society.

Over this history there seems to be little disagreement. The dispute arises from how one views what happened after the blacks reached this continent. The integrationist would focus on their transformation into imitators of the European civilization. European clothing was imposed on the slaves, eventually their languages were forgotten, the African homeland receded ever further into the background.

Certainly after 1808, when the slave trade was officially terminated, thus cutting off fresh injections of African culture, the Europeanizing of the blacks proceeded apace. With emancipation, the Federal Constitution recognized the legal manhood of the blacks, citizenship was conferred on the ex-slave, and the Negro began his arduous struggle for social, economic and political acceptance into the American mainstream.

The separatist, however, takes the position that the cultural transformation of the black man was not complete. Whereas the integrationist more or less accepts the destruction of the original culture of the African slaves as a *fait accompli*—whether he feels it to have been morally reprehensible or not—the separatist is likely to harbor a vague resentment toward the whites for having perpetrated this cultural genocide; he would nurture whatever vestiges may have survived the North American experience and would encourage a renaissance of these lost characteristics. In effect, he is sensitive to an identity crisis which presumably does not exist in the mind of the integrationist.

The separatist appears to be romantic and even reactionary to many observers. On the other hand, his viewpoint squares with mankind's most fundamental instinct—the instinct for survival. With so powerful a stimulus, and with the oppressive tendencies of white society, one could have almost predicted the emergence of the black separatist movement. Millions of black parents have been confronted with the poignant agony of raising black, kinky-haired children in a society where the standard of beauty is a milk-white skin and long, straight hair. To convince a black child that she is beautiful when every channel of value formation in the society is telling her the opposite is a heart-rending and well-nigh impossible task.

It is a challenge which confronts all Negroes, irrespective of their social and economic class, but the difficulty of dealing with it is likely to vary with the degree to which the family leads an integrated existence. A black child in a predominantly black school may realize that she doesn't look like the pictures in the books, magazines and TV advertisements, but at least she looks like her schoolmates and neighbors. The black child in a predominantly white school and neighborhood lacks even this basis for identification.

This identity problem is, of course, not peculiar to the Negro, nor is it limited to questions of physical appearance. Minorities of all sorts encounter it in one form or another—the immigrant who speaks with an accent, the Jewish child who doesn't celebrate Christmas, the vegetarian who shuns meat. But for the Negro the problem has a special dimension, for in the

American ethos a black man is not only "different," he is classed as ugly and inferior.

This is not an easy situation to deal with, and the manner in which a Negro chooses to handle it will be both determined by, and a determinant of, his larger political outlook. He can deal with it as an integrationist, accepting his child as being ugly by prevailing standards and urging him to excel in other ways to prove his worth; or he can deal with it as a black nationalist, telling the child that he is not a freak but rather part of a larger international community of black-skinned, kinky-haired people who have a beauty of their own, a glorious history and a great future.

In short, he can replace shame with pride, inferiority with dignity, by imbuing the child with what is coming to be known as black nationalism. The growing popularity of this latter viewpoint is evidenced by the appearance of "natural" hair styles among Negro youth and the surge of interest in African and Negro culture and history.

Black Power may not be the ideal slogan to describe this new self-image the black American is developing, for to guilt-ridden whites the slogan conjures up violence, anarchy and revenge. To frustrated blacks, however, it symbolizes unity and a newly found pride in the blackness with which the Creator endowed us and which we realize must always be our mark of identification. Heretofore this blackness has been a stigma, a curse with which we were born. Black Power means that this curse will henceforth be a badge of pride rather than of scorn. It marks the end of an era in which black men devoted themselves to pathetic attempts to be white men and inaugurates an era in which black people will set their own standards of beauty, conduct and accomplishment.

Is this new black consciousness in irreconcilable conflict with the larger American society? In a sense, the heart of the American cultural problem has always been the need to harmonize the inherent contradiction between racial (or national) identity and integration into the melting pot which was America. In the century since the Civil War, the society has made little effort to afford the black minority a sense of racial pride and independence while at the same time accepting it as a full participant. Now that the implications of this failure are becoming apparent, the black community seems to be saying, "Forget it! We'll solve our own problems." Integration, which never had a high priority among the black masses, is now being written off by them as not only unattainable but actually harmful, driving a wedge between them and the so-called Negro elite.

To these developments has been added the momentous realization by many of the "integrated" Negroes that, in the U.S., full integration can only mean full assimilation—a loss of racial identity. This sobering prospect has caused many a black integra-tionist to pause and reflect, even as have his similarly challenged Jewish counterparts.

Thus, within the black community there are two separate challenges to the traditional integration policy which has long constituted the major objective of established Negro leadership. There is general skepticism that the Negro will enjoy full acceptance into American society even after having transformed himself into a white blackman; and there is the longer-range doubt that complete integration would prove to be really desirable, even if it should somehow be achieved, for its price might be the total absorption and disappearance of the race—a sort of painless genocide.

Understandably, it is the black masses who have most vociferously articulated the dangers of assimilation, for they have watched with alarm as the more fortunate among their ranks have gradually risen to the top only to be promptly "integrated" into the white community—absorbed into another culture, often with undis-guised contempt for all that had previously constituted their racial and cultural heritage.

Also, it was the black masses who first perceived that integration actually increases the white community's control over the black one by destroying black institutions, absorbing black leader-ship and making its interests coincide with those of the white community. The international "brain drain" has its counterpart in the black community, which is constantly being denuded of its best-trained people and many of its natural leaders. Black institutions of all sorts—colleges, newspapers, banks, even community organizations—are all losing their better people to the newly available openings in white establishments. This lowers the quality of the Negro organizations and in some cases causes their demise or increases their dependence on whites for survival. Such injurious, if unintended, side effects of integration have been felt in almost every layer of the black community.

If this analysis of the integrationist-separatist conflict exhausted the case, we might conclude that the problems have all been dealt with before by other immigrant groups in America. (It would be an erroneous conclusion, for while other groups may have encountered similar problems, their solutions do not work for us, alas.) But there remains yet another factor which is cooling the Negro's enthusiasm for the integrationist path—he is becoming distrustful of his fellow Americans.

The American culture is one of the youngest in the world. Furthermore, as has been pointed out repeatedly in recent years, it is essentially a culture which approves of violence, indeed enjoys it. Military expenditures absorb roughly half of the national budget.

Violence predominates on the TV screen, and toys of violence are best-selling items during the annual rites for the much praised but little imitated Prince of Peace. In Vietnam the zeal with which America has pursued its effort to destroy a poor and illiterate peasantry has astonished civilized people around the globe.

In such an atmosphere the Negro is understandably apprehensive about the fate his white compatriots might have in store for him. The veiled threat by President Johnson at the time of the 1966 riots, suggesting that riots might beget pogroms and pointing out that Negroes are only 10 per cent of the population, was not lost on most blacks. It enraged them, but it was a sobering thought.

The manner in which Germany herded the Jews into concentration camps and ultimately into ovens was a solemn warning to minority peoples everywhere. The casualness with which America exterminated the Indians and later interned the Japanese suggests that there is no cause for the Negro to feel complacent about his security in the U.S. He finds little consolation in the assurance that if it does become necessary to place him in concentration camps it will only be to protect him from uncontrollable whites. "Protective incarceration," to use governmental jargon.

The very fact that such alternatives are becoming serious topics of discussion has exposed the Negro's already raw and sensitive psyche to yet another heretofore unfelt vulnerability—the insecurity which he suffers as a result of having no homeland which he can honestly feel is his own. Among the major ethno-cultural groups in the world, he is unique in this respect.

As the Jewish drama during and following World War II painfully demonstrated, a national homeland is a primordial and urgent need for a people, even though its benefits are not always readily measured. For some, the homeland is a vital place of refuge from the strains of a life led too long in a foreign environment. For others, the need to live in the homeland is considerably less intense than the need for merely knowing that such a homeland exists. The benefit to the expatriate is psychological, a sense of security in knowing that he belongs to a culturally and politically identifiable community. No doubt this phenomenon largely accounts for the fact that both the West Indian Negro and the Puerto Rican exhibit considerably more self-assurance than the American Negro, for both West Indian and Puerto Rican have ties to identifiable homelands which honor and preserve their cultural heritage.

It has been marveled that we American Negroes, almost alone among the cultural groups of the world, exhibit no sense of nationhood. Perhaps it is true that we lack this sense, but there seems little doubt that the absence of a homeland exacts a severe if unconscious price from our psyche. Theoretically our homeland is the U.S.A. We pledge allegiance to the Stars and Stripes and sing the national anthem. But from the age when we first begin to sense that we are somehow "different," that we are victimized, these rituals begin to mean less to us than to our white compatriots. For many of us they become form without substance; for others they become a cruel and bitter mockery of our dignity and good sense; for relatively few of us do they retain a significance in any way comparable to their hold on our white brethren.

The recent coming into independence of many African states stimulated some speculation among Negroes that independent Africa might become the homeland they so desperately needed. A few made the journey and experienced a newly found sense of community and racial dignity. For many who went, however, the gratifying racial fraternity which they experienced was insufficient to compensate for the cultural estrangement accompanying it. They had been away from Africa too long and the differences in language, food and custom barred them from the "at home" feeling they were eagerly seeking. Symbolically, independent Africa could serve them as a homeland; practically, it could not. Their search continues—a search for a place where they can experience the security which comes from being a part of the majority culture, free at last from the inhibiting effects of cultural repression, from cultural timidity and shame.

If we have been separated from Africa for so long that we are no longer quite at ease there, we are left with only one place to make our home, and that is in this land to which we were brought in chains. Justice would indicate such a solution in any case, for it is North America, not Africa, into which our toil and effort have been poured. This land is our rightful home and we are well within our rights in demanding an opportunity to enjoy it on the same terms as the other immigrants who have helped to develop it. Since few whites will deny the justice of this claim, it is paradoxical that we are offered the option of exercising this birthright only on the condition that we abandon our culture, deny our race and integrate ourselves into the white community.

The "accepted" Negro, the "integrated" Negro are mere euphemisms which hide a cruel and relentless cultural destruction that is sometimes agonizing to the middle-class Negro but is becoming intolerable to the black masses. A Negro who refuses to yield his identity and to ape the white model finds he can survive in dignity only by rejecting the entire white society, which must ultimately mean challenging the law and the law-enforcement mechanisms. On the other hand, if he abandons his cultural heritage and succumbs to the lure of integration, he risks certain rejection and humiliation along the way, with absolutely no guarantee of ever achieving complete acceptance. That such unsatisfactory options are leading to almost continuous disruption and dislocation of our society should hardly be cause for surprise.

A formal partitioning of the United States into two totally separate and independent nations, one white and one black, offers one way out of this tragic situation. Many will condemn it as a defeatist solution, but what they see as defeatism may better be described as a frank facing up to the realities of American society. A society is stable only to the extent that there exists a basic core of value judgments that are unthinkingly accepted by the great bulk of its members. Increasingly, Negroes are demonstrating that they do not accept the common core of values which underlies America, either because they had little to do with drafting it or because they feel it is weighted against their interests. The alleged disproportionately large number of Negro law violators, of unwed mothers, of illegitimate children, of nonworking adults *may* be indicators that there is no community of values such as has been supposed, although I am not unaware of racial socio-economic reasons for these statistics also.

But whatever the reason for observed behavioral differences, there is clearly no reason *why* the Negro should not have his own ideas about what the societal organization should be. The Anglo-Saxon system of organizing human relationships has certainly not proved itself to be superior to all other systems, and the Negro is likely to be more acutely aware of this fact than are most Americans.

Certainly partition would entail enormous initial hardships. But these difficulties and these hardships should be weighed against the prospects of prolonged and intensified racial strife stretching for years into the future. Indeed, the social fabric of America is far more likely to be able to withstand the strains of a partitioning of the country than those of an extended race war.

On the other hand, if it happened that the principle of partition were accepted by most Americans without a period of prolonged violence, it is possible that only voluntary transfers of population would be necessary. No one need be forced to move against his will.

This unprecedented challenging of the "conventional wisdom" on the racial question is causing considerable consternation within the white community, especially the white liberal community, which has long felt itself to be the sponsor and guardian of the blacks. The situation is further confused because the challenges to the orthodox integrationist views are being projected by persons whose roots are authentically within the black community—whereas the integrationist spokesmen of the past have often been persons whose credentials were partly white-bestowed. This situation is further aggravated by the classical intergenerational problem—with black youth seizing the lead in speaking out for nationalism and separatism whereas their elders look on askance, a development which has at least a partial parallel in the contemporary white community, where youth is increasingly strident in its demands for thoroughgoing revision of our social institutions.

If one inquires about the spokesmen for the new black nationalism, or for separatism, one discovers that the movement is locally based rather than nationally organized. In the San Francisco Bay area the Black Panther party is well known as a leader in winning recognition for the black community. Its tactic is to operate via a separate political party for black people, a strategy I suspect we will hear a great deal more of in the future. The work of the Black Muslims is well known and perhaps more national in scope than that of any other black-nationalist group. Out of Detroit there is the Malcolm X Society, led by attorney Milton Henry, whose members reject their U.S. citizenship and are claiming five Southern states for the creation of a new black republic. Another major leader in Detroit is the Rev. Albert Cleage, who is developing a considerable following for his preachings of black dignity and who has also experimented with a black political party, thus far without success.

The black students at white colleges are one highly articulate group seeking for some national organizational form. A growing number of black educators are also groping toward some sort of nationally coordinated body to lend strength to their local efforts to develop educational systems better tailored to the needs of the black child. Under the name of Association of Afro-American Educators, they recently held a national conference in Chicago which was attended by several hundred public school teachers and college and community workers from all over the country.

This is not to say that every black teacher or parent-teacher group which favors community control of schools is necessarily sympathetic to black separatism. Nevertheless, the move toward decentralized control over public schools, at least in the larger urban areas, derives from an abandoning of the idea of integration in the schools and a decision to bring to the ghetto the best education that can be obtained.

Similarly, a growing number of community-based organizations are being formed to facilitate the economic development of the ghetto, to replace absentee business proprietors and landlords with black entrepreneurs and resident owners. Again, these efforts are not totally separatist, for they operate within the framework of the present national society, but they build on the separatism which already exists in the society rather than attempt to eliminate it.

To a black who sees salvation for the black man only in a complete divorce of the two races, these efforts at ghetto improvement appear futile, perhaps even harmful. To others, convinced that coexistence with white America is possible within the national framework if only the whites permit the Negro to develop as he wishes (and by his own hand rather than in accordance with a white-conceived and white-administered pattern), such physically and economically upgraded black enclaves will be viewed as desirable steps forward.

Finally, those blacks who still feel that integration is in some sense both acceptable and possible will continue to strive for the color-blind society. When, if ever, these three strands of thought will converge, I cannot predict. Meanwhile, however, concerned whites wishing to work with the black community should be prepared to encounter many rebuffs. They should keep ever in mind that the black community does not have a homogenous vision of its own predicament at this crucial juncture.

TOWARD INTEGRATION

Bayard Rustin

Mr. Rustin is Executive Director of the A. Phillip Randolph Educational Fund. The contents derive from a reply to Robert S. Browne before the National Community Relations Advisory Council.

. . . The proposition that separation may be the best solution of America's racial problems has been recurrent in American Negro history. Let us look at the syndrome that has given rise to it.

Separation, in one form or another, has been proposed and widely discussed among American Negroes in three different periods. Each time, it was put forward in response to an identical combination of economic and social factors that induced despair among Negroes. The syndrome consists of three elements: great expectations, followed by dashed hopes, followed by despair and discussion of separation.

Separatism or Integration: Which Way for America? (New York: A. Philip Randolph Educational Fund, October 1968), pp. 16-21.

The first serious suggestion that Negroes should separate came in the aftermath of the Civil War. During that war many Negroes had not only been strongly in favor of freedom but had fought for the Union. It was a period of tremendous expectations. Great numbers of Negroes left the farms and followed the Union Army as General Sherman marched across Georgia to the sea; they believed that when he got to the sea they would be not only free but also given land—"forty acres and a mule." However, the compromise of 1876 and the withdrawal of the Union Army from the South dashed those expectations. Instead of forty acres and a mule all they got was a new form of slavery.

Out of the ruins of those hopes emerged Booker T. Washington, saying in essence to Negroes: "There is no hope in your attempting to vote, no hope in attempting to play any part in the political or social processes of the nation. Separate yourself from all that, and give your attention to your innards: that you are men, that you maintain dignity, that you drop your buckets where they are, that you become excellent of character."

Of course, it did not work. It could not work. Because human beings have stomachs, as well as minds and hearts, and equate dignity, first of all, not with caste, but with class. I preached the dignity of black skin color and wore my hair Afro style long before it became popular; I taught Negro history in the old Benjamin Franklin High School, where I first got my teaching experience, long before it became popular. But in spite of all that it is my conviction that there are three fundamental ways in which a group of people can maintain their dignity: one, by gradual advancement in the economic order; two, by being a participating element of the democratic process; and three, through the sense of dignity that emerges from their struggle. For instance, Negroes never had more dignity than when Martin Luther King won the boycott in Montgomery or at the bridge in Selma.

This is not to say that all the values of self-image and identification are not important and should not be stimulated; but they should be given secondary or tertiary emphasis; for, unless they rest on a sound economic and social base, they are likely only to create more frustration by raising expectation or hopes with no ability truly to follow through.

The second period of frustration and the call for separation came after World War I. During that war, 300,000 Negro troops went to France—not for the reason Mr. Wilson thought he was sending them, but because they felt that if they fought for their country they would be able to return and say: "We have fought and fought well. Now give us at home what we fought for abroad."

Again, this great expectation collapsed in total despair, as a result of post-war developments: Lynchings in the United States reached their height in the early twenties; the Palmer raids did not affect Negroes directly but had such a terrifying effect on civil liberties that no one paid any attention to what was happening to Negroes; the Ku Klux Klan moved its headquarters from Georgia to Indianapolis, the heart of the so-called North; and unemployment among Negroes was higher at that period than it had ever been before. It was at that time, too, the Negroes began their great migration to the North, not from choice but because they were being driven off the land in the South by changed economic conditions.

The war having created great expectations, and the conditions following the war having shattered them, a really great movement for separation ensued—a much more significant movement than the current one. Marcus Garvey organized over 2,000,000 Negroes, four times the number the NAACP has ever organized, to pay dues to buy ships to return to Africa.

Today, we are experiencing the familiar syndrome again. The Civil Rights Acts of 1964 and 1965 and the Supreme Court decisions all led people seriously to believe that progress was forthcoming, as they believed the day Martin Luther King said, "I have a dream." What made the March on Washington in 1963 great was the fact that it was the culmination of a period of great hope and anticipation.

But what has happened since? The ghettoes are fuller than they have ever been, with 500,000 people moving into them each year and only some 40,000 moving out. They are the same old Bedford-Stuyvesant, Harlem, Detroit, and Watts, only they are much bigger, with more rats, more roaches, and more despair. There are more Negro youngsters in segregated schoolrooms than there were in 1954—not all due to segregation or discrimination, perhaps, but a fact. The number of youngsters who have fallen back in their reading, writing, and arithmetic since 1954 has increased, not decreased, and unemployment for Negro young women is up to 35, 40, and 50 percent in the ghettoes. For young men in the ghettoes, it is up to 20 percent and this is a conservative figure. For family men, the unemployment is twice that of whites. Having built up hopes, and suffered the despair which followed, we are again in a period where separation is being discussed.

I maintain that, in all three periods, the turn to separation has been a frustration reaction to objective political, social and economic circumstances. I believe that it is fully justified, for it would be the most egregious wishful thinking to suppose that people can be subjected to deep frustration and yet not act in a frustrated manner. But however justified and inevitable the frustration, it is totally unrealistic to divert the attention of young Negroes at this time either to the idea of a separate state in the United States, or to going back to Africa, or to setting up a black capitalism (as Mr. Nixon and CORE are now advocating), or to talk about any other possibility of economic separation, when those Negroes who are well off are the 2,000,000 Negroes who are integrated into the trade union movement of this country.

This is not to belittle in any way the desirability of fostering a sense of ethnic unity or racial pride among Negroes or relationships to other black people around the world. This is all to the good, but the ability to do this in a healthy rather than a frustrated way will depend upon the economic viability of the Negro community, the degree to which it can participate in the democratic process here rather than separate from it, and the degree to which it accepts methods of struggle that are productive.

I would not want to leave this subject without observing that while social and economic conditions have precipitated thoughts of separation, it would be an over-simplification to attribute the present agitation of that idea exclusively to those causes. A good deal of the talk about separation today reflects a class problem within the Negro community.

I submit that it is not the *lumpen-proletariat*, the Negro working classes, the Negro working poor, who are proclaiming: "We want Negro principals, we want Negro supervisors, we want Negro teachers in our schools." It is the educated Negroes. If you name a leader of that movement, you will put your finger on a man with a Master's or a Ph.D. degree. Being blocked from moving up, he becomes not only interested in Negro children, but in getting those teaching jobs, supervisory jobs, and principal jobs for his own economic interest. While this is understandable, it is not true that only teachers who are of the same color can teach pupils effectively. Two teachers had an effect upon me; one was black, and the other was white, and it was the white teacher who had the most profound effect, not because she was white, but because she was who she was.

Negroes have been taught that we are inferior, and many Negroes believe that themselves, and have believed it for a long time. That is to say, sociologically we were made children. What is now evident is that the entire black community is rebelling against that concept in behalf of manhood and dignity. This process of rebellion will have as many ugly things in it as beautiful things. Like young people on the verge of maturity many Negroes now say, "We don't want help; we'll do it ourselves. Roll over, Whitey. If we break our necks, okay."

Also, while rebelling, there is rejection of those who used to be loved most. Every teen-ager has to go through hating mother and father, precisely because he loves them. Now he's got to make it on his own. Thus, Martin Luther King and A. Philip Randolph and Roy Wilkins and Bayard Rustin and all the people who marched in the streets are all "finks" now. And the liberals, and the Jews who have done most among the liberals, are also told to get the hell out of the way.

The mythology involved here can be very confusing. Jews may want now to tell their children that they lifted themselves in this society by their bootstraps. And when Negroes have made it, they will preach that ridiculous mythology too. That kind of foolishness is only good after the fact. It is not a dynamism by which the struggle can take place.

But to return to separation and nationalism. We must distinguish within this movement that which is unsound from that which is sound, for ultimately no propaganda can work for social change which is not based in absolute psychological truth.

There is an aspect of the present thrust toward black nationalism that I call reverse-ism. This is dangerous. Black people now want to argue that their hair is beautiful. All right. It is truthful and useful. But, to the degree that the nationalist movement takes concepts of reaction and turns them upside down and paints them glorious for no other reason than that they are black, we're in trouble—morally and politically. The Ku Klux Klan used to say: "If you're white, you're right; if you're black, no matter who you are, you're no good." And there are those among us who are now saying the opposite of the Ku Klux Klan: "He's a whitey, he's no good. Those white politicians, they both stink, don't vote for either of them. Go fishing because they're white."

The Ku Klux Klan said: "You know, we can't have black people teaching," and they put up a big fight when the first Negro was hired in a white school in North Carolina. Now, for all kinds of "glorious" reasons, we're turning the old idea upside down and saying: "Well, somehow or other, there's soul involved, and only black teachers can teach black children." But it is not true. Good teachers can teach children. The Ku Klux Klan said: "We don't want you in our community; get out." Now there are blacks saying: "We don't want any whites in our community for business or anything; get out." The Ku Klux Klan said: "We will be violent as a means of impressing our will on the situation." And now, in conference after conference a small number of black people use violence and threats to attempt to obstruct the democratic process.

What is essential and what we must not lose sight of is that true self-respect and true sense of image are the results of a social process and not merely a psychological state of mind.

It is utterly unrealistic to expect the Negro middle class to behave on the basis alone of color. They will behave, first of all, as middle-class people. The minute Jews got enough money to move off Allen Street, they went to West End Avenue. As soon as the Irish could get out of Hell's Kitchen, they beat it to what is now Harlem.

Who thinks the Negro middle classes are going to stay in Harlem? I believe that the fundamental mistake of the nationalist movement is that it does not comprehend that class ultimately is a more driving force than color, and that any effort to build a society for American Negroes that is based on color alone is doomed to failure.

Now, there are several possibilities. One possibility is that we can stay here and continue the struggle; sometimes things will be better, sometimes they will be worse. Another is to separate ourselves into our own state in America. But I reject that because I do not believe that the American government will ever accept it. Thirdly, there is a possibility of going back to Africa, and that is out for me, because I've had enough experience with the Africans to know that they will not accept that.

There is a kind of in-between position—stay here and try to separate, and yet not separate. I tend to believe that both have to go on simultaneously. That is to say there has to be a move on the part of Negroes to develop black institutions and a black image, and all this has to go on while they are going downtown into integrated work situations, while they are trying to get into the suburbs if they can, while they are doing what all other Americans do in their economic and social grasshopping. That is precisely what the Jew has done. He has held on to that which is Jewish, and nobody has made a better effort at integrating out there and making sure that he's out there where the action is. It makes for tensions, but I don't believe there's any other viable reality.

Furthermore, I believe that the most important thing for those of us in the trade union movement, in the religious communities, and in the universities is not to be taken in by methods that appeal to people's viscera but do not in fact solve the problems that stimulated their viscera.

We must fight and work for a social and economic program which will lift America's poor, whereby the Negro who is most grievously poor will be lifted to that position where he will be able to have dignity.

Secondly, we must fight vigorously for Negroes to engage in the political process, since there is only one way to have maximum feasible participation—and that is not by silly little committees deciding what they're going to do with a half million dollars, but by getting out into the real world of politics and making their weight felt. The most important thing that we have to do is to restore a sense of dignity to the Negro people. The most immediate task is for every one of us to get out and work between now and November so that we can create the kind of administration and the kind of Congress which will indeed bring about what the Freedom Budget and the Poor People's Campaign called for.

If that can happen, the intense frustration around the problem of separation will decrease as equal opportunities—economic, political, and social—increase. And that is the choice before us.

THE NEGRO'S STAKE IN AMERICA'S FUTURE

Nathan Glazer

Nathan Glazer is Professor of Education and Social Structure in the Department of Social Sciences, Graduate School of Education, Harvard University.

Something very strange is happening in the American racial crisis. On the one hand, the concrete situation of Negro Americans is rapidly improving. This is not only true when we look at economics—for we all know this is an inadequate measure of group progress, and that a people that feels oppressed will not be satisfied with the argument, "you never had it so good." But it is also true that things are improving when we look at political participation and power, and even when we look at the critical area of police behavior. Despite recent instances of police violence against black militants, there is no question that the police in city after city are becoming more careful in how they address Negro Americans and in the use of force and firearms. The history of police response to the riots alone demonstrates that.

On the other hand, as the Negro's situation improves, his political attitudes are becoming more extreme. The riots are called rebellions, and hardly any Negro leader bothers to deplore them these days. Militant groups become larger and their language and demands more shocking, even to a demand for political separation. This is sobering, for we know what may happen when a country begins to break up; look at Nigeria.

"The Negro's Stake in America's Future," *The New York Times Magazine* (September 22, 1968), pp. 30, 31ff. © 1968 by The New York Times Company. Reprinted by permission.

Social policy faces a dilemma; most of us—black and white, liberals and conservatives—believe that political and social attitudes reflect concrete conditions (when things get better people become more satisfied and less violent) and that we can change attitudes by changing conditions. When political attitudes become more extreme as conditions are improving, we resort to two explanations: the well-known revolution of rising expectations and the theory of Alexis de Tocqueville that the improvement of conditions increases the desire for change because people begin to feel stronger and more potent.

Both of these theories undoubtedly have some validity, but one's attitude toward them must depend upon one's attitude toward society. One who looks upon American society as the French looked upon their Old Regime—as conservative, sclerotic, repressive, irrational and selfish—will look favorably upon the rise of extreme opinion and the crash of the American Old Regime. But one who sees American society as fundamentally democratic and responsive to people's wishes will be deeply concerned about its fate. That expectations rise is good; that they rise so fast that no policy of any type carried out by anybody can satisfy them is bad. That people feel powerful and free to express their resentments is good; that their resentment may overthrow a system capable of satisfying their needs and hopes is bad. There must be a point at which improvement will moderate extremism despite the revolution of rising expectations and the Tocquevillian hypothesis. But if such a point exists, we are getting further away from it rather than closer to it.

There is, of course, another possible explanation for what is happening: that the Negro is no longer interested in advancing within the American social system. The theory here is that Negroes have begun to see themselves as a subject people, and—like all such people—will be satisfied only by independent political existence. This is the direction that militant Negro demands have now begun to take, and if Negroes follow them this nation will have to use all its political ingenuity and creativity to avoid being torn apart. It is this rise of Negro separatism, and how we might respond to it, that I wish to explore here.

First, let us show briefly that things *are* getting better. Many liberal shapers of opinion insist that the situation of the Negro has not changed or has grown worse. . . . Some who insist that the Negro's economic situation is getting worse point to the rising *absolute* gap between Negro and white incomes and ignore the fact that the *percentage* gap is diminishing. According to their logic, if at some fortunate time median white incomes are $10,000 and median nonwhite incomes are $8,000, one might conclude that Negroes are worse off than they were when whites made $5,000 and they made $3,250.

In October, 1967, the Bureau of Labor Statistics and the Bureau of the Census published a compendium of statistics on the social and economic conditions of the Negro. Here are some of the major findings:

Income. In 1966, 23 per cent of the nonwhite families had incomes of more than $7,000, and 53 per cent of white families made that much or more. Ten years earlier, using dollars of the same value, the figures were only 9 per cent for nonwhite families and 31 per cent for white families. Outside the South, Negroes did better: 38 per cent of nonwhite families had incomes above $7,000, against 59 per cent of white families.

Occupation. Between 1960 and 1966, the number of non whites in the better-paying and more secure job categories rose faster than the number of whites. There was a 50 per cent increase for non whites in professional, technical and managerial work, and a 13 per cent increase for whites; in clerical jobs the increases were 48 per cent for nonwhites and 19 per cent for whites; in sales, the changes were 32 per cent and 7 per cent, and among foremen and craftsmen they were 45 per cent and 10 per cent. During the same period, the proportion of nonwhites employed as laborers and in private households dropped.

Education. In 1960 there was a gap of 1.9 years between nonwhite and white males over 25 in median years of schooling; by 1966, there was a gap of only 0.5 years. In 1960, 36 per cent of nonwhite males and 63 per cent of white males over 25 had completed high school; by 1966, the figures were 53 per cent for nonwhite males and 73 per cent for white males. In 1960, 3.9 per cent of Negro males and 15.7 per cent of white males had completed college; in 1966, college graduates included 7.4 per cent of Negro males and 17.9 per cent of white males. This represents a 90 per cent increase in nonwhite college graduates and an increase of only 14 per cent among whites.

Housing. Between 1960 and 1966, there was a 25 per cent drop in the number of substandard housing units occupied by nonwhites (from 2.26 million to 1.69 million) and a 44 per cent increase in the number of standard units (from 2.88 million to 4.13 million).

Political participation. Negro voter registration in the South increased from 2.16 million in March, 1964, to 3.07 million in May, 1968, while Negro population remained stable. And the National Advisory Commission on Civil Disorders reported after a survey of 20 cities that they averaged 16 per cent in Negro population while Negroes accounted for 10 per cent of the elected political representatives. This figure must be interpreted in light of the fact that

Negroes of voting age are generally a smaller fraction in the total Negro population than whites of voting age are in the white population; Negroes in cities have a higher proportion of young families and children, whites a higher proportion of the aged.

The police. Even on this sorest point of black-white relations, the Kerner Commission reports progress in one significant respect: there are now substantial numbers of Negroes on many city police forces. In Washington, 21 per cent of the force is Negro; in Philadelphia, 20 per cent; in Chicago, 17; St. Louis, 11; Hartford, 11; Newark, 10; and Atlanta, 10.

These are simply over-all measures. When one considers the number of programs devoted to getting Negroes into colleges, graduate schools and corporations, to raising their grades in the civil service and to moderating police attitudes, one must conclude that the situation of the Negro is improving.

Of course all these figures can be argued with. For instance, we have recently become aware that 14 per cent of Negro males and only 2 per cent of white males were not counted in the 1960 census, and if they were counted they would probably lower the average figures for Negro earnings, education, employment, housing. On the other hand, we probably have not been counting similar proportions of white and Negro males in earlier censuses, so any improvement indicated by change from one census or sample census survey to another is real.

It can also be argued that the quality of jobs held by Negroes, even if they are in white-collar and skilled-labor categories, is lower than that of the whites' jobs, and this is true. But the quality of jobs held by Negroes certainly has not decreased on the average. Fewer Negro professionals today are preachers, more are engineers.

Some people argue that the improvement in economic, educational and housing conditions is largely a result of the Negro's migration from the South to the North and West and from small towns and rural areas to big cities; if we were to study Negroes in the North and West alone, we would not find such marked changes over the last few years. But the statistics show improvement in every section.

Another argument is that these over-all measures of improvement apply only to the Negro middle class and stable working class, that the lower working class has shown no progress. But an unpublished analysis by Albert Wohlstetter of the University of Chicago indicates that the Negro lower-income group has recently made greater progress relative to the white lower-income group than have upper-income Negroes relative to the corresponding white group. It is true, however, that such other measures of social condition as the proportion of broken homes and illegitimacy continue to show worsening conditions among low-income Negroes.

Finally, one may argue that much of the advance to which I have pointed has taken place since the Vietnam War expanded in 1965, just as the previous economic advance of the Negro took place during the Korean War and ended with it. Though there was a relative decline or stagnation between the wars, the advances were not fully wiped out; it was rather that the rate of advance was not maintained. By now the build-up of Negro political power and national programs is so great, and the scale of recent achievements is so massive, that I cannot believe they will not continue after the war—provided there is not a radical change in the political situation.

More striking, however, than the advance itself is that on the basis of our present statistics we cannot single out the Negro as a group which suffers unique deprivation as compared to other ethnic and racial groups which suffer from the effects of poor education, depressed rural background and recent migration to urban areas. Social scientists disagree on how to view Negroes in the context of the ethnic and racial history of the United States. One tendency is to emphasize the many unique things: the manner of their arrival (by force and in chains); the condition in which they lived for 200 years (slavery); the condition in which they have lived for the last 100 years (legal inferiority in much of the country); and the special role of the Negro in helping shape American culture and imagination.

But one can also view Negroes in the American context as part of a series of ethnic and racial groups that have moved into society and become a part of it. There is a new illusion which asserts that all white ethnic groups moving into American society have quickly achieved respectable levels of income, good living conditions and political power; that all racially distinct groups have been held back, and that the Negro, because of the unique character of slavery, is furthest back. The truth is nothing like this. Some white ethnic groups—the Jews, for instance—have shown a rapid economic rise; others have been much slower to achieve in this area. One of the economically backward white ethnic groups, the Irish, has been politically gifted, and its members are among elected officials at all levels in almost every part of the country. Other ethnic groups, such as Italians and Poles, have done poorly both economically and politically. Some racially distinct groups—the Japanese, for example —have done remarkably well in education and occupation; most others have done badly.

The Negro's situation is more complex than the gross simplification of having started at the bottom and having stayed there. By some measures, Puerto Ricans do worse in New York and Mexican Americans do worse in the Southwest. One can argue that the Negro is worse off than other groups in this country, but the difference is not great enough to explain by itself the special quality of despair and hysteria that dominates much Negro political discourse. Of course we must realize that our national obligation to improve the Negro's position is much greater than our obligation to those who came here voluntarily. The Negro is aware of this, and the inferiority of his position is thus more grating than it would be to other groups.

Regardless of how we view their social position, a growing number of the 22 million United States Negroes believe that Americans are racists and that the only solution is some form of separate political existence. One indication of how far this trend has gone is in the use of words—"genocide," for example. . . . By now even moderate leaders use the term "genocide," perhaps feeling they have to show they are not Toms. And by now, of course, white men who want to demonstrate their sympathy for Negroes also use the term. . . .

The public-opinion polls report rapid changes of attitude among Negroes. A Harris poll conducted *before* Martin Luther King's assassination concluded that the number of Negroes alienated rose from 34 per cent in 1966 to 56 per cent in 1968. The proportion of respondents who agreed with the statement "Few people really understand how it is to live like I live" rose from 32 per cent to 66 per cent; those who agreed that "People running the country don't really care what happens to people like ourselves" rose from 32 per cent to 52 per cent. Yet in the same poll, 73 per cent of the respondents agreed that there had been more racial progress in recent years than previously.

More impressive than attitudes and the use of words, however, is action—the rioting, the expectation of guerrilla warfare, the rise of such groups as the Black Panthers, who call for armed resistance to the police, the freeing of black prisoners and—ultimately—a separate national political existence.

There are three points of view on what to do about rising extremism in the face of social improvement. One group contends that we must strengthen the police, create riot-control forces and put down extremism. A second holds that we must increase the rate of social improvement in the hope of creating a harmonious nation. The third position is that social improvement is no longer the issue, that separate political power for Negroes is the only thing that will satisfy them.

The majority of white Americans, I think, reject the first point of view, though most of them believe that the maintenance of civil order must be part of the national response to the crisis. The second position is the one for which the Kerner Commission has written a brief and to which, undoubtedly, most liberals subscribe. It is almost the only position open to one who believes, as I do, that our society is on the whole a success and that it can handle the complex and frightening problems of an advanced technology better than such alternatives as the varied assortment of Communist authoritarian states or the unexplicated utopia that is the vague hope of the New Left. The liberal position does, however, have at least one basic difficulty.

It is that we have already carried out social programs on an ever-expanding scale without any movement toward the reward of a united and peaceful nation that is the Kerner Commission's hope. Take the commission's own figures:

> Federal expenditures for manpower development and training have increased from less than $60-million in 1963 to $1.6-billion in 1968. The President has proposed a further increase, to $2.1-billion, in 1969. . . . Federal expenditures for education, training and related services have increased from $4.7-billion in fiscal 1964 to $12.3-billion in fiscal 1969. . . . Direct Federal expenditures for housing and community development have increased from $600-million in fiscal 1964 to nearly $3-billion in fiscal 1969.

There have been similar increases in health and welfare expenditures.

I am left with the uneasy feeling that if these increases have taken place at the same time as the spread of urban riots and political extremism, it is questionable whether a further expansion will stem them. I am for expanding and improving the programs because they are our major means for achieving equality in education, housing and the like, but I do not think we can count on them to moderate attitudes; political attitudes have a life of their own and are not simply reflections of economic and social conditions. The demand for separatism will not easily be moderated by social programs. We must face up to it on its own terms.

White America must recognize that separatism means a host of things, many of them—positive identification with the group, greater political representation and economic power for the black man, the teaching of black history and arts in the schools—valuable and healthy for Negroes and American society. The major problem is the demand for territorial autonomy—a group of states set aside as a black nation or black enclaves in the cities with certain rights and powers. Certainly most white Americans will resist these demands for territorial autonomy and extraterritoriality.[1] One war has been fought to keep the nation united, and the sense of what all

[1] Greater local community control—over schools, police, urban renewal—is a definite possibility and even likelihood. It is territorial autonomy for black areas as such which raises the major issue.

Americans gain from a united nation and what they might lose from a divided one is strong enough to insure that these demands will continue to be resisted. Nor is it clear that any substantial number of Negroes want autonomy. The leaders who demand it are powerfully supported, I think, not by the realities of the Negro condition and the hope they offer of improving it, but by powerful ideologies, in particular by the belief that American Negroes are a colonial people who must be freed from their colonial status even if they enjoy all the rights of every other American.

If the demand for territorial independence captures the minds of Negroes, it will be because Americans—black and white—have failed to understand the relationship between their society and the groups that make it up. Many people see society as far more monolithic and homogeneous than it has ever been. I am afraid that whites will fight to retain something that has never existed and blacks will fight because they do not realize the enormous scope the society grants for group diversity and self-fulfillment.

Almost every group that has settled in this country has been nationalistic and separatist, and the laws have permitted for most of them a degree of separatism not yet reached by Negroes. Many groups have supported—sometimes with armed volunteers—nationalist leaders intent upon freeing or revolutionizing their homelands, even when this was a matter of great embarrassment to the United States. Most groups have maintained schools in their own languages and have tried to foster their religious and ethnic customs and beliefs among their children. The major outer limits set on the development of racial and ethnic groups in this country have been an insistence on political loyalty to the United States and a denial of territorial autonomy.

All Americans are aware of the prejudice almost all immigrant and racial groups have faced, but we tend to be less aware of the adjustments our society has eventually made to accommodate them. We have, for instance, developed a political system in which groups of any substantial number are represented among appointed or elected officials; the system has worked well without any laws specifying how much or what kind of recognition should be given. The general freedom this country grants to business enterprises has aided the economic integration of minority groups. (Unfortunately, the ability to create independent economic bases is now considerably limited by—among other things—state and local licensing requirements, union regulations and Federal tax and accounting procedures. This, of course, makes it more difficult for the less sophisticated and literate to become successful in business.) We have granted full freedom to religious organization, and under its protection a wide range of educational, cultural, political and social activities is carried on.

Compared with most countries that have tried to create themselves out of a mixed population, there has been a certain genius in the American style of handling this problem. The principle has been that there is no formal recognition of an ethnic or racial group, but there is every informal recognition of the right to self-development and integration at the group's own rate and to independence in social, religious and political matters. The principle has often been ignored; we have enacted laws that discriminate against some groups—most notably Negroes, but also American Indians and Orientals—and we have often restricted the development of certain groups through "Americanization" movements. But most breaks with these principles—from slavery to immigration quotas by race—have in the end been recognized as un-American and over-turned by the courts and legislatures and, in the most important case, war.

To say that Negroes have been a part of this pattern may seem to be no more than a refusal to face the evil in American society. Prof. Robert Blauner of the University of California at Berkeley has argued forcefully that there are "colonized" peoples in the United States who do not fit the ethnic pattern I have described; among them, he says, are Negroes, American Indians and, to some extent, Mexican Americans. According to this argument, the self-regulated rate of integration prevailed only for European immigrants and, to a much more modest degree, prevails now for the Chinese and Japanese. Blauner contends that there has been a different pattern for peoples we have conquered or brought here as slaves: this is a pattern of internal colonization, whereby these groups have been made inferior to the "settlers" politically, economically, socially and culturally; for them the only meaningful course is the colonial one: rebellion, resistance and, conceivably, forceful overthrow of the "settler." If Professor Blauner is right, we settlers must figure out how to grant to the colonized the independence that will make them whole or how to resist their effort to take it and perhaps destroy the society in doing so.

For one basic reason, I think the Blauner argument is wrong. Whatever relevance the colonization theory may have had in the past—when Negroes lived as agricultural workers in the South, Mexican Americans in villages in the Southwest and Indians on their reservations—it is scarcely relevant today, when three-quarters of American Negroes have moved to cities to become not only workers and servants but skilled workers, foremen, civil servants, profes-sionals and white-collar workers of all types; when at a slower rate the same thing is happening to Mexican Americans, and when even Indians can free themselves from any politically inferior status by giving up the reservation and moving to the city, as more and more are doing. These moves are voluntary—or if involuntary to some extent, no more so than the migration of many other groups escaping political persecution and economic misery. They lead to the creation of a voluntary community of self-help institutions. They lead to a largely self-regulated rate at which group cultural patterns are given up and new ones adopted. It is all quite comparable to what happened to the European immigrant.

The existence of prejudice and discrimination does not make the colonial analogy fit. They occur wherever different groups interact socially. Are the Algerian workers in the slum settlements around Paris and the Spanish and Turkish immigrant workers in Europe "colonized"? Or are they simply immigrants facing the discrimination that is so often the lot of immigrants? Nor are prejudice and discrimination insuperable obstacles to political and economic advancement. The important questions rather, are the *level* of discrimination, how it is reflected in *harmful policies*, what *state assistance* it gets and to what extent the *state acts against it*. Tested this way, the colonial analogy becomes meaningless. There has been a steady decline in all forms of expressed prejudice against Negroes; it is indicated by opinion polls and by everyday behavior. There is ever-stronger state action against prejudice and discrimination, even in parts of the South.

The colonial pattern makes sense if there is a *legal* inferiority of the colonized, or if, even in the case of *formal* equality, in fact only tiny proportions of the colonized can reach high statuses. But this is not true of the Negro Americans—nor will it be true shortly of the Mexican Americans and, if they so choose, of American Indians. The fact is that instead of keeping these groups out of privileged statuses, most public policy and the policy of most large private institutions is to bring them in larger and larger numbers into privileged statuses—what else is the meaning of the work of the Federal Civil Service in upgrading minority employees, of the colleges in recruiting minority students in greater numbers than could normally qualify, of the various corporation programs for increasing numbers of minority-group executives and franchise holders? The scale of most of this effort is still much too small, but its aim is to speed up the incorporation of the minority groups into the mixed American society rather than to slow it down.

The question of whether American Negroes are "colonized" is ultimately to be answered only by the Negroes. If they see themselves as being prevented by the American pattern from achieving the independence they want, they will do everything in their power to break the pattern. Then all Americans may have to choose between the suffering of another war of national unity and the dangers of separatism.

Three factors still argue against the eventual victory of the colonial theory. The first is the large number of Negroes who *are* integrated—civil servants, white-collar workers, union members, party members and elected officials. Second, there is the possibility that moderate social change may still pacify the militants. While they demand independence, they might be satisfied with more and better jobs, more political power, better schools and housing and as much institutional identity and control as the American society can allow. Finally, there is the enormous practical difficulty of satisfying the demand of a scattered people for territorial separation or of finding acceptable alternatives.

Among the factors working toward the success of the colonial analogy among Negroes is the importance to them of their experience in the South, where they were indeed colonized and where there remains in large sections the most unrelenting resistance to black equality. The colonial imagery of the South has been transported to the cities of East and West, which are largely free of colonialism. There it struggles against the immigrant analogy, and on the whole it is losing.

The second factor working for the colonial analogy is our failure to adopt rapidly enough new approaches to achieving effective equality for the Negro. Negro businesses must be created, subsidized, sustained and advised; job programs must become more meaningful; colleges must learn how to incorporate large numbers of minority students, and urban schools must undergo a transformation (though which one it is hard to say). All this is so demanding we may not succeed. Mayor Lindsay of New York, perhaps the dominant liberal member of the Kerner Commission, told businessmen what they must do to make the hard-core unemployed effective:

> You've got to literally adopt this kind of employee, be responsible for his total condition 24 hours a day, 7 days a week. . . . Adopt their families, a piece of the block where they live, a chunk of the city and its future. Know where they live, their economic condition, how their children are, whether there's a police problem, what the neighborhood pressures are. . . .
> The businessman who does hire the hard-core unemployed is going to be confronted with absenteeism, poor working habits, deficiencies in reading and writing, negative attitudes. . . .

If this is what businessmen—and perhaps teachers—must do to employ and educate a substantial part of our minority population, we may not have the compassion, commitment and capacity to succeed.

The third reason that the colonial analogy may win out is the inability of both blacks and whites to understand the American pattern of group incorporation. On the white side, there is a fear of Negro separatism and Negro power that is based on a failure to understand that every group has gone through—and some have maintained—a substantial degree of separatism; all have demanded, and many won, political representation in appointive and elected office and control over pieces of the political action.

As long as we do not succumb to the temptation to become a society of fixed quotas and compartments, we can go some distance in meeting separatist demands. If suburban towns can have their own school systems and police forces, then I can see no reason why parts of a larger city cannot have them. In any case, when the authority of teachers and policemen has been destroyed—and it has in large measure been destroyed in ghetto areas—there is no alternative to some pragmatic adjustment to the creation of new social forms.

Among the blacks, too—and here they are joined by many whites—there is a failure to understand the relationship of the group to society, to understand that, even while prejudice and discrimination exist, those discriminated against can achieve their goals and a respected place in society. There is a failure to understand that different groups vary in their cultural characteristics and in the area and character of their achievements and that an owlish insistence on equality in every area and every characteristic denies the significance of special characteristics and achievements. There may come a time when the special gifts of the American Negro will mean a massive representation in politics or the arts, even if today they mean only an overrepresentation in such fields as professional sports. The special character of American group life—its acceptance of individual merit and its flexible arrangements for group character and pride—should not be destroyed by a demand for fixed quotas and their incorporation into legal and semilegal arrangements.

Above all, I think, black militants and their too-complaisant white allies fail to understand that there *is* an American society with tremendous power to incorporate new groups—to their advantage and its own—and that this is not a *white* society. There is nothing so sad as to hear the Government, the universities and the corporations denounced as white racist institutions. A hundred years ago the same reasoning would have branded them English institutions, but the Germans and Irish became a part of them; 50 years ago they might have been called Christian institutions, but Jews became a part of them. They are not essentially white institutions today any more than they were essentially Christian 50 years ago or English a century ago. They will become white institutions only if Negro Americans insist on full political separation and decide for themselves that the American pattern of group life cannot include them.

4

Crime

Early in 1968 a Gallup Poll revealed that, for the first time since the beginning of scientific polling in the mid-1930s, the American public viewed "crime and lawlessness" as the top domestic problem facing the nation and the local community. A study in Boston by political scientist James Q. Wilson confirmed that, for the majority of people, the urban crisis is not identified with such "conventional" urban problems as housing, urban renewal, transportation, and pollution but rather with lawlessness.[1]

According to both the Gallup and Wilson surveys, the general uneasiness was not caused solely by the increase in muggings, rape, burglaries, and so on. The Gallup category includes riots, looting, and juvenile delinquency. Wilson reports that people were disturbed about the growth in racial tension, public immorality, and rebellious youth as well as crime and violence; and he further notes that "the common theme seemed to be a concern for improper behavior in public places," underlying which was "a sense of the failure of community." So the real issue may be more fundamental than crime as such. The problem may be a general anxiety about the impending breakdown of the social order threatened by the current challenge from many sources to prevailing values and behavioral norms.

Still, reported figures on crime per se show disturbing increases. According to the FBI, from 1960 to 1968 crime

[1] "The Urban Unease: Community vs. City," *The Public Interest*, No. 12 (Summer 1968), p. 26.

had increased 122%, though police solutions of serious crimes dropped 32% in the same period. This contributed to the fact that "law and order" became an increasingly potent political slogan in national, state, and local political campaigns.

This chapter on the issue of crime begins with excerpts from a key public document, quoted by all subsequent writers on the subject: the report of the President's Commission on Law Enforcement and Administration of Justice, *The Challenge of Crime in a Free Society,* in which more than 200 recommendations for change were offered. This is followed by material gathered by the Commission's Task Force on Organized Crime, which indicates that the problem is not limited to the individual law-breaker but is in part a highly organized conspiracy.

In the light of the Crime Commission findings, the statistics on rising crime, and a forthcoming presidential election, it was inevitable that President Johnson would propose legislation in this field. His bill was designed to strengthen local law enforcement by providing modest amounts of federal aid to programs for recruiting and training police, modernizing and reorganizing law enforcement agencies, improving rehabilitation techniques and court systems, and setting up crime-prevention activities in welfare and educational agencies. To congressional leaders like Senator John L. McClellan, Chairman of the Senate Subcommittee on Criminal Laws and Procedure, the President's proposal was mere shadow play. In McClellan's view, the police lacked the tools with which to do the job society had entrusted to them. Since the major handicaps had been inflicted by the Supreme Court, the only recourse was for Congress to countermand the Court. Thus the *Mallory* and *Miranda* decisions, setting stringent conditions before a confession could be accepted in court, must be challenged by new legislation. While electronic eavesdropping by private parties should be banned, the use of wiretap and electronic surveillance devices by law enforcement officers must be legitimized, subject to an appropriate court order. These proposals, together with others strengthening the hands of the police, were embodied in the Senate Judiciary Committee's bill, S. 917, in April 1968.

The proposals were strenuously debated in the Senate. Opponents presented a number of arguments. First, they suggested that, while there was undoubtedly an increase in crime, the crisis had been vastly exaggerated; part of the increase was attributable to a fuller reporting of crimes and an enlargement of the definition of what constituted a crime.[2]

Second, the critics claimed that the real remedies for crime were not to be found in tougher enforcement and more severe penalties but in curing the social ailments that breed crime. As the Crime Commission put it:

> Warring on poverty, inadequate housing, and unemployment is warring on crime. A civil rights law is a law against crime. Money for schools is money against crime. Medical, psychiatric, and family-counselling services are services against crime. More broadly and most importantly every effort to improve life in America's "inner cities" is an effort against crime.

Next, it was suggested that the legislation proposed by the conservatives contained a double standard, for it said little about the white-collar crime rampant in American business. Robert M. Morgenthau, then a U.S. Attorney from New York, attacked "persons who publicly denounce crimes of violence while privately committing more 'socially acceptable' white-collar crimes": men who use secret numbered Swiss bank accounts for tax evasion and stock manipulation, "all too frequently highly respectable corporation executives, businessmen, brokers, accountants and lawyers—men who would be the first to complain about a robbery or a mugging in their neighborhood."

Finally, opponents of S. 917 protested that *Mallory* and *Miranda* were necessary protections of the accused against police power. In the *Miranda* case Chief Justice Warren had quoted from several police manuals on interrogation, in which it was suggested that questioning take place in

---

[2]Some skepticism has also been expressed about the extent of the danger represented by organized crime. In 1961 Daniel Bell suggested that organized crime's share of the economy was not growing but shrinking. ("The Myth of Crime Waves" in *The End of Ideology* [Glencoe, Ill.: Free Press], ch. 8.) Murray Kempton has pointed to the vagueness of the estimates contained in studies of the subject (note that the Task Force cites estimates of gambling revenues ranging from $7 billion to $50 billion) and contends that the power and resources of the Mafia have been exaggerated. ("Crime Does Not Pay," *New York Review of Books* [September 11, 1969], pp. 5-10.) It is an important question, for much of the case for giving police the right to wiretap is based on the assumption that organized crime represents a massive threat to the public order.

a police station rather than in a suspect's home. As one of these manuals pointed out, the home provides a supportive atmosphere, whereas "in his own office, the investigator possesses all the advantages." The same manual advises the questioner to "interrogate without relent, leaving the subject no prospect of surcease." Various devices are also suggested to encourage a confession, including the mention of other unrelated crimes and a line-up with a coached witness, in the hope that "the subject will become desperate and confess to the offense under investigation in order to escape from the false accusations." The critics claimed that leaving the police unchecked to do this kind of thing, and in addition giving them the right to eavesdrop, would lead us in the direction of a police state.

The Senate listened to these arguments but then voted overwhelmingly against them. While the conservative coalition sponsoring S. 917 was defeated on proposals that would go so far as to deny the Supreme Court's jurisdiction over some state court determinations, the proposals debated in this chapter were accepted by overwhelming margins; and the final bill was approved with only four dissenting votes in the Senate and seventeen in the House. President Johnson declared his unhappiness with the product, but he signed it in June 1968.[3] He would not stand against the unmistakable mood of the country, and the legislation contained a very limited regulation of gun sales which he could get only by accepting the entire bill.

The Nixon Administration has displayed no reluctance at all to accept the principles built into the legislation. Attorney General Mitchell approves of the wiretapping provisions, and he has instructed federal law enforcement officials to proceed under the congressional mandate on voluntary confessions until the Supreme Court expresses itself again on the matter. While the Court is the final arbiter of the Constitution (short of a Constitutional amendment), *Miranda* was a 5-4 decision; and there are new Nixon-appointed members on the Supreme Court.

At the center of these controversies stand the local police forces. Seymour Lipset shows that they tend to adopt conservative, sometimes right-wing positions. They are the target of attacks by liberals, by the New Left, by minority groups. They have been scathingly indicted in Daniel Walker's

[3]Omnibus Crime Control and Safe Streets Act of 1968, Public Law 90-351.

report to the National Violence Commission on the events surrounding the Democratic National Convention in 1968.[4] Still, as Lipset points out, there is objectively a problem of crime and lawlessness in America today. The police—low in salaries, status, and numbers—are asked to cope with that problem. And, as James Q. Wilson has observed,[5] even if all of the more than 200 recommendations of the Crime Commission are implemented, the problem of crime will not be resolved in the 70s.

[4] *Rights in Conflict* (New York: Signet Books, The New American Library, 1968).
[5] "What Makes a Better Policeman," *The Atlantic,* Vol. 223, No. 3 (March 1969), pp. 129-135.

THE CHALLENGE OF CRIME IN A FREE SOCIETY

President's Commission on Law Enforcement and Administration of Justice

Nicholas deB. Katzenbach was Chairman of the Commission, which was appointed by President Johnson.

. . . Many Americans take comfort in the view that crime is the vice of a handful of people. This view is inaccurate. In the United States today, one boy in six is referred to the juvenile court. A Commission survey shows that in 1965 more than two million Americans were received in prisons or juvenile training schools, or placed on probation. Another Commission study suggests that about 40 percent of all male children now living in the United States will be arrested for a nontraffic offense during their lives. An independent survey of 1,700 persons found that 91 percent of the sample

President's Commission on Law Enforcement and Administration of Justice, *The Challenge of Crime in a Free Society, A Report* (Washington, D.C.: Government Printing Office, February 1967), pp. v-xi.

admitted they had committed acts for which they might have received jail or prison sentences.

Many Americans also think of crime as a very narrow range of behavior. It is not. An enormous variety of acts make up the "crime problem." Crime is not just a tough teenager snatching a lady's purse. It is a professional thief stealing cars "on order." It is a well-heeled loan shark taking over a previously legitimate business for organized crime. It is a polite young man who suddenly and inexplicably murders his family. It is a corporation executive conspiring with competitors to keep prices high. No single formula, no single theory, no single generalization can explain the vast range of behavior called crime.

Many Americans think controlling crime is solely the task of the police, the courts, and correction agencies. In fact . . . crime cannot be controlled without the interest and participation of schools, businesses, social agencies, private groups, and individual citizens.

What, then, is America's experience with crime and how has this experience shaped the Nation's way of living? A new insight into these two questions is furnished by the Commission's National Survey of Criminal Victims. In this survey, the first of its kind conducted on such a scope, 10,000 representative American households were asked about their experiences with crime, whether they reported those experiences to the police, and how those experiences affected their lives.

An important finding of the survey is that for the Nation as a whole there is far more crime than ever is reported. Burglaries occur about three times more often than they are reported to police. Aggravated assaults and larcenies over $50 occur twice as often as they are reported. There are 50 percent more robberies than are reported. In some areas, only one-tenth of the total number of certain kinds of crimes are reported to the police. Seventy-four percent of the neighborhood commercial establishments surveyed do not report to police the thefts committed by their employees.

The existence of crime, the talk about crime, the reports of crime, and the fear of crime have eroded the basic quality of life of many Americans. A Commission study conducted in high crime areas of two large cities found that:

43 percent of the respondents say they stay off the streets at night because of their fear of crime.

35 percent say they do not speak to strangers any more because of their fear of crime.

21 percent say they use cars and cabs at night because of their fear of crime.

20 percent say they would like to move to another neighborhood because of their fear of crime.

The findings of the Commission's national survey generally support those of the local surveys. One-third of a representative sample of all Americans say it is unsafe to walk alone at night in their neighborhoods. Slightly more than one-third say they keep firearms in the house for protection against criminals. Twenty-eight percent say they keep watchdogs for the same reason.

Under any circumstance, developing an effective response to the problem of crime in America is exceedingly difficult. And because of the changes expected in the population in the next decade, in years to come it will be more difficult. Young people commit a disproportionate share of crime and the number of young people in our society is growing at a much faster rate than the total population. Although the 15- to 17-year-old age group represents only 5.4 percent of the population, it accounts for 12.8 percent of all arrests. Fifteen and sixteen year olds have the highest arrest rate in the United States. The problem in the years ahead is dramatically foretold by the fact that 23 percent of the population is 10 or under.

Despite the seriousness of the problem today and the increasing challenge in the years ahead, the central conclusion of the Commission is that a significant reduction in crime is possible if the following objectives are vigorously pursued:

First, society must seek to prevent crime before it happens by assuring all Americans a stake in the benefits and responsibilities of American life, by strengthening law enforcement, and by reducing criminal opportunities.

Second, society's aim of reducing crime would be better served if the system of criminal justice developed a far broader range of techniques with which to deal with individual offenders.

Third, the system of criminal justice must eliminate existing injustices if it is to achieve its ideals and win the respect and cooperation of all citizens.

Fourth, the system of criminal justice must attract more people and better people—police, prosecutors, judges, defense attorneys, probation and parole officers, and corrections officials with more knowledge, expertise, initiative, and integrity.

Fifth, there must be much more operational and basic research into the problems of crime and criminal administration, by those both within and without the system of criminal justice.

Sixth, the police, courts, and correctional agencies must be given substantially greater amounts of money if they are to improve their ability to control crime.

Seventh, individual citizens, civic and business organizations, religious institutions, and all levels of government must take responsibility for planning and implementing the changes that must be made in the criminal justice system if crime is to be reduced.

In terms of specific recommendations, what do these seven objectives mean?

1. Preventing Crime

The prevention of crime covers a wide range of activities: Eliminating social conditions closely associated with crime; improving the ability of the criminal justice system to detect, apprehend, judge, and reintegrate into their communities those who commit crimes; and reducing the situations in which crimes are most likely to be committed.

Every effort must be made to strengthen the family, now often shattered by the grinding pressures of urban slums.

Slum schools must be given enough resources to make them as good as schools elsewhere and to enable them to compensate for the various handicaps suffered by the slum child—to rescue him from his environment.

Present efforts to combat school segregation, and the housing segregation that underlies it, must be continued and expanded.

Employment opportunities must be enlarged and young people provided with more effective vocational training and individual job counseling. Programs to create new kinds of jobs—such as probation aides, medical assistants, and teacher helpers—seem particularly promising and should be expanded.

The problem of increasing the ability of the police to detect and apprehend criminals is complicated. In one effort to find out how this objective could be achieved, the Commission conducted an analysis of 1,905 crimes reported to the Los Angeles Police Department during a recent month. The study showed the importance of identifying the perpetrator at the scene of the crime. Eighty-six percent of the crimes with named suspects were solved, but only 12 percent of the unnamed suspect crimes were solved. Another finding of the study was that there is a relationship between the speed of response and certainty of apprehension. On the average, response to emergency calls resulting in arrests was 50 percent faster than response to emergency calls not resulting in arrest. On the basis of this finding, and a cost effectiveness study to discover the best means to reduce response time, the Commission recommends an experimental program to develop computer-aided command-and-control systems for large police departments. . . .

Another way to prevent crime is to reduce the opportunity to commit it. Many crimes would not be committed, indeed many criminal careers would not begin, if there were fewer opportunities for crime.

Auto theft is a good example. According to FBI statistics, the key had been left in the ignition or the ignition had been left unlocked in 42 percent of all stolen cars. Even in those cars taken when the ignition was locked, at least 20 percent were stolen simply by shorting the ignition with such simple devices as paper clips or tinfoil. In one city, the elimination of the unlocked "off" position on the 1965 Chevrolet resulted in 50 percent fewer of those models being stolen in 1965 than were stolen in 1964.

On the basis of these findings, it appears that an important reduction in auto theft could be achieved simply by installing an ignition system that automatically ejects the key when the engine is turned off.

A major reason that it is important to reduce auto theft is that stealing a car is very often the criminal act that starts a boy on a course of lawbreaking.

Stricter gun controls also would reduce some kinds of crime. Here, the Commission recommends a strengthening of the Federal law governing the interstate shipment of firearms and enactment of State laws requiring the registration of all handguns, rifles, and shotguns, and prohibiting the sale or ownership of firearms by certain categories of persons—dangerous criminals, habitual drunkards, and drug addicts. After 5 years, the Commission recommends that Congress pass a Federal registration law applying to those States that have not passed their own registration laws.

2. New Ways of Dealing with Offenders

The Commission's second objective—the development of a far broader range of alternatives for dealing with offenders—is based on the belief that, while there are some who must be completely segregated from society, there are many instances in which segregation does more harm than good. Furthermore, by concentrating the resources of the police, the courts, and correctional agencies on the smaller number of offenders who really need them, it should be possible to give all offenders more effective treatment.

A specific and important example of this principle is the Commission's recommendation that every community consider establishing a Youth Services Bureau, a community-based center to which juveniles could be referred by the police, the courts, parents, schools, and social agencies for counseling, education, work, or recreation programs and job placement. . . .

To make community-based treatment possible for both adults and juveniles, the Commission recommends the development of an entirely new kind of correctional institution: located close to population centers; maintaining close relations with schools, employers, and universities; housing as few as 50 inmates; serving as a classification center, as the center for various kinds of community programs and as a port of reentry to the community for those difficult and dangerous offenders who have required treatment in facilities with tighter custody.

Such institutions would be useful in the operation of programs—strongly recommended by the Commission—that permit selected inmates to work or study in the community during the day and return to control at night, and programs that permit long-term inmates to become adjusted to society gradually rather than being discharged directly from maximum security institutions to the streets.

Another aspect of the Commission's conviction that different offenders with different problems should be treated in different ways, is its recommendation about the handling of public drunkenness, which, in 1965, accounted for one out of every three arrests in America. The great number of these arrests—some 2 million—burdens the police, clogs the lower courts and crowds the penal institutions. The Commission therefore recommends that communities develop civil detoxification units and comprehensive aftercare programs, and that with the development of such programs, drunkenness, not accompanied by other unlawful conduct, should not be a criminal offense.

Similarly, the Commission recommends the expanded use of civil commitment for drug addicts.

3. Eliminating Unfairness

The third objective is to eliminate injustices so that the system of criminal justice can win the respect and cooperation of all citizens. Our society must give the police, the courts, and correctional agencies the resources and the mandate to provide fair and dignified treatment for all.

The Commission found overwhelming evidence of institutional shortcomings in almost every part of the United States.

A survey of the lower court operations in a number of large American cities found cramped and noisy courtrooms, undignified and perfunctory procedures, badly trained personnel overwhelmed by enormous caseloads. In short, the Commission found assembly line justice.

The Commission found that in at least three States, justices of the peace are paid only if they convict and collect a fee from the defendant, a practice held unconstitutional by the Supreme Court 40 years ago.

The Commission found that approximately one-fourth of the 400,000 children detained in 1965—for a variety of causes but including truancy, smoking, and running away from home—were held in adult jails and lockups, often with hardened criminals.

In addition to the creation of new kinds of institutions—such as the Youth Services Bureau and the small, community-based correctional centers—the Commission recommends several important procedural changes. It recommends counsel at various points in the criminal process.

For juveniles, the Commission recommends providing counsel whenever coercive action is a possibility.

For adults, the Commission recommends providing counsel to any criminal defendant who faces a significant penalty—excluding traffic and similar petty charges—if he cannot afford to provide counsel for himself.

In connection with this recommendation, the Commission asks each State to finance regular, statewide assigned counsel and defender systems for the indigent.

Counsel also should be provided in parole and probation revocation hearings.

Another kind of broad procedural change that the Commission recommends is that every State, county, and local jurisdiction provide judicial officers with sufficient information about individual defendants to permit the release without money bail of those who can be safely released.

In addition to eliminating the injustice of holding persons charged with a crime merely because they cannot afford bail, this recommendation also would save a good deal of money. New York City alone, for example, spends approximately $10 million a year holding persons who have not yet been found guilty of any crime.

Besides institutional injustices, the Commission found that while the great majority of criminal justice and law enforcement personnel perform their duties with fairness and understanding, even under the most trying circumstances, some take advantage of their official positions and act in a callous, corrupt, or brutal manner. . . .

The relations between the police and urban poor deserve special mention. Here the Commission recommends that every large department—especially in communities with substantial minority populations—should have community-relations machinery consisting of a headquarters planning and supervising unit and precinct units to carry out recommended programs. Effective citizen advisory committees should be established in minority group neighborhoods. All departments with substantial minority populations should make special efforts to recruit minority group officers and to deploy and promote them fairly. They should have rigorous internal investigation units to examine complaints of misconduct. The Commission believes it is of the utmost importance to insure that complaints of unfair treatment are fairly dealt with.

Fair treatment of every individual—fair in fact and also perceived to be fair by those affected—is an essential element of justice and a principal objective of the American criminal justice system.

4. Personnel

The fourth objective is that higher levels of knowledge, expertise, initiative, and integrity be achieved by police, judges, prosecutors, defense attorneys, and correctional authorities so that the system of criminal justice can improve its ability to control crime.

The Commission found one obstacle to recruiting better police officers was the standard requirement that all candidates—regardless of qualifications—begin their careers at the lowest level and normally remain at this level from 2 to 5 years before being eligible for promotion. Thus, a college graduate must enter a department at the same rank and pay and perform the same tasks as a person who enters with only a high school diploma or less.

The Commission recommends that police departments give up single entry and establish three levels at which candidates may begin their police careers. The Commission calls these three levels the "community service officer," the "police officer," and the "police agent."

This division, in addition to providing an entry place for the better educated, also would permit police departments to tap the special knowledge, skills, and understanding of those brought up in the slums.

The community service officer would be a uniformed but unarmed member of the police department. Two of his major responsibilities would be to maintain close relations with juveniles in the area where he works and to be especially alert to crime-breeding conditions that other city agencies had not dealt with. Typically, the CSO might be under 21, might not be required to meet conventional education requirements, and might work out of a store-front office. Serving as an apprentice policeman—a substitute for the police cadet—the CSO would work as a member of a team with the police officer and police agent.

The police officer would respond to calls for service, perform routine patrol, render emergency services, make preliminary investigations, and enforce traffic regulations. In order to qualify as a police officer at the present time, a candidate should possess a high school diploma and should demonstrate a capacity for college work.

The police agent would do whatever police jobs were most complicated, most sensitive, and most demanding. He might be a specialist in police community-relations or juvenile delinquency. He might be in uniform patrolling a high-crime neighborhood. He might have staff duties. To become a police agent would require at least 2 years of college work and preferably a baccalaureate degree in the liberal arts or social sciences.

As an ultimate goal, the Commission recommends that all police personnel with general enforcement powers have baccalaureate degrees.

While candidates could enter the police service at any one of the three levels, they also could work their way up through the different categories as they met the basic education and other requirements.

In many jurisdictions there is a critical need for additional police personnel. Studies by the Commission indicate a recruiting need of 50,000 policemen in 1967 just to fill positions already authorized. In order to increase police effectiveness, additional staff specialists will be required, and when the community service officers are added manpower needs will be even greater. . . .

In order to improve the quality of judges, prosecutors, and defense attorneys, the Commission recommends a variety of steps: Taking the selection of judges out of partisan politics; the more regular use of seminars, conferences, and institutes to train sitting judges; the establishment of judicial commissions to excuse physically or mentally incapacitated judges from their duties without public humiliation; the general abolition of part-time district attorneys and assistant district attorneys; and a broad range of measures to develop a greatly enlarged and better trained pool of defense attorneys.

In the correctional system there is a critical shortage of probation and parole officers, teachers, caseworkers, vocational instructors, and group workers. . . .

To meet the requirements of both the correctional agencies and the courts, the Commission has found an immediate need to double the Nation's pool of juvenile probation officers, triple the number of probation officers working with adult felons, and increase sevenfold the number of officers working with misdemeanants.

Another area with a critical need for large numbers of expert criminal justice officers is the complex one of controlling organized crime. Here, the Commission recommends that prosecutors and police in every State and city where organized crime is known to, or may, exist develop special organized crime units.

5. Research

The fifth objective is that every segment of the system of criminal justice devote a significant part of its resources for research to insure the development of new and effective methods of controlling crime. . . .

A small fraction of 1 percent of the criminal justice system's total budget is spent on research. This figure could be multiplied many times without approaching the 3 percent industry spends on research, much less the 15 percent the Defense Department spends. The Commission believes it should be multiplied many times. . . .

6. Money

Sixth, the police, the courts, and correctional agencies will require substantially more money if they are to control crime better.

Almost all of the specific recommendations made by the Commission will involve increased budgets. Substantially higher salaries must be offered to attract top-flight candidates to the system of criminal justice. . . .

The Commission also recommends new kinds of programs that will require additional funds: Youth Services Bureaus, greatly enlarged misdemeanant probation services and increased levels of research, for example.

The commission believes some of the additional resources—especially those devoted to innovative programs and to training, education, and research—should be contributed by the Federal Government. . . .

7. Responsibility for Change

Seventh, individual citizens, social-service agencies, universities, religious institutions, civic and business groups, and all kinds of governmental agencies at all levels must become involved in planning and executing changes in the criminal justice system. . . .

While this report has concentrated on recommendations for action by governments, the Commission is convinced that governmental actions will not be enough. Crime is a social problem that is interwoven with almost every aspect of American life. Controlling it involves improving the quality of family life, the way schools are run, the way cities are planned, the way workers are hired. Controlling crime is the business of every American institution. Controlling crime is the business of every American.

Universities should increase their research on the problems of crime; private social welfare organizations and religious institutions should continue to experiment with advanced techniques of helping slum children overcome their environment; labor unions and businesses can enlarge their programs to provide prisoners with vocational training; professional and community organizations can help probation and parole workers with their work.

The responsibility of the individual citizen runs far deeper than cooperating with the police or accepting jury duty or insuring the safety of his family by installing adequate locks—important as they are. He must respect the law, refuse to cut corners, reject the cynical argument that "anything goes as long as you don't get caught."

Most important of all, he must, on his own and through the organizations he belongs to, interest himself in the problems of crime and criminal justice, seek information, express his views, use his vote wisely, get involved.

In sum, the Commission is sure that the Nation can control crime if it will.

ORGANIZED CRIME

Task Force of the President's Commission on Law Enforcement and Administration of Justice

The Task Force on Organized Crime included Kingman Brewster, Thomas J. Cahill, and Lewis F. Powell, Jr. Consultants were G. Robert Blakey, Donald R. Cressey, John Gardiner, Rufus King, Ralph Salerno, and Gus Tyler.

Organized crime is a society that seeks to operate outside the control of the American people and their governments. It involves thousands of criminals, working within structures as complex as those of any large corporation, subject to laws more rigidly enforced than those of legitimate governments. Its actions are not impulsive

President's Commission on Law Enforcement and Administration of Justice, *Task Force Report: Organized Crime* (Washington, D.C.: U.S. Government Printing Office, 1967), pp. 1-6, 24.

but rather the result of intricate conspiracies, carried on over many years and aimed at gaining control over whole fields of activity in order to amass huge profits.

The core of organized crime activity is the supplying of illegal goods and services—gambling, loan sharking, narcotics, and other forms of vice—to countless numbers of citizen customers. But organized crime is also extensively and deeply involved in legitimate business and in labor unions. Here it employs illegitimate methods—monopolization, terrorism, extortion, tax evasion—to drive out or control lawful ownership and leadership and to exact illegal profits from the public. And to carry on its many activities secure from governmental interference, organized crime corrupts public officials.

Former Attorney General Robert F. Kennedy illustrated its power simply and vividly. He testified before a Senate subcommittee in 1963 that the physical protection of witnesses who had cooperated with the Federal Government in organized crime cases often required that those witnesses change their appearances, change their names, or even leave the country. When the government of a powerful country is unable to protect its friends from its enemies by means less extreme than obliterating their identities surely it is being seriously challenged, if not threatened.

What organized crime wants is money and power. What makes it different from law-abiding organizations and individuals with those same objectives is that the ethical and moral standards the criminals adhere to, the laws and regulations they obey, the procedures they use are private and secret ones that they devise themselves, change when they see fit, and administer summarily and invisibly. Organized crime affects the lives of millions of Americans, but because it desperately preserves its invisibility many, perhaps most, Americans are not aware how they are affected, or even that they are affected at all. The price of a loaf of bread may go up one cent as the result of an organized crime conspiracy, but a housewife has no way of knowing why she is paying more. If organized criminals paid income tax on every cent of their vast earnings everybody's tax bill would go down, but no one knows how much.

But to discuss the impact of organized crime in terms of whatever direct, personal, everyday effect it has on individuals is to miss most of the point. Most individuals are not affected, in this sense, very much. Much of the money organized crime accumulates comes from innumerable petty transactions: 50-cent bets, $3-a-month private garbage collection services, quarters dropped into racketeer-owned jukeboxes, or small price rises resulting from protection rackets. A one-cent-a-loaf rise in bread may annoy housewives, but it certainly does not impoverish them.

Sometimes organized crime's activities do not directly affect individuals at all. Smuggled cigarettes in a vending machine cost consumers no more than tax-paid cigarettes, but they enrich the leaders of organized crime. Sometimes these activities actually reduce prices for a short period of time, as can happen when organized crime, in an attempt to take over an industry, starts a price war against legitimate businessmen. Even when organized crime engages in a large transaction, individuals may not be directly affected. A large sum of money may be diverted from a union pension fund to finance a business venture without immediate and direct effect upon the individual members of the union.

It is organized crime's accumulation of money, not the individual transactions by which the money is accumulated, that has a great and threatening impact on America. A quarter in a jukebox means nothing and results in nothing. But millions of quarters in thousands of jukeboxes can provide both a strong motive for murder and the means to commit murder with impunity. Organized crime exists by virtue of the power it purchases with its money. The millions of dollars it can invest in narcotics or use for payoff money give it power over the lives of thousands of people and over the quality of life in whole neighborhoods. The millions of dollars it can throw into the legitimate economic system give it power to manipulate the price of shares on the stock market, to raise or lower the price of retail merchandise, to determine whether entire industries are union or nonunion, to make it easier or harder for businessmen to continue in business.

The millions of dollars it can spend on corrupting public officials may give it power to maim or murder people inside or outside the organization with impunity; to extort money from businessmen; to conduct businesses in such fields as liquor, meat, or drugs without regard to administrative regulations; to avoid payment of income taxes or to secure public works contracts without competitive bidding.

The purpose of organized crime is not competition with visible, legal government but nullification of it. When organized crime places an official in public office, it nullifies the political process. When it bribes a police official, it nullifies law enforcement.

There is another, more subtle way in which organized crime has an impact on American life. Consider the former way of life of Frank Costello, a man who has repeatedly been called a leader of organized crime. He lived in an expensive apartment on the corner of 72d Street and Central Park West in New York. He was often seen dining in well-known restaurants in the company of judges, public officials, and prominent businessmen. Every morning he was shaved in the barbershop of the Waldorf Astoria Hotel. On many weekends he played golf at a country club on the fashionable North Shore of Long Island. In short, though his reputation was common knowledge, he moved around New York conspicuously and unashamedly, perhaps ostracized by some people but more often accepted, greeted by journalists, recognized by children, accorded all the freedoms of a prosperous and successful man. On a society that treats such a man in such a manner, organized crime has had an impact.

And yet the public remains indifferent. Few Americans seem to comprehend how the phenomenon of organized crime affects their lives. They do not see how gambling with bookmakers, or borrowing money from loan sharks, forwards the interests of great criminal cartels. Businessmen looking for labor harmony or nonunion status through irregular channels rationalize away any suspicions that organized crime is thereby spreading its influence. When an ambitious political candidate accepts substantial cash contributions from unknown sources, he suspects but dismisses the fact that organized crime will dictate some of his actions when he assumes office. . . .

The Types of Organized Criminal Activities

Organized criminal groups participate in any illegal activity that offers maximum profit at minimum risk of law enforcement interference. They offer goods and services that millions of Americans desire even though declared illegal by their legislatures.

Gambling. Law enforcement officials agree almost unanimously that gambling is the greatest source of revenue for organized crime. It ranges from lotteries, such as "numbers" or "bolita," to off-track horse betting, bets on sporting events, large dice games and illegal casinos. In large cities where organized criminal groups exist, very few of the gambling operators are independent of a large organization. Anyone whose independent operation becomes successful is likely to receive a visit from an organization representative who convinces the independent, through fear or promise of greater profit, to share his revenue with the organization. . . .

There is no accurate way of ascertaining organized crime's gross revenue from gambling in the United States. Estimates of the annual intake have varied from $7 to $50 billion. Legal betting at racetracks reaches a gross annual figure of almost $5 billion, and most enforcement officials believe that illegal wagering on horse races, lotteries, and sporting events totals at least $20 billion each year. Analysis of organized criminal betting operations indicates that the profit is as high as one-third of gross revenue—or $6 to $7 billion each year. While the Commission cannot judge the accuracy of these figures, even the most conservative estimates place substantial capital in the hands of organized crime leaders.

Loan sharking.   In the view of most law enforcement officials loan sharking, the lending of money at higher rates than the legally prescribed limit, is the second largest source of revenue for organized crime. Gambling profits provide the initial capital for loan-shark operations.

No comprehensive analysis has ever been made of what kinds of customers loan sharks have, or of how much or how often each kind borrows. Enforcement officials and other investigators do have some information. Gamblers borrow to pay gambling losses; narcotics users borrow to purchase heroin. Some small businessmen borrow from loan sharks when legitimate credit channels are closed. The same men who take bets from employees in mass employment industries also serve at times as loan sharks, whose money enables the employees to pay off their gambling debts or meet household needs.

Interest rates vary from 1 to 150 percent a week, according to the relationship between the lender and borrower, the intended use of the money, the size of the loan, and the repayment potential. The classic "6-for-5" loan, 20 percent a week, is common with small borrowers. Payments may be due by a certain hour on a certain day, and even a few minutes' default may result in a rise in interest rates. The lender is more interested in perpetuating interest payments than collecting principal; and force, or threats of force of the most brutal kind, are used to effect interest collection, eliminate protest when interest rates are raised, and prevent the beleaguered borrower from reporting the activity to enforcement officials. No reliable estimates exist of the gross revenue from organized loan sharking, but profit margins are higher than for gambling operations, and many officials classify the business in the multi-billion-dollar range.

Narcotics.   The sale of narcotics is organized like a legitimate importing-wholesaling-retailing business. The distribution of heroin, for example, requires movement of the drug through four or five levels between the importer and the street peddler. Many enforcement officials believe that the severity of mandatory Federal narcotics penalties has caused organized criminals to restrict their activities to importing and wholesale distribution. They stay away from smaller-scale wholesale transactions or dealing at the retail level. Transactions with addicts are handled by independent narcotics pushers using drugs imported by organized crime.

The large amounts of cash and the international connections necessary for large, long-term heroin supplies can be provided only by organized crime. Conservative estimates of the number of addicts in the Nation and the average daily expenditure for heroin indicate that the gross heroin trade is $350 million annually, of which $21 million are probably profits to the importer and distributor. Most of this profit goes to organized crime groups in those few cities in which almost all heroin consumption occurs.

Other goods and services. Prostitution and bootlegging play a small and declining role in organized crime's operations. Production of illegal alcohol is a risky business. The destruction of stills and supplies by law enforcement officers during the initial stages means the loss of heavy initial investment capital. Prostitution is difficult to organize and discipline is hard to maintain. Several important convictions of organized crime figures in prostitution cases in the 1930's and 1940's made the criminal executives wary of further participation.

Infiltration of legitimate business. A legitimate business enables the racket executive to acquire respectability in the community and to establish a source of funds that appears legal and upon which just enough taxes may be paid to avoid income tax prosecution. Organized crime invests the profit it has made from illegal service activities in a variety of businesses throughout the country. To succeed in such ventures, it uses accountants, attorneys, and business consultants, who in some instances work exclusively on its affairs. Too often, because of the reciprocal benefits involved in organized crime's dealings with the business world, or because of fear, the legitimate sector of society helps the illegitimate sector. . . .

Because business ownership is so easily concealed, it is difficult to determine all the types of businesses that organized crime has penetrated. Of the 75 or so racket leaders who met at Apalachin, N.Y., in 1957, at least 9 were in the coin-operated machine industry, 16 were in the garment industry, 10 owned grocery stores, 17 owned bars or restaurants, 11 were in the olive oil and cheese business, and 9 were in the construction business. Others were involved in automobile agencies, coal companies, entertainment, funeral homes, ownership of horses and race tracks, linen and laundry enterprises, trucking, waterfront activities, and bakeries.

Today, the kinds of production and service industries and businesses that organized crime controls or has invested in range from accounting firms to yeast manufacturing. One criminal syndicate alone has real estate interests with an estimated value of $300 million. In a few instances, racketeers control nationwide manufacturing and service industries with known and respected brand names.

Control of business concerns has usually been acquired through one of four methods: (1) investing concealed profits acquired from gambling and other illegal activities; (2) accepting business interests in payment of the owner's gambling debts; (3) foreclosing on usurious loans; and (4) using various forms of extortion. . . .

. . . The ordinary businessman is hard pressed to compete with a syndicate enterprise. From its gambling and other illegal revenue—on most of which no taxes are paid—the criminal group always has a ready source of cash with which to enter any business. Through union connections, the business run by organized crime either prevents unionization or secures "sweetheart" contracts from existing unions. These tactics are used effectively in combination. In one city, organized crime gained a monopoly in garbage collection by preserving the business's nonunion status and by using cash reserves to offset temporary losses incurred when the criminal group lowered prices to drive competitors out of business.

Strong-arm tactics are used to enforce unfair business policy and to obtain customers. . . .

The cumulative effect of the infiltration of legitimate business in America cannot be measured. Law enforcement officials agree that entry into legitimate business is continually increasing and that it has not decreased organized crime's control over gambling, usury and other profitable, low-risk criminal enterprises.

Labor racketeering. Control of labor supply and infiltration of labor unions by organized crime prevent unionization of some industries, provide opportunities for stealing from union funds and extorting money by threats of possible labor strife, and provide funds from the enormous union pension and welfare systems for business ventures controlled by organized criminals. Union control also may enhance other illegal activities. Trucking, construction, and waterfront shipping entrepreneurs, in return for assurance that business operations will not be interrupted by labor discord, countenance gambling, loan sharking, and pilferage on company property. Organized criminals either direct these activities or grant "concessions" to others in return for a percentage of the profits. . . .

Location of Organized Crime Activities

Organized criminal groups are known to operate in all sections of the Nation. In response to a Commission survey of 71 cities, the police departments in 80 percent of the cities with over 1 million residents, in 20 percent of the cities with a population between one-half million and a million, in 20 percent of the cities with between 250,000 and 500,000 population, and in over 50 percent of the cities between 100,000 and 250,000 indicated that organized criminal groups exist in their cities. In some instances Federal agency intelligence indicated the presence of organized crime where local reports denied it. Of the nine cities not responding to the Commission survey, six are known to Federal agencies to have extensive organized crime problems. Where the existence of organized crime was acknowledged, all police departments indicated that the criminal group would continue even though a top leader died or was incarcerated.

Organized crime in small cities is more difficult to assess. Law enforcement personnel are aware of many instances in which local racket figures controlled crime in a smaller city and received aid from and paid tribute to organized criminal groups located in a nearby large city. . . . Organized crime cannot be seen as merely a big-city problem.

Corruption of the Enforcement and Political Systems

Today's corruption is less visible, more subtle, and therefore more difficult to detect and assess than the corruption of the prohibition era. All available data indicate that organized crime flourishes only where it has corrupted local officials. As the scope and variety of organized crime's activities have expanded, its need to involve public officials at every level of local government has grown. And as government regulation expands into more and more areas of private and business activity, the power to corrupt likewise affords the corrupter more control over matters affecting the everyday life of each citizen.

Contrast, for example, the way governmental action in contract procurement or zoning functions today with the way it functioned only a few years ago. The potential harm of corruption is greater today if only because the scope of governmental activity is greater. In different places at different times, organized crime has corrupted police officials, prosecutors, legislators, judges, regulatory agency officials, mayors, councilmen, and other public officials, whose legitimate exercise of duties would block organized crime and whose illegal exercise of duties helps it.

Neutralizing local law enforcement is central to organized crime's operations. What can the public do if no one investigates the investigators, and the political figures are neutralized by their alliance with organized crime? Anyone reporting corrupt activities may merely be telling his story to the corrupted; in a recent "investigation" of widespread corruption, the prosecutor announced that any citizen coming forward with evidence of payments to public officials to secure government action would be prosecuted for participating in such unlawful conduct.

In recent years some local governments have been dominated by criminal groups. Today, no large city is completely controlled by organized crime, but in many there is a considerable degree of corruption.

Organized crime currently is directing its efforts to corrupt law enforcement at the chief or at least middle-level supervisory officials. The corrupt political executive who ties the hands of police officials who want to act against organized crime is even more effective for organized crime's purposes. To secure political power organized crime tries by bribes or political contributions to corrupt the nonoffice-holding political leaders to whom judges, mayors, prosecuting attorneys, and correctional officials may be responsive.

It is impossible to determine how extensive the corruption of public officials by organized crime has been. We do know that there must be more vigilance against such corruption, and we know that there must be better ways for the public to communicate information about corruption to appropriate governmental personnel. . . .

National Scope of Organized Crime

. . . Today the core of organized crime in the United States consists of 24 groups operating as criminal cartels in large cities across the Nation. Their membership is exclusively men of Italian descent, they are in frequent communication with each other, and their smooth functioning is insured by a national body of overseers. To date, only the Federal Bureau of Investigation has been able to document fully the national scope of these groups, and FBI intelligence indicates that the organization as a whole has changed its name from the Mafia to La Cosa Nostra. . . .

. . . In many ways organized crime is the most sinister kind of crime in America. The men who control it have become rich and powerful by encouraging the needy to gamble, by luring the troubled to destroy themselves with drugs, by extorting the profits of honest and hardworking businessmen, by collecting usury from those in financial plight, by maiming or murdering those who oppose them, by bribing those who are sworn to destroy them. Organized crime is not merely a few preying upon a few. In a very real sense it is dedicated to subverting not only American institutions, but the very decency and integrity that are the most cherished attributes of a free society. As the leaders of Cosa Nostra and their racketeering allies pursue their conspiracy unmolested, in open and continuous defiance of the law, they preach a sermon that all too many Americans heed: The government is for sale; lawlessness is the road to wealth; honesty is a pitfall and morality a trap for suckers.

The extraordinary thing about organized crime is that America has tolerated it for so long.

CONFESSIONS AS EVIDENCE

Senate Judiciary Committee

Chairman of the Committee was Senator John L. McClellan (D., Ark.).

Majority Report

. . . Voluntary confessions have been admissible in evidence since the early days of our Republic. These inculpatory statements have long been recognized as strong and convincing evidence—often called the best evidence of guilt. In *Mallory* v. *United States*, 354 U.S. 449 (1957), the U.S. Supreme Court declared inadmissible voluntary confessions made during a period of unnecessary delay between the time of arrest and the time the suspect is taken before a committing magistrate. . . . The Honorable Alexander Holtzoff, U.S. district judge for the District of Columbia, testified before the subcommittee as follows:

> . . . In my humble judgment, . . . (the *Mallory* rule) was one of the contributing causes to the difficulty in enforcing the criminal law and in the increasing rate of crime. Washington has become a crime-ridden city. The grapevine of the underworld travels fast, and members of the underworld, while not familiar with the intricacies of the law, know the general tendencies, and the result is that they become bolder, feeling that there will be some technicality or other which will save them from punishment.
> We get fewer pleas of guilty than we ever did before, because experienced and sophisticated criminals feel that, well, they will take

From the Senate Committee on the Judiciary, *Report on the Omnibus Crime Control and Safe Streets Act of 1967,* 90th Congress, 2nd Session, April 28, 1968: Majority Report, pp. 38-42, 46-48, 50; Minority Views, pp. 150-152.

a chance. The chances are very great that eventually, if they are found guilty, the conviction may be reversed.

Not only have we had a diminution in the percentage of pleas of guilty, but trials take longer, because instead of concentrating on the real issue of the case—namely, did the defendant commit the crime, that is what we should be trying—we have to try a great many tangential issues, such as did the policeman take his prisoner promptly enough to a magistrate. Should he have questioned him? Should he have searched him? And more time is devoted to these tangential issues than to the real issue that has to be tried.

The question of guilt or innocence becomes relegated to the background, because in many of these instances guilt isn't seriously in dispute. The only matters that are tried nowadays are these side issues. And I must say that sometimes I feel, when I am trying a criminal case, as though I am in a topsy-turvy world—I am not trying the accused, I am trying the policeman—did he break any rule? . . .

The case of *Escobedo* v. *Illinois*, 378 U.S. 478 (1964), set the stage for another most disastrous blow to the cause of law enforcement in this country.[1] This case, along with others, formed the basis for the decision in *Miranda* v. *Arizona*, 384 U.S. 436 (1966). In *Miranda*, the Supreme Court held that an otherwise voluntary confession made after the suspect was taken into police custody could not be used in evidence unless a fourfold warning had been given prior to any questioning. The majority opinion in this respect reads:

> Prior to any questioning, the person must be warned that he has a right to remain silent, that any statement he does make may be used as evidence against him, and that he has a right to the presence of an attorney, either retained or appointed. The defendant may waive effectuation of these rights, provided the waiver is made voluntarily, knowingly, and intelligently. If, however, he indicates in any manner and at any stage of the process that he wishes to consult with an attorney before speaking, there can be no questioning. Likewise, if the individual is alone and indicates in any manner that he does not wish to be interrogated, the police may not question him. The mere fact that he may have answered some questions or volunteered some statements on his own does not deprive him of the right to refrain from answering any further inquiries until he has consulted with an attorney and thereafter consents to be questioned (384 U.S. at 444).

[1]*Escobedo* held that where "the investigation is no longer a general inquiry into an unsolved crime but has begun to focus on a particular suspect, the suspect has been taken into police custody, the police carry out a process of interrogations that lends itself to eliciting incriminating statements, the suspect has requested and been denied an opportunity to consult with his lawyer, and the police have not effectively warned him of his absolute constitutional right to remain silent, the accused has been denied 'the assistance of counsel' in violation of the sixth amendment to the Constitution as 'made obligatory upon the States by the 14th amendment: (cit. omitted) and that no statement elicited by the police during the interrogation may be used against him at a criminal trial."

After considering the testimony of many witnesses, and statements and letters of many other interested parties, the committee found that there is a need for legislation to offset the harmful effects of the Court decisions mentioned above. These decisions have resulted in the release of criminals whose guilt is virtually beyond question. This has had a demoralizing effect on law-enforcement officials whose efforts to investigate crimes and interrogate suspects have been stymied by the technical roadblocks thrown up by the Court. The general public is becoming frightened and angered by the many reports of depraved criminals being released to roam the streets in search of other victims. For example, the infamous Mallory was convicted on another rape charge shortly after his first rape conviction was reversed by the Supreme Court.

The Honorable John Stennis, a U.S. Senator from the State of Mississippi, stated in subcommittee hearings that recent Supreme Court decisions dealing with interrogation procedures have demoralized policemen and threatened to lessen their effectiveness in combating crime. He feels that a change from the approach of the *Miranda* case is essential and significant in the fight against crime. The *Miranda* rule goes to the very heart of the investigative process—custodial interrogation. If *Miranda* is not challenged, its harmful effect will gain momentum when the lower Federal courts begin expanding its doctrine and result in many extended interpretations of the case.

The Honorable Alexander Holtzoff . . . also discussed the harmful effects of *Miranda*. He said the case would result in reducing the use of voluntary confessions in a very large percentage of cases. This hinders the quick and efficient enforcement of the criminal law.

Quinn Tamm, executive director of the International Association of Chiefs of Police, agreed that the *Miranda* case will materially reduce the number of confessions from defendants.

Statistical evidence further indicates the harmful effects of the *Miranda* decision. During the subcommittee hearings, Arlen Specter, district attorney of the city of Philadelphia, revealed a study on the effects of *Miranda* conducted by his office. The results indicated that prior to the *Escobedo* case, 90 percent of the suspects would make a statement, often not incriminating on their face, but valuable in investigating the crime. After *Escobedo*, only 80 percent would give statements. After the second circuit *Russo* case, only 68 percent of suspects would give statements. Then came the *Miranda* case in June 1966. For a period after *Miranda*, out of 5,220 suspects arrested for serious crimes, 3,095 refused to give a statement. This is a percentage of only 41 percent who would give statements, a decrease of 49 percent since *Escobedo*. These statistics are inclined to become more alarming as more criminals become more familiar with *Miranda*.

Aaron Koota, district attorney for Kings County, N.Y., conducted a similar survey, indicating that prior to *Miranda*, approximately 10 percent of the suspects involved in serious crimes refused to make statements or confessions to police. After *Miranda*, 41 percent refused to make statements or confessions. Specifically, between June and September of 1966, Mr. Koota revealed that 130 of 316 suspects refused to make any statement at all. In only 30 of these 130 cases did Mr. Koota have sufficient evidence to prosecute apart from the confession. Mr. Koota was unequivocal in stating that confessions are helpful in securing convictions.

Charles E. Moylan, Jr., State's attorney for the city of Baltimore, Md., reports more disturbing statistics. Mr. Moylan said:

> . . . [W]e used to get . . . (confessions) in 20 to 25 percent of our cases, and now we are getting . . . (them) in 2 percent of our cases. The confession as a law-enforcement instrument has been virtually eliminated.

Mr. Moylan noted that the *Miranda* case has encouraged criminals, discouraged the police, and disappointed the public that depends on the courts for protection.

Frank S. Hogan, New York County district attorney, reported similar findings. In the 6 months prior to the *Miranda* case, 49 percent of the nonhomicide felony defendants in New York County made incriminating statements. In the 6 months after this decision, only 15 percent of the defendants gave incriminating statements. Mr. Hogan characterized it as being most harmful to efforts to convict criminals who roam our streets and assault our citizens. . . .

The committee is convinced from the mass of evidence heard by the subcommittee . . . that the rigid and inflexible requirements of the majority opinion in the *Miranda* case are unreasonable, unrealistic, and extremely harmful to law enforcement. Instance after instance is documented in the transcript where the most vicious criminals have gone unpunished, even though they had voluntarily confessed their guilt. The transcript and subcommittee files contain testimony and statements from district attorneys, police chiefs, and other law enforcement officers in cities and towns all over the country, demonstrating beyond doubt the devastating effect upon the rights of society of the *Miranda* decision. The unsoundness of the majority opinion was forcefully shown by the four dissenting justices, who also predicted the dire consequences of overruling what theretofore had been the law of the land, confirmed in 1896 in *Wilson* v. *U.S.*, 162 U.S. 613, and in 1912 in *Powers* v. *U.S.*, 223 U.S. 303, and in other more recent Supreme Court decisions. . . .

One of the most damaging aspects of the *Miranda* decision is its apparent holding that, absent waiver, no suspect can be interrogated at all without the benefit of counsel. It is widely known that counsel will advise the suspect to make no statement at all. The police are virtually hamstrung. This is much more serious than the barring from evidence of a confession—the suspect may refuse to make *any statement whatever*.

Hearings before the subcommittee revealed further defects in the *Miranda* reasoning. Mr. Specter pointed out that the so-called third-degree methods deplored by the Supreme Court and cited as a basis for their opinion in *Miranda* is not a correct portrayal of what actually goes on in police stations across the country. While there are isolated cases of police using coercive tactics, this is the exception rather than the rule. Mr. Tamm agrees, stating that while these coercive practices might have been approved 30 years ago, they have no place in modern police techniques. The committee is convinced that the Court overreacted to defense claims that police brutality is widespread. . . .

The Committee is of the view that it simply makes no sense to exclude from a jury what has traditionally been considered the very highest type of evidence, and the most convincing evidence of guilt, that is, a voluntary confession or incriminating statement by the accused. This view is borne out by common experience and general acceptation, and by almost 200 years of precedent in the courts of this country.

The Committee also feels that the majority opinion not only runs counter to practically all the precedent in the State and Federal courts, but that it misconstrues the Constitution. The Committee aligns itself wholeheartedly with the view expressed by the dissenting Justices and with what it feels are the views of the vast majority of judges, lawyers and plain citizens of our country who are so obviously aroused at the unrealistic opinions such as the *Miranda* decision which are having the effect of daily releasing upon the public vicious criminals who have voluntarily confessed their guilt. . . .

Minority Views

. . . The fault in the *Miranda* decision, if any, lies not with the Supreme Court, but with the fifth amendment itself. Long ago, our Founding Fathers enshrined in the Bill of Rights the ancient maxim, nemo tenetur seipsum accusare. In the words of the fifth amendment, no person "shall be compelled in any criminal case to be a witness against himself." At the very heart of the privilege against self-incrimination lies one of the fundamental principles of our system of criminal justice, that the Government must produce evidence against an individual by its own independent labors, rather than by the cruel simple expedient of compelling it from his own mouth. *Chambers v. Florida* (309 U.S. 227, 235-238 [1940]). As Sir James Fitzjames Stephen commented almost a century ago on the use of interrogation by law enforcement officers:

> There is a great deal of laziness in it. It is far pleasanter to sit comfortably in the shade rubbing red pepper into a poor devil's eyes than to go about in the sun hunting up evidence (1 Stephen, "A History of the Criminal Law in England," 442 (1883)).

In *Miranda*, the Supreme Court breathed life into the privilege as applied to police interrogation. The basic thrust of the Court's decision was to place the poor and inexperienced suspect on an equal footing with the wealthy and most sophisticated suspect by informing all suspects of their constitutional right to silence and assuring them of a continuous opportunity to exercise it.

As Justice Walter Schaefer, of the Supreme Court of Illinois, one of our most distinguished jurists, has eloquently stated, the quality of a nation's civilization can be largely measured by the methods it uses in the enforcement of its criminal law. See Schaefer "Federalism and State Criminal Procedure" (70 Harv. L. Rev. 1, 26 (1956)). To allow the Government in the administration of justice to take advantage of the ignorance or indigence of an accused would violate the most elementary principles of our constitutional jurisprudence.

Forty years ago, Justice Brandeis forcefully answered the recurrent argument that the needs of law enforcement outweigh the rights of the individual. In *Olmstead* v. *United States*, he said:

> Decency, security, and liberty alike demand that Government officials shall be subjected to the same rules of conduct that are commands to the citizen. In a government of laws, existence of the Government will be imperiled if it fails to observe the law scrupulously. Our Government is the potent, the omnipresent teacher. For good or for ill, it teaches the whole people by its example. Crime is contagious. If the Government becomes a lawbreaker, it breeds contempt for law; it invites every man to become a law unto himself; it invites anarchy. To declare that in the administration of the criminal law the end justifies the means . . . would bring terrible retribution. Against that pernicious doctrine this Court should resolutely set its face (277 U.S. 438, 485 (1928) (dissenting opinion)).

Contrary to the suggestion of the proponents of title II, it can hardly be said with authority that the *Miranda* decision has seriously hampered law enforcement. Essentially the same warnings required by the Supreme Court in *Miranda* were being used by the

FBI 14 years before the decision in that case. As Chief Justice Warren stated in delivering the opinion of the Court in *Miranda*:

> Over the years the Federal Bureau of Investigation has compiled an exemplary record of effective law enforcement while advising any suspect or arrested person, at the outset of an interview, that he is not required to make a statement, that any statement may be used against him in court, that the individual may obtain the services of an attorney of his own choice and, more recently, that he has a right to free counsel if he is unable to pay . . . [T] he present pattern of warnings and respect for the rights of the individual followed as a practice by the FBI is consistent with the procedure which we delineate today (384 U.S. at 483-484).

Equally important, each of the two major field studies published to date on the impact of *Miranda* on law enforcement has concluded that the impact has been small and that the decision has had little effect on police practices or the clearance of crime. What is by far the most comprehensive of these studies was conducted by the student editors of the Yale Law Journal and faculty members of the Yale Law School. See "Interrogations in New Haven: The Impact of Miranda" (76 Yale L.J. 1519 (1967)). Over a period of 3 months, the Yale investigators observed every stationhouse interrogation undertaken by the New Haven police force. One of the basic conclusions reached by the study was that interrogation of suspects by police was unnecessary in the overwhelming majority—87 percent—of the cases observed, since the police had already obtained enough evidence against a suspect at the time of his arrest to assure his conviction. In the typical case, either the police already had enough evidence to convict a suspect without interrogation, or they did not even have enough evidence to arrest him in the first place.

The second major study of the impact of *Miranda* was a statistical survey by two law professors at the University of Pittsburgh Law School. See Seeburger and Wettick, "Miranda in Pittsburgh—A Statistical Study" (29 U. Pittsburgh L.R 1 (1967)). Using files made available by the Pittsburgh Detective Bureau, the authors found that the incidence of confessions declined by almost 20 percent in the period following the *Miranda* decision. But—and this is the crucial finding of the study—the decline in the incidence of confessions was accompanied by no substantial decline in the arrest rate, the conviction rate, the rate of crime clearance, or the court backlog.

The Yale and Pittsburgh studies point up the crucial defect in many of the studies relied upon by the proponents of title II to support the provisions of section 3501. It is not enough to study the impact of *Miranda* on law enforcement by the crude measure of the incidence of confessions. The real impact can be determined only by measuring the effect on convictions and crime clearance. By this scale, the only true scale, the much-ballyhooed deleterious impact of *Miranda* on law enforcement has been extremely small, if not illusory.

Indeed, *Miranda* itself and its three companion cases[2] present graphic examples of the overstatement of the "need" for confessions in law enforcement. In each case, law-enforcement officers had developed substantial other evidence against the defendants before conducting the interrogations held invalid by the Supreme Court. Thus, Miranda, Vignera, and Westover had been identified by eyewitnesses. Marked bills from the robbed bank had been found in Westover's car. Articles stolen from several robbery victims had been found in Stewart's home.

The overstatement of the "need" for confessions becomes even more obvious when the subsequent history of the four *Miranda* defendants is considered. Miranda himself was convicted in Arizona in February 1967 on the same two counts of kidnapping and rape with which he was originally charged, and received the same sentence of concurrent prison terms of 20 to 30 years on each count. Vignera pleaded guilty in New York to an indictment charging a lesser robbery offense, and was sentenced to a prison term of 7 1/2 to 10 years. Westover was convicted in February 1967 on the same two counts of bank robbery, and received the same sentence of consecutive 15-year prison terms on each count. Stewart has not yet been retried on the original charges of robbery and murder, for which he was convicted and sentenced to death. However, a motion to suppress evidence in the case was denied in November 1967; after several continuances, the trial has been set for May 1968.

One specter raised by the proponents of title II that is easily put to rest is the suggestion that *Miranda* and like decisions are daily releasing vicious, and confessed criminals upon the public streets. This suggestion stems from the brief and unfortunate period immediately following the *Miranda* decision. In *Johnson* v. *New Jersey*, 384 U.S. 719 (1966), decided 1 week after *Miranda*, the Supreme Court held that the rules approved in *Miranda*, would apply to all defendants tried after June 13, 1966, the date of the *Miranda* decision. Thus, in a number of cases awaiting trial at that time, seemingly voluntary confessions obtained prior to the date of *Miranda* were inadmissible in evidence, and some cases involving heinous crimes were dismissed, amid great publicity. That situation

[2]In the *Miranda* opinion, the Supreme Court actually decided four separate cases—*Miranda* v. *Arizona*, *Vignera* v. *New York*, *Westover* v. *United States*, and *California* v. *Stewart*. See 384 U.S. 436 (1966).

was temporary, however, and is no longer a serious problem. So long as the procedures of *Miranda* are followed, any truly voluntary confession can still be made and will still be admissible in evidence. As the studies of the impact of *Miranda* suggest, most of the confessions lost in the wake of *Miranda* could today be saved. . . .

WIRETAPPING AND ELECTRONIC SURVEILLANCE

Senate Judiciary Committee

Presenting an independent view is Philip A. Hart, a Democratic Senator from Michigan.

Majority Report

. . .Title III has as its dual purpose (1) protecting the privacy of wire and oral communications, and (2) delineating on a uniform basis the circumstances and conditions under which the interception of wire and oral communications may be authorized. To assure the privacy of oral and wire communications, title III prohibits all wiretapping and electronic surveillance by persons other than duly authorized law enforcement officers engaged in the investigation or prevention of specified types of serious crimes, and only after authorization of a court order obtained after a showing and finding of probable cause. The only exceptions to the above prohibition are: (1) the power of the President to obtain information by such means as he may deem necessary to protect the Nation from attack or hostile acts of a foreign power, to obtain intelligence information essential to the Nation's security, and to protect the internal security of the United States from those who advocate its overthrow by force or other unlawful means; (2) employees of the Federal Communications Commission may, in the normal course of employment,

From the Senate Committee on the Judiciary, *Report on the Omnibus Crime Control and Safe Streets Act of 1967*, 90th Congress, 2nd Session, April 28, 1968: Majority Report, pp. 66-74; Individual Views, pp. 170-174, 176-77.

intercept and disclose wire communications in the discharge of the monitoring responsibilities discharged by the Commission in the enforcement of chapter 5 of title 47 of the United States Code; and (3) employees of a communication common carrier may intercept and disclose wire communications in the normal course of their employment while engaged in any activity necessary to the rendition of service, or protection of the rights or property of the carrier of such communication.

The tremendous scientific and technological developments that have taken place in the last century have made possible today the widespread use and abuse of electronic surveillance techniques. As a result of these developments, privacy of communication is seriously jeopardized by these techniques of surveillance. Commercial and employer-labor espionage is becoming widespread. It is becoming increasingly difficult to conduct business meetings in private. Trade secrets are betrayed. Labor and management plans are revealed. No longer is it possible, in short, for each man to retreat into his home and be left alone. Every spoken word relating to each man's personal, marital, religious, political, or commercial concerns can be intercepted by an unseen auditor and turned against the speaker to the auditor's advantage.

The Report of the President's Commission on Law Enforcement and Administration of Justice, "The Challenge of Crime in a Free Society" (1967), concluded that "the present status of the law (relating to wiretapping and electronic surveilliance) is intolerable." "It serves," the Report observed, "neither the interests of privacy nor of law enforcement."

Both proponents and opponents of wiretapping and electronic surveillance agree that the present state of the law in this area is extremely unsatisfactory and that the Congress should act to clarify the resulting confusion. . . .

. . . The Supreme Court has effectively prevented the use in both Federal and State courts of intercepted communications by wiretapping, as well as the fruits thereof. State officers would be subject to Federal prosecution and, therefore, most State prosecutors do not use such evidence, although it is authorized by their State statutes.

Supreme Court cases, to some extent, prior to the *Berger* decision . . . had clarified a few complex problems in the area of "bugging." That case, by a divided Court, held unconstitutional the New York statute authorizing electronic surveillance, but in doing so has laid out guidelines for the Congress and State legislatures to follow in enacting wiretapping and electronic eavesdropping statutes which would meet constitutional requirements. . . .

Virtually all concede that the use of wiretapping or electronic surveillance techniques by private unauthorized hands has little justification where communications are intercepted without the consent of one of the participants. No one quarrels with the proposition that the unauthorized use of these techniques by law enforcement agents should be prohibited. It is not enough, however, just to prohibit the unjustifiable interception, disclosure, or use of any wire or oral communications. An attack must also be made on the possession, distribution, manufacture, and advertising of intercepting devices. All too often the invasion of privacy itself will go unknown. Only by striking at all aspects of the problem can privacy be adequately protected. The prohibition, too, must be enforced with all appropriate sanctions. Criminal penalties have their part to play. But other remedies must be afforded the victim of an unlawful invasion of privacy. Provision must be made for civil recourse for damages. The perpetrator must be denied the fruits of his unlawful actions in civil and criminal proceedings. Each of these objectives is sought by the proposed legislation.

It is obvious that whatever means are necessary should and must be taken to protect the national security interest. Wiretapping and electronic surveillance techniques are proper means for the acquisition of counterintelligence against the hostile action of foreign powers. Nothing in the proposed legislation seeks to disturb the power of the President to act in this area. Limitations that may be deemed proper in the field of domestic affairs of a nation become artificial when international relations and internal security are at stake.

The major purpose of title III is to combat organized crime. To consider the question of the need for wiretapping and electronic surveillance techniques in the administration of justice, it is necessary first to consider the historical development of our system of criminal law and procedure and the challenge put to it today by modern organized crime. We inherited from England a medieval system, devised originally for a stable, homogeneous, primarily agrarian community. In our formative years, we had no professional police force. Today, however, we are a mobile, modern, heterogeneous, urban industrial community. Our Nation, moreover, is no longer small. Our traditional methods in the administration of justice, too, were fashioned in response to the problems of our Nation as they were in its formative years. In years past it was not possible to investigate crime aided by science. Today it is not only possible but necessary, in the development of evidence, to subject it to analysis by the hands of those trained in the scientific disciplines. Even so, scientific "crime detection, popular fiction to the contrary notwithstanding, at present is a limited tool" ("The Challenge of Crime in a Free Society" (1967)). In our formative years, offenses usually occurred between neighbors. No specialized law enforcement force was thought necessary to bring such crimes into the system of justice. Ignored entirely in the development of our system of justice, therefore, was the possibility of the growth of a phenomenon such as modern organized crime with its attendant corruption of our political and law enforcement processes.

We have always had forms of organized crime and corruption. But there has grown up in our society today highly organized, structured and formalized groups of criminal cartels, whose existence transcends the crime known yesterday, for which our criminal laws and procedures were primarily designed. The "American system was not designed with (organized crime). . . in mind," the President's Crime Commission noted in its report "The Challenge of Crime in a Free Society" (1967), "and it has been notably unsuccessful to date in preventing such organizations from preying on society." These hard-core groups have become more than just loose associations of criminals. They have developed into corporations of corruption, indeed, quasi-governments within our society, presenting a unique challenge to the administration of justice. . . .

In discussing the use of electronic surveillance as a weapon against organized crime, the President's Crime Commission states:

> . . . communication is essential to the operation of any business enterprise. In legitimate business this is accomplished with written and oral exchanges. In organized crime enterprises, however, the possibility of loss or seizure of an incriminating document demands a minimum of written communication. Because of the varied character of organized crime enterprises, the large numbers of persons employed in them, and frequently the distances separating elements of the organization, the telephone remains an essential vehicle for communication.

Victims, complainants, or witnesses are unwilling to testify because of apathy, fear, or self-interest, and the top figures in the rackets are protected by layers of insulation and direct participation in criminal acts. Information received from paid informants is often unreliable, and a stern code of discipline inhibits the development of informants against organized criminals. In short, intercepting the communications of organized criminals is the only effective method of learning about their activities.

District Attorney Frank Hogan, a recognized national authority, who has served in the New York District Attorney's office for 32 years, states that wiretapping is an indispensable weapon in the fight against organized crime. The President's Commission on Law Enforcement and Administration of Justice had this to say about the organized crime problem in New York:

Over the years New York has faced one of the Nation's most aggravated organized crime problems. Only in New York have law enforcement officials achieved some level of continuous success in bringing prosecutions against organized crime. For over 20 years, New York has authorized wiretapping on court order. Since 1957 "bugging" has been similarly authorized. Wiretapping was the mainstay of the New York attack against organized crime until Federal court decisions intervened.

The principal argument of those who oppose wiretapping and electronic surveillance by law enforcement officers on court order is that it will destroy our right of privacy. Wiretapping and electronic surveillance as practiced by law enforcement officers has been subject to much confusion and misunderstanding. As District Attorney Frank Hogan so aptly put it when testifying before the subcommittee:

This is a field that produces the most extravagant accusations of abusive practices, as ill-founded and unsupported as they are shocking, and as irresponsible as they are inaccurate.

When the facts are brought to light, statistics show that extremely few telephones are tapped by law enforcement officers—and that even fewer electronic surveillance devices are installed. Testimony at the subcommittee hearings revealed the following statistics: In Kings County, N.Y., with over 3,000,000 people, 47 wiretap orders were obtained the first 11 months of 1966. In Nassau County, N.Y., which has a population of approximately 1,500,000 persons, 78 wiretap orders were obtained in 1966. In New York County, N.Y., with a population of nearly 3,200,000 persons, 73 wiretap orders were obtained in 1966. In 1966 in New York County, 23 orders granting installations of electronic surveillance devices were entered. Since 1958, when the law permitting this type of eavesdropping by law enforcement authorities under court order was enacted, the average in New York County has been less than 19 orders a year.

In his testimony before the subcommittee, District Attorney Frank Hogan referred to a study conducted by the New York Legislature which reinforces the above figures and shows that the danger that law enforcement officials may listen in on conversations that do not concern some criminal enterprise is exceedingly remote. According to Mr. Hogan, starting in 1955 a joint legislative committee conducted a 5-year study in the State of New York inquiring particularly into possible abuses by law enforcement officers. In its report the committee explicitly declared that no abuses whatever by any district attorney had been found in the use of the wiretapping privilege. Quite the contrary is true. The committee concluded that the system of legalized telephonic interception had worked well in New York for over 20 years, that it had popular approval, and that it enjoyed the overwhelming support of New York's highest State officers, executive, legislative, and judicial. There was unanimous agreement that law enforcement in New York had used this investigative weapon fairly, sparingly, and with the most selective discrimination. Law enforcement officers simply have too much to do to be listening in on conversations of law-abiding citizens. Available manpower just does not permit such abuse. It is idle to contend otherwise.

"From a legal standpoint, organized crime," the President's Crime Commission noted . . . "continues to grow because of defects in the evidence gathering process." . . . The . . . Crime Commission found . . . that under "present procedures too few witnesses have been produced to prove the link between criminal group members and the illicit activities that they sponsor." Victims do not normally testify for they are already in bodily fear or they are compliant, that is, the narcotic addict in desperate need of a "fix" does not usually turn in his "pusher." What victim of extortion will unsolicitedly risk his body by cooperation with law enforcement? Insiders are kept quiet by an idealogy of silence underwritten by a fear, quite realistic, that death comes to him who talks.

All of this is not to say that significant cases have not been developed by law enforcement agents using conventional techniques and based upon the testimony of brave martyr-witnesses. The most successful drive ever launched against organized crime begun by the U.S. Department of Justice in 1961 had by 1966 raised the number of federally secured convictions in the area of organized crime from 73 to 477. Yet against the hard-core little real progress was made. The estimated number of members of the leading groups today is put at 5,000. During the 1961-66 period, only 185 of these individuals were indicted and 102 convicted. Six gained acquittals and dismissals and four secured reversals. A conviction rate of 5 percent per 5-year period hardly constitutes more than a harassing action. The effect is negligible.

Organized criminals must hold meetings to lay plans. Where the geographical area over which they operate is large, they must use telephones. Wiretapping and electronic surveillance techniques can intercept these wire and oral communications. This is not, however, the whole situation. More than the securing of an evidentiary substitute for live testimony, which is not subject to being eliminated or tampered with by fear or favor, is necessary. To realize the potential possible from the use of criminal sanctions, it will be necessary to commit to the system more than legal tools. Time, talent, and personnel are required. Nevertheless, no amount of time, talent, or personnel—without the necessary legal tools—will work, and authorized wiretapping and electronic surveillance techniques by law enforcement officials are indispensable legal tools. . . .

Individual Views of Senator Hart

. . . Wiretapping and other forms of eavesdropping are recognized by even their most zealous advocates as encroachments on a man's right to privacy, characterized by Justice Brandeis as "the most comprehensive of rights and the right most valued by civilized men."

In yesteryear, a man could retire into his home or office free from the prying eye or ear. That time is now long past. Transmitting microphones the size of a sugar cube can be bought for less than $10. Other gadgets now enable a would-be snooper in New York to eavesdrop in Los Angeles merely by dialing a telephone number. This is done by attaching to the telephone in Los Angeles a beeper which converts the telephone into a transmitter without its ever leaving its cradle.

Directional microphones of the "shotgun" and parabolic mike type make it possible, by aiming the mike at a subject, to overhear conversations several hundred feet away. Laser beams permit an eavesdropper to monitor conversations in rooms up to half a mile away by aiming the beam at a thin wall or window. And the experts now tell us that in the years to come, as the methods of eavesdropping technology surge forward, the problems of protecting personal privacy will even further intensify.

Against this backdrop of diminishing individual privacy, proponents of title III now want to legitimate law enforcement wiretapping and eavesdropping. Clearly, if such an effort is successful, today's narrowing enclave of individual privacy will shrink to the vanishing point.

Personal privacy is not the only basic right wiretapping and eavesdropping circumscribe.

Private property is a basic institution in our democratic country. Without it, individualism and freedom wither and die, no matter how democratic a government purports to be. One of the major purposes of our Constitution and Bill of Rights was to safeguard private property.

One of the most important characteristics of private property is the right to possess it exclusively—to keep all strangers out. The house-holder may shut his door against the world.

This right of a citizen to shut the door against anyone, even the king himself, is part of our ancient heritage. One of the great ends for which men entered into society was to protect their property. Under common law, every invasion of private property, no matter how minute, was a trespass, even if no damage was done. And the king's man, entering without sanction of law, was as much a trespasser as the ordinary citizen.

Make no mistake about it: Eavesdropping and wiretapping are trespasses against the home. They are more serious trespasses than an unlawful search of the premises because they continue over long periods of time unknown to the householder. Thus to those who value the institution of private property, eavesdropping and wiretapping have always been regarded as unacceptable. That property shall not be immune from all control and entry, however, long has been accepted. Overriding claims of public health and safety needs, for example, have justified carefully defined limitations on freedom and use of private property.

Is there such an overriding claim here? Is there so great a need for wiretapping as to allow it as title III proposes, assuming it is constitutionally permitted?

Despite the clear-cut invasion of privacy, there is a great clamor for wiretapping and bugging from certain of the law enforcement community. Yet there is in fact serious doubt and disagreement as to the need for such authority in dealing with crime. According to this Nation's highest ranking law enforcement officer, U.S. Attorney General Ramsey Clark:

> Public safety will not be found in wiretapping. Security is to be found in excellence in law enforcement, in courts and in corrections. . . . Nothing so mocks privacy as the wiretap and electronic surveillance. They are incompatible with a free society. *Only the most urgent need can justify wiretapping and other electronic surveillance. Proponents of authorization have failed to make a case—much less meet the heavy burden of proof our values require. Where is the evidence that this is an efficient police technique? Might not more crime be prevented and detected by other uses of the same manpower without the large scale, unfocused intrusions on personal privacy that electronic surveillance involves?* [Emphasis added.]

Ray Girardin, speaking as police commissioner of Detroit, said:

> . . . from the evidence at hand as to wiretapping, I feel that it is an outrageous tactic and that it is not necessary and has no place in law enforcement.

Nor are the Attorney General and Commissioner Girardin alone in their views. Back in the twenties, thirties, and forties, when we also had a serious crime problem, Attorneys General Harlan F. Stone and Robert H. Jackson condemned wiretapping as inefficient and unnecessary.

As Attorney General Robert H. Jackson said before World War II:

> The discredit and suspicion of the law-enforcing branch which arises from the occasional use of wiretapping *more than offsets the good* which is likely to come of it. [Emphasis added.]

It is far from clear that crime cannot be fought without wiretapping and eavesdropping. Rifling the mails and reading private correspondence, suspension of the fifth amendment's privilege against self-incrimination and judicious use of the thumbscrew and rack would probably help the police secure more convictions. This country, however, has wisely seen fit to forbid the police from using such techniques; for the past 34 years Congress also wisely classified wiretapping as a forbidden police method because the dangers inherent in it to innocent persons far outweigh any benefit it may yield to law enforcement. As Justice Holmes said in the first eavesdropping case to confront the Supreme Court:

> For my part I think it is a less evil that some criminals should escape than that a government should play an ignoble part (dissent, *Olmstead* v. *U.S.*, 277 U.S. 438).

When the Government overhears clients talking to their attorneys, husbands to their wives, ministers to their penitents, patients to their doctors, or just innocent people talking to other innocent people, it is clearly playing an "ignoble part." . . .

Even for those who favor legalizing wiretapping, title III could present certain problems.

Section 2510(11) of title III gives standing to challenge a surveillance order only to a person who was either a party to an intercepted communication or against whom the interception was directed.

Section 2510(11) is thus likely to encourage illegal surveillance in cases where the parties to a communication are not the real objects of the surveillance. For example, section 2510(11) may encourage illegal surveillance of petty hoodlums to gain intelligence against their bosses. As section 2510(11) now stands, it is an open invitation to law enforcement officers to engage in illegal electronic surveillance. So long as the illegally obtained evidence is not used against the parties to the intercepted communications, no person will have standing to challenge its introduction in evidence. Although section 2510(11) gives standing to the person against whom an interception is directed, whether or not he was a party to the communication, it will be difficult in many cases to determine that the surveillance was directed against anyone other than the parties to the communication.

In their report, proponents of title III state:

> Applications for orders authorizing the interception of wire or oral communications may be made only in the investigation of *certain major offenses*. . . . Each offense has been chosen *because it is intrinsically serious* or because *it is characteristic of the operations of organized crime*. [Emphasis added.]

Section 2516 of title III then goes on to authorize Federal wiretapping for such crimes as bribery of union officials (sec. 186, title 29), embezzlement of union assets (sec. 501(c), title 29), bribery of public officials and witnesses (sec. 201, title 18), offering or soliciting kickbacks to influence the operation of employee benefit plans (sec. 1954 of title 18), and "any offense involving the manufacture, importation, receiving, concealment, buying, selling, or otherwise dealing in narcotic drugs, marihuana, or other dangerous drugs."

Even the most zealous advocate of wiretapping might be hard-pressed to establish some of the preceding crimes as "major offenses."

Under the list of offenses spelled out in section 2516, every high school or college student who takes a puff of marihuana could be tapped or bugged; every union activity, too.

One should be able to be against union corruption and illegal drug usage without inaugurating the big brother state which could result if the present list of Federal crimes for which tapping and bugging are authorized is allowed to stand.

It is hard to conceive how the range of State offenses for which such a serious invasion of privacy as wiretapping is authorized could be broader than the Federal offenses, but such is the case.

Section 2516(2) permits wiretapping and eavesdropping for *any state crime* punishable by more then *one year* in prison *and* dangerous to "life, limb or property." Nothing in section 2516(2) thus prohibits the use of bugging or tapping in such sensitive areas as state income tax violations.

Likewise in many states numerous petty offenses will qualify under section 2516(2) as crimes for which wiretapping and bugging orders may be issued.

Section 2511(3) of title III permits the President to authorize, without first seeking a court order, wiretapping and eavesdropping in "national security cases." In section 2511(3), however, it states:

> Nor should anything contained in this chapter be deemed to limit the constitutional power of the President to take such measures as he deems necessary to protect the United States . . . *against any other clear and present danger to the structure of existence of the Government.* [Emphasis added.]

This language leaves too much discretion in the hands of a President. Under 2511(3) a President on his own motion could declare a militant right wing political group (i.e., the Minutemen) or left wing group (i.e., Black Nationalists), a national labor dispute, a concerted tax avoidance campaign, draft protesters, the Mafia, civil rights demonstrations, a "clear and present danger to the structure of the Government." Such a declaration would allow unlimited unsupervised bugging and tapping. Section 2516 limits federal tapping and bugging to certain crimes and places such eavesdropping under judicial supervision. As drafted, however, section 2511(3) gives the President a blank check to tap or bug without judicial supervision, whenever he finds, on his motion, that an activity poses a "clear and present danger to the Government." Further, section 2511(3) permits the introduction into evidence any bug or tap the President authorizes.

Section 2511(3) vests power in a President to utilize bugging and tapping in many areas totally unconnected with our traditional concept of "national security." . . .

For nearly four decades Congress wisely has rejected numerous bills similar to title III.

In 1948, Orwell wrote a book, *1984*, in which he painted a bleak prophecy of what life would be like 16 years from now:

> The telescreen received and transmitted simultaneously. Any sound that Winston made, above the level of a very low whisper, would be picked up by it; moreover, so long as he remained within the field of vision which the metal plaque commanded, he could be seen as well as heard. There was of course no way of knowing whether you were being watched at any given moment. . . . You had to live—did live, from habit that became instinct—in the assumption that every sound you made was overheard and, except in darkness, every movement scrutinized.

In terms of the technological advances in the field of electronic eavesdropping, 1984 is clearly upon us. I, for one, however, do not want to see the Government given the right to use, especially when their use will have little or no effect in lessening crime, 1984's tools against its citizens.

Therefore, I oppose Senate adoption of title III.

WHY COPS HATE LIBERALS—AND VICE VERSA

Seymour Martin Lipset

Seymour Lipset is Professor of Government and Social Relations, Center for International Affairs, Harvard University.

There is an increasing body of evidence which suggests an affinity between police work and support for radical-right politics, particularly when linked to racial unrest. During the presidential campaign, George Wallace was unmistakably a hero to many policemen. John Harrington, the president of the Fraternal Order of Police, the largest police organization in America, with over 90,000 members and affiliates in more than 900 communities, publicly endorsed him. And Wallace has reciprocated this affection for some time. While governor of Alabama, he placed the slogan, popularized by the Birch Society, "Support Your Local Police" on the automobile license plates of the state of Alabama. During the 1964 and 1968 presidential campaigns, he frequently referred to the heroic activities of the police, and denounced the Supreme Court, and bleeding heart liberals and intellectuals, for undermining the police efforts to maintain law and order. The police were pictured as the victims of an Establishment conspiracy to foster confrontationist forms of protest and law violation, particularly on the part of Negroes and student activists.

Similar reports concerning police support for right-wing or conservative candidates who have campaigned against civil rights and integration proposals have appeared frequently in the press. Thus in 1967, Boston journalists commented on the general support for Louise Day Hicks among the police of that city. Mrs. Hicks had won her political spurs in the fight which she waged as chairman of the Boston School Committee against school integration. And when she ran for mayor, the police were seemingly among her most enthusiastic backers. In New York City, police have stood out among the constituency of the Conservative Party, an organization which also has opposed public efforts to enforce school integration. The New York Conservative Party was the one partisan group in the city to fight a civilian review board of the police department, an issue which has come up in many other communities.

Jerome Skolnick . . . made a study of the Oakland, California, police in 1964 based on interviews with many of them. He concluded that "a Goldwater type of conservatism was the dominant political and emotional persuasion of the police." During the 1964 campaign, a broadcaster on the New York City police radio suddenly made an emotional appeal for support of Senator Goldwater. Many police called in to endorse this talk. Almost no one out in police cars that night phoned in to back Lyndon Johnson, or to complain about the use of the police radio for partisan purposes. In Los Angeles, an official order had to be issued in 1964 telling the police that they could not have bumper stickers or other campaign materials on their police cars, because of the large number who had publicly so supported Goldwater. The late chief of police of the city, William H. Parker, stated his belief that the majority of the nation's peace officers were "conservative, ultraconservative, and very right wing," a description which fit his own orientation.

There is also evidence of strong support and sympathy among the police for the John Birch Society. In 1964, John Rousselot, then national director of the Society, claimed that "substantial numbers" of its members were policemen, and a study of the national membership of the Society by Fred Grupp, a political scientist at Louisiana State, confirms this contention. Mr. Grupp sent out a questionnaire to a random sample of the Birch membership with the help of the Society and found that over 3 percent of those who reported their occupations were policemen, a figure which is over four times the proportion of police in the national labor force. In New York City in July, 1965, a reporter judged that the majority of the audience at a large rally in Town Hall sponsored by the Birch Society's Speakers Bureau wore "Patrolmen's Benevolent Association badges." The Society itself "estimates that it has five hundred members in the New York City Police Department." In Philadelphia, the mayor placed a number of police on limited duty because of their membership in the Society. In a recent interview, Richard MacEachern, head of the Boston Police Patrolmen's Association, frequently referred to Birch Society material as the source of his information concerning "The Plan" of black militants to destroy the police through use of deliberate violence.

That peace officers in high places are sympathetic with the Society may be seen in the fact that former Sheriff James Clark of Selma, Alabama, who not only played a major role in suppressing civil rights demonstrations in his city but also has been a frequent speaker for the Birch Society, was elected president of the national organization of sheriffs. While serving as chief of the Los Angeles Police Department, William H. Parker took part in the Manion

Forum, a right-wing radio discussion program run by Clarence Manion, a leader of the Birch Society. According to William Turner, in his book *The Police Establishment*, Louis Neese, the police chief of Trenton, New Jersey, "incorporated sections of a Birch 'Support Your Local Police' circular into a declaration of departmental policy."

All this is no new development. The identification between the police and right-wing extremism is not simply a reflection of recent tensions. During the 1930s, investigations of the Black Legion, a neofascist organization in the industrial Midwest, which engaged in terror and vigilante activities, indicated that it appealed to police. Not only did it include many patrolmen in Michigan and elsewhere, but a grand jury in Oakland County, Michigan, reported that the chief of police in Pontiac was an active member. The Legion, it should be noted, engaged in kidnapping, flogging, and even murder of suspected Communists. Father Coughlin, who was probably the most important profascist leader of the 1930s, also found heavy backing within police ranks. An investigation of his organization, the Christian Front, revealed that 407 of New York's finest belonged to it.

Gunnar Myrdal, in his classic study of the race problem in America, *An American Dilemma*, conducted in the late thirties and early forties, asserted that one of the principal sources of Ku Klux Klan activity in the South at that time came from law enforcement officers. This finding jibed with reports of the membership of the Klan during the early 1920s when it was at the height of its power, controlling politics in many Northern as well as Southern states. Klan leaders according to one account "took particular pride in emphasizing the large number of law enforcement officers . . . that had joined their order." Typical of Klan propaganda which attracted police support was the plank in the program of the Chicago Klan which called for "Supporting Officials in all Phases of Law Enforcement," a slogan close to the "Support Your Local Police" campaign waged by the Birch Society and George Wallace four decades later. According to Charles Jackson, membership lists seized in different parts of California indicated that "roughly 10 percent of the . . . policemen in practically every California city," including the chiefs of police in Los Angeles and Bakersfield and the sheriff of Los Angeles County, belonged to the Klan. In Atlanta, the home base of the organization, a study reports that "a very high percentage" of the police were members. Considerable police backing for the Klan was also reported in analyses of its operation in cities as diverse as Portland (Oregon), Tulsa, Madison, and Memphis.

Looking back through the history of religious bigotry in this country, we find that the anti-Catholic nativist American Protective

Association (APA), which flourished in the early 1890s, also appears to have been supported by the police. My own researches on this movement and its membership indicate that the police were considerably overrepresented among APA members. In Minneapolis 6.5 percent were policemen, in Sacramento 8 percent, and in San Jose 7 percent.

Although there is a general understanding that the police should be politically neutral, their role as public employees has inevitably involved them in local politics. Prior to the emergence of civil service examinations, appointment to the force was a political plum in most cities. And once a man was hired, chances for promotion often depended on access to local officeholders. In many communities, the police were part of the machine organization. The widespread pattern of toleration of corruption and the rackets which characterized urban political life until the 1940s usually depended on the cooperation, if not direct participation, of the police. Those who controlled the rackets paid special attention to municipal politics, to those who dominated city hall, in order to make sure that they would not be interfered with by the authorities.

Although machine and racketeer domination of local government is largely a thing of the past in most cities, the police are of necessity still deeply interested in local politics. High-level appointments are almost invariably made by elected officials, and those who control city politics determine police pay and working conditions. Hence, the police as individuals and as a body must be actively concerned with access to the political power structure. They must be prepared to adjust their law enforcement policies in ways which are acceptable to the political leaders.

Such assumptions would lead us to believe that police would avoid any contact with radical groups, with those who seek to change the existing structures of political power or community leadership. Thus the evidence that significant minorities of police have been moved to join or openly back right-wing and bigoted movements is particularly impressive. For every policeman who has taken part in such activities, we may assume that there were many others who sympathized, but refrained from such behavior so as to avoid endangering their job prospects. (This comment, of course, does not apply to those communities which were actually dominated by extremist movements.)

The propensity of policemen to support rightist activities derives from a number of elements in their occupational role and social background. Many of the police are not much different in their social outlook from others in the lower middle class or working class. Twenty-five years ago, Gunnar Myrdal noted that police in the South were prone to express deep-seated anti-Negro feelings in brutal actions against Negroes and thus undo "much of what Northern philanthropy and Southern state governments are trying to accomplish through education and other means." He accounted for the phenomenon as resulting from the fact that the police generally had the prejudices of the poor whites. "The average Southern policeman is a promoted poor white with a legal sanction to use a weapon. His social heritage has taught him to despise the Negroes, and he has had little education which could have changed him." A recent study of the New York City police by Arthur Niederhoffer, a former member of the Department, reports that "for the past fifteen years, during a cycle of prosperity, the bulk of police candidates has been upper lower class with a sprinkling of lower middle class; about ninety-five percent has had no college training." In a survey of the occupations of the fathers of 12,000 recruits who graduated from the New York Police Academy, he found that more than three quarters of them were manual or service workers.

The Birch Society apart, movements of ethnic intolerance and right-wing radicalism have tended to recruit from the more conservative segments of the lower and less-educated strata. On the whole, the less education people have, the more likely they are to be intolerant of those who differ from themselves, whether in opinions, modes of culturally and morally relevant behavior, religion, ethnic background, or race. The police, who are recruited from the conservative, less-educated groups, reflect the background from which they come. John H. McNamara recently found that when he separated the New York police recruits into two status groups on the basis of their fathers' occupations, those "with fathers in the higher skill classification were less likely to feel that the leniency of courts and laws account for assaults on the police" than those who came from lower socioeconomic origins.

Once they are employed as policemen, their job experiences enhance the possibility that whatever authoritarian traits they bring from their social background will increase rather than decrease. McNamara found a sizable increase in the proportion of police recruits who resented legal restrictions on their authority or propensity to use force. At the beginning of recruit training, only 6 percent agreed with the statement "The present system of state and local laws has undermined the patrolman's authority to a dangerous extent," while 46 percent disagreed. After one year in field assignments, 25 percent of the same group of men agreed with the statement, and only 19 percent disagreed. Similar changes in attitudes occurred with respect to the proposition "If patrolmen working in tough neighborhoods had more leeway and fewer restrictions on the use of force many of the serious police problems in these neighborhoods would be greatly reduced." Fourteen percent agreed with the statement at the beginning of their career, as compared with 30 percent after one year in the field, and 39 percent among a different group of policemen who had been employed for two years.

In general, the policeman's job requires him to be suspicious of people, to prefer conventional behavior, to value toughness. A policeman must be suspicious and cynical about human behavior. As Niederhoffer points out, "He needs the intuitive ability to sense plots and conspiracies on the basis of embryonic evidence." The political counterpart of such an outlook is a monistic theory which simplifies political conflict into a black-and-white fight, and which is ready to accept a conspiratorial view of the sources of evil, terms which basically describe the outlook of extremist groups, whether of the left or right.

The propensity of police to support a radical political posture is also related to their sense of being a low-status out-group in American society. The Oakland study revealed that when police were asked to rank the most serious problems they have, the category most frequently selected was "lack of respect for the police. . . . Of the two hundred and eighty-two . . . policemen who rated the prestige police work receives from others, 70 per cent ranked it as only fair or poor." The New York City study also indicated that the majority of the police did not feel that they enjoyed the respect of the public. James Q. Wilson found that a majority of Chicago police sergeants who completed questionnaires in 1960 and 1965 felt that the public did not cooperate with or respect the police. Many articles in police journals comment on the alleged antagonism to the police voiced by the mass media. Studies of police opinion have indicated that some police conceal their occupation from their neighbors because many people do not like to associate with policemen.

If policemen judge their social worth by their incomes, they are right in rating it low. A recent article in *Fortune* reports that "the patrolman's pay in major cities now averages about $7,500 per year—33 percent less than is needed to sustain a family of four in moderate circumstances in a large city, according to the U.S. Bureau of Labor Statistics." As a result, many are forced to moonlight to earn a living. Fletcher Knebel cites an expert estimate that from a third to half of all the patrolmen in the country have a second job. The relative socioeconomic status of the police has worsened over time. Richard Wade, an urban historian at the University of Chicago, points out that the situation has changed considerably from that of fifty years ago when "policemen had an income higher than other trades and there were more applicants than there were jobs." John H. McNamara, who has studied the New York Department, concludes:

During the Depression the department was able to recruit from a population which included many unemployed or low-paid college graduates. . . . As general economic conditions have improved, however, the job of police officer has become less attractive to college graduates.

In his surveys of police opinion in Chicago, Boston, and Washington, D.C., Albert J. Reiss reports that 59 percent believe that the prestige of police work is lower than it was twenty years ago. Lower police morale is not simply a function of a relative decline in income or in perceived status. The police believe their conditions of work have also worsened. Eighty percent state that "police work [is] more hazardous today than five years ago." Sixty percent believe that the way the public behaves toward the police has changed for the worse since they joined the force.

The policeman's role is particularly subject to fostering feelings of resentment against society, which flow from a typical source of radical politics, "status discrepancies." This term refers to a sociological concept which is used to describe the positions of individuals or groups who are ranked relatively high on one status attribute and low on another.

Presumably the fact of having a claim to some deference makes people indignantly resent as morally improper any evidence that they are held in low regard because of some other factor in their background or activities. In the case of the police, they are given considerable authority by society to enforce its laws and are expected to risk their lives if necessary; on the other hand, they feel they receive little prestige, and they get a relatively low salary as compared with that of other occupational groups which have much less authority.

Many police have consciously come to look upon themselves as an oppressed minority, subject to the same kind of prejudice as other minorities. Thus Chief Parker explained some of the bitterness of the police as stemming from the "shell of minorityism" within which they lived. This view was given eloquent voice in 1965 by the then New York City Police Commissioner, Michael J. Murphy:

The police officer, too, belongs to a minority group—a highly visible minority group, and is also subject to stereotyping and mass attack. Yet he, like every member of every minority, is entitled to be judged as an individual and on the basis of his individual acts, not as a group.

Clearly, the police appear to be a deprived group, one which feels deep resentment about the public's lack of appreciation for the risks it takes for the community's safety. These risks are not negligible in the United States. In 1967, for example, one out of every eight policemen was assaulted. This rate is considerably higher than in any other developed democratic country.

The belief that police are rejected by the public results, as Wilson argues, in a "sense of alienation from society" which presses the police to develop their own "sub-culture" with norms which can provide them with "a basis for self-respect independent to some degree of civilian attitudes." Given the assumption of the police that they are unappreciated even by the honest middle-class citizenry, they are prone to accept a cynical view of society and its institutions, and social isolation and alienation can lead to political alienation.

The police have faced overt hostility and even contempt from spokesmen for liberal and leftist groups, racial minorities, and intellectuals generally. The only ones who appreciate their contribution to society and the risks they take are the conservatives, and particularly the extreme right. The radical left has almost invariably been hostile, the radical right friendly. It is not surprising therefore that police are more likely to be found in the ranks of the right.

In the larger context, American politics tends to press the police to support conservative or rightist politics. Liberals and leftists have been more concerned than conservatives with the legal rights of the less powerful and the underprivileged. They have tried to limit the power of the police to deal with suspects and have sought to enlarge the scope of due process. Efforts to enhance the rights of defendants, to guarantee them legal representation, to prevent the authorities from unduly pressuring those taken into police custody, have largely concerned liberals. The American Civil Liberties Union and other comparable groups have fought hard to weaken the discretionary power of the police. To many policemen, the liberals' constant struggle is to make their job more difficult, to increase the physical danger to which they are subject. Many are convinced that dangerous criminals or revolutionists are freely walking the streets because of the efforts of softhearted liberals. To police, who are constantly exposed to the seamy side of life, who view many deviants and lawbreakers as outside the protection of the law, the constant concern for the civil rights of such people makes little sense, unless it reflects moral weakness on the part of the liberals, or more dangerously, is an aspect of a plot to undermine legitimate authority. And the fact that the Supreme Court has sided with the civil-libertarian interpretations of individual rights in recent years on issues concerning police tactics in securing confessions—the use of wiretaps, and the like—constitutes evidence as to how far moral corruption has reached into high places. Reiss's survey of police opinion found that 90 percent of the police interviewed felt that the Supreme Court "has gone too far in making rules favoring and protecting criminal offenders." The liberal world, then, is perceived as an enemy, an enemy which may attack directly in demonstrations or riots, or indirectly through its pressure on the courts.

The fights over the establishment of civilian police review boards which have occurred in many cities have largely taken the form of a struggle between the liberal political forces which favor creating such checks over the power of police departments to discipline their own members and the conservatives who oppose these. In the best-publicized case, the referendum in New York City of November, 1966, to repeal the law creating such a board, the ideological lineup was clear-cut. The Patrolmen's Benevolent Association was supported in its successful efforts by the Conservative Party of New York and the John Birch Society. It was opposed by New York's liberal Republican mayor, John Lindsay, as well as by Robert Kennedy, the reform Democrats, the Liberal Party, the New York *Times*, and the New York *Post*. There can be little doubt that this struggle has helped to strengthen the police backing for the Conservative Party.

The greater willingness of police to join or back groups which have been antagonistic to religious (Catholics in the nineteenth century, Jews in the twentieth) and racial minorities also may be a function of concrete job experience, as well as of the degree of prejudice present in their social milieu. Ethnic slums character-istically have been centers of crime, violence, and vice. Most immigrant groups living in urban America in the past, as well as more recent Negro migrants, have contributed disproportionately to the ranks of criminals and racketeers. Hence, the police have often found that their experience confirmed the negative cultural stereotypes which have existed about such groups while they lived in the crowded, dirty, slum conditions. The ethnic minorities have, in fact, often appeared as sympathetic to criminals, as supporters of violence directed against the police. The ethnic slum historically has been an enemy stronghold, a place of considerable insecurity. Right-wing political groupings which define minorities or leftist radicals as conspiratorial corrupters of American morality have strongly appealed to the morally outraged police.

In evaluating the disposition of the police to participate in the radical right, it is important to note that only a minority of the police are involved in most communities. Most police, though relatively conservative and conventional, are normally more concerned with the politics of collective bargaining, with getting more for themselves, than with the politics of right-wing extremism. The Patrolmen's Benevolent Association is basically a trade union which seeks alliances with other labor unions, particularly those within the civil service, and with the powerful within the dominant political parties. Police have struck for higher wages, much as other groups have done. There have been occasions when they have shown sympathy for striking workers on the picket line, particularly when the workers and the police have belonged to the same ethnic groups. One of the main attractions of police work is the lifelong economic security and early pensions which it gives. In this sense, the policeman, like others from low-income backgrounds, is concerned for the expansion of the welfare state.

Like all others, the police are interested in upgrading the public image of their job. They do not like being attacked as thugs, as authoritarians, as lusting for power. Some cities have successfully sought to increase the educational level of new recruits and to have a continuing education program for those on the force. The academic quality of the courses given at police academies and colleges in various communities has been improving, and there is much that is hopeful going on.

Yet the fact remains that recent events have sorely strained the tempers of many police. Almost two thirds of the police interviewed in Reiss's study feel that "demonstrations are a main cause of violence these days." The reactions of police organizations around the country suggest that Ortega y Gasset was correct when he suggested in his book *The Revolt of the Masses*, published in 1930, that free societies would come to fear their police. He predicted that those who rely on the police to maintain order are foolish if they imagine that the police "are always going to be content to preserve ... order [as defined by government]. . . . Inevitably they [the police] will end by themselves defining and deciding on the order they are going to impose—which, naturally, will be that which suits them best." In some cities, leaders of police organizations have openly threatened that the police will disobey orders to be permissive when dealing with black or student demonstrators. The Boston Police Patrolmen's Association has stated that the police there will enforce the law, no matter what politicians say. The president of the New York Patrolmen's Benevolent Association has announced that his members "will enforce the law 100 percent," even when ordered not to do so.

This "rebellion of the police" is a response to their being faced with "confrontation tactics" by student and black radical militants. New Left radicals and black nationalists openly advocate confrontation tactics. They seek deliberately to inflame the police so as to enrage them into engaging in various forms of brutality. Stokely Carmichael has declared that a demonstration which does not result in police action against the participants is a failure. The events at Chicago during the Democratic Convention constitute the best recent example of the way in which a major police force can completely lose its head when faced by a confrontationist demonstration. Some black and white New Radicals openly declare that the killing of police in the ghetto area is not murder, that it is an inherent form of self-defense. But police have been shot at and occasionally killed in ambush.

The current tensions between the police and New Left student and black nationalist radicals probably involve the most extreme example of deliberate provocation which the police have ever faced. The tactics of the campus-based opposition rouse the most deep-seated feelings of class resentment. Most policemen are conservative, conventional, upwardly mobile working-class supporters of the American Way, who aspire for a better life for their families. Many of them seek to send their children to college. To find the scions of the upper middle class in the best universities denouncing them as "pigs," hurling insults which involve use of the most aggressive sexual language, such as "Up against the wall, Mother F———," throwing bricks and bags of feces at them, is much more difficult to accept than any other situation which they have faced. Police understand as normal the problems of dealing with crime or vice. They may resent violence stemming from minority ghettos, but this, too, is understandable and part of police work. But to take provocative behavior from youths who are socially and economically much better off than they and their children is more than the average policeman can tolerate.

The deliberate effort to bait and provoke the police by contemporary New Left radicals is rather new in the history of leftist movements. The American Socialist Party in its early history actually pointed to the police department as a good example of the way the government could provide needed services efficiently. The Communists, of course, never described the police in this fashion, but in the twenties, European Communists concerned with attaining power rather than with symbolic demonstrations defined the police, like the rank and file of the military, as exploited working-class groups who should either be converted to the revolution or at least be neutralized. They directed propaganda to the self-interests of the police, calling on them to refuse to serve the interests of the ruling class during strikes or demonstrations. The European left has often sought to organize the police in trade unions, although it is, of course, also true that they have had an ambivalent attitude toward them. The police have been involved in brutal suppression of left-wing and trade-union demonstrations in Europe, which have made them the target of left-wing criticism and counterviolence. Nevertheless, the left there remembers that the police come from proletarian origins. During the May, 1968, student demonstrations and strikes in Italy, a leading Communist intellectual, Pier Paolo

Pasolini, told the new Left students that in a conflict between them and the police, he stood with the police:

> Your faces are those of sons of good families, and I hate you as I hate your fathers. The good breeding comes through. . . . Yesterday when you had your battle in the Valle Giulia with the police, my sympathies were with the police, because they are the sons of the poor. . . .

Given the interest shown in the welfare of the police by sections of the European left, their membership in trade unions, and their working-class origins, it is not surprising that the political behavior of European police has been more ambivalent than that of their American compeers. On various occasions, segments of the police in Europe have shown sympathy for left and working-class forces, particularly where they have been serving under leftist governments for some time. This was true in Social Democratic Berlin and Prussia generally before 1932, in Vienna before 1934, and in parts of Republican Spain before 1936. The ambivalent attitudes of the police have shown up most recently in France, where a number of police unions issued statements after the May, 1968, events, denying responsibility for use of force against student demonstrators. The police organizations wanted it known that the government, not the police, was responsible for the vigor of the actions taken.

It is doubtful that the American New Left students will ever come to see the police in a sympathetic light, as exploited, insecure, alienated members of the underprivileged classes. As members of the first leftist youth movement which is unaffiliated with any adult party, they are unconcerned with the consequences of their actions on the political strength of the larger left-wing movement. To a large extent, their provocative efforts reflect the biases of the educated upper middle class. Lacking a theory of society and any concern for the complexities of the "road to power" which have characterized the revolutionary Marxist movement, they are prepared to alienate the police, as well as conventional working-class opinion, in order to provoke police brutality, which in turn will validate their total rejection of all social institutions. Hence, we may expect a continuation of the vicious circle of confrontation and police terror tactics.

Liberal moderates properly react to this situation by demanding that the police act toward deviant behavior much as all other professionals do, that they have no more right to react aggressively toward provocative acts than psychiatrists faced by maniacal and dangerous patients, that no matter what extremists do, the police should not lose their self-control. Such a policy is easy to advocate; it is difficult to carry out.

Furthermore, it ignores the fact that most of the police are "working-class" professionals, not the products of postgraduate education. As James Q. Wilson points out, "This means they bring to the job some of the focal concerns of working-class men—a preoccupation with maintaining self-respect, proving one's masculinity, 'not taking any crap,' and not being 'taken in.' Having to rely on personal qualities rather than on formal routines . . . means that the officer's behavior will depend crucially on how much deference he is shown, on how manageable the situation seems to be, and on what the participants in it seem to 'deserve.' " If society wants police to behave like psychiatrists, then it must be willing to treat and train them like psychiatrists rather than like pariahs engaged in dirty work. At present, it treats their job like a semiskilled position which requires, at best, a few weeks' training. Norman Kassoff of the research staff of the International Association of Chiefs of Police has compared the legal minimum training requirements for various occupations in the different American states. Calculated in terms of hours, the median minimums are 11,000 for physicians, 5000 for embalmers, 4000 for barbers, 1200 for beauticians, and less than 200 for policemen. The vast majority of policemen begin carrying guns and enforcing the law with less than five weeks' training of any kind.

The new tensions have increased the old conflict between the police and the liberals. For it must be said that liberals are prejudiced against police, much as many white police are biased against Negroes. Most liberals are ready to assume that all charges of police brutality are true. They tend to refuse to give the police the benefit of any doubt. They rarely denounce the extreme black groups and left radicals for their confrontationist efforts. They do not face up to the need for tactics to deal with deliberate incitement to mob violence. If the liberal and intellectual communities are to have any impact on the police, if they are to play any role in reducing the growing political alienation of many police, they must show some recognition that the police force is also composed of human beings, seeking to earn a living. They must be willing to engage in a dialogue with the police concerning their problems.

5

The Environment

Suddenly, just before the 1970s began, another issue emerged, full-blown, demanding and receiving a speedy political response. The issue was the degradation and threatened destruction of several aspects of the environment.

The problem had been there for a long time—ever since the beginning of human technology. And during the 1960s urgent warnings were sounded by scientists, conservation organizations, Senator Edmund Muskie and a few other members of Congress, and writers like Rachel Carson. Government leaders took up the theme, and some steps were taken by the Administration, Congress, and state and local governments during the Kennedy and Johnson years. But it was not until 1969, when off-shore drilling by the Union Oil Company spilled vast quantities of oil along the Santa Barbara coast, that the indignation of a larger public was aroused.

President Nixon then seized the issue. In February 1970, he presented a 37-point program aimed at purifying rivers and lakes, cleaning up the landscape and the air, and enlarging the amount of land available for recreation. These goals were to be accomplished by harnessing the efforts of all levels of government and private industry. Democrats in Congress complained that the proposals were belated and inadequate. However, all across the political spectrum, from conservatives to the radical left, everyone agreed that something—and something big—must be done to deal with the various dangers described in this chapter by John Burke and Barry Commoner.

Yet it is questionable that this consensus will remain so complete once the attack on the problem moves from generalities to specifics. The possibilities for intense controversy are many:

What will it cost? Vast expenditures are required if the trend toward pollution is to be reversed. The President's message indicated that Washington would contribute $4 billion in four years toward the construction of municipal sewage-treatment plants and would underwrite municipal financing of the remaining $6 billion. But this is only one of the many areas touched upon in the message, and there was no indication of what the total expense might be. Moreover, the cost of attacking pollution cannot be measured only in terms of direct financial outlays. Alternative benefits might have to be surrendered. For example, the banning of a new power plant from a metropolitan area would prevent additional pollution, but it might also delay the construction of new facilities so long as to cause power breakdowns.

Who will pay? Some, including Congressmen Farbstein and Brown, contend that the fault is largely with private industry and that industry should foot the bill. Max Ways, on the other hand, argues that there is no one guilty party, that the blame must be accepted by all of us. In any case, it is obvious the costs will be shared among industry, the consumer, and the general taxpayer. Thus, in 1970 the Department of Health, Education, and Welfare promulgated new regulations on air pollution, including the first federal limits on emissions of nitrogen oxides. This would move faster in the direction proposed here by Congressman Farbstein. Also, private industry announced plans to design cars that would run on lead-free gasoline.[1] It is clear, however, that at least some part of the increased costs incurred would be passed along to consumers. A number of other anti-pollution programs would have to be paid for largely out of taxes. In a time of strong resistance to higher tax rates, would this money be provided without cuts in other government programs—such as those addressed to the problems of race and poverty? (There are some, in fact, who argue that the issue of the environment is a convenient

[1]In case these various methods fail to end pollution, President Nixon included in his February 1970 message a proposal for a federally supported research effort aimed at producing "an unconventionally powered, virtually pollution-free automobile within five years."

distraction of energies and resources from more important and more intense issues in American society.)

Where do we draw the line? Today's consensus is that we are doing altogether too much damage to our environment. Yet, as the House Subcommittee on Science, Research, and Development points out, we cannot live without running some risk of doing damage to the environment and to ourselves. The problem in this, as in so many public issues, is where to draw the line. Stewart Udall admits that in the Santa Barbara affair—the "conservation 'Bay of Pigs' "—he drew the line too far away from safety. Yet, at the time when he granted the leases, it appeared to him and his advisers that the risks were minimal and the revenue gains great. It was a tragic mistake for a man who had been in the forefront of the fight for conservation of natural resources, but he indicates that it may have been one of those catastrophes we need if our arrogance and apathy are to give way to wisdom. At the same time, the House subcommittee report suggests we may have learned our lesson too well and that the necessary reordering of our priorities in favor of the environment could cause us to forego very large benefits in order to avoid very small risks.

How many people? As we pointed out in Chapter 1, the growth of world population alone is putting great pressure on the environment. Over-population is usually regarded as a threat primarily to the poorer nations. But, as a United Nations Commission points out, when we return to the environmental problem in Chapter 10, it is the advanced technology of the United States that does totally disproportionate damage to the environment. Every American, no matter how ardent a conservationist, depletes several times the resources, imposes several times the strain on the environment, as every Indian or Egyptian. Thus, the question of population increase in the United States becomes a matter of concern for the world as well as for our own country; and while the birth rate has declined recently, some projections point to a population of 300 million by the end of the century. President Nixon's February 1970 message on the environment said nothing about this problem. However, the President's chief science adviser, Dr. Lee DuBridge, has commended the notion of a sharp reduction, perhaps to zero, in population growth and the development of public policies designed to accomplish this. In the American cultural and political climate, could this be achieved? And if it could, what are the costs of moving toward a stable—some would say stagnant—population? Here again there are major issues which must soon be faced as we move on from the new consensus over the environment to emerging arenas of conflict.

TECHNOLOGY AND NATURE

John G. Burke

John G. Burke is Associate Professor in the Department of History, UCLA.

. . . Advancing technology has by now interfered with our natural environment to such a deleterious extent that it has become imperative to take action not only to retard but also to reverse this process. The future of man is threatened as well as other forms of life. Further, man's gradual estrangement from nature, his retreat into teeming urban metropolises, and his preoccupation with a scientific-technological culture have resulted in an impairment of the quality of human life, despite increased longevity and material abundance. In the long-range view, these problems are the most pressing of our time.

Man, of course, has been influencing his environment since prehistoric times. Early nomadic communities hunted by setting forests on fire, which drove the animals into the open where they could be more easily tracked and killed. The ancient agricultural civilizations of Mesopotamia and Egypt depended upon the waters of the Tigris and Euphrates rivers and the Nile, respectively. They dredged canals and constructed dams to divert the water and irrigate the fields efficiently. Overfishing of the Baltic and North seas during the medieval period resulted in the near-extinction of herring in those areas, just as certain species of whale are threatened today. Prior to the successful utilization of coal in metallurgical processes in the eighteenth century, the forests of England were almost depleted

From "Technology and Values," *The Great Ideas Today 1969*, pp. 208-215. Reprinted from *The Great Ideas Today 1969*, Supplement to Great Books of the Western World. ©1969 by Encyclopaedia Britannica, Inc. Reprinted by permission of the publisher.

because of the demand for charcoal. Complaints about the noxious and nauseous fumes from inefficiently burned sulfur-bearing coal in London appear about 1285.

That mining methods had generated vociferous criticism by the mid-sixteenth century is attested to by a passage from Agricola's *De Re Metallica:*

> . . . the strongest argument of the detractors is that the fields are devastated by mining operations, . . . Also they argue that the woods and groves are cut down, for there is need of an endless amount of wood for timbers, machines, and the smelting of metals. And when the woods and groves are felled, then are exterminated the beasts and birds, very many of which furnish a pleasant and agreeable food for man. Further, when the ores are washed, the water which has been used poisons the brooks and streams, and either destroys the fish or drives them away.[1]

A modern conservationist could hardly raise more cogent objections to unrestrained mining operations. Agricola, as an advocate of technological progress, brushes aside these objections by demonstrating that metals are necessary for the advance of civilization, and by asserting that mining operations, in fact, result in either very slight damage or none at all. His statements also have their modern counterparts.

Real environmental pollution, however, commenced during the Industrial Revolution in the nineteenth century. Hydrogen chloride gas, for example, was a by-product of the Leblanc process for producing inexpensive alkali. The pioneer manufacturers, finding no use for it, passed it up tall chimneys to the atmosphere. Its fallout caused such widespread destruction to vegetation, and property damage, that manufacturers were arraigned for creating a public nuisance. The development of techniques for absorbing the hydrogen chloride, and the later recognition of its economic value, prevented even greater environmental pollution.

Rapidly advancing technology from that time to the present, however, has resulted in our air, land, and water being increasingly polluted by industrial and radioactive wastes, pesticides, herbicides, detergents, and fumes. Analyses of the catches of fish show the rapid spread of agricultural pesticides into the oceans. Effluents from nuclear reactors, which concentrate in various organisms, are accumulating at the mouths of rivers. Water pollution from industrial wastes is harmfully affecting marine life on the shores of all major industrial nations. Indeed, Lake Erie has become such an open sewer

---

[1]Georgius Agricola, *De Re Metallica,* trans. Herbert C. and Lou Henry Hoover (New York: Dover Publications, 1950), p. 8.

that limnologists agree that it is unlikely that anyone will ever again see it clean and clear.

In August, 1968, sixty members of the medical faculty of the University of California, Los Angeles, asserted that air pollution had become a major health hazard to most of Los Angeles County during much of the year. Almost all pollution experts agree that automobile exhaust fumes are the chief source of noxious pollutants in the atmosphere, but as yet the automobile industry has been unwilling to mount the necessary effort to reduce materially these dangerous by-products of the internal combustion engine. Neither the industry nor the federal government has moved to institute a program of scientific research required to solve this problem. Nor will the government subsidize research on steam-powered or battery-operated vehicles, which offer a possible alternative. Tons of carbon, sulfur, and nitrogen compounds, as well as oil, soot, and dust, are dumped into the air in the United States every year. The phosphate companies of western America lay down a screen of choking smoke where the skies were formerly clear. From the pulp mills of Idaho and Oregon and from the processing and rendering plants of the eastern seaboard there is emitted an ever increasing stench of nauseating or highly offensive odors.

The ecological balance is delicate and at present only imperfectly understood. Nature, conquered in one respect, retaliates in another. Thus, the technological efficiency of intensive agriculture resulting in single-crop farms also creates favorable conditions for the spread of a particular pest. The boll weevil diffused rapidly over the southern cotton fields when it migrated from Mexico in the late nineteenth century. Similarly, San Jose scale attacked the bark, leaves, and fruit of most deciduous fruit trees in California, and phylloxera, the plant louse, infected grapevines. Specific pesticides alleviate these infestations, but the long-range effects of the chemical components after use and breakdown are unknown.

Yet we continue to act with surprising temerity. The United States armed forces are using herbicidal chemicals in a widespread attempt to destroy deliberately the crops and forest vegetation of certain areas of Vietnam. After protests concerning the wisdom of this decision, the Department of Defense finally produced the ecological studies which were used as a basis for the decision. The majority of the members of a committee of the American Association for the Advancement of Science, which reviewed these reports, considered them scientifically insufficient.[2]

[2]*Science,* July 19, 1968, pp. 253-56.

But even if we were to eliminate the most flagrant abuses, continued progress at our present rate will pose new environmental problems. The seriousness of overpopulation has been emphasized so widely that it will not be mentioned here. But a continued population rise together with an increase in the per capita use of energy means that the growth rate of the electric power industry, presently about 6 percent per year, will continue unchanged for years to come. Should the use of nuclear power become more extensive, as is commonly expected, there will be a major problem in the disposal of dangerous radioactive wastes. In addition, power plants must get rid of large quantities of heat, which pollutes the cooling water and adversely affects marine life. Nearby residents of Lake Cayuga in northern New York are now questioning the siting of an electric power plant at the lake because of the danger of thermal pollution. Such controversies will undoubtedly become more common in the future.

Leaving aside future problems for present realities, why is it that man continues heedlessly to pollute the environment in the face of clear danger signals? We may condemn the ubiquitous littering of beaches, parks, and playgrounds, or the careless use of fire in forest preserves, as acts of thoughtlessness, but an increase in the number or proximity of trash barrels or the posting of entreaties to preserve the beauties of nature have little effect. Similarly, we may blame the more serious pollution damage on industrialists who tolerate the visible effects or are insensible to forecasts of a deteriorating environment because of short-term monetary profits. Such attitudes are not new.

It is probable that the exploitation and consequent despoliation of nature is not a superficial problem but, rather, has deep psychological or religious roots. If one views nature as antithetical to human purposes and goals, one may consciously or subconsciously attempt to control and overcome the forces of nature, regardless of the ensuing costs to the environment. On the other hand, if one regards nature as neutral, or as beautiful and beneficent, one would be less likely to destroy its beauty for sheer material benefit but rather attempt to work with nature as a partner. The recent controversies between lumber barons and conservationists concerning the centuries-old redwood forests in California may be cited as an example of this basic difference in psychological outlook.

There is a technological bond as well as an aesthetic one between man and nature. Man must exploit nature in order to survive. But must the exploitation be so savage and the despoliation so irreparable? Was this the relationship in all ages and places?

Lynn White has answered the latter question in the negative.[3] "What people do about their ecology," White states, "depends on what they think about themselves in relation to things around them. Human ecology is deeply conditioned by beliefs about our nature and destiny—that is, by religion." Christianity, White believes, is responsible in no small measure for our ecologic crisis, because Christian teaching emphasized that God created the earth for man's enjoyment and use. Some Christians, as St. Francis of Assisi, venerated all of the objects of God's creation, but many became activists and exploited nature mercilessly with religious sanction. This creed was novel, and it was diametrically opposed to the beliefs of ancient paganism and of nearly every Asiatic religion concerning the environment. White's analysis appears to be substantiated by later historical developments. The vision of continual and unlimited progress, instituted by Sir Francis Bacon and his contemporaries, omitted consideration of the natural environment because the Christian tradition had already made it subservient to man and merely the object of his exploitative activities. . . .

In modern civilization we face a gradually increasing level of noise, from automobile traffic, riveters, electronically amplified rock-and-roll music in restaurants, and jet aircraft. In the environs of our airports, the decibel level approaches a deafening 90 inside of buildings and an ear-splitting 120 in the open air. . . .

It is now known that sonic booms are responsible for rock falls that have occurred in several national parks. Some have irreparably damaged prehistoric Indian dwellings. But beyond this, if supersonic transports are permitted to make night transcontinental flights across the United States, it is estimated that more than ten million persons will have their sleep violently disturbed. Yet the Federal Aviation Agency, without prolonged consideration, made the decision to fund the supersonic transport, brushing aside opposition with vague assurances that there would be no noise problem. Leading the opposition to a noise abatement bill in Congress were senators who had a clear political stake in the advancement of the supersonic transport program.

Our cities which supposedly exist to create and nurture civilization present an entirely different aspect. They contain miles of grease-stained concrete and asphalt, forests of electric power lines and smokestacks, tawdry gasoline stations, unsightly junkyards, and massive advertising billboards. They are not only unsafe but aesthetically repulsive. Buckminster Fuller states that "the almost totally anarchistic piecemeal development and remodification of

[3]*Science*, March 10, 1967, pp. 1203-7.

cities exclusively for the benefit of the prime investors and without comprehensive consideration of the total welfare of all mankind for all future time is getting us into ever greater trouble."[4] Flight to the suburbs is an escape from the ugliness of the artificial environment, and the spirits of those left behind in the ghettos fester in the squalor of their surroundings. . . .

[4]*Joint House-Senate Colloquium to Discuss a National Folicy for the Environment,* 99th Congress, 2nd session, July 17, 1968, p. 198.

CAN WE SURVIVE?

Barry Commoner

Barry Commoner is Director of the Center for the Biology of Natural Systems at Washington University, St. Louis, Missouri.

No one can escape the enormous fact that California has changed. What was once desert has become the most productive land in the world. The once-lonely mountain tops are crisscrossed with humming power lines. Powerful industries, from old ones like steel to the most modern aerospace and electronic operations, have been built. California has become one of the most fruitful, one of the richest places on the surface of the earth. This is all change, and it is good.

But there are other changes in California. Its vigorous growth has been achieved by many men and women who came to give their children a healthy place to live. Now, however, when school children in Los Angeles run out to the playing fields, they are confronted by the warning: "Do not exercise strenuously or breathe too deeply during heavy smog conditions." For the sunshine that once bathed the land in golden light has been blotted out by deadly smog. In a number of California towns the water supplies now contain levels of nitrate above the limit recommended by the U. S. Public Health Service; given to infants, nitrate can cause a fatal disorder, methemoglobenemia, and pediatricians have recommended the use of bottled water for infant formulas. The natural resources of California, once a magnet that attracted thousands who sought a good life, now harbor threats to health. Beaches that once sparkled in the sun are polluted with oil and foul-smelling deposits. Rivers that once teemed with fish run sluggishly to the sea. The once famous crabs in San Francisco Bay are dying. Redwoods are toppling from the banks of eroding streams. All this, too, is change, and it is bad.

Thus, much of the good that has been produced in California, through the intelligence and hard work of its people, has been won at a terrible cost. That cost is the possible destruction of the very capital which has been invested to create the wealth of the state—its environment.

The environment makes up a huge, enormously complex living machine—an ecosystem—and every human activity depends on the integrity and proper functioning of that machine. Without the ecosystem's green plants, there would be no oxygen for smelters and furnaces, let alone to support human and animal life. Without the action of plants and animals in aquatic systems, there would be no pure water to supply agriculture, industry, and the cities. Without the biological processes that have gone on in the soil for thousands of years, there would be neither food crops, oil, nor coal. This machine is our biological capital, the basic apparatus on which our total productivity depends. If it is destroyed, agriculture and industry will come to naught; yet the greatest threats to the environmental system are due to agricultural and industrial activities. If the ecosystem is destroyed, man will go down with it; yet it is man who is destroying it. For in the eager search for the benefits of modern science and technology, we have become enticed into a nearly fatal illusion: that we have at last escaped from the dependence of man on the rest of nature. The truth is tragically different. We have become not less dependent on the balance of nature, but more dependent on it. Modern technology has so stressed the web of processes in the living environment at its most vulnerable points that there is little leeway left in the system. We are approaching the point of no return; our survival is at stake.

These are grim, alarming conclusions; but they are forced on us, I am convinced, by the evidence. Let us look at some of that evidence.

A good place to begin is the farm—on which so much of California's prosperity is based. The wealth created by agriculture is derived from the soil. In it we grow crops which convert inorganic materials—nitrogen, phosphorus, carbon, oxygen, and the other elements required by life—into organic materials—proteins, carbohydrates, fats, and vitamins—which comprise our food.

The soil, the plants that grow in it, the livestock raised on the land, and we ourselves are parts of a huge web of natural processes—endless, self-perpetuating cycles. Consider, for example, the behavior of nitrogen, an element of enormous nutritional importance, forming as it does the basis of proteins and other vital life substances. Most of the earth's available nitrogen is in the air, as nitrogen gas. This can enter the soil through nitrogen fixation, a process carried out by various bacteria, some of them living free in the soil and others associated with the roots of legumes such as clover. In nature, nitrogen also enters the soil from the wastes produced by animals. In both cases the nitrogen becomes incorporated into a complex organic material in the soil—humus. The humus slowly releases nitrogen through the action of soil microorganisms which finally convert it into nitrate. In turn, the nitrate is taken up by the roots of plants and is made into protein and other vital parts of the crop. In a natural situation the plant becomes food for animals, their wastes are returned to the soil, and the cycle is complete.

This cycle is an example of the biological capital that sustains us. How has this capital been used in California?

The huge success of agriculture in California is a matter of record; it forms the largest single element in the state's economy. To achieve this wealth a vast area in the center of the state has been transformed from a bare desert into the richest agricultural land in the nation. How has this been done? How has this transformation affected the continued usefulness of the soil system, especially the nitrogen cycle?

When the first farmers came to the San Joaquin Valley, they found fertile soil and sunshine; only water was needed to make the valley bloom. This was obtained first from local streams and later, increasingly, from wells which tapped the huge store of water that lay beneath the entire Central Valley. As the bountiful crops were taken, the soil, originally rich in nitrogen, became impoverished. To sustain crop productivity, inorganic nitrogen fertilizers were added to the soil. But with the loss of natural soil nitrogen, humus was depleted; as a result the soil became less porous, and less oxygen reached the roots, which were then less efficient in taking up the needed nutrients from the soil. The answer: more nitrogen fertilizer, for even if a smaller proportion is taken up by the crop, this can be overcome by using more fertilizer to begin with. California now uses more nitrogen fertilizer than any other state—an average of about 450 pounds per acre in 1959.

One of the rules of environmental biology is: "Everything has to go somewhere," and we may ask: Where did the extra nitrate added to the soil, but not taken up by the crops, go? The answer is clear: The unused nitrate was carried down into the soil, accumulating at greater and greater depths as the water table fell due to the continual pumping of irrigation water.

With the water table falling, agriculture in the Central Valley was headed for disaster; recognizing this fact, the state constructed the Friant-Kern Canal, which began to supply the valley with above-ground irrigation water beginning in 1951. Irrigation water must always be supplied to soil in amounts greater than that which is lost by evaporation; otherwise salts accumulate in the soil and the plants are killed. So, following the opening of the new canal, the valley water table began to rise toward its original level—carrying with it the long-accumulated nitrates in the soil.

Now there is another simple rule of environmental biology that is appropriate here: "Everything is connected to everything else." The valley towns soon learned this truth, as their drinking water supplies—which were taken from wells that tapped the rising level of underground water—began to show increasing concentrations of nitrate. In the 1950's, the Bureau of Sanitary Engineering of the California Department of Public Health began to analyze the nitrate content of city water supplies in the area. They had good reason for this action, for in July, 1950, an article in the *Journal of the American Water Works Association* had described 139 cases of infant methemoglobenemia in the United States identified since 1947; 14 cases were fatal; all were attributed to farm well water contaminated with more than 45 ppm of nitrate.

At first, only a few scattered instances of high nitrate levels were found in valley water supplies. However, a study of 800 wells in southern California counties in 1960 showed that 88 of them exceeded the 45 ppm limit; 188 wells had reached half that level. In that year, the U. S. Public Health Service recommended that a nitrate level of 45 ppm should not be exceeded, warning:

> Cases of infantile nitrate poisoning have been reported to arise from concentrations ranging from 66 to 1100 ppm. . . .Nitrate poisoning appears to be confined to infants during their first few months of life; adults drinking the same water are not affected, but breast-fed infants of mothers drinking such water may be poisoned. Cows drinking water containing nitrate may produce milk sufficiently high in nitrate to result in infant poisoning.

In Delano, a 1952 analysis showed only traces of nitrate in the city water supply; in 1966, analyses of three town wells obtained by the Delano Junior Chamber of Commerce showed nitrate levels of 70-78 ppm. In 1968, a study by the Water Resources Board, made in reply to a request by State Senator Walter W. Stiern, showed:

> Nitrate concentrations in groundwater underlying the vicinity of Delano are currently in excess of the limit . . . recommended by the

U. S. Public Health Service. . .similar geologic and hydrologic conditions occur in other areas of the San Joaquin Valley and the state generally.

So agricultural wealth of the Central Valley has been gained, but at a cost that does not appear in the farmers' balance sheets—the general pollution of the state's huge underground water reserves with nitrate. Fortunately, there appear to be no reports of widespread acute infant methemoglobenemia in the area as yet. However, the effects of chronic exposure to nitrates are poorly understood. We do know that in animals nitrate may interfere with thyroid metabolism, reduce the availability of vitamin A, and cause abortions. Moreover, there is evidence that even small reductions in the oxygen available to a developing human fetus—which might occur when the mother is exposed to subcritical levels of nitrate—result in permanent damage to the brain. In sum, the success of agriculture in the Central Valley has been won at a cost which risks the health of the people.

Nor does the nitrogen problem end there. Much of the nitrogen fertilizer applied to the soil of the Central Valley finds its way into the San Joaquin River, which drains the irrigated fields. As a result, the river carries a huge load of nitrate into the San Francisco Bay-Delta area. Here the added nitrate intrudes on another environmental cycle—the self-purifying biological processes of natural waters—bringing in its wake a new round of environmental destruction. The excess nitrate—along with excess phosphate from agricultural drainage and municipal wastes—stimulates the growth of algae in the waters of the Bay, causing the massive green scums that have become so common in the area. Such heavy overgrowths of algae soon die off, releasing organic matter which overwhelms the biological purification processes that normally remove it. As a result, the natural balance is destroyed; the water loses its oxygen; fish die; the water becomes foul with putrefying material. In the cooler words of the Department of Interior report on the San Joaquin Master Drain, "Problems resulting from nutrient enrichment and associated periodic dissolved oxygen depression are numerous in the Bay-Delta area."

So the agricultural practices of the great Central Valley have overwhelmed the natural nitrogen cycle of the soil with massive amounts of fertilizer; once this cycle was broken, the rivers were contaminated with nitrate. Reaching the Bay-Delta area, the excess nitrate has destroyed the natural balance of the self-purifying processes in these waters, with the foul results that are only too well known to those who live in that once-sparkling natural area.

This much is known fact. But once the natural cycles of the Bay-Delta waters are disrupted, other biological disasters may soon follow. At the present time, in a number of regions of the Bay-Delta waters, the bacterial count exceeds the limit recommended by the

California Department of Public Health for water contact sports. This may be due to the entry of too much untreated sewage. But experience with the waters of New York harbor suggests another, more ominous, possibility which connects this problem, too, to the drainage of nutrients from agricultural areas, as well as from treated sewage. In New York harbor, in the period 1948-1968, there has been a 10-20-fold increase in the bacterial count despite a marked *improvement* in the sewage treatment facilities that drain into the bay. Here too there has been an increase in nitrate and phosphate nutrients, in this case largely from treated sewage effluent. The possibility exists that bacteria, entering the water from sewage or the soil, are now able to *grow* in the enriched waters of the bay. If this should prove to be the case, changes in water quality such as those which have occurred in the Bay-Delta area may lead to new, quite unexpected, health hazards. The soil contains many microorganisms which cause disease in human beings when they are first allowed to grow in a nutrient medium. There is a danger, then, that as the Bay-Delta waters become laden with organic matter released by dying algae (resulting from overgrowths stimulated by agricultural and municipal wastes), disease-producing microorganisms may find conditions suitable for growth, resulting in outbreaks of hitherto unknown types of water-borne disease.

Nor does the nitrogen story quite end here. We now know that a good deal of the excess nitrogen added to the soil by intensive fertilization practices may be released to the air in the form of ammonia or nitrogen oxides. In the air, these materials are gradually converted to nitrate and carried back to the ground by rain. In 1957, a national study of the nitrate content of rainfall showed excessively high levels in three heavily fertilized regions: the Corn Belt, Texas, and the Central Valley of California. There is increasing evidence that nitrate dissolved in rain can carry enough nutrient into even remote mountain lakes to cause algal overgrowths and so pollute waters still largely free of the effects of human wastes. Recent pollution problems in Lake Tahoe may originate in this way.

I cite these details in order to make clear a profound and inescapable fact of life: that the environment is a vast system of interlocking connections—among the soil, the water, the air, plants, animals, and ourselves—which forms an endless, dynamically interacting web. This network is the product of millions of years of evolution; each of its connections has been tested against the trial of time to achieve a balance which is stable and long-lasting. But the balance, the fine fabric of physical, chemical, and biological interconnections in the environment, is a delicate one; it hangs together only as a whole. Tear into it in one place—such as the soil of the Central Valley—and the fabric begins to unravel, spreading chaos from the soil to the rivers, to the Bay, to remote mountain lakes, to the mother and her infant child. The great Central Valley has become rich with the fruits of the land, but at a cost which has already been felt across the breadth of the state and which is yet to be fully paid.

Nor do we yet know how the destructive process can be halted, or if indeed it can be. In Lake Erie, where the natural balance of the water system has already been largely overwhelmed by excessive nutrients, no one has yet been able to devise a scheme to restore its original condition. The Bay-Delta waters may suffer the same fate. The recently released Kaiser Engineers' report on the San Francisco Bay-Delta Water Quality Control Program predicts that the drainage of agricultural nutrients (nitrogen and phosphorus) from the San Joaquin will continue unabated for at least the next 50 years if present agricultural practices persist. The report proposes a system which, to control only the deleterious effects of the drainage in the Bay-Delta area, will cost about $5 billion in that period. And even at that cost the plan will only transfer the problem to the ocean—where the waste nutrients are to be discharged—which can only bring disaster to this last remaining natural resource, on which so many of our future hopes must rest.

The root of the problem remains in the soil, for if the disrupted balance is not restored there, its destructive effects will only spread into further reaches of the environment. Tragically, each year of continued over-fertilization of the soil may make recovery increasingly difficult. For example, we know that inorganic nitrogen nutrients stop the nitrogen-fixing activity of microorganisms and may eventually kill them off or at least encourage them to mutate into non-fixing forms. If the natural fertility of the soil is ever to be restored, we may have to rely heavily on these microbial agents; but this becomes less and less possible as we continue to use massive amounts of fertilizer. In effect, like a drug addict, we may become "hooked" on continued heavy nitrogen fertilization and so become inescapably locked into a self-destructive course.

This same tragic tale of environmental disaster can be told of another prominent feature of California agriculture—insecticides. One important aspect of the biological capital on which agricultural productivity depends is the network of ecological relationships that relate insect pests to the plants on which they feed, and to the other insects that, in turn, prey on the pests. These natural relations serve to keep pest populations in check. Pests which require a particular plant as food are kept in check by their inability to spread onto other plants; the other insects which parasitize and prey upon them exert important biological control over the pest population.

What has happened in attempts to control cotton pests— where the great bulk of synthetic insecticide is used in the United

States—shows how we have destroyed these natural relations and have allowed the natural pest-regulating machinery to break down. The massive use of the new insecticides has controlled some of the pests that once attacked cotton. But now the cotton plants are being attacked instead by new insects that were never previously known as pests of cotton. Moreover, the new pests are becoming increasingly resistant to insecticide, through the natural biological process of selection, in the course of inheritance, of resistant types. In Texas cotton fields, for example, in 1963 it took 50 times as much DDT to control insect pests as it did in 1961. The tobacco budworm, which now attacks cotton, has been found to be nearly immune to methylparathion, the most powerful of the widely used modern insecticides.

California, too, has begun to experience environmental disaster from the intensive use of insecticides. Consider only a single recent example. In 1965 the rich cotton fields of the Imperial Valley were invaded by the Pink Bollworm from Arizona. The Department of Agriculture began an "eradication" program based on a fixed schedule of repeated, heavy, insecticide sprays. The Pink Bollworm was controlled (but by no means "eradicated"); however, the cotton plants were then attacked by other insects which had previously caused no appreciable damage—the beet army worm and the cotton leaf perforator. The insecticide had killed off insects that were natural enemies of the army worms and perforators, which had in the meantime become resistant to the sprays. Catastrophic losses resulted. The problem is now so serious that Imperial Valley farmers have proposed the elimination of cotton plantings for a year in order to kill off the new pests, which cannot survive a year without food.

California is beginning to experience the kind of insecticide-induced disaster already common in Latin American experience. In the Cañete Valley of Peru, for example, DDT was used for the first time in 1949 to control cotton pests. Yields increased—temporarily. For soon the number of insects attacking the cotton grew from 7 to 13 and several of them had become resistant to the insecticides. By 1965, the cotton yields had dropped to half their previous value, and despite 15-25 insecticide applications, pest control was impossible. Productivity was restored only when massive insecticide application was halted and biological control was reestablished by importing insects to attack the pests.

These instances are, again, a warning that present agricultural practices may be destroying the biological capital which is essential to agricultural productivity—in this case, the natural population of insects that attack insect pests and keep them under the control of a natural balance. Again, if the ecologically blind practice of massive insecticide treatment is allowed to continue, there is a danger of permanently losing the natural protective insects—and agriculture may become "hooked" on insecticides.

And here too we see disaster spreading through the environmental network. In 1969, the Food and Drug Administration seized two shipments of canned jack mackerel, an ocean fish originating from Terminal Island, Los Angeles, because of excessive residues of DDT and related insecticides. Insecticides draining off agricultural lands into the Bay-Delta area have caused levels of DDT which exceed the amount allowed by the FDA to appear in the bodies of striped bass and sturgeon. It is possible that the recent decline in San Francisco Bay crabs may be due to the same cause. Spreading through the food chain, DDT has begun to cause disastrous declines in the population of birds of prey, and there is some evidence that gulls are being affected as well. The latter would extend the web of disaster even further, for the gulls are vital in controlling waste in shoreline waters.

Now let me follow the track of environmental disaster from the farm to the cities of California. Again, nitrogen is a valuable guide, this time, surprisingly enough, to the smog problem. This problem originates with the production of nitrogen oxides by gasoline engines. Released to the air, these oxides, upon absorption of sunlight, react with waste hydrocarbon fuel to produce the noxious constituents of smog. This problem is the direct outcome of the technological *improvement* of gasoline engines: the development of the modern high-compression engine. Such engines operate at higher temperatures than older ones; at these elevated temperatures the oxygen and nitrogen of the air taken into the engine tend to combine rapidly, with the resultant production of nitrogen oxides. Once released into the air, nitrogen oxides are activated by sunlight. They then react with waste hydrocarbon fuel, forming eventually the notorious PAN—the toxic agent of the smog made famous by Los Angeles.

The present smog-control technique—reduction of waste fuel emission—by diminishing the interaction of nitrogen oxides with hydrocarbon wastes, enhances the level of airborne nitrogen oxides, which are themselves toxic substances. In the air, nitrogen oxides are readily converted to nitrates, which are then brought down by rain and snow to the land and surface waters. There they add to the growing burden of nitrogen fertilizer, which, as I have already indicated, is an important aspect of water pollution. What is surprising is the amount of nitrogen oxides that are generated by automotive traffic: more than one-third of the nitrogen contained in the fertilizer currently employed on U.S. farms. One calculation shows that farms in New Jersey receive about 25 pounds of nitrogen fertilizer per year (a significant amount in agricultural practice) from the trucks and cars that travel the New Jersey highways. Another recent study shows that in the heavily populated eastern section of the country, the nitrate content of local rainfall is proportional to the local rate of gasoline consumption.

Thus, the emergence of a new technology—the modern gasoline engine—is itself responsible for most of the smog problem and for an appreciable part of the pollution of surface waters with nitrate. And no one needs to be reminded that smog is a serious hazard to health. Again we see the endless web of environmental processes at work. Get the engines too hot—for the sake of generating the power needed to drive a huge car at destructive speeds—and you set off a chain of events that keeps kids off the playground, sends older people to a premature death, and, in passing, adds to the already excessive burden of water pollutants.

This is some of the tragic destruction that lies hidden in the great panorama of the changing California environment—costs to the people of the state that do not appear as entries in the balance sheets of industry and agriculture. These are some of the great debts which must be paid if the state's environment is to be saved from ultimate destruction. The debts are so embedded in every feature of the state's economy that it is almost impossible to calculate them. Their scale, at least, can be secured from the figure produced for the water quality-control system which will transfer the pollution problem of the Bay-Delta area to the ocean: $5 billion over 50 years, and continuing at $100 million a year.

At what cost can the smog that envelops Los Angeles be cleared up—as it surely must if the city is to survive? Start with the price of rolling back air pollution that risks the health and well-being of the citizens of the Bay area, the Peninsula, and San Diego. And do not neglect the damage already done by smog to the pine forests in the area of Lake Arrowhead. Nitrogen oxides have just been detected in Yosemite Park; what will it cost if the state's magnificent forests begin to die, unleashing enormous flood problems? How shall we reckon the cost of huge redwoods on the North Coast, which need for their secure footing the soil built up around their roots during annual floods, when these floods are stopped by the new dams and the trees begin to topple? How shall we determine the cost of the urban spread which has covered the richest soil in the state? What will it cost to restore this soil to agriculture when the state is forced to limit intensive, pollution-generating fertilization, and new lands have to be used to sustain food production? What is the price of those massive walls of concrete, those freeways, which slice across the land, disrupting drainage patterns and upsetting the delicate balance of forces that keeps the land from sliding into ravines? Against the value of the new real-estate developments on landfills in

San Francisco Bay, calculate the cost of the resulting changes in tidal movements, which have decreased the dilution of the polluting nutrients by fresh water from the sea and have worsened the algal overgrowths. Or balance against the value of the offshore oil the cost of a constant risk of beach and ocean pollution until the offending wells are pumped dry. Finally, figure, if possible, what it will cost to restore the natural fertility of the soil in central California, to keep the nitrogen in the soil, where it belongs, and to develop a new, more mixed form of agriculture that will make it possible to get rid of most insecticides and make better use of the natural biological controls.

If the magnitude of the state's environmental problems is staggering, perhaps there is some consolation in the fact that California is not alone. Most of Lake Erie has been lost to pollution. In Illinois, every major river has been overburdened with fertilizer drainage and has lost its powers of self-purification. Automobile smog hangs like a pall over even Denver and Phoenix. Every major city is experiencing worsening air pollution. The entire nation is in the grip of the environmental crisis.

What is to be done? What can be done? Although we are, I believe, on a path which can only lead to self-destruction, I am also convinced that we have not yet passed the point of no return. We have time—perhaps a generation—in which to save the environment from the final effects of the violence we have already done to it, and to save ourselves from our own suicidal folly. But this is a very short time to achieve the massive environmental repair that is needed. We will need to start, now, on a new path. And the first action is to recognize how badly we have gone wrong in the use of the environment and to mobilize every available resource for the huge task of saving it.

Yet all the marvelous knowledge in our universities and laboratories seems now to stand helpless, while the air becomes fouler every day, beaches covered with oil, and precious water and soil more heavily laden with pollutants.

But there is another crisis—one that has struck the nation's entire scientific community. This crisis, like the environmental one, is also man-made and disastrously short-sighted; it is the drastic curtailment of the funds for research and education.

What a tragedy! At the very moment that the nation has begun to sense the urgency of the environmental crisis, when the first steps in the large and urgent task must be taken in the laboratories and classrooms of our universities, the tools are denied the men who would use them.

The huge undertakings listed here cannot even be begun unless we drastically reorganize our priorities. We cannot continue to devote the talent of our engineers and the competence of our workers to the production of overpowered, pollution-generating cars that do violence on the road and in the ecosystem. We cannot burden our productive resources with a monstrous device like the SST—which, if used in the U.S., will bring the violence of airport noise to 60 million Americans. We cannot continue to waste manpower and resources on weapons that become obsolete before they are produced—and which, if ever used, will destroy this planet as a place for human life. In a crisis of survival, business as usual is suicide.

The environmental crisis has brought us to a great turning point in this nation's history. We have become a nation that wields the greatest power in the history of man: power in the form of food, industrial plants, vehicles, and the weapons of war. We have also become a nation beset by violence: on the battlefield, on the highways, in personal encounters, and, more fundamentally, in the destruction of the natural, harmonious fabric of the environmental system which supports us. It is this fundamental violence to the world in which we live which divides us, as we compete among ourselves for the earth's goods, unaware that each of us, in our own way, is thereby contributing to the destruction of the whole that supports us all.

The time has come to forge a great alliance in this nation: All of us now know that if we are to survive, the environment must be maintained as a balanced, harmonious whole. We must all work together to preserve it. If we fail, we shall abandon the place where we must live—the thin skin of air, water, soil, and living things on the planet Earth—to destruction. The obligation which our technological society forces upon all of us, young and old, black and white, right and left, scientist and citizen alike, is to discover how humanity can survive the new power which science has given it. Every major advance in the technological competence of man has enforced new obligations on human society. The present age of technology is no exception to this rule of history. We already know the enormous benefits it can bestow, and we have begun to perceive its frightful threats. The crisis generated by this knowledge is upon us.

We are enormously fortunate that our young people—the first generation to carry strontium 90 in their bones and DDT in their fat—have become particularly sensitive to this ominous paradox of the modern world. For it is they who face the frightful task of seeking humane knowledge in a world which has, with cunning perversity, transformed the power that knowledge generates into an instrument of catastrophe.

The environmental crisis is a grim challenge. It also is a great opportunity. From it we may yet learn that the proper use of science is not to conquer nature, but to live in it. We may yet learn that to save ourselves we must save the world that is our habitat. We may yet discover how to devote the wisdom of science and the power of technology to the welfare, the survival of man.

HOW TO THINK ABOUT THE ENVIRONMENT

Max Ways

Max Ways is a member of Fortune's Board of Editors.

. . . Although environmental issues do have a grave moral content, there's little sense in the tendency to present the case in the dominant art form of a TV horse opera. This isn't, really, a confrontation between "the polluters" and the good guys in the white hats. Nevertheless, casting for the villainous roles proceeds briskly. "Greed" is to blame. "Man, the dirtiest animal," is to blame, especially because his numbers are increasing. "Technology" is to blame—and this charge, as we shall see, contains much truth, though far less than the whole truth. "Capitalism" is to blame. "The poor," who throw garbage in the streets, are to blame. "Democracy," which seems unable to find remedies, is to blame. And, of course, "the establishment," everyone's goat of atonement, is to blame.

In general, the nomination of villains follows the familiar pattern of dumping the ashes of contrition on somebody else's head. A Columbia law-school senior this year was reported to have boasted that he told recruiters for law firms he "would not defend a client who was a polluter—and most of the clients who pollute are the big ones," a remark indicating that even law-school seniors may have something to learn.

For all men are polluters—and all living Americans are big polluters. The greedy and the ungreedy alike befoul the air with

Originally from "How to Think about the Environment," *Fortune*, Vol. LXXXI, No. 2 (February 1970), pp. 100ff. © 1970 by Time, Inc. This issue of *Fortune* is available in a $1.25 paperback, *How to Think about the Environment*, by the Editors of *Fortune*. © 1970 by Harper & Row.

automobile exhaust fumes, the humble 1960 jalopy contributing somewhat more poison than the arrogant 1970 Cadillac. So long as our laws and habits of land use foster chaos, the homes of saints will aggress as rudely upon nature as the haunts of sinners. Who killed the rivers of Illinois by extinguishing perhaps forever their ability to cleanse and renew themselves? The effluents of big industries did a substantial part of the damage. Sewage from towns did part. But most of the damage to the rivers of Illinois came from farms onto which decent and well-meaning "little" men, in the pursuit of the legitimate aim of increasing crop yields, poured nitrogen fertilizers. The result bears the mellifluous name of "eutrophication"; algae, slimy green gunk, rampantly feed upon the fertilizer drained into the rivers; the decay of dead algae consumes so much of the available oxygen as to destroy the bacterial action that once cleansed the rivers of organic wastes.

At the root of our environmental troubles we will not find a cause so simple as the greed of a few men. The wastes that besmirch our land are produced in the course of fulfilling widespread human wants that are in the main reasonable and defensible. Nor will we find capitalism at the root of the trouble. The Soviet Union, organized around central planning, has constructed some of the most terrifyingly hideous cityscapes on earth, while raping the countryside with strip mines, industrial pollutants, and all the other atrocities that in the U.S. are ascribed to selfish proprietary interest. Aware, as well they might be, of American environmental mistakes in handling the mass use of the automobile, Russians keep saying they will do it better; but today, as automobiles become more numerous in the U.S.S.R., it is hard to find in city or highway planning, in automobile design, or in any other tangible area signs that they are in fact better prepared for the automobile onslaught than the U.S. was in 1920.

The Japanese, though their basic culture lays great stress on harmony between man and nature, are not handling their environmental relations significantly better than the Americans or the Russians. Japan's economy, combining private enterprise with government central planning, seems able to do anything—except cherish the material beauty and order that the people value so highly.

If we wish to think seriously about the environment, we have to give up indulgence in barefoot moralism and the devil theory of what's wrong. We have to identify a root cause that explains the environmental failures of systems as different as the American, the Russian, and the Japanese. Obviously, all three are high-powered, industrialized, technologized societies, and our quest for a root cause can start by tentatively picking technology as the villain.

For Every Man, 500 "Slaves"

Despite billions of words on the subject, we still under-estimate the magnitude of technological advance and its implications. Thirty years ago in *Fortune's* tenth anniversary issue, R. Buckminster Fuller found an apt way of expressing what had occurred. He calculated the total energy generated in the U.S. as equal to the muscular energy that would be generated if every American had 153 slaves working for him. Today a similar calculation would indicate about 500 "slaves" for every American man, woman, and child.

These slaves enable us to increase our own mobility hundreds of times and to toss around incredible masses of materials, altering not only their location and external shapes but their very molecules. Excluding construction, earth moving, and many other operations, the U.S. economy, according to one estimate, uses 2,500,000,000 tons of material a year. That's nearly thirteen tons per person.

These figures explain a lot of environmental woes that are otherwise mysterious. Although our cities are not more densely populated, they produce more maddening and wasteful congestion than any cities of the past. Our crowding is not basically a matter of too many human beings to the square mile but of the enormous retinue of energy and material that accompanies each of us. Like King Lear with his hundred riotous knights and squires, we strain the hospitality of our dwelling space, and from our situation, as from Lear's, much grief may follow.

Two hundred million of us are bustling about the U.S., every one sheathed in a mass-and-energy nimbus very much bigger, noiser, dirtier, smellier, clumsier, and deadlier than he is. The paper, plastics, scrap, ash, soot, dust, sludge, slag, fumes, and weird compounds thrown off by the mass-and-energy nimbus exceed by many magnitudes our own bodily wastes. If ten billion mere people, sans technological nimbus, inhabited the U.S., they could not create more congestion, blight, and confusion. The three million high-technology U.S. farmers put more adverse pressure on their land and rivers than the hundred and fifty million low-productivity peasant families of China put upon their land and rivers.

The Rats Who Rule the Elephants

How should a city be designed and its circulatory system arranged to accommodate a people that employs energy and mass at present American levels? The past offers only wisps of inspiration, but no usable models. Consistently we have failed to face the sheer physical challenge of the contemporary city, assuming that old urban forms would be adequate if we amended them a little to meet one crisis after another.

Along with all kinds of congestion, our cities produce a paradoxical effect of isolation and desolation. Not rationally shaped for the needs of this society, the cities may be shaping us toward irrationality. Frequently mentioned in environmentalist circles these days is a research project carried out by John Calhoun at Bethesda, Maryland. He placed Norway rats in a closed area ample for the original population. As they multiplied, the crowded animals, though well fed, developed most distressing psychoses, which, out of a decent respect for the privacy of rats, will not be here detailed. Many who have heard of this project see a close parallel with our cities.

But the analogy is not quite true to the situation of contemporary urban man. It would be better to find a strain of rats each one of which had the services of a half-house-broken elephant to do its work, run its errands, and cater to its wants. In an ill-organized space these lordly rats, even if they did not multiply, might go crazier quicker than did their cousins in Bethesda.

People who center their anxiety on "the population explosion" see the challenge much too narrowly. In the U.S. and other advanced countries, population has been increasing less rapidly by far than the explosive acceleration of the total energy and total mass deployed. If the population declined and technology continued to breed, without any improvement in the arrangements for its prudent use, a small fraction of the present U.S. population could complete the destruction of the physical environment while jostling one another for room.

A Retreat to Poverty?

We come, then, to the question of whether a headlong retreat from technology would be the right strategy. This option needs to be honestly appraised, not toyed with as it is every day by nostalgic romanticists wiggling their toes in secondhand memories of Thoreau's Walden Pond.

The casualties of a withdrawal from technology would be heavier than many suppose. Everybody, of course, has his own examples of unnecessary technologies, unnecessary products, unnecessary activities. But because we are, thank God, diverse in our wants, the lists do not agree. The man who has since childhood said to hell with spinach has a ready-made response to the news that a high incidence of "blue babies" recorded in Germany has been attributed to heavy use of nitrogen fertilizer on the spinach crop. But other consumers will have good reasons for wishing spinach yields to increase. We will not improve our environmental situation by recommending a technological retreat on the basis of what each of us considers the superfluous items in the households of his neighbors.

To be effective in protecting the environment a technological retreat would extend over a wide front and go back a long, long way. A century ago we had already slaughtered the bison, felled the eastern forests, and degraded the colonial cities. Retreat to the 1870 level of technology, while not giving long-range protection to the environment, would place the median American standard of living far below the 1970 poverty line. Among the consequences of such a retreat would be the closing of 75 percent of the present colleges and most of the high schools. We would give up not only automobiles and airplanes but also mass education and social services. Grandpa would return to living in the abandoned hencoop.

Since we are not going to choose such a retreat from technology as a deliberate social policy, sheer practicality forces us to seek another way out. In that quest we have to ask seriously why the U.S. and all the other advanced countries have failed so dismally in handling the unwanted effects of technology.

Modern technology did not spring out of the void. It did not well up simultaneously in all the world's peoples. It appears first in European culture, and, although it is now disseminated over the whole globe, its main generative fonts remain to this day Western.

The Western origin and leadership in technology, the main agent of environmental destruction, inevitably raises uncomfortable questions about Western culture itself. The Judeo-Christian religious formation is not essentially "anti-nature," as some angry men now aver. But in contrast to Oriental religions, it does sharply separate its idea of God from its idea of nature and does look upon man as having a special relationship with the Creator and a unique place within creation.

The Western tendency to objectify nature—to see it "from outside"—is undoubtedly responsible for much arrogant and insensitive handling of the material world. But it ought not be forgotten that this same attitudinal "separation" of man from nature forms the basis of man's ever increasing knowledge of nature. In recent centuries, especially, Western man has empirically confirmed his ancient notion of himself as unique among the creatures: no other species possesses a glimmer of his ability to learn about nature and to operate, for better or worse, upon it.

Surely it can be no accident that four centuries of science are attributable almost entirely to Western culture. Extending the pattern of Western religion and philosophy, which had drawn sharp distinctions between ideas of God, of man, and of nature, the scientific method began to separate one aspect of nature from another for purposes of study. This superlatively effective way of discovering solidly verifiable truths tends, precisely because it is sharply focused, to ignore whatever lies outside its periphery of attention.

Science, seeking only to know, is guiltless of direct aggression against the environment. But technology, devoted to action, feeds ravenously upon the discoveries of science. Although its categories are not the same as those of science, technology in its own way is also highly specialized, directed toward narrowly defined aims. As its power rises, technology's "side effects," the consequences lying outside its tunneled field of purpose, proliferate with disastrous consequences to the environment—among other unintended victims.

Millions of Pharaohs Complicate Life

Modern Western man has advanced the principle of separation or differentiation also in areas of life, such as psychology and politics, that are seemingly remote from science and technology. These trends, too, have contributed to our environmental diseases.

The undifferentiated human mass, say of ancient Egypt, has been replaced by modern men who regard themselves—and in fact are—highly individuated. The long trend to individualism, which has Greek as well as Judeo-Christian origins, has sharply accelerated during the modern centuries. One of its aspects, democracy, is based on the assumption that the diverse wants, skills, interests, and opinions of individuals should not be ignored or rudely aggregated from above, but must be somehow coordinated from below. The latter process is clearly the more difficult, especially when applied to such large questions as how to protect the physical environment from human misuse.

The pharaonic society employed its most potent technology, irrigation, on the premise that everybody shared a common desire to eat. The knowledge required to operate the system was closely held in a group of priestly intellectuals, and the decision-making power was concentrated in the will of Pharaoh. With its technology under unified control, with few conflicts or complications arising from a diversity of skills, interests, rights, and powers within the community, the pharaonic society could maintain for centuries a stable, harmonious relation with nature and could also achieve stylistic and functional coherence within its man-made environment—such as it was.

One can hear today in environmentalist circles half-serious remarks that every city needs a king and every country an all-powerful planner to unify decisions affecting the environment. Such suggestions underestimate the human cost of the reversal, as do proposals for a retreat from technology. We will not voluntarily abandon the view that society should be made up of highly individuated men pursuing their own aims by their own lights.

We have permitted the free combination of individuals on the basis of shared specific aims. By means of such groups, mainly corporations, we have organized and stimulated technological advance, matching techniques to particular group aims. Though this pattern all too often ignores the undesirable side effects of its single-minded thrusts, it fits so closely with the evolution toward human diversity and freedom that we would shrink from a return to the pharaonic kind of harmony and stability. We are not fellahin, and the road back to that condition might be more arduous and more disorderly than the road we have traveled.

What the Garbage Specialists Overlook

Western culture has never denied that a society stressing the individuality of its members needs the restraint and to some degree the positive leadership of government. But the character of government has also been affected by the trend toward differentiation. The Lord's annointed, with unspecified and even "absolute" power, has been split up into sharply segregated bureaucratic functions.

These, too, generate undesirable side effects. A highway department's mission is defined by statute and by specific appropriations. As it goes about its assigned task of building the most road for the least measured cost, it rips up neighborhoods and landscapes, creating enormous social disutilities that never get into the department's benefit-cost calculations. A sanitation department, told to dispose of garbage, may tow it offshore and dump it. When the refuse washes back upon the beaches and into the estuaries, the problem belongs to some other department. Or the specialists in solid-waste disposal may burn trash and garbage in places and in ways that transfer the pollution to the air.

Fragmentation of modern government occurs even in "totalitarian" countries. Administration of the Soviet economy is divided among fifty-odd ministries for the sake of efficiency. If a paper mill is needed, the men told off for that responsibility look around, like any capitalist, for plentiful timber, plentiful water, and cheap electric power. One paper mill was placed on the shore of beautiful Lake Baikal because the protection of this unique body of water lay outside the field of assigned vision of the men in charge of paper production. They were not being "greedy" or even "stupid" in the ordinary meaning of those words. They were wearing the blinkers of concentration, using the great Western device of fixing attention on the job at hand, of dealing intelligently with one segment of reality at a time.

A Problem of Balance

Though the principle of segregated attention proves gloriously successful—in research, in work, and in government—it can collide disastrously with the principle of unity. For each man is a unit though his skills and wants may be various. A society is a unit as well as a multitude. Nature, most marvelously connected throughout all its diversities, is a unit. Violation of these unities invites penalties and poses formidable tasks of reintegration.

Here we come to the root cause of our abuse of the environment: *in modern society the principle of fragmentation, outrunning the principle of unity, is producing a higher and higher degree of disorder and disutility.*

How can balance be restored? Since it is profoundly unrealistic to believe that we will or should retreat from such bastions of diversity as science, technology, and human individuality, then we have to seek improved methods of coordinating our fragmented thought and action.

During recent centuries, institutions of coordination, though lagging behind diversity, have not stood still. In economic affairs the market performs, albeit imperfectly, a stupendous job of mediating disparate wants, skills, resources. Government, amidst its bureaucratic fragments, has not completely lost the notion that it is supposed to serve such unitary purposes as "the general welfare." Specialized knowledge has a medium of transfer in the great modern webs of information, particularly the universities where all the sciences meet even if they do not fluently communicate.

How might such integrative agencies as market, government, and university be used, separately or in combination, so as to minimize the damage that fragmented action now does to the environment? This is the question on which the chance of actual reform, as distinguished from alarm and breast-beating, depends.

Subsidizing Destruction

In two areas, air and water pollution, a moment's reflection should convince anybody that the market, as now set up, is rigged against the environment. A hundred and fifty years ago it was almost unimaginable that clean water, much less clean air, could become scarce in the U.S. economy. Rightly, these resources were then considered common property and used without charge. The price of everything else the economy uses—land, minerals, food, labor, time—becomes dearer. But clean air and water, though now precious, are still left out of the pricing system, still free of charge.

Because the market has failed to keep pace with changing economic reality, the pricing system, expressing relative demand and supply, works against the conservation of clean air and water. A manufacturer is under great pressure to offset rising labor and material costs by developing new techniques. He has been under no comparable pressure with respect to clean air and water. Not surprisingly, techniques for conserving these resources have developed very slowly. The effect of omitting free resources from the pricing system is to make the economy as a whole pay a high subsidy to those activities that put above average pressure on free resources. In short, we are now providing a huge, unintentional market incentive to pollution.

The most direct and logical way of getting clean air and water into the market system is by a federal tax graduated in respect to the quantity and undesirability of the pollutants. Such a tax, escalating over the first five or ten years so as not to destroy industries whose cost structures are based on the present system, would stimulate the development of antipollution techniques.

Taxes on the abuse of water and air would not replace the present trend toward stricter antipollution measures enforced by police power. Radioactive wastes, for instance, can be dangerous in very small quantities because they concentrate as they move up the food chain. The strictest control of such wastes is required—and may prove expensive. Nuclear power will be better able to absorb such costs if its competitor, fossil fuel, is forced to pay for the clean air and water it displaces. By such combination of government police power and taxing power we can turn the market toward protection of the environment—or at least achieve its "neutrality."

Correcting the market is much more difficult in that growing class of cases where the bad environmental side effects do not occur until the product is in the hands of the consumer or even until after he has disposed of it. It is by no means clear that automobiles, for instance, now carry taxes equivalent to the true social costs incurred by their use and disposal. If we become serious about the preservation or restoration of public transport in American cities the first step would be to make sure that public policy is not subsidizing the automobile.

Still more difficult to deal with is the product that is innocent until it interferes with some technique of protecting the

environment. Many plastics give trouble in this indirect way. The
polyvinyl chloride bottle causes no problems unless it is burned in a
trash incinerator that is equipped with a scrubber designed to catch
soot and fly ash. The burning PVC causes hydrochloric acid to form
in the scrubber, destroying its metal casing. Some companies that
hoped to sell more scrubbers for smaller incinerators have given up
because they cannot guarantee their devices against the increasing
incidence of PVC in trash. A small tax based on the nuisance side
effect of certain plastics would either drive them off the market or
encourage a new technology that abated the nuisance. As technology
advances into more and more esoteric compounds, each carefully
designed for a particular use, protection of the environment will
require public policies that force innovators to pay more attention to
the side effects of their products.

With gratifying frequency and emphasis, business spokesmen
these days are expressing their determination to exercise greater care
of the environment. If business greed lay at the root of our
environmental troubles then this repentance would itself signal the
great turnaround. In fact, a more sensitive and socially responsible
business attitude will be of very limited help—unless it is accompanied by new ground rules. Under the present set of rules, if one
corporation is environmentally a good citizen, incurring heavy costs
to fight pollution, and if its competitor operates on an environment-
be-damned basis, then the first corporation will be punished and the
second rewarded. The market will practice selection against the
environment.

Instead of getting on with the formidable job of rewriting the
rules, public discussion wastes time and energy on irrelevant
questions, such as how much of business profit should be diverted to
environmental betterment. The problems have become so huge that
we would not necessarily make a dent in them with *all* the profits of
American business. . . .

How to Locate a Power Plant

. . . At a meeting in New York last month, various environmental ills, including the appalling mess of the Jersey Meadows, were
excoriated. Said one of the guests, a businessman: "Jersey Standard's
officers should have been shot for putting a refinery there in the first
place." Another guest asked: "Where should they have put it—in the
Rocky Mountains?" The businessman was appalled by this sacri-
legious suggestion, but he refused to deal seriously with the question
of a refinery's location.

So do most conservationists. Everybody wants ample electric power, for instance, but more and more communities are prepared to resist the presence of a power plant. Decisions on plant location are being made in a basically disorderly way with each fragmented community interest in turn poised against the fragmented interest of the power company. More and more of these cases are getting into courts. But the courts, operating in the narrow dualism of adversary proceedings, are hardly in a position to say where a power plant ought to go. In this decision system the most apathetic or careless community would get stuck with the power plant or refinery—and this might be exactly the worst place to put it from either a business or an environmental viewpoint.

Obviously, a high-technology society needs, and its government should provide, forums for the rational resolution of such questions. Carl E. Bagge, a member of the Federal Power Commission, argues that regional planning bodies should become the forums for deciding on such questions as the location of new power plants and power transmission facilities.

Better handling of the environment is going to require lots of legal innovation to shape the integrative forums and regulatory bodies where our new-found environmental concerns may be given concrete reality. These new legal devices will extend all the way from treaties forbidding oil pollution on the high seas down to the minute concerns of local government. But the present wave of conservationist interest among lawyers and law students does not seem to be headed along that constructive path. Rather, it appears intent on multiplying two-party conflicts between "polluters" and victims. . . .

To Put the World Together Again

. . .A key contribution to the environmental future can be made by the university, the most significant institution in the whole communication network. Indignation concerning the environment is now at a very high pitch among students and faculty. Not all of this emotion, however, is translated into efforts within the university to balance specialized fragmentation with integrated studies.

An interesting view of faculty attitudes toward the environment was elicited from Robert Wood, Undersecretary (and briefly Secretary) of Housing and Urban Development in the Johnson Administration and now director of the Joint Center for Urban Studies of M.I.T. and Harvard. On his return to academia, Wood found that, throughout the faculties, interest in environmental affairs had suddenly become emotionally intense. "They are a little like the atomic scientists after Hiroshima," he says. "They had assumed that science was automatically improving the world. Confronted with contrary evidence, they feel guilt. But they tend to become impatient when their condemnations of what is happening are not immediately followed by correction."

Many faculty members who are most indignant about the environment would be unwilling to direct their own research or teaching effort to environmental questions. Urban-affairs centers and institutes of ecology are proliferating on campuses but in many cases they are not allowed, because of the jealousy of the entrenched disciplines, to give credit courses or degrees. In the academic structure, such interdisciplinary institutes are looked down upon much as a mongrel would be regarded at a show sponsored by the American Kennel Club.

U.S. society is going to need tens of thousands of "integrators," men who can handle environmental material from several natural sciences in combination with material from several of the social sciences. These men will utilize very high technologies, such as computers and space satellites, to diagnose and cure the side effects of other technologies. Tomorrow's integrators, moreover, must be able to deal with broad questions of human value, purpose, and law that lie beyond (and between) the sciences. The universities that produced the specialists who taught us how to take the world apart will now have to train the men who will take the lead in putting it together again.

Can We Afford It All?

Environmental damage is so widespread and is continuing so rapidly that there is a serious question as to whether we can afford reform—a question that is not necessarily answered by the glib truth that we cannot afford to go on as we are. . . .

If certain twentieth century trends such as population growth and, especially, the enlargement of the per capita mass-and-energy nimbus are simply extrapolated into the future, it's obvious that at some point we will destroy ourselves by consuming the earth. But these rates may not soar on forever. After ten years of falling U.S. birthrates, it has become possible to believe that the U.S. population may stabilize between the years 2000 and 2020 at not much above its present level, as a few demographers have predicted.

Limits of growth are also in sight for the more important rate of mass-and-energy used. The heavy environmental pressures come from agriculture and manufacturing (including mining). We are already producing more food than we consume and more than we would need to feed all the hungry in the U.S. The total value of manufactured goods will probably continue to rise for several decades, although substantial reductions in this demand could result from better environmental policies. Many things (e.g., the second family car, the second home) that we now buy are made "necessary" by wasteful environmental arrangements. The U.S. will probably reach saturation in manufactured goods in any event at some point in the next fifty years, if only because the time to use all the things we buy is becoming scarce.

Meanwhile, this economy will be very hard pressed to keep up with its increasing needs on the "services" front. A society that is both highly specialized and rapidly changing requires, as ours has already demonstrated, an elaborate "nerve system," employing millions, to maintain its cohesion and determine its direction. Among the elements of the "nerve system" are education, communications, law, finance, etc., which burn little fuel and consume small tonnages of materials.

We Won't Snuggle Back

The probability that gross pressure on the environment is due to stabilize does not of itself constitute a ground for optimism. It merely indicates that our prospect is not hopeless, and that by a huge and intelligent effort we might reverse the present devastation.

Whether that effort will be made depends primarily on how we think about the challenge. We did not get into this mess through such vices as gluttony, but rather through our virtues, our unbalanced and uncoordinated strengths. If we do not succeed in bringing under control our new-found powers, the failure will be attributable to the father of all vices, inattention to the consequences of our actions.

Modern man, Western or Westernized, is not going to snuggle back into the bosom of nature, perceiving all reality as a blurred continuum. That possibility of innocence we lost long ago in—of all places—a garden. We have understood differentiation, specialization, individuation; we have known the glories of action concentrated upon a specific purpose. Our path toward unity lies *through* diversity and specialization, not in recoil from them. A high-technology society without adequate institutions of coordination will produce either chaos or tyranny or both. Freedom will become meaningless because individual men will cease to believe that what they want has any relevance to what they get. But a high-technology society that can innovate adequate structures of decision will expand the freedom of individual choice far beyond any dream of the low-technology centuries.

The chief product of the future society is destined to be not food, not things, but the quality of the society itself. High on the list of what we mean by quality stands the question of how we deal with the material world, related as that is to how we deal with one another. That we have the wealth and the power to achieve a better environment is sure. That we will have the wisdom and charity to do so remains—and must always remain—uncertain.

THE NEED FOR CAREFUL ASSESSMENT

House Subcommittee on Science, Research, and Development

Chairman of the Subcommittee was Emilio Q. Daddario, a Democratic Representative from Connecticut.

. . . Objectivity and a balance of viewpoints in discussing environmental quality are goals of the subcommittee. These have proved extremely difficult to obtain. Human ecology is, after all, a personal as well as a collective affair. Each witness or member could draw upon subjective experiences which often assumed a greater importance than secondhand observations and statistical compilations, when these were available. Further, in many cases, hard facts and completed studies do not exist. Anecdotes and visceral feelings make amateur ecologists of us all. This explains both why the issue of environmental quality commands so much attention and why it is so difficult to obtain agreement on what is to be done.

A major lesson is being taught today on the relationship of man and his environment. It is the lesson of systematic ecology or the "web of life." The interdependency of all living things and the environment is so complex that the "cut and try" or reactive practical approach to nature has been the only possible method for centuries. The time tested practices of farmers, fishermen, hunters, explorers, and naturalists have a great ecological base whether or not it is recognized. To paraphrase: environments manage men even as men manage environments.

From the House Committee on Science and Astronautics, Subcommittee on Science, Research, and Development, *Report: Managing the Environment*, 90th Congress, 2nd Session, 1968, pp. 12-13, 20-22, 25-27.

Without becoming unduly philosophical, it can be stated that man *is* the dominant species and that mankind's intentions of using nature to further his own wellbeing *are* correct. Even the best of intentions may bring environmental degradation if they are clumsily executed with insufficient information. Past mistakes have impaired environmental quality, but nature was resilient and possessed an enormous momentum in comparison with man's capabilities to change it.

The lesson today is that man's powers rival those of the biosphere. In certain ways, the environment may have Achilles' heels which can lead to unwanted changes very rapidly. There is very little room for mistakes in an over-populated and underfed world. The more that is learned about ecology today, the clearer it becomes that the management of the environment is a crucial task, rivaling the search for peace in the world. . . .

Protection via Regulation

The political popularity of consumer protection legislation in recent years has erected a diverse if somewhat spotty array of regulations. Automobile exhaust emissions, automobile safety gear, flammable fabrics, cigarettes, patent medicines, pesticides, and so forth, are a few examples of products and services which receive federal scrutiny in the form of standards, warning labels, or other restrictions in use.

Powers which are normally legislative are delegated to administrative bodies. Regulations are established after a hearings process and become law. Enforcement begins, and the standards thus set are not themselves subject to adjudication. Often the only challenge allowed is on the constitutional ground of taking property without due process.

The ancient warning of "buyer beware" is useless in the present technological era. The public as a whole "buys" a system of municipal trash collection and incineration, or nuclear electric power, with little opportunity to analyze the intricacies of the operation. Consumers are offered products such as garden sprays which may drift toxic chemicals into food supplies and television sets which can emit X-rays. The caveats of "read the label" or "follow instructions closely" are not complete guards against misuse when these highly complex products diffuse into society. Even the increased technical literacy of the American public is far from adequate to make judgments.

The extent to which governmental regulation might be carried is suggested in the recent "action goal" of an advisory group to the Secretary of Health, Education, and Welfare.[1]

> A materials, trace metals, and chemicals control effort to establish, by 1970, human safety levels for synthetic materials, trace metals, and chemicals currently in use, and prohibit after 1970 general use of any new synthetic material, trace metal, or chemical until approved by the Department of Health, Education, and Welfare.

The laboratory effort, both in government and industry, to meet such a goal would be enormous and very costly.

Aside from governmental regulation, there are a number of other institutional forces at work in the public interest in environmental health and consumer protection. It is easy to be skeptical about the altruism of business, but enlightened free enterprise has demonstrated a due regard for the consequences of its products and services. Product liability laws are as old as "caveat emptor." Trade associations, the American Standard Association, the American Society for Testing Materials, the Underwriters Laboratory, and insurance-related agencies are a few examples of private sector technology assessment functions.

And yet, Dr. Rene Dubos wrote to the subcommittee:

> Unfortunately it will always remain impossible to predict from laboratory experiments all the threats to health that can arise from technological innovations. Unforeseeable accidents will happen, as was the case with exposure to ionizing radiations or with chain cigarette smoking, or with the use of thalidomide during the first 3 months of pregnancy. Since it is impossible to test all the effects of all technological innovations, some of them will inevitably have pathological consequences.
>
> We must abandon, in fact, the utopian hope that regulations can protect us completely from all health dangers in the modern world. For this reason, the science of environmental biomedicine should be complemented by a prospective kind of epidemiology, designed to detect as early as possible early manifestations of abnormality in the population at large so as to guide efforts to trace such abnormalities to technological and social changes. Seen in this light, prospective epidemiology would constitute a kind of protective social organ, as essential to disease control as are the safety regulations designed to protect the public against known dangers.[2]

---

[1] *A Strategy for a Livable Environment*, Report to the Secretary of Health, Education, and Welfare by the Task Force on Environmental Health and Related Problems, June 1967, p. xvii.

[2] *The Adequacy of Technology for Pollution Abatement*, Hearings before the Subcommittee on Science, Research, and Development of the Committee on Science and Astronautics, U.S. House of Representatives, 89th Congress, 2nd Session, Vol. II, p. 846.

Prospective epidemiology would substitute understanding for regulations which today are often based on opinion and judgment of a few persons. Regulations cannot promise absolute protection.

Despite this limitation of protection via regulation there is a tendency for public policy to react to vague charges of impending consequences and tenuous cause-effect relationships. The decision is to "err on the safe side." Commercial interests have learned through bitter experience that they cannot escape unscathed from a public relations battle over the balance of risks and benefits of new technology. Rather than presenting a defensive case with additional facts, data, and cost estimates, industry often takes the position that if the regulatory agency sets definite standards, they will propose to meet them. Thus the consumer public is often presented with new regulations which have an inadequate factual base and little analysis of the costs incurred to gain the benefits of protection. The costs are paid, of course, by the customer.

For example, New York State, acting on the basis of limited monitoring data and the proposed sulfur oxide criterion of the U.S. Public Health Service, passed a law calling for a sulfur content in fuel oil of no more than 0.37 percent. At least one oil supplier proceeded with capital investments to meet this specification. After months of analysis, Commissioner Heller of the New York City Department of Air Pollution Control testified:

> It may well be that the reduction of the sulfur content of all fuel to 1 percent will result in a satisfactory air quality with respect to sulfur dioxide. At any rate, such fuel is available in the near future. Its wholesale use, together with the accurate profile from our network, will place us in a much better situation to take intelligent abatement action. I might add that careful statistical analysis of data obtained over a 10-year period has indicated to us the possibility that the use of 1 percent sulfur fuel may reduce the average sulfur dioxide concentration close to 0.1 ppm.

Using the 1 percent fuel specification will result in a 1.5 percent increase in electricity costs to New York residents and a 2.5 percent increase for space heating customers, according to Consolidated Edison.

A New Approach to Hazard Evaluation

The dilemma involves insufficient protection of a public which cannot judge for itself, versus an overprotection which costs more than it is worth, slows innovation, and reduces personal freedom. It will not be easy to resolve. One obvious step in the right direction would be to improve the climate of discussion of these problems by depolarizing the regulating agency-industry arguments. The public and the consumer interest would be served by an assessment process in which all the facts could be put on the table for examination without fear that the efficiency of public relations rather than the authenticity and pertinence of the data would determine their weight. Perhaps a quasi-judicial arrangement could be devised where adversary positions are presented to a court which itself has access to and understanding of the technology involved.

Another contribution to assessment would be a great expansion of research work in human toxicology and environmental epidemiology. Scientists do not always agree, even when examining the same raw information. But the scientific procedure yields a more and more accurate picture of the situation by insisting on free publication of experimental results, replication of experiments, and extension of research to prospective studies which will fill in the gaps in information. The few scientists who are schooled in human health effects have been most attracted to specific disease programs rather than to the difficult environmental hazards area. An analysis of the relative importance of these fields to public health might very well result in a higher priority being given to environmental epidemiology. . . .

Whose Health Is Protected?

Environmental health legislation must face the question of what proportion of the total population is to be assured protection from a given hazard. This decision follows from the fact that the level of a pollutant must be reduced to a much greater extent (and at consequent greater cost) to protect the most sensitive, susceptible persons in the population.

The Air Quality Act of 1967, for example, states in section 108(a): "The pollution of the air in any State or States which endangers the health or welfare of any persons shall be subject to abatement as provided in this section."

A literal interpretation of this language would lead to an ambient air quality standard of zero contamination, for it is likely that some persons would be found who were endangered by the most minute exposure.

The adaptability of the human being as a species is well known. Man exists comfortably and productively in a variety of climates, altitudes, and landscapes. However, individual members of the race may have particular adaptive problems such as disease, allergy, old age, et cetera, which restrict the environment in which they can live. Other persons may predispose themselves to pollutant effects because of personal habits such as cigarette smoking. It is questionable as to how far society should go in extra abatement action to protect this group. Public health policy does not suggest that the government should control ragweed pollen for hay fever sufferers, or modify climate extremes such as heat waves or blizzards.

But pollution is manmade, not a natural, environmental stress, and therefore the argument does not hold that nothing should be done about its added effect on the susceptible fraction of the population.

In a practical sense, however, the choice of what may be done for this group can be approached rationally. With any environmental contaminant there will be an increasing cost of control as the concentration is reduced. At very low ambient levels, this cost may become so great that further reductions cannot be justified. If some persons are still adversely affected, alternative relief is available. They may use special air filters or water supplies. They may move to an area free of that particular pollutant. They may be given a counteracting medication.

Standards and Goals

The practical limit to pollution abatement occurs because it is a manmade phenomenon. Ingredients of the natural environment are numerous and varied (salt and dust in air, minerals in water, etc.) but the evolution of mankind has been in this same environment so that adaptation to minor fluctuations is relatively easy. Man uses and changes the environment for his benefit and accepts certain degradative effects in the process.

It is perfectly rational to have a goal of zero contamination and yet recognize that it may be in direct conflict with other goals in a technologic society. The result is a management choice of an optimum compromise position—the environmental quality standard. Even this expression need not be chosen once and for all time as a certain number. It appears possible to choose interim standards which would give immediate objectives for improving environmental quality. At the same time, ultimate standards could be discussed, which appear desirable to achieve but beyond the reach of present technology. As the abatement effort goes on, more information will be obtained on effects, and more efficient waste treatment technology will be developed. Then, a progressive reduction in the allowable contamination can be expressed in more stringent standards if desirable.

It is confusing and oversimplifying to discuss environmental quality only in terms of a pristine state and the total population. Public policy should recognize at least four distinct conditions of the environment.

1. Existing contamination measured frequently in densely populated areas which adversely affects most persons.

2. Interim standards which would assure a reduction of contamination concentration and frequency of occurrence so that health and welfare effects were substantially lessened for most persons. Economic and technical feasibility would set the stringency limit of interim standards.

3. Ultimate standards which would assure no adverse health and welfare effects on most persons. The exact levels of no effect (for, say, 90% of the population) are usually not known at present but prospective epidemiological research would yeild refined numerical values. The technology to reach the ultimate standards would be developed under the motivation that a market would exist once the techniques become economically feasible.

4. A pristine or zero contamination (with respect to any one pollutant) state of the environment may be necessary to protect all persons. This state may be found in nature at certain localities or it may be artifically contrived in controlled chambers. For the common contaminants in an industrial civilization it is unlikely to be possible of achievement in urban areas. . . .

THE SANTA BARBARA OIL SPILL

Senate Subcommittee on Air and Water Pollution

Fred Hartley is President of the Union Oil Co. of California. Charles A. O'Brien is Chief Deputy Attorney General, State of California. Stewart L. Udall was Secretary of the Interior in the Johnson administration.

. . . *Mr. Hartley*: I would like to first stress that we do have here a Federal Government-industry partnership involved in the development of offshore oil on the Outer Continental Shelf. It has to

From testimony before the Senate Committee on Public Works, Subcommittee on Air and Water Pollution, *Hearings*, 91st Congress, 1st Session, February-June 1969: Part 2, pp. 320-321, 326-328, 331, 342-343; Part 3, pp. 454-457; Part 4, pp. 1278-1282.

do basically, this partnership, with the desire of all concerned, both those in and out of Government, for the development of oil resources for the supply of the energy requirements of this country. It certainly is a long historical relationship.

At the present time there are approximately 6,000 wells operating in Federal waters in offshore Louisiana and Texas. . . .I mention this because this relationship to the Federal Government is one that has gone on for many years now and after a long, long period of time this relationship was extended to the area offshore from the State of California. That is basically quite recent, only a year ago this month other than a drainage sale in the Federal area that was put up prior to that time. Obviously it is a partnership. The Federal Government in the offshore sale in California collected about $602 million and on block 402 where platform A is located the four company group of which we own 25 percent paid $61.2 million approximately. Further to that partnership there were questions asked this morning that make it perhaps relevant to indicate that we do enter into a lease agreement in which the language has been clearly worked out by members of the legal profession. The section on diligence, I think, is pertinent. . . .

> To exercise reasonable diligence in drilling and producing the wells herein provided for, to carry on all operations in accordance with approved methods and practices including those provided in the operating and conservation regulations for the Outer Continental Shelf; to remove all structures when no longer required for operations under the lease to sufficient depth beneath the surface of the waters to prevent them from being a hazard to navigation; to carry out at expense of the Lessee all lawful and reasonable orders of the Lessor relative to the matters in this paragraph, and that on failure of the Lessee so to do the Lessor shall have the right to enter on the property and to accomplish the purpose of such orders at the Lessee's cost: *Provided,* That the Lessee shall not be held responsible for delays or casualties occasioned by causes beyond the Lessee's control.

I am sure when this language was written that we never thought we would have the case at hand today, because we do have a situation in the Santa Barbara Channel which certainly has not occurred in America, which I guess could be described as caused by causes beyond the lessee's control. . . .

. . . We have operated in accordance with the conditions of the lease and have produced an unfortunate result in so doing so that, since both the Federal Government and the companies are interested in producing this wealth from underground, the Government to improve its income position, and each company to hopefully receive some reward for its time and investment that it is incurring, it seems that we perhaps have something in common at this time. . . .

. . . I would certainly feel here that in this partnership with the Federal Government everyone has used due diligence in proceeding in the offshore Santa Barbara Channel. Obviously, in life you only stand as tall as the information of those who have gone before you. Mother Nature, if you have had much contact with her, you will find is always teaching us new things. Certainly we have learned to date that it is possible for the first time in our experience to end up with a well bore some 12 inches in diameter, which is what this one is, open from the 500[1] foot level where the first casing was placed in position down to the bottom of the well bore which is 3,500 feet, to have in effect a side rupture on that well, which then allows oil to escape through communication channels that we can only guess at at the moment. . . .

One other document here I think is pertinent. This document we are going to present to you was put together by our west coast oil organization known as the Western Oil & Gas Association back in December 1968. When the Outer Continental Shelf leases were made available for bidding by the Federal Government, the oil industry at that time, the producing and exploration men, who form one of the sections of the Western Oil & Gas Association, saw fit to put together in effect a handbook or bible, a statement of policy and action on the problem of water pollution control for drilling and producing operations in the Santa Barbara Channel and this, in effect, is the position statement of the men in the industry. I quote here on the scope that

> Each operating company will design, construct and conduct operations in strict compliance with all local, State and Federal laws governing such activity, including pollution control. Every operation will be programmed to prevent pollution; however, should accidental contamination occur, the operator will control and report such an occurrence in cooperation with the appropriate authority.

In that case, incidentally, it was the U.S. Geological Survey and also the Coast Guard and they were so notified. I am not quite certain whether there was a delay in getting that information into the area of the Santa Barbara Board of Supervisors referred to by Mr. Clyde this morning, but certainly the information was available. Then in this document there is a statement on the immediate pollution control action program.

---

[1] Measured from the rotary drilling table on the platform. There were 239 feet of casing below the ocean floor.

The following two statements provide the essence of an immediate pollution control action program developed by the Western Oil and Gas Association Offshore Operators Committee:

1. A company which has a spill and asks for assistance from nearby operators in cleaning it up will reimburse those providing assistance for boat, chemical, and any unusual costs incurred.

2. Clean-up of oil slicks from an undetermined source will be undertaken only on direction of the U.S.G.S. If cleanup is undertaken, responsibility for the other costs will be pro rated on an equitable basis among companies with interests in the Channel.

I quote these things to you hopefully to convey to you that we did not take our obligations lightly, that there has been pre-thought and responsibility on the subject of potential oil pollution. . . .

. . .I think we have to look at these problems relatively. I am always tremendously impressed at the publicity that death of birds receives versus the loss of people in our country in this day and age. . . .

One article was reported back East that there were as many as 15,000 birds who met their demise by actual count of the Fish and Game organization of California. As of last night, 163 birds had been recovered and more than 100 of those birds are still alive.

We set up, on the third day of this incident, a bird sanctuary, set up with appropriate scientists and cleaning chemicals to try to do our best to save our feathered friends, but I do say to you that relative to the number of deaths that have occurred in this fair city due to crime and all the accidents that occurred, relative to that problem of our Nation, this desecration to the offshore area of Santa Barbara, although important and certainly one which we are fully devoted to taking care of, relatively it does seem that we should give this thing a little perspective.

I think, on the basis of other experiences of oil spills on beaches, that this is a problem which, although it has been referred to as a disaster, is not a disaster to people. There is no one being killed. If we keep following good procedures, we don't expect anyone to be killed. We know that these beaches can be cleaned up. This experience society does have almost regardless of its magnitude. . . .

Mr. O'Brien: . . .The question of Federal-State authority in this entire area seems to us to be clouded by a larger issue: namely, governmental schizophrenia within the Department of Interior and other Federal agencies.

The Federal Government appears one day as Mr. Clean—the foe of dirty water. The next day, the same Government puts on its black hat and pollutes our waters.

An example of this Jekyll and Hyde syndrome is seen in our problems with the U.S. Navy. At the same time that the Federal Water Pollution Control Administration was demanding new high State standards for interstate and coastal water, the U.S. Navy persisted in polluting our harbors with oil.

With no help from the Federal pollution agency, our State department of fish and game convinced the Navy to improve its practices. By the time this occurred, however, a new problem emerged: The Navy was damaging the harbor environment with the chemicals that it uses to disperse the oils which it dumps. . . .

This same sort of problem arose on interstate waters when the Bureau of Indian Affairs, a Department of the Interior agency, proposed that the Fort Mojave Indian Reservation should dump its raw sewage into the Colorado River, at the same time that the Secretary of the Interior was prohibiting local agencies from doing just that. . . .

Perhaps this schizophrenia at the Federal level is best seen in the words of former Secretary of the Interior Stewart Udall. The man who approved the drilling in Santa Barbara Channel was Stewart Udall. He was also the man who stated: "With respect to all questions involved in the administration of the water quality standards program, we are operating on the policy that it is better to be safe than sorry. By that, I mean that if we err on any question, we want to err on the side of safety."

Of course, the water quality experts in Secretary Udall's Department were excluded from offshore wells by the oil and gas man in his Department.

To his credit, Secretary Udall is the only person to stand up and assume responsibility for this disaster. The drillers themselves and other officials of the Interior Department discuss it in theological rather than geological and ecological terms. . . .

New legislation must provide for higher standards of care on the part of those operating on the Outer Continental Shelf. It must more clearly set forth the responsibilities and liabilities of such operators for pollution which they cause. Finally, it must provide for a program of assuring that no drilling is done until there is the greatest assurance of safety to the surrounding environment.

A final fundamental question remains. Is offshore drilling worth the total cost? I speak not only of the cost of potential pollution which we see offshore here today. I speak also of the oil derricks strung along a coastline which is unique in the world.

When we speak of Federal offshore oil drilling, we are also speaking of State drilling. There are areas of the coastline which the State does not intend to allow to be despoiled by drilling.

If the Federal Government allows drilling on its side of the invisible line in the ocean, however, the State government will be forced to protect its revenues by allowing drilling on its tidelands. And, from every indication—until this disaster—the Federal Government intended to sell oil rights the length of the California coast.

Is it the best way to balance the Federal budget?

The California coastline is a unique national asset. How is its worth diminished by erecting offshore structures the size of 20-story apartments between the ocean sunset and the people who come to view the sunset?

I speak not solely of water pollution. I am now discussing environmental pollution. How much money does this country need? Are we so impoverished that we must turn our coastal waters into an industrial area?

Blessed as we are with natural resources, we long ago began to treat these nature assets as a sort of national pawnshop. Whenever the United States felt the financial pinch, we cashiered a few million more acres of our unique irreplaceable environment.

Are we in such bad shape that we now have to cashier our coastlines?

Our beaches, our sea birds, our fish, our view of the ocean—shall we pawn these for a few hundred million, in a paltry effort to pay off a $200 billion national budget?

If we are going to start selling things, I could think of a few things I'd sell in Washington before I'd sell the California coastline. . . .

Mr. Udall: . . .We are a high-energy country and use more energy than any other nation in the world, by far. We are apparently committed to go down that road through the development of nuclear energy and through the development of fossil fuel energy, and therefore, I think the subject of these hearings is very vital for the long-term future of the country. Maybe, although none of us likes to see things like Santa Barbara happen, it could have been a lot worse than it was. But if this serves as a warning to us, and if we can pass laws now to prevent a repetition, I think it may have been—out of the tragedy—a very good thing for the country. . . .

I want the committee to understand that this was from the beginning, for me, a troublesome decision, and one that I was uneasy about. We made the decision on Santa Barbara with the *Torrey Canyon* disaster as a background, and we testified before your committee subsequent to the *Torrey Canyon* disaster because you were at that time trying to use the alarm aroused by that accident to get legislation of the type that we needed but didn't get.

I was concerned, too, because I don't think there is any finer, more magnificent coastline in the world than the Santa Barbara coastline, and the whole country takes an interest and pride in it. I was also concerned because I think now that we have a Redwoods National Park, the other final national park opportunity that California has, and the west coast, is the Channel Islands off California. I have been interested in this for several years. . . .

As I look at the record, and we did take from the time we began nearly a year, more than a year, and there were many hearings that were held, I think I can say one thing—this was not a snap judgment. There was a great deal of argument that went on within the Department.

It is clear from the record, too, that there were several considerations that entered in and became a part of the decision-making process.

One was that the west coast was a crude oil deficit area and therefore we were interested in additional production. Incidentally, let me say one thing, now that we have the benefit of hindsight. The big major discovery that has been made in the Arctic and Alaska promises to eliminate that deficit, and if this had occurred only a few months earlier, it might have made a substantial difference in the making of the decision that was made. But, of course, this is hindsight.

It is also true, I think, that the industry was interested in this area. We had let them do exploratory drilling. They had expanded considerable money on this. It is true, I think, from the record, that there were some people within my Department who were eager to go ahead and were pressing for action.

It is true also, and some of the correspondence was not directed to me, but to my under-secretaries, that the Bureau of the Budget was in the picture because they were hungry for revenues.

If you will recall late 1967 and early 1968 before the surtax, when the big deficit was in existence, they were interested in having us move forward. But we did proceed in a rather thorough and deliberate approach. I usually insisted when I saw any decision of this kind headed toward me, that above all everyone be heard, and the wildlife people were certainly heard from.

My science adviser happened to be at that time one of the Nation's best oceanographers, from California, a man connected with the University of California at La Jolla. I put him in it and asked him to look at the entire picture and to advise me. But when I look back at the way we approached this problem, it does seem to me that we were overconfident concerning the risks that were involved.

The question I kept raising with my people was about earthquakes, because this is an earthquake prone area. My concern was in the technology of drilling and extracting oil as well as the possibility of fissures that might be breached by a major earthquake. What was the magnitude of the risk, because the main risk that we had run in the drilling of the 15 years previous on the gulf coast was hurricanes—would hurricanes come along and damage the platforms and equipment and cause spills?

Well, we had gone through several hurricanes and apparently the conclusion was that not only did the platforms stand, but in any event you could control oil flow by shutting off the wells.

I have to say, and I think the record shows that, that at the time we made the Santa Barbara decision there was no dissent in the Department. This was a sort of conservation "Bay of Pigs," you might say, and at least I have found myself in somewhat the same position, after the event, as President Kennedy. I made the decision, and I made it getting the best advice I could get in the Department, but there was nobody hammering on the door and there is nothing in the record in the weeks or months immediately before the decision that would indicate someone was saying, "This is a mistake," and predicting that what occurred would occur.

In fact much of the record shows, and this was my own recollection of it, that many of the local people, rather than saying, "There will be major spills," were objecting primarily to the esthetics of platforms, and they were also concerned, and I went along with them on this, that we put a buffer zone in the State sanctuary and push the platforms farther out. If we didn't do this, we all felt the State would have a very sound pretext then for saying, "Well, the sanctuary doesn't make any sense because you are going to drain the oil in the pool into the sanctuary and we will have to go ahead and drill in the sanctuary."

I think it is clear, too, that we needed more geologic data and the question brought up by Senator Cooper and others here, earlier, that perhaps the method that we presently use with regard to each company keeping its own data until after the leasing, that this needs to be reviewed.

In any event, however, it is hard for me to not feel that under the circumstances that existed at that time with the sort of cockiness, one might describe it that way, that existed with regard to our ability to prevent major oil spills, that if the same fact situation existed you would probably make the same decision, lacking the hindsight that we now have.

What are the lessons and remedies with regard to offshore oil drilling? It seems to me there are several. One is that we not only need tighter regulations but tougher enforcement of them because, as I understand it, there were waivers granted that we see now probably should not have been granted, and I think this whole area needs to be reviewed both in terms of administrative management as well as perhaps with regard to the act setting up the Outer Continental Shelf program as well.

It seems to me also that the Geological Survey, itself, needs to have the funds available to carry out studies on its own and I should advise the committee, because this Nation, the United States, is very rich in that it has a very big Continental Shelf, that the largest part of that Continental Shelf is off Alaska in the gulf, Alaska in the Bering Sea. This is a shallow shelf and there are at least some indications that caused the geologists to report to me over a year ago that there appear to be very promising strata on the Alaska Continental Shelf.

Now before we even open this up for exploratory drilling, I have been asking myself the question: Should the Geological Survey itself do some drilling to ascertain certain basic things about the geological factors that are present?

At the present time they have had very limited budgets with regard to their role. In fact, they played pretty much a passive rather than an active role. It is clear, too, that the Federal Water Pollution Control Administration needs more funds so that, working with industry, cleanup techniques can be perfected.

This we learned when we saw the *Torrey Canyon* disaster. It was a disaster not only because the spill occurred, but it was even more disastrous afterwards because they bombed the tanker and tried to set the oil on fire, and they used the wrong kind of chemicals and the ship went to the floor and did enormous ecological damage. We were aware of this, and yet we still found that we really weren't ready off Santa Barbara. We don't have an effective technique or system to clean up this sort of pollution once it has occurred, whether it is on a small or a large scale.

It seems also to me one of the lessons for the managers of our resources is that we should always err on the side of protection where a mistake can do great damage to other resources.

As I have tried to say, I think we approached the Santa Barbara problem with some misgivings that we might not have in other areas because of the value of the other resources that were there. But still, we probably should have been even more cautious and more careful.

It is very clear to me, and the committee of course is wrestling with this problem, that we must have laws to insure that when these mistakes are made, whether it is in transportation—a *Torrey Canyon* type situation—whether it is in the drilling and extracting of petroleum, that we have the funds and that we have a remedy, and that we have a system that works. And I believe if the committee provided for nothing except this in the legislation it writes as a result of the Santa Barbara disaster, that this would be a great service to the country. Because, if we had the funds and we have a system that fixes responsibility, and if we can't fix responsibility, we still have funds to carry out a cleanup program, then the national interest is protected as best we can.

Finally, I would like to point out, and I notice the committee is already exploring this area, my own feelings with regard to national policy concerning the overall management of resources. I came to believe in my last year as Secretary that it was very wise to flow back into resource management revenues from resources, and I could boast, because of some of the recent offshore sales, the last two times I went before my Appropriations Committee, that mine was the only Department other than the Department of the Treasury—which happens to have the Internal Revenue Service in it—that had larger revenues than appropriations.

Our resource management problems all interlock and it seems to me that it is wise to earmark or use revenues from resource development on achieving better conservation of our other resources. . . .

AIR POLLUTION AND THE AUTOMOBILE

House of Representatives

The following contributors are Democratic Representatives: John Jarman (Oklahoma), Leonard Farbstein (New York), Ken Hechler (West Virginia), Harley O. Staggers (West Virginia), and George E. Brown, Jr. (California). James Harvey is a Republican Representative from Michigan. Representative Farbstein's amendment was defeated.

. . .*Mr. Jarman:* Mr. Chairman, it is my pleasure to speak in favor of passage of H.R. 12085, the purpose of which is to extend for 1 year—fiscal 1970—the authority contained in section 104 of the Clean Air Act, as amended. This section authorizes research and development by the Department of Health, Education, and Welfare

From *Congressional Record*, House of Representatives, September 4, 1969, pp. H7507, H7511-7512, H7517-H7520.

on the prevention and control of air pollution resulting from the combustion of fuels and the operation of motor vehicles.

In adopting the Air Quality Act of 1967, the Congress set up an intergovernmental system for dealing with the problems of air pollution on a regional basis. State and local governments were given a major share of responsibility in making this system work, by dealing with air pollution arising from industrial, commercial, and other stationary sources located in virtually every urban community in this Nation, as well as in many small towns and rural areas.

The activities of State and local agencies in preventing and controlling these stationary sources of air pollution depend in large part on the availability of practical and economic techniques. Similarly, the national program of regulatory action to control motor vehicle pollution depends on progress in developing appropriate control techniques.

It is essential that the Department of Health, Education, and Welfare continue the research and development activities authorized by the Air Quality Act, especially those activities under section 104 relating to air pollution problems caused by the combustion of fossil fuels to produce electric heat and power and from the operation of motor vehicles. These sources account for more than two-thirds of the Nation's yearly air pollution.

Section 104 also reflects the need for extensive involvement of the private sector in the search for solutions to these problems. For example, the effort to develop and demonstrate techniques for sulfur oxides pollution control under section 104 is a coordinated Government-industry program which involves the National Air Pollution Control Administration, several other Federal agencies, and more than 40 organizations in the private sector. Also, under section 104, the National Air Pollution Control Administration is conducting research and development on motor vehicle pollution control. This effort includes continued attempts to develop improved emissions control from the internal combustion engine as well as initial work on the development of alternative propulsion systems for motor vehicles. . . .

Favorable action on H.R. 12085 would reaffirm the Federal Government's commitment to providing leadership in the Nation's efforts to develop ways to overcome the growing threat of air pollution. The Federal Government cannot and should not be expected to take all the responsibility, but it must continue to lead the attack. Enactment of H.R. 12085 will show that the Federal commitment to clean air remains as strong as ever. . . .

Mr. Farbstein: Mr. Chairman, I offer an amendment to H.R. 12085 to prohibit the manufacture and sale of cars powered by internal combustion engines after January 1, 1978. This ban would not apply to engines which meet the equivalent of the pollution emission standard for automobiles purchased by the State of California which are 0.5 gram per mile of reactive hydrocarbons, 11 grams per mile of carbon monoxide, and 0.75 gram per mile of oxides of nitrogen. The Federal standards for the 1970 models, which are the most stringent to date, are 23 grams per mile of carbon monoxide and 2.2 grams per mile of hydrocarbons.

I offer this amendment because I represent the city which the Public Health Service has ranked as the most polluted in the country. I represent a city which has suffered from inversions in the air, periods when the winds failed to blow away the carbon monoxide, the lead particles, the hydrocarbons, and the other deadly pollutants which were produced by the internal combustion engine automobile with the result that many died.

I come from a city where 2 million autos daily crowd into the city spouting forth dirt and heavy smoke which corrodes every material with which it comes into touch.

I offer this amendment because I want to do something about this situation.

Until now, most of the effort to combat auto-caused air pollution has come through utilization of emission control devices attached to the crankcase or tailpipe. The use of such devices has brought a noticeable reduction in emission levels of certain auto pollutants. However, these devices can only partially reduce the level of pollution emission. As the Air Pollution Control Administration projection of the level of auto pollution suggests, the increasing number of cars will begin to offset the decrease in pollution brought about by exhaust emissions control devices after 1980.

Pollution Level from Automobiles Based on 1970-71 Air Pollution Control Administration

Hydrocarbons (in millions of tons per year)					
	1968	1972	1975	1980	1990
Urban	7.0	6.0	5.0	4.5	7.0
Total emissions, nationwide	12.0	10.0	8.5	7.0	10.0
Carbon Monoxide					
Urban	47.5	40.0	32.5	27.5	43.0
Total emissions, nationwide	68.0	55.0	45.0	37.5	58.0
Oxides of Nitrogen*					
Urban	3.0	4.0	4.5	6.0	10.5
Total emissions, nationwide	6.5	8.5	9.5	12.0	19.5

*There are no current emissions standards.

The primary source of pollution is the internal combustion engine. Since it cannot uniformly burn all of the gasoline it consumes, it inherently must produce a certain level of pollutant emission. Control devices can modify its output, but they cannot prevent it. Other types of propulsion systems are capable of being emission free. They can operate with little or no release of deadly pollutants into the atmosphere.

The need to seek alternatives to the internal combustion engines which do not have to pollute was recognized by the President and his Environmental Quality Council last week when they viewed alternatives to the internal combustion engine and heard a warning from Dr. Lee A. DuBridge, the Presidential science adviser, that if we do not ban the internal combustion engine sometime in the future, we would no longer be able to breathe anything but noxious air.

In spite of this, the auto industry has resisted all efforts to reduce air pollution by developing an alternative to the internal combustion engine—just as it resisted efforts to place safety belts and other safety equipment in the American car and just as it resisted efforts to install pollutant reduction equipment.

This is dramatically demonstrated by the recent Justice Department suit against the big three auto companies, charging them with combination and conspiracy to develop and manufacture motor vehicle air pollutant equipment. Two years of Los Angeles Federal grand jury hearings has brought out auto company activity going back to 1953, one year after the link between the auto and air pollution was first established. The auto companies agreed at that time to install pollution abatement equipment only if all companies agreed to install such equipment at the same time. And on at least three subsequent occasions, the companies met and agreed to attempt to delay installation of pollution abatement equipment. In 1961, they agreed to delay the installation of the positive crankcase until the 1963 model. In late 1962 and early 1963, they agreed to delay the adoption of an improvement to the crankcase ventilating device, and in early 1964, the introduction of a new exhaust emission control measure until the 1967 model year. In 1964 the auto companies agreed to tell the State of California the technology would not exist to install tail emission devices until the 1967 model year although they had the technological know-how and devices to do so.

What we are hearing today is the same thing. Dr. Fred Bowditch, director of GM's emission control engineering, told a panel of the California State Assembly, which was then considering the Senate-passed bill to ban the internal combustion engine by 1976, that "The know-how isn't there to do the job by 1976." (*Los Angeles Times*, August 1, 1969.)

I do not believe Dr. Bowditch was under oath for at a press conference given by GM at its research laboratory, after the California bill had been safely killed, he answered a reporter's query of "What would you have done if the panel had passed the bill?" with the statement: "We would have complied, and of course, General Motors would have remained in the business of producing automobiles." (*San Fernando Valley News*, August 7, 1969.)

Apparently the big three just do not want to tell the American public the truth. Hearings by the Senate Commerce Committee have revealed that low-cost, low-emission vehicles can be produced today but that none of the big three is actively moving toward this goal because they are satisfied with the market status quo. Only American Motors, which is not satisfied with its share of the current market, is moving to explore alternative methods of propulsion. . . .

It took congressional action to make the auto safer. It took congressional action to get antipollution devices installed in the auto. It will take congressional action to make the air breathable again by doing something about the major source of air pollution—the internal combustion engine.

It is generally recognized that the automobile represents the most important single source of air pollution in the United States. It currently is responsible for 60 percent of all air pollution in the country and in many urban areas for well over 90 percent. This air pollution is a cause of pulmonary emphysema, chronic bronchitis, lung cancer, genetic mutation, degeneration of pulmonary functions, increased sensitivity of various allergic conditions, accelerations of preexisting heart disease, numerous other kinds of respiratory and circulatory diseases, cancer, and even the common cold.

Even aside from the lethal and safety hazards, the dollar loss resulting from air pollution is staggering. It is estimated at $11 billion a year or $600 per family.

The amendment would not take effect for 9 years. I feel certain that within that period, the industry can come up with a motor which will greatly reduce, if not totally eliminate, pollution emission.

I believe that passage or even a respectable number of votes for it will demonstrate to the automobile producers that the Congress is serious in its desire to do something about automobile-caused air pollution. . . .

Mr. Hechler: Mr. Chairman, is it not true that a period of only 8 years elapsed between 1961 when President Kennedy announced the goal of landing on the moon and the time when we achieved it in 1969? The gentleman from New York is giving 1 additional year beyond the 8, he is giving 9 years for the industry to meet this goal. I wonder if the gentleman feels, if we set a goal like this, it might possibly be the kind of challenge American industry could meet?

Mr. Farbstein: Very frankly I think American industry can meet this prior to that date, but my purpose in using that date, was to remove from the industry any suggestion that we are pressing industry to the wall and not giving industry an opportunity to do something about air pollution.

Mr. Staggers: Mr. Chairman, will the gentleman yield?

Mr. Farbstein: I yield to the gentleman from West Virginia.

Mr. Staggers: Mr. Chairman, I would like to answer the gentleman from West Virginia and say that the Federal Government is not spending $50 billion, or anything near that, to correct this very large danger we have here today, but the Federal Government did spend $50 billion to put a man on the moon, and it took 9 years. If we were to spend that kind of money, we could buy every car in the United States and clean it up and run it on some superfuel. We do not have that much money to spend.

Mr. Farbstein: Mr. Chairman, I would like to tell the chairman of the committee, apropos of what the chairman just said, it seems to me those who are earning not millions but billions of dollars on the production and sale of automobiles are the ones who should assume the responsibility for clearing up the pollution by manufacturing engines that will not produce the pollution or the smog that is harmful to people.

I do not believe the onus should be on the Federal Government to spend $50 billion, although, of course, I favor the legislation before us today. I do believe the automobile companies should do this, and very frankly, I believe they can do it. They have the technology today. As a matter of fact, different types of fuels can be used by existing engines which greatly reduce pollution. I understand in Florida, for example, a large firm uses natural gas to run its trucks. There are electrical cars, steam cars, and other cars using other fuels. They can be produced without contributing further to the smog problem. . . .

Mr. Staggers: Mr. Chairman, I rise in opposition to the amendment offered by the gentleman from New York.

The amendment offered by the gentleman is unnecessary. Existing law says the Department may ban new motor vehicles from sale unless they meet the emissions standards set by the Secretary. This requires that the Secretary take into account several factors which were written into the original law. This can be done at any time.

This amendment would instead have the Congress set emission standards, and we are not equipped to do that. This is the kind of a job we created the air pollution agency to handle, and we expect them to do the job with the authority we have given them, which in our opinion is adequate. . . .

Mr. Harvey: Mr. Chairman, I rise in opposition to the amendment.

I wish to join in what the distinguished chairman of the committee has already said. Obviously that authority is already vested.

Also, I wish to reply to the gentleman from New York, who has said, I believe, and I quote: "They have the technology today" to do this sort of thing. Dr. Lee DuBridge, who is the President's science adviser, spoke on this very problem just a few days ago and he said that the development of a new automobile engine is a big job, and then he went on to say, and I quote: "We must depend upon the gasoline engine and its improvements during the next 10 or 20 years."

He went on after that to discuss the problems of air pollution from the automobile, and to point out that progress has been made in this regard.

After hearing some of the talk here in the House, one would get the impression that progress is not going forward. But it is.

Let me point out what Dr. DuBridge said, for example, on progress on the control of hydrocarbons. He said that the control thus far achieved—and I quote again—"has gone from 900 parts per million of hydrocarbons before 1965 to less than 275 parts per million of hydrocarbons today," and that with the introduction of the 1970 models in the auto industry that figure will be reduced to less than 120 parts per million of hydrocarbons.

This, Mr. Chairman, represents a reduction of more than 80 percent being achieved by the industry today. I would say to the House that in my judgment this represents real and substantial progress in attempting to comply with the requirement to meet a very serious and recognized health condition.

In the field of carbon monoxide he went on to point out that more than a 65-percent reduction had already been made in that field. This again I say is substantial evidence of progress in this particular field.

We do not say that more progress cannot be made, but we say they are going ahead just as fast as they possibly can in recognition of a very serious problem. . . .

Mr. Staggers: As the gentleman stated, they are making great progress, and have plans for research in the future.

The great and overwhelming amount of this material which is being put in the air now is put there by used cars which are not equipped with the equipment to prevent this from going into the atmosphere. Those are the older cars. The newer ones are meeting the standards as set by the Secretary.

I am sure the cars in California are meeting the standards set by that State. In fact, California is the only State in the Union, out of the 50, that we exempted from the motor vehicles law. We said that the problem is so serious in California they should be permitted to do their own job out there. It is up to the States to do it, because we exempted the State of California, as to going ahead and making higher standards.

The fact is that it is the older cars which are now on the roads which are doing most of the polluting of the air.

Mr. Harvey: I thank the gentleman.

I want to say to the gentleman from New York that in my judgment to blindly set a date such as 1978 when cars with internal combustion engines can no longer be produced except under these conditions is ridiculous.

The gentleman from West Virginia pointed out that we could go to the moon in less time than that. That may be true, but as Dr. DuBridge pointed out, the problem has not yet been solved, the technology does not yet exist to do these things. Nor are we spending the sums of money, as the chairman pointed out, to do these things.

But we are making substantial progress.

I would point out to my colleagues that, yes, I do speak as one who represents a district in which the automobile industry is very important. There are more than 25,000 workers in the one city alone in my district who work directly for one company in the auto industry. I would point out to the Members that in this Nation of ours one out of every seven workers' jobs is traceable to the auto industry in some way or another; one out of every seven workers.

I would point out to you that there are more than a million directly employed by the industry itself, not to mention the dealers, the suppliers, and all of their employees. I point out to you that the net sales of autos last year came to over $19 billion and that out of our balance of payments more than $1 billion came from the sale of autos alone. So I say to you that the industry has significance. You can knock it all you want to and say that it is not doing a good enough job in getting rid of air pollution. But this industry means an awful lot to an awful lot of people in America, and I would consider that very carefully before we tamper with writing standards that would affect it on the floor of this House.

Thus far we in our committee, although we have held lengthy hearings on the entire matter, have never seen fit to write in standards either in auto safety, toy safety, or air pollution devices. We do not claim to have that sort of expertise and, as a result, we have instead given the authority in all cases to the Secretary, or someone in the administration. Never have we written such standards. This is precisely what this amendment would do, and that is why I ask it be defeated. . . .

Mr. Brown: . . . I have been deeply concerned about this problem for, roughly, 15 years. It was at least 15 years ago that I became involved in efforts to control pollution in Los Angeles. As a local government official at that time I was told then that it could be done with the effort we were then devoting to research, and that progress was good. However, what has happened? Essentially nothing. Smog today in Los Angeles is worse than it was 15 years ago. There is no question about that. Yet, all the time we have been told that the automobile industry is doing everything possible to correct the situation.

Then, Mr. Chairman, as a member of the State legislature I conducted hearings 10 years ago—hearings on the problem of smog and more particularly lead and its contamination of the atmosphere. We had before that committee the best possible witnesses that the petroleum industry could produce at that time. The reaction I had after the hearing was that not only was my concern with regard to lead in the atmosphere unnecessary, but actually the more lead put into the atmosphere the healthier it was for the people of the area. The experts have the statistics to prove it. Of course, it does not take a very intelligent person to know that lead is a cumulative poison and that the more there is in the atmosphere the worse it is for the people.

I think industries which are concerned with the production of lead—and it is a very big industry, at least one quarter of a billion dollars a year—will state that it is unnecessary to control the emission of lead and, in effect, that the more you ingest the better it is for you. However, I am not sold on the proposition that progress is being made because in my opinion the exact opposite is true.

The gentleman from Michigan has made reference to what we have done with regard to a lunar landing in recent years. I can understand the simple logic of the gentleman from New York in offering this amendment and in placing the time for the correction of this problem into a period roughly equal to what it took us to reach the moon.

The cost of this lunar operation was not $50 billion, but was essentially $25 billion from the time that the goal was set until the time it was achieved. It has been pointed out how large and important the automobile industry is, and this is very true. The very size of that industry makes it possible for the industry at the expenditure of perhaps $10 per unit sold, for example, to have a fund of $100 million a year for research. Yet they have not begun to do this.

At much less than the cost of the new model changeover each year, which runs to something like $4 or $5 billion a year, they could have produced a completely redesigned automobile which would not pollute the atmosphere. At the price of 1 cent per gallon of gasoline sold they could have a fund of a quarter of a billion dollars per year for researching into how to eliminate pollution.

Have we seen the automobile industry or the petroleum industry offer to do these things? Absolutely not.

What we have seen . . . is that the automobile companies and the manufacturers' association are now the subject of an antitrust suit because they have failed to take any action with regard to the question of emission controls and pollution. They have actually conspired over the last 10 years, according to the complaint of the Justice Department, to avoid doing anything about controlling this problem.

Hence I believe that the only practical thing to do is that which was suggested by the amendment offered by the gentleman from New York—which I frankly consider to be too moderate—and that we should, if anything, cut off completely the manufacture of automobiles with internal combustion engines, probably within 3 years. Given that stimulus, and given the vast resources which these companies possess, I have no doubt but what they could find a solution to this problem. I have no doubt but what they could find a solution. And the argument that we should not tamper with the automobile industry because one person out of six in this country is engaged in the business just does not appeal to me. What if one person in every six were engaged in the sale of heroin in this country? Would you argue that we should do nothing about heroin either? I doubt that very seriously. And yet, in view of the adverse impact of automobile air pollution upon this country, there is no question whatsoever but what the automobile industry and the petroleum industry and the poisons which they are emitting into the atmosphere are having a far worse effect upon the health of our country than heroin is. And that will continue to be the result of these emissions as they continue to concentrate in the atmosphere, because we refuse to control an $80 billion-per-year industry in this country. . . .

6

Power and Its Distribution

The cry that power in America is excessively and increasingly concentrated in the hands of the federal government has traditionally been associated with the conservative ideology. But in the 1960s a similar complaint began to emerge from a different direction. Thus, in 1967 Richard Goodwin, a Kennedy adviser, wrote an article in which he argued that liberals should no longer put their faith in the ability of Washington agencies to solve public problems.[1] It is true that Goodwin, unlike the conservatives, favored larger federal outlays and advocated a strong central government role in promoting new and significant social purposes. Nonetheless, decentralization was Goodwin's central theme; and in a later article, excerpted in this chapter, he continued to advance it as a necessary response to the growing sense of frustration and powerlessness afflicting the American people.

This idea has an inevitable attraction in an age of growing bureaucratization and centralized, remote decision-making. Yet, if power is to be diffused from the central government, a critical question presents itself. Who shall inherit the power?

The usual conservative answer is: the states. When Walter Heller, President Kennedy's Chairman of the Council of Economic Advisers, proposed that the federal government share its future budget surpluses with the states, it appeared that a consensus on the issue might be emerging. Then

[1] "The Shape of American Politics," *Commentary* (June 1967), pp. 25-40.

President Nixon took up the refrain. In his address on welfare reform in August 1969, he declared: "After a third of a century of power flowing from the people and the states to Washington, it is time for a new federalism in which power, funds, and responsibility will flow from Washington to the states and to the people." Subsequently he proposed to Congress a plan whereby state, city, and county governments would automatically get a portion of federal tax revenues with no strings attached. In the first year of the plan $500 million would be available, climbing in five years to a permanent level of 1% of the nation's taxable personal income, which could produce about $5 billion in 1976. Accordingly, the 70s will probably see the introduction of some kind of federal-state tax sharing plan. However, it will not come without opposition, and it will not dispose of all the dilemmas of allocating and distributing governmental power. For one thing, the deficiencies of state government are notorious. Then, too, the most critical domestic issues are concentrated in the great metropolitan areas. And typically, big city mayors are skeptical that the larger share of monies flowing from the federal government to the states will be allocated by the states to the cities.

If the states are not the panacea, what about the cities? Sociologist Scott Greer is an apostle of the city, but his article describes some of the many defects of local government. He suggests some possibilities of improvement but still foresees a "shaky future."

Is hope to be found in the assumption of more responsibility by local community organizations? Goodwin thinks so, and there is a strong demand in ghetto communities for local control of local institutions, especially the schools. Irving Kristol suggests that it is the wrong time to press for this kind of decentralization, for the result will be to end the prospects for racial integration. Of course, the separatists whose case was presented by Robert Browne in Chapter 3 will hardly be moved by Kristol's argument. And Nathan Glazer, whose essay in the same chapter took a position very different from Browne's, has nonetheless argued elsewhere that the blacks' demand for community control of the schools is not very different from what white suburbanites have long enjoyed.[2] Glazer is also among those who claim that the "maximum feasible participation" provisions of the antipoverty programs, disdained by Kristol and attacked by many mayors, have created community action agencies that are effective examples of what can be accomplished by decentralization and community control. Even Daniel Moynihan, whose book on the subject is entitled *Maximum Feasible Misunderstanding,* concedes that—despite a great deal of muddle, failure, and disappointment—community action agencies have survived, have added a new kind of institution to our governmental system, and have developed an important stratum of community leadership.

Whatever the merits of the case for more community control, there are some major national decisions, such as the direction of the total economy, which can hardly be determined by community agencies. Peter Drucker believes that, as a manager of economic enterprises, government has been a dismal failure; and he suggests that business organizations are a much more effective instrument of innovative management than governmental agencies. Those who disagree with Drucker tend to respond with three different kinds of arguments. The first is that government does not always fail: the moon landing, after all, though contributed to by private corporations, was the triumph of a government agency. Second, examples of massive inefficiency and waste can be found throughout the private as well as the public sector of the economy. Third, it is not only the federal government that represents the danger of an excessive concentration of power. Anti-trust legislation and litigation have failed to stop the accumulation of economic power in the hands of giant corporations. And the warnings on this subject do not come only from the New Left. In June 1969 Attorney General John Mitchell pointed out that, through a process of acquisitions and mergers, the 200 largest manufacturing companies now control more than 58% of the nation's manufacturing assets. Conceivably that figure could be reduced by smaller companies using new technologies to challenge the position of the great corporations in some

[2]"For White and Black, Community Control Is the Issue," *New York Times Magazine* (April 27, 1969), p. 37ff. In this article Glazer agrees with Kristol that there is a real danger that local control could mean the teaching of race hatred and the oppression of those who dissent from the views of the leadership of the community. But he believes that this is a risk we will have to run.

fields. But this development is by no means certain; in fact, the recent trend has been toward more concentration. And as Theodore Lowi further demonstrates, there are other power-ful private structures, like trade associations, in those areas of economic activity not dominated by huge corporations. If government power is decentralized, there will be nothing to offset the impact of these concentrations of private power.

Still, if there are more problems in decentralization than suggested in Goodwin's article, the attack on the federal government's power will undoubtedly continue as a reflec-tion of general dissatisfaction with the remoteness of the decision-making process from the ordinary individual. Indeed, this attack is so multifaceted that it could not be contained within the confines of any one chapter. Thus, the attempt by Congress to limit the power of the President in the all-important field of foreign policy is discussed in Chapter 9. And the selections in Chapter 7 show that the power of the military, or military-industrial, establishment is now being seriously questioned for the first time in many years.

SOURCES OF THE PUBLIC UNHAPPINESS

Richard N. Goodwin

Mr. Goodwin was formerly a special assistant to Presidents Kennedy and Johnson.

All political movements are efforts to redistribute power. That's all politics can do. It can't create wealth or bestow happiness. It can, however, grant to people and institutions the power to decide public issues that can affect our economic welfare, the physical setting of our lives, and even our personal contentment. The character of men chosen to hold office, the nature of the office, and

From "Sources of the Public Unhappiness," *The New Yorker* (January 4, 1969), pp. 38, 40-42, 44, 47-50. Copyright ©1969 by Richard N. Goodwin. Reprinted by permission of The Sterling Lord Agency.

the limits placed on the range of the officeholders' public actions often determine the substance of those decisions. That's why politics is important. The United States government has been unusually stable partly because political issues have rarely been discussed in terms of power. Candidates promise to help the poor or suppress them, to end wars or escalate them, to reduce spending or rebuild cities, and sometimes to do all these things at once. Rarely do they challenge the distribution of power directly, even though their policies may compel large shifts. (For example, in the course of fighting a depression the Roosevelt Administration took much of the power of economic decision away from scattered private centers.) This observation yields at least one useful dividing line between the blending concepts of evolution and revolution. Evolution occurs when power shifts in the course of an attack on particular problems. A revolution is a direct and explicit assault on those people or institutions that hold power in favor of those that want it. (Of course, particular grievances help trigger revolutions, as, in our own, opposition to British taxation became opposition to British rule.)

The temperament we brought from Britain, combined with extraordinary resources taken from nature and the Indians, has made us a rational and pragmatic people—the creators of an evolutionary nation. (That is not the whole story, of course, since it is possible to be rational and pragmatic in pursuit of foolish or monstrous goals, but one source of values is an acute sense of possibility.) Generally, we become aware of a problem, decide to solve it, and, in doing so, find that reason or expediency requires some change in the structure of power. We may set up a new government bureau or pass a law. Today, however, we are in one of those rare periods in our history marked by a large and serious revolutionary movement. There is serious discontent not only with what we as a nation are doing but with who is doing it. There is a challenge to the "power structure" itself, which means simply the methods, institutions, and people by which decisions affecting the public are made. We see this explicitly in the recent pronouncements by George Wallace, the manifestos of the New Left, and the demands of black militants. However, it is also a principal focus for the new politics of the middle class, as the response to Eugene McCarthy and Robert Kennedy revealed. Although this "movement" takes its tone and its issues from the nature of modern life, it returns us to the seminal debate between the forces of Alexander Hamilton and those of Thomas Jefferson. That, too, was a debate about power. Putting aside the relative merits of Jefferson's agrarianism and Hamilton's capitalism—both largely irrelevant—one side of the argument called for the centralization of power, in the interests of order and the economy, and the other, Jefferson's side, demanded the diffusion of power and the right of the citizen to participate in decisions, even at the price of economic efficiency. (Today's conservatives are trapped in the insoluble dilemma of demanding more order, even on a world scale, and less power for government, but when a choice is forced, they invariably prefer order; this is why the new conservatives, like Goldwater, are rejected by the old conservatives, like George Aiken, of Vermont—one lives by fear and the other by trust.) For years, textbooks have routinely praised Jefferson's idealism while asserting that Hamilton's view was the wave of the future, bound to dominate American development for all time to come; Jefferson was a wonderful romantic, and Hamilton was the realist, and in proof of this historians invoke Jefferson's own conduct in the Presidency, which aggrandized the nation.

Whatever modern revisionists do to this traditional analysis, it appears that Jefferson's day may yet come. Much that he said, if it were stripped of eighteenth-century stateliness and equipped with one or two four-letter words, could be incorporated into an S.D.S. manifesto or shouted at a Yippie rally. For example, he warned, "Were we directed from Washington when to sow, and when to reap, we should soon want bread," and "When all government . . . shall be drawn to Washington as the centre of all power, it . . . will become as venal and oppressive as the government from which we separated," and "If ever this vast country is brought under a single government, it will be one of the most extensive corruption, indifferent and incapable of a wholesome care." And he stated his general principle of government by asserting, "It is not by the consolidation, or concentration of powers, but by their distribution, that good government is effected." (Almost a century later, Emerson added the advice to "do your thing" to this political theory, which also contained warnings against a military establishment, foreign involvements, and any use of coercive power.) Today, these Jeffersonian ideas have a greater vitality than at any other time since they were written. If anything, their relevance has been increased by modern technology, for it has stripped us of the protections of distance and time, which once compelled a certain diffusion of power.

The issue of power—who shall have it and how it shall be exercised—is the overwhelming political issue of modern times. In fact, it is far more than a political issue; it penetrates our social, economic, and personal life. Nor is it simply an American problem; it plagues the entire affluent West. And if it is different in the developing countries, that is only because they are preoccupied with urgent difficulties of poverty and oppression which we have largely overcome. . . .

It would be hard to overstate the extent to which the malaise of powerlessness has eaten its way into our society, evoking an aimless unease, frustration, and fury. It is probably least pervasive among the poor urban blacks, around whom so much of the surface debate about local control and Black Power now revolves. Their grievances are, for the most part, closer to the classic ills that the New Deal was designed to solve. They want jobs and decent homes, a higher standard of living, and freedom from the welfare bureaucracy. If a beneficent government were to provide these rudimentary components of the just life, it would meet most of the present demands of the black community. Of course, even among America's poor, questions of power are more important than they were thirty years ago. For the poor of today are inevitably caught up in the main currents of our society and partake of the general atmosphere of helplessness and drift, and the resistant nature of racial feelings is forcing black Americans toward a kind of separatism as an alternative to the assimilation that was their initial goal. However, these questions can be seen most acutely among those who are neither poor nor black—the American middle class, or the American majority. Their psychological plight is both worse and more dangerous than that of the black militant leading a slum riot. For he at least has a cause and a purpose, an enemy, and comrades in the struggle. No such outlets and no human connections so satisfying are available to the man who lives in a middle-class suburb or a lower-income city apartment. And his discontents, unlike those of the poor, have real political weight.

It is impossible to provide an accurate and uniform description of a group of people as large and varied as non-poor Americans. For the most part, such an American commutes to a job that he may like or hate but is most probably indifferent to—indifferent not to the income or status it provides but to the products of his labor. It is the job that counts, not the refrigerators or vacuum tubes he produces. He would be among a minority if he felt that his work made an improving difference to the life of his country or his neighbors. At home, he can either sit amid his many purchases or get back into his car and drive to visit friends. There is probably no place for him to talk, and, almost certainly, no neighborhood gathering place where he can meet with friends, discuss the day's events, and share in the satisfactions and concerns of community. If he stays home, he probably watches television, wishing both that he had something better to do and that he could buy the goods that float alluringly across the screen. It is this increasingly atomized and insulated existence that we have created with our wealth. And if this is the suburban man's life, how much less exciting is that of his wife. Perhaps she has gone to college. Yet she does not have a job, nor are there many outlets for her intelligence or her energies. She is expected to stay home, care for children, and shop and clean house, even though hospitals and schools and many other vital services are deteriorating for want of the skills she could provide. What an incredible monster women's education has become. We spend decades instilling the same values of competition and achievement in girls as in boys, even though we can clearly foresee an ultimate collision with the socially imposed responsibilities of housewife and mother and with the mythic compulsions of lover and servant-helpmate. Some of the most ambitious women in the world hasten to confide that they have an "Oriental" streak, as well they may have. The society that sets up this clash of desires provides neither day-care centers for children nor opportunities for the use and development by women of their wasted skills. The frustrations thus generated are aggravated by the absence, especially in our better suburbs, of any communal park or neighborhood center where women can naturally meet and share experiences.

The life of the lower-income urban white shares many characteristics with that of the suburban citizen. However, the urban white is also trapped in a no man's land between black poverty and what he sees or imagines of middle-class affluence. He has the advantage of being able to express many of his wants in traditional economic terms. However, his discontent is fed both by envy of the more prosperous and by anger at the blacks—not just because he fears the blacks but also because their problems, and not his, seem to be the focus of national concern. That is why it was possible for many members of this group to support Wallace after having supported Robert Kennedy: both men, in very different ways, could be identified with their wants, and both conveyed a deeply emotional sympathy with the importance of their fears and their plight.

The unexciting and envy-producing tone of the non-poor citizen's private life is heightened by the growing remoteness of public life. The air around him is poisoned, parkland disappears under relentless bulldozers, traffic stalls and jams, airplanes cannot land, and even his own streets are unsafe and, increasingly, streaked with terror. Yet he cannot remember having decided that these things should happen, or even having wished them. He has no sense that there is anything he can do to arrest the tide. He does not know whom to blame. Somehow, the crucial aspects of his environment seem in the grip of forces that are too huge and impersonal to attack. You cannot vote them out of office or shout them down. Even the speeches of mayors and governors are filled with exculpatory claims that the problems are too big, that there is not enough power or enough money to cope with them, and our commentators sympathize, readily agreeing that this city or that state is really ungovernable. Even when a source of authority can be identified, it seems hopelessly detached from the desires or actions of individual citizens. Thus . . . we find ourselves in a major war, and our young people shipped off to battle, without any formal expression of consent or support, even by the members of Congress. And we are also aware, in some dim psychic recess, that our President, along with a few people whose names we can't remember, can blow us all up.

This powerlessness, in large measure a product of the complexity and the sheer size of modern society, is a problem in itself. It is a problem in the same way that lack of money or of useful work is a problem. For individuals have a fundamental, instinctive need for a degree of personal mastery over their lives and their environment. The sense of powerlessness is, moreover, greatly aggravated by the failure of our institutions and our social processes to respond to more specific ills. If we were providing good schools, inspiring cities, and safe streets, the degree of public discontent would be far less. If the quality of individual life were being steadily raised, we would be less concerned that we had little share in the process. But that is not the case. The desire to increase our national wealth and distribute it more broadly—a desire that was idealistic in origin and welcome in its consequences—led us to create machinery for both stimulating and regulating the economy. It is not simply that power was withdrawn from private centers and brought to Washington. It is that the use of that power was judged in terms of economic growth, which meant that construction, technology, and expansion were made into self-sufficient virtues. Build a better mousetrap or a bigger housing development and you not only made money, you were a hero of the Republic. Added to this were the exigencies of the Cold War, which persuaded us of the necessity of a large standing army. This was a historic decision, constituting the first irrevocable departure from almost two centuries of compliance with the warning of the founding fathers that such a military force would be a danger to democracy. The military-budget cutting of President Truman marked the last effort to return to the earlier tradition, and the farewell speech of President Eisenhower was an echo of those early warnings. The half peace of the past twenty years has made military forces essential, yet we are victims of some of the consequences against which we were warned. The military establishment has assumed a life of its own, developing more weapons and new ones, often unrelated to rational considerations of security, and, more subtly, leading policymakers to look at diplomatic problems in terms of force. After all, if you are the strongest kid on the block, any passionate argument is bound to evoke at least the passing thought that you could end it with a couple of blows.

Unfortunately, the policies and the institutions we evolved to make ourselves wealthy are not appropriate to the needs of a society in which lack of wealth is not the problem either for the country as a whole or for most of the people. It is not simply that we need new values but that our institutions are facing demands they were never shaped to meet. A classic example is the federal housing programs, which were designed to stimulate construction and avoid a postwar depression, and which have failed miserably under the pressure of social demands for slum clearance and the creation of livable neighborhoods. These programs can do a job, but it is not the job we now need done. Moreover, many of our institutions, including our political parties themselves, are led by men who developed their ideas in response to earlier demands, and are therefore unable to understand or cope with a new set of problems. The worst of these men no longer care for anything except the power and influence they have won, and the best of them are angry because their beneficent and humane intentions are not appreciated. The occasional violence of their response to opposition shows their unawareness that time and change, not particular individuals have been their remorseless critics.

Asking many of today's institutions to respond to new needs is a little like putting a man on a windowsill and asking him to fly. Not only was he not built for flight but if you keep insisting he's likely to turn around and punch you in the nose. When institutions and leaders are faced with demands they barely understand, their reaction is often to become rigid and defensive, and even angry. Perhaps the ultimate symbol of this reaction was the contorted fury of Mayor Daley at the Chicago Democratic Convention, lashing out at a group whose values and aims were totally alien to his experience. It is precisely this phenomenon that led Thomas Jefferson to assert the necessity of periodic rebellion. It seems almost inevitable that the repositories of power and control will react to changing circumstances and a changing environment by hardening their attitudes, narrowing the avenues of access for new ideas and men, and losing the flexibility that gave them their initial glow and effectiveness. What is even more ominous, beliefs that were once tentative and responsive to changes in circumstance tend to stiffen into dogma when confronted by conceptual challenge. When this happened in the nineteen-thirties, we were fortunate enough to get Franklin Roosevelt and a peaceful revolution. When it happened in the eighteen-fifties—a period like our own in many ways—the system collapsed in civil war. Unfortunately, the profound nature of modern change resembles the eighteen-fifties more than it does the nineteen-thirties, and there is no Roosevelt in sight.

The same stiffening of established patterns invades the relationship between private institutions and the public interest. The basic pattern of government regulation of business has hardly changed for decades, although much of it is irrelevant, some is oppressive, and many new abuses are unrestrained . . . .

. . . In almost every aspect of life, men are confronted by institutions and processes that seem unresponsive to their needs. There is, for example, no way in which the citizen can even begin to create a community—a place where he can both work and play in some kind of shared fellowship with neighbors. Our society is simply not equipped to deal with such a demand, and our political leaders are not even able to articulate it, since it transcends their own professional assumptions.

Powerlessness is made more acute by the seeming opposite of rigidity—by the swirling inconstancies of modern life. We are like boats tied to a riverbank with the rapid waters constantly seething beneath us while rope after rope breaks away. It is now common-place to observe the weakening of the ties of family and community. However, it is not merely that we are being deprived of important values. These institutions, and others, gave us a resting spot, an association within which we could have some secure sense of our own value and place regardless of our fate in the world outside. In a more subtle and profound way, the increasing incredibility of religious doctrines and the complexities of science, which have made it impossible to understand the natural world, have deprived us of anchors against the storm of events. Even our physical environment has betrayed our memories. The other day, I drove through Harvard Square, where I had gone to school ten years before. There were new buildings, shops, and roads. The familiar place of law-school days had changed beyond recognition. In fact, it did not exist. There was no place for the past, and the present, one knew, would also fade. Yet man has nearly always anchored his sense of reality, his sense of himself, to a fixed place, amid familiar landmarks. Our world has become nomadic as the scenery of our life is constantly shifted. It is small wonder if we sometimes feel as unreal as actors moving from part to part.

To all this is added the torrent of events: wars and riots, inventions and spaceships. One day we are informed that we must fear a man called Castro, on the next day that our security requires the end of strife in the Congo, and on the next that de Gaulle menaces the grandeur of our nation. And we pass through all this tumult, great and small, seated before the inexorable shadows of a television set—certainly the greatest psychic disturber ever created by man. Only it is capable of producing unrest, fear, and unbridled envy, and, at the same time, of numbing us to the human reality of that which disturbs us.

A people suffering from institutions that can't respond, problems that are virtually left untouched, and the myriad uncertainties of their own private and public existence must inevitably rise in protest. That is just what is happening in America. Frustration breeds anger, and anger has increasingly become a feature of our national life. Even people on the streets and in stores seem more easily provoked and more sullen. The most widespread reaction is a demand for change, coupled with an increasing dislike and contempt for those responsible for the present. Few people can be expected to have any clear idea of the direction that change should take. The problems are too far-reaching and profound. So they look for leadership. And precisely at this point in our history we lack the necessary leadership . . . .

We have always placed certain abstract values—those which cannot be measured or weighed—above economic, logical, or physically tangible goals. Confronted with the overwhelming and uncertain complexities of modern life, and informed by a greatly increased awareness of our limited ability to predict or control the forces loosed by our obsessive industry and invention, we must add to the list of such values. They have traditionally included not only the rights mentioned in the Bill of Rights and allied civil liberties but equality of opportunity, the freedom to develop individual talent, and, more recently, freedom from starvation and destitution. And all these, imperfectly realized though they may be, still exert a powerful hold on our national thinking and shape our political rhetoric and policy. I have no wish to coin a new set of slogans, but certainly the individual must also have the freedom to share in those public decisions which affect his private life beyond merely casting a vote in periodic elections. This does not mean a plebiscite on every problem but, rather, a distinct prejudice in favor of community and neighborhood control. We should also be guided by a desire to preserve freedom from isolation, which means, at least, that environmental decisions should be shaped to re-create the possibilities of community and neighborhood life. It is equally important that the individual be given freedom to participate in the important enterprises of our society, from working in the underdeveloped world to improving the life of the ghettos. If citizens are to find a purpose beyond their daily lives, it will come from having a personal share in important public causes, and the causes must be large and worthy enough to tap moral will and energy. Only in this way can we combat the increasing isolation and remoteness that are eroding the moral drive of our society.

Much of this resolves itself into a widening of one of the oldest staples of political language: freedom of choice. For all the talk about our permissive society, that freedom has steadily narrowed. In fact, much of the release of inhibitions on private behavior is surely a reaction to the confinements imposed by our ideology and social structure. (Successful revolutions tend to be puritanical.) When a young man sees no alternative to spending his youth in a classroom and his manhood in a modern suburb, he may want to assert himself by growing a beard. Conversely, the students who turned out to work for McCarthy cut their hair and shaved not because of adult dictates but through self-organization and self-discipline. They were involved in something more important than this kind of assertion. These are trivial things, but they are tokens of the fact that much frantic liberation of private behavior is a futile effort to alter or escape the hardening mold that envelops social man. We virtually demand, for example, that a young man go to college, and beyond, if he is to have a job that uses his abilities. At one time, a boy could go to sea or go West or start working in a factory and still aspire to success in a wide range of demanding tasks. The fact is that a lot of young men would develop more fully outside the regular educational system. The answer is not simply providing more and better schools but making alternative institutions, training, and experience available, and making them acceptable to those who guard the gates to achievement. Similarly, by huddling industry, commerce, and even intellectual life together in great urban areas we have seriously limited the kinds of places in which a man can live. Much of this is a product of the obsessive urge toward system and order, and of the fact that as systems grow larger they swiftly outpace the individual imagination or intelligence and assume a conforming life of their own. It is almost as if our society were afflicted with some kind of compulsive neatness, which it equated with efficiency or high purpose.

The fact is that organizational neatness and central control not only limit human scope but are often inefficient. Government programs break down or prove inadequate not merely because they are badly conceived but because the problems they seek to deal with are far too large for the limited abilities of a few administrators. Even a genius philosopher-king equipped by I.B.M. could not hope to deal with the varied complexities of dozens of American cities. Central direction is inefficient in a more profound way, too. Given human nature in the context of our society, such oppressive structures are bound to breed discontent. This discontent necessarily impairs our ability to solve problems and maintain traditional values. Restless and unhappy people cannot easily be persuaded to join in enterprises of high purpose, especially those involving sacrifice.

Unless we are to move toward repression, the political platform of the future must contain words still alien to serious public dialogue—words such as "community," "power," and "purpose." This does not mean we will no longer worry about matters like economic policy and defense. For large elements of our population, economic questions are still critical, although they are increasingly fused with other desires. However, since poverty or a low standard of living is not the root of much of our unhappiness, wealth and its distribution do not point the way toward a solution. Words like "community," "power," and "purpose" seem rather abstract and vague, but then so do more traditional goals, such as "liberty" and "opportunity." And, like these more familiar terms, they can be given concrete content, yielding specific and tangible programs. Effective government action toward these ends will respond to the demands of the subject matter, and not to any master plan for their attainment, just as devotion to liberty does not tell you what kind of speech can be restricted or whether the State Department can limit travel to Cuba. Without trying to anticipate a report by a future Presidential task force, I would like to discuss some specific examples, simply to show that they do exist.

Many of the programs designed to re-create community will concern the physical environment, although the power to act as a community and the consequent sense of shared purpose are also critical. This will require that we concentrate not on the quantity of construction but on assembling the components of daily living within an area that a man can comprehend and easily traverse. Along with housing should go hospitals and government services, recreation and meeting centers, parks, and, to the extent that this is possible, places of work. This does not mean breaking up our cities but restoring the concept of neighborhood under modern conditions—a place where a man can live with other men. Some of this is happening by itself under pressures of growth, as shopping centers move to the suburbs and industry seeks sites outside the city. This beginning can proliferate and expand through programs ranging from tax incentives for businesses resettling in residential areas to the construction of new satellite cities. Much can be done, for example, simply by changing and enforcing zoning ordinances, building codes, and tax laws, without a cent of public expenditure. There is a lot more to community than this. Its roots go into the powerful cementing emotions of pride, belonging, friendship, and shared concern, yet these, in turn, depend on the physical possibilities. Not only is it within our power to create those possibilities but it is probably a more practical course than our present unthinking and hopelessly scattered mixture of government programs and private enterprise.

Increasing the individual's power over the conditions of his life involves the blended methods of transferring authority, creating it where it does not exist, and lessening the coercive weight of the state. At other times, I have discussed the need for decentralizing the operations of government—allowing communities, private groups, cities, and states to make public decisions that are now vested in the central government. Although the Constitution contains a prescriptive mandate for a federal system, the actual distribution of authority and responsibility has been worked out over two centuries and is constantly changing. Today, for example, the federal government exerts a power over the economy that would have been inconceivable only a few decades ago. Decentralization is another remodelling of the federal system, and to achieve it will require a patient pragmatism. The state may be the logical unit for dealing with river pollution, the metropolitan area for transportation programs, the neighborhood for schools and even post offices. *The general guide should be to transfer power to the smallest unit consistent with the scale of the problem.* Many conservatives have welcomed the idea of decentralization, hearing in it comforting echoes of old battle cries about states' rights. They are mistaken, for decentralization, if it is to work, will require even larger public programs and even more money for public needs. Otherwise, the momentum on which local interest and involvement depend will be lost. Nor does decentralization mean the absence of rigorous national standards for the use of national revenues. For example, money given for education must in fact be used for education open to all. Such standards are necessary to protect citizens against unresponsive government, and local government against the pressures of private interests. Of course, even with decentralization, most people will not actually make decisions. Still, those who do make them will be within reach of their fellow-residents of the community, and thus will be far more familiar and readily accessible than federal officials. This, in itself, will yield at least the potential of influence and effective protest, which may be as close as we can come to the ideal of the town meeting.

Power is conferred in other ways: by a government that feels compelled to explain its policies and intentions with candor, that seeks the counsel of informed private groups and citizens, and that adheres to an honorable observance of the separation of powers. It will also be yielded by increased citizen control over the private institutions and processes that often determine the quality of our private lives. It is incredible, for example, that private builders, acting out of purely economic considerations, should be allowed to determine the shape of our urban environment—that individuals unresponsive to the public will should decide how the public will live. In addition, the expanding machinery of secret police, investigation, bugging, and wire-tapping must be halted and dismantled. Fear and suspicion are the most paralyzing agents of all, and the most likely to provoke unrest. . . .

THE SHAKY FUTURE OF LOCAL GOVERNMENT

Scott Greer

Scott Allen Greer is Professor of Political Science and Sociology and Director of the Center for Metropolitan Studies at Northwestern University.

We have, in terms of technological and economic capabilities, the power to do anything we want with our cities. But we do not have a policy capable of deciding in unambiguous and effective terms what it is that we want. This political incapacity derives from the inescapable dilemmas of power distribution that have been built into the American system of local governments. And the dilemma of power distribution is what a considerable portion of the urban crisis is all about.

History, according to Robert McIver, is largely the story of conflict between the larger and the smaller community. McIver, writing before World War I with an evolutionary background of thought, saw the larger community always winning in the long run: from increasing interdependence among local groups evolves the dominant center, for one must coordinate behavior if people are truly independent. The next-door neighbor cannot be allowed to poison the water supply.

But Emile Durkheim, looking at this proposition from a democratic socialist point of view, underlined the great danger. If there are no groups with real power between the individual and the state, the individual is helpless and the result is tyranny. Therefore Durkheim urged the creation and maintenance of separate power centers which may represent the individual against the state. Then, because he saw how easily such groups may also tyrannize, he urged the state act as counterbalance. Out of the tensions between sub-group (city, labor union, corporation) and the nation-state, he saw the possibilities for maximizing and protecting individual freedom.

"The Shaky Future of Local Government" in *Psychology Today* (August 1968), pp. 64-69. Reprinted from *Psychology Today* Magazine, August 1968. Copyright © Communications/Research/Machines/Inc.

American politics, and the politics of the American city, are concrete applications of Durkheim's theory. We have systematically divided power between state and local governments. We have also, and importantly, divided power between the freely choosing individual or group (maximizing their chances as best they can) and the public purpose, whether at municipal, state or local level. In short, we have encouraged a plethora of sub-groups between individual and nation-state. In the process we encourage not only areas of potential innovation and leadership, but coercive veto groups. We have built in conservatism. Thus the very limited kinds of government American cities get are no accidents. The dialectic of city government goes thus: Limit discretion and you limit action; allow discretion and you allow the opportunity for chicanery and the corruption of purpose. Protect interests by checks and balances, and you increase the probability of stalemate. Too many cooks not only spoil the stew—they may prevent its ever being assembled in the pot.

Consequently, the fiasco of a national program such as Urban Renewal must be seen as chiefly a *political* failure. Splitting powers between cities and national agencies, between public purpose and private marketplace, Urban Renewal turns out to be a super rivers-and-harbors bill, or a conventional American movement to "beautify downtown" (at whose expense and for what purpose seldom are questions raised by the actors involved).

Our local democracies, our cities, are the arenas of politics most accessible to the individual citizen, and they are the areas most easily studied by the social scientist. What do we know about them? Some cities are weak in their formal governmental power, fragmented and conflicted in formal terms, but strong in their political structure. Chicago is a case in point; the Democratic machine makes possible government where it is theoretically improbable if not impossible. Other cities are strong in their governmental powers but practically impotent because of the weakness of their political system; many new cities of the West Coast and Southwest are cases in point. And many lie in between.

A recent study by Claire Gilbert of Florida Atlantic University gives us a summary picture, not of all American city political structures, but of all that have been studied. Using the 167 studies in "Community Power Structure" in the United States, she was able to make certain conclusions despite the variation in background of the observer, quality of research, and nature of the city studied.

Using the data-quality-control technique, she concluded that *most* small towns studied were dominated by the formally elected political officials; most of the towns ranging from 20,000 to 50,000 population were dominated by non-political persons or coalitions between such persons and elected officials, while most cities of real size were ruled, not by a sinister power elite lurking behind the arras, but by the men who held formal political office and power. Thus the American image of the city government as, in Marx's terms, "the executive committee of the *bourgeoisie*" applies precisely to the outmoded American city, the city of *Main Street*.

But government of the small towns is chiefly housekeeping government, with major decisions postponed indefinitely. As Arthur Vidich and Joseph Bensman show, in their study of *Small Town in Mass Society*, the purpose of local government is to maintain a *status quo*, while all real forces affecting the community are generated far from its boundaries—in Albany, Washington or New York City. Local government is of little practical interest to the citizens.

In the small cities there is contact and coalition between elected officials and the "non-political" economic and organizational leaders. Under such circumstances it is possible to aggregate enough consent, among those representing enough interests, to use the powers of government positively. They may be used in ways one does not approve, of course; the point is that power can be used.

In the great cities, our metropolitan complexes, mapping the power grid is a much more complex matter. There is first, of course, the complex maze of formal jurisdictions; "too many governments and not enough government" is the slogan. The old center city from which the complex takes its name usually includes less than half the population of the metropolitan area; the rest lives in the suburbs and in the unincorporated fringe. There is no government for the metropolis as a whole.

I have said that the great cities are governed by elected officials. It is more correct to say that what government occurs passes through their hands, yet how much they can initiate and execute is problematic. Because of the near unbeatable Democratic organization in Chicago, Mayor Richard Daley has considerable power, yet as Edward Banfield argues, he may use it only at a cost, and he generally prefers to endorse whatever the major forces from outside impinge upon the city, as with pressure and bribes (grants) from Washington, one may see action. And, when scandal of such proportions as to threaten the party breaks, when police officers are hiring burglars and sharing the loot, one may see action. The government of Chicago is primarily a response mechanism, not an initiator.

When one turns to other politically less organized cities, the situation is even more ambiguous. In New York, according to Wallace Sayre and Herbert Kaufman, there is not even a real job for the Mayor as referee among contending interests. Nor can he wield the patronage power available to Daley, for the great bureaucracies have developed near complete autonomy from the general government of the city. His major power lies in his newsworthiness: he can project his own image and his concerns and aspirations for the city through the great magnifier, the mass media. . . .

The cost of a reactive, rather than an active, government is obvious and it is high. It means that prevention of ills, planning of long-term improvements—even a coherent image of what the city is and should be—are impossible. It is a view of government as broker among conflicting interests—not of government as expressing the common purpose of the citizenry. In the past we could afford it, at least in the sense that our cities have survived and many citizens have prospered.

Perhaps we can continue with do-nothing local governments. But, if there is no radical change in American urban government (and I do not expect it in the near future); if we continue to operate within the frozen framework of our political culture and our legal structure; I see this future. Major conflicts within the city between Negroes and Whites, between the vested interests of labor unions and public bureaucracies, between the prosperous and the poor, will continue and indeed the fever will rise. Mayors of Lindsay's talent will do their best to ameliorate, temporize, buy time. But time for what? Essentially, time to be bailed out by the national government.

Meanwhile, in many of our great cities there will be a quiet revolution. City Hall will go black. In the process, Negroes will have formal political power, patronage and, most important, *symbolic representation* in the power elite. The big screen will be available, the megaphone of the press, the charisma of office. Our public landscape as reflected in the media rarely includes Negroes as anything other than "problems" to be solved. As problem solvers they may look better to the indifferent, scared or hostile Whites, *who are the major social problem of American society*. Thus I consider the elections of last Fall in Gary and Cleveland a sign of hope—not because they show a breakdown in bigotry among Whites, for they do not. What they show is that our inability to re-form the boundaries of our cities has created an opportunity for Negroes to gain major political power where it counts, and that they are able and willing to do so.

There are, however, two developing trends which must be considered. Neither points to radical, short-term change, but each suggests some alternatives to do-nothing government. The first of these is, simply, the increasing professionalization and bureaucratization of local government. It is the concrete expression of that American yearning to take politics out of government which so degrades our public life. Yet it also reflects the sheer increase in organizational scale of the society as a whole and the cities within it. The command posts of large city government require highly qualified people; the decisions to be made with respect to traffic planning or the abolition of poverty are just too complex and technical for the "average citizen" to have a responsible opinion. Even the Mayor is, typically, endorsing or rejecting programs which he may understand only in terms of their short-run usefulness for his regime.

Thus we are moving towards the administrative state, the administered city. Not so much because of the active thrust for power among the bureaucrats as because of the functional requirements of large-scale government. And indeed, in my more pessimistic moments, I sometimes believe that the country would be in better shape to face its problems if we abolished local democracy altogether, putting decision-making at the state and national levels, and running the cities with men from elsewhere appointed by the higher-level governments. The danger, of course, is the one Durkheim points out: to remove the groups that protect citizens from a national government agency is to gamble individual rights. . . .

A second important trend in our cities is the burgeoning of neighborhood and community organizations. It is an old tradition, growing out of the concentration of those with similar life style and life chances in given areas; we find it in the activities of Jane Addams and the other pioneers of the "settlement house movement." It had fallen into disarray during the '40s and '50s, largely because of the surge of prosperity in the United States and the acculturation of most immigrant groups to the lower middle-class American culture. Its rebirth was due in part to liberals such as Saul Alinsky, searching for a more direct and radical mode of attacking the problems of the powerless. It has been greatly accelerated by the increased awareness among those excluded from the affluent society—Negroes, Puerto Ricans, Mexicans, rural migrants and the other poor—that they are indeed outsiders.

Such organization works best, as Alinsky notes, when it is focused on an enemy. And enemies are available in plenty for the urban poor. (It should not be forgotten that neighborhoods of the more prosperous can be organized in a similar way *against* the poor, to keep them out.) Thus some of the strength of the "Back of the Yards" movement was the fear among Polish residents that the Negroes would move in as the area declined.

Let it not be forgotten that, when one organizes *against*, he is generating and structuring intergroup hostility.

What are the consequences of such organization? There is, first, the hope for redevelopment (or at least maintenance at the same level) of the declining neighborhood. While such possibilities are limited, they are real. And this is particularly important when the goal is combined with a confrontation of the race problem—when the effort is made to achieve a stable, integrated neighborhood. As long as such neighborhoods are rare, as long as good neighborhoods which admit Negroes are in such short supply, the long-run promise of such efforts is not great. Only with a quota system could it work, and this has been declared unconstitutional by the Supreme Court.

A more important task for the community organization is what I call the "labor-union function." The local organization can survey and evaluate the goods and services provided in the area by local government; it can represent the citizens before the elected officials; it can arbitrate and negotiate between individuals and the welfare workers, the school administrators and the police. Thus the West Side Organization in Chicago, led by men including those whose background was often in the underworld before they became devoted to the cause of their community, has in the last three years helped over 1,000 welfare recipients in their dealings with the Cook County Department of Public Aid.

The original Economic Opportunity Act included substantial plans and some funds for the encouragement of community organizations. However, it was discovered that such organization was potentially political and, therefore, dangerous to the existing party organizations. These men began working either to: (1) preempt the organization, or (2) prevent it, or (3) destroy it if it existed. We might consider the costs of community organization. I have already noted their potential for creating and structuring intergroup hostility. While this may have healthy side-effects, as in the increase of self-respect among the insulted and injured of the society, it may also accelerate the tendency towards intergroup violence in the city. It may create a small order within the immediate community at the cost of greater disorder in the city. And if it is effective, we might very well face the impingement of power groups, made up of ignorant and, in the larger sense, irresponsible people, upon the educational, welfare and police functions of the society. Nobody can countenance a school board which refuses to allow Darwin's theory to be taught; by the same token, one cannot allow radicals, black or white, to rewrite American history for polemical reasons.

We have some data on a nation which has really tried participatory democracy on a large scale. The Yugoslavian system of local government gives separate representation not only to neighborhoods, but also to age groups, to ethnic groups, to the workers in factories, and many others. The individual belongs to many cross-cutting organizations which are democratically controlled; thus plant managers are appointed and serve at the pleasure of an executive committee of workers, as in our city-manager governments. The results are, of course, more participation. But there is still less than one would have expected and there are certain costs: (1) the situation builds uncertainty and therefore anxiety into the role of, say, manager; (2) one can only have so much uncertainty if a system is to function (and if managers are to stay sane); (3) therefore one moves toward preemption of the executive board by the manager—or staff domination. But there is, at any rate, a residue of power for the individual to fall back upon in his confrontation with administrative rule; perhaps this is the most that can be expected of participatory democracy.

A more important cost the Yugoslavian system has in common with our own community organizations is that the subgroups fractionate the society. Thus the cleavages in Yugoslavian society, particularly ethnic schisms which are very great, are structured for good by the present arrangement. Yet they are cleavages within a larger order, and perhaps the lesson we could learn is the necessity for some formalization of the hundreds of community organizations in a large metropolis. People belong to a "society" only through their group affiliations. American society is highly race conscious, if not racist; if we believe in local democracy we must expect local groups to express what they are. Thus we should build an organizational framework to contain, arbitrate and organize at a larger level than, say, the West Side Organization. . . .

DECENTRALIZATION FOR WHAT?

Irving Kristol

Irving Kristol is co-editor of The Public Interest. *The article was an expanded version of a paper prepared for a conference by the Rand Corporation on urban problems.*

. . . Americans have never taken questions of public administration too seriously. To do so is to suggest that there may be inherent limitations on the execution of the popular will (and our democratic ideology discourages such a notion) or that the natural capacities of the average American may be inadequate to the detailed tasks of government (a national heresy since the days of Andrew

From "Decentralization for What?" in *The Public Interest*, No. 11 (Spring 1968), pp. 17-25. Copyright © National Affairs, Inc., 1968.

Jackson). But the experience of liberals during the Kennedy Administration was a critical one. Whereas they had previously scoffed at criticisms of "bureaucracy"—by conservatives in general, and businessmen in particular—they soon discovered that there really was such a thing and that its power to thwart or distort social programs was never to be underestimated. Just as most intellectuals only get interested in education when their children start going to school, so the liberal intellectuals around John F. Kennedy suddenly found themselves getting interested in public administration when they discovered that their good ideas and fine intentions got mangled on the way to achieving reality.

The simple fact, they learned, is that the number of programs the political and sociological imagination is capable of inventing always exceeds the number of available people who can realize these programs *as intended.* You always end up with programs being carried out by a bureaucratic hierarchy that understands them only imperfectly and possibly may not even be much interested in them at all.

So it became proper for liberals to talk about the problems of "bureaucracy" and of "centralization," and many started doing so. As a matter of fact "decentralization" has in general become a very fashionable idea. Thus, where political scientists used to argue that municipal government was incapable of coping with the problems of the city and that larger, more comprehensive metropolitan governments were needed, this argument has suddenly been reversed. In his recent presidential address to the American Political Science Association, Robert Dahl pointed out that the population of New York City is about the same as that of Sweden, and that New York is "badly in need of being broken up into smaller units for purposes of local government." Indeed, Professor Dahl took a dim view of any unit of local government that encompasses more than 200,000 souls.

So far, so good. We have become keenly aware—and it's about time, too—of the deficiencies of overly centralized planning and overly centralized government. We are all decentralists now. But, unfortunately, liberal intellectuals do seem to have an uncanny knack for focusing on the right problem at the wrong time, and in the wrong way. They have opted for decentralization with the same kind of enthusiastic abstractness they once brought to centralization. They have slighted, when they have not entirely ignored, the supreme political consideration—circumstance. For, as Edmund Burke long ago observed, "Circumstances. . . give in reality to every political principle its distinguishing colour and discriminating effect. The circumstances are what render every civil and political scheme beneficial or noxious. . . ."

I shall have something to say later about the most significant "circumstance" that today affects (or should affect) our efforts at decentralization. But, first of all, it is worth taking a look at the way the *idea* of decentralization became the *ideology* of decentralization.

We have, during this past decade, witnessed a mounting anxiety about the fate of democracy in a mass, industrialized society. We have simultaneously witnessed a sharp upsurge of populism in American feeling—both on the left and (to a somewhat lesser extent) on the right. A "credibility gap" has emerged which separates the citizen, not merely from any particular administration, but from government itself. As a result, the need for "visible government" (in Mayor Lindsay's phrase) and the importance of "participation" (in just about everyone's phrase) has become widely accepted among social critics and social reformers. The vision of the American people regaining a lost political heritage through a revival of "the town meeting" within our large urban centers has become exceedingly attractive. And, since there is no blinking the fact that ours is a complex and interdependent society, the constituency for such "town meetings" is frequently redefined along "functional" lines, so as to transcend mere locality and encompass all those involved with one governmental program or another. Has not Sargeant Shriver roundly announced that "welfare without representation is tyranny"?

At about the same time, various sociologists, psychologists, anthropologists, and social theorists came to the conclusion that conventional populism was not enough. The people had not merely to be "involved" or "consulted" so as to gain their active consent. The people had to "participate" in their democracy in a very special way—i.e., through "social conflict." What these social critics had in mind was no reconstituted New England town meeting of any kind: *that* was a vehicle for consensus. Rather, they entertained images of mass picketing, rent strikes, organized boycotts of local merchants, harassment of all official bureaucracies, etc. Activities such as these, it was insisted, were necessary to the mental health and spiritual uplift of the people, and especially the poor and dispossessed among them.

Just where this particular ideology came from, and how it achieved its popularity, is an interesting question but, for our purposes, an irrelevant one. (Obviously, it had more to do with an initial animus against the status quo than with any ripe sagacity about the difficulties of public administration in a large democracy.) In any event, it came to be accepted by many eminent authorities and respectable institutions. The Ford Foundation has been a leader in stimulating this novel version of populism. A group of scholars at the Columbia School of Social Work has also played a notable role in sponsoring a neo-populist rebellion against "the welfare establish-ment." The New Left has made it clear that, in its eyes, "participatory democracy" was essentially connected with the class struggle. And black nationalism in the ghettos has learned to insist that true democracy is essentially connected with race conflict, and indeed is quite simply Black Power.

The whole business has by now become a thoroughly confusing tragi-comedy of errors. And no group has been more confused than our governing authorities. Congressmen who voted for Community Action Programs and all sorts of "maximum participa-tion" clauses, thinking they were striking a blow against "bureau-crats" and in favor of "the grass roots," are beginning to wonder what they have wrought. In desperation, they resort to the only kind of defensive action they can think of: indiscriminately cutting the budget for social services.

Meanwhile, the impulse to decentralization, oblivious to its own ideological muddle and blind to circumstance, gathers momentum. The most sensational venture of the "new decentraliza-tion" is the Ford Foundation's program for turning over New York's public schools to locally elected school boards. This is not the occasion to go into a detailed critique of the Ford plan. Suffice it to say that in my opinion—and it is not mine alone—Ford's plan will drive white parents out of integrated (i.e., mixed) neighborhoods, white children out of public schools, and white teachers out of the city altogether. It will have the same effect on many middle-class Negroes. In addition, it will certainly result in inferior education for Negro children in the central city, as experienced white teachers move (or are moved) elsewhere. All this will be accomplished in the name of "decentralization" and "neighborhood self-government"—which, in reality, will mean school boards that polarize and intensify all latent racial and political conflicts in any particular section of the city. . . .

To criticisms of this kind, which have been directed against its plan for reorganizing public education in New York, the Ford Foundation has only one strong rejoinder: the present system doesn't work. It would be more accurate and more candid to say that the system "works" no less well than it ever did, but that it has not been able to cope with lower-class Negroes as it previously coped with, say, lower-class Italians. (Essentially the same thing can be said about our welfare system.) Still, it is clear enough that New York's public education system, even when and where it works, is very efficient in enforcing petty regulations, extremely inefficient in coping with new problems or new opportunities. There is indeed, then, *in the abstract*, a valid case for decentralization. But, even in the abstract, what kind of decentralization?

It is always a good idea, when reforming an institution or a program, to take guidance, not only from general principles or preconceived opinions, but from comparable institutions and programs that do seem to work. Now, not all of education in New York City is out of popular favor. The affluent private schools, on the whole, are well regarded by parents, students, and teachers. So are the anything-but-affluent parochial schools, which the majority of Negro parents would be delighted to send their children to, were there room for them. What is it that makes these schools acceptable at the least, desirable at the best?

The answer has nothing to do with these schools being run on principles of local democracy, which they are not. It has everything to do with these schools being run on principles of *delegated authority*. Specifically, the reason these schools "work" better is that they are governed by headmasters who have considerable managerial power, managerial discretion, managerial immunity to outside pressures (*including* parental pressures). From what I have seen of public school principals in New York City, they compare favorably enough to private school headmasters. What they lack is any kind of real power to do a good job.

I am not unaware of the difficulties involved in conceding to them this power. Indeed, the difficulties are just about identical with those the Ford Foundation program is likely to encounter, but with the tumult swirling around the choice of principal instead of the school board. In any case, I am not here interested in arguing the case for one particular kind of educational reform as against another. I wish only to stress a significant, and frequently misconceived, point: decentralization is one thing, democracy is another. The government of Sweden is far more decentralized than the government of New York City, but it is not thereby more democratic. Indeed, the Swedish government is probably *less* democratic than is New York's—and better governed.

Or, to put it another way: *decentralization, if it is to work, must create stronger local authorities, not weaker ones. Effective decentralization does not diffuse authority; it takes the power that is diffused throughout a large bureaucracy and concentrates it into new nuclei of authority.* Before we commit ourselves to any scheme of decentralization, we ought to make certain that this particular reconstitution of authority is what we really want. And I find it instructive to note that many of those who favor radical decentralization of education in our Northern urban regions are simultaneously demanding the extension of federal bureaucratic controls over education in the South.

In the United States today, the key "circumstance" that ought to affect one's attitude toward decentralization is the

relationship between black and white—the present racial tensions we dare not ignore, the future integration we dare not despair of. Every reforming enterprise must, first of all and above all, take its bearings from this circumstance. It is always useful to inquire to what extent we can decentralize our cumbersome service bureaucracies (in education, welfare, housing, perhaps even policing). But it is even more useful to inquire to what extent we can decentralize our services *without fractioning our heterogeneous political community*. I am not saying that, under present circumstances, such decentralization is always undesirable. I am saying simply that we must always ask *whether* it is, in the light of these circumstances.

Indeed, were it not for the racial heterogeneity of this nation, the organization of our social services would be a relatively superficial problem. Politicians, of course, might kick up a big fuss about one thing or another. But whichever way the issue were resolved, it wouldn't make all that amount of difference. Take education, for instance. To begin with, were it not for the race issue, it might not be widely regarded as a "problem" at all. (In the all-white neighborhoods of Brooklyn, Queens, and Staten Island there isn't even as much dissatisfaction with the New York public school system as, in my opinion, there ought to be.) Second, if one wished to experiment with various forms of "decentralization," one easily could—whatever controversies they engendered would not be more damaging than, say, present controversies in smaller communities over local school board issues. (In these controversies, feelings run high—but only temporarily.) Third, one could even contemplate experimenting with quite radical reforms that go beyond "decentralization"—such as extending "consumer sovereignty" to the educational sector by abolishing "free" schools and distributing educational expenditures (in either cash or vouchers) to parents, who could then shop for schools as they please. The important thing is that, whatever was tried or not tried, whatever worked or didn't work, would not seriously affect the shape of the American republic or its ultimate destiny.

But we *are* a racially heterogeneous nation. And we *are* committed to creating a racially integrated society. This fact and this commitment are—and ought to be—dominant in our minds. It is therefore of great importance that the major impulses toward "decentralization" now come from the white segregationists in the South and the black nationalists (together with their white, radical allies) in the North. Should these impulses prevail, the task of molding this country into one nation will be made infinitely more difficult, and perhaps impossible. The statesman's responsibility is to resist these impulses where he can, to "contain" them where he cannot resist. "Decentralization," in practice, has come too often to mean the hasty "appeasement" of these tendencies.

There are two further—and not unimportant points—to be made:

1. "Decentralization" is not likely to solve any of the problems of education in our Northern ghettos.

The sociological evidence seems to be conclusive that the schools themselves have only a partial—maybe only marginal—impact on broad educational achievements. What we glibly call the "problem of education in the ghetto" is probably little more than an aspect of the problem of poverty. Though a devoted, imaginative, and inspiring teacher can always make a difference, in any school, any time, there's not much point in asserting that what the ghetto needs is masses of such teachers: they just don't exist in the mass. Nor is there any evidence that changes in the curriculum matter much; or new school buildings as against old; or even smaller classes as against larger ones. What does count is the environment, as established by home and community. The basic fact is that middle-class Negroes, living in middle-class neighborhoods (whether integrated or not), do *not* have a "crisis in education." Centering one's attention on the schools is an effective way of distracting one's attention from the far more important realities of poverty and discrimination.

One can understand why residents of the slums should be tempted to make the schools scapegoats for all of their frustrations. One can even understand—though with less tolerance—why government officials should join in this witch hunt, denouncing the schools for failing to achieve what no schools can achieve. But it is less easy to understand why social scientists in general should wish to participate in this demagogic campaign. Perhaps they do so for the same reason right-wing groups also tend to make the school a center of controversy: they feel impotent to engender controversy about anything else.

2. It is an accidental fact, but an important one, that *our large and cumbersome bureaucracies, in such fields as education, welfare, and in the civil service generally, happen to play a crucial role in integrating large numbers of middle-class Negroes into American society*. These bureaucracies are, in truth, the best-integrated sectors of American society. To this end, they "work" exceedingly well. Decentralization of these bureaucracies will almost certainly mean disintegrating them. We shall end up with only Negro teachers in Negro schools, only Negro police in Negro neighborhoods, only Negro social workers handling Negro clients, etc. That, in my view, would be a major step backward. . . .

Decentralizing these bureaucracies remains a valid and important long-term objective. But in these times, under these circumstances, it is precisely the wrong objective.

THE SICKNESS OF GOVERNMENT

Peter F. Drucker

Mr. Drucker is a lecturer, management consultant, and author of a number of books and articles.

Government surely has never been more prominent than today. The most despotic government of 1900 would not have dared probe into the private affairs of its citizens as income tax collectors now do routinely in the freest society. Even the tsar's secret police did not go in for the security investigations we now take for granted. Nor could any bureaucrat of 1900 have imagined the questionnaires that governments now expect businesses, universities, or citizens to fill out in ever-mounting number and ever-increasing detail. At the same time, government has everywhere become the largest employer in the society.

Government is certainly all-pervasive. But is it truly strong? Or is it only big?

There is mounting evidence that government is big rather than strong; that it is fat and flabby rather than powerful; that it costs a great deal but does not achieve much. There is mounting evidence also that the citizen less and less believes in government and is increasingly disenchanted with it. Indeed, government is sick—and just at the time when we need a strong, healthy, and vigorous government.

There is obviously little respect for government among the young—but the adults, the taxpayers, are also increasingly disenchanted. They want still more services from government. But they are everywhere approaching the point where they balk at paying for a bigger government, even though they may still want what government promises to give.

The disenchantment with government cuts across national boundaries and ideological lines. It is as prevalent in Communist as in democratic societies, as common in white as in nonwhite countries. This disenchantment may well be the most profound discontinuity in the world around us. It marks a sharp change in mood and attitude between this generation and its predecessors. For seventy years or so—from the 1890's to the 1960's—mankind, especially in the developed countries, was hypnotized by government. We were in love with it and saw no limits to its abilities, or to its good intentions. Rarely has there been a more torrid political love affair than that between government and the generations that reached manhood between 1918 and 1960. Anything that anyone felt needed doing during this period was to be turned over to government—and this, everyone seemed to believe, made sure that the job was already done.

The Fabians in Great Britain or the German Social Democrats started their love affair with government before 1900. It became general with World War I when government, using taxation and the printing press, had mobilized social resources way beyond what anyone earlier would have thought possible. When the Great Depression hit, a decade later, everyone immediately turned to government as the savior. It is pathetic to recall the naïve belief that prevailed in the late 1930's—such, for instance, as was preached in one of the best-sellers of the depression years, *To Plan or Not to Plan*, by the British Labour economist Barbara Wooton. The book's author, honored by the British government with a life peerage as Lady Wooton, is still alive and active; but nothing is more remote from us today, or less appealing, than the messianic innocence of this fervent love letter to government. All it says, and it says it on every page, is: "Utopia is here—all that's needed is to take everything away from the wicked, selfish interests and to turn it over to government." World War II reinforced this belief. Again, government proved itself incredibly effective in organizing the energies of society for warfare.

Disenchantment

But now our attitudes are in transition. We are rapidly moving to doubt and distrust of government and, in the case of the young, even to rebellion against it. We still, if only out of habit, turn social tasks over to government. We still revise unsuccessful programs over and over again, and assert that nothing is wrong with them that a change in procedures or a "competent administrator" will not cure.

But we no longer really believe these promises when we reform a bungled program for the third time. Who, for instance, any longer believes that administrative changes in the foreign aid program of the United States (or of the United Nations) will really produce rapid world-wide development? Who really believes that the War on Poverty will vanquish poverty in the cities? Who in France believes that one more commission on administrative reform will really change the system? Or who, in Russia, really believes that a new program of incentives will make the collective farm productive?

We still repeat the slogans of yesteryear. Indeed, we still act on them. But we no longer believe in them. We no longer expect results from government. What was torrid romance between the people and government for so very long has now become a tired, middle-aged liaison which we do not quite know how to break off but which only becomes exacerbated by being dragged out.

What explains this disenchantment with government?

We expected miracles—and that always produces disillusionment. Government, it was widely believed (though only subconsciously) would produce a great many things for nothing. Cost was thought to be a function of who did something rather than of what was being attempted. There is little doubt, for instance, that the British, in adopting the "free health service," believed that medical care would cost nothing. All that such a health service can be, of course, is a form of "pre-paid" medical care. Nurses, doctors, hospitals, drugs, and so on have to be paid for by somebody. But everybody expected this "somebody" to be somebody else. At the least, everyone expected that under a "free" health service the taxes of the rich would pay for the health care of the poor. But there never are enough rich people around to carry the burden of any general service.

All such plans are, in effect, taxation and compulsory saving that force the individual to pay for something whether he wants it or not. This is their whole rationale, and it is not necessarily a bad rationale. But the illusion persisted that government could somehow make costs go away and produce a great deal for nothing—or at the expense of only an affluent minority.

Abolishing "Vested Interests"

This belief has been, in effect, only one facet of a much more general illusion from which the educated and the intellectuals in particular have suffered: that by turning tasks over to government, conflict and decision would be made to go away. Once the "wicked private interests" had been eliminated, a decision as to the right course of action would be rational and automatic. There would be neither selfishness nor political passion. Belief in government was thus largely a romantic escape from politics and from responsibility.

One root of this argument was a hatred of business, of profit, and, above all, of wealth. That motives other than the desire for monetary gain could underlie self-interests and that values other than financial values could underlie conflict did not occur to the generation of the 1930's. Theirs was a world in which economics seemed to be the one obstacle to the millennium. Power did not appear in their vision—though this blindness in the decade of Hitler and Stalin is hard to imagine, let alone to understand. C. P. Snow's description in *The Masters* (1951) of the conflict for power within the "self-less" and "disinterested" small community of an Oxbridge college profoundly shocked the sensibilities of a generation that had grown up believing that conflicts were always motivated by economic self-interest and could be avoided by eliminating gain, that is, by nationalizing the economy.

One need not be in favor of free enterprise—let alone a friend of wealth—to see the fallacy in this argument. But reason had little to do with the belief in government ownership as the panacea. The argument was simply: "private business and profits are bad—*ergo* government ownership must be good." We may still believe in the premise; but we no longer accept the *"ergo."* Thus, the Labour government felt committed in 1967 to renationalize the British steel industry (just at the time when, ironically, the industry was on the verge of long-term decline, and when, therefore, take-over by government meant the highest possible windfall profit for the shareholders). But it immediately declared that the industry would have to be run for profit. It put in as chief executive the purest of arch-capitalists, Lord Melchett, heir to one of the world's greatest industrial fortunes (his grandfather and father founded and built Imperial Chemical Industries), a hereditary peer and a top-flight investment banker, in addition to being a life-long Tory! By contrast, less than twenty years earlier, when steel was first nationalized in Britain by an earlier Labour government, an ideologically "pure" trade-union stalwart had been the chief-executive-designate.

There is still a good deal of resistance to the responsibility of politics, and resentment of the burden of political decision. Indeed, the young today want to "drop out" altogether—in a frightening revival of the hostility to responsibility that made an earlier young generation, forty years ago, so receptive to totalitarian promises and slogans. But no one, least of all the young, believes any longer that the conflicts, the decisions, the problems would be eliminated by turning things over to government. Government, on the contrary, has itself become one of the wicked "vested interests" for the young.

A Case of Nonperformance

The greatest factor in the disenchantment with government is that government has not performed. The record over these last thirty or forty years has been dismal. Government has proven itself capable of doing only two things with great effectiveness. It can wage war. And it can inflate the currency. Other things it can promise, but only rarely accomplish. Its record as an industrial manager, in the satellite countries of Eastern Europe as well as in the nationalized industries of Great Britain, has been unimpressive. Whether private enterprise would have done worse is not even relevant. For we expected near-perfection from government as industrial manager. Instead we only rarely obtained even below-average mediocrity.

Government as a planner has hardly done much better (whether in Communist Czechoslovakia or in de Gaulle's capitalist France). But the greatest disappointment, the great letdown, is the fiasco of the welfare state. Not many people would want to do without the social services and welfare benefits of an affluent, modern, industrial society. But the welfare state promised to do far more than to provide social services. It promised to create a new and happy society. It promised to release creative energies. It promised to do away with ugliness and envy and strife. No matter how well it is doing its jobs—and in some areas, in some countries, some jobs are being done very well—the welfare state turns out at best to be just another big insurance company, as exciting, as creative, and as inspiring as insurance companies tend to be. This explains why President Johnson's spectacular performance in enacting the unfinished welfare tasks of the New Deal failed to make him a hero with the public.

The best we get from government in the welfare state is competent mediocrity. More often we do not even get that; we get incompetence such as we would not tolerate in an insurance company. In every country, there are big areas of government administration where there is no performance whatever—only costs. This is true not only of the mess of the big cities, which no government—United States, British, Japanese, or Russian—has been able to handle. It is true in education. It is true in transportation. And the more we expand the welfare state, the less capable even of routine mediocrity does it seem to become.

I do not know whether Americans are particularly inept at public administration—though they are hardly particularly gifted for it. Perhaps, we are only more sensitive than other people to incompetence and arrogance of bureaucracy because we have had, until recently, comparatively so much less of it than other people. In any case, we are now appalled to realize that, during the past three decades, federal payments to the big cities have increased almost a hundred-fold for all kinds of programs, whereas results from this incredible dollar-flood are singularly unimpressive. What *is* impressive is the administrative incompetence. We now have ten times as many government agencies concerned with city problems as we had in 1939. We have increased by a factor of a thousand or so the number of reports and papers that have to be filled out before anything can be done in the city. Social workers in New York City spend some 70 or 80 percent of their time filling out papers for Washington, for the state government in Albany, and for New York City. No more than 20 or 30 per cent of their time, that is, almost an hour and a half a day, is available for their clients, the poor. As James Reston reported in *The New York Times* (November 23, 1966), there were then 170 different federal aid programs on the books, financed by over 400 separate appropriations and administered by 21 federal departments and agencies aided by 150 Washington bureaus and over 400 regional offices. One Congressional session alone passed 20 health programs, 17 new educational programs, 15 new economic development programs, 12 new programs for the cities, 17 new resource development programs, and 4 new manpower training programs, each with its own administrative machinery.

This is not perhaps a fair example—even of American administrative incompetence. That we speak of "urban crisis," when we face a problem of race, explains a lot of our troubles. But in other areas, the welfare state has not performed much better. Nor is the administrative mess a peculiarly American phenomenon. The daily press in Great Britain, in Germany, in Japan, in France, in Scandinavia—and increasingly in the Communist countries as well—reports the same confusion, the same lack of performance, the same proliferation of agencies, of programs, of forms—and the same triumph of accounting rules over results. Everywhere, rivalry between various agencies is replacing concern with results and with responsibility. . . .

What Government Can Be

The purpose of government is to make fundamental decisions, and to make them effectively. The purpose of government is to focus the political energies of society. It is to dramatize issues. It is to present fundamental choices. The purpose of government, in other words, is to govern. This, as we have learned in other institutions, is incompatible with "doing." Any attempt to combine government with "doing" on a large scale paralyzes the decision-making capacity.

There is reason today why soldiers, civil servants, and hospital administrators look to business management for concepts, principles, and practices. For business, during the last thirty years, has had to face, on a much smaller scale, the problem that government now faces: the incompatibility between "governing" and "doing." Business management learned that the two have to be separated, and that the top organ, the decision-maker, has to be detached from "doing." Otherwise he does not make decisions, and the "doing" does not get done either.

In business this goes by the name of "decentralization." The term is misleading. It implies a weakening of the central organ, the top management of a business. The true purpose of decentralization, however, is to make the center, the top management of business, strong and capable of performing the central, the top-management task. The purpose is to make it possible for top management to concentrate on decision-making and direction, to slough off the "doing" to operating managements, each with its own mission and goals, and with its own sphere of action and autonomy.

If this lesson were applied to government, the other institutions of society would then rightly become the "doers." "Decentralization" applied to government would not be just another form of "federalism" in which local rather than central government discharges the "doing" tasks. It would rather be a systematic policy of using the other, *the nongovernmental* institutions of the society— the hospital as well as the university, business as well as labor unions—for the actual "doing," i.e., for performance, operations, execution.

Such a policy might more properly be called "reprivatization." The tasks that flowed to government in the last century, because the family could not discharge them, would be turned over to the new, nongovernmental institutions that have sprung up and grown these last sixty to seventy years.

Reprivatization

Government would start out by asking the question: "How do these institutions work and what can they do?" It would then ask: "How can political and social objectives be formulated and organized in such a manner as to become opportunities for performance for these institutions?" It would also ask: "And what opportunities for accomplishment of political objectives do the abilities and capacities of these institutions offer to government?"

This would be a very different role for government from that it plays in traditional political theory. In all our theories government is *the* institution. If "reprivatization" were to be applied, however, government would become *one* institution—albeit the central, the top, institution.

Reprivatization would give us a different society from any our *social* theories now assume. In these theories, government does not exist. It is outside of society. Under reprivatization, government would become the central social institution. Political theory and social theory, for the last two hundred and fifty years, have been separate. If we applied to government and to society what we have learned about organization these last fifty years, the two would again come together. The nongovernmental institutions—university, business, and hospital, for instance—would be seen as organs for the accomplishment of results. Government would be seen as society's resource for the determination of major objectives, and as the "conductor" of social diversity.

I have deliberately used the term "conductor." It might not be too fanciful to compare the situation today with the development of music 200 years ago. The dominant musical figure of the early eighteenth century was the great organ virtuoso, especially in the Protestant North. In organ music, as a Buxtehude or a Bach practiced it, one instrument with one performer expressed the total range of music. But as a result, it required almost superhuman virtuosity to be a musician.

By the end of the century, the organ virtuoso had disappeared. In his place was the modern orchestra. There, each instrument played only one part, and a conductor up front pulled together all these diverse and divergent instruments into one score and one performance. As a result, what had seemed to be absolute limits to music suddenly disappeared. Even the small orchestra of Haydn could express a musical range far beyond the reach of the greatest organ virtuoso of a generation earlier.

The conductor himself does not play an instrument. He need not even know how to play an instrument. His job is to know the capacity of each instrument and to evoke optimal performance from each. Instead of "performing," he "conducts." Instead of "doing," he leads.

The next major development in politics, and the one needed to make this middle-aged failure—our tired, overextended, flabby, and impotent government—effective again, might therefore be the reprivatization of the "doing," of the performance of society's tasks. This need not mean "return to private ownership." Indeed what is going on in the Communist satellite countries of Eastern Europe today—especially in Yugoslavia—is reprivatization in which ownership is not involved at all. Instead, autonomous businesses depend on the market for the sale of goods, the supply of labor, and even the supply of capital. That their "ownership" is in the hands of the government is a legal rather than an economic fact—though, of course, an important one. Yet to some Yugoslavs it does not even appear to be incompatible with that ultra-bourgeois institution, a stock exchange.

What matters, in other words, is that institutions not be run by government, but be autonomous. Cooperatives, for instance, are not considered "capitalist" in the Anglo-American countries, although they are "private" in that they are not run by government. And the same applies to "private" hospitals and the "private" universities. On the other hand, the German university has traditionally been almost as autonomous as the American "private" university, even though—as is the case with European universities generally—it is a state institution.

Reprivatization, therefore, may create social structures that are strikingly similar, though the laws in respect to ownership differ greatly from one country to another and from one institution to another. *What they would have in common is a principle of performance rather than a principle of authority.* In all of them the autonomous institution created for the performance of a major social task would be the "doer." Government would become increasingly the decision-maker, the vision-maker. It would try to figure out how to structure a given political objective so as to make it attractive to one of the autonomous institutions. It would, in other words, be the "conductor" that tries to think through what each instrument is best designed to do. And just as we praise a composer for his ability to write "playable" music, which best uses the specific performance characteristic of French horn, violin, or flute, we may come to praise the lawmaker who best structures a particular task so as to make it most congenial for this one or that of the autonomous, self-governing, private institutions of a pluralist society.

The Special Role of Business

Business is likely to be only one—but a very important—institution in such a structure. Whether it be owned by the capitalist, that is, by the investor, or by a cooperative or a government might even become a secondary consideration. For even if owned by government, it would have to be independent of government and autonomous—as the Yugoslavs show—not only in its day-to-day management, but, perhaps more important, in its position in the market, and especially in a competitive capital market.

What makes business particularly appropriate for reprivatization is that it is predominantly an organ of innovation; of all social institutions, it is the only one created for the express purpose of making and managing change. All other institutions were originally created to prevent, or at least to slow down, change. They become innovators only by necessity and most reluctantly.

Specifically, business has two advantages where government has major weaknesses. Business can abandon an activity. Indeed it is forced to do so if it operates in a market—and even more, if it depends on a market for its supply of capital. There is a limit beyond which even the most stubborn businessman cannot argue with the market test, no matter how rich he may be himself. Even Henry Ford had to abandon the Model T when it no longer could be sold. Even his grandson had to abandon the Edsel.

What is more: Of all our institutions, *business is the only one that society will permit to disappear*. It takes a major catastrophe, a war or a great revolution, to allow the disappearance of a university or of a hospital, no matter how superfluous and unproductive they might have become. Again and again, for instance, the Catholic Church in the United States attempts to close down hospitals that have ceased to be useful. In almost every case, a storm of community nostalgia forces the supposedly absolute bishop to retract his decision.

But when the best-known airplane manufacturer in the United States, the Douglas Company, designer and producer of the DC3 was in difficulty in 1967, neither the American public nor American government rushed to its rescue. If a competitor had not bought the company and merged it into his operations, we would have accepted the disappearance of Douglas—with regret, to be sure, and with a good deal of nostalgic rhetoric, but also with the feeling: "It's their own fault, after all."

Precisely because business can make a profit, it *must* run the risk of loss. This risk, in turn, goes back to the second strength of business: alone among all institutions it has a test of performance. No matter how inadequate profitability may be as an indicator, in certain respects, it is a test for all to see. One can argue that this or that obsolete hospital is really needed in the community or that it will one day again be needed. One can argue that even the poorest university is better than none. The alumni or the community always have a "moral duty" to save "dear old Siwash." The consumer, however, is unsentimental. It leaves him singularly unmoved to be told that he has a duty to buy the products of a company because it has been around a long time. The consumer always asks: "And what will the product do for me tomorrow?" If his answer is "nothing," he will see its manufacturer disappear without the slightest regret. And so does the investor.

This is the strength of business as in institution. It is the best reason for keeping it in private ownership. The argument that the capitalist should not be allowed to make profits is a popular one. But the real role of the capitalist is to be expendable. His role is to take risks and to take losses as a result. This role the private investor is much better equipped to discharge than the public one. We want privately owned business precisely because we want institutions that can go bankrupt and can disappear. We want at least one institution that, from the beginning, is adapted to change, one institution that has to prove its right to survival again and again.

If we want a really strong and effective government, therefore, we should want businesses that are not owned by government. We should want businesses in which private investors, motivated by their own self-interest and deciding on the basis of their own best judgment, take the risk of failure. The strongest argument for "private enterprise" is not the function of profit. The strongest argument is the function of loss. Because of it, business is the most adaptable, and the most flexible of the institutions around. Therefore, it is the one best equipped to manage.

International Reprivatization

Reprivatization is still heretical doctrine. But it is no longer heretical practice. Reprivatization is hardly a creed of "fat cat millionaires" when Black Power advocates seriously propose making education in the slums "competitive" by turning it over to private enterprise, competing for the tax dollar on the basis of proven performance in teaching ghetto children. It may be argued that the problems of the Black Ghetto in the American city are very peculiar problems—and so they are. They are extreme malfunctions of modern government. But if reprivatization works in the extreme case, it is likely to work even better in less desperate ones.

One instance of reprivatization in the international sphere is the World Bank. Though founded by governments, it is autonomous. It finances itself directly through selling its own securities on the capital market. The International Monetary Fund, too, is a case of reprivatization. Indeed, if we develop the money and credit system we need for the world economy, we will have effectively reprivatized the creation and management of money and credit that for millennia have been considered the prime attributes of sovereignty.

Again, business is well equipped to become the "doer" in the international sphere. The multinational corporation, for instance, is our best organ for rapid social and economic development. In the Communications Satellite Corporation (COMSAT) we are organizing world-wide communications (another traditional prerogative of the sovereign) as a multinational corporation. A socialist government, the Labour government of Britain, has used reprivatization to bring cheap energy to Britain—in contracts with the multinational oil

companies for the exploration and development of the natural gas
fields under the North Atlantic Ocean. And the multinational
corporation may be the only institution equipped to get performance
where the fragmentation into tribal splinter units, such as in the
"mini-states" of Equatorial Africa, makes performance by government impossible.

But domestically as well as internationally, business is, of
course, only one institution and equipped to do only one task, the
economic one. Indeed it is important to confine business—and every
other institution—to its own task. Reprivatization will, therefore,
entail using other nongovernmental institutions—the hospital, for
instance, or the university—for other, noneconomic "doing" tasks.
Indeed, the design of new nongovernmental, autonomous institutions
as agents of social performance under reprivatization may well
become a central job for tomorrow's political architects.

Toward a New Politics

We do not face a "withering away of the state." On the
contrary, we need a vigorous, a strong, and a very active government.
But we do face a choice between big but impotent government and a
government that is strong because it confines itself to decision and
direction and leaves the "doing" to others. We do not face a "return
of laissez-faire" in which the economy is left alone. The economic
sphere cannot and will not be considered to lie outside the public
domain. But the choices of economy—as well as for all other
sectors—are no longer *either* complete governmental indifference or
complete governmental control. In all major areas, we have a new
choice: an organic diversity in which institutions are used to do what
they are best equipped to do. In this society all sectors are "affected
with the public interest," whereas in each sector a specific
institution, under its own management and dedicated to its own job,
emerges as the organ of action and performance.

This is a difficult and complex structure. Such symbiosis
between institutions can work only if each disciplines itself to strict
concentration on its own sphere and to strict respect for the integrity
of the other institutions. Each, to use again the analogy of the
orchestra, must be content to play its own part. This will come
hardest to government, especially after the last fifty years in which it
had been encouraged in the belief of the eighteenth-century organ
virtuosos that it could—and should—play all parts simultaneously.
But every institution will have to learn the same lesson.

Reprivatization will not weaken government. Indeed, its main
purpose is to restore strength to sick government. We cannot go
much further along the road on which government has been traveling

these last fifty years. All we can get this way is more bureaucracy but not more performance. We can impose higher taxes, but we cannot get dedication, support, and faith on the part of the public. Government can gain greater girth and more weight, but it cannot gain strength or intelligence. All that can happen, if we keep on going the way we have been going, is a worsening sickness of government and growing disenchantment with it. And this is the prescription for tyranny, that is, for a government organized against its own society.

This can happen. It has happened often enough in history. But in a society of pluralist institutions it is not likely to be effective too long. The Communists tried it, and after fifty years have shown—though they have not yet fully learned—that the structure of modern society and its tasks are incompatible with monolithic government. Monolithic government requires absolute dictatorship, which no one has ever been able to prolong much beyond the lifetime of any one dictator.

Ultimately we will need new political theory and probably very new constitutional law. We will need new concepts and new social theory. Whether we will get these and what they will look like, we cannot know today. But we can know that we are disenchanted with government—primarily because it does not perform. We can say that we need, in a pluralist society, a government that can and does govern. This is not a government that "does"; it is not a government that "administers"; it is a government that governs.

DECENTRALIZATION—TO WHOM?

Theodore J. Lowi

Theodore J. Lowi is Associate Professor of Political Science at the University of Chicago.

Americans are by tradition, habit, culture, and ideology fearful of power. Yet they see power only in certain places and not

"Decentralization—To Whom? For What?" in *Midway*, Volume 9, Number 3 (Winter 1969), pp. 45-57. © 1969 by The University of Chicago.

in others. They are prepared to defend themselves against certain kinds of power, but against other kinds of power they provide themselves with no safeguards whatsoever. The primary source of power to Americans—and therefore the direction against which they orient their safeguards—is the state. For more than a century after its founding, the Constitution of the United States was written and interpreted so as to prevent as effectively as possible the development of a strong state. The very word itself tended to be replaced with such euphemisms as "government," "the public sector," and so on, as if to avoid development of undue respect toward *l'état*.

Eventually *l'état* did expand, so that by the middle of the twentieth century the "public sector" equaled in proportionate size that of any of the western European and Commonwealth democracies. But even after the expansion the Americans never ceased worrying about it. Each stage in government expansion came only after lengthy and elaborate constitutional debates in Congress and in the courts. Moreover, each expansion of government power was accompanied by expansions in the mechanisms of representation. The first expansions of Federal power, between 1888 and 1892 and between 1910 and 1914, were accompanied by spectacular social movements—populism and progressivism—each of which was strongly oriented toward enhanced representation. Their goals included congressional reform, direct election of senators, reform in methods of nominating candidates for public office, adoption of the "secret ballot," and so on. Further expansions of government before and during the period of Woodrow Wilson were accompanied by further dramatic reforms in Congress, amending the Constitution to admit female suffrage, drastic reforms in the system of balloting, and major reforms in the structure of local government. During the Roosevelt period, the doctrine of "interest representation" became a dominating force in American political thought. The corporativistic structure of the famous National Recovery Administration (NRA) is but one small example of the effort of political leaders to extend representation as a safeguard against the extension of the state. Since Roosevelt, the expansion of the state has been regular rather than by revolution; and since that time, the expansion of representative devices has been equally regular. Interest representation continues to be seriously demanded in the United States even as demands for it are declining in Europe. Significant advances have been made in suffrage and in methods of nomination. Even more significant reforms have taken place in methods of apportioning population in election districts.

But the state has not merely expanded. The expansion has taken on newer forms that may not be met at all by expansion of the mechanisms of representation. Americans, for example, always look with some consternation upon the Western European democracies because of the degree to which central state administration enters into private processes. The decrees and prefects in France, the aristocratic civil servant governing by discretion in England, the aloof civil servant governing by routine in Germany, the apolitical bureaucracies with their benevolent ombudsman in Sweden all seem too heavy-handed. *Etatism* has negative connotations in the United States because it means administrative intervention. Administration has inevitably and unavoidably expanded in the United States, and it has excited all sorts of efforts to "solve the problem."

The latest cry is for decentralization. Related cries are for "interest representation" and "cooperation" and "partnership" and "creative federalism" by the old left, and for "participatory democracy" and "community action" by the new. All of these cries are related in that their aim is for some means of conserving the creative and directive power of the state without losing the grip of localized popular control on that power. Since these cries are inappropriate, all reforms responding to them are self-defeating.

The Administrative State in the United States

Resistance to the development of centralized and bureaucratized administrative structures in the public sector is a policy upon which most American liberals tend to agree with American conservatives. There has been an almost permanent consensus among political leaders in the United States in favor of expanding the state while dreading expansion of centralized and formal administrative intervention in private affairs. American trade unions have consistently throughout modern history opposed federal intervention in collective bargaining, once the collective bargaining process was established. Farmers have been traditionally in favor of state intervention, but only on the basis of various forms of "cooperation." Most of the new Great Society programs have resulted at one and the same time in a large net expansion of state power and an incredibly intense effort to avoid giving the impression that there has been a net increase in bureaucratic power.

This concern for administrative power in the public sector has been matched by a singular lack of concern for the same thing in the private sector. There may be a large body of criticism concerning the over-centralization of capitalist wealth. There may be widespread recognition that some safeguards must be erected against this kind of "economic power." However, criticisms are rarely directed to the extent to which the "private sector" is now governed by an administrative state.

The rise of the private administrative state began early and has been dramatic. For example, in less than half a century, between 1900 and 1950, administrative employees in the United States increased from below 6 percent to nearly 25 percent of all industrial employees. These rates are comparable to those of Great Britain and Sweden. According to Reinhard Bendix, the rate of increase has been lower in Germany (from 5 percent to nearly 12 percent), and considerably lower in France (a static level of about 12 percent). The latter two cases are particularly significant, because these two countries are known to have had the largest and most authoritative state apparatus. This suggests that the quantum of administrative need is about the same in all industrial states. The bureaucratization of the private sector is less understood in the United States, but its existence and its influence on private life are impossible to deny. Many an American giant corporation had a five-year plan before the concept was invented in the Soviet Union. As of 1956 white-collar workers in the United States outnumbered blue-collar workers, suggesting the extent to which work and workers have been reduced to shuffling papers, handling routines, and supervising the conduct of others.

A more direct view of private life in modern industrial society is the trade association. It is a slightly extreme case of the typical. Thus it is a good introduction into the realities of politics after decentralization.

The trade association is basically an administrative structure whose quintessential mission in life is to regularize relations among potential competitors in the same industry, trade, or economic sector. In history and in theory, the law of the commercial marketplace is competition. The trade association seeks to replace this with an administrative process.

Trade associations have been widely misunderstood, much to their own advantage in public relations. Social scientists tend to treat them as a form of "interest group" or "pressure group," suggesting that the trade association is primarily a category of political activity. Within this rubric the trade association is merely a means of efficient representation of certain economic interests. This means of course that the trade association is a good thing insofar as there are always several trade associations each representing other economic interests. Under such conditions no concern need be given to life within any of the respective associations.

It is true that Washington and every state capital and city hall abound with trade associations and their political representatives, the lobbyists. However, political activity is only marginal and occasional with any trade association. In the first place, there are thousands of issues being faced by the legislatures of the country in any given year, and only a very few of these issues will be salient to any one trade association. On public housing, for example, the National Association of Home Builders is intensely active; but new public housing legislation is not even an annual affair. In the second place, political activity is a functional specialization inside each major trade association. This responsibility is turned over to one bureau among many bureaus inside the association. The other bureaus are meanwhile intensively active making their respective contributions to the other administrative responsibilities of the association. These responsibilities include research and development or subsidies therefor, information on pricing and costs, market research, joint advertising campaigns and other promotions, collection and dissemination of political information, and information regarding civic duties.

The population of trade associations began to mushroom in the late nineteenth century and was given special impetus during and after World War I. From a few guilds and rate bureaus as late as 1850, the trade association effort to formalize economic relations expanded until, by 1940, when an official census was taken, there were at least 12,000 national, state, and local trade associations. Over a quarter of these were national or international in scope. No recent census has been taken, but there is no reason to expect that the number or importance of trade associations has declined. It is probable that no production or service facility in the nation exists without a trade association to serve it by controlling the behavior of its members. Single businesses of more than modest size usually find it desirable to belong to several such associations.

If trade associations are not primarily political but administrative animals, neither are they the mere expressions of centralized and oligopolized economic sectors. The fact is that the more decentralized and potentially competitive sectors and industries need the trade associations and their administrative functions most of all. Where the number of firms is greater, the fear of competition is stronger; the need for research and marketing information is greater; the need for systems of recruiting trained personnel and sharing the results of research and technological advances is far greater. Such services are often provided from within by the giant corporations, but they must be provided solely by trade associations among the smaller operations. Thus, many of the most famous American trade associations serve highly decentralized economic sectors. Examples include the National Association of Real Estate Boards, the National Association of Retail Druggists, and the American Medical Association.

But life in industrial society is not administered only by trade associations. There are at least three categories of groups not, strictly speaking, trade associations that perform most of the functions of a trade association. The first of these is the "peak association." The second, and a formidable type indeed, is the organization of agricultural commodities. The third, of course, is the trade union.

The peak association is a group formed primarily by other groups and associations which join together in order to cooperate on a front larger than an individual trade or sector, yet far narrower than a whole class. Robert Brady reports on the same phenomenon in many countries, in particular, the *Spitzenverbande* in Germany. Probably the best-known European example was the pre-Vichy French Confédération générale de la production française. In the United States the National Association of Manufacturers is probably the best-known example. The American Farm Bureau Federation is another. Each has a large staff in Washington, the NAM has still another large staff in New York, and the AFBF has an impressive staff in every agricultural state in the country. Their research and educational services are impressive. The AFBF offers various types of insurance along with its other services. The United States Chamber of Commerce is another example, and there are nearly four thousand local chambers which perform admirably as peak associations for city and regional groups.

Every major commodity in the United States is represented by a commodity organization. These range from immense and aged groups, such as those organized around cotton, tobacco, and wool interests, to very narrow groups, such as one organized by the cranberry growers. Each of these groups is deeply involved in politics, because agriculture is highly politicized. But most of the year's reality for all these commodity groups is administrative. They not only must keep their members informed of the complex price system in agriculture but are deeply involved in the actual implementation of federal and state agriculture programs.

The trade union in the United States was almost self-consciously modeled after business associations. The founder of modern unionism, Samuel Gompers, was considered a success largely because he espoused the principle of "business unionism" against the alternatives of class solidarity and political action. Unions act politically from time to time, and unions do compete in the labor market in a political process called collective bargaining. But collective bargaining is itself highly bureaucratized, involving elaborate studies of business profits, national economic conditions, prospects for gains outside the wages areas ("fringe benefits"), and problems of jurisdiction. Moreover, most of the year union staffs are busy administering the labor-management contract, not bargaining or campaigning for it. Still other union responsibilities, most particularly job classification, must be bureaucratized if they are to succeed.

The trade association and related types of groups became a factor of still greater importance in the economy of the United States because of the antitrust laws. Certain kinds of direct business cooperation and coordination were considered to be illegal restraints upon trade. Trusts were clearly illegal. Pools and market-sharing devices were highly vulnerable to civil and criminal prosecution. Any consolidation that involved a potential competitor was illegal. Private contracts to stabilize markets, even if not illegal, were almost completely unenforceable in the courts. In contrast, the trade association was a structure against which Americans had no particular defenses. Cooperation for advertising, exchange of information, collaborative research, standardization of sizes and grades, and campaigns to discourage "cutthroat competition" all seemed far enough removed from the problem of excessive economic power or the ideal of the free and unencumbered market. Some associations—for example, the Linseed Crushers' Council and the American Hardwood Manufacturers' Association—have been successfully prosecuted for coercing their members or helping members conspire to influence prices directly; but as time passed, the trade associations have become more and more legitimate. This is the basis for practices of today and begins to suggest why decentralization means delegation of power to these groups.

These are the primary types of interest groups in the country, but they are by no means the only ones. There are multitudes of noneconomic groups—special interest and general interests groups—and being less economic in interest makes them no less oligarchic in internal structure. To stress this character of the organization of private interest groups as strongly as possible, Grant McConnell prefers to refer to them as "private governments." This aspect of life is as true of local health and welfare councils as it is of the National Association of Manufacturers. It is as true of the League of Women Voters as it is of the local commerce and industry association. Groups are run by the few on behalf of the many, and the richer and larger the group the more staff it will have to assume organizational responsibilities. Newer groups, although less bureaucratized, tend to be extremely oligarchic. Many such groups are no more than the leader, a small cadre, and a collection of affiliates of varying degrees of affiliation.

The phenomenon of the formally organized group is a distinguishing mark of modernity. This means also that the administration of social relationships is also a prime condition of modern life. If one defines administration properly—as a relatively formal means of social control through the use of the most rational possible ordering of means to ends—it is obvious that modern men prefer administration, for they are constantly in search of rational controls, on human as well as physical environments. All of this must mean increases in routine, in hierarchy, in oligarchy, in inequality. The phenomenon of the organized group is also a mark of what social scientists call the pluralist system, another mark of modernity. It is true that groups introduce an important element of competition into large-scale society. It is true that groups can interact with each other in a manner which increases the dynamism of such a society. However, it romanticizes the notion to pretend that life inside established groups is egalitarian, flexible—in a word, democratic. Leading contemporary students of groups such as David B. Truman, as well as such predecessors as Roberto Michels, look at the constitution and the myths of groups and provide for them such appellations as "the iron law of oligarchy" (Michels) and "the democratic mold" (Truman).

Groups and the Problem of Governing

Parallel to the development of formal groups was the increased recognition of such groups as legitimate units of representation. As syndicalism and corporatism were making their mark in Europe, so pluralism, interest representation, and more contemporary variants were gaining ground in the United States. The precedents were established by government cooperation with trade associations and commodity associations beginning in the late nineteenth century. Formal cooperation spread to other types of groups and became more and more systematic as more and more interest groups established themselves on a national scale. The Department of Commerce considered trade associations indispensable in the collection of business statistics. Agencies in the Department of Agriculture had been working for a long time directly with a rather large number of commodity associations and the local "farm bureaus" of the young Chamber of Commerce. Eventually it became government policy to encourage groups in areas where no such groups existed. The Departments of Commerce and Agriculture were instrumental, for example, in the creation of the Chamber of Commerce and the American Farm Bureau Federation, respectively. Various kinds of employer and employee associations were encouraged and brought into the interior processes of government as a fundamental part of war mobilization after 1914. But the zenith of popularity for business and nonbusiness groups in the eyes of government came not during war or during reactionary Republican administrations but during the height of the Roosevelt administration. The essential instrument of New Deal industrial planning was the National Industrial Recovery Act of 1933 and its administrative apparatus, the National Recovery Administration. In good corporativistic fashion, NRA worked through the activities of officially recognized trade organizations. Each sector and service industry and agricultural commodity organized into governing committees of trade association representatives. These representatives developed elaborate codes of fair competition—dealing with prices, wages, exchanges, health conditions, and so on—and, once approved, these codes were officially promulgated as federal law.

The NRA was eventually declared unconstitutional as an excessive delegation of law-making power to private groups and government agencies. However, the practice of government controls in cooperation with trade associations did not end; it simply became somewhat less formal and explicit. At present, the Federal Trade Commission could not carry on its business without the regular cooperation of the trade associations and other interest groups. The Interstate Commerce Commission depends almost totally upon the information and administration of the associations of railroads to achieve any regulation at all in the railroad industry. Almost the same pattern of government-supported self-government by trade association is true in the more ancient trade of shipping and the more recently developed airline industry. The vital role of the commodity associations in the administration of agricultural policy has been identified. In other fields, such as coal mining, insurance rate regulation, the export trade, space industries, and defense research and development, the official role of trade associations is somewhat more difficult to assess exactly, but their importance in each of these fields is undoubtedly the same.

The official and semiofficial role of the well-organized groups in government in the past half-century merely proves their legitimacy. Their actual scope and significance in American life are far greater. The stamp of governmental legitimacy has had the effect of blinding the American citizen to the real extent to which his life is being controlled irresponsibly. To anyone with any juridical concerns at all, the trade association represents a dilemma, because it is an exercise in control against which there is no regular defense governed by law. This is also true of the trade union. In more subtle forms it is also true of many noneconomic groups. When a person with an LL.B. degree is denied membership in a state bar association on the grounds that he refuses to reveal his political activities, he has no recourse as a citizen although the denial results in a severe deprivation. When a person with an M.D. degree is denied membership in a state medical society solely on the grounds that he is black, he too has no recourse in the courts. When a minority member of a trade union seeks to organize a competing union in the shop, he is very likely to run afoul of prohibitions against such a thing in legislation enacted and supported even by liberals.

Due to some colossal misunderstanding or misplacement of liberal sympathies, the most poetic and sympathetic defenses of groups and their official and semiofficial access have come from liberals whose concerns are otherwise for equality and justice. Treating groups as mere interest groups—and disregarding the degree of internal and administrative control of the members—political scientists tend to elevate such associations to an essentially democratic form. When the economist and philosopher-prince John Kenneth Galbraith created the economic model called "countervailing power," he elevated the trade association to a general principle of virtue, so precious in our society that he could propose that "support of countervailing power has become in modern times a major peacetime function of the Federal government."

These considerations have almost everything to do with any realistic evaluation of the drive for decentralization. If one sincerely wishes to implement such a goal, he is faced with two possibilities—and two only. One possibility for decentralization is the absence of government altogether, in the spirit of *laissez faire*. But in our day and age, and to the very ones who cry for decentralization, this solution is not acceptable, for it appears to mean abdication to all sorts of forces which have already come to be considered evil. The only other possible way of implementing the notions of decentralization is to use direct and positive government involvement on the basis of *delegation of power*. This is undoubtedly what most of the decentralization campaigners have in mind. But this leads precisely to the group domination and the oligarchic pattern of control which have already been described.

When a government program is deliberately and carefully decentralized, it begins with a grant of power and responsibility to an administrative agency. This is called "enabling legislation." This enabling legislation leads to a decentralization through what is called "delegation of power." The delegating authority—Congress at the national level—must carefully avoid accompanying that delegation of power with any clear standards of guidance in law. If such clear standards were present in the law, Congress would in effect be giving with one hand what it takes back with the other, and that would not be considered sincere decentralization. This is because clear standards at law limit the discretion of the administrator, and the ultimate choices which guide conduct would then be left with the decisions made by congressional authority and the presidential authorities at the center.

Delegation of power, and decentralization by this process, is the very jurisprudence of the modern liberal state: Give the agency and its agents sufficient discretion by keeping the rules of law broad and permissive so that agencies can enter into a true policy-making relationship with their clientele. True decentralization would then be consonant with liberal belief in the pluralistic process of bargaining. This is seriously the process of decentralization as it is widely described in the professional literature and as it is understood by the campaigners for real decentralization. The traditional notion of rule of law has in effect been replaced by a rule of bargaining. The rule of bargaining is in turn justified in the name of representation, decentralization, and participatory democracy.

But can we ennoble such practices by calling them true representation or effective participatory democracy or applying to them any other halo-laden words in the democratic lexicon? When the law passed and promulgated at the center sets no central directions, all the advantages in eventual implementation rest with those elements of the community which are best organized and most sensitive to what is going on. That in turn obviously means the trade associations and all their organized cousins. Sometimes a government program sets out deliberately to create new groups in order to equalize the access a bit. This was done in the War on Poverty, but it was not new there, for it had been done many years ago with the Chamber of Commerce and the American Farm Bureau Federation. In any of those cases the effort to create the new groups to improve "countervailing power" affects the political situation mainly on the first round of organization, if at all. That is to say, once new groups have been formed, they take on all the oligarchic trappings of previously organized groups, and the character of true representation in the society has hardly been affected at all.

Decentralization through delegation of power to lower levels, therefore, almost always results in unequal access and group domination of the public situation. However, the situation is far worse when these arrangements for access are formalized. This is true in the case of the War on Poverty as in the case of COMSAT. It is also true of agriculture policy-making vis-à-vis the commodity organizations. It is incredible that this pattern of policy-making could ever be supported by any person sincerely espousing the values of true representation and true political equality. Formal recognition of groups and their representatives for purposes of such participatory democracy converts each of the groups so honored into official components of government. Such recognition converts what is already an oligarchic situation into an involuntary situation. One of the saving characteristics of oligarchy in groups is that a person may have alternative group memberships and therefore may choose among them. This may even give him a kind of consumer influence over the activities and policies of each of the groups. But when groups are officially recognized for purposes of being included in the interior processes of policy-making, the virtues of multiple membership pass out of existence.

Thus, public recognition of a private group gives that group an involuntary character and increases the degree to which persons are subject to hierarchy, and even at that price does not increase the sum total of real representation. Whether the recognition is formal or merely clear and *de facto*, social control by irresponsible processes is the result. The notion of the "voluntary association" becomes more and more an absurdity. On the South Side of Chicago there is a group called the Blackstone Rangers. The group is feared by many because it forces teen-agers to be members. However, the differences between the Blackstone Rangers and some other local groups participating in the War on Poverty or some educational program becomes less and less easy to make as that group becomes more and more the officially recognized channel of access to public policy-making. The Blackstone Ranger organizer may say, "Join our organization or I will beat your head in." But how different is this from the community organizer who say, "Join our organization or you will have very little say in community policy-making"?

Increasing demands in the country for decentralization are a reflection of increasing distrust of public programs. But direct response to those pleas through *apparent* decentralization—by further spreading the pattern of devolving programs upon organized interest groups—is a complete misunderstanding of the nature of the demand and of the nature of the problem. Decentralizing in these terms and along these lines as a response to the present crisis of public authority in the United States is comparable to the practice of bleeding in medieval medicine. For the physician the only answer to noxious blood was its elimination, at the very time when the patient could hardly spare any blood of whatever character. Further decentralization at the federal level at a time when so much power has already devolved upon private structures is an almost certain way of perpetuating the very crisis decentralization is supposed to cure.

Thus, the real question was never one of centralization versus decentralization. Decentralization was always a question of to whom and for what. Decentralization through delegation of power merely meant conversion from government control to a far more irresponsible and enigmatic and unpredictable group control. The only apparent way out of the present crisis is not to yield directly to private claims but quite independently to determine the clear injustices and inequities that are involved and to exercise control over them through clear laws that do not depend upon the good wishes or the participatory practices of any of the subjects of those laws. If such laws were for a time properly and vigorously administered by duly constituted governmental administrative bodies—and this has not happened for many years—one might at some point thereafter anticipate a proper and effective decentralization. Until such time as true federal power and a clear national commitment to racial equality and economic equity have been established beyond doubt, decentralization is abdication.

7

The University

No contemporary issue is generating more anger than the turmoil that has enveloped so many university campuses. To some extent the reaction in the outside community has racial overtones, for the demands of black and brown students have raised the kind of issues discussed in Chapter 3 of this book. But the uproar on the campuses began before the ethnic studies issue was introduced; and it is the attack on the university by children of white, affluent America that is so bewildering to the majority of adults. In the popular imagination there can be only one explanation for the agony of the universities: it is the work of a tiny minority of troublemakers.

It is true that the activists comprise but a small proportion of the student body. Yet the trouble cannot be dismissed as the aberration of the few. The activists have become a significant force because, on several campuses, they have been able to command the tacit approval and occasional involvement of much larger numbers of students. The Gallup survey reproduced here shows why this is so. While the majority disapprove of violent and disruptive tactics, it is clear that attitudes critical of society in general and the university in particular are widely held on our campuses today.

The Gallup article is followed by three statements sympathetic to the dissident movement. Michael Miles, while recognizing the limitations of some radical left ideas, supports the allegation that the university is the captive instrument of reactionary outside interests.

Wolin and Schaar's essay is particularly relevant to some of the questions of technology and bureaucracy touched on in Chapter 1 of this reader. They begin with the confrontation that occurred in Berkeley in April 1969, when a vacant lot owned by the University of California was taken over by a number of people, most of them unconnected with the university, and transformed into a "People's Park." The occupants were asked to leave, they refused, the area was surrounded by police, a rally on the Berkeley campus was followed by a march on the area by a large crowd. Rocks and bottles were thrown at the police, gunfire by the police resulted in one death and several injuries. Before peace was restored and the lot taken over again by the university, chaos reigned, National Guardsmen were brought in, and there was tear gas all over campus, some of it sprayed from a helicopter. In exploring the meaning of these melancholy events in the selection included here, Wolin and Schaar conclude that much of the blame must be placed on the university, which has allowed itself to become a bureaucratized expression of the technological society, unable to relate to human impulse and spontaneity.

Kenneth Keniston, in his discussion of drug use by students, rejects the view that this phenomenon can be explained primarily in pathological terms. Even among the "heads," the frequent users of hallucinogens, he finds that there are only a few whose drug use is part of a pattern of serious psychopathology. Beyond the heads, who are the most alienated students and the most likely to be attracted to the hippie world, there are the "seekers," who use drugs periodically as part of a general experimental attitude toward life. Heads and seekers together still represent a small proportion of all students; but, as the Gallup survey reveals, a significant number have at least tried marijuana. (Keniston has noted that the proportion is very much higher on certain campuses, those with an "intellectual climate," and in certain disciplines, particularly the arts and humanities.) In the selection reprinted in this chapter, Keniston suggests that the use of drugs on campus has an important relationship to student attitudes on the state of American society.

The next three selections are far less sympathetically inclined toward the student dissenters. Bruno Bettelheim asks that we try to understand the grievances of students today; but, unlike Keniston, he believes it is the technological society that is rejecting the students rather than vice versa. And he calls for stern measures against campus disorder. Robert Brustein is dismayed by what he interprets as an onslaught on standards and academic excellence. Stephen Tonsor's essay, according to the *National Review*, has been commended by President Nixon as "the most significant and perceptive analysis of what is wrong with our approach to higher education...I want everybody who has anything to do with education to read this piece." What is wrong, according to Tonsor, is that universities have become too ready to forsake their teaching responsibilities to do the work of society at large; that we need more variety among our educational institutions; and that there is a growing tendency toward uniformity of approach and doctrine—a problem exacerbated of late by New Left pressure.

Even if there is less uproar on the campuses in the future, the prospect is that the university will continue to be a prime subject of controversy. Daniel Bell and John Kenneth Galbraith have observed that the university is emerging as a key institution in the post-industrial society, embodying great potential power. And, as Chapter 5 made clear, in the American system any center of power becomes a source of anxiety and conflict.

STUDENT ATTITUDES

George Gallup

Dr. George Gallup is Director of the American Institute of Public Opinion. The findings reported were based on a nationwide survey on 55 college campuses and personal interviews with 1030 students representing private and public institutions.

From polls taken April 23 through May 17, 1969, by the American Institute of Public Opinion. © 1969, American Institute of Public Opinion. (See *Gallup Opinion Index* [June 1969].)

The Militants and the Majority

Those who comfort themselves that the trouble on the college campuses of America is caused by only a "handful of students" and that the majority is completely out of sympathy with the goals of the militant few would be disabused of this view if they were to talk to students across the nation, as 75 representatives of the Gallup Poll did recently.

The opinions of a Rutgers University sophomore represent those of many students reached in this survey:

> The militants on campus may have gone too far, but society needs to wake up. Students are genuinely concerned with the way things are on campus and in the community and they want these things changed.

Attitudes vary from college to college and region to region on specific issues such as the ROTC, special courses and facilities for Negroes and college defense contracts, but at the heart of the discontent over these and other matters is the feeling that society as a whole is seriously ill and that changes are imperative.

"The causes for unrest go much deeper than simple dissatisfaction with our colleges," explained a premedical student at Yale:

> We all feel the sting of an immoral war, prejudice against Negroes and widespread poverty. We want to do something about these problems. We use our colleges as a sounding board, and to most of us, colleges and college administrators stand as symbols of why nothing gets changed.

The important difference between college students of today and those of earlier years is their great desire for change, supported by the conviction that change can be brought about without waiting for years or decades.

Although college students are impatient for change, they deplore violence and are repelled by the episode at Cornell. One student said, "I'm for complaining, not destroying."

A Columbia University coed said:

> Students raised a fuss about the war and they proved their point with the McCarthy campaign. Now, they're using their new-found power to fight what they consider to be sicknesses of society. But I'm fed up with the creeps who get violent and ruin things for the others. They have a right to dissent, but the violence part is absurd.

This campus study shows that 28% of all students say they have participated in a demonstration of some kind, while 72% say they have not. But even among "demonstrators," only a very few support the tactics of the militants.

Deploring violence, students nevertheless are in sympathy with the basic goals of those who create the noise on campus and many accept the precept, "the end justifies the means."

Answers to one of the many Gallup Poll queries included in the survey provide some basis for this observation. No fewer than four college students in every 10—and six in 10 among those who have participated in demonstrations—say that students who break laws while demonstrating should not be punished by being expelled.

A Yale graduate student, whose tweed coat and regimental tie contrasted sharply with his long hair and sideburns, said:

> If an institution has the power to improve a situation and does not
> take action, then it loses its moral authority and students have no
> choice but to take matters into their own hands.

The findings reported here are based on a nationwide survey on 55 college campuses and personal interviews with 1,030 students representing the proper proportion of private, public and denominational institutions. . . .

Students are in widespread agreement that they should have a greater say in the running of their colleges. Eighty-one per cent of all students interviewed hold this view as do 92% of demonstrators.

An equally high proportion of students as a whole (75%) and demonstrators (86%) say they should also have a greater say concerning the academic side of college courses, examinations and class requirements.

The views of the general public stand out in stark contrast. Only 25% of adults of all ages think students should have a greater say in the running of colleges and only 33% hold this view in regard to academic matters, as seen in the tables below:

Do you think college students should or should not
have a greater say in the running of colleges?

	All Students	Demonstrators	General Public
Yes, should	81%	92%	25%
No, should not	17	6	70
No opinion	2	2	5

Do you think college students should or should not have a greater
say concerning the academic side of colleges—that is
the courses, examinations, and so forth?

	All Students	Demonstrators	General Public
Yes, should	75%	86%	33%
No, should not	23	13	55
No opinion	2	1	12

A generation gap is also apparent in a comparison of the views of students and the general public on campus lawbreakers, as seen in the following table:

Do you think college students who break laws while participating in campus demonstrations should be expelled, or not?

	All Students	Demon- strators	Gen. Public
Yes	54%	31%	82%
No	40	62	11
No opinion	6	7	7

Students attending denominational colleges are less likely to say students should have a greater say in running colleges and in determining the curriculum. They are somewhat more likely (than are public and private college students) to favor expelling campus lawbreakers.

All students in the survey were asked to name what they believed to be the biggest gripes of the college population today. These are shown in the following table:

Why do you think students in many schools around the country are demonstrating—that is, what do you think is their biggest gripe?

	All Students %
Not enough say in running of college	42
Current inadequacies of society	22
Adult and governmental authority	16
The Vietnam war	11
Want to have their voices heard	7
Civil rights	6
They have no real gripe	8
Other responses	5
	117%*

*Table adds to more than 100% due to multiple responses.

All persons interviewed were then asked if they agree or disagree with the complaints named. In each case large majorities expressed agreement.

The demonstrator is sometimes pictured as a maverick, perversely out of step with the rest of the student body. A comparison of the profiles of demonstrators and non-demonstrators, however, shows both similarities and contrasts. Demonstrators tend to be far more liberal in their political philosophy than non-demonstrators.

Following is a full profile of the demonstrator and the non-demonstrator:

	Have Demonstrated	Have Not Demonstrated
All students	28%	72%
Sex		
Men	31	69
Women	24	76
Age		
18 years and under	27	73
19 years	24	76
20 years	33	67
21-23 years	28	72
24 and older	32	68
Region of college		
East	34	66
Midwest	29	71
South	22	78
West	28	72
Politics		
Republicans	13	87
Democrats	31	69
Independents	34	66
Political philosophy		
Extremely conservative	22	78
Fairly conservative	16	84
Middle road	15	85
Fairly liberal	33	67
Extremely liberal	61	39
Parents' income		
$15,000 and over	32	68
$10,000-$15,000	27	73
$7,000-$10,000	31	69
Under $7,000	30	70
Class		
Freshmen	28	72
Sophomores	28	72
Juniors	25	75
Seniors	24	76
Graduate students	41	59
Type of college		
Public	28	72
Private	30	70
Denominational	27	73

A Swing to the Left

If the political views of the present generation of college students are indicative of a trend that will gain momentum during the next decade, the two major parties need to do a lot of new thinking and planning.

The trend on the campus is strongly toward the left. . . .

The desire to get out of the war in Vietnam and the need for social reform have led so many students to the left that the appellation, "conservative," is almost a dirty name on U.S. campuses today. Students for a Democratic Society (SDS) has taken the play away from the Young Americans for Freedom and other right wing groups.

In the survey only two students in 100 describe their political beliefs as "extremely conservative," even though most college students come from middle and upper income homes.

The question asked [was] *How would you describe your political beliefs—as extremely conservative, moderately conservative, middle-of-the-road, moderately liberal or extremely liberal?* The following table shows political beliefs leaning heavily to the left. It also reveals that students who have participated in demonstrations are far more liberal in their political beliefs than non-demonstrators.

	All Students	Demonstrators	Non-Demonstrators
Extremely conservative	2%	2%	2%
Moderately conservative	19	10	22
Middle-of-road	24	12	29
Moderately liberal	41	48	39
Extremely liberal	12	25	6
No opinion	2	3	2

Party labels have far less appeal on campus than they do with the general public.

Here is the question asked of both college students and the general public: *In politics as of today do you consider yourself a Republican, Democrat or Independent?* The following table compares the present party affiliation of college students with that of the general public (adults 21 and older):

	Students	General Public
Republicans	23%	29%
Democrats	33	42
Independents	44	29

Students who describe themselves as independents lean decidedly left in their political beliefs. Four times as many in this group say they are "moderately liberal" or "extremely liberal" as say they are "moderately conservative" or "extremely conservative."

In looking to the future, this important fact should be borne in mind: college juniors, sophomores and freshmen at this time bear a close resemblance to this year's graduating seniors in terms of habits and beliefs and in their desire for radical change on campus and in society.

A New Breed

Results of a nationwide survey of college students leave little doubt that students today are indeed a new breed.

Representative of this new breed is a highly vocal Yale student who said, "We are disenchanted with the ideologies of the adult population today, with their belief that a large Buick says something important about one's self. The urge of people for self-aggrandizement repels us. Furthermore, we don't go along with the 'hard work mystique'—the notion that if one works hard he is therefore a good person."

Interviews with college students across the nation—in private institutions, such as Harvard University, in state-supported institutions, such as Ohio State University, and in denominational or church-related colleges, such as Notre Dame University—provide ample evidence that students today are different from earlier generations of college students in these six important respects:

1. *Use of drugs.* One student in every five (22%) says he has *tried* marijuana. Less stigma seems to be attached to the use of marijuana now than one year ago—many students admit to taking marijuana as readily as they do to drinking beer.

Those who have used marijuana are far more likely to be men than women, and are more likely to come from higher income families.

A large majority of students (73%) think that a student found taking drugs such as marijuana should *not* be expelled. "I can't see anything wrong with taking pot," a Rutgers freshman said, brushing a lock of hair from his face. "People do a lot worse things when they're drunk than when they're 'high' on marijuana."

One student in 10 (10%) says he has taken a barbiturate and four in one hundred have tried LSD. As for expelling students found taking LSD, a slight majority say "no" (53%), with some saying that such students should be helped, not expelled.

2. *Attitude toward sex.*   Two out of every three college students (66%) think it is not wrong for men and women to have pre-marital sex relations, with 72% of college males holding this view and 55% of women.

A majority of students in both public and private colleges say sex before marriage is not wrong, but a majority of denominational college students hold the opposite view.

3. *Dress and appearance.*   The most obvious difference between today's students and students of previous years is in their dress and appearance. Many students consciously affect a slovenly appearance to drive home their anti-Establishment, nonconformist point of view.

Historians of the future, who will want to take account of the customs and foibles of college students in 1969, will find the following facts about dress and appearance helpful (based on tabulations by interviewers):

6% of college males have beards.
28% of college males have long sideburns.
13% of all students dress in a slovenly manner (19% of men and 6% of women).

Beards, sideburns, and sloppy clothes appear to be somewhat more prevalent in the East than in other major regions of the country and are much more likely to be found among students in public and private colleges than on denominational campuses.

Not only are beards, sideburns, sloppy clothing and long hair the current mode, they also tend to be symbols. A Yale student explained, "To a certain extent, long hair and casual clothes are a badge telling people that we are part of the new and swinging generation—that we are out to conquer great wrongs in the world." Another student suggested that the longer the hair, the more radical the person's politics.

Is the present college vogue of beards, sideburns, long hair and sloppy clothes just a fad, or is it a trend that will continue?

When this question was put to the sample of college students, 51% answered "Just a fad" while 41% held the opposite opinion. "These things go in cycles," said one student.

4. *Interest in social work.*   It wasn't so long ago that doing extra-curricular social work while in college was considered in some quarters to be "square." Now, working among the poor and underprivileged is frequently a normal and expected part of one's college experience.

A majority of all students (51%) say they have done social work. The percentage is 58% among women and 47% among men. A higher proportion of denominational college students (60%) than private college students (52%) and students in state-supported colleges (50%) have engaged in this type of service.

Evidence that demonstrators are willing to do more to try to change society than march and carry placards is seen in the fact that 65% of this group have done social work as opposed to 45% among non-demonstrators.

5.   *Future occupation, goals in life.*   An uncertainty about the immediate future hangs over the campus today. Some students are not sure what route they will take in life. One student said, "We need time to think, to really figure out who we are and where we want to go. Not many of us are eager to plunge into the fast pace of society and be forced to conform to the usual pattern."

The traditional goals of earning a great deal of money and making one's mark in the world have lost some of their charm. An extraordinarily high proportion of students today are interested in going into the "helping" professions, notably teaching.

The following question was asked of all students interviewed in the survey: *What field or occupation do you expect to be in when you are age 40?* Here are the results:

Occupation by Age 40?

Teaching	29%
Business, management	8
Housewife	8
Law	5
Clergy	5
Engineering	4
Social work	4
Medicine	2
Others	24
Don't know	11

6.   *Attitudes toward society.*   Today's student looks at society with a coldly critical eye. Angered by the Vietnam war, he has turned his ire on the closest representative of "the Establishment"—his own college. He has learned about demonstrations from the civil rights movement and about the effectiveness of "student power" from Sen. Eugene McCarthy's campaign last year.

A much larger percentage of demonstrators than non-demonstrators have gotten drunk, taken drugs and done social work. The following table shows the habits of college students today and differences between demonstrators and non-demonstrators:

Have You Ever . . .

	All Students	Per Cent "Yes" Demonstrators	Non-Demonstrators
Drunk more than you should?	57%	67%	53%
Done social work?	51	65	45
Tried marijuana?	22	40	15
Taken barbiturates?	10	21	6
Tried LSD?	4	7	3
Tried all these?	2	1	3
Tried none of these?	13	—	18

Seven in ten college students think a "generation gap" exists, and the same proportion of older persons in the populace hold this view. College students complain about parents being "too set in their ways" and "unwilling to listen to us," while older persons criticize young persons for being "unruly" and "irresponsible." A full comparison follows:

Biggest Gripe of Students about Parent's Generation?

Too set in their ways	36%
A lack of communication ("they won't listen to us")	18
Too conservative	8
Indifferent, apathetic	8
Materialistic	6
Too strict	6
Their views on morals	4
Racial prejudice	4
They stereotype young people	4
Other responses	6
No gripe about them	11
No opinion	3
	114%*

*Total adds to more than 100% since some persons gave more than one response.

Biggest Gripe of Parents about Young People?

Undisciplined behavior	30%
Lack respect for authority	16
Youth are overindulged	10
Irresponsible	7
Parents too permissive	7
Smug, too self-assured	6
Use of drugs	4
Too idealistic, naive	2
Other responses	4
No gripe about them	12
No opinion	6
	104%*

*Total adds to more than 100% since some persons gave more than one response.

Today's college students have succeeded in enraging large segments of the American public. A strong backlash is evident in recent Gallup surveys showing large majorities in favor of expelling campus lawbreakers and for a stronger hand on the part of college administrators.

Many in the public are offended by the appearance and dress of students, demonstrations, their drug habits and attitudes toward sex. But sometimes overlooked in the furore over the campus situation is the solid record of students in terms of actually working to improve society by helping the poor and underprivileged as well as their interest in teaching and other "helping" professions as a career.

WHOSE UNIVERSITY?

Michael Miles

Michael Miles is an analyst of young radicals; he frequently contributes to The New Republic.

According to radical students, university faculty are not the university; they only *work* for the university. The university, say the students, is the management and the trustees who run what amounts to a research-and-development corporation, a major "growth industry." The faculty, they say, is a privileged class, bought off with good salaries, long vacations, leaves of absence, fringe benefits, opportunities for lucrative consultantships, and most important of all, control of their immediate affairs such as curriculum and the state of their guilds. The faculty is privileged but not powerful—because it is cut out of the crucial matters of *institutional* concern, such as investment decisions, budget priorities, and product innovation.

This rude revision of their image (no "community of scholars" engaged in the "disinterested pursuit of truth"?) is hard for

"Whose University? A View from the Other Side of the Fence" in *The New Republic* (April 12, 1969), pp. 17-19. Reprinted by permission of *The New Republic*, © 1969, Harrison-Blaine of New Jersey, Inc.

the faculty to bear—especially hard, because some professors have suspected as much, even discussed it over coffee but, of course, never expounded it over public address systems. It is, then, because of student radicals—those wretched, scruffy student leftists—that faculty have been cursed with the worst of existential afflictions: self-doubt.

After the first university crisis has passed and then a second and a third, the professoriate must resolve its crisis of confidence in one way or another. And since, as Populists used to say, "self-interest controls," the faculty, especially the tenured gentry, turns against the students. Although its law-and-order dalliance with the administration goes some distance in disposing of the student movement as a political force on campus, it does not eliminate it as a tumor in the brain. For the evil spirit to be exorcised, for student radicalism to be truly dismissed, it must be *explained*. Thus, in a great ink wave welling up from the San Francisco Bay Area in 1964, rolling across the plains to the Hudson River and Columbia in 1968, sociologists, historians, and political scientists have analyzed the students in the scholarly journals, the intellectual magazines and their books. This enterprise is not only counterattack; it is group therapy. It relies heavily on historical analogies. Cultural historians, for instance, are fond of comparing the modern student left to the Russian Nihilists of the late nineteenth century. They point out that the Nihilists were politically isolated, university-based, revolutionary, unprogrammatic, and of course nihilistic. Social historians, however (and Bruno Bettleheim), prefer to compare the "neo-fascist" student movement to the Nazi paramilitary organizations of the 1920's. There is, they say, the same obsession with direct action, the myth of violence, the revolutionary claims without substance. Another recent favorite is comparison to the revolutionaries of 1848—international, middle-class, university-based and somewhat inept.

When the critics of the student movement attempt political analysis, which is not often, they generally caricature what they observe in terms of student obsession with conspiracy theories (the "Establishment," the "power structure," "corporate capitalism" and so forth). A theory of conspiracy would attribute enormous discretionary power to certain circles of politicians, corporate executives and bureaucrats. But the radical viewpoint is precisely the opposite of this. It is that the men of power are creatures, not rulers, of the institutions they inhabit; policy decisions are the results of choices among a narrow range of options determined by the structure of institutions, bureaucracies and finally of the corporate capitalist system itself. If anything, the fault of this radical student viewpoint is not that it is conspiratorial but that it is rigidly deterministic. A social theory which ascribes all manifestations of a society to the nature of its social structure is impaled on its own horns when it attempts to develop an alternative social vision based on freedom.

Young radicals have tended to swing from the issue-oriented pragmatism of some years ago to a comic-book Marxism in which they connect the Vietnam war to corporate capitalism as a system, not by analysis, but by a leap of faith. This connection, especially if thought of as a purely economic relation, is clearly false in the case of the Vietnam war. Still, an entire generation of US policy-makers *has* intervened against social revolutions in Guatemala, Iran, Cuba, the Dominican Republic, Vietnam on the basis of some conception of "vital national interests." One ought to examine the social system which invites this counter-revolutionary formulation of national interest, rather than falling back on a "politics of inadvertence," in which policy-makers happen to roll snake-eyes every two or three years.

The pluralists and end-of-ideologists who attribute a conspiracy theory to the student left often employ its family cousin, a theory of elite manipulation, in their analysis of student revolts. For example, in an article in *The Public Interest* on Columbia, Daniel Bell, a Columbia sociologist, discovered that SDS with a membership of a hundred not only precipitated but effectively directed the occupation by 2,000 students. Furthermore, a small Maoist Progressive Labor faction "increasingly dominated" SDS as events proceeded. By implication, a small band of pop revolutionaries led a student rebellion involving thousands—through a coordinating committee "bureaucracy'" no less. The *Cox Commission Report* was a pleasant surprise to radical students and a rude shock to the Columbia administration and its faculty allies, when it rejected this "conspiracy of student revolutionaries."

For academic analysts who have spent their careers studying structures, organizations, economies and social mechanisms, it is exceedingly difficult to grasp the character of the student left as a *movement*. As such, the student left draws unto its bosom an infinite variety of SDS New Leftists, left-liberals, old leftists, frauds, hippies, social democrats, freaks, pacifists, humanitarians, anarchists, opportunists, idealists, adventurers. Every critic of the movement is able to confirm his own worst fears with some set of incidents, publications and individuals. Because there are among the student left, young representatives of old left sects, often of left-wing parentage, the anti-communist liberals are out in force to do battle with what they take to be the sons of Frankenstein. Because the Pop Left is expert at "media theater," professors feel themselves under imminent threat of invasion by mind-blown barbarians and may be hardly aware of the role in radical politics played by their own graduate students.

SDS, old left sects, and the Pop Left are and are not the student movement. People reared in leftist traditions are significant as leaders and spokesmen because of their schooling in leftist politics. Their influence will diminish as the radical student movement grows and its members acquire greater political sophistication. There are, no doubt, cases of elite manipulation by steering committees. Manipulation is not characteristic, however, because the student movement does not organize; it materializes around some issue, then vanishes. Without mass organizations or disciplined cadres (SDS hardly qualifies as the latter), elitists are left groping for something to control. The really successful campus revolts have been unplanned, spontaneous creations of events, dominated not by individuals but by a mood. Columbia SDS, for instance, was notoriously weak *ante-bellum*.

The strength of the student movement lies in this spontaneity and a common rejection of a social order. It is also this spontaneity, variety, amphorousness—an almost spectral quality—which make it so hard to distinguish between what is transient and what is enduring, what is accidental and what is essential in the movement. It suffers the fault peculiar to any radical movement—a psychology of radical one-upmanship, which strengthens the position of political adventurers, pop revolutionaries, and ultra-leftists. Despite this, the movement's development over what is, after all, a very short span of time—five years or so—has been toward a more, rather than less rational assessment of American society. Nor is there any iron law of leftward momentum that requires that the student movement hurtle over the edge into an abyss of revolutionary nihilism. At Berkeley, which has the longest history, there is an open split between radicalism with a rational analysis and program and "militancy" empty of political content, according to which it's not whether you win or lose, but how you play the game. There is no consensus on the relevance of "guerrilla warfare" or the imminence of "revolution." It has not entirely escaped student radicals that the requirements of military organization for revolutionary warfare would undermine the conditions for the construction of the free society they want.

What appalls the faculty, ultimately, is not any particular failing of the student movement but simply direct action politics in a university setting. Since most faculty feel that order and quietude are basic requirements for research and the making of their names, they are natural allies of the university *status quo*. The English professor who did not want Columbia transformed into "some, scruffy Latin

American university" expressed with more passion than logic the faculty consensus on this point. Faculty often claim that "free inquiry" is threatened by student strikes and campus disruptions, but the temporary closing of a university and such disruption of classes as has taken place have not been directed against any particular forms of inquiry. Except in the case of war research (hardly an academic field of inquiry), disruptions have not been *selective* against points of view. It is as if employers were accusing unions of threatening the right of "free production" by strikes, picket lines and scuffles arising from them. The object of these disruptions is not to destroy the manufacturing plant or the university but to effect changes in them.

Senior faculty are prone to take student talk of democratic control of the university as a threat to professional guild control of teaching, curriculum and personnel. White students *are* somewhat interested in sharing control of teaching and curriculum, hardly interested in hiring and firing faculty, and mainly concerned with the institutional policies of the university in regard to war research, race and institutional expansion. Black students, however, in their call for black studies programs at Wisconsin, San Francisco State and elsewhere have demanded total autonomy within the university and student/faculty control of curriculum and personnel. These demands are less a function of political theory or educational principles than of race and the blacks' perception of white universities and society as essentially hostile.

Faculty are generally committed to the "natural hierarchy of knowledge," a notion which students would concede up to a point in regard to curriculum, where they would generally be content with a minority voice. It is less clear how this "natural hierarchy" affects general university policy. As it stands, most university faculties are either powerless to affect university policy, or they influence it only in an advisory capacity, or in the administration of decisions made elsewhere. The more politically sophisticated faculty justify such arrangements as "functional differentiation," in which the knowledgeable parties determine policy in their spheres of interest. Administrators "naturally" control university policy. Faculty are "naturally" autonomous in the area of curriculum and promotion. And the students—quite unnaturally—are powerless, although the consistent exponents of this view are willing to concede student control of curfews, lunch-lines, dormitory regulations and the like. This Great Chain of Being—a place for everyone and everyone in his place—is appropriate ideology for the faculty, who will often cite the importance of the medieval traditions of the university. The radical students, they will say, are wrong in claiming that the university is enmeshed in the operations of the society at large. Like the medieval

Church, these presbyterian professors will say that the university is in, but not of society. Otherwise, it could not serve Pure Reason.

The explanation fails at several points. It hardly explains the ultimate authority of boards of governors, who usually know little about the university. It assumes that men in power are disinterested in their use of authority, as it affects those to whom they are not accountable—especially students. It ignores politics.

The otherworldly justification of the university is also used in extremely disingenuous ways. The Academic Freedom Committee of the Berkeley faculty justified *un*-classified war research on grounds of academic freedom that protects "scholarly work from having to pass moral or political tests." The committee noted, "Results of striking importance and vast benefit to mankind have emerged from work that appeared at the outset to be mundane or morally suspect—even from research into instruments of warfare." In maintaining a view of the university as sanctuary, professors have simply not read their Clark Kerr. The University of California receives over $200 million from the Atomic Energy Commission—nearly as much as the entire amount appropriated by the state of California—to do work on nuclear explosives. In terms of dollar volume of contracts, MIT and Johns Hopkins are among the one hundred major military/aerospace corporations in the United States. As of 1966, Stanford, Columbia, and Michigan had over $10 million in Defense contracts. In relation to the universities, the military/ industrial complex is not "conspiracy theory"; it is reality.

The more imperially-minded of the academic mandarins extend their functionalist vision of the university to the point that the university becomes future society in microcosm. In some future time of astonishing technological and economic development, the whole world will be one vast, transistorized automated university As education is the "new factor of production," society will be rationalized beyond the ken of politicians, corporate executives and the like who currently rule it. The technocrats and men of intellect will finally come into their own: men of power instead of mere intellectual auxiliaries. It is a questionable vision. But as Zbigniew Brzezinski has said, "many intellectuals tend to be frustrated power-seekers."

Because student radicals will have no place in the new order and already attempt to frustrate its realization, these academicians continue, the student revolution is actually reaction, not in time with these forthcoming profound social and economic transformations.

It is characteristic of these academics that they should expect a mass movement of students to be moveable seminars in social theory. In fact, the radical students' failure to develop a refined analysis and detailed program is the failure of academicians and intellectuals whose job that is. In any case students base their hopes for a free society, just as the scholar/bureaucrats base their expectations of a new medieval synthesis, on fundamental transformations. These students assume, as their critics do not, that the replacement of an economics of scarcity by an economics of abundance will create new possibilities for social freedom. They assume that advances in communications and transportation technology require not only organization and bureaucracy, but also increase the opportunities for decentralization and democratic control. And they assume that all of these possibilities will be obstructed by political interests, grounded in past necessities and oppressions. As a new generation of scholars and thinkers begins to appear, as it has, the development of program and the refinement of analysis will accelerate. In preinvasion Czechoslovakia and Yugoslavia, this momentum was expressed in philosophy by a "socialist humanism" founded on a concept of human freedom. In economics, it was expressed by "market socialism" which expounded means to reduce the authority of the state and to decentralize power; in politics, by the desire to construct "socialist democracy" in which people may speak and act freely and in which industrial enterprises are controlled by workers' councils. In this country and in Western Europe, the formulations of philosophy and politics are not so far advanced. But the student movement is international and the spirit is the same.

THE BATTLE OF PEOPLE'S PARK

Sheldon Wolin and John Schaar

Sheldon Wolin and John Schaar are Professors of Political Science at the University of California, Berkeley.

. . . The bureaucratic nature of the multiversity and its disastrous consequences for education are by now familiar and beyond dispute. So, too, is the web of interdependence between it

From "Berkeley: The Battle of People's Park" in *The New York Review of Books* (June 19, 1969), pp. 29-31. Reprinted with permission from *The New York Review of Books.* Copyright © 1969 The New York Review.

and the dominant military, industrial, and political institutions of our society. These explain much about the response of the University to the absurd, yet hopeful, experiment of People's Park.

What needs further comment is the increasingly ineffectual quality of the University's responses, particularly when its organizational apparatus attempts to cope with what is spontaneous, ambiguous, and disturbingly human. It is significant that the Berkeley administration repeatedly expressed irritation with the failure of the Park people to "organize" a "responsible committee" or to select "representatives" who might "negotiate." The life-styles and values of the Park people were forever escaping the categories and procedures of those who administer the academic plant.

Likewise the issue itself: the occupants of the Park wanted to use the land for a variety of projects, strange but deeply natural, which defied customary forms and expectations, whereas, at worst, the University saw the land as something to be fenced, soil-tested, processed through a score of experts and maze of committees, and finally encased in the tight and tidy form of a rational design. At best, the most imaginative use of the land which the University could contemplate was as a "field-experiment station" where faculty and graduate students could observe their fellow beings coping with their "environment." In brief, the educational bureaucracy, like bureaucracies elsewhere, is experiencing increasing difficulty, because human life is manifesting itself in forms which are unrecognizable to the mentality of the technological age.

This suggests that part of the problem lies in the very way bureaucracies perceive the world and process information from it. It was this "bureaucratic epistemology" which largely determined how the University responded to the People's Park. Bureaucracy is both an expression of the drive for rationality and predictability, and one of the chief agencies in making the world ever more rational and predictable, for the bureaucratic mode of knowing and behaving comes to constitute the things known and done themselves.

Now this rational form of organizing human efforts employs a conception of knowledge which is also rational in specific ways (cf. Kenneth Keniston's analysis in *The Uncommitted: Alienated Youth in American Society*, 1967, pp. 253-272). The only legitimate instrument of knowledge is systematic cognition, and the only acceptable mode of discourse is the cognitive mode. Other paths to knowledge are suspect. Everything tainted with the personal, the subjective, and the passionate is suppressed, or dismissed as prejudice or pathology. A bureaucrat who based his decisions upon, say, intuition, dialectical reason, empathic awareness, or even common sense, would be guilty of misconduct.

The bureaucratic search for "understanding" does not begin in wonder, but in the reduction of the world to the ordinary and the manageable. In order to deal with the world in the cognitive mode, the world must first be approached as an exercise in "problem-solving." To say there is a problem is to imply there is a solution; and finding the solution largely means devising the right technique. Since most problems are "complex," they must be broken down by bureaucrats into their component parts before the right solution can be found. Reality is parsed into an ensemble of discrete though related parts, and each part is assigned to the expert specially qualified to deal with that part. Wholes can appear as nothing more than assemblages of parts, just as a whole automobile is an assemblage of parts. But in order for wholes to be broken into parts, things that are dissimilar in appearance and quality must be made similar.

This is done by abstracting from the objects dealt with those aspects as though they were the whole. Abstraction and grouping by common attributes require measuring tools that yield comparable units for analysis: favorite ones are units of money, time, space, and power; income, occupation, and party affiliation. All such measurements and comparisons subordinate qualitative dimensions, natural context, and unique and variable properties to the common, stable, external, and reproducible. This way of thinking becomes real when campus administrators define "recreation" in fixed and restrictive terms so that it may accord with the abstract demands of "lead-time." In a way Hegel might barely recognize, the Rational becomes the Real and the Real the Rational.

When men treat themselves this way, they increasingly become this way, or they desperately try to escape the "mind-forged manacles," as Blake called them, of the bureaucratic mentality and mode of conduct. In the broadest view, these two trends increasingly dominate the advanced states of our day. On the one side, we see the march toward uniformity, predictability, and the attempt to define all variety as dissent and then to force dissent into the "regular channels"—toward that state whose model citizen is Tocqueville's "industrious sheep," that state whose only greatness is its collective power.

On the other side we see an assertion of spontaneity, self-realization, and do-your-own-thing as the sum and substance of life and liberty. And this assertion, in its extreme form, does approach either madness or infantilism, for the only social institutions in which each member is really free to do his own thing are Bedlam and the nursery, where the condition may be tolerated because there is a keeper with ultimate control over the inmates. The opposing forces were not quite that pure in the confrontation over the People's Park, but the University and public officials nearly managed to make them so. That they could not do so is a comforting measure of the basic vitality of those who built the Park and who have sacrificed to preserve it.

But this still does not account for the frenzy of violence which fell on Berkeley. To understand that, we must shift focus.

Clark Kerr was perceptive when he defined the multiversity as "a mechanism held together by administrative rules and powered by money." But it is important to understand that the last few years in the University have seen more and more rules and less and less money. The money is drying up because the rules are being broken. The rules are being broken because University authorities, administrators and faculty alike, have lost the respect of very many of the students. When authority leaves, power enters—first in the form of more and tougher rules, then as sheer physical force, and finally as violence, which is force unrestrained by any thought of healing and saving, force whose aim is to cleanse by devastation.

Pressed from above by politicians and from below by students, the University Administration simultaneously imposes more rules and makes continual appeals to the faculty for more support in its efforts to cope with permanent emergency. It pleads with the faculty for more "elbow room," more discretionary space in which to make the hard decisions needed when money runs short and students run amuck. That same Administration is right now conducting time-and-motion studies of faculty work and "productivity." Simultaneously, both faculty and Administration make spasmodic efforts to give the students some voice in the governance of the institution. But those efforts are always too little, too late, too grudging.

Besides, as soon as the students get some power, unseemly things happen. Admit the Blacks on campus and they demand their own autonomous departments. Give the students limited power to initiate courses and they bring in Eldridge Cleaver and Tom Hayden. The faculty sees student initiative as a revolting mixture of Agitprop and denial of professional prerogatives. The Administration sees it as a deadly threat to its own precarious standing within the University and before the public. The politicians see it as concession to anarchy and revolution. The result is more rules and less trust all around— more centralization, bureaucratization, and force on one side, more despair and anger on the other.

Under these conditions, the organized system must strive to extend its control and reduce the space in which spontaneous and unpredictable actions are possible. The subjects, on the other hand, come to identify spontaneity and unpredictability with all that is human and alive, and rule and control with all that is inhuman and dead. Order and liberty stand in fatal opposition. No positive synthesis can emerge from this dialectic unless those who now feel themselves pushed out and put down are admitted as full partici-pants. But that is not happening. More and more, we are seeing in this country a reappearance of that stage in the breakdown of political societies where one segment of the whole—in this case still the larger segment—determines to dominate by force and terror other segments which reject and challenge its legitimacy.

This dynamic largely accounts for the crushing violence and terror that hit Berkeley. When spontaneity appeared in People's Park, it was first met by a re-statement of the rules governing possession and control of land. When that re-statement did not have the desired effect, the University failed to take the next step dictated by rule-governed behavior—seeking an injunction. Nor did it take the step which would have acknowledged itself as being in a political situation—talking on a plane of equality, and acting in a spirit of generosity, with the other parties. Instead, it regressed immediately to the use of physical measures. In the eyes of the Administration, the building of People's Park was an "unjustified aggression," and the right of self-defense was promptly invoked.

Once force was called into play, it quickly intensified, and the University cannot evade its share of responsibility for what followed. He who wills the end wills the means; and no University official could have been unaware of the means necessary to keep that fence standing. But the administrators did not quite understand that their chosen agents of force, the police, would not limit their attention only to the students and street-people, who were expend-able, but would turn against the University and the city as well.

Ronald Reagan reached Sacramento through Berkeley because, in the eyes of his frightened and furious supporters, Berkeley is daily the scene of events that would have shocked Sodom and revolutionary Moscow. All this came into intense focus in the behavior of the cops who were on the scene.

The police were numerous and armed with all the weapons a fertile technology can provide and an increasingly frightened citizenry will permit. Their superiority of force is overwhelming, and they are convinced they could "solve the problem" overnight if they were permitted to do it their own way: one instant crushing blow, and then license for dealing with the remaining recalcitrants. All the troublemakers are known to the police, either by dossier and record or by appearance and attitude. But the police are kept under some restraints, and those restraints produce greater and greater rage.

The rage comes from another source as well. Demands for a different future have been welling up in this society for some years now, and while those demands have not been unheard they have gone unheeded. Vietnam, racism, poverty, the degradation of the natural and manmade environment, the bureaucratization of the academy and its active collaboration with the military and industrial state, unrepresentative and unreachable structures of domination—all these grow apace. It seems increasingly clear to those who reject this American future that the forces of "law and order" intend to defend it by any means necessary. It becomes increasingly clear to the forces of law and order that extreme means will be necessary, and that the longer they are delayed the more extreme they will have to be.

Those two futures met at People's Park. It should be clear that what is happening this time is qualitatively different from 1964 and the Free Speech Movement. The difference in the amount of violence is the most striking, but this is largely a symptom of underlying differences. In 1964, the issues centered around questions of civil liberties and due process within the University. The issues now are political in the largest sense.

The appearance of People's Park raised questions of property and the nature of meaningful work. It raised questions about how people can begin to make a livable environment for themselves; about why both the defenders and critics of established authority today agree that authority can be considered only in terms of repression, never in terms of genuine respect and affection. These questions cannot be evaded. Those who honestly and courageously ask them are not imperiling the general happiness but are working for the common redemption.

It is increasingly clear that legitimate authority is declining in the modern state. In a real sense, "law and order" *is* the basic question of our day. This crisis of legitimacy has been visible for some time in just about all of the non-political sectors of life—family, economy, religion, education—and is now spreading rapidly into the political realm. The gigantic and seemingly impregnable organizations that surround and dominate men in the modern states are seen by more and more people to have at their center not a vital principle of authority, but a hollow space, a moral vacuum. Increasingly, among the young and the rejected, obedience is mainly a matter of lingering habit, or expediency, or necessity, but not a matter of conviction and deepest sentiment.

The groups who are most persistently raising these questions are, of course, white middle-class youth and the racial and ethnic minorities. The origins of protest are different in the two cases: the former have largely seen through the American Dream of meaning in power and wealth and have found it a nightmare; the latter have been pushed aside and denied even the minimal goods of the Dream. But the ends of the protest are remarkably similar: both are fighting against distortions and denials of their humanity. Both reject the programmed future of an America whose only imperative now seems to be: more.

The people who built the Park (there will be more People's Parks, more and more occasions for seemingly bizarre, perverse, and wild behavior) have pretty much seen through the collective ideals and disciplines that have bound this nation together in its conquest of nature and power. Having been victimized by the restraints and authorities of the past, these people are suspicious of all authorities and most collective ideals. Some of them seem ready to attempt a life built upon no other ideal than self-gratification. They sometimes talk as though they had found the secret which has lain hidden through all the past ages of man: that the individual can live fully and freely with no authority other than his desires, absorbed completely in the development of all his capacities except two—the capacity for memory and the capacity for faith.

No one can say where this will lead. Perhaps new prophets will appear. Perhaps the old faith will be reborn. Perhaps we really shall see the new technological Garden tended by children—kind, sincere innocents, barbarians with good hearts. The great danger at present is that the established and the respectable are more and more disposed to see all this as chaos and outrage. They seem prepared to follow the most profoundly nihilistic denial possible, which is the denial of the future through denial of their own children, the bearers of the future.

In such times as these, hope is not a luxury but a necessity. The hope which we see is in the revival of a sense of shared destiny, of some common fate which can bind us into a people we have never been. Even to sketch out that fate one must first decide that it does not lie with the power of technology or the stability of organizational society. It lies, instead, in something more elemental, in our common fears that scientific weapons may destroy all life; that technology will increasingly disfigure men who live in the city, just as it has already debased the earth and obscured the sky; that the "progress" of industry will destroy the possibility of interesting work; and that "communications" will obliterate the last traces of the varied cultures which have been the inheritance of all but the most benighted societies.

If hope is to be born of these despairs it must be given political direction, a new politics devoted to nurturing life and work. There can be no political direction without political education, yet America from its beginnings has never confronted the question of how to care for men's souls while helping them to see the world politically. Seeing the world politically is preparatory to acting in it politically; and to act politically is not to be tempted by the puerile attraction of power or be content with the formalism of a politics of compromise. It is, instead, a politics which seeks always to discover what men can share—and how what they share can be enlarged and yet rise beyond the banal.

People's Park is not banal. If only the same could be said of those who build and guard the fences around all of us.

DRUGS AS A COMMENTARY ON SOCIETY

Kenneth Keniston

Kenneth Keniston teaches in the Department of Psychiatry at the Yale University School of Medicine.

. . .It is widely feared that student drug use is a commentary upon American society; words like degeneracy, addiction, thrill-seeking and irresponsibility are eventually introduced into most popular discussions of student drug use. So, too, student drug use is said to be related to the excessive permissiveness of parents, to the laxness of adult standards, to breaches in law enforcement, to disrespect for law and order, and to an impending breakdown of our social fabric.

Although these particular interpretations of the social implications of drug use are incorrect, drug use *is* importantly influenced by social, political and historical factors. Those students who lust after significance or reject the prevalent values of American society are in fact reacting to and within a societal context. The sense of being locked-off and enclosed in an impermeable shell is related not only to individual psychological states like depression, but to broader cultural phenomena. And the fact that a considerable number of the most able students have become convinced that significance and relevant experience are largely to be found within their own skulls is

From "Heads and Seekers" in *The American Scholar* (Winter 1968-69), pp. 107-112. Reprinted from *The American Scholar*, Volume 38, Number 1, Winter 1968-69. Copyright ©1968 by the United Chapters of Phi Beta Kappa. By permission of the publishers.

indirectly related to their perception of the other possibilities for fulfillment in the social and political world. In a variety of ways, then, student drug use is a commentary on American society, although a different kind of commentary than most discussions of youthful "thrill-seeking" would lead us to believe.

To single out a small number of social changes as especially relevant to understanding student drug use is to make a highly arbitrary decision. A variety of factors, including rapid social change, the unprecedented possibilities for total destruction in the modern world, the prevalence of violence both domestic and international, the high degree of specialization and bureaucratization of American life, and a host of others are relevant to creating the context of values and expectations within which drug use has become increasingly legitimate. But of all the factors that could be discussed, three seem particularly relevant: first, the effect of modern communications and transportation in producing an overwhelming inundation of experience, which I will term *stimulus flooding*; second, the effect of *automatic affluence* in changing the values and outlooks of the young; third, the importance of recent social and historical events in producing a kind of *social and political disenchantment* that leads many students to seek salvation through withdrawal and inner life rather than through engagement and societal involvement.

Stimulus Flooding and Psychological Numbing

Every society subjects its members to pressures and demands that they simply take for granted. Such pressures are woven into the fabric of social existence, are assumed to be a natural part of life, and become the object of automatic accommodation. These accommodations are rarely examined, yet they may profoundly alter the quality of human experience. Such is the case with the quantity, variety and intensity of external stimulation, imagery and excitation to which most Americans are subjected. As Robert J. Lifton has pointed out, modern man in advanced societies is subjected to a flood of unpredictable stimulation of the most varied kinds; by newspapers, television, radio and rapid travel, he continually exposes himself to novel and unanticipatable experience. This stimulus inundation, in turn, produces a self-protective reaction which, following Lifton, we can term psychic numbing.

Most individuals in most societies have at some point in their lives had the experience of being so overcome by external stimulation and internal feelings that they gradually find themselves growing numb and unfeeling. Medical students commonly report that after their first, often intense reactions to the cadaver, they simply "stop feeling anything" with regard to the object of their dissection. And we have all had the experience of listening to so much good music, seeing so many fine paintings, being so overwhelmed by excellent cooking that we find ourselves simply unable to respond further. Similarly, at moments of extreme psychic pain and anguish, most individuals "go numb," no longer perceiving the full implications of a catastrophic situation or no longer experiencing the full range of their own feelings. This lowered responsiveness, this psychological numbing, seems causally related to the variety, persistence and intensity of stimulation and emotion.

Most Americans have had the experience of returning to urban life from a calm and pastoral setting. Initially, we respond by being virtually deluged with the clamor of people, sights, sounds, images and colors that demand our attention and response. The beauty and the ugliness of the landscape continually strike us; each of the millions of faces in our great cities has written on it the tragicomic record of a unique life history; each sound evokes a resonant chord within us. Such periods, however, tend to be transient and fleeting; and they usually give way to a sense of numbness, of nonresponsiveness, and of profound inattention to the very stimuli that earlier evoked so much in us. We settle in, we do not notice anymore.

This psychological numbing operates at a great variety of levels for modern man. Our experience, from childhood onward, with the constantly flickering images and sounds of television, films, radio, newspapers, paperbacks, neon signs, advertisements and sound trucks numbs us to the sights and sounds of our civilization. Our continual exposure to a vast variety of ideologies, value systems, philosophies, political creeds, superstitions, religions and faiths numbs us to the unique claims to validity and the special spiritual and intellectual values of each one: we move among values and ideologies as in a two-dimensional landscape. Similarly, the availability to us in novels, films, television, theater and opera of moments of high passion, tragedy, joy, exaltation and sadness often ends by numbing us to our own feelings and the feelings of others.

Modern men thus confront the difficult problem of keeping "stimulation" from without to a manageable level, while also protecting themselves against being overwhelmed by their own inner responses to the stimuli from the outer world. Defenses or barriers against both external and internal stimulation are, of course, essential in order for us to preserve our intactness and integrity as personalities. From earliest childhood, children develop thresholds of responsiveness and barriers against stimulation in order to protect themselves against being overwhelmed by inner or outer excitement. Similarly, in adulthood, comparable barriers, thresholds and defenses are necessary, especially when we find ourselves in situations of intense stimulation.

A problem arises, however, if the barriers we erect to protect ourselves from the clamors of the inner and outer world prove harder and less permeable than we had originally wanted. In at least a minority of Americans, the normal capacity to defend oneself against undue stimulation and inner excitation is exaggerated and automatized, so that it not only protects, but walls off the individual from inner and outer experience. In such individuals, there develops an acute sense of being trapped in their own shells, unable to break through their defenses to make "contact" with experience or with other people, a sense of being excessively armored, separated from their own activities as by an invisible screen, estranged from their own feelings and from potentially emotion-arousing experiences in the world. Most of us have had some inkling of this feeling of inner deadness and outer flatness, especially in times of great fatigue, letdown, or depression. The world seems cold and two-dimensional; food and life have lost their savor; our activities are merely "going through the motions," our experiences lack vividness, three-dimensionality, and intensity. Above all, we feel trapped or shut in our own subjectivity.

The continual flooding of stimulation to which modern men are subjected is thus related not only to the psychological conditions and institutional pressures that help create the feelings of numbness, but, indirectly, to the nature of perception and experience in an advanced technological society. One problem every modern American faces is how to avoid becoming entrapped in the protective shell he must construct to defend himself against being overwhelmed by stimulation. And the use of drugs, especially in the context of the experiential counter-culture, becomes more attractive to youth precisely because the drugs preferred by students often have the effect of dissipating, blurring, or breaking down the boundaries of individual selfhood and personality.

Automatic Affluence

No society in world history has ever provided its citizens with the automatic abundance that our society provides to a majority of Americans. In over ten years of interviewing students from middle-class and upper-middle-class backgrounds, I have yet to find one who was worried about finding a job, and have met relatively few who were worried about finding a *good* job. Whatever their levels of aspiration, today's advantaged youth rarely think in terms of getting ahead in the world, acquiring increasing status, or struggling to "succeed." These goals, both relevant and important to their parents (products of the 1920's and the Great Depression), are largely irrelevant to today's youth. Like youth in every era, they turn from the successes of the past to the problems of the present and future. Thus, paradoxically, although they live in a society more affluent than any before it, they are far more outraged at poverty, injustice, inequality, exploitation and cruelty than were their parents, who lived in a more impoverished society. Indeed, one of the central demands of today's politically active youth is that everyone have the benefits which they themselves have always taken for granted.

One of the undeniable benefits of affluence is that it brings increased opportunities for enjoyment and leisure, and destroys the need to devote oneself to a life of unrelenting toil in order to prosper. Affluence permits a de-emphasis of hard work, self-control and renunciation, and makes possible the development of new cultures of leisure. As work, success and achievement decline in relative importance, new values are beginning to replace them, and new patterns of consumption are beginning already to reflect these new values. As "getting ahead in the world" no longer suffices to define the meaning of life, today's advantaged students turn increasingly to explore *other* meanings of life.

Two rather different alternatives have so far been tried. The first is the solution of the political activist, who remains primarily concerned with the fact that his own affluence and freedom have not been extended to all. Within America, his concern is with the poor, the deprived, the excluded and the disadvantaged. Abroad, he focuses on the many failures of American foreign policy, failures that in his eyes involve a catastrophic gap between the values of a democratic society and the foreign policies that purportedly implement them. The activist would have us support rather than oppose movements of national liberation, and use our affluence not in military engagements but in programs of assistance to the developing nations. The activist is most likely to accept the traditional values of American society, especially those emphasizing justice, equality, opportunity and freedom, and to insist that these values be more thoroughly practiced.

The second response to the question, "What lies beyond affluence?," while not incompatible with the first, looks in a different area for an answer. This second response turns to a more fundamental critique of the premises and assumptions upon which technological America has been based. Instead of equality, it champions diversity; instead of pressing for the extension of affluence, it questions the meaning of affluence. Associated with a long tradition of romantic criticism of industrial and postindustrial society, this response points to the price of affluence— dehumanization, professionalization, bureaucracy, a loss of power over society, the absence of a sense of small scale, and the erosion of traditional community. For the romantic critic of American society, fulfillment and personal wholeness are more important than abundance and achievement. The life of the affluent middle class in America is seen as empty, spiritually impoverished, driven and neurotic; the vaguely defined alternative involves expressiveness, self-knowledge, involvement with the small group of others, the fulfillment of nonmaterial artistic, spiritual and psychological needs. "Self-actualization" is the goal; "let each man do his thing" is the motto.

Automatic affluence, then, inevitably means that many of those who experience abundance as routine, attempt to create goals beyond affluence. These goals may involve a reform of the world so as to extend affluence to all, or a critique of the technological assumptions upon which affluence itself was based. Insofar as the individual's main effort is to extend affluence, he is relatively immune to the appeals of the experiential, drug-using world, for his energies are oriented toward changing the world rather than himself. But insofar as his primary focus is antitechnological—upon self-fulfillment, personal change, and spiritual or humanistic fulfillment—this focus is highly consistent with the use of drugs. For drug use among college students is closely related to the effort to change oneself, to become more creative, to be more expressive, more emotionally open and more genuinely in contact with the world. And the use of drugs is associated with a questioning or rejection of the traditional success ethic of American life, and with a search for new styles of living more oriented to leisure, to intimate personal relationships, and to spiritual expression. Thus, affluence indirectly produces a mood among some of its recipients that makes them receptive to drug use and other forms of personal experimentation.

Socio-Political Disenchantment

In juxtaposing two answers to the quest for meaning beyond abundance, I have implied a certain tension between them. It is not accidental that full-time and committed political activists are rarely intensive drug users; it is also important that the full-time denizens of the drug-using hippie subculture are rarely capable of sustained political activity. Sustained engagement in an effort to change the world is rarely compatible with the kind of self-absorption and inwardness that results from intensive and regular drug use; conversely, however strongly the committed drug user may feel about the inequities of American society, his primary efforts are usually directed toward self-change, rather than changing the world around him. Although some individuals alternate at different times in their lives between activism and alienation, it is very difficult to be an active social reformer and a "head" at the same time.

This argument suggests that disenchantment with the possibilities of meaningful social action is related to the development of an outlook conducive to drug use. To trace student drug use directly to such factors as racial injustices or the war in Vietnam would, of course, be a major oversimplification. But disenchantment with meaningful and honorable political activity creates a general climate of opinion that *is*, in turn, favorable to drug use. Specifically, the change in student attitudes toward political life and social reform since the assassination of President Kennedy seems importantly connected to the rise of drug use.

The influence of Kennedy upon the attitudes of youth is often exaggerated or stated in an oversimplified way. Many of the young, of course, disliked Kennedy, as did many of their parents. Furthermore, most of those who admired Kennedy personally had no intention whatsoever of entering public life. Kennedy's impact on the attitudes of youth was indirect: he and the group around him symbolized the conviction that it was possible for young, idealistic and intelligent men and women to enter the political world and to "make a difference." Such Kennedy ventures as the Peace Corps further provided an outlet—and more importantly a symbol—for the idealistic energies of activist youth. Although Kennedy himself in fact rarely listened to the advice of students, such symbolic Kennedy acts as pots of coffee for peace marchers in front of the White House indicated at least an awareness of the opinion of the dedicated young.

The image of political life conveyed by the Johnson Administration, especially from 1966 to 1968, was vastly different. Not only have older views of politics as a form of horse trading, "compromising," and "wheeling and dealing" been reinstated, but large numbers of American college students have come to associate political involvement with gross immorality and even with genocide. In this context, such revelations as that of covert C.I.A. funding of liberal student organizations like the National Students Association have the effect of convincing many intelligent and idealistic youth that politics—and, by extension, efforts to work to change the System from within—are dishonorable or pointless occupations.

The demise of the Civil Rights Movement and the collapse of the War on Poverty have also helped change the climate of opinion about political reform. In the early 1960's, the Civil Rights Movement was the chief catalyst for the rising tide of student political involvement. Sit-ins, Freedom Rides, the work of S.N.C.C. and other groups in the Deep South helped convince students that their efforts at social change would be honored, recognized and responded to by the society at large. Students in the early 1960's saw themselves not so much in opposition to the policies of the nation as in the vanguard of these policies; and the passage of major Civil Rights legislation in 1964, followed by the promise of a major "War on Poverty," gave support to this conviction. Thus there arose a hope that "American society would crash through" in remedying its own inequities. This hope had a widespread impact, not only upon that small minority of students who were actively involved in civil rights work, but upon others who were indirectly encouraged to plan careers of responsible social involvement.

But the events of subsequent years have altered this initial hope. The "white backlash" has made legislators extremely reluctant to assist the Negro revolution. The war in Vietnam drained funds away from domestic programs just when federal assistance was needed most. The student Civil Rights Movement for its part discovered that legal reforms exposed more clearly the depths of the problem of black Americans, and pointed toward more far-reaching psychological, social and economic changes that were more difficult to legislate from Washington. The War on Poverty collapsed into a small skirmish. Equally important, the rising militancy of black radicals has pushed white students out of organizations like S.N.C.C. and CORE with the demand, "Go home and organize your own people." Lacking national support, and "rejected" by their former black allies, white activists have increasingly despaired of working within the System, have become more radical, and are talking more militantly about "changing the System."

The changing image of political involvement has had two effects. On the one hand, it has contributed to the "radicalization" of those individuals who have remained activists: especially now among such students, disaffection with the established system is at a high that has not been reached in this country since the 1930's. But equally important, the revitalized image of the political process as dishonest, reprehensible, immoral and unresponsive to both the ideals of America and the rights of the deprived has created a climate in which it is more and more possible to argue that salvation—if it can be found at all—must be found within the self or the counter-community, rather than within the wider society. Given this belief, the individual in search of meaningful engagement with the world must either create new political institutions (as stressed by the rhetoric of the New Left), or else abandon political struggle altogether in a search for meaning within small groups of other disaffected people. It is in these latter groups that drug use is most common. If the world outside is corrupt, dehumanized, violent and immoral, the world within—the almost infinitely malleable world of perception, sensation, communication and consciousness—seems more controllable, more immediate, less corrupting, and ofttimes more pleasant. To be sure, there is a price to be paid for exclusive involvement in the interior world, but, for many young Americans, there simply seems to be no alternative.

Political and historical events do not have a direct, one-to-one relationship with drug use: the war in Vietnam does not *cause* students to smoke marijuana or experiment with LSD. But the political climate of the past few years has created a negative view of the possibility of meaningful involvement within the established institutions of the society, at the same time that it has convinced many students that society is in desperate need of reform. This climate of opinion in turn contributes to the assumption that if meaning, excitement and dignity are to be found in the world, they must be found within one's own cranium. Drug use can indeed be a kind of cop-out, not from perversity or laziness, but simply because there seems to be no other alternative. Student drug use is indeed a commentary upon American society, but it is above all an indirect criticism of our society's inability to offer the young exciting, honorable and effective ways of using their intelligence and idealism to reform our society.

THE DANGERS OF CAMPUS DISORDERS

Bruno Bettelheim

Bruno Bettelheim is a professor at the University of Chicago, teaching educational psychology.

Most of us have come to recognize that the rebellious students—as opposed to those who express their often justified dissatisfaction in non-disruptive ways—are a serious danger to the country. Not because I fear that they can bring about a successful revolution. For that they lack the necessary mass following and a

From testimony before the Senate Committee on Government Operations, Permanent Subcommittee on Investigations, *Hearings on Riots, Civil and Criminal Disorders*, 91st Congress, 1st Session, May 9, 13, and 14, 1969, Part 16, pp. 3069-3079.

program for positive actions during and after the revolution, conditions without which no revolution can succeed. I believe their dangerousness originates, firstly, in the fact that they may indeed seriously damage our universities, and with it deprive us of the high level intellectual training centers which an advanced society needs to continue its progress.

They indeed may politicize our universities to such a degree that they may then become centers of social and political unrest rather than of research and training. If this happens, then society will be deprived of the intellectual leadership we need to continue our scientific, economic and social progress. Typically, the countries where the universities were thus politicized fell far behind in these and all other respects.

Secondly, because of the advanced nature of our society, we have come to expect leadership of our universities, that they set examples to be emulated. If they become centers in which decisions are based on who can intimidate whom, then this indeed becomes a most dangerous example. If the leaders of our intellectual establishment are so unsure of their values that they cave in under threats, rather than being guided by democratic values, then the trust in rational process, so important for a democratic system of government, becomes destroyed.

Worst of all, if students, because they are so advantaged socially and economically, can get away with breaking the law, and even when apprehended are given special amnesties, then the country begins to feel that these students are above the law, which undermines everybody's respect for it.

Universities lend a prestige to the claims of revolutionary students they would otherwise never enjoy. . . .

Thus, in themselves, a couple of hundred demonstrators somewhere in New York or Chicago would mean very little. But if they take over a large lecture hall and broadcast their ideas to people who came to hear something quite different, then they have made news. And this is where the function of political phraseology becomes operative. Thus, if girls dress up as witches and put the curse on professors, as they did in Chicago, or undress in public and walk around naked as they did on other campuses, but without reference to the "sickness" of society, everyone would conclude it was they who were sick in their minds. But if they do so as a condemnation of the Vietnam war, they have the support of many of the older liberals who will inevitably consider it all to be very socially significant. If these youngsters are wrestling with the police and say they are doing it because of their moral conviction that ours is a vile social order, nobody wonders whether they could create a better one. Instead of asking them to demonstrate what they are doing on the positive side to improve conditions, they get the sympathetic attention of the mass media for their disruptive behavior rather than of psychiatrists and social workers.

The ritualistic invocation of ideology is thus used by them and accepted by large groups of society, both as an alibi and a defense.

Finally, and worst of all, violence breeds violence, and every instance in which violence is rewarded by gaining the group that engages in it what it asked for, encourages all of society to rely ever more on violence rather than on the democratic process for gaining one's goals. In this sense, I think these rebellious students are a real danger to the universities and the intellectual life of our society.

But they are a serious danger also in another fashion. The provocative behavior of a very small group of students will arouse a dangerous counter-reaction. . . . This is what I consider most dangerous about the student attempts to create chaos, to prove democratic procedures ineffectual in containing them. Because such a demonstration does undermine trust in the democratic way and sends their opponents toward fascist solutions of their own. And if this should happen it could indeed swell the ranks of the still insignificant fascists of the right, give them a mass following that would constitute a very real danger.

In desperation, and to prevent chaos, repressive measures might then be taken that would seriously threaten our domestic institutions. (And the tactics of left radical students, designed as they are to test and exhaust the patience of what they call the establishment, do create desperation, particularly since the student movement has no positive program and since revolution without a definite picture of what the future would be like when the revolution is over, creates well-founded anxiety.) It is because of this danger that I believe we must deal with student rebellions. And the only way we can do this is by not permitting the militants to disrupt the workings of the universities, or to intimidate them so that they accede to demands they would reject if not forced or intimidated, and by paying serious attention, and by removing in constructive ways the causes of widespread unrest among college youth.

To understand that unrest, one has to begin by asking oneself: "What do all dissenting youth have in common, round the globe?" In the United States, students point first to Vietnam and the Negro problem. Because of the war, they say, "we have no future so that the education we get is not relevant"; and because society has failed to solve the race problem, it should be destroyed. Even if some do not go quite so far, they distrust a society, they say, which does nothing to end the war, racial injustice, urban decay, air and water pollution, et cetera. But in Germany, there is no Negro problem; in

Japan, there is no Vietnam; in Italy and France, no one threatens to make nuclear war. What, then, is common to so wide a cross section of world youth?

It is my conviction that Vietnam and the bomb serve youth as a screen for what really ails them: Their feeling that youth has no future because modern technology has made them obsolete—socially irrelevant, and, as persons, insignificant. Youth feels its future is bleak not with the prospect of nuclear war, as biologist Wald told MIT students recently, and for which they gave him a standing ovation, but because of their feeling that nobody needs them, that society can do nicely without them. This is the even bleaker anxiety behind their feeling that youth has no future. Because, if a young man does not feel it is he who will be building the future, is sorely needed to bring it about, then the feeling is that he has none. That is why, in hopes of denying such an anxious conviction, students insist that their mission is to build a wholly new and different future. Their anxiety is not—as they claim—about a future atomic war. It is not that society has no future. Their existential anxiety is that they have no future in a society that does not need them to go on existing.

It makes sense, then, that so much of their battle is fought in and around schools, be it the grammar and high schools where blacks are concerned, or the colleges and universities where whites and blacks are concerned. Actually, I believe the problems of black students in America are entirely different from those of white students, though time prevents my discussing them here.

Because it is education that prepares us for our place in the work of society, and if education today prepares us only to be replaceable items in the production machine, to program its computers, then it seems to prepare us not for a chance to emerge in importance as persons, but only to serve the machine better.

Behind all this lie more fundamental reasons why adolescent malaise grows so widespread. These begin to emerge when we look in quite another direction—when we recognize that adolescent revolt is not a stage of development that follows automatically from our natural makeup, because what makes for adolescent revolt is the fact that a society keeps the next generation too long dependent in terms of mature responsibility and a striving for independence. This, I believe, is the common denominator wherever student rebellion occurs. And the fact that it occurs only where affluence exists, only in the modern, industrial state, is merely the same common denominator as seen from the outside.

Years ago, when schooling ended for the vast majority at 14 or 15, and thereafter one became self-supporting, got married and had children, there was no need for adolescent revolt. Because while puberty is a biological fact, adolescence as we know it with its identity crises is not. All children grow up and become pubertal. By no means do they all become adolescents. To be adolescent means that one has reached and even passed the age of puberty, is at the very height of one's physical development—healthier, stronger, even handsomer than one has been, or will be, for the rest of one's life—but must nevertheless postpone full adulthood till long beyond what any other period in history has considered reasonable.

With no more open frontiers left, our society has no special place for adolescence today, with the single exception of our colleges and universities. Moreover, we push our young people toward maturity nowadays even while overextending the years of their dependence. We start them sooner and sooner in school and make a farce of graduations—even from kindergarten now—until school becomes a rat race with never a home stretch in sight. And, so, by the time they get to college, they have had it. I doubt whether life was ever less of a rat race than today. But it only became a senseless rat race when more and more people got to feeling they were racing after goals that were not really worthwhile or urgent, because survival seems assured by the affluent state.

At the same time, the educational experience today, whether in the home or the school, prepares only a small minority of youth well, for such a prolonged waiting, for controlling their angry impatience. Here we should not overlook the symbolic meaning of the student's invading the office of the president or dean, violently, or through sit-ins. Big in size and age, those who sit in feel like little boys with a need to play big by sitting in papa's big chair. They want to sit in the driver's seat, want to have a say in how things are run, not because they feel competent to do so, but because they cannot bear to feel incompetent a moment longer.

I think it is unnatural to keep a young person in dependence for some 20 years attending school. This may be a way of life for that small elite which would always have chosen it in the past. There were always those who could go to school for 20 years, but they were never more than a small percentage of the population—even of the university population which included those attending as a matter of caste. Now the tremendous push on everyone to go to college has brought incredibly large numbers to the university who do not find their self-realization through study or the intellectual adventure—or not at that point in their lives. What they still want urgently, however, is to find their manhood.

To make matters worse, our institutions of higher learning have expanded too fast. Under public pressure for more education for all, they have steadily increased enrollment without the means to make parallel adjustments in the learning situation. One result is far too large classes. Another is the anonymity, the impersonal nature of student-faculty contacts that students rightly complain of.

But essentially it is the waiting for things—for the real life to come—that creates a climate in which a sizable segment of students are chronically seduced into following the lead of a small group of militants. In the words of Jerry Rubin, yippie organizer, "Who the hell wants to 'make it' in America any more? The American economy no longer needs young whites and blacks. We are waste material. We fulfill our destiny in life by rejecting a system which rejects us."

Campus rebellion seems to offer youth a chance to shortcut the empty waiting and prove themselves real adults. This can be seen from the fact that most rebellious students, here and abroad, are either undergraduates or those studying the social sciences and humanities. There are precious few militants among students of medicine, chemistry, engineering, the natural sciences. Student power has no meaning in the laboratory; there no one doubts the need for leadership by the most experienced of the less experienced. Moreover, while the social science student can easily convince himself that he knows precisely what is wrong with society, particularly if his friends all agree, it is impossible for the medical student to fool himself that he knows what went wrong in the cancerous cell. Nor can such a student believe that what he is doing, or the discipline it demands, is irrelevant.

Those who cannot find themselves in their studies or their work are hence the most vocal in finding the university irrelevant. Typically, the militant finds his largest following among the newcomers, those with least time or chance as yet to find a place for themselves at the university. This place some try to find quickly by plunging into active, even violent, battle against the existing order. Except that if they should win they would be changing the university into an institution that no longer serves inquiry and study, but a belligerent reshaping of society.

I maintain that, despite the high-sounding moral charges against the sins of our society, those sins—in the hearts and minds of youth—are not the destruction of youth in Vietnam but of neglecting youth on the home front, of finding them "waste material" so that they must "reject a system that rejects us." This is the socio-psychological situation which permits the extremist leaders to find a mass following without which their efforts at disruption would soon collapse or could readily be contained.

Which takes me to the small group of the militant leaders. Their psychological makeup I found very different from that of those serious students who are deeply concerned with what is wrong in our universities and in society, who try for better ways of doing things, but who know that violence only leads to destruction and who, therefore, work hard for a better world, and who respect themselves and others too much to push them around or to prevent others from doing their work. The militant leaders have very different motives. Most of them I found consumed by a self-hatred they try to escape from by fighting any establishment. Many of these extremists are highly intelligent and very verbal. Unfortunately, their claim to act out of high motives, and their often attacking real evils, has misled many well-meaning people to overlook that their true motif is hate, not desire for a better world. This is not to say that much in our society is not overdue for reform. But only that hatred and desire for destruction never lead to an improvement of things.

Here we should not overlook how many, for how long, were taken in by Hitler's pointing to the suffering of the German people as a mainspring of his actions, and hoped he would indeed create better conditions in Germany, overlooking that the only motif for his claim was his hatreds.

Still, it is their hatred of society that makes it so easy for the small group of militant leaders to make common cause with two other small groups that provide temporary leadership for some rebellions: Those persons who suffer from extreme isolation, and those who are clearly paranoid. I do not believe the number of paranoids among students is greater than their number would be in any comparable group of the population. They become dangerous because their high intelligence makes them more successful at hiding their disturbance from the layman. . . .

Having worked professionally with some extremists for years, I know that student revolt permits the social isolate to feel himself part of a community for a while, and the paranoid to act out his paranoia, as could happen in no other niche of society. How understandable, then, that all extreme isolates and paranoids who can, quickly flock to the ranks of the militants.

Unfortunately, most nonprofessionals do not know how persuasive paranoids can be in their unconscious appeal to the vague and fleeting paranoia of the immature and disgruntled. And they always are able to make an excellent case for their accusations, as if they were based on just causes, and not on their hatreds and delusions of persecution. The justness of their complaints is then taken erroneously as the cause of their disruptive actions. Paranoids are always persuasive in their appeal to any group of the population who rightly or wrongly feel persecuted. They seek out such groups as most likely to take their paranoia for a true understanding of the particular dilemma the group suffers.

Political activity for such persons enables them to escape a complete break with reality. Though they interpret reality in line with their delusions, they at least remain in touch with isolated aspects of reality, while the support and admiration of their followers is another, though most tenuous, contact. . . .

But even if some of these rebellious students are paranoid, and others desperate isolates, both pathologies have existed in all societies and can hardly explain our problem. Certainly, it does not explain the seriousness or the magnitude of the present student revolt. For our deepest concern should not be so much with the activist leaders, quite a few of whom are in need of professional help, but rather with their followers. Because it is that larger and ever-changing body of students whom the leaders can attract and enlist, once they have set up a confrontation that seems to pit the world of the fathers against the world of the sons, which poses the biggest problem to society.

My thesis is that more than anything else it is the seeming vacuum to which we graduate so many of your young in the modern industrial state, which so convinces them that ours is a society that cannot make sense. . . .

However varied the origins and motives, these rebellions can and do paralyze universities. Not only because classes are interrupted and buildings occupied, not only because the faculty must devote all their energies to calming things down, but because all the time and energy that should go to more lasting achievements are diverted to forestalling the next confrontation.

In our universities today, we see faculty members who strive to remain aloof from it all, while others try to anticipate even the most radical of student demands to avoid still another confrontation. Unfortunately, too little is done to activate more constructive attempts at reform or to mobilize alternative student groups. Yet, what this age group needs and wants is the chance to be active. Even if student representatives were to sit on all faculty committees, take part in all their ponderous deliberations, this is not the active life youth hankers for. Much as they now clamor for it, they would soon enough lose all interest. Instead of searching, however, for new modes of bringing action to student life, faculties seem to spend their time worrying about what the militants may do next or in anxious efforts to give them no offense. Worst of all, many are so intimidated that they cave in before the students have ever begun to exert pressure.

All this saps the universities of their strength to the point of paralysis. This anxious avoidance of taking a firm stand gives militants the feeling—but also many noncommitted students—that they have the faculty on the run. And this chance seems irresistibly attractive to youth.

If the colleges and universities felt sure of their values, took a determined stand against coercive intimidation—while open to and inviting reasonable discussion of much needed improvements—I believe student rebellions would cease to be a threat. And here, I believe, lies the true challenge to our universities—the chance to lead the intellectual, and with it the establishment, itself.

American liberals have made all too much of a fetish out of formal democracy. They are so afraid they may turn undemocratic, that they have become helpless at the threat of mob rule. True, no system of government is more vulnerable than democracy. If it should ever lose its ability to right itself by adapting to emergencies without losing its democratic way, it will indeed perish: Destroyed either by fascism of the right or the left, or by its own defensive recourse to repressions that would destroy it just as effectively.

But the day seems gone when we could rely on our institutions remaining unchallenged because those who had a voice in them were part of a once broad consensus, part of the only establishment that counted and ran things. From now on, all institutions will be challenged—through force and intimidation, if the challengers can get away with it; through superior reasoning, if we are strong enough to permit nothing less. The more we invite and take advantage of sound reasons for and against change, and the more firmly we protect ourselves from coercion, the better off everyone will be.

At this moment in history both seem equally needed. If proposed changes are bad they should be rejected, violence or not. If they are better than what exists, why should they be dragged into being under duress? That merely legitimizes the effectiveness of violence. On both counts universities would do better to recapture the initiative they have lost; to furnish ideas for change.

I think it should be obvious by now what I believe some of these much needed improvements might be. First, all too many who now go to college have little interest, ability, or use for what now constitutes a college education. They would be better off with a high level education in the professions and the services, closely linked to a work program. This would give scope to their need to be active, while enjoying tangible achievement in the immediate present. Their complaint is that nobody needs them. Since they feel themselves parasites of society, they come to hate a society which gives them such a feeling. But nothing so balances the sense of being still an apprentice as to already be actively serving in the profession one is training at. . . .

Youth needs some romantic ideas and even romantic actions. They want to do things, and if we will not let them, they will destroy things. They want to be able to serve where they and it counts.

I would, therefore, suggest a youth service program of a few years' duration—something on the order of a civilian peace corps—in which young people would work on socially relevant projects while earning pay, and getting higher professional training as they go. After this period, only those would go to universities who really wanted to. But by that time most young adults would have acquired a real stake in society because they had been helping to shape it. At the very least, they would be better prepared for permanent jobs because of the training received.

So long as the need for an army draft continues, civilian service could be an alternative choice. Only those young people who preferred it would serve in the Armed Forces, making it a voluntary Army. I am convinced that if every able-bodied person had to serve 2 years in one program or the other, there would be no scarcity of those with a preference for 2 years of military service. This would do away with the draft exemption of college students which further provokes student unrest. Because if I am exempt from serving in Vietnam when others are not, I can only live in peace with myself by believing that an immoral war—as if there was ever a moral war.

As for the very small group who led the student rebellion, I have little to add here. Without the current widespread discontent among youth, they would find scant enough following, which might force them to more constructive channels themselves. I would favor most our providing for them those emotional experiences which would help them out of their desperate isolation. For some, that could be provided most effectively by psychotherapy. And if some of them did seriously break the law, without followers they could readily be contained. It is the mass following they arouse because of the general unrest among youth which alone makes them dangerous.

I therefore think it would be wrong to concentrate, in our thinking and planning for youth, in or out of college, on these very few. Our focus belongs on how to provide our young people with the age-correct satisfactions they need. And these satisfactions are very different from the ones that their largely unconscious motives will keep pushing them toward, for want of better direction.

THE CASE FOR PROFESSIONALISM

Robert Brustein

Robert Brustein is dean of the drama school at Yale University; he has been a drama critic for The New Republic *since 1960.*

In such a state of society [a state of democratic anarchy] , the master fears and flatters his scholars, and the scholars despise their masters and tutors; young and old are alike; and the young man is on a level with the old, and is ready to compete with him in word and deed; and old men condescend to the young and are full of pleasantry and gaiety; they are loth to be thought morose and authoritative, and therefore they adopt the manners of the young. . . .

Plato, *The Republic*, Book VIII

Among the many valuable things on the verge of disintegration in contemporary America is the concept of professionalism—by which I mean to suggest a condition determined by training, experience, skill, and achievement (by remuneration, too, but this is secondary). In our intensely Romantic age, where so many activities are being politicized and objective judgments are continually colliding with subjective demands, the amateur is exalted as a kind of democratic culture hero, subject to no standards or restrictions. This development has been of concern to me because of its impact upon my immediate areas of interest—the theater and theater training—but its consequences can be seen everywhere, most conspicuously in the field of liberal education. If the amateur is coequal—and some would say, superior—to the professional, then the student is coequal or superior to the professor, and "the young man," as Plato puts it in his discourse on the conditions that lead to tyranny, "is on a level with the old, and is ready to compete with him in word and deed."

As recently as five years ago, this proposition would have seemed remote; today, it has virtually become established dogma, and its implementation is absorbing much of the energy of the young. Although student unrest was originally stimulated, and rightly so, by such external issues as the war in Vietnam and the

"The Case for Professionalism" in *The New Republic* (April 26, 1969), pp. 16-18. Reprinted by permission of *The New Republic*, ©1969, Harrison-Blaine of New Jersey, Inc.

social grievances of the blacks and the poor, it is now more often aroused over internal issues of power and influence in the university itself. Making an analogy between democratic political systems and the university structure, students begin by demanding a representative voice in the "decisions that affect our lives," including questions of faculty tenure, curriculum changes, grading, and academic discipline. As universities begin to grant some of these demands, thus tacitly accepting the analogy, the demands escalate to the point where students are now insisting on a voice in electing the university president, a role in choosing the faculty, and even a place on the board of trustees.

I do not wish to comment here on the validity of individual student demands—certainly, a student role in university affairs is both practical and desirable, as long as that role remains advisory. Nor will I take the time to repeat the familiar litany of admiration for the current student generation—it has, to my mind, already been sufficiently praised, even overpraised, since for all its intrinsic passion, intelligence, and commitment, the proportion of serious, gifted, hardworking students remains about what it always was (if not actually dwindling for reasons I hope soon to develop). I do want, however, to examine the analogy which is now helping to politicize the university, and scholarship itself, because it seems to me full of falsehood.

Clearly, it is absurd to identify electoral with educational institutions. To compare the state with the academy is to assume that the primary function of the university is to govern and to rule. While the relationship between the administration and the faculty does have certain political overtones, the faculty and administration can no more be considered the elected representatives of the student body than the students—who were admitted after voluntary application on a selective and competitive basis—can be considered freeborn citizens of a democratic state: the relationship between teacher and student is strictly tutorial. Thus, the faculty member functions not to represent the student's interests in relation to the administration, but rather to communicate knowledge from one who knows to one who doesn't. That the reasoning behind this analogy has not been more frequently questioned indicates the extent to which some teachers are refusing to exercise their roles as professionals. During a time when all authority is being radically questioned, faculty members are becoming more reluctant to accept the responsibility of their wisdom and experience and are, therefore, often willing to abandon their authoritative position in order to placate the young.

The issue of authority is a crucial one here, and once again we can see how the concept of professionalism is being vitiated by false analogies. Because *some* authority is cruel, callow, or indifferent (notably the government in its treatment of certain urgent issues of the day), the Platonic *idea* of authority comes under attack. Because some faculty members are remote and pedantic, the credentials of distinguished scholars, artists, and intellectuals are ignored or rejected, and anyone taking charge of a classroom or a seminar is open to charges of "authoritarianism." This explains the hostility of many students towards the lecture course—where an "authority" communicates the fruits of his research, elaborating on unclear points when prodded by student questioning (still a valuable pedagogical technique, especially for beginning students, along with seminars and tutorials). Preferred to this, and therefore replacing it in some departments, is the discussion group or "bull session," where the student's opinion about the material receives more attention than the material itself, if indeed the material is still being treated. The idea—so central to scholarship—that there is an inherited body of knowledge to be transmitted from one generation to another—loses favor because it puts the student in an unacceptably subordinate position, with the result that the learning process gives way to a general free-for-all in which one man's opinion is as good as another's.

The problem is exacerbated in the humanities and social sciences with their more subjective criteria of judgment; one hardly senses the same difficulties in the clinical sciences. It is unlikely (though anything is possible these days) that medical students will insist on making a diagnosis through majority vote, or that students entering surgery will refuse anaesthesia because they want to participate in decisions that affect their lives, and, therefore, demand to choose the surgeon's instruments or tell him where to cut. Obviously, some forms of authority are still respected, and some professionals remain untouched by the incursions of the amateur. In liberal education, however, where the development of the individual assumes such weight and importance, the subordination of mind to material is often looked on as some kind of repression. One begins to understand the current loss of interest in the past, which offers a literature and history verified to some extent by time, and the passionate concern with the immediate present, whose works still remain to be objectively evaluated. When one's educational concerns are contemporary, the material can be subordinated to one's own interests, whether political or aesthetic, as the contemporary literary journalist is often more occupied with his own ideas than with the book he reviews.

Allied to this problem, and compounding it, is the problem of the black students, who are sometimes inclined to reject the customary university curriculum as "irrelevant" to their interests, largely because of its orientation towards "white" culture and history. . . .

On the one hand, the demand for "relevance" is an effort to make the university undertake the reparations that society should be paying. On the other, it is a form of solipsism, among both black students and white. And such solipsism is a serious threat to that "disinterestedness" that Matthew Arnold claimed to be the legitimate function of the scholar and the critic. The proper study of mankind becomes contemporary or future man; and the student focuses not on the outside world, past or present, so much as on a parochial corner of his own immediate needs. But this is childish, in addition to being Romantic, reflecting as it does the student's unwillingness to examine or conceive a world beyond the self. And here, the university seems to be paying a debt not of its own making—a debt incurred in the permissive home and progressive school, where knowledge was usually of considerably less importance than self-expression.

In the schools, particularly, techniques of education always seemed to take precedence over the material to be communicated; lessons in democracy were frequently substituted for training in subjects; and everyone learned to be concerned citizens, often at the sacrifice of a solid education. I remember applying for a position many years ago in such a school. I was prepared to teach English literature, but was told no such subject was being offered. Instead, the students had a course called *Core*, which was meant to provide the essence of literature, history, civics, and the like. The students sat together at a round table to dramatize their essential equality with their instructor; the instructor—or rather, the coordinator, as he was called—remained completely unobtrusive; and instead of determining answers by investigation or the teacher's authority, they were decided upon by majority vote. I took my leave in haste, convinced that I was witnessing democracy totally misunderstood. That misunderstanding has invaded our institutions of higher learning.

For the scholastic habits of childhood and adolescence are now being extended into adulthood. The graduates of the *Core* course, and courses like it, are concentrating on the development of their "life styles," chafing against restrictions of all kinds (words like "coercion" and "co-option" are the current jargon), and demanding that all courses be geared to their personal requirements and individual interests. But this is not at all the function of the university. As Paul Goodman has observed, in *The Community of Scholars*, when you teach the child, you teach the person; when you teach the adolescent, you teach the subject through the person; *but when you teach the adult, you teach the subject*. Behind Goodman's observation lies the assumption that the university student is, or should already be, a developed personality, that he comes to the academy not to investigate his "life style" but to absorb what knowledge he can, and that he is, therefore, preparing himself, through study, research, and contemplation, to enter the community of professional scholars. In resisting this notion, some students reveal their desire to maintain the conditions of childhood, to preserve the liberty they enjoyed in their homes and secondary schools, to extend the privileges of a child- and youth-oriented culture into their mature years. They wish to remain amateurs.

One can see why Goodman has concluded that many of the university young do not deserve the name of students: they are creating conditions in which it is becoming virtually impossible to do intellectual work. In turning their political wrath from the social world, which is in serious need of reform (partly because of a breakdown in professionalism), to the academic world, which still has considerable value as a learning institution, they have determined, on the one hand, that society will remain as venal, as corrupt, as retrogressive as ever, and, on the other hand, that the university will no longer be able to proceed with the work of free inquiry for which it was founded. As an added irony, students, despite their professed distaste for the bureaucratic administration of the university, are now helping to construct—through the insane proliferation of student-faculty committees—a far vaster network of bureaucracy than ever before existed. This, added to their continual meetings, confrontations, and demonstrations—not to mention occupations and sit-ins—is leaving precious little time or energy either for their intellectual development, or for that of the faculty. As a result, attendance at classes has dropped drastically; exams are frequently skipped; and papers and reports are either late, under-researched, or permanently postponed. That the university needs improvement goes without saying. And students have been very helpful in breaking down its excesses of impersonality and attempting to sever its ties with the military-industrial complex. But students need improvement too, which they are hardly receiving through all this self-righteous bustle over power. That students should pay so much attention to this activity creates an even more serious problem: the specter of an ignorant, uninformed group of graduates or dropouts who (when they finally leave the academic sanctuary) are incompetent to deal with society's real evils or to function properly in professions they have chosen to enter.

It is often observed that the word *amateur* comes from the Latin verb, to love—presumably because the amateur is motivated by passion rather than money. Today's amateur, however, seems to love not his subject but himself. And his assault on authority—on the application of professional standards in judgment of his intellectual development—is a strategy to keep this self-love unalloyed. The permanent dream of this nation, a dream still to be realized, has been a dream of equal opportunity—the right of each man to discover wherein he might excel. But this is quite different from that sentimental egalitarianism which assumes that each man excels in everything. There is no blinking the fact that some people are brighter than others, some more beautiful, some more gifted. Any other conclusion is a degradation of the democratic dogma and promises a bleak future if universally insisted on—a future of monochromatic amateurism in which everybody has opinions, few have facts, nobody has an idea.

ALIENATION AND RELEVANCE

Stephen J. Tonsor

Stephen Tonsor is Professor of History at the University of Michigan.

There is a striking parallel between the crisis in government at the national level in America and the crisis in the universities. In both cases the institutional structure has recently increased gigantically in size and in the scale of operation. Along with this increase in size has gone a tremendous augmentation of power both real and potential. However, it is a characteristic of this power that it is diffuse and focused only with difficulty: that it is all but impossible to bring this power to bear effectively on the problems of the state and the university. The problems which bedevil both the state and the university are frequently not problems which can be solved by the application of power. Along with the augmentation of size and power has gone a singular inability to match commitments with resources so that the state and the universities in spite of megadollar budgets find themselves perennially impoverished. Finally, and most importantly, each finds itself alienated from its constituency. Each has discovered that it is increasingly difficult for it to project an

From "Alienation and Relevance" in *National Review*, Vol. 21, No. 35 (July 1, 1969), pp. 636-638, 661. Copyright ©National Review, Inc., 1969.

objective which will move men to its single-minded pursuit. It is not that men no longer believe in government and education. Indeed, they believe passionately in both. It is rather that they no longer understand either the purpose or the designs of big government or big education. While the power of both institutions has steadily increased, their authority has declined. Ultimately authority is far more important to education than power, and power without authority in the state soon gives way to tyranny. This parallel between the state and the university is instructive.

What is necessary in order to restore the institutional authority of higher education? How can higher education regain the confidence of those over thirty and command the respect of those under thirty who listen with reluctance and dissent without debate?

It would be false to assume that all our difficulties are institutional in origin, that they arise from the fact that the university has either done too much or done too little. It must be said at the outset, and the fact faced with candor and resolution, that the most important problem which higher education faces today is the growing wave of irrationality and anti-intellectualism which has caught up large numbers of both students and professors. Student and professor activists inside the university and certain ideological groups outside the university no longer believe that truth must be the essential consideration in the academy.

Both the extreme Right and the extreme Left hold the same destructive view. Both Mark Rudd of Columbia and Governor Wallace of Alabama stand in the schoolroom door and, seen from the vantage point of the academy, they both hold the same low view of reasoned discourse. They believe that force ought to be substituted for sweet reason, that power ought to replace persuasion and that only "socially approved" voices and views should be heard. They believe that toleration is a weakness rather than a strength in intellectual enquiry and they are in the deepest sense of the word anti-intellectual. They aim at nothing less than the destruction of the life of reason. The university and the parent society have no alternative to repression. These groups cannot be permitted to disrupt and destroy the institutions they so obviously do not understand. They constitute a small minority and it is possible that had university administrations not been long accustomed by their faculties to bearing fools gladly, these groups would already have disappeared from the campus scene. Their disappearance, however, will not restore the authority of the university.

If the institutional aspirations of education are once more to become credible, universities must regain a sense of modesty and selectivity in the formulation of their objectives. They cannot be all things to all men. The notion of the multiversity is rejected with justice by students and by perceptive faculty. They reject it not simply because it is impossible to administer but because it is an institution without goals. It does not know its own mind. The able administrator in the setting of the multiversity is not a man characterized by unusual educational vision but someone whose social acoustical equipment is highly refined and who acutely senses all the many needs of his society. He is committed to servicing those needs and adjusting and compromising between these many conflicting interests. Little wonder that in such circumstances the teacher feels he is an unwanted encumbrance and the student senses that he is a forgotten man. To compound the problem now by expecting the university to become a court of last resort for the solution of the major social problems of our time will only deepen the crisis which the university faces.

Until there is a restoration of genuine educational purpose there will be no restoration of confidence by society in its institutions of higher education. Higher education has as its chief goals the education of young men and women in such a way as to make them capable participants in our complicated technological civilization, sophisticated and creative members of our common culture, and active and concerned citizens.

In order to ensure circumstances in which teaching rather than research or community service is the primary objective of the university, government at all levels must forgo the temptation of easy recourse to the enormous resources of the university. Recently there has been a great deal of debate concerning the use of the talent and facilities available in the university for defense research. It is not inconsistent to argue that under very exceptional circumstances the university ought freely to use its talent in the defense of society, and still maintain that both the government and the university would be better served under most circumstances were both basic and applied research in the national defense area done in autonomous research institutes. The same case can be made against the use of the facilities of the university for the solution of social problems. Finally, business and industry should look to sources other than the university for their pure and applied research.

Much of the debate concerning university research at the present time misses the point. War research is no more illicit or licit than peace research. The only sound test is whether or not research enhances or diminishes the primary teaching function of the university. And it must be confessed that in spite of the brave talk to the contrary and considerable administrative legerdemain, research has become the tail that in many instances wags the dog. Faculty members on fractional appointments who spend the greater part of their time in other than teaching activities distort and confuse the educational purpose of the university. Foundation grants for centers and programs which are often inconsistent with the needs and basic educational directions of the institution are as dangerous to the university as government, civic and business research for which there is no clear-cut teaching mandate.

. . . The possibility for educational diversity in America is immense; but in reality American education is homogenous and uniform. The privately endowed colleges do poorly what the state universities do only a little better, and a handful of determinative major universities, as alike as peas in a pod, set the tone and direction for the whole educational enterprise. . . .

Among the most important functions of education are those of widening the options available to men in the solution of their problems and in the improvement of the quality of their lives, yet our universities steadily diminish and dilute the differences between themselves. Students are still able to choose the quality of their educations; they are unable, however, to do much through their own choice about the kind of education they receive. It is important that we re-establish a free market in education. It is important that the church-related school survive, not as a secularized ghost of its former self but as a school with a genuinely religious vision of the world, a school in which men learn to serve God and their fellow men rather than themselves. It is important that private humanistic colleges with their commitment to civilization and decorum and their quiet emphasis on freedom remain an important constituent of our educational system. It is essential that we have genuine experimentation in curriculum and method and not the pseudo-experiments hatched by administrators and departmental chairmen who need an excuse for hitting the foundations or the legislators once again for funds.

We cannot have this diversity, however, until the federal and the state governments drastically alter the role they play in financing higher education. American education will become diverse and relevant to the needs of both the student and the nation when, and only when, the student is forced to pay a very substantial portion of the total cost of his education. Privilege without responsibility is a very dangerous condition; privilege without either responsibility or choice generates unbearable tensions in the society, which makes such privilege possible. State schools which compete unfairly with private schools through discriminatory tuition rates have been the chief force in leveling and homogenizing American education. If we genuinely desire diversity we will do all in our power to encourage students to pay for their education through a tax on future earnings. If we genuinely wish diversity, we will insist that such educational grants as are made by the Federal Government will be made directly to the student rather than to institutions of higher education.

. . .The growing sense of alienation among students arises in substantial measure from their inability to choose the quality and kind of education they believe relevant to their lives.

Not only should there be a diversification in the kind of college and university training available, but diversification should bring into existence a wide range of educational alternatives. Apprenticeship programs, proprietary schools, technical institutes operated by industry for the training of specifically needed talents, a strengthening and broadening of the junior and community college programs are all of considerable importance in the problem of making education relevant to the needs of the student and the needs of society. The American public must be disabused of the notion that the AB degree holds some sort of magic. For some time it has not been a mark of status and certainly it is not a guaranteed pass to higher income.

The right of entry into a craft union is often more difficult to achieve than entry into the most exclusive college. It strikes me as odd that the New Left which has been so concerned with the indiscriminate admission of all minority-group students into our colleges irrespective of their qualifications has had little or nothing to say of the restrictive practices which deny the right of entry, of many of these same minority groups, into those favored unions which possess monopoly advantages in our economy and society. Someone should say clearly that the way to status and achievement in our society is not through learning Swahili but through learning English. Someone needs to say clearly that the way to affluence does not lie through an AB degree, granted by yesterday's second-rate normal college, but a marketable skill which will secure for its holder and his family the dignity of achievement.

Nearly every professor has in the past several years encountered, in what he thought a rather sober discussion of an academic question, a sudden denunciation by a student member of his audience. The student does not challenge the professor's method or even question his data but simply rejects his position as immoral, as fascist or racist, or as simply irrelevant. There is no debate or discussion, no attempt to identify the question or purposefully expose the issue. It is assumed that absolute right prevails on one side and that moral obtuseness, Marxian false consciousness or plain wrongdoing characterizes the other side. The issue is not joined; it is not even discussed. Question periods at lectures are not occasions for refining the position of the lecturer but are seen as opportunities to present long, rambling denunciations and counter-lectures. The student usually ends his harangue with a plea for relevance and the lecturer, if he is smart enough, gathers that the young man or young lady (it is sometimes difficult to tell just which it is), is alienated.

Last fall the *London Times* reported an international meeting of philosophers in Vienna in the following words:

> While their elders and betters solemnly discuss the epistemological significance of the phrases 'Johnny has lost his pen. I have found a pen. I know Johnny lost it,' the students are racing through the corridors, shouting 'What about the Soviet invasion [of Czechoslovakia] ,' burning Russian and American flags, and wrestling with their professors for microphones during debates.
>
> It is disgusting, say the students, that three thousand of the wisest men from every country of the world should have gathered together in the largest philosophical talk-in in history and have nothing forceful to say about the Russian tanks on the Czech border less than fifty miles away. If philosophy has any real function it should be performing it now.

Clearly, what the student seeks is a relevant orthodoxy rather than an agonizing enquiry. Faced with some of the toughest choices in history, and living in a period when traditional certainties and traditional values have been challenged and opposed by alternatives, the student is really calling upon his professor for a clear and definitive answer and one preferably couched in a currently fashionable vocabulary and bearing the marks of current social concerns. To the student, education is irrelevant if it cannot provide a solution; preferably, of course, a solution which costs the student nothing and whose weight is born by the non-student sectors of society. The student wants to know what to think rather than how to think.

And the student has far too many professors who are willing to tell him what to think rather than attempt to teach him how to think for himself. The student has learned his lessons only too well. His professors, expecially in the humanities and the social sciences, have all too often been exponents of an established orthodoxy rather than masters in the art of reasoned enquiry.

The situation is not to be mended by diversifying orthodoxies. That is the student's solution. He wishes to replace the liberal orthodoxy with a New Left orthodoxy, a WASP orthodoxy with a black orthodoxy, a permissive and tolerant orthodoxy with a repressive orthodoxy. What the student wishes is a substitution of orthodoxies rather than an end to all closed systems. His efforts will only compound the problem, for the liberal ascendancy in today's colleges and universities is like the pre-1918 Austrian Empire—"an autocracy ameliorated by inefficiency"—while the student Maoist dictatorships would end altogether the life of reason.

The professor, if he is to re-establish the authority of reason must not only admit of the possibility of his being wrong but must have the openness of mind necessary to, as Lord Acton said, "make out the best possible case for error." He must actively court diversity and contradiction rather than seek a world of like-minded men. He must continuously engage in a great debate not only with his students and his colleagues but above all with himself, and as President Truman said: "If he can't stand the heat, he should get out of the kitchen."

The ideological and cultural uniformity of higher education in America is a disgrace. Why is it that our colleges and universities have conformed themselves over the past two decades to the orthodoxy of secular liberalism? Why has the atmosphere been so increasingly hostile to open debate? Why does it take the crisis of the exclusion of the Negro from the university to make us see that not only people, but ideas have been excluded by higher education?

The authority and the relevance of the university lie in its ability as an institution to explore systematically and rationally the problems men face. Its success is not dependent upon current fashions in ideas or current solutions to particular problems. Its success derives from its ability to take the long view and ask the hard questions, and the hardest of these is the question the professor asks of himself, of his colleagues and of his society, about the possibility of being wrong.

Part Two

International Issues

8

The Arms Race

Despite the declared existence of a state of "peaceful coexistence" between the two superpowers, both the United States and the Soviet Union maintain vast stockpiles of thermonuclear weapons, poised for delivery against the other's territory. Since neither can launch a "first strike" effective enough to prevent a massive retaliatory blow, the condition of peace is a "balance of terror" in which, in Winston Churchill's graphic phrase, "by a process of sublime irony, survival is the twin brother of annihilation."

The balance is a precarious one. The terror could be unleashed by an electronic error or a human aberration; the United States has an elaborate system of checks and balances built into its nuclear weapons systems, but we are not sure that the other nuclear powers have taken such precautions. As the Cuban missile crisis of 1962 made clear, there is also a risk that one power could make a bold strategic move based on a miscalculation of the other side's response. Or a non-nuclear war could escalate by stages into a nuclear holocaust—a danger implicit in Vietnam before March 1968. All of these dangers would multiply if more of the several countries which now have the technological capacity to build nuclear weapons were to do so. The final problem making the balance of terror so unstable is the possibility that one of the superpowers, by a sudden build-up of its forces or a technological breakthrough in either offensive or defensive weapons, could establish an overwhelming superiority, if not invulnerability; the military on both sides are constantly afraid that the rival power is close to accomplishing this. It is this fear that has caused a continual build-up of armaments by America and the Soviet Union, leading us now into the era of the defensive ABM (anti-ballistic missile) and the offensive MIRV (multiple independently targetable reentry vehicles). The latter is a kind of "space bus," which packs several H-bombs into one missile, either a land-based Minuteman III or a submarine-based Poseidon, and releases them over enemy territory toward separate targets; it makes possible a large increase in destructive power with the same number of missiles.

In the first selection of this chapter, ex-Defense Secretary Robert McNamara presents the basic doctrine of peace through deterrence. He believes it to have been a necessary and valid doctrine but pleads for a greater readiness by the major powers to seek agreement on controlling and then reversing the arms race. General McConnell, however, presents the case for a further build-up, based on the premise that the Soviets are accelerating their arms expenditures and that our former superiority is fast disappearing.[1] The excerpts from McConnell's testimony include his major requests for weapons expenditures but by no means cover his full list. Moreover, McConnell is speaking only for the Air Force, and the other services were also asking Congress for support on an extensive range of nuclear and "conventional" weapons systems.

Seymour Melman's statement calls for drastic reductions in these expenditures. There is no prospect in the near future that cuts on the scale demanded by Melman will be accepted. Nonetheless, it now appears that annual increases in military outlays are no longer automatic and that the power of the military and the military committees of the Congress will be fiercely contested. Thus, although Defense Secretary Laird's case for the ABM prevailed over that

---

[1] Indeed, in 1967 a subcommittee of the American Security Council—including retired Generals Bernard A. Schriever, Curtis E. LeMay, Thomas S. Power, and Albert C. Wedemeyer and Professors Edward Teller and Stefan T. Possony—disagreed with McNamara's contention that America was securely ahead in nuclear forces and insisted that by 1971 "a massive megatonnage gap will have developed" in favor of the Soviet Union. This would enable the Soviets to use "nuclear blackmail" against us, compelling us to back down in situations similar to that in Cuba in 1962. See "The Changing Strategic Military Balance," prepared at the request of the Committee on Armed Services, House of Representatives, 90th Congress, 1st Session, July 1967.

opposition of Herbert York and many others,[2] the Senate vote was 51-50. Moreover, in August 1969, Secretary Laird announced a cut in the 1970 defense budget from $80 billion to $77 billion, which, among other things, would halt work on the Air Force's Manned Orbiting Laboratory and the Army's Cheyenne helicopter-gunship. Nor did this put an end to demands for cuts.[3]

Arguments about specific weapons stem from a more fundamental question about the alleged power of the "military-industrial complex." That issue is debated here by Senator Fulbright and Admiral Colwell.

The concluding selection, a speech by George Wald at the Massachusetts Institute of Technology, presents the view that the human race cannot coexist with nuclear weapons. It is not surprising that the speech was received with passionate approval by the audience of students. As long as the stockpiles exist, the world is in deadly danger. To build civilizations under a perpetual burden of terror is fundamentally absurd and vicious. Yet, if we survive the 70s, it will not be because nuclear weapons were all abolished. As long as national rivalries and deep mutual suspicions persist, none of the big powers will take a chance on unilateral disarmament. Indeed, despite the intense opposition to further increases in armaments, large expenditures for old and new weapons systems were finally approved by Congress in 1969; and military expenditures are likely to remain very high for some time to come. The best hope is that we will be able to build on the negotiated agreements on nuclear weapons achieved in the 60s—covering atmospheric testing, outer space, and proliferation to other nations—and arrive at new, more far-reaching understandings. The big question for the future

[2] Jerome B. Wiesner, George B. Kistiakowsky, and Wolfgang K. H. Panofsky were among the scientists who joined York in opposing both the Johnson Administration's Sentinel (designed to protect large cities) and the Nixon Administration's Safeguard (emphasizing the protection of missile sites). However, the scientific community was by no means unanimous on the issue. The University of Chicago's authority on military strategy, Albert Wohlstetter, and Nobel-Laureate Eugene Wigner of Princeton University offered strong support of the Safeguard system, suggesting that the only way to work out any unresolved technical questions was to get started on the ABM at once.

[3] An August 1969 Gallup Poll showed that 52% of the public thought we were spending too much on defense, 31% were satisfied with the present outlays, and 8% thought we were spending too little.

is whether SALT (strategic arms limitation talks between the United States and the Soviet Union) can be made more significant than MIRV and all of the other grim acronyms that are the focus of attention in this chapter.

THE ESSENCE OF SECURITY

Robert S. McNamara

Robert S. McNamara, former Secretary of Defense, is currently President of the World Bank.

. . . The cornerstone of our strategic policy continues to be to deter deliberate nuclear attack upon the United States or its allies. We do this by maintaining a highly reliable ability to inflict unacceptable damage upon any single aggressor or combination of aggressors at any time during the course of a strategic nuclear exchange, even after absorbing a surprise first strike. This can be defined as our *assured-destruction capability.*

It is important to understand that assured destruction is the very essence of the whole deterrence concept. We must possess an actual assured-destruction capability, and that capability also must be credible. The point is that a potential aggressor must believe that our assured-destruction capability is in fact actual, and that our will to use it in retaliation to an attack is in fact unwavering. The conclusion, then, is clear: if the United States is to deter a nuclear attack on itself or its allies, it must possess an actual and a credible assured-destruction capability.

When calculating the force required, we must be conservative in all our estimates of both a potential aggressor's capabilities and his intentions. Security depends upon assuming a worst plausible case, and having the ability to cope with it. In that eventuality we must be able to absorb the total weight of nuclear attack on our country—on our retaliatory forces, on our command and control apparatus, on our industrial capacity, on our cities, and on our population—and still be capable of damaging the aggressor to the point that his society would be simply no longer viable in twentieth-century terms. That is what deterrence of nuclear aggression means. It means the certainty of suicide to the aggressor, not merely to his military forces, but to his society as a whole.

Let us consider another term: *first-strike capability*. This is a somewhat ambiguous term, since it could mean simply the ability of one nation to attack another nation with nuclear forces first. But as it is normally used, it connotes much more: the elimination of the attacked nation's retaliatory second-strike forces. This is the sense in which it should be understood.

Clearly, first-strike capability is an important strategic concept. The United States must not and will not permit itself ever to get into a position in which another nation, or combination of nations, would possess a first-strike capability against it. Such a position not only would constitute an intolerable threat to our security, but it obviously would remove our ability to deter nuclear aggression.

We are not in that position today, and there is no foreseeable danger of our ever getting into that position. Our strategic offensive forces are immense: 1,000 Minuteman missile launchers, carefully protected belowground; 41 Polaris submarines, carrying 656 missile launchers, with the majority hidden beneath the seas at all times; and about 600 long-range bombers, approximately 40 percent of which are kept always in a high state of alert.

Our alert forces alone carry more than 2,200 weapons, each averaging more than the explosive equivalent of one megaton of TNT. Four hundred of these delivered on the Soviet Union would be sufficient to destroy over one-third of her population and one-half of her industry. All these flexible and highly reliable forces are equipped with devices that ensure their penetration of Soviet defenses.

Now what about the Soviet Union? Does it today possess a powerful nuclear arsenal? The answer is that it does. Does it possess a first-strike capability against the United States? The answer is that it does not. Can the Soviet Union in the foreseeable future acquire such a first-strike capability against the United States? The answer is that it cannot. It cannot because we are determined to remain fully alert and we will never permit our own assured-destruction capability to drop to a point at which a Soviet first-strike capability is even remotely feasible.

Is the Soviet Union seriously attempting to acquire a first-strike capability against the United States? Although this is a question we cannot answer with absolute certainty, we believe the answer is no. In any event, the question itself is—in a sense— irrelevant; for the United States will maintain and, where necessary, strengthen its retaliatory forces so that, whatever the Soviet Union's intentions or actions, we will continue to have an assured-destruction capability vis-à-vis their society.

But there is another question that is most relevant. Does the United States, then, possess a first-strike capability against the Soviet Union? The answer is that we do not. We do not have this capability, not because we have neglected our nuclear strength; on the contrary, we have increased it to a point that we possess a clear superiority over the Soviet Union. We do not possess first-strike capability against the Soviet Union for precisely the same reason that they do not possess it against us. Quite simply, we have both built up our second-strike capability—in effect, retaliatory power—to the point that a first-strike capability on either side has become unattainable.

There is, of course, no way by which the United States could have prevented the Soviet Union from acquiring its present second-strike capability, short of a massive preemptive first strike in the 1950s. The fact is, then, that neither the Soviet Union nor the United States can attack the other without being destroyed in retaliation; nor can either of us attain a first-strike capability in the foreseeable future. Further, both the Soviet Union and the United States now possess an actual and credible second-strike capability against one another, and it is precisely this mutual capability that provides us both with the strongest possible motive to avoid a nuclear war.

The most frequent question that arises in this connection is whether or not the United States possesses nuclear superiority over the Soviet Union. The answer is that we do.

But the answer, like everything else in this matter, is technically complex. The complexity arises in part out of what measurement of superiority is most meaningful and realistic. Many commentators on the matter tend to define nuclear superiority in terms of gross megatonnage, or in terms of the number of missile launchers available. By both these standards the United States does have a substantial superiority over the Soviet Union in the weapons targeted against each other. But it is precisely these two standards of measurement that are themselves misleading. Instead, the most meaningful and realistic measurement of nuclear capability is the number of separate warheads that can be delivered accurately on individual high-priority targets with sufficient power to destroy them.

Gross megatonnage alone is an inadequate indicator of assured-destruction capability since it is unrelated to survivability, accuracy or penetrability, and poorly related to effective elimination of multiple high-priority targets. There obviously is no advantage in overdestroying one target at the expense of leaving undamaged other targets of equal importance. Further, the number of missile launchers available is also an inadequate indicator of assured-destruction capability since many of our launchers will carry multiple warheads.

But using the realistic measurement of the number of warheads available, those which could be delivered with accuracy and effectiveness on appropriate targets in the United States or Soviet Union, the United States currently possesses a superiority over the Soviet Union of at least three or four to one. Furthermore, we will maintain superiority by these same realistic criteria for as far ahead as we can realistically plan.

One point should be made quite clear, however: our current numerical superiority over the Soviet Union in reliable, accurate and effective warheads is both greater than we had originally planned and more than we require. In the larger equation of security our superiority is of limited significance, for even with our current superiority, or indeed with any numerical superiority realistically attainable, the blunt, inescapable fact remains that the Soviet Union, with its present forces, could still effectively destroy the United States, even after absorbing the full weight of an American first strike.

I have noted that our present superiority is greater than we had planned. How this came about is a significant illustration of the intrinsic dynamics of the nuclear arms race.

In 1961 when I became Secretary of Defense, the Soviet Union had a very small operational arsenal of intercontinental missiles. However, it did possess the technological and industrial capacity to enlarge that arsenal very substantially over the succeeding several years. We had no evidence that the Soviets did plan, in fact, fully to use that capability. But, as I have pointed out, a strategic planner must be conservative in his calculations; that is, he must prepare for the worst plausible case and not be content to hope and prepare merely for the most probable.

Since we could not be certain of Soviet intentions, since we could not be sure that they would not undertake a massive build-up, we had to insure against such an eventuality by undertaking a major build-up of our own Minuteman and Polaris forces. Thus, in the course of hedging against what was then only a theoretically possible Soviet build-up, we took decisions which have resulted in our current superiority in numbers of warheads and deliverable megatons. But the blunt fact remains that if we had had more accurate information about planned Soviet strategic forces, we simply would not have needed to build as large a nuclear arsenal as we have today.

Let me be absolutely clear. I am not saying that our decision in 1961 was unjustified; I am saying that it was necessitated by a lack of accurate information. Furthermore, that decision in itself, justified as it was, in the end could not possibly have left unaffected the Soviet Union's future nuclear plans.

What is essential to understand here is that the Soviet Union and the United States mutually influence one another's strategic plans. Whatever their intentions or our intentions, actions—or even realistically potential actions—on either side relating to the build-up of nuclear forces necessarily trigger reactions on the other side. It is precisely this action-reaction phenomenon that fuels an arms race.

In strategic nuclear weaponry the arms race involves a particular irony. Unlike any other era in military history, a substantial numerical superiority of weapons today does not effectively translate into political control or diplomatic leverage. While thermonuclear power is almost inconceivably awesome and represents virtually unlimited potential destructiveness, it has proven to be a limited diplomatic instrument. Its uniqueness lies in the fact that it is at the same time an all-powerful weapon and a very inadequate weapon.

The fact that the Soviet Union and the United States can mutually destroy one another regardless of who strikes first narrows the range of Soviet aggression which our nuclear forces can effectively deter. Even with our nuclear monopoly in the early postwar period, we were unable to deter the Soviet pressures against Berlin or their support of aggression in Korea. Today our nuclear superiority does not deter all forms of Soviet support of Communist insurgency in Southeast Asia. What all of this has meant is that we, and our allies as well, require substantial non-nuclear forces in order to cope with levels of aggression that massive strategic forces do not, in fact, deter.

This has been a difficult lesson both for us and for our allies to accept. There is a strong psychological tendency to regard superior nuclear forces as a simple and unfailing solution to security and an assurance of victory under any set of circumstances. What must be understood is that our nuclear strategic forces play a vital and absolutely necessary role in our security and that of our allies, but it is an intrinsically limited role. Therefore we and our allies must maintain substantial conventional forces, fully capable of dealing with a wide spectrum of lesser forms of political and military aggression. This is a level of aggression against which the use of strategic nuclear forces would not be to our advantage, and thus a level of aggression which these strategic nuclear forces by themselves cannot effectively deter. One cannot fashion a credible deterrent out of an incredible action. Thus security for the United States and its allies can only arise from the possession of a range of graduated deterrents, each of them fully credible in its own context.

In recent years the Soviets have substantially increased their offensive forces. We have been watching and evaluating this very carefully, of course; clearly the Soviet build-up is in part a reaction to our own build-up since the beginning of the 1960s. Soviet strategic planners undoubtedly reasoned that if our build-up were to continue at its accelerated pace, we might conceivably reach in time a credible first-strike capability against the Soviet Union.

That was not, in fact, our intention. Our goal was to ensure that they, with their theoretical capacity to reach such a first-strike capability, would not outdistance us. But they could not read our intentions with any greater accuracy than we could read theirs. The result has been that we have both built up our forces to a point that far exceeds a credible second-strike capability against the forces we each started with. In doing so neither of us has reached a first-strike capability. And the realities of the situation being what they are—whatever we believe their intentions to be, and whatever they believe our intentions to be—each of us can deny the other a first-strike capability in the foreseeable future.

How can we be so confident that this is the case? How can we be so certain that the Soviets cannot gradually outdistance us, either by some dramatic technological breakthrough or simply through our imperceptibly lagging behind, for whatever reason: reluctance to spend the requisite funds, distraction with military problems elsewhere, faulty intelligence, or simple negligence and naïveté? All of these reasons and others have been suggested by some commentators in this country who fear that we are, in fact, falling behind to a dangerous degree.

The answer is simple and straightforward. We are not going to permit the Soviets to outdistance us, because to do so would be to jeopardize our very viability as a nation. No President, no Secretary of Defense, no Congress of the United States of whatever political persuasion is going to permit this nation to take that risk. We do not want a nuclear arms race with the Soviet Union, primarily because the action-reaction phenomenon makes it foolish and futile. But if the only way to prevent the Soviet Union from obtaining first-strike capability over us is to engage in such a race, the United States possesses in ample abundance the resources, the technology and the will to run faster in that race for whatever distance is required.

What we would much prefer to do is to come to a realistic and reasonably riskless agreement with the Soviet Union which would effectively prevent such an arms race. We both have strategic nuclear arsenals greatly in excess of a credible assured-destruction capability. These arsenals have reached that point of excess in each case for precisely the same reason: we each have reacted to the other's build-up with very conservative calculations. We have, that is, each built a greater arsenal than either of us needed for a second-strike capability, simply because both wanted to be able to cope with the worst plausible case.

Since we each now possess a deterrent in excess of our individual needs, both of our nations would benefit from a properly safeguarded agreement first to limit and later to reduce both our offensive and defensive strategic nuclear forces. We believe such an agreement is fully feasible since it is clearly in the interests of both our nations. But formal agreement or not, we can be sure that neither the Soviets nor we are going to risk the other's obtaining a first-strike capability. On the contrary, we can be sure that we are both going to maintain a maximum effort to preserve an assured-destruction capability.

It would not be sensible for either side to launch a maximum effort to achieve a first-strike capability. The intelligence-gathering capability of each side being what it is, and the realities of lead-time from technological breakthrough to operational readiness being what they are, neither of us would be able to acquire a first-strike capability in secret. . . .

The road leading from the stone age to the ICBM, though it may have been more than a million years in the building, seems to have run in a single direction. If one is inclined to be cynical, one might conclude that man's history seems to be characterized not so much by consistent periods of peace, occasionally punctuated by warfare, as by persistent outbreaks of warfare, wearily put aside from time to time for periods of exhaustion and recovery that parade under the name of peace.

I do not view man's history with that degree of cynicism, but I do believe that man's wisdom in avoiding war is often surpassed by his folly in promoting it. However foolish unlimited war may have been in the past, it is now no longer merely foolish, but suicidal as well. It is said that nothing can prevent a man from suicide if he is sufficiently determined to commit it. The question is: what is our determination in an era when unlimited war will mean the death of hundreds of millions and the possible genetic impairment of a million generations to follow?

Man is clearly a compound of folly and wisdom, and history is clearly a consequence of the admixture of those two contradictory traits. History has placed our particular lives in an era when the consequences of human folly are waxing more and more catastrophic in the matters of war and peace. In the end, the root of man's security does not lie in his weaponry, it lies in his mind. What the world requires in its third decade of the Atomic Age is not a new race toward armament, but a new race toward reasonableness.

We had all better run that race.

AMERICAN WEAPONS AND THE SOVIET THREAT

John P. McConnell

General John P. McConnell is Chief of Staff, United States Air Force.

Threat

The threat to U.S. security and interests—now and in the foreseeable future—arises from the dedication of Communist leaders to the expansion of their power and influence and from the increasing capabilities of their military forces.

The focus of Soviet military policy is on strategic and political relations with the United States. Despite the sizeable military capabilities of the Far Eastern and Eastern European Communist countries, it is the resources and military power of the U.S.S.R. which represent the primary threat to the United States.

It now seems clear that the primary Soviet goal is, at a minimum, to draw even with the United States in strategic offensive weapons, and if possible to gain and maintain a lead in intercontinental attack capabilities. Already the U.S.S.R. has created formidable deterrent forces and is making strenuous efforts to improve its defenses. The strategic posture of the Soviets, now more impressive than at any time since 1945, will continue to grow as present programs add to their assured destruction and damage-limiting capabilities.

Soviet achievement of a significant nuclear deterrent, increased free world focus on nonnuclear military capabilities, the potential of huge ongoing military research and development (R. & D.) programs, and other recent developments have raised a greater possibility of significant changes in Soviet military policy than at any time since the fall of Khrushchev. The collective leadership now faces major decisions concerning both the strategic

From the Senate Committee on Armed Services, *Hearings on Authorization for Military Procurement, Research and Development, Fiscal Year 1970, and Reserve Strength*; 91st Congress, 1st Session, March and April, 1969, Part 1, pp. 924-933, 936, 943-944, 948, 952-957. (Hereafter referred to as *Hearings on Authorization for Military Procurement.*)

and general purpose forces. Decisions now being made within the U.S.S.R., and those to be made over the next several years, will depend on an interaction of several factors: the power balance in Soviet leadership circles, priorities given to the various demands on finite resources, and external developments and their interpretation within the Kremlin. Neither we nor they can confidently predict what the outcome will be.

The announced 1969 Soviet budget again showed a sizeable increase in defense/space spending. Outlays for science—which include major expenditures for military/space programs—will increase by 14 percent. The continuing emphasis on R. & D., in addition to costly deployment of offensive and defensive weapon systems, is intended to provide new and improved weapons for the future.

The Soviet Inter-Continental Ballistic Missile (ICBM) force continues to expand at a rapid rate with no indication that force goals have been reached. Further qualitative improvements in this force are likely—changes that would make their ICBM's more accurate, more reliable, and more survivable.

Although ballistic missile systems now comprise the major element in the Soviet nuclear strike force, manned bombers remain an important part of that force. Production continues on a supersonic dash medium bomber, and a reconnaissance version of a heavy bomber is being manufactured in limited numbers. The Soviets are capable of equipping these aircraft with improved air-to-surface missiles. They could also initiate production of new heavy and medium bombers employing some of the technological advances from their supersonic transport which made its first test flight on December 31, 1968.

The Medium Range and Intermediate Range Ballistic Missile (MRBM/IRBM) force probably is being qualitatively upgraded also. Mobile launchers and additional hardening of fixed sites seem likely developments in the modernization of this Eurasian-oriented force.

The size and capabilities of the Soviet submarine-launched ballistic and cruise missile force continue to increase. It must be anticipated that Soviet ability to maintain submarines on station off U.S. shores will improve, and that they will place great emphasis on increasing their antisubmarine warfare capabilities against the Polaris fleet. . . .

Communist China, still plagued by the dislocations of Mao's "Cultural Revolution," has apparently shielded its strategic weapons development efforts from the worst effects of the turmoil. This is most clearly evident in the December 1968 test of another thermonuclear device, which yielded some three megatons. While some setbacks may have occurred in Communist China's drive to achieve an operational ballistic missile force, there is no doubt that

Peking is determined to expend the necessary resources to have long-range nuclear forces at the earliest possible date. We must be prepared to deal effectively with this forthcoming Chinese capability. . . .

Neither Moscow nor Peking makes any secret of its support for Communist revolutionary forces. Both have continued to funnel economic and military aid to such groups, and each will undoubtedly persevere in its efforts to alter the world power equation in its favor. The total threat to the United States and our allies is complex, dynamic, and unrelenting.

The events of the past year have reinforced our view that the threat posed to our security by growing Communist power is increasing across the entire conflict spectrum. The Soviets and the Chinese Communists appear determined to materially improve their respective strategic positions relative to that of the United States. Considerable progress has been made toward this end, particularly by the Soviet Union. The Soviets' improved strategic posture has not been made at the expense of their general purpose forces which have continued their rather substantial improvements aimed at meeting contingencies short of strategic nuclear war. These general purpose forces represent a means by which the Soviets can and do effectively project their power in support of nations distant from their periphery. There is no indication that the Soviets or the Chinese intend to abandon their policy of promoting subversion and insurgency. "Wars of liberation" continue to be part of the doctrine and strategy of both major Communist powers.

To summarize the threat, our security is being increasingly challenged by the improving military capabilities of the Communist powers across the spectrum of nuclear and conventional conflict, and by their demonstrated willingness to use these military forces. Our proposed forces must be designed to counter this threat.

Strategic Offense

Our primary strategic objective is to deter nuclear aggression. The success or failure of this deterrence is determined by the enemy's evaluation of our strategic forces and of our willingness to use them. Thus the United States must possess a quantity and quality of mixed strategic forces which make it explicitly clear that nuclear war with the United States will result in unacceptable damage to any adversary.

Attempts are frequently made to define deterrence by identifying specific tasks to be performed in terms of urban fatalities or industrial capacity destroyed; however, these are still subjective judgments because we are dealing with the enemy's concept of the price he is willing to pay. To cover this uncertainty, the United States must possess forces against which no rational enemy could ever believe that he would emerge victorious.

In the past, the United States has had these forces. As an example, at the time of the Cuban missile crisis the overwhelming nuclear superiority possessed by the United States—no matter how defined or evaluated—served to emphasize to the Communist world that its military and political goals in the Western Hemisphere could not be achieved. Such experiences reinforce our conviction that we must maintain sufficient military power to defend our interests and maintain our commitments worldwide.

In our strategic forces, we have become increasingly dependent on missiles as the manned bomber force continues to be phased down. The current Air Force strategic missile force consists of 54 Titan II's and 1,000 Minuteman I's and II's. The Titan, which is programmed at the current level through fiscal year 1973, can deliver the largest warhead in the missile inventory and is equipped with penetration aids. As planned, we have maintained our 1,000 missile Minuteman force throughout the past year while continuing to improve this force qualitatively. We are replacing Minuteman I with Minuteman II to obtain an increased throw weight, greater accuracy, and a larger number of selectable target options.

Minuteman III will further improve our missile force through the first operational use of Multiple Independent Reentry Vehicles (MIRVs). With MIRV, Minuteman III will be able to carry multiple warheads and penetration aids to confuse the enemy. We are now proceeding with Minuteman III flight testing and expect to continue Minuteman force modernization as currently planned. . . .

As we deploy Minuteman II and III, we are making improvements in their launch control centers and facilities. Additionally, we are now capable of controlling the launch of a major portion of our Minuteman force from Airborne Launch Control Centers (ALCCs). In the near future, these ALCCs will be able to control the launch of the entire Minuteman force should these missiles become isolated from their ground launch control facilities. . . .

In my report last year, I indicated that we had begun the design and development of a dual capable Hard Rock Silo, hardened against higher overpressures than our present silos and compatible with either Minuteman III or an advanced intercontinental ballistic missile (ICBM). To insure the balanced survival of the entire system, we hope to achieve even higher hardness for the more critical launch control and associated command and control facilities.

We are also continuing efforts to develop an advanced ICBM system. Extensive studies conclude that a missile with increased throw weight, greater accuracy, and improved survivability over those currently programmed will be required to meet the long-term threat. Although we are not proceeding with contract definition for this system, we are pursuing several technology programs which include a new guidance system. These advanced ICBM technology programs will permit us to start developing those elements of the overall system which are critical to reduced leadtime, technical risk, and cost. These initial R. & D. efforts will be applicable to either additional Minuteman improvements or the development of an advanced ICBM, and they will enable us to respond appropriately to the threat as it evolves.

Another essential element of our capability for strategic offense is the manned bomber force. This portion of our strategic force mix is capable of flexible, discriminating, and highly controllable actions which are responsive to changing combat environments and to the requirements of the National Command Authority. Although the current bomber program calls for a continuing reduction, we are examining the possibility of retaining existing forces in light of the rapidly increasing threat.

The B-52 force remains the major portion of our current manned bomber force. . . .

We will begin to modernize our bomber force this year by introducing the FB-111, and the phasein of this new interim medium bomber is planned to be completed by the end of fiscal year 1971. However, a recent decision has lowered the procurement rate and reduced total procurement from the previously approved level of 210 aircraft in 14 squadrons. This reduced procurement decision requires that we retain older model aircraft in order to maintain total bomber force capabilities.

We believe that a new bomber is required to accomplish the strategic tasks of the future and we are very pleased with the recent decision to proceed with full-scale engineering development of the Advanced Manned Strategic Aircraft (AMSA). Our assessment of the tasks assigned to the bomber force, and the capabilities required, indicates that we must continue advanced bomber development in order to maintain a deployment option in the late 1970's. Our current schedule, in light of the recent approval for AMSA development, calls for the award of full-scale engineering development contracts late this year leading to first flight in mid-1973. If all subsequent decisions are favorable, we should be able to achieve an initial deployment in the mid-1970's.

Our analyses have shown that over the long term and against the higher levels of the Soviet threat, the addition of the AMSA would be a cost effective option compared to the approved forces, even though the approved forces are equipped with penetration aids.

Also bearing on this problem are the Soviets' aggressive research and development program and their intense emphasis on strategic defensive systems. These factors have convinced us that an advanced bomber possessing penetration and weapon delivery capabilities far superior to those of the existing bomber force will be necessary in the late 1970's and beyond. . . .

In the interim period, prior to AMSA deployment, we must maintain the capability of our programmed bomber force to penetrate improved enemy defenses. To this end we are developing and testing the Short Range Attack Missile (SRAM) on the FB-111 and B-52 aircraft in accordance with the recent SRAM program decision. This decision delayed full-scale production of the SRAM. The production funding included in the fiscal year 1970 budget will allow us to initiate long leadtime procurement of SRAM weapon system equipment and establish tooling to support the planned production program. The SRAM will permit us to stand off and suppress the Soviet low altitude surface-to-air missile (SAM) defenses postulated for the early 1970's and will be an excellent weapon against many other targets as well.

It should be noted that the projected equipping of the B-52 with SRAM will complement, rather than replace, our existing Hound Dog missiles. Each type of missile has individual characteristics which enhance bomber capabilities for penetration and target destruction. The Hound Dog provides longer range and higher yield against area defenses and soft targets, while the SRAM provides improved capabilities against point defenses and other military or urban/industrial targets.

We believe the Soviet air defense environment of the 1970's will require other penetration aids for our bomber force in addition to SRAM. If the Soviets deploy an Airborne Warning and Control System (AWACS) and improved interceptors, we must provide new and effective means of countering them. To do so the Air Force is proceeding with development of improved Electronic Countermeasures (ECM) equipment as well as the Subsonic Cruise Armed Decoy (SCAD) which will contribute to acceptable bomber penetration by diluting Soviet air defenses.

To further aid bomber penetration, we are examining the feasibility of equipping the bomber force with a Bomber Defense Missile (BDM) which would be used by our bombers to offset the effectiveness of the Soviet forces. Our current R. & D. studies will provide data relative to critical design factors, development risk, and operational feasibility upon which we can base future development and deployment decisions. . . .

We realize that the degree of strategic superiority the United States once enjoyed may never be fully regained. We do consider it essential, however, that our strategic forces be structured to provide capabilities clearly able to counter the threat from the Soviets or any other potential enemy. Therefore, in responding to all elements of the Soviet threat, we are attempting to make near term improvements to our existing forces and to provide imaginative development of new forces.

Strategic Defense

The primary purpose of our strategic defense is to strengthen our deterrent posture. Effective defenses accomplish this by convincing the enemy that, following nuclear war, ratios of surviving population, industry, and military forces would be favorable to the United States. Effective defenses also augment our offensive forces by introducing uncertainty into the enemy's planning, compounding his targeting problems, and causing him to divert resources from other essential tasks. If our forces fail to deter an enemy, then our defensive forces must perform their classic roles of protecting offensive forces and limiting damage to our country.

The possibility that deterrence might fail requires the United States to possess defensive forces in sufficient quantity and quality to be effective against an evolving threat of missile, space, and aircraft systems. To manage these forces in a wartime environment, provisions must be made for their controlled employment against a single vehicle or as a totally integrated system to defend against a massive attack. At the same time, the interaction of our defenses with our strategic offensive forces must be accommodated to prohibit interference between the two.

During peacetime our strategic defense forces discourage Soviet nuclear attack and provide mobile defense capabilities for contingency operations. In addition, they identify airborne and space vehicles whose origins and intentions are uncertain, and they furnish warning that alerts our other strategic forces and the National Command Authority.

The primary military threat to the United States continues to be the Intercontinental Ballistic Missile (ICBM) force of the Soviets and, to a lesser degree, their bombers and Sea-Launched Ballistic Missiles (SLBM's). They also have the capability to employ a Fractional Orbit Bombardment System (FOBS) and a Depressed-trajectory ICBM (DICBM). Each of these threats presents a difficult defense problem for the United States should the Soviets increase the quantity and sophistication of these systems—and they have the capacity to do both.

We are now primarily dependent on the Ballistic Missile Early Warning System (BMEWS) to warn us of attack by ICBM's. To provide a warning of a Soviet FOBS or DICBM attack, we have obtained an interim capability with an Over-the-Horizon (OTH) forward-scatter radar system designated "440L." This system takes advantage of the radio energy reflecting properties of the ionosphere. Our improved detection capability, communications, and system automation are programmed to provide the earliest and most comprehensive notification possible to our combat operations centers.

Our seven-site SLBM warning system is scheduled to attain an Initial Operational Capability (IOC) in the near future. This system can detect and track SLBM's launched off U.S. coastlines along the Atlantic and Pacific Oceans and the Gulf of Mexico. We are using radar systems that formerly were part of our air defense ground environment but have been modified to perform the missile detection and tracking function. This system will assist in reducing the effectiveness of the rapidly growing Soviet capability to launch missiles against the United States from peripheral waters.

Despite these improvements in our ground-based surveillance systems, we are still concerned that our ability to detect and provide warning of missile attack should be improved. To accomplish this we are developing an early warning system which will utilize advanced sensors, data processing, and communications techniques. . . .

Last year I noted that the number of objects in orbit had reached 1,275, and the cumulative number recorded over the years had exceeded 3,000. The number of objects in orbit now totals more than 1,600, and our total catalog count exceeds 3,700. To insure that we retain our capability to detect, track, and maintain an up-to-the-minute catalog of all objects in space, we will be expanding our spacetrack capability during the next 2 years.

Our defensive efforts to counter the bomber threat of the Soviets continue to complicate their strategic planning and make their offensive efforts more costly. The enemy suffers a considerable decrease in his bomber force capability by the mere existence of our air defenses. Because our existing bomber defenses are able to intercept and destroy high-flying bombers, the Soviets have been forced to plan for low-level penetration at a significant cost in payload. They have also been forced to equip many of their bombers with Air-to-Surface Missiles (ASM's) rather than gravity bombs in order to release their payload outside our defenses. The combined effect of low-level attack and ASM equipage has served to reduce significantly the payloads Soviet bombers can deliver.

Thus, our current bomber defenses can exact a toll on U.S.S.R. bombers by depriving them of optimum tactics. However, if we continue to reduce our air defense capabilities, the enemy will certainly reevaluate the situation and revise his tactics accordingly.

These revised tactics could include resumption of high-altitude penetrations from random directions permitting more effective use of the Soviet bombers, including the large medium-bomber force. . . .

Considering the magnitude and diversity of the entire atmospheric and space threat, it is quite clear that high priority near-term and long-term efforts are required to eliminate present defense deficiencies and provide required future capabilities. These efforts should include retention of our present defense forces until adequate replacement forces are in being. The number of lives that could be saved by effective defense of the United States argues for the employment of a strong damage limiting capability, and we consider this essential to the preservation of our deterrent posture.

General Purpose Forces

General purpose or tactical offensive forces must be capable of responding to any level of conflict, including high-intensity nuclear warfare. However, their most likely use will be in conflicts which require the employment of conventional weapons. This broad range of possible contingencies over widely scattered reaches of the globe calls for flexible general purpose forces that can deploy rapidly and respond with adequate force to any possible contingency, as directed by national authority. With on-going improvements in weapon delivery systems, conventional ordnance, and unit deploya-bility, we are confident of our growing ability to counter limited aggression anywhere in the world.

To achieve maximum effectiveness with our modern weapon systems, we must integrate the employment of all elements of the tactical forces, including strike, reconnaissance, electronic warfare, airlift, special operations, and command and control. Each element must be able to perform its own function extremely well while, at the same time, reinforcing the effectiveness of the other components. In addition, because the nature and location of future contingencies cannot be accurately predicted, tactical air forces must be capable of deploying to and rapidly operating from austere as well as established operating bases. . . .

. . .We are striving for an expanded, modernized, and bal-anced force of tactical fighters and fighter-bombers, each designed to do one mission extremely well and one or more missions reasonably well.

To counter the growing Soviet air-to-air threat of the mid-seventies, we believe the development and deployment of the F-15 air superiority fighter should receive the highest priority. Additionally, we need a more effective close air support aircraft with high survivability, the A-X, to provide combat troops with improved fire support.

Finally, we must have the capability to deploy and resupply these tactical forces anywhere in the world and conduct round-the-clock all-weather operations from austere bases. . .

Airlift Forces

Airlift plays an increasingly critical role in our military force posture. By exploiting speed, range, and accessibility to any land area, airlift provides flexibility and precision to the global maneuverability of both land and air forces.

Today, our airlift force planning is based on the need to support worldwide operations of the Department of Defense and to respond rapidly to politico-military crises in various parts of the world. Projected improvements in the airlift force over the next few years stem from continuing analyses of requirements based on our overseas posture and strategy. The airlift forces, together with selective forward basing, prepositioning and sealift, must be able to support multiple contingencies while providing continued lift for other deployed U.S. forces. . . .

. . .We now possess airlift forces capable of performing the critical tasks of both strategic and tactical airlift at varied levels of conflict. In the near future we will have an all-jet strategic airlift force, but we also need a larger tactical airlift force, modernized and augmented by new equipment. These modernized forces, complemented by updated CRAF, Guard, and Reserve airlift capabilities, as well as improved aerial port facilities, will enable us to maintain an effective global airlift system. With such a system we can immediately respond to, and indefinitely sustain, a wide range of emergency and wartime airlift requirements at the lowest practicable cost. . . .

Research and Development

. . .The Air Force has always devoted substantial resources to achieve a well-balanced R. & D. effort capable of providing qualitative superiority over any current or future enemy force.

But I would like to point out that our R. & D. program has proceeded under considerable restraint. Because of the high cost of modern weapon systems, we have withheld effort not only on new systems that appeared promising but also on some that we considered necessary. We have, in effect, limited our R. & D. program to those developments which offered significant improvements to our existing forces or which responded directly to the known capabilities of possible enemies.

This approach, however, has left little room to accommodate to the uncertainties of the potential threat. Despite our best intelligence efforts, both the capabilities and intentions of the Communists frequently remain obscure. Even when we do detect the testing of a major system a few years before it becomes operational, our ability to produce an effective counterweapon is dependent upon the technology already in hand.

In order to survive in such an environment, we must support a broad-based R. & D. program which assures the right technology at the right time. Also, we must do this in the context that our adversaries are equally aware that military superiority has a technological foundation. The record of the Soviets in doubling their budget for R. & D. and space during the period from 1960 through 1968 speaks for itself. In contrast, our national R. & D. effort (including space expenditures) has leveled off in the past few years. The Air Force R. & D. program, in particular, has remained essentially constant for the past 8 years.[1] While we have kept pace with the Soviets in many fields, we have not, in my view, done so in all of our mission areas.

In strategic offense and defense, R. & D. can produce perhaps the greatest changes in relative national strength. For this reason, we have characteristically devoted a major portion of our R. & D. effort to these areas. I discussed earlier the requirements for the Advanced Manned Strategic Aircraft (AMSA) and the recent full-scale engineering development decision rendered on this system, the Hard Rock Silo, the advanced Inter-Continental Ballistic Missile (ICBM), an Airborne Warning and Control System (AWACS), Over-the-Horizon (OTH) radars, to mention only a few. All of these are, or could be, products of our R. & D. program.

In the strategic missile area, we are making satisfactory progress in the development of Minuteman III. The first Minuteman III R. & D. missile was successfully launched last August. . . .

Our development programs for the tactical area are also very important, and many of these are being combat tested in Southeast Asia. Overall, we are meeting the immediate requirements of the battlefield, and we are also identifying new requirements to improve the capabilities of our tactical forces worldwide. One such requirement which I described earlier is the F-15.

The F-15 development program and its related avionics and weapon developments are designed to ensure a timely, systematic approach for obtaining an air superiority fighter. . . .

Another vital tactical requirement which I mentioned previously is the specialized close air support aircraft, the A-X. This

---

[1]Constant in dollar expenditures, but declining in purchasing power.

system, optimized for support of friendly ground forces, will stress increased responsiveness and it will be the first aircraft weapon system to include high survivability as a primary design objective. It will have such high survival features as manual and redundant flight controls, fully foamed fuel system remote from all ignition sources, "go-home" fuel in self-sealing fuel tanks, blast-resistant and redundant structure, extensive armor provisions for the pilot, and subsystem and engine protection. . . .

. . .We have been making progress in applying space technology to defense requirements. Two of the more important of these space efforts are the Satellite Communications and Manned Orbiting Laboratory (MOL) programs.

Much of the effectiveness of a modern military establishment is dependent upon its ability to communicate, and the DOD Satellite Communications Program is intended to exploit the advantages of satellite communications for strategic and tactical functions. The strategic and tactical aspects are handled by the Defense Satellite Communications System (DSCS) and the Tactical Satellite Communications Program (TSCP), respectively. . . .

In my statement last year, I discussed the MOL program for which the Air Force has both development and operational responsibility. Full-scale development of all of the major components continued during the past year as the program approached the period of peak activity. Significant progress was made in the development of each segment of the basic vehicle configuration as well as the major sub-systems and support activities. . . .

I would summarize our R. & D. efforts as a balance between current developments, new systems developments to meet longer range requirements, and the technology necessary to maintain military superiority for years to come. The fiscal year 1970 R. & D. program represents the best such balance that we can achieve within the current budget. This program provides for progress toward AMSA and a new air-superiority fighter and the initial step on the A-X. It also includes continued development of the Minuteman, the Hard Rock Silo, and the MOL. . . .

REDUCTIONS IN OVERKILL

Seymour Melman

Seymour Melman, Professor of Industrial Engineering at Columbia University, spoke on behalf of SANE.

Proposed Reductions in Military Overkill and Waste

The proposed budgets for national defense for fiscal year 1970 amount to $80,815 million (allowing for proposed modifications in the Johnson administration budget by Secretary of Defense Laird, March 16, 1969). This is the largest item in the federal budget and exceeds annual spending for military purposes except those at the peak of the Second World War.

In his first official press conference in January 1969, President Nixon announced that, in his view, what the United States required is sufficiency in the realm of defense. Sufficiency means adequacy. Definite, explicit criteria are required in order to define what is enough.

Since 1961 the design of the armed forces of the United States has been oriented towards a three-fold requirement: a war in the NATO area, a war in the China area, a lesser military action in Latin America.

Further, the requirement has been that U.S. armed forces should be capable of fighting wars in each of these areas at the same time. This means the conduct of one nuclear war and two conventional wars at once.

This combination of military operations does not refer to the defense of the United States. A nuclear war is an end-of-society war. The war in Vietnam, as a model of conventional far-Eastern war is clearly a military, political, economic and moral disaster—a major drain on American society and highly destructive of this nation both materially and morally. Such wars, in combination, are the military requirements in terms of which the Congress has voted funds from 1961 to 1969: to prepare 18 Army Divisions as against 11 in 1961; 11,000 deliverable nuclear warheads for intercontinental effect, as against 1,100 in 1961; 34,000 aircraft, as against 30,000 aircraft in 1961.

Statement before the Senate Committee on Armed Services, *Hearings on Authorization for Military Procurement*, April, May, June, 1969, Part 2, pp. 1378-1382.

An evaluation of "sufficiency" for the armed forces of the United States requires a basic definition of the nature of security commitment that is to be served by U.S. military power. The following are alternative criteria of sufficiency for U.S. armed forces: operation of a strategic deterrence force, guarding the shores of the United States, capability for participation in International peacekeeping operations.

This memorandum proposes a set of modifications in the Fiscal Year 1970 budget for U.S. military forces on the ground that the above criteria are a sound basis for judging sufficiency of U.S. military security forces. It should be underscored that these criteria do *not* include war plan elements of the following sort: there is no intention here of preparing a nuclear force in such numbers and of such powers as to be calculably competent for a first strike operation against another nuclear power; these criteria for military sufficiency exclude the intention of preparing armed forces for wars of intervention as in Vietnam.

It is emphasized that *after* the substantial reductions recommended here are made for reasons of merit, the armed forces of the U.S. would consist of 2,300,000 men, and would operate missile, aircraft and naval forces of staggering power. *These reductions are directed toward deescalating additions to already massive overkill forces.*

Proposed Reductions of Department of Defense and Related Spending by Deescalation of Present Overkill Forces and Other Wasteful Practices

Incremental costs of the Vietnam War

The additional military spending owing to the operation of the Vietnam war refers to the using up of ammunition, material, and people directly or indirectly connected with the Vietnam war. This amounts to $20 billion per year. The Congress should reduce the budget of the Department of Defense by this amount as an instruction to the Department and to the President to terminate this war. ($20 billion.)

Reducing Additions to Strategic Overkill

It is generally appreciated that no present or foreseeable research effort will make it possible for the armed forces of the United States, or any other nation, to destroy a person or a community more than once. Nevertheless, the nuclear forces and delivery systems of the United States have been built up with multiples of overkill. The exact number is, of course, unknown since we have not observed a full-scale nuclear war. Such observation is not required, however, to understand that the present capability for delivering 11,000 nuclear warheads to the territory of the Soviet Union refers mainly to 156 Soviet cities of 100,000 or over. The systems include various long and short-range missile systems, aircraft and submarines. To continue a buildup of these forces is grossly wasteful, not to mention irrational. Accordingly the following reductions in proposed budgeted expenditures are recommended:

1. *New nuclear weapons production.* The proposed budget for the Atomic Energy Commission includes funds for further production of nuclear materials and for further production of nuclear weapons. This activity should simply be stopped as being militarily and humanly irrational. . . . ($1,518 million.)

2. *Research, development, test and evaluations.* The descriptive material in the Budget . . . indicates that the major part of new military research activity is oriented to new strategic weapons delivery systems. This is part of the proliferation of overkill forces which has no rational justification whatsoever (except to keep managerial-industrial empires intact). Accordingly a substantial reduction is recommended in this budget line. ($5,000 million.)

3. *Poseidon and Minuteman III.* These "new generation" intercontinental missiles would make possible a multiplication of nuclear warheads beyond the present 11,000, and perhaps allow for an increased calculated accuracy. A few hundred yards closer to calculated target in such weapons should be appreciated against the fact that their destructive power extends over miles. Accordingly, a reduction is recommended to cut off this enlargement of overkill forces. ($1,000 million.)

4. *ABM.* The proposed antiballistic missile system has been the subject of exhaustive debate. The technical workability of the system is under grave doubt on the grounds of complexity and in terms of the experience with an unsuccessful attempt to build an anti-aircraft defense system. . . . Accordingly, the budgeted items for their purpose . . . are recommended for elimination. ($904 million.)

5. *Chemical and biological warfare.* Since 1961 the United States has been producing and stockpiling increasing quantities of these lethal materials. Outside Denver, 100 million doses of nerve gas have been placed in open storage in steel containers. The mass production of these and biological warfare materials mean more overkill weapons systems. In addition, the very existence of these materials in quantities expose the people of the United States itself to grave hazards because of possible accidents in the handling of lethal, self-propagating organisms. It is therefore recommended that this production be stopped. ($350 million.)

6. *Advanced manned strategic aircraft.* In the face of already existing massive overkill capability the proposal to build

additional and new highspeed bombers is organizational and industrial empire building and little else. This should be terminated. ($102 million.)

7. *Bomber defense system (SAGE)*. It has long been understood that the Soviets do not have meaningful long-range bomber capability. When this is coupled with the known defects in the operation of the SAGE-type system there is no reason for incurring the large cost that building this would involve since it would apparently add nothing meaningful to the defense of the United States. . . . ($1,000 million.)

8. *Surface to air missiles*. Former Pentagon staff have indicated that substantial savings could be made by holding back on major spending for ineffective anti-aircraft missiles, and deferring production on apparently inadequate designs. . . . ($850 million.)

9. *The Manned Orbiting Laboratory*. This is an Air Force venture that is NASA's task on the scientific side, and an addition to overkill if used to add to nuclear delivery. Hence, reduction is recommended. . . . ($576 million.)

Reduction in Additions to Conventional War Overkill

1. *Vietnam war manpower*. The Vietnam war now uses 639,000 soldiers, sailors, airmen. As the Congress instructs the Department of Defense and the President to refrain from operating wars of intervention, these 639,000 men would not be required. Their termination (annual cost of about $10,000 per man) would leave the United States with armed forces of 2,900,000 and an opportunity to effect a major reduction in an unnecessary military outlay. ($6,390 million.)

2. *Surplus military manpower*. Analysts in the Department of Defense have reported . . . that substantial savings could be made in manpower in all the services by a 10 percent cut in "support" forces which use a lion's share of military manpower, and have been unjustifiably large compared with other armies of the world. In addition manpower savings could be effected by imposing a requirement to reduce the large category of "transient" personnel. These combined reductions in the Army, Navy and Air Force would make possible a reduction of $4.2 billion, allowing for a cost of $10,000 per man year. ($4,200 million.)

3. *Tactical aircraft programs*. Specialists in the aviation field have indicated that elimination of overly-elaborate and impractical electronic systems, and concentration on simpler (hence more reliable) aircraft would make possible savings on a large scale. . . . ($1,800 million.)

4. *Attack carriers*. The United States now operates 15 attack carrier forces. Their justification is based on the assumption of fighting three wars at once. Even a beginning of reasonable economy in the use of these forces . . . makes possible substantial budget reductions. ($360 million.)

5. *Anti-submarine carrier forces*. These forces are known to have severely limited capability in their military function, casting grave doubt on the worth of continuing them, according to Pentagon specialists. . . . ($400 million.)

6. *Amphibious forces and Fast Deployment Logistics ships (FDL)*. The amphibious forces are massively overbuilt . . . and are presumably oriented to a Western hemisphere war mission. These could be substantially reduced without reducing a massive military capability. The FDL's are part of an expanded Vietnam War program that should be stopped by the Congress. . . . ($500 million.)

7. *C5-A jet transport*. This plane has been specifically designed to transport large numbers of troops for the Pentagon's world-wide policing and Vietnam War program. This capability should be curtailed. ($500 million.)

8. *Military assistance*. For some time it has been apparent that the U.S. military assistance program has been a major factor in encouraging and sustaining dictatorial and backward regimes in many countries. This outlay has no demonstrable relation to the defense of the United States and should therefore be eliminated. ($610 million.)

9. *New naval ship construction*. We are informed in the Budget for FY 1970 . . . that "The largest single 1970 increase proposed for General Purpose Forces is for a new ship construction program for our naval forces of $2.4 billion total obligational authority." Such massive expenditures for naval forces is justifiable only in terms of the 3-wars-at-once military perspective. Even first steps towards building a military sufficiency force, as against a military overkill force for 3-wars-at-once requires elimination of this item. ($2,400 million.)

10. *Economics in training*. A former Pentagon staffer (Office of Comptroller) recommends changes in training methods that would save an appreciable sum as against present methods and costs. . . . ($50 million.)

11. *Improved buying procedures*. A series of straight-forward steps can apparently produce major savings in Pentagon buying—by curtailing the pattern of costly cost-overruns. . . . Therefore the following Procurement reduction is indicated. ($2,700 million.)

12. *U.S. NATO forces*. Pentagon staff indicate feasibility of reducing forces in Europe by 125,000 and their backup by

50,000. . . . At $10,000 cost per man, this justifies budget
reduction of $1,750 million.

Miscellaneous Economies

1. *Military construction*. The Budget for FY 1970 . . .
enumerates diverse purposes for which new military construction has
been scheduled. Secretary of Defense Laird proposed a reduction of
the $1,948 million military construction item by $634 million,
leaving $1,314 million. This should be further reduced in order to
limit the further over-expansion of unnecessary military forces
within the United States and abroad—in terms of the requirements of
defense sufficiency. ($1,000 million.)

2. *F-14 aircraft*. The Navy has announced a program for
constructing a new class of fighter planes to be carried by its major
aircraft carriers. These fighter planes are of doubtful worth since
there is no present or potential opposing force with fleets of carriers
against which U.S. carrier forces and fighter planes will conceivably
be operated. Furthermore, the enlargement of the carrier aircraft
force involves a major addition to preparations for further Vietnam-
type wars. This alone is the issue with respect to this aircraft (not
whether the design is right, or whether the contractor is competent).
The Budget for FY 1970 . . . suggests the amount intended for this
purpose. This should be eliminated. ($834 million.)

*The sum of these proposed savings in the military spending of
the United States for FY 1970 is $54,794 million. . . .*
The recommendations given above for savings in Fiscal Year
1970 military programs of the United States are justified on the
following grounds:

1. Present forces are more than sufficient to serve as a
competent security force for the United States.
2. The Congress should stop the armed forces from adding
to overkill.
3. The Congress should stop preparation for more Vietnam
wars.
4. No conceivable armed forces can do more than help to
secure the U.S. in a military sense. Defense as a literal shield is no
longer purchaseable. The Joint Chiefs do not promise to defend the
U.S.—they cannot do it. Neither can they promise a nuclear war
"victory," for a "successful first-strike" without one's own destruction is not achievable.
5. The Congress, through these budget reductions, can make
available a large fund that is needed for productive, life-serving
purposes within the United States.

6. Only by these means can the American people cope constructively with the nation's massive problems of economic development and forestall the dread prospect of racial confrontation in this land. . . .

The application of recommended savings to these purposes could probably be accomplished, swiftly, by translating these savings into major tax reductions. This would permit the cities and the states to use their existing taxing mechanisms for tapping this new source of tax power and applying these funds to the urgent needs of our own people.

FOR THE ABM

Melvin R. Laird

Melvin R. Laird is Secretary of Defense.

. . . I believe we can all agree that our nuclear deterrent must be made as secure as is technically and economically feasible. Our nuclear forces defend not only ourselves, but our allies. Accordingly, we must take whatever steps are practicable to insure that our strategic retaliatory forces can survive a Soviet attack.

After examining the available alternatives, we have concluded that a combination of approaches provides the most realistic means of safeguarding our retaliatory capability.

This combination consists of beginning a measured deployment of an active defense of our retaliatory forces, structured to expand as circumstances may dictate, and preserving the option, if we later find it necessary, to harden further our land-based missiles. The combination is necessary because our studies show that hardening alone would not provide adequate protection against foreseeable advances in the accuracy of Soviet missiles.

The ABM defense system we now propose to deploy will use components previously developed for Sentinel. However, if the

Statement before the Senate Committee on Armed Services, *Hearings on Authorization for Military Procurement*, Part 1, pp. 98, 123, 154-157.

system is fully installed, these components will be deployed in such a way as to provide:

1.   A local defense of the Minuteman missile silos
2.   Early warning and area defense of our bomber bases and command and control system
3.   A defense of the continental United States against the kind of attack which the Chinese Communists may be able to launch in the mid-1970's
4.   Protection against an accidental or small attack from any source

This system will not require the emplacement of missiles or radars in or near our major cities, except for the protection of the national command authorities in Washington, D.C. . . .

The basic deployment plan would include a total of 12 sites, compared with 17 sites in the previous plan. These 12 sites would be in the continental United States. Two others, Alaska and Hawaii, could be added if required. (The Chicago, New York, and Salt Lake City sites have been eliminated.) The first two sites—Grand Forks Air Force Base and Malmstrom Air Force Base—which have been proposed for initial deployment, will each have one 4-face Missile Site Radar (MSR), one 1-face Perimeter Acquisition Radar (PAR), Standard Spartans and Sprints.* The schedule on which the remaining sites will be deployed will be determined year by year in step with the emergence of the threat. . . .

. . . The Sprint missile has been tested. The Spartan missile has been tested. The missile site radar has also been tested. The only item that has not been tested as far as the hardware is concerned is the PAR radar, and, of course, as you know, we have not tested the warhead of the Spartan missile. Although we have tested R. & D. warheads of a lower megatonnage, we have not tested the kind of operational warhead that would be necessary for the Spartan missile.

But these tests can move forward, we believe, in keeping with the nuclear test ban, and we have facilities where these tests will be carried forward. . . .

The modified ABM system has been designed so that its defensive intent is unmistakable. It is not an escalation of the arms race. The original Sentinel plan could have been interpreted as a first

*The Spartan missile is designed to intercept an incoming missile at a point high above the atmosphere. If it fails to do so, the Sprint missile is fired in an effort to destroy the incoming weapon at a point close to the target and within the atmosphere (ed.'s note).

step toward the construction of a heavy system for the defense of our cities. Indeed it could have been used for that purpose.

The Safeguard system, both in fact and in appearance, is a protection for our retaliatory force, it is an essential safeguard for the U.S. interests against the nature of the threat we face from the Soviet Union and from Red China.

The potential threat from the Soviet Union lies in the growing missile force which could destroy a portion of our deterrent, or destroy a portion of our retaliatory force.

We cannot stop a massive Soviet attack on our cities. Technically we just don't have the know-how. We must rely on our deterrent to insure that a nuclear attack doesn't start in the first place. This system truly protects people by protecting our deterrent force, which maintains the peace in the world today.

In order to deter an attack, we must be positive, and the Soviet Union must be positive, that a substantial number of our long-range missiles and bombers will survive, that they will survive any attack, and then that they can destroy the attacker.

The Soviet Union today is building at a rapid rate the kinds of weapons which could be used to erode our essential deterrent force, and as recently as December, they went forward with further installations of large ICBM's within the Soviet Union.

They are installing many SS—9 Intercontinental Ballistic Missiles. This is a large and an accurate weapon. With improvements in accuracy and a continued increase in numbers, the Soviet missile force could gain real effectiveness against our Minuteman.

The Soviets also could build nuclear submarines at a rate of one a month, which could come into a very close proximity to our shores, and attack at short range many of our missile and bomber bases. They are also working hard on the FOBS system, the Fractional Orbit Bombardment System, also designed to reduce the warning time to our bombers, so that they will not have sufficient time to become airborne.

Communist China is another potential threat to us. It cannot threaten our retaliatory weapons system for many years, but by the mid-1970's China could pose a threat to our people and to our property.

The Government of Communist China is devoting an astonishing portion of its national resources to the development of nuclear weapons, particularly the ICBM's, the Intercontinental Ballistic Missiles. The Safeguard ABM system proposed by President Nixon is carefully designed to meet these threats adequately, without overreacting.

Continuing research and development without any initial deployment would leave us with no option to provide defense for our deterrent on the schedule that might be required by the Soviet threat, if we do not reach agreement with the Soviets on limiting strategic forces.

Under the new concept outlined by the President of phased and measured installation, we give added insurance that our ballistic missile defense will be adequate but not wasteful.

If further threats do not develop, we can stop the installation with the two sites that will be constructed under phase 1 of our program that we are presenting to you in the 1970 budget. If either the Soviet or the Chinese threat continues to grow, we can meet that threat with added installations.

Our obviously thin protection of cities and added protection of our deterrent forces will require no reaction at all from the Soviet Union, providing the Soviet Union has a responsible deterrent nuclear war policy as we in the United States do.

. . . The Safeguard system is not a stumbling block to arms limiting talks with the Soviet Union. On the contrary, under the type of deployment we have chosen, this measured deployment, the Soviet Union is given an added incentive to negotiate a meaningful agreement on limitation of both offensive and defensive weapons.

First, the modified ABM program would show the Soviets that we are quite serious about protecting our deterrent forces, about assuring all enemies that they cannot achieve an effective low-risk first strike against the United States.

Second, it would show the Soviets that we are preparing so that we will not be in a position for a low-risk attack on them, and that it is worthwhile to negotiate limits on strategic arms.

. . . Under the proposed Safeguard program, even the first two installations will not be operating before 1973. This gives ample time for the two countries to negotiate agreements on these and on other weapons. Thus the modified ABM opens the door wider to mutual arms control.

But, if the Soviet Union should slam the door on an agreement, the modified ABM would permit us to continue steps toward the protection of our retaliatory force. . . .

Our studies showed that while we could not defend our cities effectively against a missile attack of a massive nature, only a small attack, we could defend our Minuteman missiles and bombers to a significant degree against any size of threat. The problems here are different.

In defending cities, our minimum objective must be to intercept all incoming warheads. If one gets through, the city and most of its people are destroyed. But in the case of the Minuteman missiles, and our alert bombers, we do not have to preserve every one of them. We must preserve only a certain minimum essential number, enough to guarantee immense destruction in the aggressor's own country. . . .

. . . My technical advisers are convinced, and they have convinced me, that this limited ballistic missile defense system is feasible. Mr. Packard, the Deputy Secretary of Defense, and service Secretaries, the Chairman of the Joint Chiefs, and all members of the Joint Chiefs and I agree unanimously that the recommended program will be adequate, will be timely, and will be an appropriate counter to the threat that we in the United States face as a people. . . .

AGAINST THE ABM

Herbert F. York

Herbert F. York is Professor of Physics, University of California, San Diego

. . . I do not doubt the statements of the Secretary of Defense that the Soviets are now rapidly building up their offensive forces. . . . What is difficult to understand about this matter is why the Soviets settled for being such a poor second in intercontinental nuclear arms for such a long time. Conceivably, the suggestion that the Soviets are reaching for a first strike capability may be true, but their actions can be easily understood without appealing to such a notion. In any event, I doubt the wisdom of the proposed U.S. response because (1) the Safeguard system is technically questionable and (2) the deployment of Safeguard would accelerate the arms race.

For our purposes today it is important to note that the Defense Department has in these last few weeks reintroduced the objective of providing an ABM defense capable of coping with a large and sophisticated offense. True, the defense of selected hard points now being proposed for Safeguard is theoretically somewhat easier than the defense of large soft targets such as cities, the goal of

Statement before Senate Committee on Armed Services, *Hearings on Authorization for Military Procurement*, Part 2, pp. 1115-1119.

Sentinel and its predecessors. However, the designers are now again required to cope with that large variety of very difficult technical problems which defense designers tried unsuccessfully to solve in the days of Nike-Zeus and Nike-X. I am referring to that large group of quantifiable technical problems which includes radar blackout, penetration aids of all sorts (decoys, chaff, electronic counter-measures and multiple warheads), warhead kill mechanisms and the defenses against them, as well as offensive tactics such as "roll back" and saturation techniques. Fortunately, these matters have been much discussed in public in recent years and especially in recent months. As a result, I think it has become clear to most interested persons that while defense designers have sometimes been on the verge of solving one or two of these problems when they treat them separately and in isolation, they have never come close to coping with them in the complex combinations that even a moderately sophisticated offense can present. I see no reason to suppose that this situation will change.

I should like now to turn to two technical problems that pertain to all the forms of ABM so far proposed, but which unfortunately are not so simple to discuss nor so easy to quantify as that class of problems I have just mentioned.

Any active defense system such as the ABM must sit in readiness for 2 or 4 or 8 years and then fire at precisely the correct second following a warning time of only a few minutes. This warning time is so short that many systems designers would like to eliminate human decisionmakers, even at low command levels, from the decisionmaking system. Further, the precision needed for the firing time is so fine that machines must be used to choose the precise instant of firing no matter how the decision to fire is made. In the case of offensive missiles the situation is different in an essential way; although maintaining readiness throughout a long indefinite period is necessary, the moment of firing is not so precisely controlled in general and hence human decisionmakers, including even those at high levels, may readily be permitted to play a part in the decisionmaking process. Thus if we wish to be certain that the defense will respond under conditions of surprise, the trigger of the ABM, unlike the triggers of the ICBMs and Polarises, must be continuously sensitive and ready, in short a "hair" trigger for indefinitely long periods of time.

On the other hand, it is obvious that we cannot afford to have an ABM fire by mistake or in response to a false alarm. Indeed the Army went to some pains to assure residents of areas near proposed Sentinel sites that it was imposing requirements to insure against the accidental launching of the missile and the subsequent detonation of the nuclear warhead it carries. Moreover Army R. & D.

officials have assured the public that no ABMs would ever be launched without the specific approval of very high authorities. These two requirements, a "hair" trigger so that it can cope with a surprise attack and a "stiff" trigger so that it will never go off accidentally or without proper authorization are, I believe, contradictory requirements. In saying this I am not expressing doubt as to the stated intentions of the present Army R. & D. leaders, and I strongly endorse the restrictions implied in their statements. However, I am saying that if the system cannot be fired without approval of the highest authorities, then the probability of its being fired under conditions of surprise is less than it would be otherwise. Furthermore, when control over the system passes from the present R. & D. oriented officers to operations oriented officers, it is not at all clear that these latter will approach the problem with the same degree of sensitivity.

It is important to emphasize that this problem exists only in the real world and not on the test range; on the test range there need be no such concern about accidental misfires, the interceptions do not involve the use of nuclear weapons and the day, if not the second, of the mock attack is known. Another essential—but again difficult to quantify—difference between the real world and the test range lies in the fact that the deployed defensive equipment will, normally, never have been fully and realistically exercised and even the supposedly identical test range equipment will never have been tested against the precise target or targets that the deployed equipment would ultimately have to face. In the case of other defense systems which have worked after a fashion, practice using the actual deployed equipment against real targets has been possible and has been a major element in increasing their effectiveness. Thus, the Soviet SAMs in North Vietnam work as well as they do because both the equipment designers and the operating crews have had plenty of opportunities to practice against U.S. targets equipped with real countermeasures and employing real tactics.

For all these reasons, I continue to have the gravest doubts as to the capability of any ABM system I have heard of, whether or not the problem has been defined into being "easy" and whether or not it "works" on a test range. I stress that I am not just talking about some percentage failure inherent in the mathematical distribution of miss distances, or statistically predictable failures in system components, but rather about possible catastrophic failure in which at the moment of truth either the system doesn't fire at all, or all interceptions fail for some unforeseen reason.

Let us now move from technical to political matters concerning the relationship between the ABM and the arms race. It is frequently said that the ABM, or at least some versions of it, does not have serious arms control implications. The reasons advanced have to do with its intrinsically defensive character. In my opinion such a belief is based on an error which may be called the fallacy of the last move. It is indeed true that if the last move ever made in the arms race consisted in deploying an ABM system, then deploying the ABM would by definition not have any arms race implications. But in the real world of constant change in both the technology and the deployed numbers of all kinds of strategic weapon systems, ABMs are accelerating elements in the arms race. In support of this, let us consider a relevant bit of recent history.

At the beginning of this decade, we began to hear about a possible Soviet ABM and we became concerned about its potential effects on our ICBM and Polaris systems. It was then that we began seriously to consider various penetration aid ideas, among them that of placing more than one warhead on a single offensive missile. This idea has since grown in complexity, as these things do, and has resulted in the MIRV concept (multiple independently targeted reentry vehicles). There are now additional justifications for MIRV besides penetration, but that is how it all started. As others have pointed out, the MIRV concept is a very important element in accelerating the arms race, and potentially seriously destabilizing. In fact, the possibility of a Soviet MIRV is used as one of the main arguments in support of the idea of hard-point defense and thus we have come one full turn around the arms race spiral. No one in 1960-61 thought through the potential destabilizing effects of multiple warheads, and certainly no one predicted, or even could have predicted, that the inexorable logic of the arms race would carry us directly from Soviet talk in 1960 about defending Moscow against missiles, to a requirement for hard-point defense of offensive missile sites in the United States in 1969. Likewise, I am sure the Russians did not foresee the large increase in deployed U.S. warheads that will ultimately result from their ABM deployment.

Similarly no one today can describe in detail the chain reaction which the Safeguard deployment would lead to. The response of our Defense Establishment to the Soviet ABM, which I have outlined above, was not the result of our being provoked and I emphasize this because we hear so much discussion about what is a provocative move and what is not. Rather, our response was motivated by a deep-seated belief that the only appropriate response to any new technical development on the other side is further technical complexity of our own. The arms race is not so much a series of political provocation followed by hot emotional reactions, as it is a series of technical challenges followed by cool, calculated responses in the form of ever more costly, more complex, and more fully automated devices. I believe that this endless, seemingly uncontrollable process was one of the principal things President Eisenhower had in mind when he made his other, usually forgotten, warning: "We must be alert to the . . . danger that public policy could itself become the captive of a scientific-technological elite." He placed this other warning, also from his farewell address, on the same level as the much more familiar warning about the military-industrial complex.

It may be that the present Soviet offensive buildup is in part a response to one of the earlier versions of our ABM. The Soviet "Pentagonologists" may simply have concluded in the midsixties that the U.S. military-industrial complex eventually would succeed in foisting an ABM on the American people, and the Soviet technologists felt a need to provide a technical response to it, just as we did earlier in the reverse case. Just how correct this hypothetical analysis of our future action was, still remains to be seen.

Thus, although I cannot be sure of the mechanism, I believe that either Sentinel or Safeguard will produce further acceleration of the arms race. It is possible that the deployment of these ABMs will lead to a new round of penetration aid developments with further consequences of the magnitude of those produced by MIRV. It is indeed probable that deployment of these ABMs would lead to greater numbers of deployed offensive warheads on both sides. We may further expect deployment of these ABMs to lead to the persistent query, "But how do you know it really works?" and thus to increase the pressures against the current Partial Test Ban Treaty. Finally, it is certain that deployment of these ABMs will lead to placing greater reliance on automatic devices for making that ultimate decision about whether or not doomsday had arrived.

Perhaps the worst implication of the ABM with regard to arms control is that the people and the Congress may be deceived into believing that we are finally on the track of a technical solution to the dilemma of the steady decrease in our national security which has accompanied the steady increase in our military power over the last two decades. Such a false hope would be extremely dangerous if it diverted any of us from searching for a solution in the only place it may be found: in a political search for peace combined with arms control and disarmament measures.

Let me close on a more positive note by saying that I do believe there are circumstances in which an ABM could play a beneficial role. Such a circumstance would be one in which, as part of a bold and strong arms control agreement, at least one offensive missile was eliminated for each defense missile deployed. Under such circumstances, deployment of an ABM would receive very wide support indeed. But, unfortunately, that's not what we're talking about; instead, the only serious proposals before us seem to involve more of everything.

MILITARISM AND AMERICAN DEMOCRACY

J. William Fulbright

Senator J. Fulbright is Chairman of the Senate Committee on Foreign Relations and a member of the Senate Finance Committee and Joint Economic Committee. The speech was delivered as Owens-Corning Lecture, Denison University, Granville, Ohio, on April 8, 1969.

. . . Dangerous though it may be, the arms race is also exceedingly profitable. It is profitable not only to the "Strangeloves of the military-industrial complex," as I. F. Stone calls them, but to millions of honest, decent Americans whose primary concern is with nothing more than earning a decent living for their families. The industries and businesses which fill military orders have become the largest single producer of goods and services in the United States, pouring some $45 billion a year into over five thousand communities where more than eight million Americans, including members of the armed forces, and comprising 10 per cent of the labor force, earn their living from defense spending.

Violence has become the nation's leading industry. We are now spending about $80 billion a year on the military, which is more than the profits of all American business, or, to make another comparison, is almost as much as the total spending of federal, state, and local governments for health, education, old age and retirement benefits, housing and agriculture. Drawing their income from the $80 billion military budget, the defense industry forms what amounts to a giant concentration of socialism in our nominally free enterprise economy. . . .

It is not an enthusiasm for war but simple economic self-interest that has drawn millions of workers, their labor unions and their elected representatives into the military-industrial complex. For all of them the anti-ballistic missile means prosperity not war. For the industrialist it means higher profits not war; for the worker new jobs and the prospect of higher wages; for the politician a new

Excerpts from "Militarism and American Democracy" in *Vital Speeches of the Day* (May 15, 1969), pp. 455-460.

installation or defense order with which to ingratiate himself with his constituents. These benefits, once obtained, are not easily parted with. Every new weapons system or military installation soon acquires a constituency—a process which is aided and abetted by the perspicacity with which Pentagon officials award lucrative contracts and establish new plants and installations in the districts of influential members of Congress. I have not the slightest doubt that, if the anti-ballistic missile is deployed, "thick" or "thin," it will soon acquire its own powerful constituency, whereupon we will be saddled with it—for reasons wholly independent of its ostensible military utility.

The defense industry and the military establishment are coming under a kind of interlocking directorate. According to a survey made for the Subcommittee on Economy and Government of the Joint Economic Committee under the chairmanship of Senator Proxmire of Wisconsin, the one hundred biggest defense contractors now employ 2,072 former high-ranking military officers. Among these the ten largest companies, which received $11.6 billion in defense contracts last year, now employ 1,065 former high-ranking officers. The nine major producers of the Sentinel anti-ballistic missiles, as initiated by the Johnson Administration, employ 465 former military officers. All this, as Senator Proxmire said in something of an understatement, points to "the increasing influence of the big contractors with the military and the military with the big contractors."

Spawned by our global military involvements, the military-industrial complex has become a powerful force for the perpetuation of those involvements. Millions of Americans have acquired a vested interest in the expensive weapons systems which provide their livelihood and, indirectly therefore, in a foreign policy that has plunged the United States into a spiraling arms race with the Soviet Union; made us the world's major salesman of armaments; and committed us to the defense of "freedom"—very loosely defined—in almost fifty countries, including Vietnam, Spain and Greece with their "freedom-loving" regimes.

I would not equate the vested interest of the Pentagon generals and the leaders of the aerospace industry with that of the ordinary wage-earner but, lest we become too sanctimonious about the fat-cats, it is well to remember that it is not the price received but the service rendered that gives a profession its name. And that brings me to the role of the universities in the military-industrial complex. . . .

To a far greater extent than its European counterparts the American university has always had a penchant, in Alfred North

Whitehead's phrase, for "mating itself with action," and this has contributed both to the welfare of the country and the vitality of the university. But, coupled with an unprecedented need for funds in the years since World War II, the penchant for action has also turned out to be a serious weakness of our universities. Tempted by lucrative government contracts, many universities—especially the big and famous ones—have become neglectful of their paramount responsibilities and have gone dangerously far toward becoming servants of the state. Because the major source by far of government contract funds is the military establishment, the universities have been drawn primarily into military, or militarily useful, research in the physical and social sciences, becoming in the process card-carrying members of the military-industrial complex. . . .

In a society whose leading industry is violence, one of the leading professions, inevitably, is soldiering. Chronically at war, or threatening war, or being threatened with war, with a million and a half American military people stationed outside of our own borders, with a huge and costly military establishment and a gigantic defense industry, "America," as former Marine Corps Commandant David M. Shoup recently wrote, "has become a militaristic and aggressive nation."

Militarism is new to America. Prior to World War II we never maintained more than a token peacetime army; even in 1940, on the eve of World War II, there were less than half a million men in the armed forces. In those days the military had little prestige or influence. . . . Nor, in those years, was there anything resembling the military-industrial complex which looms so large in our affairs today. Allegations made in the thirties to the effect that the United States had been maneuvered into World War I by munitions makers, by the "merchants of death" as they were called, turned out to be unfounded.

World War II gave birth to American militarism, and the cold war, the Korean War and the Vietnamese war nourished it into the giant force of today. These wars conferred upon military leaders the power and prestige which previously they had been denied. Military leaders, as General Shoup points out, became not only popular heroes but respected opinion makers.

In addition we have become a nation of veterans—over twenty-three million as of 1968. This means that one-fifth of our adult population have been subjected to some degree of indoctrination in military values and attitudes. The great veterans organizations, with over four million members, have grown into one of the most powerful lobbies in Washington primarily working for veterans' benefits but, often too, lobbying for chauvinist and belligerent foreign policies.

There is much that is valuable in military experience: it encourages loyalty, honor and courage. But it also fosters less wholesome attitudes—conformism, elitism, authoritarianism, and a certain romanticism about war. As time passes, memories are revised, and the veteran is likely to remember the comradeship and excitement while forgetting the killing and the fear; he may remember the music and pageantry while forgetting how hot and smelly and boring it is in a column of marching men. Most of all, as nostalgia sets in, the veteran is likely to remember the thrill of adventure while forgetting its lethal purpose. . . .

At the core of the new American militarism is the professional officers' corps made up of a few thousand high-ranking officers of unusual ability and energy. Marked as men of talent by their rise to the highest ranks through the rigorous competitiveness of the military services, they bring to bear a strength of conviction and near unanimity of outlook that gives them an influence on public policy disproportionate to their numbers. Disciplined and loyal to their respective services, with added prestige in the case of many of them deriving from heroic combat records, they operate with an efficiency and effectiveness not often found among civilian officials. In addition, as General Shoup points out, they always have a plan in an emergency, and that can be very beguiling to anxious politicians and frightened people.

The danger arises from the narrowness of outlook of so many professional soldiers, an outlook amounting to an inveterate preference for the use of force. As one social psychologist, Professor Ralph K. White of George Washington University, points out, every profession tends to overvalue its own stock in trade and it is only natural that soldiers lay great stress on theirs, which happens to be weapons. To the "professional" soldier it is axiomatic that, if you make the enemy "hurt" enough, he will eventually give in. If, as in Vietnam, the enemy does not give in to superior power, that is attributed to an insufficiency of force and can be remedied by applying more force. To this military prototype, there is "no substitute for victory" and the failure to apply the necessary force to achieve it is taken as the result of a failure of will, a lack of courage, and even a deficiency of virility. Excluded from serious consideration is the possibility that force may fail, as in Vietnam, not because you didn't use enough of it, but because it was the wrong thing to use in the first place. . . .

Just as force is the professional soldier's stock in trade, war is his best opportunity for advancement. I do not think that military professionals consciously seek or yearn for war, but they can hardly be blamed if they do not abhor it as civilians do. Peace-time duty is dull. An army in peace-time is like Congress during adjournment—without the same opportunities for travel. Combat provides a soldier with the opportunity for distinction, advancement and command. . . .

The military have become ardent and dangerous competitors for power in American society. The services compete with each other for funds, for the control of new weapons systems, and for the privilege of being "first to fight." Constantly improving their techniques for rapid deployment, they not only yearn to try them out but actively seek opportunities by pressing their proposals on political authorities, who all too often are tempted by the seemingly quick, "surgical" courses of action proposed by the military in preference to the endless, wearisome methods of diplomacy. For a variety of reasons—to test new plans and equipment, to try out the techniques of counterinsurgency, and, in the case of the Marines, says General Shoup, just to avoid the disgrace of being left out—all of the military services were enthusiastic about the initial involvement in Vietnam. By now they should have had their fill, but they still seem game to go on, trying out new weapons and strategies, although up to now the only military principle which has been vindicated in Vietnam is Tocqueville's maxim that, "There are two things that will always be very difficult for the democratic nation: to start a war and to end it."

Even though there is probably not a single top-ranking officer in any of the armed services who would consider an attempt to overturn constitutional government in the way of *Seven Days in May*, militarism poses a distinct threat to our democracy. At the very minimum it represents a dangerously constricted and highly influential point of view toward our foreign relations—a viewpoint which takes little account of political complexities, even less of social and economic factors, and just about none of human and psychological considerations.

But the military is more than a benign repository of parochial political views. It has become a vigorous partisan in our politics, exerting great influence on the executive, on the military committees of Congress, on the "think-tanks" and universities to which it parcels out lucrative research contracts, and on public opinion. A few weeks ago it came to my attention that the Department of the Army was planning a national publicity campaign, involving exhibits and planted magazine articles to be solicited from tame civilian scientists, in order to sell the ABM to the American public and to counteract the criticisms of Congressmen and the scientific community.

Only very rarely does a general invoke the higher loyalty of patriotism—his own concept of it, that is—over loyalty to civilian political authority, as General MacArthur did in his defiance of President Truman. But if, as time goes on, the country continues to be chronically at war, continues to sustain a huge, largely autonomous military establishment, and continues to neglect its domestic problems, militarism will surely increase, and even if the military does not take over the government directly, it could come to acquire power comparable to that of the German General Staff in the years before World War I. It may not seem likely now, but it is by no means so inconceivable that we need not warn against it and act to prevent it. . . .

INDUSTRY AND DEFENSE

J . B. Colwell

Vice Admiral J. B. Colwell is Deputy Chief of Naval Operations (Fleet Operations and Readiness); this is the text of a speech to the New York chapter of the American Ordnance Association.

The United States today has a very large military establishment. It is sizable in manpower, numbering over two million men. It is sizable in real property holdings, both here and abroad. It has a sizable inventory of aircraft, vehicles, and ships.

The cost of maintaining this force also is sizable. This year some 60 per cent of our governmental budget or 12 per cent of our gross national product will be spent in support of our defense establishment. Without debating the adequacy of this outlay, past and current, it is an obvious fact that military preparedness is an expensive business.

This military force is built upon and sustained by the largest industrial economy the world has ever known. To defend our Nation in today's environment, we must have the most advanced, most effective weapons which can be produced, and we must have them in sufficient numbers. There is no second-place prize in a military contest.

"Industry and Defense" in *Ordnance*, Volume LIV, Number 295 (July-August 1969), pp. 60-61. Copyright 1969, American Ordnance Association.

It is our industrial technology and production capacity which make it possible to put such weapons into the hands of our troops. The resulting military force safeguards our economy. Our economy, thus secure, maintains for our society the world's highest standard of living with its rights to life, liberty, and the pursuit of happiness.

This, simply stated, is the military-industrial relationship which exists in our country.

Certainly there is a so-called "military-industrial complex" in this country! Our military forces could not exist without it, and, in the international environment in which we find ourselves, our country could not long exist without the means to achieve military security.

There are those, however, who would have us believe that the military and industry operate in an entirely different manner from the normal manufacturer-consumer relationships which are accepted in other sectors of our economy.

The country has been warned of an insidious Military-Industrial Complex, controlled by an oligarchy of military and industrial leaders. The necessary teamwork between industrial management and members of the Defense Department is alleged by some to represent a form of conspiracy, generated not in the Nation's interest but for the purpose of personal power and immense profit.

The existence of this complex, we are warned, will lead to the ruination of our economy, the reduction of our democracy to a garrison state, and, finally, to our destruction through irrational war.

I am not so naive as to forget that there are historical incidents of illegal activities and collusion in the past, nor to deny that there are people in the military and in business today who would turn a dishonest dollar. But I would emphatically deny that such activity is widespread, and I submit that the possibility of activity so extensive as to approach a conspiracy is indeed remote.

Let me develop the strange kind of logic which leads to an erroneous conclusion about the military-industrial relationship. It begins with the establishment of demand which, in this supposed case, is generated by an aberration in the desires of the military leader whose mind is fixed on war and who demands all the things with which to wage war. It is never satisfied with the capability or quality of the weapons in the arsenal and is constantly striving for more and better arms.

Industry, so the story goes, always interested in a good market, responds to fill this demand. Going further, industry applies the professional hard sell, playing on the fears and egos of the anxious and easily convinced military.

By elaborate advertising and lavish entertainment, the fable continues, industry generates artificial demands for useless weapons. Once this cycle is established, the military and industry join forces and control this process for their mutual advantage. The middle-men are the retired military officers employed by the defense contractors.

How is it that such business can be carried on despite governmental controls and congressional checks? How can it be done right under the noses of a suspicious press and public? Again, the explanation is the military mind.

However, this time the critics have transformed the character of this mind. It is no longer slow and easily persuaded. The point is now made that military opinions and advice prevail because the military has produced an unending supply of distinguished, capable, articulate, and effective leaders.

Their skill, energy, and dedication make them dominant in almost every government or civic organization they may inhabit, from high position to the local PTA. They are able to dazzle the Congress by their intricate budgetary footwork.

The public at large is supposedly hoodwinked by a vast public-relations campaign (referred to in the complex as propaganda) and by what might be called the military-industrial auxiliary. This includes all those who have ever served in the military and a number of organizations and persons who are just sympathetic.

They lobby for the complex, supplement the propaganda with periodicals extolling the merits of a strong defense posture, and generally subvert the population by encouraging youth to enlist, making patriotic speeches, and organizing Fourth of July parades.

However, this is *not* the way it works in real life. You know it, I know it, and I think the great American public knows it.

Let us look at the structure which militates against the feared unholy alliance. In the first place, each service has a limited budget which it will not knowingly waste on unneeded weapons or inflated prices.

Secondly, anyone remotely familiar with Government contracting procedures knows that the restraints, checks, audits, and requirements make it extremely difficult for any collusion to take place. Also, the contractors are competing among themselves.

One might ask a contractor who has just lost a major contract-formulation/contract-definition bid, after having spent millions of his own money, what his opinion is of the military-industrial complex!

What about those retired senior officers who are employed by industry? The real reasons are very evident. It is good common sense for a company engaged in building weapons to hire individuals conversant with the operational employment of those weapons. Oil companies employ petroleum engineers, drug firms employ physicians, defense firms hire military professionals. To do otherwise would result in less effective designs and a less capable military arsenal.

If there were such a thing as a highly polished smoothly functioning military-industrial complex working for the mutual benefit of both parties, would our shipbuilding industry be in the shape it is in today? Would 58 per cent of U.S. naval combatant ships be 20 years old or older? Would our aging and overworked fleet be on the verge of obsolescence?

Consider these figures: in 1963, the gross national product was just under $600 billion—the Navy shipbuilding account was $2.8 billion; in 1966 the GNP had risen to $750 billion, but Navy ship construction had dropped to $2 billion; in 1969, with a near-$900 billion GNP, the amount allocated to building new men-of-war had dwindled to $1.2 billion.

I ask you, what has happened to the smoothly effective operation of the military-industrial complex?

And then there is the charge of militarization of American society. I would submit that, in a society which permits citizens dressed as Viet Cong to march on Easter Sunday, overemphasis on the military virtues of loyalty, patriotism, duty, discipline, and service to country is hardly the problem. If the culture is so geared to the military, if the military is so respected, admired, powerful, and influential, why is retention of officers and men one of our most serious problems?

No, I think that those who are so concerned with this danger not only have overlooked our long history, but also have closed their eyes to the present opposition to the draft, dissension over the Vietnam war, and disillusionment with structured power.

Of all the fallacious arguments, the one which personally distresses me most is the allegation that the military man essentially wants war. The charge is leveled from time to time that the leaders of the complex deliberately plan war because war justifies the existence of the establishment; that war provides experience for the military novice, challenges for the professional, and the field to exercise, prove, and perfect the industrial products. Thus war is not only welcomed but actively sought.

Well, what of these charges? What about this mythical beast?

First let me say that there is no such thing as the military mind. Military men as a group have similar inclinations, feelings, and general codes, but to assume that they think differently from any other segment of our society is ridiculous. They are products of the same schools, live in the same neighborhoods, read the same literature, and are exposed to the same pressures of domestic life as are other Americans. And as Americans they differ among themselves in their thinking just as do their neighbors.

In point of fact, the military man historically has opposed reckless, aggressive, belligerent action. He may argue that the danger of war requires more armament, but he will never argue that increased armament makes war desirable. He dreads war.

Concerning the professional associations, it is a significant point that these organizations serve a vital purpose in bringing together professionals who are engaged in a serious, expensive business critical to our national survival. Such liaison has been vastly beneficial in maintaining our defense.

I have attempted to show that fear of a massive military partnership with industry is without basis in fact. Such a thing does not now, nor did it ever, exist. Under our form of government, under the leadership of wise men imbued with an abiding love of country, it will not come to pass.

We cannot return to a simpler time when the problems of world leadership and the complexities of technological warfare did not rest upon our shoulders. The threat which we face is real, and we must have a modern strong military establishment in order to defend ourselves.

I view the military-industrial complex, if we choose to use that term, as an essential element of our national survival. An occasional self-serving individual there may be, for infallibility is a scarce commodity. But patriotism is in rich supply, and our loyalty and integrity are not for sale.

WE HAVE TO GET RID OF THOSE NUCLEAR WEAPONS

George Wald

George Wald, Higgins Professor of Biology at Harvard University and the recipient of a Nobel prize in medicine, made this extemporaneous speech before a group of scientists and students at the Massachusetts Institute of Technology.

All of you know that in the last couple of years there has been student unrest breaking at times into violence in many parts of the world: in England, Germany, Italy, Spain, Mexico and needless to say, in many parts of this country. There has been a great deal of discussion as to what it all means. Perfectly clearly it means something different in Mexico from what it does in France, and something different in France from what it does in Tokyo, and something different in Tokyo from what it does in this country. Yet unless we are to assume that students have gone crazy all over the world, or that they have just decided that it's the thing to do, there must be some common meaning.

I don't need to go so far afield to look for that meaning. I am a teacher, and at Harvard, I have a class of about 350 students—men and women—most of them freshmen and sophomores. Over these past few years I have felt increasingly that something is terribly wrong—and this year ever so much more than last. Something has gone sour, in teaching and in learning. It's almost as though there were a widespread feeling that education has become irrelevant.

A lecture is much more of a dialogue than many of you probably appreciate. As you lecture, you keep watching the faces; and information keeps coming back to you all the time. I began to feel, particularly this year, that I was missing much of what was coming back. I tried asking the students, but they didn't or couldn't help me very much.

But I think I know what's the matter, even a little better than they do. I think that this whole generation of students is beset with a

From "A Generation in Search of a Future," March 4, 1969.

profound uneasiness. I don't think that they have yet quite defined its source. I think I understand the reasons for their uneasiness even better than they do. What is more, I share their uneasiness.

What's bothering those students? Some of them tell you it's the Vietnam War. I think the Vietnam War is the most shameful episode in the whole of American history. . . .

I think we've lost that war, as a lot of other people think, too. The Vietnamese have a secret weapon. It's their willingness to die, beyond our willingness to kill. In effect they've been saying, you can kill us, but you'll have to kill a lot of us, you may have to kill all of us. And thank heavens, we are not yet ready to do that.

Yet we have come a long way—far enough to sicken many Americans, far enough even to sicken our fighting men. Far enough so that our national symbols have gone sour. How many of you can sing about "the rockets' red glare, bombs bursting in air" without thinking, those are *our* bombs and *our* rockets bursting over South Vietnamese villages? When those words were written, we were a people struggling for freedom against oppression. Now we are supporting real or thinly disguised military dictatorships all over the world, helping them to control and repress peoples struggling for their freedom.

But that Vietnam War, shameful and terrible as it is, seems to me only an immediate incident in a much larger and more stubborn situation.

Part of my trouble with students is that almost all the students I teach were born since World War II. Just after World War II, a series of new and abnormal procedures came into American life. We regarded them at the time as temporary aberrations. We thought we would get back to normal American life some day. But those procedures have stayed with us now for more than 20 years, and those students of mine have never known anything else. They think those things are normal. Students think we've always had a Pentagon, that we have always had a big army, and that we always had a draft. But those are all new things in American life; and I think that they are incompatible with what America meant before.

How many of you realize that just before World War II the entire American army including the Air Force numbered 139,000 men? Then World War II started, but we weren't yet in it; and seeing that there was great trouble in the world, we doubled this army to 268,000 men. Then in World War II it got to be 8 million. And then World War II came to an end, and we prepared to go back to a peacetime army somewhat as the American army had always been before. And indeed in 1950—you think about 1950, our international commitments, the Cold War, the Truman Doctrine, and all the rest of it—in 1950 we got down to 600,000 men.

Now we have 3.5 million men under arms: about 600,000 in Vietnam, about 300,000 more in "support areas" elsewhere in the Pacific, about 250,000 in Germany. And there are a lot at home. Some months ago we were told that 300,000 National Guardsmen and 200,000 reservists—so half a million men—had been specially trained for riot duty in the cities.

I say the Vietnam War is just an immediate incident, because so long as we keep that big an army, it will always find things to do. If the Vietnam War stopped tomorrow, with that big a military establishment, the chances are that we would be in another such adventure abroad or at home before you knew it.

As for the draft: Don't reform the draft—get rid of it.

A peacetime draft is the most un-American thing I know. All the time I was growing up I was told about oppressive Central European countries and Russia, where young men were forced into the army; and I was told what they did about it. They chopped off a finger, or shot off a couple of toes; or better still, if they could manage it, they came to this country. And we understood that, and sympathized, and were glad to welcome them.

Now by present estimates four to six thousand Americans of draft age have left this country for Canada, another two or three thousand have gone to Europe, and it looks as though many more are preparing to emigrate.

A few months ago I received a letter from the Harvard Alumni Bulletin posing a series of questions that students might ask a professor involving what to do about the draft. I was asked to write what I would tell those students. All I had to say to those students was this: If any of them had decided to evade the draft and asked my help, I would help him in any way I could. I would feel as I suppose members of the underground railway felt in pre-Civil War days, helping runaway slaves to get to Canada. It wasn't altogether a popular position then; but what do you think of it now?

A bill to stop the draft was recently introduced in the Senate (S.503), sponsored by a group of senators that ran the gamut from McGovern and Hatfield to Barry Goldwater. I hope it goes through; but any time I find that Barry Goldwater and I are in agreement, that makes me take another look.

And indeed there are choices in getting rid of the draft. I think that when we get rid of the draft, we must also cut back the size of the armed forces. It seems to me that in peacetime a total of one million men is surely enough. If there is an argument for American military forces of more than one million men in peacetime, I should like to hear that argument debated. . . .

But there is something ever so much bigger and more important than the draft. That bigger thing, of course, is the militarization of our country. Ex-President Eisenhower warned us of what he called the military-industrial complex. I am sad to say that we must begin to think of it now as the military-industrial-labor union complex. What happened under the plea of the Cold War was not alone that we built up the first big peace time army in our history, but we institutionalized it. We built, I suppose, the biggest government building in our history to run it, and we institutionalized it.

I don't think we can live with the present military establishment and its $80 billion a year budget, and keep America anything like we have known it in the past. It is corrupting the life of the whole country. It is buying up everything in sight: industries, banks, investors, universities; and lately it seems also to have bought up the labor unions.

The Defense Department is always broke; but some of the things they do with that $80 billion a year would make Buck Rogers envious. For example: the Rocky Mountain Arsenal on the outskirts of Denver was manufacturing a deadly nerve poison on such a scale that there was a problem of waste disposal. Nothing daunted, they dug a tunnel two miles deep under Denver, into which they have injected so much poisoned water that beginning a couple of years ago Denver began to experience a series of earth tremors of increasing severity. Now there is a grave fear of a major earthquake. An interesting debate is in progress as to whether Denver will be safer if that lake of poisoned water is removed or left in place. . . .

Perhaps you have read also of those 6000 sheep that suddenly died in Skull Valley, Utah, killed by another nerve poison—a strange and, I believe, still unexplained accident, since the nearest testing seems to have been 30 miles away.

As for Vietnam, the expenditure of fire power has been frightening. Some of you may still remember Khe Sanh, a hamlet just south of the Demilitarized Zone, where a force of U.S. Marines was beleaguered for a time. During that period we dropped on the perimeter of Khe Sanh more explosives than fell on Japan throughout World War II, and more than fell on the whole of Europe during the years 1942 and 1943.

One of the officers there was quoted as having said afterward, "It looks like the world caught smallpox and died." . . .

The only point of government is to safeguard and foster life. Our government has become preoccupied with death, with the business of killing and being killed. So-called Defense now absorbs 60 percent of the national budget, and about 12 percent of the Gross National Product.

A lively debate is beginning again on whether or not we should deploy antiballistic missiles, the ABM. I don't have to talk

about them, everyone else here is doing that. But I should like to
mention a curious circumstance. In September, 1967, or about
1½ years ago, we had a meeting of M.I.T. and Harvard people,
including experts on these matters, to talk about whether anything
could be done to block the Sentinel system, the deployment of
ABM's. Everyone present thought them undesirable; but a few of the
most knowledgeable persons took what seemed to be the practical
view, "Why fight about a dead issue? It has been decided, the funds
have been appropriated. Let's go on from there."

Well, fortunately, it's not a dead issue.

An ABM is a nuclear weapon. It takes a nuclear weapon to
stop a nuclear weapon. And our concern must be with the whole
issue of nuclear weapons.

There is an entire semantics ready to deal with the sort of
thing I am about to say. It involves such phrases as "those are the
facts of life." No—they are the facts of death. I don't accept them,
and I advise you not to accept them. We are under repeated pressure
to accept things that are presented to us as settled—decisions that
have been made. Always there is the thought: let's go on from there!
But this time we don't see how to go on. We will have to stick with
those issues.

We are told that the United States and Russia between them
have by now stockpiled in nuclear weapons approximately the
explosive power of 15 tons of TNT for every man, woman and child
on earth. And now it is suggested that we must make more. All very
regrettable, of course; but those are "the facts of life." We really
would like to disarm; but our new Secretary of Defense has made the
ingenious proposal that now is the time to greatly increase our
nuclear armaments so that we can disarm from a position of strength.

I think all of you know there is no adequate defense against
massive nuclear attack. It is both easier and cheaper to circumvent
any known nuclear defense system than to provide it. It's all pretty
crazy. At the very moment we talk of deploying ABM's, we are also
building the MIRV, the weapon to circumvent ABM's.

So far as I know, the most conservative estimates of
Americans killed in a major nuclear attack, with everything working
as well as can be hoped and all foreseeable precautions taken, run to
about 50 millions. We have become callous to gruesome statistics,
and this seems at first to be only another gruesome statistic. You
think, Bang!—and next morning, if you're still there, you read in the
newspapers that 50 million people were killed.

But that isn't the way it happens. When we killed close to
200,000 people with those first little, old-fashioned uranium bombs
that we dropped on Hiroshima and Nagasaki, about the same number

of persons was maimed, blinded, burned, poisoned and otherwise doomed. A lot of them took a long time to die.

That's the way it would be. Not a bang, and a certain number of corpses to bury; but a nation filled with millions of helpless, maimed, tortured and doomed persons, and the survivors of a nuclear holocaust will be huddled with their families in shelters, with guns ready to fight off their neighbors, trying to get some uncontaminated food and water.

A few months ago Sen. Richard Russell of Georgia ended a speech in the Senate with the words: "If we have to start over again with another Adam and Eve, I want them to be Americans; and I want them on this continent and not in Europe." That was a United States senator holding a patriotic speech.* Well, here is a Nobel Laureate who thinks that those words are criminally insane. [Prolonged applause.]

How real is the threat of full-scale nuclear war? I have my own very inexpert idea, but realizing how little I know and fearful that I may be a little paranoid on this subject, I take every opportunity to ask reputed experts. I asked that question of a very distinguished professor of government at Harvard about a month ago. I asked him what sort of odds he would lay on the possibility of full-scale nuclear war within the foreseeable future. "Oh," he said comfortably, I think I can give you a pretty good answer to that question. I estimate the probability of full-scale nuclear war, provided that the situation remains about as it is now, at 2 percent per year." Anybody can do the simple calculation that shows that 2 percent per year means that the chance of having that full-scale nuclear war by 1990 is about one in three, and by 2000 it is about 50-50.

I think I know what is bothering the students. I think that what we are up against is a generation that is by no means sure that it has a future.

I am growing old, and my future so to speak is already behind me. But there are those students of mine who are in my mind

---

*Seymour M. Hersh, who formerly covered the Defense Department for the Associated Press, says that this statement was made during a closed-door debate over the ABM in October 1968 with then-Senator Joseph S. Clark of Pennsylvania. According to Hersh ("The Military Committees," *The Washington Monthly,* Vol. 1, No. 3 [April 1969], p. 87), Senator Clark said: "There comes a time when the tens of millions of casualties are so enormous that civilization is destroyed, and if there are a few people living in caves after that, it does not make much difference." Senator Russell replied: "If we have to start over again with another Adam and Eve, then I want them to be Americans and not Russians, and I want them on this continent, and not in Europe." (Ed.'s note.)

always; and there are my children, two of them now 7 and 9, whose future is infinitely more precious to me than my own. So it isn't just their generation; it's mine too. We're all in it together.

Are we to have a chance to live? We don't ask for prosperity, or security; only for a reasonable chance to live, to work out our destiny in peace and decency. Not to go down in history as the apocalyptic generation.

And it isn't only nuclear war. Another overwhelming threat is the population explosion. That has not yet even begun to come under control. There is every indication that the world population will double before the year 2000; and there is a widespread expectation of famine on an unprecedented scale in many parts of the world. The experts tend to differ only in the estimates of when those famines will begin. Some think by 1980, others think they can be staved off until 1990, very few expect that they will not occur by the year 2000.

That is the problem. Unless we can be surer than we now are that this generation has a future, nothing else matters. It's not good enough to give it tender loving care, to supply it with breakfast foods, to buy it expensive educations. Those things don't mean anything unless this generation has a future. And we're not sure that it does.

I don't think that there are problems of youth, or student problems. All the real problems I know are grown-up problems.

Perhaps you will think me altogether absurd, or "academic," or hopelessly innocent—that is, until you think of the alternatives— if I say as I do to you now: we have to get rid of those nuclear weapons. There is nothing worth having that can be obtained by nuclear war: nothing material or ideological, no tradition that it can defend. It is utterly self-defeating. Those atom bombs represent an unusable weapon. The only use for an atom bomb is to keep somebody else from using one. It can give us no protection, but only the doubtful satisfaction of retaliation. Nuclear weapons offer us nothing but a balance of terror; and a balance of terror is still terror.

We have to get rid of those atomic weapons, here and everywhere. We cannot live with them.

I think we've reached a point of great decision, not just for our nation, not only for all humanity, but for life upon the Earth. I tell my students, with a feeling of pride that I hope they will share, that the carbon, nitrogen and oxygen that make up 99 percent of our living substance, were cooked in the deep interiors of earlier generations of dying stars. Gathered up from the ends of the universe, over billions of years, eventually they came to form in part the substance of our sun, its planets and ourselves. Three billion years ago life arose upon the Earth. It seems to be the only life in the solar system. Many a star has since been born and died.

About two million years ago, man appeared. He has become the dominant species on the Earth. All other living things, animal and plant, live by his sufferance. He is the custodian of life on Earth. It's a big responsibility.

The thought that we're in competition with Russians or with Chinese is all a mistake, and trivial. Only mutual destruction lies that way. We are one species, with a world to win. There's life all over this universe, but in all the universe we are the only men.

Our business is with life, not death. Our challenge is to give what account we can of what becomes of life in the solar system, this corner of the universe that is our home and, most of all, what becomes of men—all men of all nations, colors and creeds. It has become one world, a world for all men. It is only such a world that now can offer us life and the chance to go on.

9

Intervention: The Lessons of Vietnam

As Vietnam has made painfully clear, the existence of a thermonuclear balance of terror has not ruled out the possibility of wars which, if less cataclysmic than World Wars I and II, can yet involve a great deal of death and destruction. But now the question is posed: has the Vietnam war opened up the prospect that there will be no more Vietnams?

There is much that points in this direction. The war has caused a profound moral and political upheaval within this country. There is growing receptiveness to the case presented in this chapter by Henry Steele Commager and Hans Morgenthau that we have been excessively ready to intervene militarily wherever we thought Communism threatened. Vietnam has provided powerful evidence for the position developed here by Vladimir Dedijer that all the power of the United States cannot bring about a conclusive defeat of a well-organized, indigenous guerrilla movement. And it is Vietnam that has provoked the Senate into a declaration that no President should undertake future military interventions without securing the specific approval of Congress. President Nixon, a close student of what Vietnam did to Lyndon Johnson, is obviously aware of the political meaning of the hostility aroused by Vietnam. Though some of that hostility was re-kindled by his own Vietnam policy and though he declared that the United States would not withdraw its influence from Asia, he insisted that for the future the non-Communist Asian states would have to assume the prime responsibility for their defense.

Thus, it may well be that we are entering a period in which the United States will avoid intervention abroad to attend to its internal problems. This would lend support to the thesis of Frank L. Klingberg, who in a 1952 article predicted that America would by now be ready to retreat, to some extent at least, from involvement in international affairs.[1] Klingberg found that since 1776 there had been a fairly regular alternation of American attitudes toward foreign affairs between introversion and extroversion. The first period of extroversion had been from 1798 to 1824, the second from 1844 to 1871, and the third from 1891 to 1919. The fourth period of extroversion began, said Klingberg, in 1940. Since the extroverted phases have averaged 27 years (as against 21 for the introverted eras that intervened), he speculated that some time in the 1960s America would move into its fifth historical cycle with a swing toward introversion. The reaction against Vietnam since 1966 suggests that a new American mood is arriving on schedule, that we have grown tired of the exertions and frustrations consequent on three decades of massive military involvements abroad.

Nonetheless, there is no inevitability that history will repeat itself. What D. W. Brogan called "the illusion of American omnipotence" has been destroyed, but the reality of American power remains. Any American President of the 1970s will be acutely sensitive to the danger of future Vietnams. Yet the avoidance of further entanglements is not a foregone conclusion, and the pressure to intervene in various situations may come from many points on the political spectrum. In this chapter John P. East, writing in the magazine of the Young Americans for Freedom, persists in the view that we must be ready to use American military force to contain Communism. But Eugene V. Rostow, Ithiel de Sola Pool, and Gale McGee—who are not of East's conservative persuasion—also warn against a national swing toward introversion. Will America, for example, be able to avoid intervention during the 70s in the Middle East? And what if there is a major eruption in southern Africa? If we are to intervene less against Communism, should we intervene more against racism?

[1] "The Historical Alternation of Moods in American Foreign Policy," *World Politics*, Vol. IV (January 1952), pp. 239-273. See also Samuel P. Huntington's discussion of the Klingberg thesis in Richard M. Pfeffer, ed., *No More Vietnams?* (New York: Harper & Row, Publishers, 1968), pp. 40-41.

Of course, intervention does not have to be military. But, as we shall see in the next chapter, the reliance on economic and political methods produces its own set of disappointments and frustrations.

THE LIMITS OF AMERICAN POWER

Henry Steele Commager

Henry Steele Commager is Professor of History, Amherst College.

. . .It is my feeling that we do not have the resources, material, intellectual, or moral, to be at once an American power, a European power, and an Asian power. Justice Holmes used to say that the first lesson a judge had to learn was that he was not God. It is a lesson every man has to learn and a lesson every nation has to learn. For, as the great historian Herbert Butterfield has said, "The hardest strokes of Heaven fall in history upon those who imagine that they can control things in a sovereign manner, as though they were kings of the earth, playing Providence not only for themselves but for the far future, reaching out into the future with the wrong kind of farsightedness." It is not our duty to keep peace throughout the globe, to put down aggression wherever it starts up, to stop the advance of communism or other isms which we may not approve of. It is primarily the responsibility of the United Nations to keep the peace, to settle disputes, to discourage aggression, and if the organization is not strong enough to do the job we should perhaps bend our major energies to giving her the necessary authority and the tools.

We are still committed to vast but as yet unrealized reforms in Latin America; we are committing ourselves to incomparably larger responsibilities in Asia. We should not be astonished if the rest

From a statement before the Senate Committee on Foreign Relations, *Hearings on Changing American Attitudes Toward Foreign Policy*, 90th Congress, 1st Session, February 20, 1967, pp. 5-13.

of the world wonders at our ambition and our temerity, or if it asks why, if we have the power and the resources to carry through these projects, we do not use some of them to put our own house in order. Perhaps one-fifth of our population lives in poverty; we do not have the resources to wipe out that poverty. Our cities are decaying, we do not have the resources to restore them. Our educational enterprise is desperately inadequate; we do not have the resources to bring it up to the standards which we ourselves set. Our rivers and streams are polluted and the very air we breathe is poisonous but we lack the resources to cleanse these. Racial discrimination and injustice flourish in every section of the Nation but we lack the resources to eradicate them from our society or economy. Crime flaunts itself in the streets of our cities, but we lack the resources to control it. Would it not be wise, so doubtless many are asking at home and abroad, if we used our immense power and resources to wipe out poverty and injustice and waste at home before launching ourselves upon crusades to wipe out these things in distant continents?

Our problem is not primarily one of material resources or material power. It is possible that if we were to use for peaceful purposes all of the wealth we now use for war, we would, indeed, have the resources to lift standards of living in Latin America, Asia, and Africa as well as at home. What we lack, what every people lack, are the political, the intellectual, and the moral resources for such global enterprises.

One explanation of our obsession with communism and more particularly now, with "Communist aggression" in Asia is to be found, I think, in a deep and persistent trait of the American mind: the belief in Old World corruption and New World innocence. The men who won our independence from the mother country were convinced that the Old World was abandoned to tyranny, misery, ignorance, injustice, and vice and the New World was innocent of these sins. They were not altogether wrong. The commonsensical Dr. Franklin, rejecting the suggestion of an accommodation with England as late as 1775, said. . ."When I consider the extreme corruption prevalent among all orders of men in this rotten old State (of Britain), and the glorious public Virtue so predominant in our Rising Country, I cannot but apprehend more Mischief than Benefit from a closer union."

And in his first inaugural address, Jefferson—for whom this principle of New World innocence was itself almost an obsession—proclaimed that the United States was "kindly separated by Nature and a wide ocean from the exterminating havoc of one-quarter of the globe" and "too high minded to endure the degradations of the others." This theme persisted down into the 20th century and was one of the many strands that have gone into the fabric of making isolationism.

The notion of an international Communist conspiracy, which a good many Americans still cling to, fits neatly into this shibboleth of Old World wickedness and New World virtue. And so, too, our habit of throwing a mantle of morality over our own wars. We do tend, perhaps more than most other peoples, to transform our wars into crusades. The Mexican War was part of manifest destiny. The Spanish-American War was a crusade to free Cuba from Spanish tyranny. The First World War was a crusade to make the world safe for democracy. The Second World War did indeed have moral purposes, more clearly, I think, than almost any war of modern times. Our current involvement in Vietnam is cast, increasingly, into a moral mold; it is, quite simply, a war to halt Communist aggression. Indeed by a kind of circular argument this provides and embraces the "vital interest" which we have in that area, for on closer examination our "vital interest" is precisely the interest in halting communism.

Closely associated with the notion of New World virtue is the somewhat more activist notion of New World mission. This, too, is a familiar theme: Providence, or history, has put a special responsibility on the American people to spread the blessings of liberty, democracy, and equality to other peoples of the earth. Sometimes, indeed, this mission included even religion: Some of you will remember even the argument which was decisive with President McKinley when it came to the annexation of the Philippines, that "there was nothing left for us to do but to take them all, and to educate the Filipinos and uplift and Christianize them." He did not know, apparently, that most Filipinos had been Christianized before the Pilgrims—and Plymouth—landed in Cape Cod.

When other nations expanded they did so on practical and selfish grounds, but when we expanded our conduct was not only practical but highly moral. The notion of mission has permeated much of American thinking about territorial expansion; it has colored our conception of the meaning of the Monroe Doctrine; it has conditioned our relations with Europe and, more recently, with Asia. . . .

Now nations that are self-righteous and powerful are almost irresistibly prone to creating, or accepting, a double standard of conduct. Britain was guilty of this during much of the 19th century, and it is not perhaps surprising that the United States—or the American people—indulge in it today. We do think that we are better than other nations and doubtless we really are in many respects, we have been and are. We have not fought wars for the subjugation of alien peoples—except the Indians—we have not exploited colonies for our benefit. We have been magnanimous toward our foes, except perhaps the Mexicans, and generous to most other peoples. We have opened our doors to unrestricted immigration until just the other day; we have never permitted religious tyranny or class warfare; we have, for the most part, kept the military subordinate to the civilian authority. Yet even in the domestic arena we have not been beyond criticism; when we speak, as we often do, of communist slavery we might, perhaps, remember that we retained legal slavery in the United States long after most other civilized nations had abandoned it.

It is perhaps in the realm of foreign relations, where we instinctively take for granted (as other people do) the justice of our foreign policies, that we exhibit most markedly traces of a double standard. The most conspicuous example of this is doubtless in the attitude toward expansionism, aggression, and imperialism, and here we share a certain parochialism with the whole of Western Europe. The free nations of the West are greatly—and justly—disturbed by what appears to be aggressive tendencies on the part of the two great communist powers, and "Communist-aggression" has almost become (like "Damn-Yankee" of earlier days) a single word. We forget, most of us, that since the Crusades, and certainly since the Age of Discovery, aggression has been Western and European. It was Europe that expanded and conquered and laid waste, that created empires and planted colonies and ruled from afar. Christian Europe divided up Africa; it established its rule over much of Asia; it discovered America, wiped out the native civilizations here, planted colonies and ruled them as long as it was able. It was the West—not communist countries—that invented imperialism and invented colonialism.

Our own view of expansion and aggression is a distorted one. Most of us have been deeply disturbed over the prospect of Soviet expansion and are now disturbed at the prospect of Chinese aggression and expansion, and some protagonists of our war in Vietnam defend it chiefly on the ground that it is designed to put a halt to Chinese aggression. It might be good for us to remember that in the eyes of the 19th century world, it was the United States that was preeminently the expansionist and aggressive nation. In the first half of the century this new Nation with—be it remembered—an "ideology" as pernicious in the eyes of legitimatist governments as communism is in our own eyes—expanded from the Mississippi to the Pacific. We bought Louisiana, we forced Spain out of west Florida and maneuvered her out of east Florida: we annexed Texas and fought a war with Mexico which ended by stripping her of half of her territory—the Southwest and California; we ousted the British from the Pacific Northwest. Thus in half a century we trebled our territory at the expense of France, Spain, Mexico, and Britain. In the same period our Presidents announced the Monroe Doctrine and the Polk

Doctrine, proclaiming in effect American hegemony in the Western Hemisphere. If China today should put on a show of this kind we might truly be alarmed. . . .

Other examples of our double standard come readily to mind. We maintain powerful military installations in a great arc around eastern China, from Japan, Okinawa, the Philippines, Taiwan, Guam, to Vietnam and Thailand; if—this requires some stretch of the imagination—China should somehow set up powerful military installations in British Columbia, Mexico, Cuba, Bermuda and Newfoundland, we might not think very well of it. We claim, in all sincerity, a vital interest in Vietnam, though we did not tolerate a Soviet claim to a vital interest in Cuba, nor for that matter, do we accept the claim of China to a vital interest in South Vietnam which is rather closer to Peking than Saigon is to Washington. We have long asserted a sphere of influence in the Caribbean and even managed to get that sphere of influence formally accepted and recognized in the League of Nations and in the Charter of the United Nations, but we are not prepared to concede to China a comparable sphere of influence in southeast Asia. We think ourselves justified in intervening in the domestic affairs of Guatemala and Santo Domingo, but we would be very surprised if Cuba intervened in Florida to put down guerrilla organizations or Mexico in the affairs of Texas. We look with alarm on the spread of nuclear weapons, as indeed we must, and President Johnson asserted that it was "a dark day" when China detonated a nuclear bomb; we appear to forget that so far we are the only nation that has used the atomic bomb in anger, though it must not be supposed that the Japanese have forgotten this.

What I am suggesting is that we need to cultivate patience, tolerance, the long view, and even sympathy with the new nations of the globe, even if their emergence onto the crowded stage of history is turbulent and dangerous. We would do well to recover something of Jefferson's perspective on the French Revolution—which horrified most Western peoples just as communism does today. It was, he said, "the agonizing spasms of infuriated man, seeking through blood and slaughter his long-lost liberties." "Long-lost liberties" is, to be sure, not the phrase we instinctively apply to either the Russian or the Chinese revolutions, for they did not, alas, enjoy liberty in their historical past, but that they are seeking to throw off what they assume to be tyranny and exploitation—in the case of the Soviet, a homegrown brand of tyranny; in the case of China, foreign—and achieve independence and progress in their way, is, I think, beyond dispute.

This brings me. . . to a final consideration, and that is our failure, as a people and as a government, to appreciate what is probably the greatest revolution since the discovery of America and the transfer of the center of historical gravity from the Mediterranean to the Atlantic. That is the revolt of Asia and Africa against the West, and the emergence into modernity of perhaps two-thirds of the peoples of the globe. What we are witnessing seems like the breakup of the great firmament itself; the upheaval of peoples and civilizations, the throwing off of centuries of misrule and exploitation, the convulsive efforts to catch up in a single generation with the progress which the West made, painfully and with almost limitless bloodshed and war and revolution, over a period of four or five centuries.

Materially, to be sure, we have given aid to this enterprise, particularly to those peoples we sought to win to our side in the struggle against communism; but in other and, perhaps, important ways we have allowed ourselves to be maneuvered into the position of opposing revolution and what some of these peoples think of as progress. We have allowed ourselves to drift into the position that Britain occupied in much of the 19th century and France in part of the 20th—that of the champion of the status quo, the defender of the Western way of life, of Western government and ideology. We have not intended it that way, but it is difficult to doubt that most of the world looks upon us today as the leading opponent of revolutionary change.

What is sobering, and even paradoxical, is that the new, or old-new, nations of the globe, such as India and China, are trying to carry through their revolution with the tools which we have fashioned: the dynamic instrument is revolution, the political instrument is nationalism, the social instrument is equality, the economic instrument is science and technology; all of them are Western inventions.

We must inescapably bear much of the responsibility for what is going on in the underdeveloped nations of the world, even in nations like China, and we should, I think, be prepared to acknowledge our responsibility. For if we did not precisely invent any of the instruments which these new nations are now using, we did illustrate their potentialities more fully and, I think, on the whole, more happily and more successfully than any other nation.

The United States was the first nation to be founded squarely on the right of revolution—that is, the right to "alter or abolish government and institute new government." As James Madison wrote:

> If there be a principle that ought not to be questioned within the United States, it is that every nation has a right to abolish an old government and establish a new one. This principle is not only recorded in every public archive, written in every American heart,

and sealed with the blood of a host of American martyrs, but it is the only lawful tenure by which the United States hold their existence as a nation.

. . . The United States was born of rebellion and grew to greatness through revolution. No other nation has a revolutionary history so long or so comprehensive, and perhaps no other has a record that was, in the eyes of the world, so deeply subversive as ours. Certainly the Declaration of Independence is far more subversive than, let us say, the Communist Manifesto; those ardent conservatives who fear revolution everywhere might logically start by banning the Declaration from schools and textbooks. Its principles were, and are, explosive: all men are equal; all have a right to life, liberty, and happiness; the purpose of government is to secure these rights; men make government and can unmake it and make it over again.

Nor did our subversive activities come to an end with the winning of independence. We adopted other institutions and practices that were deeply subversive of existing governments and rulers: no kings, no aristocracy, no established church, no military establishment, no colonies to exploit. And the positive features of the new society were just as bad: self-government, limited government, religious freedom, universal education, and a classless society.

Next, we were the first people to create a nation, and should be infinitely sympathetic to the new nations of the world. What Lincoln said is quite literally correct: the fathers "brought forth a new nation." That had never been done before—all other nations had grown, they had not been created. But we showed the world that men could quite deliberately create a nation, and soon the peoples of Spanish America were busy following our example, and eventually scores of other nations throughout the world. Some 60 of them since 1945 have followed our example.

Third, Americans were perhaps the first people who took for granted and exploited to the full the potentialities of change. Americans not only believed in orderly progress, they even believed that human nature could be changed—that given a beneficial environment, given education, given freedom, men could throw off the shackles of the past and lift themselves by their bootstraps. Just give them a chance. Free them from tyranny, free them from superstition, free them from poverty and ignorance, free them from the curse of war, and they would write a new and more glorious chapter in the history of man. Of all peoples we should be the most ready to sympathize with those who are trying to close the desperate gap between what they are and what they might be.

And if we sometimes think, as doubtless we do, that their methods are violent and misguided and dangerous, we should recall to mind that the Old World thought our methods violent and misguided and dangerous—certainly democracy and equality were as dangerous, in the eyes of Europe, as is communism in our eyes, and in fact they proved a good deal more subversive, in the long run.

Let us have patience with revolution and even with alien ideologies. We have our revolution. We created our Nation. We formulated our ideologies of democracy and equality. We had our expansion, our territorial conquests, our manifest destiny. We established our spheres of influence and our hegemonies, and we did all of these things without serious interference from old established nations. . . .Some of us are taught to resent British sympathy for and support to those who would break up the American union in 1861, but Britain did not in fact intervene in American affairs. What would we think had Britain intervened to support the Confederacy or had she recognized an exiled Jefferson Davis as the legitimate head of a Confederate government in exile, as we persist in recognizing Chiang Kai-shek as the legitimate head not only of the government of Taiwan but of China 17 years after his expulsion?

. . . Americans—I think it a fair statement—are on the whole amiable, generous, and friendly; they do not bear grudges nor nurse animosities. Certainly this has been true in the past, and certainly, too, we made up with Germany and Japan very speedily after the end of the Great War. But our previous quarrels with other nations were national quarrels; now—for the first time, really—we are tempted not by national but by ideological animosities. These have always been deeper, more obsessive and more stubbornly ineradicable, than mere national rivalrics, as the prolonged and savage religious wars of the 16th and 17th centuries make clear. Perhaps because we have so little experience with ideological quarrels, we take them harder than we do other kinds. Monstrous as were the Nazi violations of humanity, I do not recall any obsession with the Nazi danger comparable to our prolonged obsession with communism and the communist danger.

Now hatred does a great deal of harm and never, I think, does any good. It is much worse for the hater than for the hatee; it blurs that clarity of vision so necessary for the objective calculations and decisions we must make in the conduct of foreign policy. And it leaves lasting scars. The British have forgotten their treatment of the Irish in the 18th and 19th centuries, but the Irish have not forgotten; we have forgotten the Mexican War, but the Mexicans have not forgotten; and it is a fair observation that the Negro has a longer memory of slavery than has the southern white. Even when the shoe is on the other foot, resentment lingers on; I still recall that a U. S. Senator challenged my advocacy of aid to Britain with the reminder that the British couldn't be trusted because they had burned Washington in 1814. It is a pretty safe prophecy that the Chinese will not find it easy to forget our implacable hostility over a period of 18 years, or the Vietnamese our bombing, as we will.

And in this connection we should, I think, be very cautious about encouraging or even rejoicing in mounting hostilities between the Russians and the Chinese which is so widespread now. It may seem good tactics for the moment, but I greatly doubt that it is good strategy for the long pull. Can we assert with confidence that mankind would really benefit by a clash between two of the three greatest powers on the earth—by a war between the East and the West, the colored races and the white, by a war which would involve one-third the population of the world? We do not look on the West in this naive or immoral fashion; we do not think it is a good thing if there is a war between France and Germany, or Britain and Egypt, nor do we look back with satisfaction on the religious wars that decimated Europe for over a century. National hostilities are bad enough; ideological are worse; and now that we have entered the nuclear age the prospects of war between the two great nuclear powers is one that can only cause the deepest dismay. . . .

We have achieved such power as no other nation has possessed since the Romans established a Pax Romana. Will our traditional commitment to peace triumph over the temptation to establish a Pax Americana?

AMERICAN SECURITY IN AN UNSTABLE WORLD

Eugene V. Rostow

Eugene V. Rostow was Under Secretary of State for Political Affairs in the Johnson Administration; he is Sterling Professor of Law, Yale Law School.

. . . It is of course true that our primary national mission is the improvement of our own society. But it is equally true that a

From "American Security in an Unstable World," text of an address made before the regional foreign policy conference at the University of Kansas, Lawrence, October 17, 1967, pp. 2-7, 9-18.

responsible government must protect the safety of the nation. We cannot expect to be allowed to pursue our domestic goals, vital as they are, in a world that is not reasonably safe for our democracy.

The challenge to our four postwar Presidents has been something completely new in American history—and a challenge for which we have not been particularly well prepared, intellectually or psychologically, by our earlier experience as a nation. The essence of that challenge can be summed up in this way:

In the small, unstable, nuclear world in which we live, the security of the United States depends on maintaining a tolerably stable balance of power not merely in the Western Atlantic or the Hemisphere but in the world as a whole. If we do not take the lead in maintaining that balance, no one else will. We have had to take an active part in world politics since the war only because those who used to undertake the vital tasks of maintaining an international equilibrium of power have lost the capacity to do so. This is the fact which the critics of our foreign policy ignore or evade. It is the key to our security problem today.

It is important for us all to realize the implications of this debate—both in terms of its consequences for the future and their relation to our own history and culture as a nation.

It is not a new debate. We went through one round of it in 1919 and 1920, when we decided not to join the League of Nations and tried to retreat into the comfortable cocoon of 19th-century isolation. There was another during the thirties, as we sought to determine whether German and Japanese militarism were in fact a threat to our security. . . .

After the war, eager to atone for our repudiation of President Wilson, we took an active part in building the United Nations. Some hoped the United Nations would become a new world system in which peace and our own security would be guarded through the collective action of the great powers and of the world community at large. But within a few hesitant months we all began to realize that the United Nations could not supersede our own responsibilities for the safety of the nation. The United Nations is not a separate power or sovereignty—an independent force in the world, an authority to which issues can be remitted for solution. It is an invaluable forum, a meeting place in which diplomatic business can sometimes be done and world opinion can be crystallized and brought to bear on the policies of the individual nations. It is not, however, a substitute for national responsibility but a means through which national responsibility can be expressed.

When the Soviet Union breached the Yalta and Potsdam agreements calling for free elections in Eastern Europe and Germany and began to push outward toward Iran, Turkey, and Greece, our instinct for self-preservation was stirred. Our response, in 1947, was the Truman doctrine and the Marshall Plan, expressing the two key themes of our postwar foreign policy.

The essence of the Truman doctrine has been a simple rule designed to minimize risks and miscalculations: that there be no unilateral change in the relevant frontiers of the Communist and free-world systems, no change that is achieved by force directly or indirectly applied.

This rule does not make us and our allies the universal gendarmes of the world. There are, and will doubtless continue to be, local conflicts that do not threaten the general peace and can therefore safely be left to run their course. But in areas of significance to political geography, major conflicts and extensions of the Communist sphere achieved by force do carry with them a threat to the world equilibrium and the possibility of escalation into general war. Such acts would therefore directly concern the national interests of the United States and other free nations.

Since President Truman's decision, the United States has followed what few democracies have been able to maintain: a measured, flexible policy combining firmness and restraint.

The goal of that policy is nothing less than a stable world peace. We have a national interest in world peace because wide disturbance in world politics inevitably threatens us. To achieve that goal, our foreign policy has employed four basic means to the end of stability: resistance to aggression which threatens our particular interests or the general peace; respect for the vital interests of the other side; zeal in searching for common areas of agreement and cooperation; and support for national and international programs that could lead to a more stable and decent world.

The elements of conciliation in this policy should not be overlooked. The correlative of the Truman doctrine, as I have just remarked, was the Marshall Plan—and you will recall that it was open not only to the West of Europe but to the East as well.

We have persisted for 20 years in a foreign policy which has served the nation well. That it has continued in its essentials these 20 years is something of a political miracle. According to most of the classical writers on government, a democracy is supposed never to be able to sustain a measured course in foreign affairs. Its policy, they claim, is at the mercy of every gust of sentiment. Democracies, the pundits say, are fated to oscillate between belligerence and appeasement. Once aroused, democracies are mighty in war; but dictatorships, using carrot and stick, can always defeat them in peace.

These melancholy reflections have ample support in history.

But for 20 years, the United States has defied the wisdom of the ancients. We have maintained an active, rational, and reasonably consistent foreign policy. It has rested in the end on the understanding and good sense of the American people and the leadership of Presidents Truman, Eisenhower, Kennedy, and Johnson.

The maintenance of this steady policy has not been easy for our Presidents. Every one of them has had to face threats to the stability of our policy stemming from swings of public opinion toward belligerence or indifference. The challenges come along regularly. Some Presidents have been luckier than others. President Truman had to face the full brunt of Stalinist pressure abroad. At home, he also had to fight off Henry Wallace on one side and Senator McCarthy on the other. The Truman doctrine and the Marshall Plan touched off an attack from the left that continued throughout the Korean war and the elections of 1952. At the same time, President Truman's policy of restraint also provoked a disquiet on the right that fed McCarthyism.

Today, all shades of opinion join in recognizing that President Truman's staunch policy was right. His Presidency is recalled with universal respect and admiration. At the time, however, with the casualties rising and polls falling, it was a different story. But President Truman had the character that permits a man to stand firm in a storm. The motto for his Presidency, you will recall, was "The buck stops here."

President Truman's firmness and restraint in Korea achieved nearly 12 years of relative peace. But the forces and ideas that swarmed against President Truman remain in our society. In periods of stress, leaders and arguments come forward to rally them.

Today, we are caught up in a new challenge, a new time of strain, and a new attack on our foreign policy at home recalling that led by Henry Wallace. Americans are being told not only that it is wrong for us to be in Viet-Nam, but also that we ought not to be anywhere; that the threat of Communist expansion has vanished, and that we are already living in a world of peaceful coexistence; that our postwar policy, so dramatically challenged in Viet-Nam, should not be qualified, shrunken, or abandoned. Many of the same leaders who attack our policy in Viet-Nam also urge substantial cuts in our NATO forces, even as the Soviet Union maintains its force levels in Central Europe and continues to make massive arms shipments to the Near East. . . .

The United States is no less a Pacific than an Atlantic power. Our security demands an equilibrium of power in the Far East as much as it does in Europe and in the Middle East. That equilibrium depends on Viet-Nam and the system of alliances it symbolizes. . . .

Viet-Nam is the test for a new technique of revolution. As nuclear warfare is unthinkable and massed frontal attacks of the Korean type are too dangerous to be tried, Communist leaders are drawn to "wars of national liberation." Indeed, they have developed an elaborate doctrine explaining the place of these ventures in their overall strategy. . . .

. . . Whether one believes we were right or wrong in getting into Viet-Nam in the first place, the hostilities in Viet-Nam have been made the test of America's resolve to maintain that network of security arrangements upon which the equilibrium of world power has come to depend. There would be little security to protect our interests anywhere in the world if America's promise faltered or failed when the going got rough. . . .

It is sometimes contended that it is hopeless to intervene in these explosive situations—that Asia, South America, and Africa are doomed to go through revolutionary turmoil of many kinds, and that nothing can be done to stem the flood.

The simplest answer to this counsel of despair lies in the accomplishments of many developing states, often achieved in the face of threats both from within and without: Iran, for example, and Thailand, Israel, South Korea, Taiwan, and Malaysia. Others, like Indonesia, have turned sharply from adventurism to policies of peace and economic development. All over the world, countries are seeking to apply for themselves, and in their own ways, the economic and social methods of that enlightened capitalism which has permitted the United States and the other free advanced nations to accomplish the most successful social revolution of the 20th century.

Now allow me to turn from the particular question of Viet-Nam to a deeper issue raised by the current challenge to our foreign policy. Some contemporary partisans of the foreign policy of John Quincy Adams contend, in essence, that the acceptance by America of worldwide responsibilities violates traditional American values and is therefore morally incompatible with freedom and social justice at home. There is a dichotomy, they claim, between power and goodness. The American role in the world is concerned with power; but power politics, they assert, is evil and un-American. Therefore, the United States should withdraw its concern with power abroad and concentrate on building a model society at home.

Of course we should keep in mind the dangers raised by the critics of this school. It is right for Americans to worry about the corruptions of power. It is right that we should remain careful not to pollute the springs of our own moral strength as a nation. And it is right to remember that few exhortations are as convincing as a good example.

But I cannot discover a process of thought that would permit us to move from these valid concerns to the proposition that it is wrong, indeed immoral, for America to continue in her present world role because that role supposedly violates the principles of our domestic political health. My belief is to the contrary. My belief is that America's international role and her domestic excellence not only are compatible but are mutually dependent.

What principle of ethics makes it immoral to protect the safety of the nation through methods which have the sanction of international law and the United Nations Charter? Is it wrong to oppose aggression and to uphold the principles of the United Nations Charter? In what way do we lessen our capacity to seek social justice at home by defending the cause of peace, stability, and social progress abroad?

On the contrary, I should contend that we cannot have a truly good society at home if we practice irresponsibility abroad. How is it possible to believe that there can be any security for a rich, isolated America if the world descends to chaos and disorder? Can anyone really believe, in a nuclear world, that maintaining the balance of power upon which world order depends is a sordid business for which Americans are too pure?

It is quite true, of course, that such isolationist beliefs are among America's oldest political traditions. But they form a part of our past, like the tradition of racial discrimination that should be banished.

Isolationism, and the view that a concern for the control of power is immoral, bespeak a naive utopianism which is the dark side of our idealism. I do not suggest that all the critics of our Viet-Nam policy are dominated by these traditions, but their arguments serve to rouse them throughout the land. Stirring these nostalgic yearnings for the past constitutes a real and present danger. To understand the persistence of these traditions, it is important to remind ourselves of their place in our national history.

Isolationism in general was nourished by the peculiar position of the United States in the last century. Thanks to our remoteness from Europe and the absence of a threat from Asia, we were able to enjoy the fruits of a world equilibrium without having to take an active role in maintaining it. This was a comfortable position that allowed us to get on with the immense tasks of domesticating a wild continent and defining ourselves as a nation. It even allowed us the moral luxury of complaining about the sordidness of power politics and classic diplomacy.

We were allowed the luxury of these views only because the task we found so sordid—the balanced containment of power in the world—was handled by the Europeans. We lived in peace within a world order assured by the Concert of Europe, that basic arrangement among the great states of Europe that followed the defeat of Napoleon. That system kept power under reasonable control between 1815 and 1914. It has long been fashionable to criticize the old diplomats and their methods—but theirs is a record we had better surpass before we dismiss it.

That particular system of order is gone forever. It might have been adapted and preserved had the New World really entered the mainstream of world politics in time to "redress the balance of the old"; but twice in this century America has moved too late. Some of our critics, it is interesting to note, refer to Munich as an example of the failure of the old diplomacy. But how different Munich might have been if the United States of America had been there!

Not only do today's critics draw their attitudes from the isolationist experience of the last century but from that American utopian dream, sometimes ascribed to the young Jefferson, that looked for a world that was naturally harmonious, a world where the freedom of every man to do as he pleased led to a naturally peaceful order. Jefferson had the good sense to believe that this state of affairs was not possible everywhere but only in the abundant and uncorrupted American wilderness. But even before television we knew that the reality of the American frontier was quite different. There it was quickly learned that freedom without organized power to maintain the law was a moral and practical contradiction. The arts of civilization can flourish only in an environment where force has been brought under rational and agreed control.

The lessons of history, philosophy, and psychology all teach that such peace is not the natural state of human affairs. Civilizations—above all, free civilizations—are built and maintained by struggle—by patience, work, courage, and firmness. They do not just happen.

If there was ever a country whose wealth and liberty have been built by struggle, it is this one. Struggle was the lot of the early colonists and of the later settlers who braved the perils of the frontier. Struggle has been no less the fate of the waves of later immigrants who came to build a better life in a strange and competitive New World. And struggle is still our lot in seeking at long last to make good the equality of our Negro fellow citizens.

In short, the utopian view that everything will be all right if you just go away and leave it has never been true of domestic American society, neither in the past nor today. Why should we assume it to be true of international politics? It is not.

In foreign policy, the utopian often tells us that if we can only escape from the "traditional methods of foreign policy" the problems of the world will somehow vanish. There is no substance to the argument. There is nothing wrong with the traditional methods of diplomacy. There is in fact no alternative to them in a world of nation-states. These methods fail only when men pursue them with inadequate energy, insight, and optimism. The supposed alternative between the bad old diplomacy and some hypothetical good new diplomacy is an illusion—especially when the implacable dimension of power is ignored.

Is a foreign policy, because it is concerned with the balance of power, therefore devoid of idealism and higher ends? If the utopians mean to exclude from higher ends anything short of a visionary world where there will be no struggles, where the lion will lie down with the lamb, then it must be confessed that our foreign policy lacks vision. But surely it is not a contemptible goal to preserve peace in our lifetimes and pass on to our children some reasonable prospects for a peaceful future.

Nor should anyone say that the United States seeks a sterile and static system of order for its own sake. We have viewed order not as a reactionary goal, good in itself, but as the indispensable condition of progress. From the Marshall Plan and Point 4 to our current programs of aid to the developing world, we have sought, and we are seeking, to link order with progress in every human sense—with education and economic welfare, with health and cultural advance, and with political development toward the goal of self-government.

Under the umbrella provided by American power, vitality and creative energy have, in fact, gradually returned to many parts of the world once demoralized by war, communism, and the general disruption of the times. The revival of Western Europe has encouraged great democratic nations to resume an active role in the world. In the Pacific, Japan has acquired splendid prosperity and stable democracy. These developments among old and new allies open up a new vista of possibilities for the creation of a broadly based cooperative world system. We may hope to see our efforts joined around the world as they have been for many years in Europe, by a concert of peace-loving powers conscious of a common interest in keeping force under rational control and in protecting the progress of the developing nations. In the future, the burdens that define our interests will not disappear, but we can expect more help in carrying them.

The Russians, their aggressive impulses so often thwarted, have begun, we can hope, a slow evolution to peaceableness. Eastern Europe seems to enjoy a greater measure of freedom. There has been gradual progress in the third world toward economic growth and responsibility, not only because of aid from us and other developed countries but through imaginative new institutions for international and regional cooperation and the impressive efforts of many of the developing nations themselves. Behind the protection of American power, numerous international bodies have made genuine progress toward a more rational organization of the free world's economy.

We have made progress, but we are not at the brink of utopia. The revival of Europe and the apparent mellowing of some Communist nations pose dangers as well as opportunities. Some

Europeans, like some Americans, are tempted by irresponsibility. Isolationism on one side of the ocean has reciprocal effects on the other. Aggressive propensities still lurk among the Russians, as the Near Eastern crisis amply illustrates. The simultaneous progress of Red China toward nuclear weapons and political turmoil is hardly a comforting harbinger for the future.

Above all, we should have no illusions about the gravest problem of our time—the gap between rich and poor countries. It will not be easy to close; and in any event, even if successful, development does not necessarily promise peace. The social transformation involved in economic development, at best, is a cruel and unsettling process—particularly for traditionalist societies for whom modern technology is an alien and often an unwelcome intrusion. The history of the 20th century does not suggest that prosperity leads automatically to peace. There will be plenty of occasions for conflict in the third world, apart from deliberate Communist cultivation of instability, racism, and "wars of national liberation."

In short, we shall be living in a troubled world for a long time. There will be no magic solutions abroad, as there are none at home. New ideas are always needed, but not facile panaceas and irresponsibility masquerading as idealism.

One of the dangerous tendencies of the utopian is his inclination to look for scapegoats. The world ought naturally to be perfect; if it is not, he assumes someone must be to blame. This tendency is inherent in the utopian view of domestic as well as international politics.

But there are no quick solutions for the problems of poverty, cities, and the incorporation of Negroes into the mainstream of our culture. As we all know, these are all painful and complex historical processes. They need inexhaustible idealism, dedication, patience, firmness, and hard work. All this is frustrating to the utopian mentality. If he cannot have his instant Great Society, he looks for a scapegoat.

At the moment, his favorite scapegoat is Viet-Nam. In his rush to remove this one obstacle to perfection, he seems willing to abandon what 20 years of patient labor has built into a structure that gives reasonable promise of developing into a tolerably successful world order.

The answer to America's domestic problems lies in America and not in Viet-Nam. If it is true that we cannot have a world role and a good society together, then we shall not have either one. It is no good building model cities if they are to be bombed in 20 years' time.

But we need make no such choice. We have the wealth both to build a better America at home and to protect ourselves abroad. The question is whether we have the will.

There is, in short, an unending task ahead of us, in America and in the world, in the next generation as in all the generations of the past. We are often told that the present younger generation bridles at the responsibility and at the labor that lies before them. I am suspicious of those who claim to speak for the young. As a professor, I think I have as good a right as anyone else to an opinion on the subject. As I recall my own student days, most of us were deeply and rightly disturbed by the idea of war. We felt then, I believe, very much as young people feel now.

The problem, however, is not feelings alone but thought—and whether in the end reflection will dominate feeling in the formation of policy. I have been a professor too long not to have unshakeable respect for the good sense of the young. They are fully the equals of their predecessors—probably better educated and certainly not lacking in independence of mind. The young of today know, I am certain, that the freedom and wealth they are about to inherit could not have been built without persistent effort and cannot survive without it either. I have no doubt that the great majority will reject irresponsibility and face reality. I believe that young Americans accept, in this generation as in others, the basic rule of the social contract: that as the privileges of democracy are always great, so, too, are its duties sometimes stern.

TO INTERVENE OR NOT TO INTERVENE

Hans J. Morgenthau

Hans J. Morgenthau is Albert A. Michelson Distinguished Service Professor of Political Science and Modern History at the University of Chicago and Leonard Davis Distinguished Professor of Political Science at the City University of New York.

What we have witnessed since the end of the Second World War appears . . . as a mere continuation of a tradition that was well established in the nineteenth century. There appears to be nothing new either in the contemporary confusion of doctrine or in the pragmatic use of intervention on behalf of the interests of individual nations. What Great Britain and Russia were doing in the nineteenth century, the United States and the Soviet Union seem to be doing

From *A New Foreign Policy for the United States* (New York: Frederick A. Praeger, Inc., 1969), pp. 117-129, 148-150. © 1969 by Council on Foreign Relations, Inc.

today. Thus, to cite... two spectacular examples among many, the Soviet Union intervened in Hungary in 1956 as Russia had done in 1848, and the United States intervened in Cuba at the beginning of the 1960s as it had done in the first decades of the century. Yet there are fundamental differences between the interventions of the past and those of the present. Five such differences exert an important influence upon the techniques of contemporary intervention as well as upon the peace and order of the world.

First, the process of decolonization, which started after the Second World War and is now almost completed, has more than doubled the number of sovereign nations. Many, if not most of these new nations are not viable political, military, and economic entities; they are lacking in some, if not all of the prerequisites of nationhood. Their governments need regular outside support. Thus France subsidizes its former colonies in Africa; all the major industrial nations extend economic and financial aid to the new ones, and the United States, the Soviet Union, and China do so on a competitive basis.

What makes this aid a lever for intervention is the fact that in most cases it is not just an advantage the new nations can afford to take or leave, but a condition for their survival. The Indian economy, for example, would collapse without outside support and in consequence the Indian state itself would probably disintegrate. Large masses of Egyptians would starve without the outside supply of food. What is true of these two ancient and relatively well-developed nations is of course true of most of the new nations, which are nations within their present boundaries only by virtue of the accidents of colonial policy: The supplier of foreign aid holds the power of life and death over them. If a foreign nation supplies aid, it intervenes; if it does not supply aid, it also intervenes. In the measure that the government must depend on foreign aid for its own and its nation's survival, it is inevitably exposed to political pressures from the supplying government. Many of the recipient governments have been able to minimize or even neutralize these political pressures by keeping open alternative sources of foreign aid and by playing one supplying government against the other. Some nations have developed this technique into a fine and highly successful art.

Second, our age resembles the period of history after the Napoleonic Wars, when the theory of nonintervention and the practice of intervention flourished, in that it is a revolutionary age. Many nations, new and old, are threatened by revolution or are at one time or other in the throes of it. A successful revolution frequently portends a new orientation in the country's foreign policy, as it did in the Congo, Cuba, and Indonesia. Thus the great powers, expecting gains or fearing disadvantages from the revolution, are tempted to intervene on the side of the faction favoring them.

The temptation is particularly acute when the revolution is committed to a Communist or anti-Communist position. Thus the United States and the Soviet Union often oppose each other surreptitiously through the intermediary of governments and political movements. It is at this point that the third new factor comes into play.

Of all the revolutionary changes that have occurred in world politics since the end of the Second World War, none has exerted a greater influence upon the conduct of foreign policy than the recognition on the part of the two superpowers, armed with a large arsenal of nuclear weapons, that a direct confrontation between them would entail unacceptable risks, for it could lead to their mutual destruction. Thus they have decided that they must avoid such a confrontation. This is the real political and military meaning of the slogan "peaceful coexistence."

Instead of confronting each other openly and directly, the United States and the Soviet Union have chosen to oppose and compete with each other through third parties. The internal weakness of most new and emerging nations, requiring foreign support, and the revolutionary situation in many of them give them the opportunity of doing so. Thus, aside from competing for influence upon a particular government in the traditional ways, the United States and the Soviet Union have interjected their power into the domestic conflicts of weak nations, supporting the government or the opposition as the case may be. While one might think that on ideological grounds the United States, a status-quo power, would always intervene on the side of the government and the Soviet Union, a revolutionary power, on the side of the opposition, it is characteristic for the interplay between ideology and power politics (to which we turn in a moment) that this has not always been so. Thus the Soviet Union intervened in Hungary in 1956 on the side of the government, and the United States has been intervening in Cuba on the side of the opposition. The Soviet slogan of support for "wars of national liberation" is in truth an ideological justification of Soviet support for that side in a civil conflict in which the Soviet Union happens to have an interest. In the Congo, the United States and the Soviet Union have switched their support from the government to the opposition and back again according to the fortunes of a succession of civil wars.

While contemporary interventions, serving national power interests, have sometimes been masked by the ideologies of Communism and anti-Communism, these ideologies have been an independent motivating force. This is the fourth factor we must consider. The United States and the Soviet Union face each other not only as two great powers competing for the advantage in the traditional ways. They face each other also as the fountainheads of two hostile and incompatible ideologies, systems of government, and ways of life, trying to expand the reach of their respective political values and institutions and to prevent the expansion of the other's. Thus the Cold War has been a conflict not only between two world powers but also between two secular religions. And like the religious wars of the seventeenth century, the war between Communism and democracy does not respect national boundaries. It finds enemies and allies in all countries, opposing the one and supporting the other regardless of the niceties of international law. Here is the dynamic force that has led the two superpowers to intervene all over the globe, sometimes surreptitiously, sometimes openly, sometimes with the accepted methods of diplomatic pressure and propaganda, sometimes with the frowned-upon instruments of covert subversion and open force.

These four factors favoring intervention in our time are counteracted by a fifth one, which is in a sense a counterpart to the weakness of the nations intervened in. These nations have just emerged from a colonial status or are in the process of emerging from a semicolonial one. They compensate their need for outside support with a fierce resistance to the threat of "neo-colonialism." While they cannot exist without support from stronger nations, they refuse to exchange their newly won independence for a new dependency. Hence their ambivalent reaction to outside intervention. They need it and they resent it. This ambivalence compels them to choose among several different courses of action. They can seek support from multiple outside sources, thereby canceling out dependence on one by dependence on the other. They can alternate among different sources of support, at one time relying on one, and at another time relying on another. Finally, they can choose between complete dependence and complete independence, by either becoming a client of one of the major powers or by renouncing outside support altogether.

This ambivalence of the weak nations imposes new techniques upon the intervening ones. Intervention must either be brutally direct in order to overcome resistance, or it must be surreptitious in order to be acceptable, or the two extremes may be combined. Thus the United States intervened in Cuba in 1961 through the proxy of a refugee force, and the Soviet Union intervened in Hungary in 1956 by appointing a government that asked for its intervention.

U.S. Policy of Intervention

What follows from this condition of intervention in our time for the foreign policies of the United States? Four basic conclusions can be drawn: the futility of the search for abstract principles, the error of anti-Communist intervention per se, the self-defeating

character of antirevolutionary intervention per se, and the requirement of prudence.

First, it is futile to search for an abstract principle that would
allow us to distinguish in a concrete case between legitimate and
illegitimate intervention. This was so even in the nineteenth century,
when intervention for the purpose of colonial expansion was
generally regarded to be legitimate and when the active players on
the political stage were relatively self-sufficient nation-states,
opposed to intervention as a threat to their existence. If this was so,
then, it stands to reason that in an age where large segments of whole
continents must choose between anarchy and intervention, intervention cannot be limited by abstract principles, let alone effectively
outlawed by a United Nations resolution.

Let us suppose that nation A intervenes on behalf of the
government of nation B by giving it military, economic, and
technical aid on the latter's request, and that the government of B
becomes so completely dependent upon A as to act as the latter's
satellite. Let us further suppose that the opposition calls upon C for
support against the agents of a foreign oppressor and that C heeds
that call. Which one of these interventions is legitimate? A will of
course say that its own is and C's is not, and vice versa, and the
ideologues on both sides will be kept busy justifying the one and
damning the other. This ideological shadow-boxing cannot affect the
incidence of interventions. All nations will continue to be guided in
their decisions to intervene and their choice of the means of
intervention by what they regard as their respective national
interests. There is indeed an urgent need for the governments of the
great powers to abide by certain rules according to which the game
of intervention is to be played. But these rules must be deduced not
from abstract principles which are incapable of controlling the
actions of governments, but from the interests of the nations
concerned and from their practice of foreign policy reflecting those
interests.

The failure to understand this distinction between abstract
principles and national interests as guidance for a policy of
intervention was in good measure responsible for the fiasco of the
Bay of Pigs in 1961. The United States was resolved to intervene on
behalf of its interests, but it was also resolved to intervene in such a
way as not openly to violate the principle of nonintervention. Both
resolutions were legitimate in terms of American interests. The
United States had an interest in eliminating the political and military
power of the Soviet Union, which used Cuba as a base from which to
threaten the security of the United States in the Western Hemisphere. It was also an interest of the United States to avoid
jeopardizing its prestige in the uncommitted nations through

intervention in Cuba. The United States failed to assign priorities to these two interests. In order to minimize the loss of prestige, the United States jeopardized the success of the intervention. Instead of using concern for prestige as just one interest among others in the political equation, it submitted to it as though it were an abstract principle imposing absolute limits upon the actions necessary to achieve success. In consequence, the United States failed thrice. The intervention did not succeed, and in the attempt we suffered a temporary loss of prestige as the friend of the uncommitted nations, as well as much of our prestige as a great nation able to use its power successfully on behalf of its interests.

Had the United States approached the problem of intervening in Cuba in a rational fashion, it would have asked itself which was more important: to succeed in the intervention or to prevent a temporary loss of prestige among the uncommitted nations. Had it settled upon the latter alternative, it would have refrained from intervening altogether; had it chosen the former alternative, it would have taken all the measures necessary to make the intervention a success, regardless of unfavorable reactions in the rest of the world. Instead, it sought the best of both alternatives and got the worst.

The Soviet Union's interventions in Hungary in 1956 and in Czechoslovakia in 1968 are instructive in this respect. The Soviet Union put the success of the interventions above all other considerations, and succeeded. Hungary and Czechoslovakia are today Communist states within the orbit of the Soviet Union. However, while Soviet prestige did recover from the damage it suffered in 1956, it was dealt an apparently irreparable blow in 1968.

The interventions of the United States in Cuba, the Dominican Republic, and Vietnam, and other less spectacular ones, have been justified as reactions to Communist intervention. This argument derives from the assumption that Communism everywhere in the world is not only morally unacceptable and philosophically hostile to the United States, but also detrimental to the national interests of the United States and must therefore be opposed on political and military as well as moral and philosophic grounds. I shall assume for the purposes of this discussion that, as a matter of fact, Communist intervention actually preceded ours in all these instances, and shall raise the question as to whether our national interest required our intervention against the Communist one.

Ten or twenty years ago, this question could have been answered in the positive without further examination. For then Communism anywhere in the world was a mere extension of Soviet power, controlled and used for the purposes of that power. Since we were committed to the containment of the Soviet Union, we were also committed to the containment of Communism anywhere in the world. Today however, we are faced not with one monolithic Communist bloc controlled and used by the Soviet Union, but with a variety of Communisms, whose relations with the Soviet Union and China change from country to country and from time to time and whose bearing upon the interests of the United States requires empirical examination in each instance. Communism has become polycentric, with each Communist government and movement, to a greater or lesser extent, pursuing its own national interests within the common framework of Communist ideology and institutions. The bearing which the pursuit of those interests has upon the policies of the United States must be determined in terms not of Communist ideology but of their compatibility with the interests of the United States.

Subjecting our interventions in Cuba, the Dominican Republic, and Vietnam to this empirical test, one realizes the inadequacy of the simple slogan "Stop Communism" as the rationale of our interventions. While this slogan is popular at home and makes only minimal demands upon discriminating judgment, it inspires policies that do either too much or too little in opposing Communism, and can provide no yardstick for a policy that measures the degree of its opposition to the degree of the Communist threat. Thus, on the one hand, as part of the settlement of the missile crisis of 1962, we pledged ourselves not to intervene in Cuba, which is today a military and political client of the Soviet Union and seeks to become the fountainhead of subversion and military intervention in the Western Hemisphere, and as such directly affects the interests of the United States. On the other hand, we have intervened massively in Vietnam, even at the risk of a major war, although the Communist threat to American interests emanating from Vietnam is at best remote, and in any event infinitely more remote than the Communist threat emanating from Cuba.

As concerns the intervention in the Dominican Republic, even if one takes at face value the official assessment of the facts that the revolution of April 1965 was controlled by Cuban Communists, it appears incongruous that we intervened there in a revolution that was, according to that same assessment, a mere symptom of the disease, while the disease itself—Cuban Communism—remained exempt from effective intervention.

This type of intervention against Communism per se naturally tends to blend into intervention against revolution per se. We tend to intervene against all radical revolutionary movements because we are afraid lest they be taken over by Communists, and conversely we tend to intervene on behalf of all governments and movements opposed to radical revolution, because they are also opposed to Communism. Such a policy of intervention is unsound on intellectual grounds for the reasons mentioned in our discussion of contemporary Communism; it is also bound to fail in practice.

Many nations of Asia, Africa, and Latin America are today objectively in a prerevolutionary stage, and it is likely to be only a matter of time until actual revolution breaks out in one or the other of these nations. The revolutionary movements that will then come to the fore are bound to have, to a greater or lesser degree, a Communist component—that is, they run the risk of being taken over by Communism. Nothing is simpler, in terms of both intellectual effort and, at least initially, practical execution, than to trace all these revolutions to a common conspiratorial source, to equate all revolutionary movements with world Communism, and to oppose them with indiscriminate fervor as uniformly hostile to the interests of the United States. Under this rationale, the United States would be forced to intervene against revolutions throughout the world because of the ever-present threat of a Communist take-over and would transform itself, in spite of its better insight and intentions, into an antirevolutionary power per se.

Such a policy of intervention might succeed if it had to deal with nothing more than isolated revolutionary movements that could be smothered by force of arms. But it cannot succeed, since it is faced with revolutionary situations all over the world; for even the militarily most powerful nation does not have sufficient usable resources to deal simultaneously with a number of acute revolutions. Such a policy of indiscriminate intervention is bound to fail not only with regard to the individual revolution to which it is applied, but also in terms of its own indiscriminate anti-Communism. For the very logic that would make us appear as the antirevolutionary power per se would surrender to Communism the sponsorship of revolution everywhere. Thus indiscriminate anti-Communist intervention achieves what it aims to prevent: the exploitation of the revolutions of the age by Communism.

If this analysis of our policy of intervention is correct, then we have intervened not wisely but too well. Our policy of intervention has been under the ideological spell of our opposition to Communism and to potentially Communist-led revolutions. While this ideological orientation has continued to determine our policy of intervention, the Soviet Union has continued to pay lip service to the support of "wars of national liberation" but has in practice relegated these wars to a secondary place in the struggle for the world. This softening of the Soviet ideological position has become one of the points of contention in the ideological dispute between the Soviet Union and China. In a statement of June 14, 1963, the Chinese Communist Party declared that "the whole cause of the international proletarian revolution hinges on the outcome of revolutionary struggles" in the "vast areas of Asia, Africa, and Latin America" that are today the "storm centers of world revolution dealing direct blows at imperialism." Conforming to this doctrine, China has almost indiscriminately intervened throughout the world on behalf of subversive movements, very much in the manner in which the Bolshevist government under Lenin and Trotsky tried to promote world revolution. In their reply of July 14th of the same year, the Soviet leaders opposed the " 'new theory' according to which the decisive force in the struggle against imperialism . . . is not the world system of socialism, not the struggle of the international working class, but . . . the national liberation movement." The Soviet Union's recent practice of restraint in fomenting and supporting revolution has matched this theoretical position. This ideological "revisionism" has of course not prevented the Soviet Union from intervening—as in Egypt, Somalia, and Czechoslovakia—when its national interest appeared to require intervention.

One factor that cannot have failed to influence the Soviet Union in toning down its ideological commitment to intervention has been the relative failure of ideological intervention. The United States, China, and Cuba have joined the Soviet Union in the experience of that failure. The uncommitted nations have been eager to reap the benefits of intervention, but have also been very anxious not to be tied with ideological strings to the intervening nation. After making great efforts, expending considerable resources, and running serious risks, the participants in this world-wide ideological competition are still approximately at the point from which they started: Measured against their ambitions and expectations, the uncommitted third of the world is still by and large an ideological no man's land.

This experience of failure is particularly painful, and ought to be particularly instructive, for the United States. For since the end of the Second World War we have intervened in the political, military, and economic affairs of other countries at a cost far in excess of $100 billion, and we have for some time been involved in a costly, risky war in order to build a nation in South Vietnam. Only the enemies of the United States will question the generosity of these efforts, which have no parallel in history. But have these efforts been wise? Have the commitments made and risks taken been commensurate with the results to be expected and actually achieved? The answer must be in the negative. Our economic aid has been successful in supporting economies that were already in the process of development; it has been by and large unsuccessful in creating economic development where none existed before because the moral and national preconditions for such development were lacking. Learning from this failure, we have established the principle of giving aid only to the few nations who can use it rather than to the many who need it. While this principle of selectivity is sound in theory, its consistent practical application has been thwarted by the harsh political and military realities that sometimes make it necessary to give aid when it is not economically justified, as well as by political and military considerations derived from the ideological concerns discussed above.

This principle of selectivity must be extended to the political and military sphere as well. We have come to overrate enormously what a nation can do for another nation by intervening in its affairs even with the latter's consent. This overestimation of our power to intervene is only a counterfoil to our ideological commitment, which by its very nature has no limit. Committed to intervening against Communist aggression and subversion anywhere, we have come to assume that we have the power to do so successfully. But in truth, both the need for intervention and the chances for successful intervention are much more limited than we have been led to believe. Intervene we must where our national interest requires it and where our power gives us a chance to succeed. The choice of these occasions will be determined not by sweeping ideological commitments or by blind reliance upon American power, but by a careful calculation of the interests involved and the power available. If the United States applies this standard, it will intervene less and succeed more.

Vietnam

. . . Errors in the way of thinking about foreign policy lead of necessity to wrong political judgments. There are, however, wrong political judgments which are not so occasioned but can result from a variety of intellectual errors. Three such misjudgments have had a deleterious effect upon policies in Vietnam. They concern the nature of Communism, of revolution, and of limited war.

It is one of the great ironies of history that we have tended to take Communism more seriously as a political ideology than have the major Communist governments. For Stalin and his successors in particular, Communism was first of all an ideological means to the traditional ends of imperial Russia. By contrast, we have tended to take the Communist postulates and prophecies at their face value and in consequence have been unable to divorce our political judgments from the assumption of the monolithic, conspiratorial character of Communism. Thus we have been unable to judge Vietnamese Communism on its own national merits, as an indigenous phenomenon resulting from the peculiar circumstances of time and place. Instead, Vietnamese Communism has appeared to us as a special instance of a general phenomenon which is not by accident the same regardless of time and place; for it has been created by a world-wide conspiracy whose headquarters are assumed to be in Moscow or Peking or both, and whose aim is to Communize the world. In this view, what happens in Vietnam is just an episode in that international struggle between Communism and the "free world," and consequently the outcome of the Vietnamese War has world-wide significance.

The misjudgment of revolution fits organically into this largely fictitious picture of the political world. Revolution, too, must not be understood on its own terms but must be traced to a conspiracy of foreign origin imposed upon an unwilling people. That concept of revolution is in good measure responsible for the fiasco of the Bay of Pigs. We thought of Castro as a dictator imposed by the Communist conspiracy of Moscow upon the unwilling Cubans, who, at the sight of a thousand anti-Castro refugees, would rise *en masse* against their oppressor. Similarly, the revolution in South Vietnam must be traced to a foreign conspiracy located in Hanoi and, at one remove, in Moscow and Peking. What looks like revolution, then, is really foreign aggression, and the revolution can be suppressed by thwarting that aggression.

What is inadmissible to us is the recognition that in large parts of the world there exists today an objective revolutionary situation. This revolutionary situation would exist even if Communism had never been heard of, and is in good measure a response to the Western teachings and examples of national self-determination and radical social reform. That these national and social revolutions are largely identified with Communism is primarily the result of the West's failure to identify with them morally and to support them materially. The Vietnamese revolution is a case in point. In Vietnam as elsewhere, particularly in Latin America, the Communist and anti-American orientation of revolutionary movements is directly related to the American misunderstanding of the nature both of Communism and of revolution.

While our misjudgments of Communism and revolution are organically related, our reliance upon limited war to combat them is a spectacular *non sequitur*. For if we are combating in Vietnam foreign aggression inspired and supported by the centers of world Communism, particularly Peking, and if we are serious about getting rid of the trouble, then we must strike at the source and not only at one of its outward manifestations. But for perfectly good reasons we shy away from a direct military confrontation with China, let alone the Soviet Union. Thus the means we have been employing in Vietnam are divorced from our conception of the nature of the conflict. While we conceive of the conflict as a particular manifestation of a world-wide struggle, we have tried to win that struggle through victory in a localized war.

That discrepancy also determines the nature of the localized war we have been fighting. Not only have we been fighting North Vietnam in order to suppress a South Vietnamese revolution inspired and supported by either China or the Soviet Union or both, but we have also imposed limitations upon this war against North Vietnam in order to avoid a direct military confrontation with either the Soviet Union or China or both. But these limitations have at the very least been a factor that has made military victory more difficult to attain. Thus our political misjudgments have put us into the doubly paradoxical situation in which we respond to what we consider to be the world-wide challenge of Communist revolution with a local war which is itself subject to limitations making a military victory more difficult, if not impossible, to attain. Thus we have been engaged in a war which we can neither win on the battlefield without risking a direct military confrontation with the two major Communist powers nor liquidate without giving the lie to the political assumptions on which our involvement is based. . . .

THREE LESSONS OF VIETNAM

Ithiel de Sola Pool

Ithiel de Sola Pool is Chairman of the Department of Political Science, Massachusetts Institute of Technology, and a member of the Defense Science Board, Department of Defense.

. . . Right now the anti-intellectuals—and Senator Fulbright, astonishingly enough, with them—are trying to deny policy-makers

From "Epilogue: The Lessons of Vietnam" in *No More Vietnams?* edited by Richard M. Pfeffer (New York: Harper & Row, Publishers, 1968), pp. 205-208. Copyright © 1968 by the Adlai Stevenson Institute of International Affairs. By permission of Harper & Row, Publishers.

the capability to learn what they need to know if they are to avoid the disease of overgeneralized reaction. . . Without social-science area knowledge to correct their instinctive clichés, our military officers are likely to march us into futile battles and our foreign-policy makers into repeated crises, like the Red Coats who marched according to their rule book against the embattled farmers of New England.

That has been the lesson of every recent intervention crisis. We marched into the Bay of Pigs because those area experts who did know were not consulted. In the Dominican intervention we succeeded, and successes are seldom questioned. Nonetheless, the fact of the matter in retrospect is that we did not know at the time who was on what side. Both our civilian and our military authorities needed good political analysis more than they needed anything else.

Our need for better social-science knowledge can perhaps be identified as the first lesson of Vietnam. In a world in which we will continue to be involved in a series of overseas crises located in diverse and strange cultures, the prime requirement is available social-science area experts who know the language and the country. They are needed, not only in the field, but also in the highest policy-making councils. Until the Secretary of State, the Secretary of Defense, and the President are adequately and directly served by the top experts on each country in crisis, and until we massively increase our social-science knowledge of crisis areas, we will make drastic mistakes over and over again. That is the first of three major lessons of Vietnam.

The second concerns the conduct of war by a democracy. Mankind, regrettably, has not yet reached the point of totally rejecting war. But a democracy in the present era cannot deliberately choose war as an instrument of national policy. The people in a democracy will not fight willingly for long unless they believe that combat is forced upon them by an aggressive enemy. Pearl Harbor and the North Korean invasion of the South were signal events to which the American public could and did respond. There has been no such event in Vietnam. The lesson looks clear for revolutionists or aggressors seeking to impose their will on a foreign country; the lesson is to act covertly and gradually. It would be naïve to think that the experience of Vietnam precludes an American military response to future overt dramatic aggressions against our allies. Our response, however, may well be timid if the provocation is not obvious.

To the American government the lesson is that it must find effective ways of responding to limited disruptions by means short of war. We have learned, for example, that divisions of troops are not very effective against undergrounds, and we will have to learn how to use police and intelligence operations.

Our worst mistake in Vietnam clearly was to initiate the bombing of the north. Before that started, it was my view that the United States as a democracy could not stand the moral protest that would arise if we rained death from the skies upon an area where there was no war. After the bombing started, I decided I had been in error. For a while there seemed to be no outcry of protest, but time brought it on. Now I would return to my original view with an important modification, namely, time. Public reactions do not come immediately. Many actions that public opinion would otherwise make impossible are possible if they are short-term. I believe we can fairly say that unless it is severely provoked or unless the war succeeds fast, a democracy cannot choose war as an instrument of policy. Any other sort of war will destroy the cohesion of the democratic community that wages it.

A third lesson in Vietnam is more specifically American. It is that the politics of this country will continue to be polarized between an isolationist impulse to avoid involvement in other people's problems and an internationalist impulse to promote our own values in the world. We are likely to oscillate dangerously between these extremes. . . .

Right now it is fashionable to say that the American public will accept no more Vietnams. Perhaps that is a partial truth for the moment, but it would take only another catastrophe that occurred because we sat on our hands and avoided intervention to push the pendulum back the other way. Whatever the last catastrophe was shapes the direction of the public's indignation at the incumbent administration. Just as the fall of Czechoslovakia oriented us toward the Marshall Plan and NATO, and as the fall of China shaped our response to Korea, and as Cuba conditioned us to act in the Dominican Republic, so a passive acceptance after Vietnam of some communist takeover elsewhere—or even there—would be the prelude to a revived activism in American policy.

In the long run, it seems to me sure that the isolationism now so rampant in the McCarthy campaign and in the anti-Vietnam protest is a transient thing. It is transient for two reasons. The first reason is that American money and armed power have been a major stabilizing force in the world. If we cease using them, it is fairly predictable that the result will be a catastrophe somewhere, and with that will come the revival of the internationalist impulse. The second reason is surer though more remote: it is nuclear proliferation. Treaty or no treaty, there are many in this room who will live to see several underdeveloped countries with the means to launch nuclear war. The United States, I predict, will not stay passive in the face of such a threat. When we come to realize that we can live in safety only in a world in which the political systems of all states are democratic and pacifically oriented, the immediate lessons of Vietnam—whether of success or of failure or a combination of the two—will recede into a dimly remembered image.

In the nuclear age the world has become a small place. In various ways we will all become more alike, and more like America as we know it today. People everywhere want some aspects of American culture, such as automobiles, TV sets, refrigerators, and Coca-Cola. Vietnam illustrates this trend, too. Other aspects of our value system, such as participatory politics, civil liberties, social mobility, pragmatism, and a pacific orientation, are also spreading, but less readily and universally. Were it not for the nuclear threat, the world might well remain heterogeneous in these respects. However, in the era of technological change on the edge of which we now stand, American policy-makers will not be able to view with indifference aggressive dictatorships with nuclear arms, no matter how small or remote they may be. Vietnam, therefore, is not likely to be the last case in which this nation finds itself trying to cope with dangerous armed ideologies in countries far from our area of normal concern and at the potential cost of much American sacrifice. The lesson we must learn is how to cope with such situations by better means than contests of fire power.

CONTAINMENT—THE MILITARY IMPERATIVE

John P. East

John P. East is Associate Professor of Political Science at East Carolina University; he serves on the North Carolina Young Americans for Freedom Advisory Board.

Since 1947 the primary basis of American foreign policy in response to the Communist Revolution has been the "containment" policy. It has become increasingly clear that the military aspect of this policy, particularly as regards the "soft continents" of Asia, Latin America, and Africa, has been inadequate.

Excerpts from "Containment—The Military Imperative" in *The New Guard*, Volume 9, No. 2 (February 1969), pp. 14-17, 22.

Because the Cold War is a conflict waged on economic, social, psychological (including religious), diplomatic, political, and military fronts, an effective policy of containment must be directed at *each* of these fronts. It is on the military front in the underdeveloped continents that American policy, and as a consequence Western policy, has failed most conspicuously, and because of this failure we have lost ground on the other fronts.

In Europe the policy of containment has met with a reasonable degree of success, for behind the military shield of N.A.T.O., Western Europe has been able to compete successfully to this point against Communist ideology in the nonmilitary sphere. Similar success has been less prevalent on the "soft continents."

America has been confounded in the military conduct of the Cold War for various reasons, including frequently a lack of will, but one of the greatest obstacles has been the reality of nuclear stalemate, the fact that the United States and the Soviet Union each possesses nuclear capability. This fact has imposed severe limitations on the military conduct of the Cold War. It has imposed new rules of warfare to which the Communist revolutionaries have adjusted brilliantly, while the Western World, under the leadership of the United States, continues to grope for a solution.

In the Communist camp, the desired military end is world domination, while in the case of the United States and the Free World the military end has been to contain Communist expansion. Because of American nuclear power, the Soviet Union has employed nonnuclear strategy and tactics in its military planning. Specifically, it has resorted to the exportation of guerrilla warfare, often called "wars of national liberation" by the creators of Communist double-think. Red China, because it has lacked until recently nuclear capability, has by necessity relied upon the "war of national liberation" to execute its military conquests.

The Communist revolutionaries, then, have successfully overcome the limitation imposed by nuclear parity upon the military conduct of the Cold War. America does not have a successful policy of "containment," for the simple reason that it is not "containing" the military arm of the Communist revolution. At best, the *military* policy of the United States is one of a slow rear-guard action.

Today the problem in Vietnam is precisely that America has not been able *militarily* to contain Communism. The Communist success in Cuba, and the present exportation of Castroism throughout the Western Hemisphere through guerrilla tactics, are incontrovertible evidence of America's failure to check *militarily* the Communist revolution in Latin America. Finally, American (and therefore Western) response to Communist military challenges in Africa, as the analysis to follow suggests, has not been impressive. It is in the underdeveloped continents of Asia, Latin America, and Africa where the military failure of the West, under American leadership, to halt Communist militarism has been most evident.

There is no simple solution to correct this American failure; however, there are basic approaches that could be followed to contain Communist military thrusts. No pretense is made that the proposals presented in this article are totally original and sparkling new. Some of them are "old," but because they are sound, yet untried, they merit reassertion. Where the final consequences are so grave, the cliche that "these are complex matters" can be no excuse for continuing ineptitude and ineffectiveness. America must find methods of stopping Communist militarism in the underdeveloped continents, within the limitations imposed by nuclear stalemate, or the West may well be confronted in due course with uglier alternatives than it faced with Nazism, Fascism, and Japanese imperialism three decades ago.

The first prerequisite to any policy of military containment is the will to contain, stemming from an understanding for the need to contain. Communist militarism needs to be challenged for the same reasons that the Axis powers needed to be confronted in the 1930's. Communism must be contained for the same reasons that free men always resist armed totalitarian ideologies; they prefer that they and their children shall remain free. The neoisolationists contend that America, and the Atlantic Community generally, can remain free even though the soft continents succumb to Communism. The moral enormity of this position is itself chilling, for the neoisolationists are cavalierly consigning vast numbers of human beings to oppression at best, and liquidation and genocide at worst.

On military and strategic grounds the neoisolationist position is also highly vulnerable. Certainly the events leading up to the Second World War made it clear that America cannot remain uninvolved, and yet ultimately free, in a world in which totalitarian, revolutionary predators can subvert with impunity the weak nations of the world. The will to contain Communist militarism stems from an acceptance of the assumption that Communism cannot ultimately be kept from America itself unless it is checked militarily in the underdeveloped continents. If the will to check Communism exists, then the means to express this will can be found.

Asia

Currently it is in Southeast Asia that the failure of American containment of the Communist "wars of national liberation" is most dramatically illustrated. With the success of the Communist revolution in China in 1949, it was inevitable that Communist military pressures would increase throughout Asia. In the Korean War, America became directly involved militarily, and Communism was contained, at least as regards the attempted conquest of South Korea; however, in that conflict the Red Chinese learned that at best America had a toleration for "limited wars," and they further learned that America would involve itself in a "wider war" only under the most severe provocations, if even then. The stage was set for Communist military probes into Southeast Asia.

By 1954, the French had been driven from Indochina, and the Communists had secured North Vietnam. The peace parleys had barely adjourned when the Communist revolution began to spread militarily via guerrilla warfare into Laos and South Vietnam. By 1962 Laos was "neutralized," which is the transitional phase leading to total Communist control. The success of the Communist exportation of a guerrilla war into South Vietnam brings us to the present perilous situation in that part of the world.

Is it possible to expect the evolution of a viable political, economic, and social system when that system is under direct military assault? In the American context, it is understood that desired change cannot take place in our great urban centers if violence and rioting were allowed to rampage unchecked. The problem in Vietnam is comparable. That is, political, economic, and social change cannot take place in the middle of a riot in urban America nor in a country under overt military assault, as in the case in Vietnam. Military success is the linchpin of containment, for without it no viable society or government can evolve. The current negotiations do not eliminate the need for military success; rather they underscore the necessity for it, because negotiated settlements at best can only reflect current military realities.

The exact steps to be followed to achieve military success could be provided by the highest levels of military expertise and leadership. Over a period of time, various responsible military authorities have proposed such steps as closing the port of Haiphong, effective destruction of the military-industrial complex of North Vietnam, destruction of the irrigation system, effective interdiction of supply trails through Laos and Cambodia, destruction of the railroads from South China to the Hanoi-Haiphong area, sealing off the Mu Gia Pass, and the employment of free Asian ground forces on a more expanded scale in South Vietnam. These proposals are indicative of the variety of suggestions that have been made to achieve military success; to achieve it without the use of nuclear weapons; to achieve it with minimal civilian casualties, and to achieve it with the war remaining confined to the two Vietnams. What is important is not the precise form in which such conventional military proposals might be employed, but the evidence that military victory by conventional military means is possible, if the *will* to achieve that end exists.

The standard charge will be raised that such "escalation" to achieve a military victory will precipitate the military intervention of the major Communist powers, namely, the Soviet Union and China. As for the Soviet Union, the possibility of her intervention would appear minimal. First, by confining the war to the two Vietnams and to nonnuclear means, it is difficult to believe the Soviet Union would risk a major conflagration over such limited stakes. Secondly, the logistical problems for the Soviet Union would be great in supporting her military forces in Southeast Asia, particularly with her land routes being over the territory of an often hostile China. . . .

As for Chinese intervention. . . It is unlikely that China, with her own territory not being under attack, would risk a major military confrontation with the United States, which is, it must not be forgotten, still the greatest military power in the world. . . .

. . . If the thought of escalation continually paralyzes our will, we shall ultimately be confronted with the fruits of escalation in reverse. That is, if Communist militarism can move unchecked, in time America will be faced with the spectacle of a world that is substantially Communist-dominated, and America may well be confronted with the ugly alternatives of capitulation or nuclear war. These are the nonchoices that escalation in reverse can bring to us. . . .

. . . To those who insist on a guarantee of success in South Vietnam before further military action is undertaken, one can only reply that the worst that may happen is that we will be driven into the South China Sea, which is precisely what is occurring anyway, it would appear under current policies. A military program employing Free Asian ground forces, and American air and sea power, offers a greater guarantee of success than the inadequate *status quo*.

Latin America

In Latin America, military containment of Communism has failed and is failing. America's nuclear capability, which has become in many respects the American Maginot Line, presented no hindrance to the molding of guerrilla forces in the Sierra Maestra, and, within the limitations set by the nuclear age upon the conduct of war, the Communists secured Cuba in 1959. Since that time Communist power has solidified on the island, and Cuba has become the inviolable sanctuary for the dispersion of Communist guerrilla war throughout South America, including Venezuela, Colombia, Guatemala, northeastern Brazil, Puerto Rico, and the Dominican Republic.

The basic military problem of containment in Latin America is to halt the spread of Castroism via guerrilla war. Militarily, Cuba is the Cold War in microcosm. The Communists won this territory, in spite of American nuclear capability, by flanking this nuclear strength with guerrilla warfare. As a minimum requirement, if Cuba is at least to be neutralized as an exporter of Communist militarism in this hemisphere, similar tactics—infiltrating guerrilla forces into the island—will have to be employed.

To confine Castroism militarily, the first step might be the recognition of a Free Cuban Government in Exile which would indicate *American* determination to prevail. Secondly, we must support and train the Cuban exiles in guerrilla warfare and skillfully and subtly disperse them on the island. The plan is to commence with a small force and slowly, but inexorably, build it up to proportions that may well topple Castro from power. Not only should the Free Cubans in exile be employed in this military operation, but America should, as *leader* of the West, *encourage* other Free Latins to assist. There is supporting sentiment in South America, for example, in Venezuela, and it is America's responsibility to find, nurture and develop this determination. . . .

. . . It must be remembered that the primary purpose in infiltrating military forces into Cuba is to *contain* Castroism; to prevent the further exportation of Communist military revolution from Cuba. Even if Castro is not deposed, by exporting free guerrilla forces into the island, he would be kept preoccupied defending his fortunes at home, and he could not afford to divert resources for the spreading of armed revolution throughout the hemisphere. . . .

Conclusions

Communism cannot be contained on any front in this Cold War unless it is first contained militarily. In the soft continents of Asia, Latin America, and Africa, the Free World, under the leadership of the United States, has not met this great need, and, as a consequence, we are not stopping Communist expansion. At best the West is fighting a slow rear-guard action. Within the limitations imposed by nuclear stalemate upon the conduct of warfare, the Communist World continues to export successfully via guerrilla war its militarism, and hence its ideology, throughout the underdeveloped world.

GUERRILLA WARFARE—THE POOR MAN'S POWER

Vladimir Dedijer

Vladimir Dedijer is a historian by profession; he now works in Ljubljana, Yugoslavia, and makes a special study of the nature of revolutions.

Among people in the industrially advanced countries fears about future wars tend to focus on nuclear weapons carried by long-range missiles, on other possible methods of mass destruction, and on the dangers of open conflict between major powers such as the United States and the Soviet Union, or others. But to be concerned only with the threat of world-wide thermonuclear war is to ignore the character of actual warfare since 1945. Guerrilla wars have been in progress, more or less continuously, in one part of the world or another, but always in economically underdeveloped countries. We can see such wars continuing today and, looking at the world of the future, one can only predict a series of guerrilla wars arising from the grave social unrest that is latent in large regions of the earth.

It is a potent form of warfare available to the most technically backward populations and scarcely susceptible at all to control by international treaty or other disarmament measures. If the nuclear stalemate continues between the major powers, guerrilla warfare will persist as the principal military factor of our time. As we have seen in the recent past, major powers may be drawn into antiguerrilla operations; in turn there may be intervention on behalf of the guerrillas so that, superficially, the struggle may come to resemble a conventional war. There is an ever-present risk that what begins as a revolutionary civil war may grow and grow until major powers are in open conflict. With a view both to avoiding errors in response to guerrilla outbreaks and, above all, to dispel conditions in which such outbreaks are likely to occur, it is essential to understand the character and motives of guerrilla warfare. Only on that basis, too, is it possible to approach the question of how and where guerrilla warfare may be waged in the future.

Guerrilla Wars of the Recent Past

The distinction between guerrilla warfare and other military and paramilitary activities that may resemble it is best illustrated from experiences in occupied Europe during World War II. Then, we witnessed various forms of resistance against German rule, but not all of them could be described as guerrilla warfare. In each occupied country the resistance movement had its own special style and waged war in its own way. Some of these actions assumed the character of national wars continued after military defeat, with the sole purpose of ending the German rule. Such was the case particularly in industrialized countries with good national and social cohesion (Norway, Denmark, the Netherlands, Belgium, and France). There was little or no purpose beyond the defeat of the Germans; no major change in the social patterns of these countries followed the end of German occupation. The forms of resistance in these countries could not be identified with the classical concept of guerrilla warfare, as I interpret it or as it will figure in the world of the future. To be sure, techniques used by these movements had much in common with those of guerrilla warfare: the use of irregular troops; reliance on elusiveness, knowledge of the local terrain, and sympathy from a large section of the civilian population; sabotage and ambush; capture of arms and supplies from the enemy. But both the motives and organization of these resistance activities lacked the political and revolutionary character of guerrilla warfare.

Consider now the economically underdeveloped parts of Europe during World War II. In these countries, particularly those of southern Europe, there were pre-existing social and political conflicts when the Germans or Italians occupied them. Here the resistance assumed much more clearly political forms, and in Yugoslavia, Albania, and Greece a species of guerrilla warfare appeared. Because these countries were economically backward there was little or no working class in the historical sense of that term; the guerrilla movements found their social basis in the peasantry, by far the most numerous part of the populations.

Guerrilla warfare in these countries was not exclusively military in purpose, in the technical sense of the defeat of the German occupying forces. It was also aimed at the destruction of pre-existing institutions, either domestic or foreign in origin, that represented barriers to social emancipation within the countries. The guerrilla fighter was thus, basically, a social reformer. In the very process of fighting, new institutions were created, particularly the new type of army, molded from the guerrilla units with an eye to its social and political character as well as to the special strategy and tactics of guerrilla warfare.

The nature of the guerrilla war depended as much upon circumstances as upon ideology. Although the Communist Party took the leading role in Yugoslavia, for example, the warfare there was quite different from the operations of the partisans in the occupied parts of the Soviet Union. Soviet resistance behind the German lines was the strongest in occupied Europe, both in terms of the number of partisans and in the style of the military operations, but the Soviet partisans were an auxiliary arm of the Red Army, centrally directed, with the particular task of harassing the rear of the German army and its lines of communication, in concert with the operations of the regular army and with specific tactical aims. By contrast, the guerrilla army in Yugoslavia was self-created and had no regular army on which to depend. It was a new kind of army, springing out of a revolutionary situation in occupied Yugoslavia. New civil organs of power were formed, together with the new army.

The strength of the guerrilla movements in Yugoslavia, Albania, and Greece, compared with those of other economically underdeveloped countries of occupied Europe, needs some explanation. Spontaneous resistance by the population at large is of primary importance because, without it, organized resistance cannot prosper. But spontaneous resistance is not sufficient; only when backed with ideology and organization did it bear fruit. But the guerrilla ideology had to match the mood of the majority of the population, typically in the national aim of eliminating not only German rule but also all foreign influences and the social structures linked to them. It also had to be an ideology matching the facts of life. Resistance movements survived when there was no discrepancy between ethical principles and real life; otherwise they were subject to internal crisis.

With the origins of guerrilla warfare lying in the spontaneous resistance and social discontents of the general population, on whom it depends for active support, it follows that measures of intimidation or reprisal by the opposing regular forces have the opposite effect to what is intended by them. In Europe, when political and organizational factors favored the guerrilla movement, reprisals by the Germans led, not to secure rule over docile masses, but, on the contrary, to even more determined revolt than before, with more of the population joining the guerrillas. As a general principle in guerrilla warfare, manpower is fundamental to victory, and is to be valued above control of territory. A guerrilla war is essentially a psychological and political war. The decisive role of morale in warfare is nowhere so obvious as in a guerrilla movement, which is usually confronted by strong enemy forces equipped with powerful weapons and having total command of the air.

But a guerrilla war is not a closed system, immune to other world events. Comparison of the outcome for the Yugoslav and

Greek movements shows the influence of the Soviet Union, the United Kingdom, and the United States, which had carried the main burden in the war against Germany. After 1941 the Adriatic region was not regarded by the Allies, or the Germans for that matter, as a major theater of war. The guerrilla warfare sprang up before any direct aid was delivered by the Allies; when aid came, it was of political importance but only secondarily significant from a military point of view. Yet the eventual success of the movements was settled by secret agreements between the Soviet Union, the United Kingdom, and the United States, concerning the division of influence in liberated Europe. Greece was put firmly in the Western sphere of influence, and the Soviet Union refused to intervene when British troops crushed the Greek resistance movement in December 1944; the social revolution for which the guerrillas had fought did not occur. Similar motives led Moscow to send instructions to Palmiro Togliatti that the Italian partisans were not to occupy the factories of Turin and Milan, at the end of the war. Yugoslavia, on the other hand, was "fifty-fifty" in relation to the Eastern and Western spheres of influence, and no doubt this fact was of great importance in allowing the final political success of the Yugoslav guerrilla war.

Since 1945 guerrilla warfare has exhibited almost all the features I have ascribed to it in the narrow European context. It has occurred in the economically underdeveloped countries of Africa and Southeast Asia and in Cuba, all inhabited by peasant masses. It has been nationalist in spirit, directed against colonial rule or domestic governments dominated by foreign influences. The conditions for success are still the same: for example, that the guerrilla movement cannot thrive in a countryside that does not give them active support. In Malaya most of the guerrillas were Chinese and represented a minority of the local population; they were defeated. In post-1945 guerrilla movements, as in Europe, severe retaliatory measures by the opposing forces have strengthened rather than weakened the guerrillas.

Successful guerrilla warfare is essentially an art of the undogmatic and the original-minded social reformer. The political springs of guerrilla warfare have changed since 1945; Communists have not the special place they had in the European guerrilla wars. In Cuba guerrilla warfare against the former regime was started against the wishes of the Cuban Communist Party. During the Algerian war, the French Communist Party took no strong action in support of the Algerian guerrillas, even though it was backed by one-fifth of the French electorate and could have called general strikes or sought to subvert French troops in Algeria. The party's behavior was similar during the French Army's struggle with the guerrillas in Indo-China.

It would indeed be rash to generalize about the political or geopolitical connotations of guerrilla movements, or seek to apply some conspiratorial theory of history to them. Despite many similarities of conditions and governing principles, the movements in Cuba, Algeria, and Vietnam have differed markedly in their historical, social, and international traits. The relations or conflicts between guerrilla movements and great powers are, as in the case of Europe, very important but not necessarily decisive. In particular, material aid from outside is not vital for guerrillas who are accustomed to seizing their arms from the enemy and otherwise living a very simple life. (For the same reasons, any policy of bombing supposed "lines of communication" is likely to be futile.)

On the other hand, the established rule and institutions against which guerrilla warfare is directed are characteristically dependent on foreign support—political, financial, material, and often military, too. Without such support the war could not continue because if, as we have defined it, a guerrilla movement matches the political wishes of the general populations, the existing government could not survive; in other words, the event would be a brief revolution rather than a protracted guerrilla war. There are now few nations on earth in which some great power does not have an interest in maintaining the existing regime, for the principle of "spheres of influence" now extends far from the Elbe and the Adriatic. Therefore, in many countries, one would predict that attempts at social revolution would lead to long drawn-out guerrilla wars.

The Foci of Revolution

Reformist revolutions do not occur in countries with broadly contented populations such as the industrialized "welfare states." Standards of living of the industrially advanced countries are rising continuously. These countries have good reason to feel materially contented, though perhaps their consciences should be uneasy. With one-sixth of the world's population they dispose of three-quarters of the world's wealth, as measured by gross income. The gap is widening between the developed and underdeveloped countries.

In many underdeveloped countries, in Latin America, Southeast Asia, and parts of Africa, the social tensions associated with economic backwardness are potentially explosive. Not only is the theoretical average income very low by the standards of the industrially advanced countries, but great inequalities may exist in the distribution of that income because of the social and economic structures of the nations concerned. These structures may also be a positive impediment to increase in national wealth, because the strata of society that, by virtue of conservative patriarchal, tribal, and feudal relations, controls the surplus wealth is not prepared to invest it productively in modern ways. Just as the gap between rich and poor nations is widening, so are the richer sectors of some underdeveloped countries becoming richer while the poor grow poorer. These sources of strain are compounded with the effects of the population explosion, and the outlook for the world's poor is indeed bitter. Populations will tend to grow most rapidly in the very countries where the people are poorest; in the underdeveloped regions as a whole, the rate of growth is expected to be twice as great as in the industrialized countries.

The statistics of world poverty and exploding populations, and grim evidence at times of crisis and famine of the human realities that underlie the statistics, have long been available to the great powers. Yet they have failed to agree on a common plan for massive aid without political "strings," which would accelerate development and release hundreds of millions of people from the tightening grip of despair. Relatively little aid is available from truly "neutral" sources such as the United Nations. Aid given bilaterally, even with subjectively pure and humane motives, will tend to be seen as politically motivated by dissident elements within the receiving country—as a foreign influence of the very kind that bolsters the existing regime, the kind that nationalist guerrilla wars are fought to end. Similarly, investments of foreign capital, useful though they may be in strictly economic terms, may well become a focus for nationalist and revolutionary discontent, especially if the profits are exported and if the investors form a political alliance with the regime. Many commentators treat multi-lateral (United Nations) and bilateral aid as though they were merely interchangeable sources of funds for economic development, without appreciating the great subjective differences, from the viewpoint of a nationalist rebel. In short, economic aid with conscious or unconscious political con- notations, just as much as military and political assistance, may reinforce rather than diminish the unrest in the poor countries of the world, even though massive economic aid is the only way of removing the long-term economic causes of the unrest.

Unless there is a fresh, concerted approach to world development, by the powerful and rich countries of East and West, neither the scale nor the manner of economic assistance is likely to prevent violent outbreaks of guerrilla-style warfare in country after country, as poverty and exploitation become worse than the peasantry will tolerate. I have already mentioned Latin America, Southeast Asia, and parts of Africa as the principal regions where such wars must be expected. Today, the population of Latin America is about 200 million; by the year 2000, it will be about 500 million, unless famine supervenes. It is simply not credible that such growth can occur without major social changes in the countries of Latin America. If those changes are not brought about voluntarily by the ruling strata, popular revolutions will occur. As it is unlikely that they will be allowed to take their course swiftly and without foreign intervention, long and terrible guerrilla wars will ensue.

Guerrilla Warfare and New Weapons

A general feature of guerrilla warfare is as plain in Vietnam in the 1960s as it was in Algeria in the 1950s or Yugoslavia in the 1940s. It is that technical superiority in arms and logistic support possessed by the forces opposing the guerrillas is quite unimportant in determining the outcome of the war. A second general feature is that military commanders tend to be blind to the true character of a guerrilla movement that they are fighting, and that they make the same political, psychological, and tactical mistakes over and over again. This is not the place to discuss guerrilla strategy and tactics in general, but something should be said about their relation to the fearsome new weapons that military science and technology are making available to regular forces.

From a military point of view the art of guerrilla warfare is largely a matter of improvisation and opportunism. As I have mentioned, greater importance attaches to conserving manpower than to holding ground. With this principle in mind, the guerrilla is always ready, if need be, to run away and hide. Consequently, when regular ground or air forces attack with powerful modern weapons, the guerrilla makes it his business not to be present. It is possible that areas of open country which are regularly patrolled on the ground or surveyed from the air will be entirely denied to him, unless he moves in the guise of a civilian. The use of chemical agents to defoliate trees may rob the guerrilla of cover in some places. A massive sweep through a particular area by the regular forces may force him out of it, temporarily. The important point is that, unless the regular forces are prepared to lay waste to the entire country, with nuclear weapons for example (which cannot correspond with any rational political goal), there will always be somewhere for the guerrilla to conceal himself from attack by modern weapons systems. From his hiding place he can emerge at a moment of his own choosing to attack the enemy at a vulnerable point. The only strategy open to the regular forces is to attempt to eliminate the guerrillas, one by one, in infantry engagements over a huge area and a long period of time. The war becomes uncontrollably large and costly in lives and materials for the regular forces.

If the guerrilla movement (by our earlier definition) is supported by a large section of the population, it has a reservoir of manpower on which to draw. Clumsy, destructive, and impatient action by the regular forces will always tend to drive civilians into the guerrilla camps. A characteristic of advanced and powerful weapons systems by land and air seems to be that, despite the allegedly "sophisticated" electronic systems for fire control, the impression at the target is of clumsiness and purposeless destruction. For this reason advanced weapons systems may be much more of a liability than an asset in antiguerrilla warfare. And even if some highly lethal new weapon, such as a nerve gas or an infectious microorganism, were used effectively against the guerrillas, that local military victory of the regular forces would be bought at a price of moral catastrophe that would make political victory utterly impossible.

A secondary consideration about the use of advanced or novel weapons against guerrillas is that, as the guerrillas rely largely upon captured arms, these weapons, too, are quite likely to fall into their hands and be turned upon the original owners.

To sum up, guerrilla warfare is likely to remain militarily viable, whatever weapons are used to combat it, unless those weapons are so morally indefensible or indiscriminately destructive that the user forfeits all his political purposes. The well-organized guerrilla movement in a country of reasonable size, based on popular support, is indestructible except by enormously costly and protracted infantry warfare which is almost beyond the resources of even the biggest nations. In this sense, it represents the eternal truth that you cannot destroy a political belief without killing, one by one, all the people who possess it. That is something that no scientific advances in weaponry can alter, even though they make the killing easier to accomplish.

THE NATIONAL COMMITMENTS RESOLUTION

Senate of the United States

Whereas accurate definition of the term "national commitment" in recent years has become obscured: Now, therefore be it
Resolved, That (1) a national commitment for the purpose of this resolution means the use of the Armed Forces of the United States on foreign territory, or a promise to assist a foreign country, government, or people by the use of the Armed Forces or financial resources of the United States, either immediately or upon the happening of certain events, and (2) it is the sense of the Senate that a national commitment by the United States results only from affirmative action taken by the executive and legislative branches of the United States Government by means of a treaty, statute, or concurrent resolution of both Houses of Congress specifically providing for such commitment.

Senate Resolution 85, Expressing the sense of the Senate relative to commitments to foreign powers, June 25, 1969, 91st Congress, 1st Session, 1969.
The Resolution as finally approved by the Senate was changed slightly from the version approved by the Foreign Relations Committee. The Committee's recommendation read as follows:

Whereas accurate definition of the term "national commitment" in recent years has become obscured: Now, therefore, be it *Resolved*, that it is the sense of the Senate that a national commitment by the United States to a foreign power necessarily and exclusively results from affirmative action taken by the executive and legislative branches of the United States Government through means of a treaty, convention or other legislative instrumentality specifically intended to give effect to such a commitment.

THE NATIONAL COMMITMENTS RESOLUTION

Senate Committee on Foreign Relations

Chairman of the Committee is Senator J. William Fulbright (D., Ark.). Senator Gale McGee (D., Wyoming) presents a minority view.

For the Resolution

Our country has come far toward the concentration in its national executive of unchecked power over foreign relations, particularly over the disposition and use of the Armed Forces. So far has this process advanced that, in the committee's view, it is no longer accurate to characterize our government, in matters of foreign relations, as one of separated powers checked and balanced against each other. . . .The executive has acquired virtual supremacy over the making as well as the conduct of the foreign relations of the United States.

The principal cause of the constitutional imbalance has been the circumstance of American involvement and responsibility in a violent and unstable world. Since its entry into World War II the United States has been deeply, and to a great extent involuntarily, involved in a series of crises which have revolutionized and are continuing to revolutionize the world of the 20th century. There is no end in sight to these global commotions; there is no end in sight to deep American involvement in them. Because of the indefinite duration of our country's involvement in world crisis, it is more rather than less necessary to examine the effects of this involvement on the American system of government. Unless it is believed that a government of limited and divided powers is no longer feasible, or no longer desirable, insofar as foreign relations is concerned, it is incumbent upon us to ask how such a government can be accommodated to modern world conditions.

The committee believes that changed conditions, though the principle cause of the present constitutional imbalance, are not its sole cause. It believes that events have been aided and abetted by what Justice Frankfurter called the "generative force of unchecked

From the Senate Committee on Foreign Relations, *Report Together with Minority Views on National Commitments*, 91st Congress, 1st Session, April 16, 1969: Majority Comments, pp. 7, 9, 33-34; Minority View, pp. 39-44.

disregard of the restrictions that fence in even the most disinterested assertion of authority.". . .

The committee believes that the division of powers spelled out in the Constitution is in fact compatible with our country's role as a world power. The principle purpose of that division, as Justice Brandeis noted, is liberty rather than efficiency, but, unless speed is equated with efficiency and deliberation held to be an obstacle to it, there is no reason why we cannot have under our system of government a foreign policy which is efficient as well as democratically made. Indeed, it can be argued that the division and limitation of powers are indispensable to American foreign policy. . . .

The committee does not believe that formal declarations of war are the only available means by which Congress can authorize the President to initiate limited or general hostilities. Joint resolutions such as those pertaining to Formosa, the Middle East, and the Gulf of Tonkin are a proper method of granting authority, provided that they are precise as to what is to be done and for what period of time, and provided that they do in fact *grant authority* and not merely express approval of undefined action to be taken by the President. That distinction is of the greatest importance. As used in the recent past, joint resolutions have been instruments of political control over the Congress in the hand of the President, enabling him to claim support for any action he may choose to take and so phrased as to express Congressional acquiescence in the constitutionally unsound contention that the President in his capacity as Commander in Chief has the authority to commit the country to war.

The committee therefore recommends that, in considering future resolutions involving the use or possible use of the Armed Forces, Congress—

1. debate the proposed resolution at sufficient length to establish a legislative record showing the intent of Congress;

2. use the words *authorize* or *empower* or such other language as will leave no doubt that Congress alone has the right to authorize the initiation of war and that, in granting the President authority to use the Armed Forces, Congress is granting him power that he would not otherwise have;

3. state in the resolution as explicitly as possible under the circumstances the kind of military action that is being authorized and the place and purpose of its use; and

4. put a time limit on the resolution, thereby assuring Congress the opportunity to review its decision and extend or terminate the President's authority to use military force.

Over the nearly two centuries of our constitutional history power over various aspects of our national life has shifted between the executive and legislature depending on which, at a particular time, seemed to have greater energy or competence for performing the function in question. Within limits this flexibility is desirable; it has been one important factor in the survival and adaptability of our Constitution. When, however, as in the case of the war power, a shift takes place which is so great as to transfer authority from one branch of government to the other, and in so doing to negate the intent of the Constitution, there arises a threat to democracy and constitutional government. Whether the war power is misused or not by a particular President is not the fundamental point; the danger to constitutional government arises from the fact that the President or some future President will be in a *position* to misuse power.

The committee is well aware. . .that one of the reasons for the flow of the war power out of the hands of Congress and into the hands of the President has been the failure of Congress to adapt its power over the armed forces to the circumstances of the nuclear age. Tacitly acknowledging a lack of confidence in its ability to make that adaptation, Congress has permitted its war power to be transferred to the hands of an executive which, though less susceptible to self-doubt than the Congress, is no less susceptible to error.

Already possessing vast powers over our country's foreign relations, the executive, by acquiring the authority to commit the country to war, now exercises something approaching absolute power over the life or death of every living American—to say nothing of millions of other people all over the world. There is no human being or group of human beings alive wise and competent enough to be entrusted with such vast power. Plenary powers in the hands of any man or group threaten all other men with tyranny or disaster. Recognizing the impossibility of assuring the wise exercise of power by any one man or institution, the American Constitution divided that power among many men and several institutions and, in so doing, limited the ability of any one to impose tyranny or disaster on the country. The concentration in the hands of the President of virtually unlimited authority over matters of war and peace has all but removed the limits to executive power in the most important single area of our national life. Until they are restored the American people will be threatened with tyranny or disaster.

Against the Resolution—Senator McGee

Senate Resolution 85 is an ill-advised way in which to seek to achieve some sort of balance in foreign policy matters between the executive and legislative branches. It could even jeopardize the fixing of ultimate responsibility in foreign policy decisions. . . .

The issue of executive power in foreign policy has tended to rear its head during the administrations of strong Presidents and to languish through inattention during the administrations of weak Presidents. And without exception the trend toward a stronger and stronger executive role in foreign policy has coincided with the rising preeminence of the United States in world politics during the 20th century. Presidents Theodore Roosevelt, Taft, and Wilson expanded that role materially. But the most significant changes have occurred since the beginning of World War II. Under President Franklin Roosevelt the use of executive agreements experienced a sharp increase. In particular his commitments to the transfer of destroyers for bases, the extension of the Monroe Doctrine principle to Iceland and Greenland, and the "shoot on sight" edict to American naval forces in the Atlantic are often cited as serious encroachments by the Executive Office on the assumed foreign policy "partnership" between the President and the Congress.

Concomitant with the incidents preceding American involvement in World War II was the sudden emergence of the United States as the most powerful nation in the world, largely as a result of that conflict. As a great power, American actions cause reverberations all around the globe and must, therefore, be carefully weighed and delicately executed. Not infrequently they must be carried out swiftly. The decisionmaking process may be reduced by events to a matter of a single day, or even hours. On more than one occasion the time allotted by crisis incidents to those who must make the decisions has been less than the time it would take to assemble a quorum of the Congress.

Possibly an even greater factor which presses for increasing the power of the President in making foreign policy in recent decades has been the advent of the nuclear age. We live in a time when 15 minutes could spell the difference between life and death for millions of people—possibly even for life itself on earth. In the past 25 years there have been times when the only sure thing that could be said about the next 24 hours was that no one really knew if we would live through them.

More than ever, consequently, the authority to make decisions and take action supporting them must be located in one place. From the rather meager beginnings of our constitutional system when Congress shared more directly with the President some of the policy processes, we have now come to an age when the pressure of time and the multiplicity of other issues scarcely allow the Congress more than a passing glance at some of the most important decisions in the history of mankind.

It is imperative, therefore, that in determining a judgment on Senate Resolution 85 we recast the role of the Congress—and more particularly of the Senate—in foreign affairs against the backdrop of the nuclear age. Whether the division of responsibility between the President and Senate can follow the lines of other years is a question central to the present dispute. Whether Senate Resolution 85 goes to the heart of that dispute, moreover, is also open to serious doubts. . . .

It would appear to invade areas of responsibility reserved under the Constitution for the President alone. Two areas of executive responsibility will illustrate the point:

One, the President alone under the Constitution has authority to recognize foreign governments and to enter into commitments which implement that recognition. In the conduct of the foreign relations of the United States, the President necessarily must have the power to make many commitments to foreign governments.

Two, as Commander in Chief of the Armed Forces of the United States, the President has the sole responsibility over them either within our country or outside it. Reasonable men may well disagree as to the conditions under which he should do so. The President has the constitutional power to send U.S. military forces abroad when he deems it to be in the national interest.

Because Senate Resolution 85 implies that the President and the Congress together would be the exclusive means by which the Government of the United States in the future could enter into commitments with a foreign power, it runs counter to constitutional intent.

The sponsors of Senate Resolution 85 have gone to great pains to assure us that they have no intentions of tampering with the constitutional powers of the President. Yet, the majority report on Senate Resolution 85 is replete with references to and charges against a "constitutional imbalance" which, it is asserted, has resulted from power grabs by a succession of Chief Executives. Whatever the intent of the sponsors, the mere language of the resolution calls to the forefront current constitutional misgivings loaded with serious implications. . . .

At best, Senate Resolution 85 has only the capabilities of mischief-making with the responsibilities of the President of the United States in foreign affairs, particularly in times like the present. In a world of 130-odd sovereign nations, some of the more powerful of which are monolithic in structure and capable of quick decision-making, the need for a President of the United States to act with dispatch has already arisen. It will surely recur again and again. Presidential decisionmaking in foreign policy provides a quality of leadership superior to the alternatives available under our system.

Does it strengthen the security of our country or serve the national interest to hobble the executive branch in times of crisis?

The answer must be no. Mindful as we all are of the risk involved in increasing executive power in the field of foreign affairs, there would appear to be no reasonable alternative to assuming those risks save at the price of confusion, delay, and even inaction through some series of yet unspecified procedures implied in the commitments resolution.

Much as one may hesitate to repose such frightening authority in the executive branch alone, it is necessary to acknowledge that the alternative of joint dialog with the Congress in those particular circumstances would more likely obfuscate rather than clarify the issues. To have to revert to Senate debate and discussion at a time like that would be cumbersome at the very least and disastrous to the national interest in the extreme.

It serves to point up what has happened to the foreign policymaking process in a time of instant communications. The machinery of policy decisions assembled nearly two centuries ago simply has not been able to keep pace with the changing requirements of present-day realities.

At a time when the world is getting smaller and when the problems among nations are becoming more complex, it ill behooves the leader of the free world to move away from its share of responsibility in coping with international crises. Yet, Senate Resolution 85 would have the effect of doing just that. . . .

It is conceivable, should this resolution be enacted, that some President at some time would be required to plunge into a military crisis—say of the dimensions of Lebanon or Laos—in which he reached the conclusion that it was in the national interest to commit a limited number of troops in quick order. Such a decision in the wake of passage of Senate Resolution 85 would instantly become clouded with an aura of illegitimacy. The public doubts which would quickly surface in that circumstance could only impair the efforts of the President of the United States to act with dispatch and to conclude successfully the commitment. The implications of Senate Resolution 85 are heavily laden with overtones of neoisolationism.

If the democratic process is to be salvaged, we must be prepared to move toward more clean-cut presidential authority in foreign policy. . . .

Is there, then, a meaningful role for the U.S. Senate in the shaping of foreign policy? The answer, of course, is yes. If the Senate is to succeed in achieving this new role, it, too, must update its procedures in the foreign relations field as well as upgrade its sense of responsibility by focusing more and more on larger and larger questions. The Senate could afford to address itself well in advance of crises to the broad outlines and directions of American policy. This becomes far more constructive as well as influential than in responding principally to crisis situations after the fact. . . .

10

America and the Developing Nations

As we saw in Chapter 2, there is a persisting problem of poverty in America; and the complexities of the problem become more apparent as we develop new public policies designed to dispose of it. Still, the very poor are a declining minority, and it seems reasonable to expect that a sustained effort of national will could bring domestic poverty within manageable proportions.

On the international scale, the problem is vastly more acute and difficult. The prosperous are in a minority. There are many hundreds of millions of poor people, among them great numbers who constantly live on the very edge of survival—a situation that cannot be fully comprehended by the Western imagination.

In the face of this, both morality and self-interest would seem to encourage the rich nations to give to the poor. The moral principle is self-evident. The claim of self-interest should hardly be more difficult to establish. The poor have usually envied the rich, and the population explosion means that the gap between the rich and the poor nations grows dangerously wider every year.

Yet our foreign aid program has been steadily reduced over the past few years despite the increasing affluence of America. In part, this is because the practice of foreign aid has embraced many different purposes—some military, some political, some humanitarian—and extraordinary confusion has resulted from the failure to distinguish between them. Also, the economic, social, and political systems of the underdeveloped countries are usually not well geared to Western-style industrialization, and the surge of economic growth which the givers of aid anticipate all too often fails to happen. Nor are the recipient nations grateful for the help which is given them, for they may harbor deep resentments resulting in the kind of hostile reactions noted by Mario Pei. Again, if one of the purposes of aid is to reduce the danger of revolution, this is by no means assured; as Samuel P. Huntington notes, in some cases the reforms that accompany aid programs actually increase instability and the potential for revolution. Consequently, the foreign assistance program is now under attack, not only from the conservative quarters traditionally hostile to it but also from many who have become disenchanted with the unduly hopeful claims made year after year by successive Administrations.

Faced with this growing body of criticism, it has become an invariable practice for Presidents to appoint blue-ribbon advisory committees to review the foreign aid programs. John Kennedy set up a committee under General Lucius Clay (whose report, though intended to help the program, was used by the congressional opposition to bolster its case for deep cuts in its budget). Lyndon Johnson's committee, chaired by James A. Perkins, offered a strong rebuttal to the critics and advocated increased outlays. Still, the opposition of both conservatives and non-conservatives continues. And the new Administration, of course, has had to undertake a new study; Richard Nixon has appointed the Task Force on International Development, headed by Rudolph A. Peterson, President of the Bank of America.

Robert L. Heilbroner's article examines the question of foreign assistance in the broader context of foreign policy after Vietnam. At the heart of his policy is neutrality toward the revolutionary movement emerging in many developing nations. To Heilbroner, the basic defect of our past policies has been their association with the status quo, often meaning reactionary forces and government. Huntington, on the other hand, suggests that we have given aid to a variety of systems. He believes we must pursue more cautious policies in the future, that we should encourage political stability wherever possible, and that a prime means to this end is support for the creation of effective political parties.

The essay by Harold R. Isaacs points to the fact that there is an important racial component in the distrust between the established, industrialized countries on the one hand and the "Third World" on the other. He suggests that there is a relationship between this factor and the racial crisis in America.

The final selection by the United Nations Economic and Social Council raises a disturbing question "involving developed and developing countries alike." A central purpose of most programs of development assistance is to promote technological advances and long-range, if not immediate industrialization. But already technological processes are doing serious damage to the human environment. What will happen to that environment if the programs of development assistance succeed, and more and more countries, with rapidly increasing populations, move toward our level of industrialization? This is not to suggest that we should not help other nations lift themselves out of poverty by becoming more industrialized. But it is urgently necessary to recognize that an environmental crisis is already upon us and to engage all nations in collaborative plans to deal with that crisis.

THE CASE FOR DEVELOPMENT ASSISTANCE

President's General Advisory Committee on Foreign Assistance Programs

Chairman of the Committee was James A. Perkins. Members included Dwayne O. Andreas, David E. Bell, Eugene R. Black, Josephine Young Case, Luther H. Foster, Alfred M. Gruenther, J. George Harrar, Theodore M. Hesburgh, William R. Hewlett, Edward S. Mason, Franklin D. Murphy, Rudolph A. Peterson, David Rockefeller, Frank Stanton, William J. Zellerbach. George Meany disassociated himself from the report.

Can the U.S. Afford to Assist Less Developed Countries?

Development assistance programs have been under heavy attack, particularly in the Congress, on the ground that the United

From President's General Advisory Committee on Foreign Assistance Programs, *Report on Development Assistance in the New Administration,* October 25, 1968, pp. 10, 12-16.

States cannot support development assistance and at the same time meet our overriding defense needs, make long-overdue expenditures on our cities, and stop the drain on our balance of payments.

The Committee feels that domestic budget costs of development assistance programs have not in fact been large relative to other claims... Appropriations for development assistance programs ... were only about 2 percent of Federal appropriations for all government programs. In contrast, we spend about 40 percent of our budget on defense, 8 percent paying interest on the national debt, 4 percent for veterans' benefits, and 3 percent for space programs...

Development assistance is now extremely low in its balance of payments costs. Only 6 percent of recent gross A.I.D. expenditures have added to the balance of payments deficit, and they are offset by interest and principal payments on past loans. Virtually all of the P.L. 480 expenditures are on U.S. goods and shipping.

The Committee does not wish to understate the importance of the other needs of the country, or to advise on the entire scale of priorities. The Committee does feel that development assistance has a strong claim among the nation's appropriations for living in the world, which include money for defense, military assistance, diplomatic relations, and other international programs.... This total was about $90 billion in FY 1968; development assistance was $4 billion. The Committee believes that this share should be larger in view of the benefits that the development assistance program delivers.

It is important to remember that the cost of neglecting the economic development and stability of the poor nations may be great. Had we neglected Korea economically after the armistice there, we could very well have been drawn back into a military conflict as a result of the economic and political weakness of that country.

Our conclusion that the United States can afford what is called for in development assistance is reinforced by the fact that other advanced nations much less wealthy than the U.S. are now devoting *larger* shares of their national income to official assistance than we are. In 1964, two ... nations surpassed us in the proportion of their income devoted to official development assistance. By 1967 we had become laggards, with both France and Germany ahead of us, as well as Australia, Belgium, the Netherlands, and Portugal, and we were tied with the United Kingdom. The deep appropriations cuts imposed in Fiscal Years 1968 and 1969 will cause the

United States to fall still further behind other aid suppliers unless the trends are reversed.

Does Development Assistance Lead to Military Entanglement?

In reaction to the Vietnam war, some Americans are afraid that development assistance programs may involve the country in dangerous military entanglements.

The Committee finds that the historical evidence does not support the charge. In Korea, military involvement preceded substantial development assistance. In Vietnam, U.S. activities have been security-oriented from the beginning, and the decisions made at each step of the way have not been compelled by simple development assistance relations. In the Dominican Republic our small assistance program to the Trujillo government had been ended before the revolution which led to the landing of U.S. forces.

On the other hand, armed conflicts have occurred between or within countries where we have had substantial economic assistance programs, without our becoming militarily involved. This was the case in the 1965 India-Pakistan fighting, the 1967 Arab-Israeli war, the civil wars in the Congo, and the current civil war in Nigeria. Indeed, the influence gained through development cooperation has helped our diplomats in their efforts to avert or to settle such conflicts.

Fundamentally, the Committee believes that development cooperation provides the U.S. with an alternative to military involvement for playing a continuing role in the less developed world. Doves and hawks on our military commitment in Vietnam can equally support assistance for development.

Can Development Assistance Be Effective?

Critics of development assistance often question whether it accomplishes its purposes. Certainly the experience of the last two decades includes many mistakes and disappointments. But the Committee believes that the record as a whole is one of remarkable success for such a difficult enterprise.

Sometimes the challenge of ineffectiveness is made because the goals of development assistance are misunderstood. A frequent criticism, for example, is that major recipients of aid disagree with the United States on particular foreign policy issues. But the goal of having all countries toe the line on all aspects of our foreign policy, besides being infeasible, is not a desirable one for a world community of free nations. The general pattern of our relations with most of the less developed countries has been friendly, open, and cooperative. Development assistance cannot buy agreement when the basis for it—in parallel national interests—does not exist, but where interests are not in conflict, development assistance can provide benefits in more cooperative attitudes and better working relations.

A central objective of development assistance is cooperation with friendly countries to achieve *self-sustaining* economic and political progress. There is by now a great deal of evidence that assistance programs are succeeding in promoting economic development. Gross National Products in Israel, Iran, Taiwan, and Greece have grown at annual rates of 8 or 9 percent in the 1960's, and after receiving large amounts of aid for many years, these countries have graduated from the need for assistance on easy terms. Turkey and Korea have made substantial progress, and are well on the way to self-sustaining growth. The annual growth rate of Gross National Product in all the less developed countries as a group from 1960 to 1967 has been about 5 percent, which is comparable to growth in the developed countries and in line with goals for the Development Decade of the 1960's that seemed highly optimistic when adopted.

Graduation from the need for development assistance is certainly not the only measure of success. Countries are at different stages of development, and achievements must be judged by different standards. In some cases modern institutions must be built before the country can sustain a major development program with large-scale capital assistance. Assistance programs in a good many African countries are devoted mainly to technical assistance projects aimed at building such institutions. The establishment of modern training colleges for secondary school teachers in Nigeria and Uganda are examples of crucial progress whatever the trend of GNP.

In many countries, particularly in Asia, the race between food and population must be won before self-sustaining growth can be contemplated. U.S. assistance has already had unmistakable effects on this race. Family planning programs in recent years have begun to reduce birth rates in Taiwan and Korea. The dramatic breakthroughs in wheat and rice production in India, Pakistan, and other countries of South and East Asia are perhaps the most exciting accomplishment of all. They are particularly striking because there is an influential body of opinion which holds that nations so tradition-bound cannot progress economically without long-term changes in popular attitudes. The recent experience in Asia of millions of farmers adopting fertilizers, new seeds, and improved methods demonstrates that profitable investments will be undertaken, and older methods changed, even in traditional societies. This too is an important form of success.

In still other countries, development assistance programs have been significant mainly in inducing governments to adopt economic policies that are more congenial to progress. In Brazil, for example, a U.S.-assisted program of monetary and fiscal discipline, import liberalization, and tax and savings reforms has been carried through, and though inflation continues (at lower rates) the economy is now growing again in real terms.

Development assistance is a long-term commitment, however. In a single country, under favorable circumstances, the transition to self-sustaining growth normally takes at least a decade or two. In view of the large number of countries, their diverse circumstances, and the fact that many are not yet able to make full use of capital inflows, the need for development assistance will continue. Moreover, since economic development is a disruptive process politically and socially, there may be interruptions because of political instability as well as because of economic mistakes. When we decide to assist development, we necessarily open ourselves to the risks of occasional disappointment. The Committee believes that these risks must simply be accepted, and that the over-all record is much more successful than is commonly recognized.

Can Development Assistance Be Managed Soundly?

Some of the sharpest criticisms of foreign assistance programs have focused on instances of scandal or mismanagement. In February, 1968, for example, widespread press coverage was given to the fact that about $100,000 of various luxury items was included in A.I.D. shipments to the Dominican Republic. This was true, and deplorable, but the suggestion that it indicated widespread mismanagement was grossly misleading. First, money for the questionable items was already being refunded to A.I.D. when the story broke. Second, the total involved was four-tenths of one percent of a crash program of support to the new government of the Dominican Republic. The Committee has been impressed with the vigorous efforts of A.I.D. to tighten administrative procedures and minimize the possibilities of misuse. These efforts must not flag.

This whole problem of managing the use of aid inputs must be considered in the context of what development assistance is trying to accomplish. It is true that many foreign governments do not manage their resources as efficiently as would the U.S. government if we were entirely responsible. Many do have more corruption. But A.I.D. is not a management agency in the receiving countries, and it cannot be so long as we respect the sovereignty of host governments. Indeed, if we tried to make it so, local management abilities would never be developed. The U.S. must work with host governments, with their vital knowledge of local needs, and an essential part of the process is strengthening local administration.

Economic assistance is used in some cases to assist new governments trying to lead their countries to recover from political or economic turmoil. The risks of waste in such programs are greater than in countries with an established momentum of development. Nonetheless, the Committee feels that external assistance on a proper scale at such critical times can have a very high pay-off. With the best management possible, some of these risks must simply be accepted for the sake of the potential benefits of a sizable and rapidly committed program. There was waste in Korea in the early fifties, but Korea's success since then suggests that it was right to push ahead with a crash program at that critical time. Development assistance is also sometimes criticized because it appears to benefit largely people who are already well-to-do in the host country. Appearances can be misleading. Rapid economic growth over many years benefits most people in a society even if large wealth differentials continue. The U.S. must deal with countries as they exist—so long as they are committed to economic and social development—and cannot by itself determine how the benefits of over-all economic progress should be distributed. We can, however, seize opportunities to support activities which broaden popular participation, build democratic institutions, and implement social reforms. Increasing emphasis should be given to such efforts in the future.

A CONSERVATIVE LOOKS AT FOREIGN AID

Mario Pei

Mario A. Pei is Professor of Romance Philology in the Graduate Faculties, Columbia University.

"The Issue of Foreign Aid" in *The America We Lost* (New York: New American Library, 1968), entire chapter. Reprinted by permission of The World Publishing Company from *The America We Lost* by Mario Pei. An NAL book. Copyright ©1968 by Mario Pei.

Foreign aid is probably one of the most widely misunderstood areas of government action, and the one in which the greatest misconceptions appear. Since foreign aid, both military and economic, costs the U.S. taxpayer close to five billion dollars a year, the question most frequently asked is: "Does not this huge sum weigh heavily upon the American economy, and is it not the major cause of red ink in our balance of international payments, and of the unrelenting pressure on our gold reserves?"

The answer is a qualified no. While over four billion dollars went out in foreign economic aid in 1964, less than one billion in gold actually left the country. Over three and a half billion dollars were used to purchase goods and services here. It was the goods and services, not the gold, that were exported. Our entire program of foreign economic aid meant a potential drain of little over 700 million on our gold stock. Too much, perhaps, and even the sums spent in the United States present a questionable feature that will be discussed later. But it is a far cry from being the sole, or even the major cause of our gold imbalance. The real major causes are the difference between what our tourists spend abroad and what foreign tourists spend here (over one and a half billion), and the difference between what American firms send out in the form of foreign investments and what our past investments bring back to us (nearly two billion).

As for foreign military aid, that has long been dwindling until now it amounts to less than a billion. How well spent is that sum is something for the military authorities to determine. Under any circumstances, it must be regarded as part of our defense budget, which few Americans, liberal or conservative, are willing to forgo, at least for the present. The only question involved is that of effectiveness, which in these days of high specialization is hardly for the layman to settle. If there is economic waste involved, it is for the military and the Congressional defense committees to do away with it.

Purely economic aid is different. It involves a philosophy of government, and there is a question of principle involved. Why foreign economic aid at all?

Such aid can be justified on only four grounds, each of which can legitimately be discussed by the layman: (1) Such aid is a charitable act whereby we relieve human misery abroad out of our own surplus resources; (2) foreign aid may serve to promote certain ends which the State Department judges beneficial to us in connection with our foreign policies; (3) it gains "goodwill" for us in the recipient nations, which again is beneficial to us; (4) it spurs the domestic economy by stimulating our production and exports, even if that extra production and those extra exports are entirely subsidized by their own beneficiaries, the American taxpayers. Note that point number 4 is generally muted and unpublicized, though it is doubtless very much in the back of the Administration's mind.

Point number 1, the alleviation of human misery abroad, is no doubt the most unselfish and praiseworthy. It is also the one that should regretfully be written off as not falling within the sphere of legitimate government activities, at home or abroad.

It is not the function of government to dole out charity to the needy, save perhaps on an emergency relief basis under circumstances of sudden disaster, such as an earthquake or a flood. The government's function is to promote the general welfare, not to relieve individual misery. A good case can be made out for quake and flood relief, in the same fashion that a public ambulance and a public hospital take immediate care of the victim of an automobile accident. *Chronic* poverty should not be subsidized or relieved by the government, though it should be the government's responsibility to see that it is prevented and abolished by wise policies. Its relief on a chronic basis properly pertains to charity-minded individuals and institutions, such as church agencies and foundations. If government steps into the charity field, it is compelling individuals to be charitable against their will, since government funds consist of tax moneys about contributing which the individual has no choice.

It is also argued that we should not attempt to relieve misery abroad while there is still much misery to relieve at home. This can be debated, but not on the plane of governmental philosophy. It is as wrong for the government to force me to give my money for the relief of poverty in American slums as for the relief of poverty in India. At best, it forces me to do good against my will, and robs of all its moral merit the contribution I might willingly make to the relief of misery.

Foreign economic aid can be and has been effectively used to promote our foreign policies and achieve certain desirable global ends. The Marshall Plan did much to speed the economic and military recovery of nations that it was to our advantage to set back on their feet. Here the big question is whether the aid is efficiently administered to produce maximum results with minimum expenditures. Another question is whether the aims and goals of such aid are invariably worthwhile from the American point of view.

This point is closely linked with that of building up goodwill abroad. Naturally, we stand to gain from having a foreign population feel kindly disposed or even grateful to us. But does economic aid achieve this goal?

There is considerable unrest among American taxpayers over the fact that nations that have been heavy recipients of our aid not only proclaim their neutrality or noncommittedness, but actively oppose our policies in the UN and elsewhere. Worse yet, they permit and even encourage public demonstrations against us at the slightest provocation, with attacks upon our embassies and consulates and burnings of USIA libraries. This has happened in Egypt, Algeria, Indonesia, Ghana and other countries too numerous to mention. It is not a series of sporadic incidents, nor can it be said that the demonstrations are spontaneous outbreaks on the part of a hot-headed minority, since in most of the countries where they have occurred the regime is of a dictatorial or semidictatorial type, and in a position to enforce a determined prohibition of such outbursts. Far too often the outbursts carry the imprint of government sanction and even encouragement. The question then legitimately arises in the American mind: "Shall we continue to subsidize and feed ingrates who bite the hand that feeds them?" If we do, we can no longer invoke the goodwill argument. We can only claim that regardless of the way the local population or its government feels about us and our aid, it suits our policies and furthers our interests to continue aiding these countries. The sign goes up: "Proceed at your own risk. You may be building up a potential enemy."

Is this a wise procedure? Should we shore up the econ-omy of an Indonesia or an Egypt that may, when the chips are down, turn that same economy to the advantage of our potential foes? Ought we not rather to withhold aid in these cases, while bestowing it with an even more open hand on countries whose leadership we can count on? And ought we not to do so without regard for the form of government of the country that gets our aid? The democracies (in our sense of the term) are generally with us and behind us in principle, though they may occasionally differ on minor matters of procedure. For countries that are not democratically run, is there much to choose, ideo-logically, between Franco's Spain and Salazar's Portugal on the one hand, Tito's Yugoslavia and Nasser's Egypt on the other? The real difference is that Franco and Salazar are willing to be firmly committed to our side, Tito and Nasser are not. If we must bolster dictatorships as a matter of foreign policy, is it not better to bolster those that are with us than those that are against us? Would we not have been better off siding firmly with Chiang Kai-shek and Batista than flirting with Mao Tse-tung and Castro? Foreign policy must be realistic if it is to be foreign policy and not a flight into the wild blue yonder. Let us help our friends, even if we don't approve of everything they do, particularly since by helping them we may get them to mend their ways. Let us thwart, or at least not help, those who are either our avowed foes or lose no opportunity to inform us that they consider us on a par with or beneath our avowed foes.

Outside of realism, there remains the issue of popular gratitude, the accumulation of that elusive substance known as goodwill. When we help a country, we expect the population to know about it and be properly grateful, or at the very least friendly. Here the form taken by foreign aid, its method of distribution, the publicity that accompanies it, become important. Here we get the story of how a Peruvian Andean village, or a clump of Nigerian huts, turn everlastingly thankful because of the Peace Corpsman in their midst; how the setting up of an Alliance for Progress organization wins the undying gratitude of the people of Ecuador; how the shipment of free tractors to Iran and Pakistan turns the natives into lifelong friends of the United States, ready to resist all Communist blandishments.

It is difficult to evaluate episodes or generalize from them. It was brought out not too long ago that "the best-kept secret in the United Arab Republic appears to be the U.S. aid program—specifically, our vast shipments of surplus farm commodities to the tune of nearly one billion dollars in twelve years." The Nassar regime, it appears, permits no publicity whatsoever in this respect, while highlighting Soviet arms shipments, to be turned against Israel, and Aswan Dam aid. The U.S. markings are carefully removed from food packages, and practically no one in Egypt knows that we are making huge contributions to the population's survival.

This brings us squarely back to the issue of charity *vs.* foreign policy. The purest form of charity is anonymous, and if that is what we want, well and good. But foreign policy and even popular gratitude are determined by the group in power. If Nasser doesn't like us, it matters little how many Egyptians we save from starvation; they will never know it was we who saved them, and the next time there is a chance to take part in an anti-American demonstration, they will cheerfully participate.

The disadvantages of unpublicized foreign aid, even in the case of thoroughly friendly countries and governments, were borne in upon me by a personal experience. Traveling by bus from Rome to Naples in the summer of 1959, we made a luncheon stop at Cassino, with a visit to the famous abbey, scene of the American air bombings in World War Two. The abbey itself had been beautifully reconstructed, and the town, below, reduced to rubble in the course of the battle, had been completely rebuilt, with ultramodern housing for all the inhabitants.

Professionally, I was interested in viewing the 960 A.D. Testimonial Formulas of Monte Cassino, which are the first attested documents of the Italian language, and are kept in the library's archives. To my request that they be shown to me, the archivist replied with an obdurate no. The documents were kept under lock and key, he said, and could not be exhibited save on very special occasions. My credentials as Professor of Romance Philology at Columbia University availed me nothing. Neither did the obvious fact that I was a native Italian speaker. I could have carried my plea to a higher authority, but there was no time. The bus was due to leave for the town in ten minutes.

Discussing the incident over the luncheon table with a local priest, I remarked that there had seemed to be in the archivist's attitude a note of hostility. Could this be due to the fact that I was an American citizen, I wondered? The priest allowed that it might be so. "But why?" I persisted. "Well," he said, "you recall what happened here during the war." "Indeed I do," said I, "but it was a clear-cut case of military necessity. Anyhow, we did our best to make amends. Both the abbey and the town were rebuilt with American help." "Who told you that?" he almost snarled. "They were rebuilt by the Italian government and the Banco del Mezzogiorno; there was no American participation whatsoever!" "And where did they get the money?" I countered. "Have you ever heard of the Marshall Plan? The American government gave the Italian government some billions of dollars to reconstruct Italy and get her back on her feet, and the Italian government, with that money, financed a lot of worthy enterprises, the rebuilding of Cassino among them."

This was news to the priest. He had, in a vague sort of way, heard about the Marshall Plan, but it had not occurred to him to link it with what had gone on in his own ·area. Nor had the Italian government taken the trouble to publicize the fact. It had taken all the credit.

This was, in a sense, beneficial to us, because we wanted the Christian Democrat government to be popular among the masses, and thus offset the Communist drive for voters. At the same time, it would not have hurt to let those same voters know that America was helping, too. This, apparently, we had not insisted on. The net result was that the local population gave us full credit for the bombings, but no credit for the reconstruction.

This, then, seems to be the score to date on economic foreign aid:

It can be and has been effective in promoting certain policy aims. Whether these aims were invariably well thought out is questionable.

A great question mark attaches to the publicitarian, or goodwill, aspect of foreign aid. By and large, only a fraction of what could have been brought to pass has worked out.

Charity is highly meritorious, particularly when it is anonymous. But is such charity on a chronic, long-range international basis a government function?

One additional facet of foreign aid remains to be discussed. To what extent is foreign aid used to spur our own domestic economy, create employment, swell up production and export figures, get rid of our surpluses, and generally add to our internal prosperity? Officially, very little is said about this. Unofficially, any member of the foreign service will readily admit that this is one of the most important features of foreign aid. You cannot produce and export four billion dollars' worth of extra goods and services without adding to your employment, purchasing power, and general prosperity. Viewed from this angle, foreign aid becomes a major item of internal economic policy, highly beneficial in one sense. In another sense, it becomes a major inflationary factor in our economy, like farm subsidies, minimum wage laws, union featherbedding, and pork-barrel legislation, all things which go against a free market, but on which our economy seems to thrive, at least temporarily. It is all part of pump-priming, spending ourselves into prosperity, and owing it to ourselves.

A word of caution is in order. During the Fascist regime in Italy, the Italian government issued economic reports which showed amazing excesses of exports over imports, with implications of a booming economy and wide-spread prosperity. A breakdown of the figures revealed that the exports were mainly to Ethiopia and other parts of the Fascist empire, from which there was little if any return flow. The Italians could delude themselves into viewing this as an investment for the future. It just didn't happen to work out that way.

One wonders to what extent the impressive U.S. surplus of exports over imports may include parts of the four billion dollars, more or less, that represent goods and services produced here and shipped abroad as foreign aid. With us, of course, there is no question of investment, or expectation of an eventual return (American private investments abroad and returns from past investments appear as a separate item from imports and exports in our official figures). The question then is to what extent our impressive export figures represent cash transactions of the same economic nature as our imports, and to what extent they represent fictitious "exports" that are not paid for, save by ourselves to ourselves.

Even if foreign aid "exports" are kept carefully distinct from true exports, it is nevertheless a fact that they must be paid for, on the internal market, by the American taxpayer. If those amounts go to increase the purchasing power of the producers of goods and services, they reduce the purchasing power of the American taxpayer-consumer by a like amount. We are then faced with the customary redistribution of income, with the Federal Government, as usual, determining the redistribution.

It is perhaps more difficult to outline a sound conservative policy in the matter of foreign aid than in most other areas, by reason of the number and complexity of the factors involved.

It would be an oversimplification to take a traditional isolationistic stand and declare ourselves against all forms of foreign aid save in the purely military sphere. The questions at issue involve our foreign policy, our prestige and general image abroad, even our internal economy.

A few things, however, seem clear. Foreign economic aid should be carefully reexamined, item by item and country by country, to determine whether it is really in line with the goals of a foreign policy which should be highly realistic and aimed, first and foremost, at the best interests of the United States, and only secondarily at those of recipient nations. It should be reduced where possible, never squandered with a free and reckless hand, as it too often has been in the past.

Save for sudden emergencies, it should never be based on charitable ideals, or even the recipient's need, however dire. On the other hand, there is no reason why the government should not encourage churches, private agencies and private foundations to assist in the relief of poverty and misery abroad, in their own way and on as broad a scale as possible. Americans are traditionally charitable, openhanded and openhearted. There is no doubt that they will respond to appeals, as witnessed by CARE and kindred initiatives. Private institutions also have their own way of distributing aid in such a fashion that the recipients know where it is coming from. There is all the difference in the world, psychologically, between the U.S. Government granting the government of a foreign nation one hundred million dollars to use as it chooses (there is little doubt that a good deal of it falls into the wrong hands), and a private organization which functions on the spot and knows what the immediate needs of the community are.

As a matter of general principle, official aid should be withheld from those countries and governments which display attitudes of opposition or downright hostility and animosity against us. If they want to hate us as capitalistic, colonialistic aggressors, that is their privilege; but they should not be allowed to hold out one hand for a loaf of American bread while with the other they tear down our flag to trample on it.

For the uncommitted, neutralistic nations, requests for foreign aid should be viewed with a jaundiced eye. Let them feel free to apply to Russia or China if they feel they can get a better deal that way. The friendship of certain countries, like that of certain people, is sometimes a liability rather than an asset. Unless there is strong reason to the contrary, let our opponents enjoy the liability.

Our avowed and sincere friends we should back to the limit. Nor should we worry unduly about their internal form of government. As between two dictators, better one who likes us and hates Communism than one who has Communistic leanings, despises us, and misses no opportunity to let us know it.

It would be wise, particularly in connection with foreign aid, to preach less democracy abroad and let democracy work by example. We have a form of government and a social and economic system which, with all their avowed imperfections, are nevertheless among the most satisfactory on earth. They are open for all to see and study. Unlike some of our critics, there is little if anything that we strive to conceal, whether it be racial strife in the South or crime waves in the North, election scandals in one locality or graft and corruption elsewhere. But under our system, imperfect as it is, we have achieved things that the entire world envies us—a larger measure of personal freedom, initiative and opportunity than is found elsewhere, standards of living and material prosperity that are hard to duplicate. These things speak for themselves. People who come to our land and return to their own, American films, radio and TV, industrial concerns that do business abroad, spread the gospel of American methods and viewpoints and American democracy far more effectively than all our government agencies put together. It is not the height of wisdom for us to link our aid, where it is given, to the reform of internal government structures in the recipient lands, save only insofar as those reforms may help the recipients to help themselves. Even internationally, there is such a thing as a "Mother, I'd rather do it myself!" attitude. In more cases than we care to admit, the existing political structure of a country is the one best suited for its present conditions. As those conditions change in the economic and educational spheres, there will almost inevitably be a change in the political structure, that will bring it more in line with our own ideals. We should not attempt to use foreign aid as a weapon of political reform, though it may be a useful tool for economic and educational development.

We are here reminded of an American military commander in a southern Italian area who insisted that there should be immediate and free elections. When assured by the local political leaders that such an election would be almost surely won by the Communists, he was equally insistent that they should not win. Fortunately, the Italian politicians were at least as skilled in the art of manipulating a "free" election as are the leaders of certain Chicago wards, and everything came out all right.

In conclusion:

1. For best image results, replace government-to-government aid with people-to-people aid wherever possible.

2. Insist upon appropriate publicity where the aid is still government-to-government.

3. Refuse aid to those who openly hate and oppose us.

4. Cut down aid to those who can't make up their minds whether they prefer us or our opponents.

5. Extend full aid to those who like and support us.

6. Link aid to realistic foreign policy, not to political ideologies.

I am the first to admit that these are not clear-cut solutions. But foreign aid, like foreign policy generally, does not admit of clear-cut solutions. Situations are forever shifting, and must be handled as they arise, while in foreign aid, as in foreign policy, only half the power of determination is ours, with the other half quite properly pertaining to the nation with which we are dealing at the moment.

FOREIGN POLICY AND ECONOMIC DEVELOPMENT

Robert L. Heilbroner

Robert L. Heilbroner is a professor of economics at the Graduate Faculty of the New School.

The great lesson of the Vietnam war is now clear. It is that the mightiest nation in the world has not been able to defeat the forces of revolutionary nationalism in one of the smallest nations in the world. We may even yet work out the kind of settlement that will enable us to proclaim at least some kind of victory in the struggle against "aggression," but it is quite plain that the United States has lost the war. For the ultimate purpose of our intervention in Vietnam was not to beat a *national enemy*—no one ever accused North Vietnam of threatening our territorial integrity. It was to beat

"Making a Rational Foreign Policy Now" in *Harper's Magazine*, Vol. 237, No. 1420 (September 1968), pp. 64-71. Copyright ©1968, Harper's Magazine, Inc. Reprinted from the September 1968 issue of *Harper's Magazine* by permission of the author.

a *revolutionary force*, to demonstrate beyond a doubt that "wars of national liberation" would end in disaster for the revolutionaries.

Now, by a supreme irony, we have shown just the opposite. For what the Vietnam war has revealed above all else is the extreme difficulty of defeating a determined national revolutionary group. Inevitably this must both encourage the rise of such groups elsewhere and discourage our own future willingness to meet their force with counterforce. Thus if the Philippines explodes in an outraged revolt, as seems very probable in a nation where half the customs receipts disappear between the dock and the Treasury; or if guerrilla warfare on a large scale breaks out again in Guatemala, as seems likely in view of the increased revolutionary activity there; or if India dissolves into linguistic parts and these parts are taken over by revolutionary parties, as would certainly be the case in some areas; or if the muted civil war in Venezuela or Colombia or Bolivia or Northeast Brazil again assumes major proportions, it will not be so easy for the United States to intervene on the side of the existing governments. For the first rule of American politics in the next years will be: *No more Vietnams!*

But will revolutionary activity break out in these nations? For reasons that I shall spell out in this article, I think it extremely likely, although it is easier to indicate the broad areas where revolution impends rather than the individual countries. I would think that by the year 2000 and possibly much sooner, we would find revolutionary governments installed, or formidable revolutionary armies fighting, in most of Asia, in at least a half-dozen Latin-American countries, and probably in a fair number of nations in West and Central Africa, and the Near East.

The prospect, in other words, is one of world-wide upheaval in which, retrospectively, the Vietnam war will have been only the first successful campaign. If this prospect comes about, it will present the United States with the gravest challenge of its national existence. It would entail nothing less than the risk of becoming embroiled in Vietnam-like situations in many countries at once. If it has proved almost unbearably costly to wage war against revolutionary nationalism in a nation of fifteen million, what will it be like trying to quell the forces of revolution that can call on the human resources of three continents?

There is no more pressing requirement for the American people than to consider what policies their nation can pursue to pass safely through this unprecedentedly dangerous era. But it is little use seeking to articulate policies until we have a clear idea of what it is that we are up against. And here there is a fundamental lesson that has yet to be learned about the origins of the revolution that threatens us.

We have been taught that the ultimate cause of the worldwide threat of revolution is the subversive and conspiratorial activities of communism. Now, although these activities have often been grossly exaggerated, they certainly exist, and there is no doubt that communist maneuvering can be discovered near the center of nearly every revolutionary situation. Yet to blame the danger of these explosive situations themselves on the presence of communists is like blaming the inherent danger in a huge mass of exposed combustible materials on the possible presence of arsonists. The revolutions we must come to terms with would break out even if communism as an idea and as a political force disappeared from the face of the world tomorrow. For the harsh facts we have yet to acknowledge are these: *(1) in many countries of the underdeveloped world only revolutionary activity will rescue the populace from its unending misery, and (2) the United States has consistently opposed the kinds of revolutionary action that might begin such a rescue operation.* Thus the real tragedy of the coming decades is not that revolutionary action will be necessary, but that it is likely to have a bitter anti-American flavor because of our unwillingness to allow the forces of economic development to take their essential course.

This is an assertion that seems to fly in the face of the facts. No government among wealthy nations has tried harder to promote economic development than the United States. Our foreign-aid program may not be very large in relation to our capabilities, but it towers over the efforts of other Western nations, not to mention those of Russia. Moreover the struggle for economic development has captured the natural sympathies of the vast majority of Americans; indeed, the very slogan that we ourselves have coined for development—"the revolution of rising expectations"—conveys in itself our goodwill for the peoples struggling to escape from poverty.

All this is true. But the problem is that few Americans understand what the process of "economic development" entails, or what the "revolution of rising expectations" really means. To most of us, development is merely a matter of money with which we assume economic advancement is bought. Unfortunately, money is the last, if not the least, step in the development sequence. For the long climb out of backwardness is not merely a matter of getting "richer." It is first and foremost a matter of changing an entire society in ways that must go to the roots of its ordinary life and that are bound to shake or topple its basic structure of power and prestige.

Actually, we have had a glimpse of the difficulties and dangers in trying to initiate "economic development" in the problems we have encountered at home in Harlem or Watts. We have learned, for example, that an enormous gulf must be bridged between the people who have to "develop" and those to whom the guidance of development is entrusted. The business and government leaders of Caracas or Rio or Calcutta have little or no contact with the dirty, ignorant, primitive people of the urban and rural slums of their countries—in which live, however, not 10 or 20 per cent, but 70 or 80 per cent of the population. In turn, the inhabitants of the villages and urban slums regard the upper classes as representatives of a class whose only relation with themselves has been arrogant, exploitative, patronizing, or indifferent.

Second, both the slum and the underdeveloped areas smart under the constraints of absentee domination. We know of the resentment of the "radical" Negro against white-owned stores. Far greater is the resentment of the radical Asian, African, or Latin American against the foreign ownership of the main instruments of production in his country—the utilities, the manufacturing plants, railroads, plantations, or oil fields. To be sure, one can answer that the supply of native entrepreneurship is small and that these foreign companies introduce capital and expertise that would otherwise be lacking. But they introduce as well a steady drain of earnings out of the country, and a basic orientation of business interest that is geared at least as much to the needs of the corporate home office as to the requirements of its host nation.

Last, we find another similarity between ghetto and backward land that may help us visualize the problems of economic development. This is the population problem that cuts away at both milieux. At home the rolls of relief mount steadily as the city poor produce more children than can be easily absorbed into society. Abroad, this disproportion between the rate of production of impoverished human beings and their social absorption takes on nightmarish dimensions. Each year we have watched Asia, the Near East, much of Africa and Latin America in a race between survival and starvation—a race that has already produced a devastating famine in India two years ago. By the year 2000 we shall have to run this race with twice as many human beings, and even with the brightest hopes for agricultural improvement, no one can face that prospect without flinching. President Ayub of Pakistan has put the threat succinctly: "In ten years' time, human beings will eat human beings in Pakistan."

Ten Thousand a Day

These are some of the obstacles to economic development— obstacles that are obscured behind the bright slogan of "the revolution of rising expectations." They make it clear that much more is needed to bring improvement to the backward areas than money, just as much more is needed in our slums. At home, moreover, we are dealing with a minority that is in some kind of touch with a prevailing culture into which most of its members would, if they could, gladly enter. Abroad we are dealing with an ingrown, suspicious peasantry that has little or no understanding or acceptance of the modern ways that produce "loose" women and "disrespectful" children and a snubbing disregard of the wisdom of the village elders. So, too, at home we have an upper class that, however insulated from the slums, does not find its social position fundamentally incompatible with slum clearance. Abroad the clearance of the vast rural slums requires that its beneficiaries—the landed ruling class—give up their power and position to another ruling group. And finally, whereas the population problem at home exacerbates the problem of bringing economic improvement to the slum, abroad it renders this problem unmanageable.

Thus although Harlem and Watts give us some insights into India and Brazil, the problems of the latter are a thousandfold larger and more intractable than those at home. That is why the changes needed to bring development to the backward areas are so far-reaching that they are hard to describe as "reforms." Take, for example, the question of land reform—the breakup of the vast semi-feudal land holdings that everyone, including our government, recognizes as incompatible with development. In Latin America, according to Oscar Delgado, an official in the Inter-American Committee on Agricultural Development in Washington, "There are families who own more land than is occupied by a number of sovereign states. . . . Statistically speaking, Latin America has the highest index of concentrated rural property in the world."

To urge land "reform" on such a society is tantamount to a visitor from Mars urging stock "reform" on us—telling us that great social benefits would accrue from breaking up the concentration of two-thirds to three-fourths of all privately owned corporate stock that lies in the hands of the top 2 per cent of American families. With how much enthusiasm would such a proposal be received in the U.S. and with how much carried out? Precisely the same response has greeted other proposals for land reform in Latin America.

But the trouble is not wholly that of upper classes who are unwilling to change the social system on which their power and prestige are based. There are other nations in the world—India is of course the prime example—where the terrible and persisting absence of necessary social change comes from the inability of mild men of goodwill to translate good intentions into effective deeds. Somehow a squabbling Congress, a nepotistic bureaucracy, and an over-powering atmosphere of futility have smothered every impetus to change, so that despite the intelligence and humane aspirations of the national leadership, we look with horror at the spectacle of the rotting poor who somehow cannot be housed or fed or put to work; at the world's largest collection of cattle, roaming through the country as an untouchable symbol of holiness and active agent of famine; at tens of thousands of still isolated villages where tens of millions of women remain in ignorance or fear of birth control.

It would be cruelly wrong to suggest that no progress has been made in the underdeveloped world. Compared with the past, giant strides have been taken. In Asia and Africa, millions of persons who, had you asked them to identify themselves a generation ago would have answered that they were so and so of such and such village, now answer that they are Pakistani, or Algerian, or whatever: the dangerous but necessary infection of self-conscious nationalism has become virtually pandemic. So, too, stirrings of modernization have made their way into the remote hamlets of Asia and Latin America alike: radios bring news of events in the capital city and the outer world; the cinema stirs imaginations; visitors from the cities bring new seeds which, cautiously tried, often bring better crops; there is talk of a school; a road is improved; an irrigation dam is built.

These changes are important and cumulative, but they must not be magnified out of proportion. First, were there no such changes, the Malthusian dilemma would by now have pushed even more millions below the starvation line (as it is, an estimated *10,000 people a day* die of malnutrition in the underdeveloped areas). Second, the sum total of all these changes has not been enough to accelerate the rate of economic growth. In Latin America as a whole, gross national product has grown by a *smaller* percentage in each successive five-year period between 1950 and 1965. Virtually nowhere in Asia or the Near East or Africa does output per capita show a strong steady upward trend.[1] And last and most important of all, there is no evidence that the people themselves have been roused from their torpor, no release of energies from the great stagnant reservoir of humanity that is the basic repository of backwardness itself.

[1]But what about the fabulous new agricultural techniques, such as the new seeds that yield up to twice the weight of output of present varieties? Our eager endorsement of technology as the cure for underdevelopment reveals all too clearly our failure to understand the social environment in which the process of change takes place. For the new seeds (in India and South America) are first used by the richer peasants. The poorer ones cannot afford to experiment for fear of starvation if the seed fails, or simply because, being poor, they are least "ready" for change. As a result the disparity in income between the upper stratum of peasants and the lowest widens. There is more food—but there is also more social misery.

Instead what we see in virtually every corner of the underdeveloped world is a terrible changelessness that it seems impossible to affect. What we call "economic development" is in truth little more than a holding action that has succeeded only in building up the dikes just enough to keep the mounting population from washing away everything, not a movement that has invested life with a new quality. Change, insofar as it is being introduced, comes at a pace that is discouraging even to the most dedicated enthusiast. Thus we no longer hear the trumpets sound for the Alliance for Progress or the U.N. Development Decade. The outlook is for a continuation, no doubt with some small improvements, of the prevailing misery, filth, ill-health, and hunger for as long ahead as we can see.

This is not a "pessimistic" estimate. To be pessimistic would be to suggest a *worsening* of current trends—a cut in foreign aid, a petering out of the few birth-control programs that have begun, a collapse of foreign or domestic investment in the underdeveloped world because of growing unrest there, a deterioration rather than an improvement in the caliber of governments. An optimistic appraisal would assume the contrary of these things. A realistic appraisal, I think, assumes that matters will go on much as they have gone on—a forecast that offers little room for rising expectations on our part.

To this general outlook for a continuation of the prevailing hopelessness of the backward world we must now add one final, all-important exception. It is that the sapping inertia of the underlying populace *has* been overcome within the last half-century in a very few nations.

One of these is of course Russia, whose leap into modernity has been the most extraordinarily rapid social transformation in history. Another, still more striking, is China. Even more hopeless, corrupt, and miserable than Russia, China was the source of endless horror stories of peasants eating mud when the crops failed; of the sale of daughters into prostitution to ward off starvation, of the subhuman degradation of the "coolie," the ricksha boy, the city homeless. China, in a word, was like India. But that too has changed. In China, we no longer find the homeless on the street, or forced prostitution, or children deliberately mutilated to become appealing beggars, although we still find all of these things in India. Nor do we find corruption in government, or an inability to distribute food supplies in bad times so as to provide a fair ration for all. More significant, we see an all-important redirection of Chinese life away from the endlessly static past to a new future—a redirection nowhere more dramatically expressed than in the spectacle of the youthful Red Guards indulging in the heretofore unthinkable action of defying their elders. To be sure, as the Red Guard also symbolizes,

China is a nation in a paroxysm of change that has brought much that is ugly, cruel, and mean. And yet, before we condemn it for its very obvious evils, let every reader ask himself into which society he would take his chances as an anonymous human being today—India or China?

Last, there is the case of Cuba, never so impoverished as the other two, but also afflicted with the curses of underdevelopment in an uneducated rural proletariat and a corrupt city one. Every report from Cuba emphasizes that a tremendous effort is being made to eradicate these ills. Gambling and prostitution have disappeared in Havana. A great effort is being made in the countryside to bring education and agricultural reform. And if we may believe the testimony of articles both in *Look* Magazine and in the *New York Times*, a new and genuine spirit of idealism and endeavor is to be found among the young. I do not wish to rhapsodize over these countries in which life is still hard and harsh, and if one is an intellectual, often impossibly demeaning. Nor should one slight the important fact that China has not tackled its population problem and that Cuba has not yet built a well-functioning economy. Both nations may fail to bring about economic growth. Yet I would insist on one central achievement whose importance it is impossible to overstate. It is that these nations *have* succeeded in touching and bringing to life the deadened humanity that is the despair of the underdeveloped world. Even if they fail now, they have opened the way for a future assault that can succeed. One may fault the communist nations on many grounds, not least that of morality—and on that score I will have more to say later—but one must also admit that they have brought hope, enthusiasm, and effort to the common people of their lands. *Of how many other backward nations can this be said?*

Is Communism the Answer?

Does this imply that only a communist government can bring about the revolution of rising expectations that is indeed the foundation on which development must rest?

This is not the conclusion I wish to urge. There are also a few noncommunist—although, please note, revolution-based—countries, Turkey and Mexico in particular, where at least the beginnings of a mass awakening have been carried out. Thus it is not communism, either as a system of philosophy or as a particular party, that makes the crucial difference, but a political movement that has the courage, conviction, and ruthless energy to carry through a program of modernization from top to bottom.

What is the galvanic force of such a movement? It lies first in the overthrow of an existing regime that is unable or unwilling to change the social order on which it rests. But that is only the initial stage of a developmental revolution, as contrasted with a purely political one. Next, such a movement must move with the full power of an authoritarian will to impose a program of change—often unwanted change—upon the very people in whose name the revolution has been waged—the underlying peasantry. Finally, it must bring to bear whatever economic compulsion is needed to mount the massive redeployments and concentrations of labor that will be needed to move the economy off dead center.

In this painful process, the spread and degree of development that can be accomplished depend very largely on the willingness and ability of the revolutionary group to press relentlessly for change. It is for this reason that democracy and capitalism are not instruments of the revolutionary impulse, for there are certain changes that neither one permits even when they are essential for modernization. For instance, our own national goal of racial equality—a change that might be regarded as part of our own modernization—has been seriously impeded by the democratic process of consulting the will of the majority. How fast can one bring equality when large numbers—perhaps even majorities—do not wish to have it brought? So, too, our ability to raze and rebuild the slums is crippled by our insistence on relying on a market mechanism and on deferring to prerogatives of private property, with the result that urban renewal has come to a virtual halt. It is not surprising, then, that revolutionary parties, facing emergencies of far greater seriousness than anything we must deal with at home, utilize authority and command, and do not brook democratic dissent or rely on market incentives.

Chances for Slowing Down

Thus revolution, authoritarianism, and collectivism are often the *only* instruments by which essential social changes can be made. But having stated this as a generalization, let us now modify and soften the case as it applies to many individual nations. One need hardly say, for instance, that the prognosis for revolutionary change does not apply to Europe, where communism is an agent not at all for modernization but rather for political retrogression. But even in the backward world it would be wrong to deny the possibility of a more gradual and less traumatic evolution in some instances. In Africa, for example, many new nations are now undergoing the first trials of nationhood, including above all that of creating national consciousness and loyalties where only tribal affiliations existed before. These countries may experience their share of coups and turmoil, but it is unlikely that they will constitute fertile ground for mass revolutionary activity until a genuine national community has been forged. And perhaps by that time a workable "African socialism" will permit the rigors of a revolutionary movement to be by-passed.

In Latin America the situation is much more revolution-prone, but even here some important nations may carry out their internal transformations without wholesale revolution. Argentina, with its relatively high standard of living and its low rate of population growth may be one such; Chile—provided that the reforms of President Frei are not blocked by the landholding and foreign interests—is another. As we have already said, Mexico, with a bloody revolution of national identity and foreign expropriation behind it, should be a third. In Asia, the long-run outlook is, perhaps least propitious of all, and yet even here a few nations may bring development to pass without resort to violent upheavals. Moreover, even in these most labile areas, it is unlikely that revolution impends immediately. The incumbent governments in Latin America have strong military forces at their disposal (and are using them); the peasants in Asia are as yet largely unorganized and apathetic. Hence the outlook is not for uprisings everywhere, but for a gradually mounting pressure, a growing instability, as the combination of weak and inept governments and cancerous population growth works its fatal results.

Finally, taking the world as a whole there is always the possibility that a heroic effort to bring birth control to the masses, especially through the use of the plastic intrauterine device, might slow down the Malthusian timetable sufficiently to allow slower processes of change to work their way. Yet realism tells us that such a program will take decades to carry out; 97 per cent of the world's women do not use the pill or the plastic insert.

Last, when revolution comes, the leadership may spring from many sources other than Communist party membership. Angry and disillusioned army officers, idealistic middle-class intellectuals, even peasant guerrilla leaders may provide the nuclei that seed the clouds of potential disaffection. A movement that begins as a mere palace coup may find itself carried on its own momentum into a revolutionary trajectory. Thus revolution and communism are by no means synonymous, although it is undeniably true that communists are working for and eager to lead a revolutionary thrust.

Whatever the leadership, however, it is clear that some sort of authoritarian nationalist socialism will be the vehicle of change. Whether or not this socialism will become communist—that is, whether it will accept the dogmas and doctrines of Marxism and Maoism or seek active alliance with Russia and China—depends on many events internal and external to the nation in question (including our own actions). The nationalism that is so powerful a motive force in revolutions tends to drive the leadership away from communism because of its danger of vassalage to a great state; the need for moral support and technical advice may drive it toward accepting or concocting some version of the communist catechism.

But it is important to realize that we should not expect the attitude of a noncommunist revolutionary regime toward the United States to be very different from that of a communist one. For it is the unhappy fact that the United States in recent years has thrown its support against *all* revolutions and provided its backing for *all* groups that have opposed revolutions, regardless of the merits of the one or the demerits of the other—the scandal of our Dominican invasion, our Guatemalan "success," and our Cuban "failure," our backing of the militarist Branco in Brazil, and now our intervention in Vietnam all being instances in point. In the essential process of social surgery that must be performed if many backward nations are to be brought to life, it is the United States—for good reasons or bad—that delays the necessary stroke of the blade. That is why the revolution of economic development must become an anti-American revolution unless the United States changes its ways.

In Place of Fortress America

But how to change our ways? How to cope with the forces of economic development? To date we have lived with it in a curiously schizophrenic way. On the one hand we have been the leading agent of international assistance through AID, the Peace Corps, Food for Peace, etc. On the other hand we have been the leader of the antirevolutionary forces of the world.

We have not, of course, meant to be schizophrenic. The possible connection between revolution and development has never been pointed out to us, particularly since the modernizing efforts of communism have been obscured by our steady emphasis on its repressive elements. Nor have we meant to oppose development in backing right-wing or center governments of Latin America or Asia. We continue to believe that development can take place gradually and peaceably, preferably with governments that "understand" the needs of the American business community. Hence our schizophrenia has ultimately been the price of self-deception—of unwillingness to confront the demanding process of development fearlessly or to acknowledge the inadequacies of our client governments to initiate deep and rapid social change. But now, if my prognosis is correct, this self-deception will be increasingly difficult to practice. As the pressures of revolutionary change build up, partly as a result of the bankruptcy of American policy in Vietnam, we shall have to face more squarely the harsh calculus of the developmental process. Indeed, the rise of the development revolution will force us to choose among one of three policies for the future.

The first of these is a continuation of our present policy. This will commit us to determined antirevolutionary activity, both political and military, wherever radical elements threaten to overthrow existing governments. I will not argue the consequences of this policy except to point out again that it presents the likelihood of a succession of Vietnam wars for the indefinite future.

An imaginable alternative is a volte-face in policy that would turn us away from all contact with the underdeveloped world. This would entail the creation of a fortress America, without diplomatic or economic—or direct military—contact with any revolutionary nations, defensively turned away from the inimical changes taking place in the underdeveloped continents. In the end this may be a policy to which we are forced to retreat, but it presents obvious dangers to the United States. An isolationist America, at bay in a revolutionary world, would bring forth the worst tendencies in this country, encouraging every superpatriot, fanning the fires of suspicion and fancied subversion, and submerging the humanitarian impulses that are the best side of the Amerian national character.

The third policy is by far the most difficult to pursue, but is ultimately the only constructive course to follow. It is a policy of neutrality toward the revolutionary movement—a neutrality that ceases to oppose all revolutions as such, although not ceasing to differentiate between revolutionary regimes that we can actively support and those that we cannot. Such a policy does not ask us to endorse regimes that are bitterly anti-American in utterance or intolerable in behavior, nor does it prevent the political and military support of conservative government regimes threatened by subversion or submersion from neighboring states, *provided that these governments have the support of their people as a whole.*

But it would force us to change our present attitudes and actions in several regards. First it would call for an immediate halt to military aid to reactionary regimes and for a cessation of clandestine activity against revolutionary movements. Second, it would require an acceptance of some form of revolutionary nationalist socialism as the political and economic order most suited to guide many developing nations in their desperately hard initial stages of change. Third, it would permit the continuation of humanitarian programs of food and medical aid, as well as technical assistance of a nonmilitary kind, for all governments, revolutionary or not, provided that reasonable standards of international behavior were met.

I need not point out the problems of steering such a course—of determining which revolutionary governments were acceptable and which governments under pressure warranted our support. But these problems would certainly be less than those encountered under a policy that recognized no revolutionary governments and that supported all antirevolutionary ones. Indeed, if such a pragmatic and noninterventionist policy could be pursued in the future, a kind of victory could yet be snatched from the otherwise pointless and hideous sacrifices of the Vietnam war. For then it could be said some day that this war was for American foreign policy what the Great Depression was for domestic policy.

However difficult to carry out abroad, the real difficulties of such a policy of neutrality are apt to be encountered at home. For in changing our stance from one of belligerent opposition to one of neutrality, recognition, and selective aid, we would be sure to hear two frightening accusations from many groups in America.

The first of these would be that we were aiding and abetting an international aggressive movement whose rise would eventually engulf us. Frightening though it is, this accusation could be answered with some degree of assurance. For one thing, the alternative—military action abroad—has been revealed by the Vietnam war to be a policy that can bleed us white. For another, it is increasingly evident that communism is no more of a unified world force than capitalism ever was, and that the rise of many intensely nationalistic revolutionary states is much more apt to result in internecine warfare among themselves than in military action against us. Let us recall the tensions between Russia and its satellites, between Russia and China, and between both nations and Cuba when the cry of a communist "bloc" is raised. And last, there is simply the enormous disparity in industrial and military strength between America and Europe (and perhaps Russia on our side as well), and the populous but impoverished masses of the revolutionary world. A revolutionary world will assuredly be an extraordinarily dangerous, thin-skinned and rhetorically aggressive environment in which to make our way; but the specter of concerted military action of its impoverished governments against the rich nations an ocean's distance away is a fantasy that should not be difficult to destroy.

Not so easy to allay is another alarm that would accompany a policy of neutralism. It is that in acquiescing in the rise of communist (or even noncommunist) regimes, we were condoning evil for expediency's sake.

This is not an accusation that can be readily countered by an appeal to reason. There is a strain of fundamentalism among sections of the American people that regard communism as the ultimate evil with which no compromise is imaginable and toward which no attitude but fear and loathing is possible.

It is true enough that communism has been a perpetrator of evil and it is all too likely that more evil will be committed in its name (or in whatever name is inscribed on the banners the revolutionists of development will carry). Yet if one cannot and should not seek to minimize the weight on that side of the scale of human suffering, one should also have the courage to pile up whatever weights belong on the other side.

This is not an operation we have carried out honestly. We tend to count carefully each corpse attributable to the terrorists, guerrillas, or avowed soldiers of revolutionary action, but to ignore the bodies of those who perish because of the actions of our own side, military or not. To whom, for example, should be charged the permanent and irreversible mental and physical stunting of Latin America's children that follows from an inability to alter the established social order? To whom shall we debit the grisly corpses, living and dead, in the streets of Bombay? In what account shall we enter the hunger of those who live within sight of the expensive restaurants of New Delhi or Lima or Hong Kong?

One does not know which way the scales of history would tilt if all the evils attributable to both sides were piled on their respective balances. But there is the uncomfortable suspicion that ours might not necessarily be the lighter side of the scale. What exists in most of the world beyond our borders is a condition of human indignity and degradation that verges on the unspeakable. If we are to set ourselves against a movement, however violent or cruel, that has demonstrated its ability to lead such men out of their misery for at least the first critical stage of the journey, we must at least offer something as good in its place. At this juncture it is the shameful fact that we have nothing as good, and worse than that, have ranged ourselves against nearly every movement that might have led men toward a better life, on the grounds of our opposition to communism. Now the question is whether America will take its ultimate stand on the side of humanitarianism or moralism, self-reliance or fear, open-mindedness or dogma. The challenge goes to the very core of this nation—its structure of power and economic interest, its capacity for reasoned discussion, its ultimate inarticulate values. It is not alone the life and death of anonymous multitudes that is weighed in the balance, but that of American conscience, as well.

PROMOTING POLITICAL STABILITY

Samuel P. Huntington

Samuel P. Huntington is Frank G. Thomson Professor of Government at Harvard University and a fellow at the Center for Advanced Study in the Behavioral Sciences, 1969-70.

. . . Social reform and political institutionalization are . . .two goals, the successful promotion of which in a modernizing country would reduce significantly the likelihood of United States military intervention.

Beginning in the last years of the Eisenhower Administration, there was an increasing tendency to make American economic assistance to modernizing countries contingent upon those countries embarking upon appropriate programs of social reform. In 1961, of course, the link between economic assistance and social reform was crystallized on a grand scale in the Alliance for Progress. The assumption here was quite clearly that by promoting social reform the United States would reduce the likelihood of Castroite revolutions in Latin American countries and thus avoid the dilemma of either accepting another communist state in the Western Hemisphere or intervening militarily to prevent it. After 1961 the role of social-economic reform as a means of preventing instability and violence was stressed again and again in negotiations between the United States and aid-receiving governments. . . .

There are, however, at least two major problems in emphasizing social-economic reform as an alternative to instability. The first concerns the presumed effects of such reforms. It is assumed that reform is a substitute for social revolutions. In some cases, however, reform may well be a catalyst of revolution. This was de Tocqueville's argument on the French Revolution; there are reasons to suggest its applicability to contemporary modernizing countries. Reforms aimed at urban and especially middle-class groups seem particularly likely to produce violence and disorder in their wake. Land reforms, in contrast, have usually had the effect of turning peasants from a potentially revolutionary force into a conservative bulwark of the existing order.

In Vietnam, however, even this may not have been true. For a decade Americans urged land reform as a means of countering the Viet Cong appeal to the peasants. Yet one recent study has found the Viet Cong in the 1960's to be weakest in those provinces in which no land distribution had taken place in the 1950's and much stronger in those provinces where some land reform had been implemented. In addition, the greater the inequality of current land ownership in a province, the weaker the Viet Cong was in the province. The assumptions and methods of this study can be debated. They have, indeed, been subjected to outraged criticism and passionate denunciation by AID true believers in the doctrine of "salvation through land reform." Whatever quibbles may be made, however, the conclusions suggested by this seemingly perverse statistical analysis can be bolstered by much evidence from other countries and other times. The promotion of social-economic reform may in some circumstances reduce the likelihood of civil violence; in other circumstances it may increase that likelihood.

A second problem concerns the effects of American efforts to promote social reforms. So long as American efforts remain relatively small and are limited to the carrot and the stick of economic assistance and its denial, the impact of these efforts on social change will be relatively small. Where the United States massively intervenes in a society, however, its effects on the promotion of social reform, economic change, and modernization are likely to be overwhelming and revolutionary. American liberals frequently think of United States involvement in the politics of another country as inherently biased on the side of the status quo. This is, however, only a half truth. In fact, there would appear to be a direct correlation between the scope and direction of American involvement. *The more extensive the American involvement in the politics of another country, the more progressive or reform-oriented is its impact on that country.* In those countries which it has governed militarily or colonially the impact of the United States has generally tended to undermine and destroy the traditional order, promote social and economic equality, expand human welfare, and stimulate economic development. In the years since World War II, for instance, rapid and thoroughgoing land reforms have (with one exception) been carried out under two auspices: communist revolution (China, Vietnam, Yugoslavia) and American military occupation (Japan, Korea, and, at a second remove, Taiwan). The only other country which has carried out a land reform as sweeping as these is

Bolivia, and that was done by a revolutionary government financed by the United States.

The revolutionary and modernizing impact which a massive American presence has on a foreign country is in part the result of conscious desire to promote reform and in part simply the by-product of the exposure of a traditional culture to the ways of an egalitarian, affluent, liberal, modern society. On the other hand, where the American presence is relatively limited—and in particular, of course, where the American governmental presence is limited—the net effect of the American impact tends to be much more conservative, witness most of the states of Central America. In a sense this relationship between the scale and the direction of the American impact parallels that which students of colonialism have noticed between direct and indirect colonial rule. Countries subjected to a massive and prolonged colonial rule, it is argued, were in a much better position to modernize and develop than those, such as the Middle East countries and China, which were subjected to indirect, marginal, and hence irresponsible colonial influence.

This seemingly positive relationship between intervention and reform obviously creates problems for the American liberal. On the one hand, he is against intervention; on the other, he is in favor of reform. Outside of government, he can add up the balance one way or another. In the government, however, and anxious to promote social-economic reform (and this includes, I would argue, the bulk of State, AID, and CIA personnel, despite myths to the contrary), he inevitably also finds himself promoting more and more American intervention. Vietnam is the perfect case in point. There, as in so many other non-Western societies, the forces of traditionalism, elitism, apathy, corruption, family, and self-interest were so strong as to make extremely difficult achievement of reforms through the indigenous political system. As a result the life of the American advisor was typically one of intensifying frustration. Adhering to the canons of advisorship, the new American arrival inevitably starts by attempting to become chummy with his Vietnamese counterpart and then gradually to induce him to take the actions which to the American seem obviously needed to promote social welfare. The Vietnamese smiles approvingly and does nothing. The American becomes more insistent; the Vietnamese becomes more resistant. In the end the Vietnamese eventually orders some action to be taken, but then also ensures that it will have just the opposite effects from those which the American intended. By that time the American advisor, who arrived with such idealistic hopes and progressive ideas of promoting social good *with* the Vietnamese, has come to the conclusion that if any good is to be accomplished, it must be done by Americans *to* the Vietnamese. If he still has any time left in his twelve- or eighteen-month tour of duty, he will demand five more American assistants and plunge in to do the job himself. The desire for reform thus promotes the continual expansion of the American presence; and the expansion of the American presence promotes both intended and unintended social and economic change.

This issue of reform *vs.* nonintervention is perhaps most dramatically posed by the problem of corruption. Many of those Americans who have voiced doubts about the American role in Vietnam and have argued for a decrease in the American presence there are also precisely those who have argued that we must do whatever is necessary to eliminate corruption there. Achieving the latter goal, however, would inevitably mean much greater American intervention and involvement. The United States could, for instance, simply refuse to recognize or to cooperate with GVN officials known to be more corrupt than the average. If this policy was to be effective, however, it would soon mean the exercise of a veto power by United States officials over virtually all appointments in the ARVN and the GVN. The results might well be successful, but they would be achieved at a price. Which is worse: toleration of Vietnamese corruption or expansion of American colonialism?

Many AID and CORDS provincial advisors in Vietnam have tacked up on their office walls one of those many verses from the poet laureate of the British empire which now seem peculiarly relevant to American dilemmas:

> Now it is not good for the Christian's health
>   to hustle the Aryan brown,
> For the Christian riles, and the Aryan smiles
>   and he weareth the Christian down;
> And the end of the fight is a tombstone white
>   with the name of the late deceased,
> And the epitaph drear: "A Fool lies here
>   who tried to hustle the East."

The instinct of Americans, however, is to draw quite the opposite lesson than Kipling intended. If the East cannot be hustled, it must be replaced. If the Vietnamese won't reform and change their own society, we must reform it for them. And few phenomena are more unsettling in their consequences than masses of energetic and highminded Americans intent on doing good.

If promotion of social reform seems unlikely to reduce the pressures for American military intervention, what about the promotion of political institutions capable of channeling discontent into peaceful paths? To some extent, of course, more effective political institutions are required for social reform. The assumptions about political development which underlie the American commitment to social reform, indeed, directly conflict with those which have been associated with American economic assistance programs. The latter have in part reflected the belief that economic development will create the social and economic conditions favorable to the emergence of broad-based, stable political institutions. The American commitment to social reform, on the other hand, presupposes the existence in the recipient country of a political system sufficiently well developed and authoritative as to be capable of inaugurating such reforms. As the experience of the Alliance for Progress amply demonstrates, this assumption is of questionable validity in much of Latin America. It is probably even less valid in Southeast Asia. If the United States is to make social reform a condition for economic assistance, it may also have some responsibility to help governments to develop the political institutions required to make such reforms a reality.

The development of broader-based political institutions is thus in some cases a prerequisite to reform. In other cases, of which Vietnam is probably one, the development of such institutions may well slow down the pace of reform. The concentration of power will give way to the dispersion of power, and the result will be less reform but more stability. In particular, it will mean less obvious signs of reform, which are the things that please Americans, and more toleration of Vietnamese practices and ways, many of which are abhorrent to Americans. Clearly, however, political stability in many modernizing countries will depend upon the creation of an institutional framework to provide for the peaceful participation of larger and larger groups of people in the political process. If a political system is unable to develop the organizations to serve this end, if its leaders, like Diem in South Vietnam in the late 1950's, instead attempt to close off the institutional channels for popular participation, the inevitably revolutionary leaders arise to mobilize popular participation against the political system rather than through the political system. To maintain political stability, consequently, the construction of organizations and institutions for peaceful participation in government must go hand in hand with the expansion of political awareness among the masses of the population. In particular, stability requires the development of political parties and party systems.

By and large, stable countries have strong political parties; unstable countries have weak parties. More importantly, countries which do have strong political parties can look forward to future stability with considerably greater confidence than countries with weak parties or with no parties. The future political stability of Thailand is more problematical than that of Malaysia, in part because Thailand lacks organized political parties to assimilate into the political system groups which inevitably will acquire political consciousness as the process of modernization continues. It is a bitter truth but a real one that probably the most stable government in Southeast Asia today is the government of North Vietnam. The relative political stability which has characterized that country in contrast to South Vietnam derives largely from the fact that in the north the organization of the communist party reaches out into the rural areas and provides a channel for communication of rural grievances to the center and for control of the countryside by the government.

Changes in the political stability of a country are related to changes in the strength of its party system. The emergence of South Korea from civil strife and instability after 1962 coincided with the creation by General Park and his associates of a strong political party which was able to provide effective rule and public order and at the same time promote economic growth and such needed reforms as the normalization of its relations with Japan. The contrast between India's political stability during the 1950's and the instability of Pakistan was due to the strength of the Congress party in India with its well-developed grass-roots organization, as contrasted with the weakness of the Muslim League in Pakistan, which at that time was little more than a clique of maneuvering politicians with no roots in the country which they were supposed to govern. The emergence in the 1960's of political stability in Pakistan coincided with the development of a new grass-roots political system through the Basic Democracies program and the reinvigoration of the Muslim League organization. At the same time, the decline in the strength of the Congress party threatened India with increasing political turmoil and instability.

The nature of the party system in the society largely determines whether new groups will enter politics peacefully or through revolution. After the urban intellectuals appear on the scene, the next crucial turning point in the expansion of political participation in a modernizing society is the inauguration of the rural masses into national politics. The timing, the method, and the auspices of the "green uprising" decisively shape the subsequent political evolution of the society. It may occur relatively rapidly, or it may occur slowly and proceed through several stages. In a colonial society the "green uprising" may occur under the auspices of the nationalist intellectuals who, as in India and Tunisia, mobilize peasant groups into politics within the framework of the nationalist party to support them in their struggles with the imperial power. In a competitive party system the peasant mobilization often takes the form of one segment of the urban elite developing an appeal to or making an alliance with the crucial rural voters and mobilizing them into politics so as to overwhelm at the polls the more narrowly urban based parties. If no group within the political system takes the lead in organizing peasant political participation, some group of urban intellectuals will mobilize and organize them into politics against the political system. This results in revolution. This almost happened in the Philippines. It did happen in Vietnam. It may be happening in Thailand.

The argument that the United States ought to encourage the development of more highly structured and broad-based party systems in modernizing countries always runs into at least three objections. First, many Americans question the legitimacy of governmental programs directly related to political institutionaliza-tion and party development. They recoil from any thought of "intervention," and particularly intervention in the politics of other countries. Yet the fact of the matter is that American intervention in the affairs of other countries occurs continuously in scores of ways. The United States intervenes to promote health, agriculture, land reform, industrialization, education, and military security. Why should it not also intervene to promote political development? The United States intervenes to help build civil services, police forces, universities, armies, and navies. Why should it not also intervene to help build political parties? Modernization means increasing political participation. That participation has to be organized. The principal institutional means for organizing that participation is the political party. Why should it be thought immoral or inappropriate to help strengthen these essential institutions of modern society?

Second, it is at times also argued that intervention to promote political development is bound to be ineffective or self-defeating. American support for a particular party or group, it is said, will be the kiss of death to this group. In some cases this may be true, but it should be noted that people in most countries think that the United States intervenes now to support particular groups, even when it does not do so. In many ways the United States suffers all the stigmata and disadvantages of political intervention and reaps few of the benefits. In addition, in many countries important groups have strongly urged the United States to play a more active political role, but the United States has hung back and refused to do so. It is also argued that American intervention in the politics of other countries runs counter to the general desire of the people of those countries to manage their own affairs and will consequently give rise to violently anti-American nationalism. Quite obviously, however, the control of politics, even more than that of the economy, will remain in local hands. The elites of each society will choose their own forms of political organization. All that foreigners can do is to advise them on the prerequisites and requirements of political organization, even as they do for economic development, and give them technical and material assistance in the development of political organizations.

Third, it is at times argued that the United States is so much a victim of liberal myopia that it is hopelessly incapable of understanding the political needs of foreign systems and of adapting its own goals and methods to meet those needs. Americans, it is said, will inevitably attempt to reproduce in the most unsuitable foreign soil all the characteristics of their own highly distinctive two-party, liberal, pluralistic, constitutional democracy. Obviously Americans, like anyone else, like to see the virtues of their own system and to flatter themselves by seeing it reproduced elsewhere. On the other hand, however, it is also quite clear that Americans have been able to rise above such parochialism in the past, and there is no reason why this should not be even more of a pattern in the future. Indeed, many of those critics who accuse the United States of attempting to export its own institutions, at the same time also accuse the United States of supporting reactionary and repressive personalistic dictatorships around the world. Such critics would be more persuasive if they were less inconsistent. In fact, of course, the United States has, wisely or not, supported and attempted to promote the development of the most varied types of political systems around the world. Surely few political systems differ more fundamentally from the American system than that which has existed in Iran. Yet the United States has engaged in the most active efforts to strengthen and develop this essentially authoritarian monarchy. Whether this is a wise policy or not and whether it will succeed or not are other questions, but we certainly were not inhibited in our efforts to promote monarchical development by the failure of the Iranian political system to conform to the American model. In similar fashion the United States has played an active role in promoting one-party systems in Tunisia and Bolivia, a military-led dominant party system in Korea, monarchical-bureaucratic regimes in Thailand and Nepal, and also, of course, a variety of competitive democratic systems in which the dominant groups have been socialist, Catholic, and liberal, as well as highly conservative.

Political involvements designed more effectively to promote the development of political institutions will certainly require levels of discretion and sophistication which have not always been present in our international behavior in the past. Such involvements may be designed to ward off the instabilities which could lead to military intervention, but conceivably they could in themselves become a cause and excuse for military intervention. The way to avoid this is to keep commitments to particular individuals and groups conditional and/or covert and deniable. In the past we have often felt the need to justify such commitments by saying that the future of the country rested with Mr. X or the military or some other group. In fact, however, our leverage varies inversely with our commitments. In Vietnam we became the victim of our own declarations: we talked ourselves to the point where . . . our commitment became the commitment. In the future a more detached attitude toward foreign governments and leaders may well increase rather than decrease our influence. All commitments should be conditional, and many should be covert. In the past the logic of democratic politics tended to dramatize the commitment and play down the conditions. The shift to introversion and the resulting absence of public support which requires recourse to political means in foreign policy, however, may also give our leaders greater freedom to avoid the stark commitments which they have felt compelled to make in the past. The need to substitute more discreet political action for more massive economic and military action may also create the possibility of doing so.

The United States clearly can affect the political development of other countries only in marginal ways. Yet we also clearly have some interest in doing so, if only because such action might marginally reduce the probability of more Vietnams. There are perhaps at least five things which we might do in this area.

1. We could consciously recognize, even if we did not publicize it, that a major goal of American policy is the promotion of stable political institutions in modernizing countries and particularly the development of strong political parties. Our support for and cooperation with political leaders or military juntas could depend upon their actively attempting to develop grass-roots political organization. If we do get irrevocably committed to any one leader, no matter how charismatic he may be, we could, like the Russians in Cuba, try to nudge that leader into the difficult task of building political institutions.

2. We could devote much more effort to the study of the conditions and patterns of political evolution and to the elaboration of new concepts and categories useful for the analysis of societies undergoing rapid social change.

3. We could evaluate economic and technical assistance programs in terms not only of how they contribute to economic development but also of how they affect political development. We could try to identify those types of economic assistance which may contribute to both forms of development. We could develop criteria and guidelines for balancing prospective economic gains against political losses and political gains against economic losses.

4. We could inaugurate new activities directed specifically toward political development. These might include assistance to political parties, programs to develop and train political leaders,

assistance to more broadly based and public-oriented interest groups, and more widespread support for community development programs.

5. Finally, we could create some office in our own government which would have a primary responsibility for political development. Until recently, the Agency for International Development has been, in effect, an agency for economic development. Somewhere, either inside AID or outside AID, we need an office for political development;...We need diplomats and economic planners, but we also need to recruit and train personnel skilled in the techniques of analyzing political change and promoting political organization. What we could use, perhaps, is a new-style CIA, more skilled in building governments than in subverting them.

All this may seem highly adventurous. But it is, I would suggest, a highly conservative prescription for promoting political stability and avoiding military intervention. Such a program of preventive political involvement would be less visible to both the American public and foreign publics. In an age of introversion and of hostility to massive expenditures overseas, this has much to be said for it. Stimulating political organization, in particular, would get the United States out of the job of attempting to promote social and economic changes on its own. Instead of trying to pressure a reluctant government to introduce land reform as a substitute for peasant revolution, we would focus on the promotion of peasant organizations which could then, if they wished to, put pressure on the government. Political involvements of this nature could well be more discreet, less expensive, and more productive of political stability than current reliance on economic development, social reform, and, ultimately, military intervention.

COLOR IN WORLD AFFAIRS

Harold R. Isaacs

Harold Isaacs is Professor of Political Science at the Massachusetts Institute of Technology; he was formerly a correspondent in East Asia.

Matters of race and color are not actually more important in world affairs now than they were, say, a generation ago; only the thrust and direction of their importance have changed. This has been, of course, quite a change. The world of the 1940s was still by and large a Western white-dominated world. The long-established patterns of white power and nonwhite non-power were still the generally accepted order of things. All the accompanying assumptions and mythologies about race and color were still mostly taken for granted, hardly as yet shaken even by the Japanese challenge to Western primacy in Asia or by the attempt of the Germans to make themselves masters of the master race. The world of these late 1960s is a world in which this white dominance no longer exists, certainly not in its old forms. The power system which supported it has crumbled. Its superstructure of beliefs about the superiority-inferiority patterns of races and cultures lies in pieces amid the ruins. While some people cling to chunks of the debris and stand defiantly in the door-openings of their shattered towers, most of us are stumbling blindly around trying to discern the new images, the new shapes and perspectives these changes have brought, to adjust to the painful rearrangement of identities and relationships which the new circumstances compel. This is now the pressing business of individuals, nations and whole societies, and in the cluster of matters with which they must deal, hardly any is more nettling and more difficult to handle than the matter of race, especially as symbolized by differences of physical feature and color of skin. Of all the elements involved in this wrenching rearrangement, race or color is surely one of the most visible, more important in some cases than in others but hardly in any case not important at all.

From "Color in World Affairs" in *Foreign Affairs*, Volume 47, No. 2 (January 1969), pp. 235-242, 244-248, 249-250. Excerpted by special permission from *Foreign Affairs*, January 1969. Copyright 1968, Council on Foreign Relations, Inc., New York.

Taking it in perhaps its largest aspect, we begin with the fact that the entire cluster of some 70 new states carved out of the old empires since 1945 is made up of nonwhite peoples newly out from under the political, economic and psychological domination of white rulers. Our legacy from the fallen empires is a world now often seen as divided between the northern and southern hemispheres, between have-nations and have-not-nations, and in this picture all the haves, except the Japanese, are white, and the have-nots are all nonwhite, each bearing the heavy burden of the carryover of the past with its experience of subjection or of mastery. To the political and economic tensions and conflicts that divide the world along these hemispheric and class lines, race differences and the recent history of racial behavior by whites add their own special quality of greater explosiveness. Indeed, among those who feel these differences most strongly—usually the angriest nonwhite radicals or the most frightened white conservatives—many are prone to put the race issue at the front and center of all current and prospective world conflict. Their prime threat or prime fear is the approach of a series of racial confrontations leading to a universal race war that will drive the line of color across all the other fields of conflict that now criss-cross the globe. This is commonly foreseen as an apocalyptic collision between what Sukarno used to call the OLDEFO (old established forces) under the leadership of the United States and the Soviet Union brought together by their common whitism, and NEFO (new emerging forces) led by China, mobilizing behind it all the peoples of the Third World united by their nonwhitism and their shared hatred of all whites. It would come as a crushing and catastrophic fulfillment of the famous prediction of W.E.B. DuBois of nearly 70 years ago, that the problem of the twentieth century would be "the problem of the color line—the relation of the darker to the lighter men in Asia and Africa, in America, and the islands of the sea," bringing a terrible time of reckoning for the white man called to account for his sins.

This may seem an unnecessarily feverish view of a world whose prospects under the plainest light just now are lurid enough. But it will not do to dismiss it just because it is usually held in this form by racial extremists of one kind or another. This would be like dismissing as wholly implausible the notion that the United States would not have dropped on Germany the atom bomb it did drop on Japan, or speculation over the possible reasons having to do with race why a mercy airlift to rescue a handful of Europeans in the Congo was feasible while a mercy airlift to bring succor to thousands of dying Africans in Biafra is not. Even the most cogently argued explanations in both these matters could not entirely ignore their racial components. In any case, it takes only a slight jog of the kaleidoscope to produce a view of the future held by some quite sober citizens who believe that the necessary power arrangement to come—and possibly the ultimate nuclear showdown as well—must be a Russian-American combination against the Chinese, a prospect not as far removed from the race-war view as some of these sober citizens might want to insist it is.

But it is not necessary to be overcome by overheated visions of an oncoming race war to see that issues of race and color *are* in some degree almost universally present in the great issues and problems that dominate this hemispheric set of confrontations. These are in the main issues of resources and development, population and the shaping of the political institutions—more open or more closed—that will govern the great majority of men for the next long while. Wherever the racial element is added to national, class, religious, ethnic and tribal lines of cleavage, it brings its own peculiar accretion of greater glandular involvement and emotional violence to all the other elements of conflict in which we are now entangled.

Race or color does not often appear as the central or single most critical factor in conflicts affecting international relations. As an issue of identity or relationship it is more usually present as one element among many. There are, however, some countries and situations where color does in fact figure as the core issue making for both internal and external conflict. Of these the most obvious and most important is the Union of South Africa.

The maintenance of white power by brute force in southern Africa—taking in Rhodesia and South West Africa—probably supplies the main source in current reality for the vision of a world eventually engulfed in a race war. If the actualities of power in southern Africa and in black Africa have so far belied the frequent predictions of explosive racial conflict there, this hardly means that it will not come to pass at all. The chances for that depend on whether the whites of southern Africa do finally come to their senses before it is too late, or whether the black peoples of those countries will submit indefinitely to their condition of total subjection. There is no present sign of the first outcome and no basis for expecting the second. An ultimately bloody confrontation of black and white in South Africa, with all its possible, predictable or imaginable consequences in the rest of the world and especially in the United States, is by no means the least certain of all the grim possibilities that lie ahead for us all. It may be a nightmare of a prospect, but as so much of our recent history has shown, nightmares are a good deal more likely to come true than any of our sweeter dreams.

But it is not only the possibility of future eruption that counts in this measure of things. White power in southern Africa is right now probably the sharpest of all the wedges that separate the newly emergent nonwhites of the world from its whites. It continuously mobilizes the emotions, if not yet the effective action, of the new nonwhite nations, especially in Africa, which figure so prominently and yet so insecurely in the world's politics. It may very well be that the South African mote helps them not to see their own assorted beams with respect to racism or oppression of minorities, but the fact remains nevertheless that the survival and blatant exercise of white supremacy in South Africa keeps their own experience with white racism alive and vivid. It provides them—and the communist powers who are happy to be handed an additional weapon—with a set of issues and emotions on which they can all join despite so much else that divides them. Colonialism, often used to serve the same purpose, may indeed be a dead horse—except, to be sure, in Angola and Mozambique—but there is nothing dead about white power as it is wielded in southern Africa. It has figured on the United Nations agenda every year since 1952. Pushed by the nonwhite newcomers, often to the acute discomfort especially of the British and the Americans, U.N. majorities have repeatedly denounced South African apartheid, pressed the South West Africa issue, handed down detailed indictments of oppression of blacks and Indians, and demanded international action to put down the South African and Rhodesian white racists.

The dragging reluctance of Britain and the United States to join in these indictments—much less to take the actions voted—has served as a measure in the minds of many nonwhites (American as well as others) of the value of the commitments which these governments always make on the issues of equality and justice in general. Those winds of change which blew away the British Empire have by now largely also dissipated the sentimental-romantic fog that for a while overhung Britain's relations with its ex-colonies. The influx of black and brown immigrants from the Caribbean, India and Pakistan has produced a full-fledged white backlash in England, complete with riots, liberal dismay, civil rights legislation and restrictions on immigration. This new state of affairs was dramatically underlined when the British Government recently reneged on its promise of an open door for passport-holding Asian British subjects fleeing, ironically enough, from black nationalism in Kenya. Britain's temporizing response to white Rhodesian defiance has undoubtedly been due mainly to Britain's post-imperial weakness, but African blacks and Asian browns could quite reasonably interpret Britain's behavior as not so much weak as white. In the case of the United States, the equivocation over white racism in Africa helped to cancel out the flickering sympathy the United States commanded at times during the last ten years or so for its own turbulent and only half-successful effort to do away with the survivals of white racism at home. Into this equation must also go the size and weight of Anglo-American investments and strategic-military interests in South Africa, not to speak of the demonstrated over-readiness of American power to intervene forcibly elsewhere when its vital interests were thought to be involved. The overall effect has been to reinforce in a general way the communist, radical nationalist and radical racialist views of Anglo-American realities.

Race or color is also a central or even governing factor in a number of other places and situations which may have less weight in the balance of world affairs but can hardly be seen as negligible in the working out of the next chapter of the human story.

Of these only Portugal's stubborn effort to keep power in its African colonies carries over what we might now call the old colonial pattern of things, although the Portuguese style of handling the color issue is several shades more ambiguous than that of its ex-counter- parts elsewhere. Somewhat like the French colonialists, the Portu- guese like to insist that they are a good deal more flexible in such matters, especially with nonwhites whom they coopt as willing instruments of white power, whether in bed, in politics or in business. It is rather striking to note that the colonialists who have insisted most strongly on their paternalistic or racial flexibility as masters have tried the hardest or fought the longest and bloodiest wars to hold on to their colonies: the Dutch, the French and lastly now the Portuguese. On the political side, no enduring vitality appeared in the methods and institutions by which they gave some limited voice to their colonials in their own affairs. On the racial side, there is little to support the claims of greater humanity that have often been made for themselves by the French, Dutch and Portuguese colonialists as compared, say, to the British. The differences are more a matter of style than of substance. Taking it in its most literal aspect, much waits to be learned about these differences from a comparison of the experience of the varieties of Eurasians and Eurafricans produced out of some of these colonial relationships. None of it seems likely to put any higher gloss on the picture we already have of this past. It is a matter of some suggestive relevance to our present theme, however, that the nationalist movement in Angola is reportedly split between at least two groups, one of which is said to be led by blacks, the other by mulattoes.

The other examples that fall into this category are in quite a different way part of our legacy from the colonial era. They all arise from the effort to create nations out of the often disparate and mutually hostile population groups which made up the former colonies where, as the saying went, division generally made for easier ruling. These differences are usually regional, tribal and in highly varying degrees "ethnic" or "racial," two vaguely defined terms used, for lack of more precise definition, to mark out some blurry lines between distinctions and differences that are sometimes physical, sometimes cultural, often both. Almost every "new" nation—and not a few "old" ones—is now more or less painfully hung on this kind of centrifuge.

Probably the bloodiest of these new confrontations where the difference is most distinctly racial is going on in the Sudan. Here a civil war has been under way since 1962 between the predominantly lighter-skinned Arab rulers in the north and the black non-Moslem people of the south, a clash in which this difference plays a paramount role. Another example was the heavy bloodletting between the tall Hamitic Watusi and the short Negroid Bahutu that accompanied the creation of the two small states of Burundi and Ruanda. Other situations with similar elements exist in several West African countries, like Sierra Leone, Gambia, Liberia, where coastal "creoles" of varying degrees of racial mixture or foreign origin confront indigenous tribes in contests to hold or win power. There are north-south divisions in India which are divisions of culture and language but also, to no small extent, divisions between light-skinned northerners and dark-skinned southerners with strong feelings about their lightness and darkness. Some of our "new" situations are filled with "new" anomalies that in some cases have a strong racial cast, as in the encounter between European and Oriental Jews in Israel, Arabs and Berbers in the Maghreb, Hindus and Nagas in India's northeast, Hindus and Singhalese in Ceylon, the "black" Khmers and the "yellow" Vietnamese. Also on this list must appear the bizarre reproduction of older imperialist patterns by the neo-imperialist brown Indonesians in the imposition of their rule on the black Papuans in West New Guinea.

If we were to extend this catalogue from the more distinctly "racial" to the more vaguely "ethnic" or "tribal," it would obviously be possible to multiply examples almost indefinitely. In cases where the colonial boundaries have been retained as national boundaries, again without regard for population groups, conflict has been revived or ignited, both internally and across borders, between peoples whose physical or racial differences may be much less marked but between whom the ethnic or racial clash is hardly any less intense. Consider on this score Nigeria, the Congo, India in Assam and Nagaland, Indonesia in Borneo, the Ethiopian-Somali-Kenyan irredentisms, the high permeability of the frontiers of all the countries of the Indochina peninsula, to say nothing of the presence of this factor on both sides of the lines which arbitrarily divided North and South Korea and North and South Viet Nam, with rather notable effects on American and world affairs.

Nor can we entirely fail to mention here—despite the absence of the color factor as such—the long-vibrating hostility that separates such European tribes as the Czechs and Slovaks, Serbs and Croats, Flemands and Walloons, Welsh and Scots and English, Bretons and French, French and English Canadians, Spaniards and Basques, etc. The failure of so many political systems—national, imperial, international—to satisfy the identity needs of people in these many groups has led to the powerful resurgence of their feelings about their special separateness. Some of these tribal differences have been bloodying the world's fields for ages and we are plainly not done with them yet. However else they are caused and defined, almost all are rooted in or reinforced and rationalized by those physical and cultural differences which they themselves often see as "racial" or "ethnic" and which, despite all the mixing that has been done, manage somehow still to dominate so much of man's affairs. . . .

Running far out beyond these small and localized blots of detail, changing color patterns are staining and rearranging the look of much larger areas of the new power-political map of the world. Besides the new and highly fluid patterns created by the north-south hemispheric view of the world to which we have already referred, there are also the triangular shapes created by that other hemispheric arrangement—East and West: the U.S.-Russian, Russian-Chinese and Chinese-U.S. cleavages. In each of these combinations and often spreading through and across all of them run the feelings that have to do with race and all the attitudes, fears, self-perceptions and mutual perceptions that go with it.

The Soviet Union has long had to deal with race and color problems in its effort to create a successful federation of many diverse peoples, including the many nonwhites who make up the populations of the Soviet east. The dominance of the Great Russians in Soviet affairs has often had a racial as well as national character. More recently the most visible outcropping of this kind in the Soviet Union has been the appearance of its own set of "yellow peril" fixations around its power conflict with China. The Russian-Chinese conflict has deep roots in the geography and history of these two huge continental powers. As in all such cases, mutual fears and hostilities are fed by racial differences which serve to reinforce or to rationalize politically dictated behavior. In recent years Russians have more and more openly expressed their feelings about Chinese in these terms. In conversations with Americans and Europeans, they frequently promote a common cause against the prospective Chinese threat in terms of a common "whiteness" united against Chinese "yellowness." They endow the latter with full-strength versions of all the most negative and fearsome stereotypes, bearing on numbers, limitless energy and endurance, fiendish cleverness and cruelty, deviousness and inscrutability. These are all images they already hold in common with other Westerners, especially Americans, who get them from the same sources, indeed, from the same historic experiences. That Russians also share other varieties of "white" attitudes and behavior patterns toward nonwhites is amply indicated by the testimony of African students in Russia who met with discrimination, hostility and violence at the hands of their Russian hosts and fellow students. Chinese students in Russia had similar experiences. However one might balance out the "facts" of these episodes, it is clear that some of this Russian "whiteness" is at least part of the story of the Russian failure to win allies and keep influential friends both in black Africa and yellow China.

In the case of China, its racial chauvinism has been a factor of great weight in communist Chinese political behavior, as it indeed has been in all of China's history. Chinese pride of place in the history and culture of the world is not always easily separable from pride of race in its most literal physical form. Chinese feeling about the inferiority of all non-Chinese is almost always expressed in physical terms; outsiders are often portrayed as animals or animal-like demons, or are otherwise denied the status of human beings. It took a good deal of Chinese self-pride to sustain these convictions of Chinese superiority during the last century or so of repeated humiliation at the hands of foreigners. Repairing this damage to the Chinese ego and restoring the Chinese sense of greatness to its fullest luster are among the prime purposes and driving motivations of the present communist leadership in China. Although racism, at least crude racism, is anathema in communist ideology (as it is in the American credo), the Chinese, like the Russians, play heavily on its themes. They do so mainly negatively, charging their foes with its evils. Peking's heavy-handed and largely unsuccessful efforts to whip up support for itself in Africa and in the Third World movements associated with Bandung, Cairo and Algiers were deeply—if informally—larded with racial arguments. In open propaganda the Third World formula became a code for "nonwhite world" counterposed to the white world of the United States and the Soviet Union. In their private maneuvering, it was specifically on racial grounds that the Chinese moved to keep Russia out of the councils of the Third World and to create an all-nonwhite international trade union movement which they could dominate.

The failures of this Chinese effort were, again, due to many causes: the actuality of Chinese weakness; the marked lack of enthusiasm among a great many Afro-Asians for Maoist extremism or for becoming tributaries to a new celestial empire; the counter-pulls of Western strength, resources, influence; or, often most powerfully of all, their own nationalism or their own values. But to judge from a variety of accounts, they also came about in part because the Chinese involved in these encounters could not help conveying their strong belief that, if Western whites were not superior to Africans and others, the Chinese *were*. We are far from through with Chinese chauvinism or with its racial component.

For the United States most of all—more than for any other nation, new or old—the element of race and color has finally become a matter of central and crucial concern. Its importance cannot be separately assigned or portioned out between our internal or our external affairs. In the fundamental sense that the role of the United States as a world power will be determined by the nature and quality of the American society, the United States itself has now become the principal arena of our struggle to shape the future. In that arena the principal issue, plainly put, is whether our partially opening society will open enough to include Americans who are black on the same common and equal basis as all others.

This is not to suggest that race and color did not figure importantly in our foreign affairs before this. Until 25 years or so ago, white supremacy was a generally assumed and accepted state of affairs in the United States as well as in Europe's empires. It did not begin to give way seriously in the United States until it had clearly begun to give way in the rest of the world. Up until that time, the notions of white supremacy and superiority and the subordinate position of blacks and other nonwhites in American society had been duly refracted in American affairs abroad. It showed up mainly in American relations with Asia, where in the middle of the nineteenth century we joined Europe's freebooting imperialist system, acquiring our own "little brown brothers" in the process. Our behavior in these affairs was marked by that uniquely American combination of benevolence and rapacity, attraction and repulsion, virtue and cynicism which, for a great many Chinese at least, became our special national hallmark. At home in the United States in the same period we moved into an era of remarkable bigotry and violence against nonwhites. This was in the post-Reconstruction decades when nominally freed blacks were driven into new and even deeper pits of debasement. It was a period marked by the exclusion acts aimed at the Chinese beginning in 1882 and then against the Japanese, and not long thereafter similar restrictions on all further immigration from anywhere except Anglo-Saxon northern Europe. The restrictions on Chinese and Japanese, including denial of the right to citizenship by naturalization, were continued until as recently as 1946. On the political side, we did not yield our extraterritorial position in China—won for us by European armed conquest a century earlier— until 1943. We are obviously not dealing here with matters of ancient or remote history.

The direct role of racism in these relationships and its effect on Asian-American relations during the last hundred years are almost always more or less consciously underplayed in American historical accounts. But there it is, barely out of view beneath the surface of most versions of our experience in the Philippines, where we were, to be sure, enormously benevolent, but where our soldiers sang about the monkeys who had not tails in Zamboanga. It is seen in the lynchings and other mob violence against Chinese in America; in the first anti-foreign boycott in China in 1905, which was directed specifically against U.S. maltreatment of Chinese there; in the practice of discrimination against Japanese in the United States and its effect on Japanese-American relations before and after the First World War and particularly in the negotiations at Versailles; and in the heavily race-tinted propaganda used by Japan against the United States before and during the Second World War.

Today this part of our past continues to dog us, mutedly in Japan just now, but quite explicitly in China, where communist propaganda against the United States makes heavy use of racial themes and images, not just because the Chinese are themselves racial chauvinists but because this kind of crude racism is no small part of what they had to take from us in the years of their weakness. It is still not easy for many Americans to understand that we are now simply getting quite a bit of our own thrown back at us, whether from China or Japan, from Latin America where the gringo syndrome carries its own special racial ingredient, or from Africa, in whose darkest experience of human enslavement we played such a prominent role.

But now the worms—and the wheels of history—have turned. The end of the system of white supremacy in the world, except in southern Africa, has forced the quickening of the end of white supremacy in the United States. The changes that have taken place in this country in the last twenty years have come about for many reasons and as the outcome of many slowly—oh, so slowly— converging forces and circumstances. But surely not the least of these was the sudden American need to deal as a great power with a world in which long-subordinate, submissive races had ceased to be subordinate or submissive. The racial facts of American life abruptly became vital to our success as leader, whether in pitting our claim of democratic freedom against the challenge of communist totalitarianism or in winning the trust, not to say the alliance, of the new nations. It is hardly necessary to belabor this point at this late hour in the proceedings. It does not require too much distortion by our enemies to depict our destructiveness in Viet Nam as a product of our disregard for nonwhite Asian lives. It does not require much imagination to guess how much more hopelessly untenable our position in Viet Nam would be if we were claiming to fight there for Vietnamese democratic freedom of choice with an army that was still as racially segregated as it was when we fought for democracy and freedom in World War II, and as it remained until harsh military necessity imposed battlefield integration in Korea in 1950. . . .

... The crisis now wide open in American life is a concatenation of long-unsolved problems of poverty, the cities and race, each set formidable enough in itself but woven all together now in a single massive tangle of issues, demands and circumstances.

Of the three, the most critical is clearly race. To see that this is so, one has only to imagine what our present national condition and state of mind would be if our poor, especially in our city slums, were not so largely black. Without the problem of race, we would be facing demands of the kind this society has shown itself matchlessly able to confront and solve. It is the demand that we finally resolve the place of the black man in the American society that makes this the potentially mortal climax of an issue that has been with us since the founding of the Republic. It bears on what our society is and on what we say we think it is or want it to be—namely an open society offering freedom of choice and growth and well-being to all its citizens regardless of race, creed, color or national origin.

There has been no such society on earth and the American promise of it is in fact the unique substance of the American alternative to the claims of the communist totalitarians. It is the difference between the promise of our open society and the closed society of the communists that makes the world power struggle something more than a matter of deciding an issue of brute force. It can of course be argued that American power will impinge heavily on the world no matter what is done about the place of the black man in American society. This is no doubt so. But the proposition here is that the world power role and impact of an American society on its way to becoming an open, humane society for all its members is one thing. The role and impact of an American society moving toward new forms of racial separation in a garrison state will be quite another.

THE CRISIS OF THE HUMAN ENVIRONMENT

United Nations Economic and Social Council

... For the first time in the history of mankind, there is arising a crisis of world-wide proportions involving developed and developing countries alike,—the crisis of the human environment. Portents of this crisis have long been apparent—in the explosive growth of human populations, in the poor integration of a powerful and efficient technology with environmental requirements, in the deterioration of agricultural lands, in the unplanned extension of urban areas, in the decrease of available space and the growing danger of extinction of many forms of animal and plant life. It is becoming apparent that if current trends continue, the future of life on earth could be endangered. It is urgent, therefore, to focus world attention on those problems which threaten humanity in an environment that permits the realization of the highest human aspirations, and on the action necessary to deal with them.

For most of the time that man has been on earth, his numbers have been small and his power limited. Damage to his environment was at worst local, and usually subject to repair by the regenerative powers of nature. It is estimated that only a few centuries ago in 1600 A.D., the numbers of men were no more than half a billion and much of the world was uninhabited or little affected by man's activities. In these few centuries, the numbers of mankind have increased sevenfold and all areas on the earth's surface have been to some degree modified by man. What were once local problems are now global in extent and call for concerted effort by the nations of the world if they are to be solved. With the prospect of another doubling of the world's population in less than a half century, the need for action becomes even more acute. The need to provide food, water, minerals, fuel and other necessities for such increasing numbers of people will place pressures upon virtually all areas of the earth and demand the most careful planning and

From United Nations Economic and Social Council, *Report of the Secretary-General on Problems of the Human Environment*, 47th Session, Agenda Item 10, May 26, 1969, pp. 4-6.

management of natural resources. No nation can any longer be isolated from these global pressures. It has become clear that we all live in one biosphere within which space and resources, though vast, are limited.

Accompanying the growth of populations in recent decades has been the spread of urbanization. Forty per cent of the world's people now live in urban areas. In somewhat more than half a century, if present trends continue, urbanization will have reached its maximum and the great majority of people will live in towns and cities. The rate of urbanization is more rapid in the developing nations. According to national estimates, in 1920, the urban population was 100 million in these countries. By the year 2000, it may well have increased twentyfold. In the developed nations, the urban population in the same period will have increased fourfold. Urbanization is not in principle destructive to the environment. With proper planning and control, and if it were proceeding at a slower rate, it should enhance and not detract from environmental quality—by relieving pressure on rural lands, by providing goods and services in quantity and diversity, by providing new and attractive habitats and ways of life. However, in most areas, Governments have neither prepared for, nor have they been able to cope with, the mass migration into urban areas. In the large cities, slums of the most wretched nature often become the environment of people who once lived in greater dignity and better health on rural lands. Pollution of air, water, and land, concentrated in urban areas, have become universal problems, threatening man's health. Diseases associated with urban living in developing nations have increased greatly despite advances in medicine. Noise and congestion in urban areas add to physical and mental distress.

Accompanying population growth and urbanization is the accelerated impact of industrialization, and of an advanced technology that is often poorly integrated with human needs and environmental necessities. The rate of industrial growth can be indicated by various statistics. Thus, the production of crude petroleum was negligible a century ago. By 1966, however, it amounted to 1,641 million metric tons per year. Between 1937 and 1966, the annual rate of production increased sixfold. In the same period, the passenger motor vehicle, scarcely known at the start of this century, was produced at a rate that grew from 5 million to 19 million per year. In the most recent decade, the total value of all industrial production has doubled. Virtually all measures of industrialization show an increasing rate. Industrialization is of vital importance to nations which seek to elevate the living standards of their people. Improved technology is necessary if productivity is to increase and the products of industry be provided to growing numbers of people. However, the side effects of poorly planned or uncontrolled industrialization and of the one-sided application of technology have been a direct cause of many serious environmental problems. . . . The reliance of modern technology upon the combustion of fossil fuels has brought a 10 per cent increase in atmospheric carbon dioxide over the past century. With increased rates of combustion, this could rise to 25 per cent by the year 2000 A.D. The consequence of such an increase upon world weather and climate are uncertain, but could eventually be catastrophic. The increased use of modern technology has brought major increases in the amount of waste products which serve as environmental pollutants. It has been stated that in the United States of America alone, this amounts each year to 142 million tons of smoke and noxious fumes, 7 million automobiles, 20 million tons of paper, 48,000 million cans, 26,000 million bottles and jars, 3,000 million tons of waste rock and mill tailings and 50 trillion gallons of hot water along with a variety of other waste products. Other industrialized nations make their comparable contributions of debris and toxic materials. While technology is adequate to cope with these problems of pollution, the planning and application of pollution control lags far behind what is required, often due to economic considerations.

The spread of the urban-industrial network with its associated transportation facilities is consuming open space at a rate known to be high, but not yet possible to estimate for the world as a whole. In the United Kingdom, it has been estimated that such expansion will consume one sixth of the farming land in the next three decades. Properly planned and controlled, the spread of an urban-industrial-transportation complex could enhance the human habitat. Too often, however, uncontrolled urban sprawl destroys valuable resources, landscapes and living things.

Increasing populations bring increasing demands upon the productivity of agricultural lands in order to meet needs for food and fibre. Application of technology to these lands has brought greatly increased production in developed nations so that most of the material needs of their people can be supplied. Elsewhere, however, further gains in productivity must exceed the considerable progress already achieved if human misery is to be prevented. It is of great importance, however, that such gains be not offset by environmental deterioration. Thus, increased food crop yields have accompanied the increased use of fertilizers and new varieties of pesticides produced by chemical industries. However, some of these agricultural chemicals have side effects on the environment that we are only now beginning to comprehend. Thus the maintenance of both atmospheric oxygen and the productivity of marine environments depends upon photosynthesis by marine plants, mostly the floating algae of microscopic size. Minute amounts of such pesticides as DDT have been found to inhibit photosynthesis in these algae by 75 per cent. Nevertheless, we have dumped an estimated billion pounds of DDT into our environment and are adding an estimated 100 million pounds per year. The total world production of pesticides is estimated at over 1,300 million pounds annually. The United States of America alone exports over 400 million pounds per year. Apart from their potential effects upon the productivity of the oceans, many of these have known effects upon fish, wildlife and human health, which have been of serious consequence in many areas. Such damage to the environment should be avoided. It is possible to achieve the same goals without danger to the environment by application of knowledge that is already available, or by the development of new approaches.

The land upon which man depends for his sustenance has been seriously impaired by many of his past activities and in many areas this process continues. It has been estimated that 500 million hectares of arable lands have already been lost through erosion and salinization, that two thirds of the world's forest area has been lost to production and that 150 types of birds and animals have become extinct through human agency. Approximately 1,000 species or races of wild animals are considered to be rare or endangered. Erosion, soil deterioration, deforestation, watershed damage and the destruction of animal and plant life continue and in some areas are accelerating. The loss to mankind is of serious concern.

The deterioration of the human environment may thus be related to three basic causes: accelerated population growth, increased urbanization, and an expanded and efficient new technology, with their associated increase in demands for space, food and natural resources. None of these need be damaging to the environment. However, the efforts to accommodate population, to integrate technology into complex environments, to plan and control industrialization and urbanization, and to properly manage land and resources, have fallen far short of those required. In consequence, all nations of the world face dangers which in some fields and in some areas have already achieved critical proportions. To overcome them will require carefully planned and vigorous action at the local, regional, national and international levels. . . .

11

Conclusion: The American System in Crisis

As Hugh Davis Graham and Ted Robert Gurr remind us in this chapter, America is not unaccustomed to violence. Yet the profusion of violent events in the 60s—the assassinations of two Kennedys and black leaders Martin Luther King and Malcolm X, the city riots, the campus eruptions, the rising crime rates—inflicted a severe shock on the American psyche. Still one more commission was appointed to look into the matter—the National Commission on the Causes and Prevention of Violence. At home and abroad the question was posed: is the American culture especially conducive to violence? And more fundamentally: does the violence portend an imminent breakdown of the American system because of its unfitness to handle the kind of problems discussed in this book? Are we on the verge of falling into virtual anarchy or, to prevent anarchy, of declining into a garrison state? Each of the authors represented in this final chapter agrees that we are at the outset of a critical period, though they differ in their diagnoses and prescriptions.

Jerome H. Skolnick believes that confrontations, disruptions, and riots have been a natural reaction to deep-seated grievances—grievances to which America must respond with rapid and fundamental reforms. Graham and Gurr favor reforms, too, but are skeptical of the effectiveness of violent tactics in contemporary America.

David Riesman sees America as basically a conservative country, but he still has hope that the current upheavals represent only a temporary interruption of a trend toward a healthier and more open society. Perhaps the greatest danger that he sees is the majority reaction to radical demands and tactics.

Christopher Lasch rejects the view that we are moving slowly toward a better society. He argues that liberalism has failed, that the situation calls for radical solutions, but that radicalism cannot succeed unless the Left develops a coherent program and ideology.

Richard H. Rovere makes the case for liberalism. First he defends the value of free expression against several radical left writers who dismiss such classic liberal freedoms as devices of the oppressors. Then, in the excerpt which appears here, Rovere insists that, despite the serious failings of the system, it offers the potential and the mechanisms for its own improvement.

THE POLITICS OF PROTEST

Jerome H. Skolnick

Jerome Skolnick is Professor of Sociology, University of California, San Diego.

The Anti-War Movement

. . . Two lines of development within the peace movement are especially likely to flourish. One is the increasing preference for structural analysis as opposed to moral protest. After a certain number of months and years of begging their elected leaders to take

From *The Politics of Protest* (New York: Ballantine Books, 1969), pp. 76-78, 105-109, 122-124, 210-211, 239-240, 339-346. A Report submitted by Jerome H. Skolnick, Director of the Task Force on Violent Aspects of Protest and Confrontation, the National Commission on the Causes and Prevention of Violence.

mercy on the people of Vietnam and to meet the crisis at home, protesters inevitably begin asking themselves whether they have been conceiving the problem truly. Why, protesters ask, has the United States become, in Robert Hutchins' words, "the most powerful, the most prosperous, and the most dangerous country in the world"? . . . Many protesters are questioning whether the war might not be a natural result of the bureaucratic welfare state, with its liberal rhetoric, its tendency to self-expansion, its growing military establishment, and its paternalism toward the downtrodden. Doubts like these have been gradually eroding party loyalties and creating a broad public for radical thought and dialogue. The result will not necessarily be a swelling of the ranks of Marxists, but almost certainly a thorough questioning of current institutions and political style. As John McDermott has remarked, the movement's own tactics have produced "a growing appreciation of the creative role of social conflict, and accordingly a growing rejection of the pluralist consensus views which have dominated American political and social theory for so long."

The second development has to do with the question of violence versus nonviolence. A minority of alienated activists may flirt with terrorism, but they are unlikely to cause serious damage to the "war machine" or even to gain the support of other dissenters. There seem at present to be built-in limitations on the possibilities for effective movement-initiated violence; American society is simply unready for revolutionary bloodshed. Nonviolence, on the other hand, has been making some unexpected converts within the peace movements, not because of a rising tide of pacifism, but because activists have begun to understand that their first target must be the psychology that acquiesces and delights in war. The use of "guerrilla theater"—radical sentiments expressed in songs and skits—and the bringing of anti-military culture to American soldiers in the form of coffee houses and newspapers and "GI teach-ins" thus have an importance beyond their current degree of effectiveness; they suggest that major figures in the peace movement are turning from despairing gestures to attempts to convert those who must be converted if the movement is to grow. In David Dellinger's words:

> We will come closer to achieving our goals of subverting an inhuman system and undermining its ability to rely on fascist methods when we conduct teach-ins for the police and soldiers and fraternize with them rather than insulting them by calling them "pigs" or raising their wrath by stoning them. We must make a distinction, both philosophical and tactical, between institutions and the people who have been misled into serving them. . . . The traditional pacifist has been misled by the gentility and gentleness of the men who order out armies, napalm, bombs and Mace. The

unthinking revolutionist is misled by the crudity of the actions that police and soldiers can be conditioned into performing.

There is nothing to guarantee that the peace movement will evolve further in the directions pointed here, and there is a residue of bitterness which nothing will easily erase. Yet if the Vietnam War is sustained by policy-makers in the face of worldwide indignation and the apparent apathy of the soldiers who must fight it, it seems reasonable to suppose that the movement's current mood of disenchantment with existing institutions will both generate new forms of militancy and spread into new segments of the American public, creating possibilities for social changes which neither the movement's supporters nor its opponents have yet imagined. The anti-war movement is tied inextricably to the student and black protest movements, even as its historical roots lie with the symbolic confrontations of the pacifists. . . . The war has been a significant spur to each of these movements—it has become a primary rallying point of campus protest, and it has compounded the difficulties of fulfilling promises of progress made to the black communities of America earlier in the decade. . . .

Student Protest

. . . "Resistance" and "confrontation" have come to occupy an increasingly prominent position in the strategy and tactics of the student movement. "Resistance" and "confrontation" refer to such forms of direct action as deliberate disruption of or interference with normal, routine operations of persons or institutions by large masses of persons; deliberate violation of authoritative orders to disperse; forceful retaliation against police use of clubs, chemicals, or other force; the use of barricades or "mobile tactics" to prevent or delay police efforts to disperse a crowd; the use of ridicule, rudeness, obscenity, and other uncivil forms of speech and behavior to shock, embarrass, or defy authorities; refusal to comply with orders or to accept authoritative commands or requests as legitimate.

Even so, confrontations arranged by students have been usually more "symbolic" than "disruptive" or "destructive." Much rhetoric flows in university circles, and elsewhere, about "interference with institutional functioning." Whatever the intent of radicals, however, they have usually not been successful in disrupting the routines of most university members—until massive police formations were called to campus.

Doubtless some student radicals hope for physical confrontations with the police. But there is little evidence that such a hope is widespread. Further, there is little evidence that many students are willing (much less able) to disrupt functioning, attack persons, or destroy property in the university. But they are willing to engage in symbolic protest—to symbolically "throw their bodies on the machine." This leads to showdowns with the police, and then to violence from the police—and retaliation by some students.

Many observers who have tried to understand the student movement and who express sympathy for many of its objectives find the turn toward confrontation, disruption, and incivility highly irrational and self-destructive. Increasingly, SDS and the "new left" are criticized for the style of their actions and rhetoric. Although many such critics can understand the frustration which contributes to extreme militancy, they argue that the strategy of confrontation serves only to defeat the aims of the movement, and that student radicals ought to exercise self-restraint if they sincerely wish to achieve their political and social ends. For example, it is frequently argued that confrontation tactics accomplish little more than the arousal of popular hostility, thus fueling the fires of right-wing demagoguery and increasing the likelihood of government repression. Confrontation tactics in the university, the critics argue, do not promote reform; they mainly achieve the weakening of the university's ability to withstand political pressure from outside, and consequently they threaten to undermine the one institution in society that offers dissenters full freedom of expression. Some critics conclude their arguments by assuming that since in their view the main effect of new left activity is to create disorder, intensify polarization, increase the strength of the far right, and weaken civil liberties, then these must be the results actually desired by the student radicals.

We have interviewed new left activists in an effort to understand the basis for their actions from their point of view. The following is an attempt to present the case for confrontation tactics as the militants themselves might make it.[1]

1. *Confrontation and militancy are methods of arousing moderates to action.* The creation of turmoil and disorder can

---

[1]On the rationale for resistance and confrontation tactics: informal interviews and conversations were conducted with the following new left leaders: Thomas Hayden, Rennard Davis, Todd Gitlin, Carl Davidson, Paul Potter, Clark Kissinger, Michael Rossman, Steve Halliwell, Frank Bardacke; public speeches by Mark Rudd, Michael Klonsky; conversations with Staughton Lynd and David Dellinger; a systematic monitoring of the following "new left" periodicals: *New Left Notes, The Movement, San Francisco Express Times, The Guardian, The Rat, Village Voice, Liberation. . . .*

stimulate otherwise quiescent groups to take more forceful action in their own ways. Liberals may come to support radical demands while opposing their tactics; extreme tactics may shock moderates into self-reexamination. Student radicals can claim credit for prompting Senator McCarthy's Presidential campaign, for increased senatorial opposition to the Vietnam War, and for the greater urgency for reform expressed by such moderate bodies as the Kerner Commission.

2. *Confrontation and militancy can educate the public.* Direct action is not intended to win particular reforms or to influence decision-makers, but rather to bring out a repressive response from authorities—a response rarely seen by most white Americans. When confrontation brings violent official response, uncommitted elements of the public can see for themselves the true nature of the "system." Confrontation, therefore, is a means of political education.

3. *Confrontation, militancy and resistance are ways to prepare young radicals for the possibility of greater repression.* If the movement really seriously threatens the power of political authorities, efforts to repress the movement through police state measures are inevitable. The development of resistant attitudes and action toward the police at the present time is a necessary preparation for more serious resistance in the future. Fascism is a real possibility in America; and we don't intend to be either "Jews" or "good Germans."

4. *Combative behavior with respect to the police and other authorities, although possibly alienating "respectable" adults, has the opposite effect on the movement's relationships with nonstudent youth.* Educated, middle-class, nonviolent styles of protest are poorly understood by working-class youth, black youth, and other "dropouts." Contact with these other sectors of the youth population is essential and depends upon the adoption of a tough and aggressive stance to win respect from such youth. Militant street actions attract a heterogeneous group of nonstudent youth participants who have their own sources of alienation from middle-class society and its institutions.

5. *The experience of resistance and combat may have a liberating effect on young middle-class radicals.* Most middle-class students are shocked by aggressive or violent behavior. This cultural fear of violence is psychologically damaging and may be politically inhibiting. To be a serious revolutionary, one must reject middle-class values, particularly deference toward authority. Militant confrontation gives resisters the experience of physically opposing institutional power, and it may force students to choose between "respectable" intellectual radicalism and serious commitment to revolution, violent or otherwise.

6. *The political potency of "backlash" is usually exagger-ated.* Those who point to the possibility of repression as a reaction to confrontation tactics wish to compromise demands and principles and dilute radicalism. Repression will come in any case, and to diminish one's efforts in anticipation is to give up the game before it starts.

Some movement spokesmen would add that the possibilities of polarization, repression, and reaction do require more careful attention by the movement if it wishes to win support and sympathy among middle-class adults. They would argue that such support can be obtained, even as militant action is pursued, by concerted efforts at interpretation to and education of such adult groups. The Chicago convention demonstrations are cited as an instance in which adult moderate and liberal sympathy was *enhanced* by militant action, because some care was taken to maintain good relations with these groups, and because the actual events in the street were directly observable by the general public.

We have no way of knowing how many participants in such actions share these perspectives; many rank and file participants may engage in militant or violent action for more simple and direct reasons: they have been provoked to anger, or they feel moral outrage. The rationale we have tried to depict is at least partly the result of student outbursts rather than the cause—after an event (e.g., Columbia), movement stategists try to assimilate and rationalize what occurred. Nevertheless, when movement participants maintain that confrontation and resistance are politically necessary, the arguments described above are those most frequently used.

To a large extent, acceptance of the moral or practical validity of these arguments depends on one's view of the nature of American society and of the university as an institution. Radical activists base their commitment to a politics of confrontation on a kind of negative faith in the repressive and illiberal character of American institutions, including the university. These perceptions have been augmented by an increasing sense that the American university is deeply implicated in the perpetuation of racial injustice. The increasing protest of nonwhite students has brought the issue to the foreground of campus conflict in recent months. . . .

. . . The reduction of campus disorder seems unlikely unless universities possess the means to commit themselves decisively and consistently to the autonomous resolution of political disputes. Resort to force and the unleashing of official violence against student protesters is the clearest way for an administration to effectively destroy an academic community. . . . The remarks of a University of Chicago official after the recent student occupation of the University's administration building are instructive:

> We were prepared to lose that building or any other building by occupation or by arson right down to the last stone rather than surrender the university's ability to govern itself without the police, the courts, or the Guard.

Particularly in the case of public universities, this kind of administrative response requires a similar commitment on the part of outside authorities to the value of campus self-governance. Nothing is more destructive of a university's efforts to resolve conflicts than simplistic demands for "law and order on the campus" and indiscriminate use of police and troops by public officials. . . .

White Militancy

The idea of "militancy" suggests the activities of blacks, students, anti-war demonstrators, and others who feel themselves aggrieved by the perpetuation of old, outworn, or malignant social institutions. The historical record, however, indicates that considerably more disorder and violence have come from groups whose aim has been the preservation of an existing or remembered order of social arrangements, and in whose ideology the concept of "law and order" has played a primary role. There is no adequate term to cover all of the diverse groups who have fought to preserve their neighborhoods, communities, or their country from forces considered alien or threatening. The lack of a common term for Ku Klux Klansmen, Vigilantes, Minutemen, Know-Nothing activists, and anti-Negro or anti-Catholic mobs reflects the fact that these and other similar groups have different origins, different goals, and different compositions, and arise in response to specific historical situations which repeat themselves, if at all, only in gross outline.

Still, certain patterns stand out in the history of white militancy. In the past, the white militant was usually—though not always—an Anglo-Saxon Protestant, and the targets of his protest included other white ethnic groups. Today, while the WASP remains a major figure in the overall picture of white militancy, much of the white protest, especially in the urban North, comes from ethnic groups—especially Southern and Eastern European—which were themselves former targets of nativist agitation. Another change is more subtle. Until recently, the violent white militant acted, very frequently, with the assistance, encouragement, or at least acquiescence of more "stable" elements of the population, and quite often in concert with the militant and nativist aims of the American political and legal order. Today this is considerably less true. With the exception of some areas of the country—notably parts of the South—the violent white militant has become a minority, and operates beyond the pale of the law and the polity, both of which he tends to distrust in proportion to his lack of political efficacy or influence. . . .

. . . Still, a significant minority of white Americans feel driven to the use or contemplation of violence in support of similar aims. Their protest reflects the failure of American society to eradicate the underlying causes of the disaffection of both blacks and whites. On the one hand, the failure to deal with the roots of racism has meant the rise of violent black protest in the cities, which the working-class white fears will spill over into his own neighborhood along with rising crime and sinking property values. On the other hand, the failure to deal with the institutional roots of white marginality has left many whites in a critical state of bitterness and political alienation as they perceive the government passing them by.

For the Minutemen, the Klan, and similar groups, adrift and overwhelmed by the processes of the modern corporate state, the language of racism or anti-Communism structures all discontents and points to drastic solutions. Politically immature groups define the source of their problems in terms provided for them. This should not obscure the fact that their problems are genuine.

Continued political exclusion and organizational fragmentation render such groups increasingly prone to violence as a last political language. An effective response to these groups must transcend mere surveillance and condemnation, which can only aggravate their frame of mind without providing redress of their situation.

For the most part, the political response to white militancy has been either repressive or self-servingly encouraging. The current emphasis on "law and order" partakes of both elements. A continued repressive response to the militancy of both blacks and whites could conceivably lead to a state of guerrilla warfare between the races. There are precedents for such warfare in some of the race riots of the first half of the century, and in recent clashes between armed black and white militants in the South.

Of more immediate importance is the growing militancy among white policemen, as evidenced by the recent activity of the Law Enforcement Group in New York, the beating of black youths by policemen in Detroit, and the revelation of Ku Klux Klan activity in the Chicago police force. The new militancy of the police has obvious and ominous implications for the American racial situation, indeed for the future character of all forms of group protest in America. The policing of protest takes on a new aspect when the policeman carries with him the militant white's racist and anti-radical worldview. . . .

Official Conceptions of Riot

. . . The ghetto riots of the 1960's were participated in by a cross section of the ghetto communities, and given wide sympathy or support by those communities. Given these facts, few serious official treatments of riots now attempt to explain the resulting violence purely in terms of a criminal or "riffraff" element. Nevertheless, some official commissions, while generally appreciating that riots attract some popular support and participation, argue that riots are invariably aggravated or instigated by the criminal activities of a small group of provocateurs who take advantage of human weakness and transform basically nonviolent individuals into an irrational mob.

Thus, riots are widely characterized as outlets for pent-up frustrations and grievances sparked by a few. . . . The Watts riot was characterized as an "insensate rage of destruction," a "spasm," and a "formless, quite senseless, all but hopeless violent protest."[2] Similarly, the riots of 1968 were viewed as the product of a "sense of rage" and "years of frustration born and bred in poverty."[3]

Implicit in this concept of frustration-aggression is the idea that riots are without purpose or direction. Though it is granted that "rioters" have some objective justification for their unhappiness and anger, it is also argued that they tend to exaggerate the importance of underlying grievances. According to the recent Chicago Commission, for example, "There is a conviction on the part of a clear majority of our black citizens that [political] representation is entirely unsatisfactory and must be improved. This conviction, *whether or not or to what extent it is true* [our emphasis], is of critical importance to the continued health of our city."[4]

The essential problem with this perspective is that it neglects the intrinsically political and rational aspects of collective protest and fails to take seriously the grievances that motivate riots. Looting, for example, which distinguishes the riots of the 1960's, is a form of group protest and not merely individualistic or expressive action. Looting is widespread, collective, public, and undertaken by a cross section of local residents whose behavior is perceived by most of the community as a legitimate form of protest. The instrumental nature of looting is evident in its selective character: stores and supermarkets with a reputation for discrimination and exploitation are

[2]Governor's Commission on the Los Angeles Riots, *Violence in the City—An End or a Beginning?* (Los Angeles: College Book Store, 1965), pp. 1, 4-5; hereafter cited as *Violence in the City*.

[3]See, e.g., Chicago Riot Study Committee, *Report* (Chicago, 1968), p. 3; Mayor's Special Task Force, *Progress Report* (Pittsburgh, 1968), p. 4.

[4]Chicago Riot Study Committee, *Report*, p. 112.

usually singled out by looters. It is not accurate, therefore, to conceive of looting as merely random or senseless violence.

Finally, the emphasis on the irrational and "hypnotic"[5] aspects of rioting tends to obscure the interactional nature of riots. It is misleading to ignore the part played by social control agencies in aggravating and sometimes creating a riot. It is not unusual, as the Kerner Commission observed, for a riot to begin *and* end with police violence.

Abnormality. Almost every official riot commission has pointed out that riots are abnormal and useless:

The problem will not be solved by methods of violence.[6]
The avenue of violence and lawlessness leads to a dead end.[7]
[There] can be no justification in our democratic society for a resort to violence as a means of seeking social justice.[8]
[Unless] order is fully preserved, . . . no meaningful, orderly, and rational physical, economic or social progress can occur.[9]
Violence cannot build a better society.[10]

This "violence doesn't pay" argument is misleading on two counts. First, it refers only to the domestic violence of disaffected groups, while ignoring the fact that systematic official violence for social ends is widely upheld in other spheres. . . . It is a matter of moral judgment to attribute "normality" to one kind of violence—such as overseas war—but not to another. And it may be a glaring example of motivated obtuseness to ignore the possible connection between the public celebration of heroic military violence "over there" and the sporadic appearance of rebellious violence "back home." The breakdown of peaceful restraint during periods of war is among the most firmly established findings of social science.

Second, whether or not violence is "useless" is a problem for historical analysis, not a certainty. In any event, rioting has not been a particularly novel or unusual technique for expressing grievances.

[5] Federal Bureau of Investigation, *Prevention and Control of Mobs and Riots* (Department of Justice, April 3, 1967), p. 86.

[6] Chicago Commission on Race Relations, *The Negro in Chicago: A Study of Race Relations and a Race Riot* (Chicago: University of Chicago Press, 1922), p. xiii.

[7] *Violence in the City*, p. 9.

[8] Chicago Riot Study Committee, *Report*, p. 3.

[9] Mayor's Special Task Force, Pittsburgh, p. 5.

[10] National Advisory Commission on Civil Disorders, *Report* (New York: Bantam, 1968), Chapter 2.

Instances of such rioting by both the respectable and disreputable poor in eighteenth- and nineteenth-century Europe have been well documented by historians. As Hobsbawm has noted, the preindustrial city mob "did not merely riot as a protest, but because it expected to achieve something by its riot. It assumed that the authorities would be sensitive to its movements, and probably also that they would make some sort of immediate concession." Like the modern riot, the classical mob was composed of a cross section of "the ordinary urban poor, and not simply of the scum."[11] Moreover, one need not be fond of revolutions to observe that riots are sometimes the preface to an even more organized overthrow of existing arrangements with the substitution of new regimes. And one need not admire the consequence of the Russian Revolution to appreciate those of America or France. All three began with rioting. There is no intention here of making dire predictions. Our only point is that the viewpoint that holds that rioting is "useless" lacks a certain foundation in reality. At the same time, rioting is a "primitive" form of political action, which may lead to consequences undesired by the rioters.

Collective violence by powerless groups acts as a "signaling device" to those in power that concessions must be made or violence will prevail. Hobsbawm gives the example of the Luddites, whose "collective bargaining by rioting was at least as effective as any other means of bringing trade union pressure, and probably *more* effective than any other means available before the era of national trade unions." . . .

The available evidence, then, suggests that contemporary urban riots are participated in by a predominantly youthful cross section of the lower-class black community, that they are supported (usually passively) by other segments of that community, that they are often instrumental and purposive, and that they are not a historically unique form of social protest.

Social Control of Riots

Official and academic conceptions of riots have strongly influenced the assumptions underlying governmental response to civil disorders in the past. We have argued that these conceptions seriously misconstrue the meaning of riots on several counts. It follows that riot-control efforts based on these conceptions may be inadequate and often self-defeating.

[11] Eric Hobsbawm, *Primitive Rebels* (New York: Norton, 1959), p. 114.

No recent treatment advocates a purely repressive approach to riot control. On the contrary, official conceptions of riots have usually been translated into recommendations combining a program for the reduction of social tensions with a call for the development of strategy and technology to contain disruption. On its face, this dual approach seems both reasonable and feasible. It suggests sympathetic response to legitimate grievances, and at the same time it offers the prospect of sophisticated, measured, and controlled force to protect civic order. After considerable analysis, however, we have come to question whether this two-pronged approach is ultimately workable.

Prospects of support. First, implicit in the two-pronged theory is the assumption that, in practice, reform measures have about the same prospect of gaining executive and legislative support as control and firepower measures. Historical experience, however, suggests no such parity. On the contrary, commissions from the Chicago Commission of 1919 to the Kerner Commission have adopted the dual approach and have lived to observe control recommendations being implemented without concomitant implementation of social reform measures. Although it has generally been recognized that riots are motivated in part by legitimate grievances, the ensuing political response clearly reveals that order has been given priority over justice. . . . The Kerner Commission reported . . . that "in several cities, the principal official response has been to train and equip the police with more sophisticated weapons." Following the Kerner Commission, there has been considerable development of riot-control weapons and programs in urban areas, without similar efforts, recommended by the Commission, to meet underlying and legitimate grievances. From the evidence, it appears that it has been found more expedient to implement recommendations for control than recommendations for altering the social structure. There is little evidence that a call for social reform, on the one hand, and for the development of sophisticated riot-control techniques and weaponry, on the other, will not suffer the same fate today.

We may suggest as a general rule that a society which must contemplate massive expenditures for social control is one which, virtually by definition, has not grappled with the necessity of massive social reform. There are various possible levels of social reform, ranging from merely token and symbolic amelioration of fundamental problems to significant changes in the allocation of resources—including political power. We feel that contemporary efforts at reform in this country remain largely at the first level. Precisely because society leaves untouched the basic problems, the cycle of hostility spirals: there is protest, violence, and increased commitment to social control: as we spiral in this direction, the

"need" for massive social control outstrips the capacity of democratic institutions to maintain both social order and democratic
values. Little by little, we move toward an armed society which,
while not clearly totalitarian, could no longer be called consensual.

We need to reverse the spiral. A genuine commitment to
fundamental reform will have positive effects, both reducing the
need for massive social control and altering the quality and character
of social control. We do not, of course, suggest that every demand of
every protester or protest group be met. We do suggest, however,
that a distinction be drawn between *demands* and *underlying
grievances* and that grievances be considered on their merits. Too
often attention is paid to disruption, but not to the reasons for it.

Law enforcement should be taken seriously. By this we mean
to suggest that policing should take place within the framework of
due process of law, using the minimum force required to effect the
establishment of order. When actual crimes are committed, suspects
should be arrested, charged and tried in a court of law, not beaten in
the streets. . . . We should support reform of control agencies, not
simply the addition of weaponry. The reduction and reformation of
control should also occasion positive benefits by reducing polarization and hostility; that, in turn, should decrease disaffection, thus
decreasing the need for force, and so forth. Only if the roots of
disorder are attacked can the spiral be reversed and the problem of
social order rendered manageable within a democratic framework.

The ramifications of reducing force and reforming the social
structure, including the established policing services, are evident if we
examine the connection between anti-war, student, and black
protest. For example, a reduction of military spending and involvement overseas would reduce the level of anti-war and student protest,
freeing resources that could then be used to combat the problems of
the black communities. A greater understanding of black problems
by control agents—a sympathetic understanding—would, in turn, also
reduce the need for massive force.

Strategies of control. The escalation of violence is related to
strategies of social control. Our evidence suggests that a diversion of
resources into domestic force and away from redress of social
grievances is not only costly but self-defeating, since the heightening
of force is likely to be a factor in creating still more violence. . . .

Because the police are received with hostility in the black
communities of America . . . the introduction of more and
better-armed police will, we believe, only aggravate the situation. The
contemporary ideology and behavior of police across America make
it difficult to think otherwise. Furthermore, the introduction of
sophisticated weaponry will likely be seen by protesting groups as

evidence of governmental duplicity. The development of "nonlethal" weapons, for example, will not be perceived by the young man in the ghetto as a humane response to his condition; to him they will still be weapons—aimed at him—and will be viewed with hostility. Finally . . . the police, the military, and other agents of social control may themselves be implicated in triggering riots and in building up long-term grievances.

The political significance of riots. The conventional approach underestimates the political significance of riots. Even given the possibility of efficient short-term control of riots, and ignoring its immediate destructive effects, the political nature of riots suggests that forceful riot-control techniques may channel expressive protest into more organized forms of political violence, thus requiring greater military and paramilitary force with its inescapable monetary and social costs. Thus it is not surprising that one expert finds that riots may be "giving way to more specific, more premeditated and more regularized uses of force."[12] What is surprising, however, is his conclusion that "only surveillance and covert penetration supplies an effective technique of management."[13]

We have learned from the Vietnam War that power and covert surveillance may well have the unanticipated effect of increasing resistance. Indeed, the literature of guerrilla warfare stresses that revolutionaries are made through violence. So, too, the young man who encounters the hostile actions of a policeman is likely to increase his hostility toward the society and to be attracted to groups that express such hostility. Moreover, in measuring the consequences of escalating domestic force, we must add the political and social dangers of depending on espionage as an instrument of social control, including its potential for eroding constitutional guarantees of political freedom.

For these reasons, we question the conventional two-pronged approach to contemporary American protest. An approach that gives equal emphasis to force and reform fails to measure the anticipated consequences of employing force; and it fails to appreciate the political significance of protest. If American society concentrates on the development of more sophisticated control techniques, it will move itself into a destructive and self-defeating position. A democratic society cannot depend upon force as its recurrent answer to longstanding and legitimate grievances. This nation cannot have it both ways: either it will carry through a firm commitment to massive

[12]Morris Janowitz, *Social Control of Escalated Riots* (Chicago: University of Chicago Center for Policy Study, 1968), p. 20.

[13]*Ibid.*

and widespread political and social reform, or it will develop into a society of garrison cities where order is enforced without due process of law and without the consent of the governed.

DOES VIOLENCE WORK?

Hugh Davis Graham and Ted Robert Gurr

Hugh Davis Graham is Associate Professor of History at Johns Hopkins University; Ted Robert Gurr is Assistant Professor of Politics of Princeton University.

. . . For all our rhetoric, we have never been a very law-abiding nation, and illegal violence has sometimes been abundantly rewarded. Hence there have developed broad normative sanctions for the expression or acting out of discontent, somewhat limited inhibitions, and—owing to Jeffersonian liberalism's legacy of fear of central public authority—very circumscribed physical controls. Public sympathy has often been with the lawbreaker—sometimes with the nightrider who punished the transgressor of community mores, sometimes with the integrationists who refused to obey racial segregation laws. Lack of full respect for law and support for violence in one's own interest have both contributed to the justifications for private violence, justifications that in turn have helped make the United States historically and at present a tumultuous society.

On the other hand, the United States also has characteristics that in other countries appear to minimize intense revolutionary conspiracies and internal wars. Thus far in our history the American political system has maintained a relatively high degree of legitimacy in the eyes of most of its citizens. American political and economic institutions are generally strong. They are not pervasive enough to provide adequate opportunities for some regional and minority groups to satisfy their expectations, but sufficiently pervasive and egalitarian that the most ambitious and talented men—if not women—can pursue the "American dream" with some chance of success. These are conditions that minimize the prospects of revolutionary movements: a majoritarian consensus on the legitimacy

From *Violence in America: Historical and Comparative Perspectives* (New York: Bantam Books, 1969), pp. 808-818. A Report submitted to the National Commission on the Causes and Prevention of Violence by Hugh Davis Graham and Ted Robert Gurr, Co-directors of the Task Force on Historical and Comparative Perspectives.

of government, and provision of opportunity for men of talent who, if intensely alienated, might otherwise provide revolutionary cadres. But if such a system is open to the majority yet partly closed to a minority, or legitimate for the majority but illegitimate for a minority, the minority is likely to create chronic tumult even though it cannot organize effective revolutionary movements.

Some consequences of patterns of social control, legitimacy, and institutional development for the processes of collective violence are examined more fully below.

Some Consequences of Violence

Does violence succeed? The inheritors of the doctrines of Frantz Fanon and "Che" Guevara assert that if those who use it are sufficiently dedicated, revolution can always be accomplished. Many vehement advocates of civil order and strategists of counterinsurgency hold essentially the same faith: that sufficient use of public violence will deter private violence. This fundamental agreement of "left" and "right" on the effectiveness of force for modifying others' behavior is striking. But to what extent is it supported by theory and by historical evidence?

The two most fundamental human responses to the use of force are to flee or to fight. This assertion rests on rather good psychological and ethological evidence about human and animal aggression. Force threatens and angers men, especially if they believe it to be illegitimate or unjust. Threatened, they will defend themselves if they can, flee if they cannot. Angered, they have an innate disposition to retaliate in kind. Thus men who fear assault attempt to arm themselves, and two-thirds or more of white Americans think that black looters and arsonists should be shot. Governments facing violent protest often regard compromise as evidence of weakness and devote additional resources to counterforce. Yet if a government responds to the threat or use of violence with greater force, its effects in many circumstances are identical with the effects that dictated its actions: its opponents will if they can resort to greater force.

There are only two inherent limitations on such an escalating spiral of force and counterforce: the exhaustion of one side's resources for force, or the attainment by one of the capacity for genocidal victory. There are societal and psychological limitations as well, but they require tacit bonds between opponents: one's acceptance of the ultimate authority of the other, arbitration of the conflict by neutral authority, recognition of mutual interest that makes bargaining possible, or the perception that acquiescence to a powerful opponent will have less harmful consequences than resisting to certain death. In the absence of such bases for cooperation, regimes and their opponents are likely to engage in violent conflict to the limit of their respective abilities.

To the extent that this argument is accurate, it suggests one kind of circumstance in which violence succeeds: that in which one group so overpowers its opponents that they have no choice short of death but to desist. When they do resist to the death, the result is a Carthaginian peace. History records many instances of successful uses of overpowering force. Not surprisingly, the list of successful governmental uses of force against opponents is much longer than the list of dissident successes against government, because most governments have much greater capacities for force, provided they keep the loyalty of their generals and soldiers. Some dissident successes. . .include the French, American, Nazi, and Cuban Revolutions. Some governmental successes include, in Britain, the suppression of the violent phases of the Luddite and Chartist movements in the 19th century; in Venezuela the Betancourt regime's elimination of revolutionary terrorism; in the United States the North's victory in the Civil War, and the quelling of riots and local rebellions, from the Whiskey Rebellion of 1794 to the ghetto riots of the 1960's.

Governmental uses of force are likely to be successful in quelling specific outbreaks of private violence except in those rare circumstances when the balance of force favors its opponents, or the military defects. But the historical evidence also suggests that governmental violence often succeeds only in the short run. The government of Imperial Russia quelled the revolution of 1905, but in doing so intensified the hostilities of its opponents, who mounted a successful revolution 12 years later, after the government was weakened by a protracted and unsuccessful war. The North "won" the Civil War, but in its very triumph created hostilities that contributed to one of the greatest and most successful waves of vigilante violence in our history. The 17,000 Klansmen of the South today are neither peaceable nor content with the outcome of the "War of Northern Aggression." State or federal troops have been dispatched to quell violent or near-violent labor conflict in more than 160 recorded instances in American history; they were immediately successful in almost every case yet did not significantly deter subsequent labor violence.

The long-range effectiveness of governmental force in maintaining civil peace seems to depend on three conditions. . .public belief that governmental use of force is legitimate; consistent use of that force; and remedial action for the grievances that give rise to private violence. The decline of violent working-class protest in 19th century England was predicated on an almost universal popular acceptance of the legitimacy of the government, accompanied by the development of an effective police system—whose popular acceptance was enhanced by its minimal reliance on violence—and by gradual resolution of working class grievances. The Cuban case was quite the opposite: the governmental response to private violence was terroristic, inconsistent public violence that alienated most Cubans from the Batista regime, with no significant attempts to reduce the grievances, mostly political, that gave rise to rebellion.

We have assumed that private violence is "successful" in those extreme cases in which a government capitulates in the face of the superiority of its opponents. This is not the only or necessarily the best criterion of "success," though. A better criterion is the extent to which the grievances that give rise to collective protest and violence are resolved. Even revolutionary victories do not necessarily lead to complete success in these terms. The American Revolution returned effective political control to the hands of the colonists, but eventually led to an expansion of state and federal authority that diminished local autonomy to the point that new rebellions broke out in many frontier areas over essentially the same kinds of grievances that had caused the revolution. The Bolshevik revolution ended Russia's participation in World War I, which was perhaps the greatest immediate grievance of the Russian people, and in the long run brought great economic and social benefits; but the contingent costs of the subsequent civil war, famine, and totalitarian political control were enormous. The middle-class political discontents that fueled the Cuban revolutionary movement, far from being remedied, were intensified when the revolutionary leaders used their power to effect a basic socioeconomic reconstruction of society that favored themselves and the rural working classes.

If revolutionary victory is unlikely in the modern state, and uncertain of resolving the grievances that give rise to revolutionary movements, are there any circumstances in which less intensive private violence is successful? We said above that the legitimacy of governmental force is one of the determinants of its effectiveness. The same principle applies to private violence: It can succeed when it is widely regarded as legitimate. The vigilante movements of the American frontier had widespread public support as a means for establishing order in the absence of adequate law enforcement agencies, and were generally successful. The Ku Klux Klan of the Reconstruction era similarly had the sympathy of most white Southerners and was largely effective in reestablishing and maintaining the prewar social and political status quo. The chronicles of American labor violence, however, suggest that violence was almost always ineffective for the workers involved. In a very few instances there was popular and state governmental support for the grievances of workers that had led to violent confrontations with employers, and in several of these cases state authority was used to impose solutions that favored the workers. But in the great majority of cases the public and officials did not accept the legitimacy of labor demands, and the more violent was conflict, the more disastrous were the consequences for the workers who took part. Union organizations involved in violent conflict seldom gained recognition, their supporters were harassed and often lost their jobs, and tens of thousands of workers and their families were forcibly deported from their homes and communities.

The same principle applies, with two qualifications, to peaceful public protest. If demonstrations are regarded as a legitimate way to express grievances, and if the grievances themselves are widely held to be justified, protest is likely to have positive effects. One of the qualifications is that if public opinion is neutral on an issue, protest demonstrations can have favorable effects. This appears to have been an initial consequence of the civil-rights demonstrations of the early 1960's in the North. If public opinion is negative, however, demonstrations are likely to exacerbate popular hostility. During World War I, for example, pacifist demonstrators were repeatedly attacked, beaten, and in some cases lynched, with widespread public approval and sometimes official sanction. Contemporary civil-rights demonstrations and activities in the South and in some northern cities have attracted similar responses.

The second qualification is that when violence occurs during protest activities, it is rather likely to alienate groups that are not fundamentally in sympathy with the protesters. We mentioned above the unfavorable consequences of labor violence for unions and their members, despite the fact that violence was more often initiated by employers than by workers. In the long run, federally enforced recognition and bargaining procedures were established, but this occurred only after labor violence had passed its climacteric, and moreover in circumstances in which no union leaders advocated violence. In England, comparably, basic political reforms were implemented not in direct response to Chartist protest, but long after its violent phase had passed.

The evidence supports one basic principle: Force and violence can be successful techniques of social control and persuasion when they have extensive popular support. If they do not, their advocacy and use are ultimately self-destructive, either as techniques of government or of opposition. The historical and contemporary evidence of the United States suggests that popular support tends to sanction violence in support of the status quo: the use of public violence to maintain public order, the use of private violence to maintain popular conceptions of social order when government cannot or will not. If these assertions are true—and not much evidence contradicts them—the prolonged use of force or violence to advance the interests of any segmental group may impede and quite possibly preclude reform. This conclusion should not be taken as an ethical judgment, despite its apparent correspondence with the "establishmentarian" viewpoint. It represents a fundamental trait of American and probably all mankind's character, one which is ignored by advocates of any political orientation at the risk of broken hopes, institutions, and lives.

To draw this conclusion is not to indict public force or all private violence as absolute social evils. In brief and obvious defense of public force, reforms cannot be made if order is wholly lacking, and reforms will not be made if those who have the means to make them feel their security constantly in jeopardy. And as for private violence, though it may bring out the worst in both its practitioners and its victims, it need not do so. Collective violence is after all a symptom of social malaise. It can be so regarded and the malaise treated as such, provided public-spirited men diagnose it correctly and have the will and means to work for a cure rather than to retaliate out of anger. Americans may be quick to self-righteous anger, but they also have retained some of the English genius for accommodation. Grudgingly and with much tumult, the dominant groups in American society have moved over enough to give the immigrant, the worker, the suffragette better—not the best—seats at the American feast of freedom and plenty. Many of them think the feast is bounteous enough for the dissatisfied students, the poor, the Indians, the blacks. Whether there is a place for the young militants who think the feast has gone rotten, no historical or comparative evidence we know of can answer, because absolute, revolutionary alienation from society has been very rare in the American past and no less rare in other pluralistic and abundant nations.

Some Alternatives to Violence

Political leaders faced with outbreaks or threats of collective violence can respond in the two general ways that we discussed above: they can strengthen systems of forceful social control, or they can exert public effort and encourage private efforts to alleviate conditions leading to discontent. Primary reliance on force has indeterminate outcomes at best. If popularly supported, public force will contain specific outbreaks of private violence, but is unlikely to prevent their recurrence. At worst, public force will so alienate a people that terrorist and revolutionary movements will arise to challenge and ultimately overthrow the regime. The teaching of comparative studies is that governments must be cautious in their reliance on force to maintain order, and consistent in the exercise of the modicum of force they choose to use. These are policies that require both appropriate leadership and well-trained, highly disciplined, and loyal military and police forces.

The effort to eliminate the conditions that lead to collective violence may tax the resources of a society, but it poses less serious problems than increased resort to force. American labor violence has been mitigated in the past 25 years partly by growing prosperity, but more consequentially because employers now have almost universally recognized unions and will negotiate wage issues and other grievances with them rather than retaliate against them. The movement toward recognition and negotiation was strongly reinforced when workers in most occupations were guaranteed the right to organize and bargain collectively in the National Labor Relations Act of 1935. Taft and Ross judge the act to have been effective not just because it established procedures but because of the concerted effort to enforce them by the National Labor Relations Board and the willingness of both employers and unions to recognize the Board's authority. Their willingness may be a testimony also to their own and public dismay at the destructiveness of earlier conflicts. It is worth emphasizing that in this situation the long-range consequences of conciliatory response was a decrease not increase in violent conflict. In fact, violence was chronic so long as union recognition was denied. The outcome suggests the inadequacy of arguments that concessions necessarily breed greater violence.

The history of English working-class protest supports these interpretations. In the 19th century, when England was transformed by an industrial revolution in which a highly competitive, laissez faire market economy disrupted traditional employment patterns and led to sweatshop conditions for many urban workers, violent public protest then became chronic. Several conditions averted to what many Englishmen then feared as a threat of working-class revolt. One was economic growth itself, which led to a significant improvement in the standard of living of urban workers and to hopeful prospects shared by all classes. A second was the acceptance by upper-class political leaders of demands for political reform, an acceptance dictated by both principle and practicality that led to the enfranchisement and assimilation of the working classes into the English body politic. A third was a trend toward grudging toleration of, and ultimately the acceptance and encouragement of, working-class organization. Recognition of the right of workers to organize and bargain led to a flourishing not only of unions but of self-help organizations, cooperatives, and religious and educational groups, all of which together provided British workers with means to work toward the resolution of their discontents.

There were and are characteristics of English society that had no direct American parallels. Expectations of English workers were less high than those of ambitious immigrants to the United States. The English class structure, though more stratified and complex than the American, was generally accepted by all classes, seldom directly challenged. The laissez faire sentiments of British employers were tempered by an acceptance of civic responsibilities that developed more quickly than it did in the United States, and as one consequence English labor violence never reached the intensity that it did in the United States. Working-class demands for political reform were predicated on the common assumption that governments could be changed and the power of the state used to ameliorate the economic grievances of workers. Though the parallels are not exact, the English experience seems to suggest some general lessons for the contemporary United States: civil peace was established through a judicious, perhaps fortuitous, combination of governmental and political reform, and institutional development among the aggrieved classes of society.

Intensely discontented men are not will-less pawns in a game of social chess. They also have alternatives, of which violence is usually the last, the most desperate, and in most circumstances least likely of success. Peaceful protest, conducted publicly and through conventional political channels, is a traditional American option. As one of the world's most pluralistic societies, we have repeatedly albeit reluctantly accommodated ourselves to discontented groups using interest and pressure-group tactics within the political process as a means of leverage for change. But it also is an American characteristic to resist demonstrative demands, however legal and peaceful, if they seem to challenge our basic beliefs and personal positions. Public protest in the United States is a slow and unwieldy instrument of social change that sometimes inspires more obdurate resistance than favorable change.

Another kind of group response to intense stresses and discontents is called "defensive adaptation" by Bernard Siegal. It is essentially an inward-turning, nonviolent response motivated by a desire to build and maintain a group's cultural integrity in the face of hostile pressures. The defensive group is characterized by centralization of authority; attempts to set the group apart by emphasizing symbols of group identity; and minimization of members' contacts with other groups. It is an especially common reaction among ethnic and religious groups whose members see their social environments as permanently hostile, depreciating, and powerful. Such adaptations are apparent, for example, among some Pueblo Indians, Black Muslims, and Amish, and many minority groups in other nations. This kind of defensive withdrawal may lead to violence when outside groups press too closely in on the defensive group, but it is typically a response that minimizes violent conflict. Although the defensive group provides its members some, essentially social and psychological, satisfactions, it seldom can provide them with substantial economic benefits or political means by which they can promote their causes vis-a-vis hostile external groups.

A third general kind of response is the development of discontented groups of positive, socially integrative means for the satisfaction of their members' unsatisfied expectations. This response has characterized most discontented groups throughout Western history. In England, social protest was institutionalized through the trade unions, cooperative societies, and other self-help activities. In continental Europe, the discontent of the urban workers and petit bourgeoisie led to the organization of fraternal societies, unions, and political parties, which provided some intrinsic satisfactions for their members and which could channel demands more or less effectively to employers and into the political system. In the United States the chronic local uprisings of the late-18th, the 19th, and the early-20th century—such as the Shays, Whiskey, Dorr, and Green Corn Rebellions—have been largely superseded by organized, conventional political manifestations of local and regional interests. Labor violence similarly declined in the United States and England once trade unions were organized and recognized.

The contemporary efforts of black Americans to develop effective community organizations, and their demands for greater control of community affairs, seem to be squarely in this tradition. So are demands of student protesters for greater participation in university affairs, attempts of white urban citizens to create new neighborhood organizations, and the impulse of middle-class Americans to move to the suburbs where they can exercise greater control over the local government.

The initial effects of the organization of functional and community groups for self-help may be increased conflict, especially if the economic and political establishments attempt to subvert their efforts. But if these new organizations receive public and private cooperation and sufficient resources to carry out their activities, the prospects for violence are likely to be reduced. The social costs of this kind of group response seem much less than those of public and private violence. The human benefits are likely to be far greater than those attained through private violence or defensive withdrawal.

AMERICA MOVES TO THE RIGHT

David Riesman

David Riesman is Henry Ford II Professor of Social Sciences at Harvard Univeristy.

When Barry Goldwater was defeated by a large majority in the electoral college in 1964, many liberals and radicals concluded that the right wing had been similarly defeated. I thought then that they were too euphoric, overlooking the substantial numbers who had voted not only for the Republican party but specifically for Goldwater, and especially the many enthusiastic young people who brought to the Goldwater crusade an intensity of passion, an anarchic attitude toward bigness in government and, often, in business, and a quasi-conspiratorial view of its enemies similar to what we see now on the extreme left. The left and right, of course, differ very much in the objects of their compassion and concern: the left cares about the non white world, about the weak and powerless and the victims of militarism at home and abroad; the crusaders of the right, far less compassionate to begin with, are concerned about William Graham Sumner's original forgotten man: the middling white man who works hard, pays taxes, likes sports more than ideas and finds the modern world bewildering. (There are also a number of extremely wealthy, though provincial, sponsors of right-wing thought who, as Daniel Bell has observed, nevertheless feel dispossessed because they have more wealth than standing or understanding.) On the right wing, there are a number of people who are psychologically predisposed to authoritarianism, admiring the strong and despising the weak, fiercely chauvinistic *vis-à-vis* their race, their country, their definition of the American way. However, people of this dispensation, although more than sufficient to staff a totalitarian regime, account for only a fraction of the support for right-wing political candidates. How, then, is one to explain the persistence and growth of right-wing sentiment in America, to the point at which a quarter of our young people have become supporters of George Wallace, a brilliant demagogue where Goldwater was genial and perhaps the most capable right-wing politician since Huey Long?

To begin with, it must be recognized that the United States through most of its history has been a profoundly conservative country. However, the conservative majority for much of our national existence has been apathetic, reasonably generous and good-natured and willing to put up with change if it did not come too fast and if it did not appear to threaten the majority's definition of what America stood for and what they themselves represented. Revisionist historians of Jacksonian America (Richard Hofstadter, Lee Benson, Marvin Meyers) have argued that, despite Populist rhetoric, neither Jackson nor his followers were radicals, nor did their movement have radical consequences, even for the civil service. Lincoln was no radical, nor was Woodrow Wilson, nor yet Franklin Roosevelt. Indeed, even in the Depression of 1929 and subsequent years, Communists, Trotskyites and national-Populists were mistaken in supposing that vast unemployment and an apparent failure of capitalism offered opportunities to mobilize people for revolutionary political change. On the whole, Americans have favored equality of opportunity, not equality of result, although there has been a slowly increasing willingness to put a floor under misery, if not a ceiling over aspiration and accomplishment.

The conservative majority has not been especially interested in politics, particularly at the national level. It has distrusted politicians, by which is meant professional politicians, not generals or celebrities whose previous reputations made it possible for them to appear to be above politics. Some national leaders, and many members of national *élites*, have been liberal or even radical; their views have gradually influenced Americans without ever establishing a permanent liberal hegemony. What has resulted is a blend of traditions: a conservatism about American values coupled with an interest in innovation and, when people have felt unthreatened, a certain measure of mutual tolerance for different ways of life. Correspondingly, when cumulative changes have presented the conservative majority with definitions of American life sharply at odds with their own, the result has often been what Prof. Joseph Gusfield terms symbolic crusades to extirpate the strange and the stranger and to set the country back on the right track.

Gusfield points out, for example, that the temperance movement was a way in which Protestant small-town America defined beer-drinking Germans in Milwaukee or whisky-drinking Irishmen in Boston not as an interesting contribution to cultural pluralism but as a threat to their America, just as the hippies appear to some today not as an exotic curiosity but as a threat to masculine dominance and family stability. Even when the national climate is moderately liberal, many such battles are fought locally, with the victory going to the conservatives. There are, for instance, the many recent referenda on the fluoridation of water in New England and elsewhere. Fluoridation comes to be defined as an interference with God's water, a conspiracy between the Communist party and the aluminum company to poison good Americans. Beyond that, it is seen as one more example of the intrusion of the national scientific *élite* into local affairs—and the vote against fluoridation has often been a vote against those well-educated, smooth people who have come into one's town and who seem to understand the modern world and even profit from it.

The natives can score similar victories over such people (and over the young as well) by voting down school bond issues or school budgets; such negative votes have been endemic in the last few years. To understand them better, one has to appreciate the fact that geographic and social mobility have the effect of forcing change on those who stay put as well as those who move. Stayputters feel threatened by new people who come from elsewhere to run the new light industries, teach at the new colleges, preach at the more liberal Catholic and Protestant churches and otherwise bring the tolerant messages of the college-educated, national upper-middle class to previously isolated locales—messages which include staying up later at night, treating children more permissively, spending more on their education and introducing foreign movies. Hence a vote against fluoridation or a school bond issue may express resentment against a style of life that is costlier and at the same time more articulately defended than that of the indigenous stay-at-homes; such a vote also may be a gesture of impotent defiance against the big and feared powers: big government, big business, big labor—and the media. In the South, a similar politics of resentment has operated on the issue of race and in many communities has permitted a counter-establishment to develop in opposition to traditional moderate upper-class and upper-middle-class paternalistic whites who do not feel endangered by Negroes but who can be pushed out of authority by less affluent segregationists.

It is only under certain conditions, such as an unsatisfactory war, that these local pockets of right-wing and defensive conservatism coalesce into any kind of national movement. Father Coughlin represented such a movement at the time of the Depression, Senator Joseph McCarthy at the time of the Korean war. Like George Wallace today, and like Huey Long, the late Joseph McCarthy espoused some Populist attitudes, speaking on behalf of the little people against all the big powers, eventually including the Army itself. Opportunistically, he sought victims, not an agenda for change or even an effort to turn America back to the point where older people could feel that things made sense again. Joseph McCarthy helped to throw liberals and the left off balance by bullying individuals and by making dramatically visible the extent of resistance to change. Furthermore, as a Republican Irish Catholic, he helped cement a new tacit alliance of Catholic and Protestant fundamentalism—an alliance that became still more evident in the Kennedy-Nixon election, when a minority of conservative Catholics opposed Kennedy and allied themselves with Southern Baptists; it is often forgotten how near they came to winning, how tenuous Kennedy's victory was.

It has been almost as difficult for the various fragments of the extreme right to unite as for those on the extreme left, thanks to the suspiciousness and distrust that is one of the characteristics of right-wing attitudes. Among many other groups, the John Birch Society has been one which, as it were, could keep in storage some of the more well-to-do secular fundamentalists during a period when the right wing was on the defensive nationally, even while the society's members could be given practice in domestic counter-insurgency in crusades against UNESCO or Earl Warren or Polish hams in supermarkets. Its extreme economic conservatism and aura of wealth deprived the society of the Populist support that Joseph McCarthy had. Its weight, along with that of other endemic right-wing sects, could be felt only locally. However, at a time when the less well-to-do working class and the lower-middle class—stirred up by the Negro revolution, South and North, and by its liberal and radical white supporters—are ready to respond to someone like Wallace, who speaks to them directly as one of them, the wealthier and already organized right-wing cadres can serve as clusters of influence, political mobilization and financial backing. George Wallace is building a mass movement as Joseph McCarthy never did.

The right wing and the more apathetic conservatives, despite what might divide them in the realm of fiscal policy, tend to react similarly to the widespread and not wholly unrealistic feeling that there is no one in charge in America—that the country faces dissolution and anarchy. Of course, they are not aware how much they contribute to this anarchy themselves, seeing only the blacks and the militants on the left as the source of dissension. . . .

. . . The conservative majority attributes the rising national noise level to the radical left and to the liberal, educated upper-middle class, which appears to tolerate if not to sponsor the radicals. The life of the blue-collar working class and the lower-middle white-collar class tends to be a neighborhood life, with friendships based on family and propinquity, savings based on real estate and much dependence on public facilities (like schools) and semi-public ones (like churches and taverns). These people often feel themselves caught in a pincers movement between the Negroes or Puerto Ricans pressing into their neighborhoods from below and the upper-class and upper-middle-class anti-Puritan snobs who admire the poor and defiant, not the square and inhibited. (Many of the poor are square and inhibited, too, but the tradition of Western romanticism closes its eyes to this). Policemen, schoolteachers, social workers, factory foremen and lower-level civil servants are all men in the middle, caught between their often-unruly clients and the liberal and tolerant mandates of the national *élite* and its media. (These mandates sometimes suffer from a credibility gap, as when they appear to deny the everyday experience of Negro crime, picturing the oppressed as victims and rarely as victimizers.)

Among the hippies and their hangers-on, there are many splinter groups, but most of them come from the affluent strata and appear to denigrate the American insistence that in a democracy everyone must strive to get ahead; they reject the advantages desperately sought by those who have risen from the working class to the lower-middle class. Hence, although some hippies celebrate the value of toil, they cannot pose as members of the "poor but honest" class who disturb nobody; on the contrary, as played up by the mass media, they contribute their share to the politics of polarization.

Some hippies share with the radicals and with many liberals the widely prevalent assumption that the country is already post-industrial, that there is no serious problem of keeping the economy going but only of redirecting its energies. This seems far-fetched to those who do not yet feel secure in the affluence they see around them, which they define as an American prerogative. Many understandably feel helpless in the face of strikes that cripple a city's transport, hospitals, schools or telephone service. I often see our society as a series of vast traffic jams, to which each idiosyncratic individual contributes his own weight, complaining about that of the others. To unsnarl America, to keep it productive, to make it so productive that it can satisfy the claims of the disinherited without aggravating the malaise of the most recent, still-undernourished heirs, is no mean task. The many intellectuals who reject industrialism and bureaucracy are tacitly assuming that it is no trick at all to keep our society's 200 million people alive, functioning and productive, and some of their discourse suggests that they would prefer a smaller country of noble frontiersmen. At this point society depends upon the ethic of production to keep going. Someday it may be possible to reject the blessings production provides, but that day cannot come until the blessings are universal, until they are fully at hand. I was mistaken in thinking at one time that abundance was assured, even though I recognized that our measure of it has depended since 1939 on a war-preparedness economy.

As vested interests can sabotage production in the economy, so each locale, each ethnic group and ideological position has in effect had its own deterrent in national politics. The anarchic right wing seeks Federal funds for its projects, but resists Federal control. In foreign affairs, however, it is the captive of its own chauvinism, and with the decline in right-wing isolationism, there have obviously been insufficient deterrents to adventurous and expensive foreign and military policies; Federal action has had many powerful friends and, despite generally declining xenophobia, few organized opponents. And since the right wing in the United States always tacitly cooperates with the right wing and militarist elsewhere, the influence of our right wing domestically grows when, for example, the Soviet military insists on the invasion of Czechoslovakia to secure the Warsaw Pact; such cooperation has also imperiled the nuclear nonproliferation treaty and other measures of arms control.

Nevertheless, despite the unintentional assistance given American chauvinism by nationalists elsewhere, the patriotic fervor of Americans has continued to decline throughout the century. America is a more open society than it has ever been. Leftist radicals point to the repression of dissent against the Vietnam war, as in the trial of Dr. Spock or in the prosecution or reclassification of draft resisters. Yet compared to the way opposition to earlier wars was treated, opposition to the somewhat tangential and patiently escalated war in Vietnam has not evoked fierce community pressures. There is little censure of those who avoid the draft, even though there is opprobrium for men who express opposition to America as well as to the war. The relative coolness and equanimity with which the majority of Americans accepted the Soviet invasion of Czechoslovakia is an indication of maturity (and, to some degree, of indifference) inconceivable a decade earlier. Even *vis-à-vis* Communist China—and despite fanaticism there—there is less fanaticism now in the United States than there was when Quemoy and Matsu seemed almost fighting words.

What Communist adversaries have not succeeded in doing to strengthen the American right wing, the provocative left is accomplishing in another tacit alliance of extremes. Some on the left regard contemporary America as basically fascist and want to develop the latent film that has already, in their view, been exposed. "America couldn't be worse" is a frequent refrain. Little do they know. Some indeed do not want to know, since the excitement and solidarity of the politics of confrontation tend to blind them to their own destructiveness. . . .

An absolute morality tends to be characteristic of people whose experience of life has not included the give-and-take of wide human contacts and the mutual tolerance and sense for compromise that these often, but not invariably, encourage. Idealistic young people on both the right and on the left are outraged at an America that does not live up to its ideals as their parents and other significant adults interpret—and evade—them. . . . When these ideals are stated as absolute demands, rather than as aims to be approximated over time, the effect is sometimes to aggravate the right without much helping the left. . . .

Incremental gains won over a long period by careful work—and capable of being easily erased by an explosion, whether nuclear or political—seem like no gains at all to impatient young people of all chronological ages. I think that one must live simultaneously on two levels; the level on which one works for incremental gains and another on which one develops the faith and vision by which to judge those gains and to evaluate both what has been accomplished and where shortcomings remain. But a sense of moral urgency has led many people on the left to an attitude a little like that of the nineteen-thirties, when left-wing radicals found in the near target of the liberals an enemy who shared enough of their own values to be despised for not sharing them *à outrance*. . . .

Yet the argument for caution has itself to be used with caution. Any liberal who counsels radicals to his left against revolutionary tactics in a situation where the only revolution that seems probable will come from the right is likely to be reminded that, in the period when Joseph McCarthy flourished, many timid liberals sacrificed the left without mollifying the radical right. The question of tactics is always an arguable one, and it is possible that self-restraint in the face of the right-wing danger may provoke and encourage the right. The extreme right, as we have already seen, is often in the anomalous position of being stronger than it feels. It feels persecuted because many positions of influence in Washington, New York and Hollywood are outside its control, but Goldwater's 27 million votes represent an enormous potential base to which the right wing can appeal. Yet many of the left, both black and white, make no assessment of their potential strength or that of their adversaries before plunging into battle. Some with whom I have talked justify this by saying not only that there is little to lose but also that prudence and calculation are less attractive and human than impulse and spontaneity, so why not express themselves, even in dubious battle? One difficulty with this cavalier approach is that the victims may be others than themselves, so that indulgence in spontaneity and a lack of calculation for oneself may have long-range consequences that limit the spontaneity of others. . . .

My own view of America is that we grow slowly more civilized, though not at a rate guaranteed to prevent catastrophe. The upper-middle, educated classes become more tolerant, less xenophobic, more willing to endure complexity. . . . Even now, more Americans are confused than are dogmatic and fanatical; more Americans are decent than are sadistic and niggardly. It is my impression from studying public-opinion polls that, except among the most militant, firm ideological polarities of left and right have not crystallized; rather the Vietnam war and the race issue overlap and combine with different constituencies to create political constellations that may not be permanent. Undoubtedly, Wallace's national showing helps make legitimate the myriad local campaigns which the right wing continuously wages. Yet other than shooting looters and bombing Haiphong, there is no coherent national right-wing program; a new long-term right-wing hegemony—as opposed to a traditional conservative one—has not been forged.

If the war should continue, a violent push to the right is likely to ensue, both abroad and at home. But if we can somehow make peace in Vietnam and survive the present era, we may discover that America's development toward further openness has been only temporarily halted.

THE AGONY OF THE AMERICAN LEFT

Christopher Lasch

Christopher Lasch is Professor of History at Northwestern University, Evanston, Illinois.

It is clearer than ever that radicalism is the only long-term hope for America. The erosion of the liberal Center makes it difficult for liberals to undertake even palliative reforms. . . . Liberalism can save itself only by making an alliance with radicalism—whether in the new party, a restructured Democratic party, or in some other form will be the subject of much debate among radical-liberals. A radicalized liberalism under a leader like Ted Kennedy or John Lindsay might force concessions to the Negroes, forestall disastrous military adventures abroad, turn back the right-wing assault against the Warren court and against civil liberties in general, and thereby postpone the collapse of liberal capitalism. In the long run, however,

From *The Agony of the American Left* (New York: Alfred A. Knopf, Inc., 1966, 1967, 1968), pp. 208-212. Copyright © 1966, 1967, 1968 by Christopher Lasch. Reprinted by permission of Alfred A. Knopf, Inc.

liberalism cannot eliminate the contradictions of that system. It cannot liquidate the overseas empire or liberate the cities, because these things require the destruction of the power of great corporations—the oil industry, the auto industry, the insurance companies, the makers of armaments, to name only a few—which profit from existing arrangements. If America is to become a democracy, the only question is whether the power of these corporations can be destroyed piecemeal—for example, by creating autonomous enclaves of socialism in the ghettos and elsewhere—or whether it will be destroyed only through some ultimate confrontation in the future. Liberalism does not address itself to this question; it proposes only an extension of the welfare state. Nor does it address itself to the disintegration of values, the alarming spread of nihilism and alienation, which is bound up with the social and economic crisis of liberal capitalism. The liberal values of self-reliance, sexual self-discipline, ambition, acquisition, and accomplishment, while often admirable in themselves, have come to be embodied in a social order resting on imperialism, elitism, racism, and inhuman acts of technological destruction. They have therefore lost their capacity to serve as a guide to any but individual conduct. As a social philosophy, liberalism is dead; and it cannot survive even as a private morality unless it is integrated into a new moral and philosophical synthesis beyond liberalism. Such a synthesis, it seems clear, will emerge only in connection with a political movement that tries to demonstrate, both in practice and theory, how the unprecedented technological achievements of postindustrial society can become the basis for a new order in which men will no longer be slaves to production.

Radicalism—socialism—is the only long-term hope; but the almost overwhelming difficulties confronting the radical movement in America are suggested, more clearly perhaps than by anything else, by the vagueness and imprecision of the term "socialism." What is "socialism," particularly in an advanced country? For most Americans, the word has ugly overtones of bureaucracy, centralization, and forcible repression. Nor is this unjustified or surprising, considering the nature of most of the existing socialist regimes. Because socialism first came to power not in the seat of industrialism, as Marxian theory assumed it would, but in countries where the material basis for a socialism of abundance did not yet exist, twentieth-century socialist regimes have had to address themselves first of all to the task of capital accumulation—a task that in the West was performed by capitalism itself. For this reason if for no other, socialist regimes in undeveloped countries cannot serve as models for advanced countries. Their very existence, however, has helped to impede the development of socialist theory and programs appropriate to advanced industrial societies, since it was always easier ... for Western socialists to import a ready-made theory than to fashion one of their own. The blinding prestige of the Russian and later the Chinese revolution tended to conceal not only the monstrous character of Stalinism but its total irrelevance to the attempt to build socialism in the West.

When they have not patterned themselves after irrelevant (and often barbarous) examples, those who call themselves socialists in the advanced countries have tended to become social democrats, indistinguishable in most essential respects from welfare liberals. Where they are in power, as in Sweden and Great Britain, social democrats not only offer no alternative to capitalism that is relevant to the needs of advanced countries—something they share with socialists in the undeveloped countries—they offer no alternative at all. Where they are out of power, the social democrats form a loyal opposition that breaks down completely at just those moments when an opposition is most needed. Beginning with the First World War, social democrats in the West have been among the staunchest defenders of imperialism; and even those who oppose imperialism have offered no plausible strategy for putting an end to it.

Socialism in the West oscillates between capitulation and a mindless revolutionary militancy based on irrelevant models. The New Left in America, in spite of its ostensible repudiation of Stalinism and other ideologies of the 1930's, is no exception to this generalization. It is true that the New Left has articulated values, derived for the most part from an indigenous tradition of radical populism, that might become the basis of a new socialism addressing itself to the needs of the twentieth century, not to those associated with the early stages of capital accumulation. In espousing decentralization, local control, and a generally antibureaucratic outlook, and by insisting that these values are the heart of radicalism, the New Left has shown American socialists the road they must follow. Until American socialism identifies itself with these values, it will have nothing to offer either to black people or to all those others whose suffering derives not merely from the private ownership of the means of production but from the dehumanizing effects of bureaucratic control.

The history of the New Left, however, shows what can happen when the values of local control and "participatory democracy" are not embodied in a coherent program and strategy for change, a theoretical understanding of postindustrial society, and an alternative culture and vision. As long as the Left merely reacts to events, exposing and disrupting the "system" without offering anything to take its place, it suffers endless defeats and frustrations out of which grows, not a consciousness of alternatives, but a rising demand for more and more militant tactics. The worst features of the Old Left then begin to reappear in the New: dogmatism, an obsession with factional purity, vilification of opponents, hysterical gestures of alienation, the cult of violence. Eventually the New Left loses sight of its own peculiar traditions of local autonomy and democratic decision-making; New Left organizations begin to resemble the autocratic bureaucracies of the Stalinist period, against which SDS and other groups originally rebelled.

The experience of the New Left already refutes one of its principal tenets, that a revolutionary movement has no need of theory because theory will spring spontaneously out of the daily struggles of the movement. Struggle itself leads only to more struggle, or—as in the case of the labor unions—to eventual absorption. Particularly in a society for which no kind of precedent exists, the problems of which, accordingly, are almost entirely novel, a theory of social change can develop only if radicals—particularly radical intellectuals—cultivate it systematically. The United States is a society in which capitalism itself, by solving the problem of capital accumulation, has created the material conditions for a humane and democratic socialism, but in which the consciousness of alternatives to capitalism, once so pervasive, has almost faded from memory. This contradiction will not disappear in the course of struggle against capitalism, unless the struggle is carried into the realm of ideology and becomes a demand not merely for equality and justice but for a new culture, absorbing but transcending the old.

ALIENATION AND THE FUTURE OF DEMOCRACY

Richard H. Rovere

Richard Rovere is a journalist and critic.

We appear to have reached a point at which there can be no communication between the alienated and those who have, as I do, a continuing commitment not only to the professed ideals of this society, many of which are dishonored every day, but to its political and legal institutions. Alienation is not, I suppose, a point of view that can be dealt with in discourse of any kind. Still, it seems to me that those who are coming to perceive the limitations of liberty owe it to themselves to confront not only the disagreeable facts about those limitations, but the facts, many of them no less disagreeable, about the nature of this society and its place in history and in the world. Such a confrontation can be dispiriting indeed, for it can produce despair not only about American possibilities but about human possibilities in general. It must begin, I think, with an acknowledgment of the fact that the United States was born in a revolution led by men of uncommon intelligence and integrity, men whose ideals were of an elevation rare in the history of revolutions. They provided us with model charters of freedom and with a governmental structure that, whatever its defects, has been workable enough to endure for almost two centuries. They achieved a political unity that was in time, though not without strife, to become continental. The continent we claimed was enormously rich and fertile, and this made easier the maintenance of the liberties for which the charters provided. In the first century and a quarter of our national existence, we attracted from a Europe unable to achieve much in the way of either liberty or unity millions of settlers eager to share the opportunities our continent offered and, for the most part, eager to share our ideals. We enjoyed, in short, good fortune of a kind unknown in the past and unlikely to be known in the future. It is not, I think, chauvinistic to say that if in the end we prove unable to make a go of democracy, there is a fair presumption that no one else will be able to do so either.

The alienated feel that the evidence is already in, that we have compromised ourselves fatally, and that the role of the individual is either to destroy the society or drop out of it. In that case, if I am right, they must concede the futility of the very idea of human community and the fatuousness not only of change but of criticism. For myself, though I have not known a time of greater anguish over our possibilities, I want this society to be preserved, and I hope for the strength to maintain my only commitment to it. Despite the horror of Vietnam, despite the squalor and hopelessness to which we have condemned generation after generation of Negro Americans, despite the vulgarity of much of our culture, we have, I think, done much to keep hope alive in this world. Until the Negro is fully franchised and represented, we cannot rebut those who are cynical about our democratic professions. Nevertheless, our history has been one of a steady extension and strengthening of democratic procedures, and this extension continues in this period. The rule of law has likewise been extended and strengthened—more in the last decade than in any period in the past. Though our economy can fairly be described as exploitative, we have, by the exercise of democracy on behalf of equality and of compassion, compelled it to distribute the product of our agriculture and technology more equitably than it is distributed in many countries which claim to have institutionalized economic egalitarianism.

As for our failures, they seem to me—to use a phrase expressive of some of our shabbier values—about par for the course. The war in Vietnam is a monstrous miscarriage of a foreign policy that may very well have been ill-conceived to begin with; but I do not think it morally more odious than similar undertakings on the part of other great powers—most notably and most recently, the French in Indochina and Algeria—who now censure us. Among the alienated, it is terribly fashionable now to say that ours is a "racist" society. Of course it is. I should like to know of an organized society anywhere of which this cannot be said. I have yet to visit a country in which the dominant majority, even where it is physically indistinguishable from any of its minorities, is not persuaded of its own innate superiority. I think it far less remarkable that we can be accurately described as racist than that we can be described as a people who have shown some eagerness to be free of this condition and have elected leaders and representatives committed to this form of liberation.

Though I have been writing here of "this society" as if it were an entity that the individual can sensibly be "for" or "against," this way of approaching the problem has never made much sense to me. There are too many loose and loosely connected phenomena here, too many currents and crosscurrents, too many forces in tension and contention, to speak of the whole thing as a machine in operation. There is plenty to be despised and rejected. There is much that stands in need of radical change or of destruction. There is at the same time much to be defended and preserved, the liberty of the individual being to my mind the first of these because it is the most needed for the realization of any possibilities. The work of any sentient individual, of anyone interested in appraising the utility or inutility of freedom, would seem to me to be to cast a discriminating eye on the nation—not to determine whether it is good or bad but to associate these qualities with the specific values and institutions that come within his field of vision. His judgment will not be reflected in Presidential cease-and-desist orders or rewarded by vast trans-formations of the economic order. But the exercise of liberty will be a defense of liberty, while its disparagement will surely lead to its atrophy and disappearance and to the end of any talk about human possibilities.

Author Index